DATE DUE FOR RETURN

This book may be recalled before the above date.

The Information Age Series
Series Editor Manuel Castells

There is a growing interest in the general audience, as well as in universities around the world, on the relationships between information technology and economic, social, geographic, and political change. Indeed, these new relationships are transforming our social, economic, and cultural landscape. Social sciences are called upon to understand this emerging society. Yet, to be up to the task social sciences must renew themselves, in their analytical tools and in their research topics, while preserving their scholarly quality.

The Information Age series is the "Nasdaq" of the social sciences – the series that introduces the topics, the findings, and many of the authors that are redefining the field. The books cover a variety of disciplines: geography, sociology, anthropology, economics, political science, history, philosophy, information sciences, communication. They are grounded on original, rigorous research and present what we really know about the Information Age.

Together, the books in *The Information Age* series aim at marking a turn in the academic literature on information technology and society.

Published

Work in the New Economy
Chris Benner

Bridging the Digital Divide
Lisa J. Servon

The Internet in Everyday Life
Barry Wellman and Caroline Haythornthwaite

Forthcoming

The Geography of the Internet
Matthew A. Zook

The Internet in Everyday Life

Edited by

Barry Wellman and Caroline Haythornthwaite

Blackwell
Publishing

© 2002 by Blackwell Publishers Ltd
a Blackwell Publishing company
except for editorial material and organization © 2002 by Barry Wellman and
Caroline Haythornthwaite

350 Main Street, Malden, MA 02148-5018, USA
108 Cowley Road, Oxford OX4 1JF, UK
550 Swanston Street, Carlton South, Melbourne, Victoria 3053, Australia
Kurfürstendamm 57, 10707 Berlin, Germany

First published 2002 by Blackwell Publishers Ltd

The Internet in everday life / edited by Barry Wellman and Caroline
Haythornthwaite.
    p. cm.
    Includes bibliographical references and index.
    ISBN 0-631-23507-8 (alk. paper) – ISBN 0-631-23508-6 (pbk. : alk. paper)
      1. Internet–Social aspects. 2. Internet users. I. Wellman, Barry.
II. Haythornthwaite, Caroline A.

HM851 .I58 2002
303.48'33–dc21

2002066638

Library of Congress Cataloging-in-Publication Data

ISBN 0-631-23507-8 (hardback); ISBN 0-631-23508-6 (paperback)

A catalogue record for this title is available from the British Library.

Set in 10.5 on 12.5 pt Palatino
by SNP Best-set Typesetter Ltd., Hong Kong
Printed and bound in the United Kingdom
by MPG Books Ltd, Bodmin, Cornwall

For further information on
Blackwell Publishing, visit our website:
http://www.blackwellpublishing.com

Contents

Some of the chapters in this book are revised and expanded versions of articles originally appearing in the *American Behavioral Scientist* 45, 3 (November 2001): the editors' introduction, and chapters 1, 3, 4, 7, 10, 11, 12, 14 and 15.

Figures

Tables

Contributors

Anthony S. Alvarez is a graduate student in Sociology at the University of Maryland, College Park and a graduate research assistant on the Internet Scholars Program, also at College Park. He has varied interests in information technology, and is currently finishing his master's thesis about the digital divide. He may be reached at aalvarez@socy.umd.edu

Ben Anderson has a B.Sc. in Biology and Computer Science (Southampton University, UK) and a Ph.D. in Computer Studies (Loughborough University, UK). He has "dabbled" extensively in cognitive psychology, anthropology, sociology, and ethnography during his time as an academic and commercial research scientist engaged in user studies, HCI and applied social research. Until recently he ran Digital Living, a program of applied social science research within BTexaCT. He is now at Chimera, a research institute at the University of Essex. His research interests include the application of behavioral science techniques to the study of human telecommunication and the co-evolution of people and the technology they use.

Sandra J. Ball-Rokeach, Ph.D. Director of the Communication Technology and Community Program, is Professor of Communication and Sociology, Annenberg School for Communication, University of Southern California. Professor Ball-Rokeach's primary areas of interest are communication technology and community, human values, inequality, strategies of social change, and collective and interpersonal violence. Her books include *Violence and the Media, Theories of Mass Communication, The Great American Values Test: Influencing Belief and Behavior through Television, Media, Audience and Society*, and the forthcoming volumes, *Paradoxes of Youth and Sport*, and *Reinventing Technology*. Her journal articles appear in communication, sociology, and psychology journals, including *Communication Research*, *Mass Communication and Society*, *American Sociological Review*, *Public Opinion Quarterly*, *Journalism Quarterly*, *Social Problems*, *Journal of Social Issues*, and *The American Psychologist*. Ball-Rokeach co-edited *Communication Research* (1992–9), is a Fellow of the Society for the Psychological Study of Social Issues, and has been a Fulbright scholar at the Hebrew University, and a Rockefeller Fellow at the Bellagio Study Center.

Jeffrey Boase is a doctoral student at the Department of Sociology, University of Toronto, an active member in NetLab, and a participant in the "Webshop" summer institute, supported by the (US) National Science Foundation. His research interests include the transfer of knowledge through networks, as mediated by the Internet. He is the co-author of "A Plague of Viruses: Biological, Computer and Marketing," *Current Sociology*, 49(6), 2002.

Bonka Boneva is a postdoctoral fellow at the Human Computer Interaction Institute at Carnegie Mellon University. She has a Ph.D. in Sociology from the University of Sofia and has done doctoral work in Psychology at the University of Pittsburgh. She has previously worked as a senior researcher at the Department of Social Psychology of the Bulgarian Academy of Sciences, a visiting researcher at the Anthropology Department at Northwestern University and at the Psychology Department at the University of Pittsburgh. She has also been an Associate Lecturer at the University of Sofia and is now a lecturer at the University of Pittsburgh. Her research and publications include personality factors in international and internal migration, reconstructing social identities under new sociocultural conditions, and power motivation – theoretical and methodological issues. Recently, she has been studying the impact of a variety of social and personality factors on computer-mediated communication.

Manuel Castells, born in Spain in 1942, is Professor of Sociology, and of City and Regional Planing at the University of California, Berkeley, where he was appointed in 1979 after teaching for twelve years at the University of Paris. He has published twenty books, including the trilogy *The Information Age: Economy, Society, and Culture* (Blackwell, 1996–2000). Among other appointments, he has been a member of the European Commission's High Level Expert Group on the Information

Society, and a member of the UN Secretary General's Advisory Board on Information and Communication Technologies.

Wenhong Chen is a doctoral student in the Department of Sociology and NetLab member at the University of Toronto. She received her BA in economics from the University of International Business and International Economics, Beijing, and studied sociology at the University of Munich. Her research interests include social stratification and social change. She is currently doing comparative studies on entrepreneurships in the new economy.

Janell I. Copher is a Research Associate at the National Center for Supercomputing Applications at the University of Illinois at Urbana–Champaign. Her interests have included more basic research into adaptive behavior and community attitudes as well as more applied research into related social issues of our times such as community integration of individuals with developmental disabilities, AIDS prevention, non-traditional vocational education for females with disabilities, and the impact of computer-based communication on communication behavior.

Theresa Davidson is a graduate student in the department of sociology at Louisiana State University. Research interests include labor market sociology, welfare reform, and the digital divide.

Lutz Erbring, earned his Ph.D. in Political Science at the University of Michigan, and is Professor of Mass Communication Studies at the Free University of Berlin, where he heads the program in Empirical Communication Research. Professor Erbring specializes in the study of mass media impact on public opinion and the role of journalistic norms and practices in different national news traditions, as well as the application of advanced statistical methods in empirical social research. His current research interests include the role of the news media in election campaigns in Germany and the contribution of the media toward converging or diverging political attitudes and behaviors of east and west Germans since German unification. As a visiting research fellow at Stanford University, he is collaborating with Professor Norman Nie in studying the societal consequences of the Internet on American society.

John P. Haisken-DeNew (né DeNew) is a research economist at the DIW Berlin. He was born in 1965, received his BA Honours in Economics at Carleton University, Ottawa, Canada, 1987, and his MA in Economics at the University of Toronto, Canada in 1988. In 1995 at the University of Munich, he received his doctorate degree in economics (*Doctor oeconomiae publicae*) with his dissertation on migration and the inter-industry wage structure in Germany. Since 1996 he has been at the DIW Berlin, Germany. He published several articles in collected volumes and in journals such as *The Review of Economics and Statistics, Labour Economics, Journal of Population Economics*, and the *Allgemeines Statistisches Archiv*. His research interests include: wage differentials, other applied labor economics topics, and econometrics.

Keith N. Hampton is Assistant Professor of Technology, Urban and Community Sociology in the Department of Urban Studies and Planning at the Massachusetts Institute of Technology. His research interests focus on the relationship between new technology, social relationships and the urban environment. Recent projects include "Netville," an ethnographic and survey-based study of how living in a highly wired broadband suburban neighborhood affects social relationships, community, and family life.

Caroline Haythornthwaite earned her Ph.D. at the University of Toronto and is an Associate Professor at the Graduate School of Library and Information Science, University of Illinois at Urbana–Champaign. Her research centers on information exchange in computer-mediated environments and the way in which media are used to support work and social interaction. Current research includes exploration of information exchange and the development of community among distance learners, and an NSF funded exploration of knowledge processes in computer-supported interdisciplinary scientific research teams. Her publications appear in the *Journal of Computer-Mediated Communication, New Media & Society, Journal of the American Society for Information Science*, in Jones's *Doing Internet Research* and forthcoming in Renninger and Shumar's *Building Virtual Community*. http://www.lis.uiuc.edu/~haythorn

D. Sunshine Hillygus is senior research assistant at the Stanford Institute for the Quantitative Study of Society and a Ph.D. candidate in the department of political science at Stanford University. Her previous research has covered such topics as survey methodology, political behavior, and American elections.

Philip E. N. Howard is completing his Ph.D. in Sociology at Northwestern University and is a research fellow at the Pew Internet and American Life Project. His dissertation research looks at the construction of modern political communication technologies – political hypermedia – and their use during the elections in 2000.

Steve Jones is Professor of Communication at the University of Illinois–Chicago, and President and co-founder of the Association of Internet Researchers. He is senior research fellow at the Pew Internet and American Life Project.

Alaina G. Kanfer is a Senior Consultant with BORN eBusiness Solutions Center in Minneapolis and a Senior Research Scientist at the National Center for Supercomputing Applications at the University of Illinois at Urbana–Champaign. She specializes in distributed knowledge processes and e-commerce from a communities and exchanges perspective.

James E. Katz (Ph.D., Rutgers University) won postdoctoral fellowships at Harvard and MIT, served on the faculties of the University of Texas, Austin, and Clarkson University, and headed the social science research unit at Bell Communication Research (Bellcore). He was also granted national and foreign patents on his inventions in telecommunication technology. Katz is the author of several books in the field of technology and society, including *Connections: Social and Cultural Studies of the Telephone in American Life*, which won an "outstanding academic title" award from a division of the American Library Association, and *Congress and National Energy Policy*, which was nominated for the American Political Science Assocation's Gladys Kammerer award. Dr Katz is Professor, Department of Communication, School of Communication, Information and Library Studies, Rutgers, The State University of New Jersey.

Andrea L. Kavanaugh, Ph.D., a Fulbright scholar and Cunningham Fellow, has worked extensively on communications systems and effects. Her areas of current research are the use and social impact of computer networking, development communication, and telecommunications policy. She has served for a number of years as Director of

Research for the Blacksburg Electronic Village, Information Systems, at Virginia Polytechnic Institute and State University (Virginia Tech). Her recent books include *The Social Control of Technology: Information in the Global Economy.* Andrea's research has been published in the *Journal of Communication, Telecommunications Policy,* and the *International Handbook of Telecommunications Economics;* she is co-editor of *Community Networks: Lessons from Blacksburg, Virginia* and *The Wired Homestead: New Views on a Web World.*

Michelle M. Kazmer received her Ph.D. from the Graduate School of Library and Information Science, University of Illinois at Urbana–Champaign, and is currently Assistant Professor at the School of Information Studies, Florida State University. Her research focus is on knowledge-building communities in which members communicate primarily through computer media and are not physically co-located. Currently, she is focusing on how individuals enter into and disengage from these communities.

Meyer Kestnbaum is an Assistant Professor in the Department of Sociology at the University of Maryland. Trained as a historical and comparative sociologist, he has worked with colleagues at Maryland and elsewhere on the social impact of the Internet. He is currently developing an analytic framework to conduct such research organized around distinct communications formats.

Robert Kraut is Herbert Simon Professor of Human Computer Interaction at Carnegie Mellon University. He has a Ph.D. in Social Psychology from Yale University, has worked as a research scientist at AT&T Bell Laboratories and Bell Communications Research, and has previously been an assistant professor at the University of Pennsylvania and Cornell University. He has broad interests in the design and social impact of computing and has conducted empirical research on office automation and employment quality, technology and home-based employment, the communication needs of collaborating scientists, the design of information technology for small-group intellectual work, and the impact of national information networks on organizations and families.

Robert J. Lunn, Ph.D. serves as a Senior Research Analyst for the UCLA Center for Communication Policy. Dr Lunn is also the principal of Eta Consulting, providing data analysis and consulting services across a wide spectrum of industries. Prior to forming Eta Consulting, he was the Executive Director of Survey Research Operations at J.D. Power and Associates. Dr. Lunn received his BA in Psychology from California State University, Northridge and his MA and Ph.D. in Cognitive Psychology from The Claremont Graduate University. He performed post-doctoral work as a National Institute of Health Fellow at the University of California, Berkeley. He is a member of the American Statistical Association, American Society for the Advancement of Science, Sigma Xi, and the New York Academy of Science. Dr. Lunn was a recent panel member at the American Statistical Association's meeting on: The Importance of Communications in the Consulting Profession.

Sorin Matei, Ph.D. is Project Manager, Communication Technology and Community Program, Annenberg School for Communication, University of Southern California. He has an MA in History and Philosophy from Bucharest University and an MA in International Relations from The Fletcher School of Diplomacy and Law, Tufts University. He has also worked as a radio producer for the BBC World Service. His most recent research interests are the relationship between online and offline social bonds in local and global contexts, and the communicative shaping of social space.

Kakuko Miyata is a professor of social psychology at Department of Sociology, Meiji Gakuin University in Tokyo. She received her graduate school education in social psychology at the University of Tokyo. She has conducted extensive empirical research on the impact of social relationships which are fostered and maintained through interactive communication technologies on individuals' psychological state and behaviors in everyday lives. Currently her works focus on a comparative study of the impact of Internet activities on social capital in Japan and North America. She is the author of *The Society of Electronic Media: Social Psychology of New Communication Technology* (in Japanese), which won the Social Science Award from the Japan Telecommunications Advancement Foundation and which was translated into Korean.

Alan Neustadtl is Associate Professor in Sociology at the University of Maryland. Previous research examined elites, networks of corporate political action, and campaign finance and reform. In addition to articles published in journals like *American Sociological Review*, *American Journal of Sociology*, and *Social Forces*, Neustadtl has published two books – *Money Talks* and *Dollars and Votes* – on organized corporate political behavior. Currently he is concerned with the impact of technology, specifically the Internet, on society. Information about ongoing research is available at *www.webuse.umd.edu*.

Norman H. Nie is a Research Professor in the Department of Political Science, Stanford University and Director of the Stanford Institute for the Quantitative Study of Society. He is Professor Emeritus, Department of Political Science, University of Chicago. He is co-author of *Education and Democratic Citizenship in America* (1997), and the *Changing American Voter* (1976), both of which won the Woodrow Wilson Award; *Participation in America* (1972) which won the Gladys Kammaner Award; and *Participation and Political Equality* (1978). He is chairman and founder of SPSS.

Scott J. Patterson, Ph.D. is an Associate Professor of Broadcast and Electronic Communication Arts at San Francisco State University where he has been teaching since 1997. Scott's work focuses explicitly on the use of interactive communication technologies in the fostering and maintenance of social relationships. His current work explores the uses and impact of high-capacity telecommunication systems on individuals and communities. Scott's recent work has been published in the *Journal of Media Economics*, the *Journal of Broadcasting and Electronic Media*, *Communication Research* and the *Electronic Journal of Communication*; he also edited *Collaborative Strategies for Developing Telecommunication Networks in Ohio*.

Rainer Pischner is a research fellow at the DIW Berlin (German Institute for Economic Research). He received his *Diplom* in economics and statistics at the Free University of Berlin. He joined the DIW Berlin in 1971 and until 1983 his research focused on input–output analysis. In 1979 he received his doctorate degree in economics with this dissertation on industrial concentration processes in Germany. Since 1983 he has been working for the German Socio-Economic Panel Study. His chief interests currently include empirical weighting problems, analysis of spell-data and software-development for the GSOEP. He has mainly published in journals of the German Institute of Economic Research.

Anabel Quan-Haase (MS, Humboldt University, 1998) is a Ph.D. student of Information Science at the Faculty of Information Studies,

University of Toronto. Before starting her Ph.D. in Toronto she completed a masters degree in psychology in the area of cognition. Quan-Haase has participated in a series of projects relating the Internet to changes in cognitive processes. Among these was the Connected Intelligence project conducted in Madeira, where school children were organized around specific tasks and encouraged to use the Internet to perform their research. Currently, her interests lie in the impact of new media on society in general and specifically on collaborative work. She is also the project manager for the Collaborative Environment Project; a collaboration between the Bell Canada University Labs and the University of Toronto with the aim of developing new tools for supporting virtual work.

Lee Rainie is Director of the Pew Internet and American Life Project, a research center fully funded by the Pew Charitable Trusts to examine the social impact of the Internet.

Howard Rheingold lives north of Silicon Valley, a distance that gives him both participation and perspective. He was an early active member in online communities, especially THE WELL. He wrote *The Virtual Community* (1993, revised 2001). He has also written *Virtual Reality* (1991), and *Tools for Thought* (1985, 2000). Rheingold edited the *Whole Earth Review* 1990–4 and *The Millennium Whole Earth Catalog* (1994). His website is http://www.rheingold.com, where many of his articles and paintings are displayed.

Ronald E. Rice (MA, Ph.D. Stanford University) has co-authored or co-edited *Accessing and Browsing Information and Communication*; *Public Communication Campaigns*; *The Internet and Health Communication*; *The New Media: Communication, Research and Technology*; *Managing Organizational Innovation*; and *Research Methods and the New Media*. He has conducted research and published widely in communication science, public communication campaigns, computer-mediated communication systems, methodology, organizational and management theory, information systems, information science and bibliometrics, and social networks. www.scils.rutgers.edu/~rrice.

John P. Robinson is a Professor of Sociology and Director of the Internet Scholars Program and the Americans Use of Time Project at the University of Maryland. He has tracked trends in time use, the impact of mass media (including the Internet) in public opinion since the

1950s and is a specialist in social science methodology. He is the author of *Time for Life* (1999), and *Measures of Personality and Psychological Attitudes* (1991).

Janet W. Salaff attended the University of California, Berkeley for her bachelor, master, and doctorate degrees in Sociology. In 1970, she joined the faculty of the Department of Sociology at the University of Toronto, and was cross-appointment to the Center for Urban and Community Studies in 1992. Salaff has spent time as a visiting scholar at the University of Hong Kong, working in the Department of Sociology, the Center for Asian Studies and the Women's Studies Research Centre, and has given keynote addresses on computing and teleworking for learned conferences in Asia. Salaff and her teleworking research team has found that work structure, rather than worker personality, determines job efficacy for teleworkers. Salaff is currently working on a monograph on the structural causes of telework.

Wesley Shrum is Professor of Sociology at Louisiana State University. Since 1993 he has studied research communication in Ghana, Kenya, and Kerala. Other scholarly interests include large scientific collaborations, cultural mediation in high and popular art, and ritual disrobement at Mardi Gras.

R. Sooryamoorthy, MA, Ph.D., is currently a senior lecturer in the post-graduate department of Sociology at Loyola College of Social Sciences, Kerala, India. His works include *NGOs in India: A Cross-sectional Study*, *Climbing Up*, *Extension in Higher Education*, *Consumption to Consumerism*, and *Science in Participatory Development*.

Michael Suman is research director of the UCLA Center for Communication Policy. In this capacity he has managed and coordinated the UCLA Television Violence Monitoring Project, the UCLA Internet Project, and the World Internet Project. Suman, a Ph.D. in sociology from UCLA, has taught sociology, anthropology, and communication studies in Japan, Korea, China, and the Marshall Islands. He is now a member of the UCLA faculty in the Department of Communication Studies. He is also editor of two books, *Religion and Prime Time Television* and *Advocacy Groups and the Entertainment Industry*.

Karina Tracey graduated from Queens University, Belfast in 1995 with a B.Sc. in Psychology. She joined BT in 1997 after completing an M.Sc.

(Eng.) in Work Design and Ergonomics at Birmingham University. She spent 5 years as a senior researcher in the Cognition and Perception Lab at BT Adastral Park working on the Digital Living research program, numerous collaborative learning projects, and leading the design of the qualitative part of a pan-European study of "The Impact of Telework on a Sustainable Social Development and Quality of Life." She is currently Business Development Manager at the Chimera research institute, University of Essex. Her interests include the diffusion of products through social networks, mobility and issues of control and identity, and the development of new qualitative methodologies.

Gert G. Wagner is Full Professor of Economics at Berlin University of Technology (TUB) and Director of the German Socio-Economic Panel Study at DIW Berlin (German Institute for Economic Research). He serves on the Advisory Board of Statistics Germany (*Statistischer Beirat*) and on the German Science Council (*Wissenschaftsrat*). From 1992–7 he was Full Professor of Public Administration at Ruhr-University Bochum and from 1997–2002 he was Full Professor of Economics at European University Viadrtina at Frankfurt (Oder). He was visiting professor at Cornell University, Syracuse University, and American University, Washington, DC. He is editor-in-chief of the *Journal of Applied Social Science Studies* (*Schmollers Jahrbuch*). He has published in journals such as *European Economic Review, Industrial and Labor Relations Review, International Migration Review, Journal of European Social Policy, Journal of Human Resources, Journal of Comparative Economics, Journal of Conflict Resolution, Journal of Public Economics, Journal of Cross-Cultural Gerontology, Journal of Ethnic and Migration Studies, Population* and *Development Review*, and *Research in Labor Economics.*

Mary Bea Walker is Associate Director of the Education, Outreach, and Training (EOT) Division at the National Center for Supercomputing Applications (NCSA), University of Illinois at Urbana–Champaign (UIUC). Prior to joining NCSA in 1996, Walker was Training Director for the US Army Corps of Engineers Construction Engineering Research Laboratory, Assistant Dean and Director of Continuing Engineering Education for the UIUC College of Engineering, and Assistant Coordinator for Undergraduate Education in the UIUC College of Education. She has been NSCA's lead for the Department of Defense's Programming Environment and Training (PET) Program, and NCSA's senior academic lead for training for the US Army Research Laboratory DoD PET program site. Walker holds an Ed.D. in Adult and Continuing Education from UIUC and a Ph.D. in French literature from the University of Kentucky. She has published more than thirty papers on continuing professional development for engineers, scientists, and other practicing professionals in academia, government, and industry.

Sociologist **Barry Wellman** learned to keypunch in a Harvard basement in 1965. He now heads the NetLab at the University of Toronto. Wellman founded the International Network for Social Network Analysis in 1976 and led it for a dozen years. He recently chaired the Community and Urban Sociology section of the American Sociology Association and was the first keynote speaker of the Association of Internet Research's keynote conference. Professor Wellman has added the study of virtual community and computer-supported cooperative work to his continuing interests in community, social support, and social networks. He recently edited *Networks in the Global Village* and co-edited *Social Structures: A Network Approach*. He is currently writing about living wired in a network society. http://www.chass.utoronto.ca/~wellman/

James C. Witte (Ph.D., Harvard University, 1991) is an Associate Professor of Sociology at Clemson University. Before moving to Clemson University, Witte was an Assistant Professor at Northwestern University and before that a postdoctoral fellow at the Carolina Population Center at the University of North Carolina at Chapel Hill. He was also a research fellow at the DIW Berlin (German Institute for Economic Research). Witte's areas of interest include the sociology of the Internet, economy and society, and research methods. Witte was the principal investigator for the National Geographic Society's web-based survey, Survey2000 and also principal investigator for the National Science Foundation funded follow-up study, Survey2001, which included a number of methodological experiments and a parallel telephone survey. Witte's other research includes work on developing multi-dimensional, longitudinal class models and analyses of the German vocational education system and declining fertility rates in East Germany after unification.

Foreword

The Virtual Community in the Real World

Howard Rheingold

Now that the authors of this volume (and many other social scientists around the world) have established a solid foundation of systematic observation and theory about the ways the Internet influences everyday life, perhaps we won't have to rely on data-free philosophizing to make policy decisions as citizens and societies.

Until recently, individuals and policy-makers have been making decisions about personal use and societal regulation of the Internet amidst a scarcity of science and abundance of rumor and sensationalism. Since the early 1990s, popular concerns, images, and delusions, as reflected in and molded by mass-media journalism and online folklore, have outpaced systematic studies of social cyberspace. The quality of contemporary cyberspace studies today leads me to suspect that social scientists have pulled ahead of anecdotal evidence and armchair theorizing to provide significant answers to some of society's most important questions about social behavior via online media.

No population that seeks to govern itself can hope to do so for long without good information and widespread debate about how to address the issues of the day. For some time, the place of the Internet in everyday life has been one of the most important issues of the day. Unfortunately, good information was hard to come by until recently, and as a consequence, the level of debate took a long time to evolve. Good information is now available, but it's still drowned out by the noise. The next step is getting that news out. Good information only becomes popular information when it diffuses beyond the population

of specialists who first find it. I hope it's not too late for more people
to raise the quality of the questions they are asking.

Since the 1990s, I have been asked the same questions in many
places:

- Does using the Internet make people happier or unhappier?
- Is the Internet empowering, or is it a tool of social control?
- Is the Internet addicting?
- Does virtual community erode face to face community?

These were natural questions. It took me years and many conversations with some of the authors of this volume to realize that the
questions themselves were the first problem to solve:

- Is the Internet empowering to which specific groups of people and
  under what circumstances, and by whose definition of "power?"
- Which people, in what contexts, are getting happier or unhappier?
  And in exactly what manner did these specified groups of people
  use the Internet?
- What do we expect from the word "community," and for whom,
  precisely, do we expect it?
- Are there more usefully specific terms than "community" to
  describe human relationships in the alphabet-printing-press-
  telephone-Internet-enabled era?
- How do we want to define "we" in this context, and who does the
  defining?
- How have previous communication technologies, from the alpha-
  bet and printing press to the telephone and Internet, enabled social
  changes in traditional (i.e., pre-new-technology) families, social
  networks, neighborhoods, villages, nations?

People and our circumstances are too different from city to city and
continent to continent to generalize about how anything affects them
in more than a general way. Most importantly, what data do we have
to support different hypotheses regarding these issues, once the issues
are stated specifically enough? What methodology was used to gather
that data?

The current volume provides useful answers. More importantly, it
frames the right kinds of questions about the ways in which the use
of Internet-enabled media affect everyday lives. Each chapter in this
volume should stimulate others to ask even more specific questions,
as all good research should.

Series Editor's Preface

The Internet and the Network Society

Manuel Castells

This book is precious. It provides us with reliable, scholarly research on the hows and whats of the Internet as it relates to people's lives. The critical importance of the Internet as a new medium of communication is only surpassed by the amount of fantasy and gossip that surround its development. At the end of 2001 the number of Internet users in the world has crossed the threshold of 500 million (up from 16 million in 1996), and in North America and Scandinavia over 60 percent of the population has access to the Internet. While the digital divide is still a fundamental source of inequality on the planet, the Internet is rapidly becoming part of the fabric of our lives, not only in advanced societies but in the core activities and dominant social groups in most of the world. Yet, its perception in the public opinion continues to be dominated by misrepresentations induced by futurologists and business consultants. It is about time for academic researchers to set the record straight, engaging into the exploration of a new society, our society, the network society.

The network society is precisely that: a social structure built on networks. But not any kind of networks, since social networks have been an important dimension of social life since the origins of humankind. The networks that characterize contemporary social organization are information networks powered by microelectronics-based information technology. This is most easily perceived in the new, global economy. It is an economy characterized by the dominance of interdependent global financial markets, operated by electronic networks processing information at high speed, handling huge volumes of transactions in a pattern of extraordinary complexity. It is also an economy where the

core activities of management, production, and distribution of goods
and services are equally organized around electronic networks that
simultaneously coordinate decision-making and decentralize production and distribution throughout the planet. Business is organized
around projects, that bring together various firms, and segments of
firms, to accomplish a given task, then reorganizing themselves to
undertake the next project, in an endless process of organizational
reconfiguration. This is the network enterprise, that brings together
intranets and extranets, that connects labor under different labor relationships, and that constitutes the operating system of the information
economy.

Cultural expressions are increasingly captured in the electronic
hypertext of the multimedia system that is at the same time global and
local: global in its interaction, local in its sources of emission and in
the destination of its messages. Multidirectional networks are the stuff
of which the media world is made, the heart of the system of collective images and representations.

Governance becomes largely irrelevant when confined within the
obsolete boundaries of the nation-state, but nation-states do not disappear: they transform themselves. They band together, forming coalitions and crystallizing these coalitions of interest into supra-national
and co-national institutions that allow them to manage the global
processes that constitute wealth and power in our world. They also
relate to their civil societies through a process of decentralization, at
the regional and local level, extended through non-governmental
organizations that become a new layer of the political system. Thus, a
new state, the network state, emerges as the form of the state in the
information age.

Social protest also comes to depend on networking capability on the
Internet, as shown by recent experiences of the women's movement,
the environmental movement, or the anti-globalization movement – a
global movement enacted by and with the Internet.

Sociability is also transformed by a combination of cultural change,
transformation of work, and technology. The crisis of patriarchalism,
and the self-centered character of personality systems in our societies,
combine with the individualization of labor and the fragmentation of
the work process to induce the rise of individualism as a predominant
pattern of behavior. But individualism is not social isolation or even
alienation, as superficial observers or nostalgic commentators often
suggest. It is a social pattern, it is a source of meaning, of meaning
constructed around the projects and desires of the individual. And it

finds in the Internet the proper technology for its expression and its organization. The emerging pattern is one of self-directed networking, both in terms of social relationships and in terms of social projects. It does not substitute for face-to-face sociability or for social participation. It adds to it, although it rarely counteracts forms of social disengagement derived from other causes. For instance, the crisis of political legitimacy is linked to the crisis of political parties and to the politics of scandal, and cannot be countered by the Internet. In fact, it may be deepened, as citizens find new forms of connection outside the institutional realm.

Thus, the Internet is the appropriate tool for networking, and for self-directed, horizontal communication. This is one the reasons (the other being technological, e.g. the worldwide web) why, after three decades of existence, it emerged from specialized communities in the world of researchers, techies, hackers, and countercultural communities, to catch fire in business and in society at large.

Furthermore, if users are producers of technology, of all technologies, this is even more clearly the case for the Internet, due to the speed of its feedback effects. Thus, many of the Internet applications, including email, chat rooms, and group lists, were serendipitously developed by early users. This continues to be the case every day. So, rather than analyzing the impact of the Internet on society, the key issue is to understand the effect of society on the Internet. However, the Internet is not just a tool, it is an essential medium for the network society to unfold its logic. This is a clear case of co-evolution between technology and society. As for the content of this co-evolution, it is by investigating along the lines suggested in this volume that we will be able to assess its contour and its implications. The network is the message, and the Internet is the messenger.

Part I

Moving the Internet out of Cyberspace

The Internet in Everyday Life

An Introduction

Caroline Haythornthwaite
and Barry Wellman

Abstract

The changing presence of the Internet from a medium for elites to one in common use in our everyday lives raises important questions about its impact on access to resources, social interaction, and commitment to local community. This book brings together studies that cover the impact of "the Internet" in everyday life in the United States, Canada, Britain, Germany, India, Japan, and globally. These studies show the Internet as a complex landscape of applications, purposes, and users. This introduction begins by summarizing results from studies in this book and other recent research to provide an overview of the Internet population and its activities – statistics that help define and articulate the nature of the digital divide. We move from there to consideration of the social consequences of adding Internet activity to our daily lives, exploring how use of the Internet affects traditional social and communal behaviors such as communication with local family and commitment to geographical communities. We conclude with a look at how these studies also reveal the integration of the Internet in our everyday lives.

Authors' note

We appreciate the help in compiling Internet data provided by Wenhong Chen, Uzma Jalaluddin, Monica Prijatelj, Uyen Quach, and Nathaniel Simpson. Our research has been supported by the Social Science and Humanities Research Council of Canada, Communications and Information Technology Ontario, IBM's Institute for Knowledge Management, the Office of Learning Technology (Human Resources Development Canada), Mitel Networks, and the University of Illinois Research Board. We give heartfelt thanks for the patience and support provided by Beverly Wellman to Barry Wellman, and by Alvan and Gillian Bregman to Caroline Haythornthwaite.

The Dazzling Light

This book is about the second age of the Internet as it descends from the firmament and becomes embedded in everyday life. In the early 1990s, the first age of the Internet was a bright light shining above everyday concerns. It was a technological marvel bringing a new Enlightenment to transform the world, just as the printing press fostered the original Enlightenment a half-millennium ago in Renaissance times (McLuhan, 1962). As John Perry Barlow wrote in 1995, a long time ago as Internet trends go,

> With the development of the Internet, and with the increasing pervasiveness of communication between networked computers, we are in the middle of the most transforming technological event since the capture of fire. I used to think that it was just the biggest thing since Gutenberg, but now I think you have to go back farther. (p. 36)

In those early days, the Internet was exciting because it was new and special. All things seemed possible. Internet initiates became avantgarde elites. While they extolled the virtues of the great changes in human endeavor to result from the Internet, others voiced grave concerns about these same changes. The very term "Internet" became a kind of "garbage can" – a receptacle for both fame and infamy relating to any electronic activity or societal change.

In the euphoria, many analysts lost their perspective. Most discussion of the Internet followed three types, making headlines even in reputable newspapers:

1 Announcements of technological developments, coupled with pronouncements of how this was going to change everybody's lives (at least the lives of everyone in Silicon Valley who could afford it, with the rest of the world following soon afterward). Travelers' tales, as if to the darkest Amazon, providing anecdotes about the weird and wonderful ways of Internet life, from cyber sex changes to the annual Burning Man ritual celebrations of technology in the Nevada desert (see http://www.zpub.com/burn/; Sterling, 1996)
2 Cautionary tales about the evils of wired life. Psychologists diagnosed "Internet addiction" on the basis of a few obsessive patients, and impersonators faked identities to "cyber-rape" online through exchanging personal secrets (e.g., Dibbell, 1993, 1996; Van Gelder, 1985, 1996)

Extolling the Internet to be such a transforming phenomenon, many analysts forgot to view it in perspective. For example, their breathless enthusiasm for the Internet led them to forget that long distance community ties had been flourishing for a generation (Wellman, 1999). They also assumed that only things that happened on the Internet were relevant to understanding the Internet. For example, "group-ware" applications for people to work together usually assumed that all interactions would be online. Similarly, early studies of media use tended to consider only one medium, in isolation, and often relating to only one social context, rather than looking at use of all media and their multiple deployments (Haythornthwaite, 2001). Analyses have also often been implicitly (and somewhat Utopianly) egalitarian, rarely taking into account how differences in power and status affect how people communicate with each other. Throughout, analysts committed the fundamental sin of *particularism*, thinking of the Internet as a lived experience distinct from the rest of life. People were supposed to be immersed in online worlds unto themselves, separate from everyday life (Rheingold, 1993). Jacked into "cyberspace" (Gibson, 1984), their "second selves" would take over (Turkle, 1984). "Avatars" (cartoon bodies) would more accurately represent their inner, cyber-expressed personas (Webb, 2001). This often shaded into elitism, as only the small percentage of the technologically adept had the equipment, knowledge, desire and leisure to plunge so fully into cyber-space. Not surprisingly, these adepts were disproportionately white, middle-class, young adult men in major universities or organizations.

The reality of the Internet is more important than the dazzle

This all occurred a long time ago as Internet time goes. Just ask the once-mesmerized investors in technology stocks, who were blinded by the hyperlight until March 2000. The light has become less blind-ing, as dot.com flames dim down, special newspaper Internet sections disappear in the wake of instantly vanishing dot.com vanity ads, and the pages of *Wired* magazine (the *Vogue* of technoid trends) shrink 25 percent, from 240 pages in September 1996 to 180 pages in September 2001. The rapid contraction of the dot.com economy has brought down to earth the once-euphoric belief in the infinite possibility of Internet life.

It is not as if the Internet disappeared. Instead, the light that dazzled overhead has become embedded in everyday things. A reality check is now underway about where the Internet fits into the ways in which people behave offline as well as online. We are moving from a world of Internet wizards to a world of ordinary people routinely using the Internet as an embedded part of their lives. It has become clear that the Internet is a very important thing, but not a special thing. In fact, it is being used more – by more people, in more countries, in more different ways (table I.1). Use is no longer dominated by white, young, North American men; access and use has diffused to the rest of the population and the rest of the world. Of these users,

- Almost all use email, with email rapidly becoming more used than the telephone.
- Almost all web surf. Moreover, web-surfers are spending more time online and using the Internet more often. In September 2001, Internet users spent an average of 10 hours and 19 minutes online, up 7 percent from the nine hours and 14 minutes recorded a year earlier (Macaluso, 2001).
- Many shop. E-commerce sales in the US for 2001 are estimated at $32.6 billion dollars, up 19 percent from 2000. However they still account for only 1.0 percent of total sales (Pastore, 2002).
- Usenet members participated in more than 80,000 topic-oriented collective discussion groups in 2000. More than eight million participants posted 151 million messages (Marc Smith, personal communication, August 10, 2001; see also Smith, 1999; Dodger, 2001). This is more than three times the number identified on January 27, 1996 (Southwick, 1996).
- Although only a smaller percentage of Internet users play online games, their sheer numbers are enough to sustain a sizeable industry.
- Although data are hard to come by, Internet telephone accounts for 5.5 percent of international traffic in 2001 (ITU, 2001). Anecdotal evidence suggests there is a growing use of Internet phones in developing countries for connectivity within the countries and to overseas diasporas (Fernández-Maldonado, 2001; Christina Courtright, personal communication).

This book is a harbinger of a new way of thinking about the Internet: not as a special system but as routinely incorporated into everyday life. Unlike the many books and articles about cyber-this and cyber-that, this book represents the more important fact that the Internet is becoming embedded in everyday life. Already, a majority

Table 1.1   The top ten most popular Internet activities in the US, 2000

Activity	% of Internet users
1 Web-surfing or browsing	81.7
2 Email	81.6
3 Finding hobby information	57.2
4 Reading news	56.6
5 Finding entertainment information	54.3
6 Buying online	50.7
7 Finding travel information	45.8
8 Using instant messaging	39.6
9 Finding medical information	36.6
10 Playing games	33.0

Source: UCLA Internet Report: Surveying the Digital Future (US)

of North Americans are using the Internet, and the rest of the developed world will soon be there. In the developing world, community centers and cybercafes are helping the Internet move from an elite preserve to a way in which ordinary people can do business and chat with friends, quickly and cheaply (Fernández-Maldonado, 2001).

This pervasive, real-world Internet does not function on its own, but is embedded in the real-life things that people do. Just as all-Internet commerce is being supplanted by "clicks-and-mortars" (physical stores integrated with online activity), so too is most online community becoming one of the many ways in which people are connected – through face-to-face, phone and even postal contact. Now, the Internet is routinely used in both old and familiar ways, and new, innovative ones.

As the Internet becomes part of everyday existence and as exploiting it no longer seems to be the key to earning zillions, it is starting to be taken for granted. It is in danger of being ignored as boring just as the telephone was ignored for half a century even while it enhanced the ability of people to work and find community with others over long distances. Ignoring the Internet is as huge a mistake as seeing it as a savior. It is the boringness and routineness that makes the Internet important because this means that it is being pervasively incorporated into people's lives. It is time for more differentiated analyses of the Internet that take into account how it has increasingly become embedded in everyday life.

The master issue in this book is whether the Internet – that brave new cyberworld – is drawing us away from everyday life or adding layers of connectivity and opportunity? Is it supporting new forms of human relationships or reproducing existing patterns of behavior?

- *Domestic relations:* Is the Internet providing new means of connectivity, or as Nie, Hillygus, and Erbring argue here, sucking people away from husbands, wives and children?
- *Community:* Is the lure of the Internet keeping people indoors so that their in-person (and even telephone) relationships with friends, neighbors, and kinfolk wither? Or is it enhancing connectivity so much that there is more interaction than ever before?
- *Civic involvements:* Does the Internet disconnect people from collective, civic enterprises so that they are connecting alone, as Robert Putnam (2000) has argued? Or is it leading people to new organizations and to increased involvement with existing organizations?
- *Alienation:* Is the Internet so stressful or disconnecting from daily life that people feel alienated? Or, does their sense of community increase because of the interactions they have online?
- *Activities:* Is the Internet replacing or enhancing everyday pursuits, be it shopping or getting companionship and social support?
- *Work:* What happens when people move home to work online? How does their connectivity with peers, clients, and their employing organizations change?

Such questions challenge us to build a picture of Internet use that separates the impact of the Internet from our existing behaviors, yet integrates its use with these behaviors. Much existing research on computer-mediated communication and online behavior has laid out differences between computer-mediated and face-to-face communication, and provided in-depth reports on online communities. While important research has been done from this perspective, the concentration on computer-mediated versus face-to-face, online versus offline, and virtual versus real, has perpetuated a dichotomized view of human behavior. Such either/or dichotomies pit one form of computer-mediated communication against another, e.g. synchronous versus asynchronous communication (e.g., chat versus email), text versus graphics, as well as one category of human endeavor against another, such as computer use at work versus home, online content for adults versus children, and computer and Internet users versus non-users. A growing body of research – including the work presented here – is now examining more integrative views of computer mediated communication, looking at how online time fits with and complements other aspects of the individual's everyday life.[1]

Important trends are intersecting with the impact of the Internet on people's everyday lives:

- *Increasing access*: A rapid increase in the number of users gaining access to and using the Internet: for example, Katz, Rice, and Aspden (2001) found 8 percent of their sample using the Internet in 1995 (sample of 2,500 adults in the US) and 65 percent in 2000 (sample of 1,305 adults).
- *Increasing commitment:* Users of the Internet are showing an increasing exposure and commitment to Internet-based activity. They are spending more time online and doing more types of things. Furthermore, the more years they use the Internet, the more involved they are (Chen, Boase, and Wellman; Howard, Rainie, and Jones; Nie, Hillygus and Erbring; see also Horrigan and Rainie, 2002). Current estimates put the average American using the Internet over nine hours a week (UCLA Center for Communication Policy (CCP), 2000; Horrigan and Rainie, 2002)
- *Domestication:* While a large proportion of Internet use is work related (UCLA CCP, 2000), the use of the Internet at home is increasing its "domestication"(Anderson and Tracey; Chen, Boase, and Wellman; Haythornthwaite and Kazmer; Nie, Hillygus, and Erbring; Salaff; see also Kraut, Kiesler, Mukhopadhyay, Scherlis, and Patterson, 1998).
- *Longer work hours:* People are not only using the Internet from home (and to a lesser extent from public places such as cybercafes), they are bringing their work home. Wired Silas Marners are increasing their work days to nights and weekends. The question remains: Is the use of the Internet at home bringing families together or diverting individuals from household relationships? (Nie, Hillygus, and Erbring; Salaff; Scabner, 2001; see also Horrigan and Rainie, 2002; Nie and Erbring, 2000).

1 For reviews of research on computer-mediated communication see DiMaggio, Hargittai, Neuman, and Robinson 2001; Haythornthwaite, Wellman, and Garton, 1998; Jones, 1995, 1998; Kiesler, 1997; Lievrouw, Bucy, Finn, Frindte, Gershon, Haythornthwaite, Kohler, Metz, and Sundar, 2001; Smith and Kollock, 1999; Wellman and Gulia, 1999; Wellman, 2001; Wellman, Salaff, Dimitrova, Garton, Gulia, and Haythornthwaite, 1996.

- *School work:* Using the Internet in conjunction with school work by adult learners, university students, and households with children (Hampton and Wellman, 2002; Haythornthwaite and Kazmer; Kraut, Kiesler, Mukhopadhyay, Scherlis, and Patterson, 1998). Presence of children in the household is cited as a key reason many adults invest in computers and Internet access. For example, Statistics Canada (2000) reports a much higher rate of interest in and connection to the Internet among households with unmarried children under 18: 59 percent of Canadian single-family households with unmarried children under 18 were connected to the Internet in 1999, compared to 39 percent for other single-family households. In 1999, 40 percent of households with children were connected from home, nearly twice the proportion in 1997.
- *Keeping up:* Dealing with a need to "keep up," reported by non-users as the number one reason for becoming an Internet user (Katz and Aspden, 1997; Katz and Rice; Kraut, Kiesler et al., 1998). For example, half of those North Americans who are not online say they would like to be if they had the funds and the ability (Reddick, Boucher, and Groseillers, 2000; Wellman, Wilkes, Fong, and Kew, 2002).
- *A networked society:* A move from a group-based society to a networked society (Castells, 2000; Putnam, 2000; Wellman, 2001). Rather than functioning in discrete, bounded groups – at home, in the community, at work, in organizations – people move as individuals between various fuzzily bounded networks.

This book brings together studies from the United States – the mother ship of the Internet – as well as Canada, Britain, Germany, India, Japan, and globally that examine the impact of "the Internet" in everyday life. The authors have in common the acceptance of the wholeness of human experience, and the idea that the Internet cannot be separated from ongoing activity. They take an integrative approach, using empirical research to assess the Internet as a social phenomenon.

The book shows that the Internet is a complex landscape of applications and purposes, and users. It helps to build a picture that situates Internet use in the rest of peoples' lives, including the friends with whom they interact, the technologies they have around them, their "lifestage and lifestyle" (Anderson and Tracey), and their offline community (see Chen, Boase, and Wellman; Hampton and Wellman; Kavanaugh and Patterson; Matei and Ball-Rokeach; Quan-Haase and Wellman). To keep things manageable in size and coherent in content, we have deliberately excluded studies of work and workplaces, except for Salaff's study of how teleworkers operate from their homes.

Understanding people's Internet use must take into account people's non-Internet attributes and behavior. For example, it is neither accidental nor trivial that men with higher incomes and higher education levels were the early adopters of the Internet, and that their lifestyles set some of the norms ("netiquette") for behavior online (see also Boneva and Kraut). Multiple interactions and responsibilities, both online and offline, compose people's activities, relationships, and community. We want to identify patterns of successful integration (see Howard, Rainie, and Jones; Haythornthwaite and Kazmer; Salaff) as well as unsuccessful patterns (e.g., Kraut, Patterson, Lundmark, Kiesler, Mukhopadhyay, and Scherlis, 1998).

Moreover, our picture and our task are not complete without also considering those who do not have access to the Internet, who use it little, or who have lost access to it (Chen, Boase, and Wellman; Katz and Rice). It is important to examine how the increasing presence and importance of the Internet in the everyday lives of those with access separates others from the ongoing social, economic, and commercial activity the Internet supports, and creates or perpetuates an existing social divide.

In the rest of this introductory chapter, we provide an overview of the Internet in everyday life based on the research presented in this book (see table I.2) and in other recent studies. We begin with a look at who is online. This also shows who is coming online and who has not yet come online, and what they are doing online. Access and use statistics help define and articulate the nature of the digital divide. We move from there to the social consequences of adding Internet activity to our daily lives, exploring how use of the Internet affects traditional social and communal behaviors, such as communication with local family and commitment to geographical communities. We conclude with a look at how the Internet is integrating into our everyday lives, and transforming them.

Concerns about the Digital Divide

The size of the Internet population

With well over 500 million Internet users (Nua, 2002) at the time of writing (early 2002; the number surely will be higher by the time you

Table I.2 Studies, countries, chapter authors, and websites

Study name	Country	Chapter authors	Website
Blacksburg Electronic Village	US	Kavanaugh and Patterson	http://www.bev.net//research/
Digital Living	UK	Anderson and Tracey	http://www.essex.ac.uk/chimera/people/ben_anderson.html
German Socio-economic Panel (GSOEP)	Germany	Wagner, Pischner, and Haisken-DeNew	http://www.diw.de/english/sop/aktuelles/stata.html
Homenet	US	Boneva and Kraut	http://homenet.hcii.cs.cmu.edu/progress/index.html
LEEP Distance Education	US	Haythornthwaite and Kazmer	http://www.lis.uiuc.edu/gslis/degrees/leep.html
Metamorphosis	US	Matei and Ball-Rokeach	http://www.metamorph.org/
National Geographic Survey 2000	Canada Global	Quan-Haase and Wellman; Chen, Boase and Wellman	http://www.nationalgeographic.com
Netville Wired Suburb	Canada	Hampton and Wellman	http://www.chass.utoronto.ca/~wellman http://web.mit.edu/knh/www/
Pew Internet and American Life	US	Howard, Rainie, and Jones; Boneva and Kraut	http://www.pewinternet.org/
Science and Technology in the Third World	India	Davidson, Sooryamoorthy, and Shrum	http://www.lsu.edu/sociology/faculty/shrum.html
Social Support for Japanese Mothers	Japan	Miyata	http://www.meijigakuin.ac.jp/~miyata/
Stanford Institute for the Quantitative Study of Society (SIQSS) Internet and Society Study	US	Nie, Hillygus, and Erbring	http://www.stanford.edu/group/siqss/
Syntopia	US	Katz and Rice	http://www.scils.rutgers.edu/~rrice/syntopia.htm
Technology Research Group	US	Copher, Kanfer, and Walker	http://archive.ncsa.uiuc.edu/edu/trg/
UCLA Center for Communication Policy World Internet	US	Lunn and Suman	http://ccp.ucla.edu/pages/internet-report.asp
University of Maryland WebUse Data Archives	US	Robinson, Kestnbaum, Neustadtl and Alvarez; Neustadtl et al.	http://www.webuse.umd.edu/

are reading this), the Internet is no longer the expensive high-tech toy of corporate elites and university professors. It has become the routine appliance of a large chunk of the developed world and a sizeable portion of the developing world (Chen, Boase, and Wellman). Even those who do not use the Internet themselves, benefit indirectly: Friends relay messages from other friends; children abroad use the Internet phone to speak to family in the home country; parents ask children to search the web for shopping information; gossip revolves around news gleaned online.

That the Internet is here to stay and spreading rapidly creates a pressing need to understand and prepare for its impact. The statistics available about the Internet, and those presented in many of the studies in this volume, document the rapid growth in use of the Internet. An "educated guess" (Nua, 2002) places the number of Internet users at 513 million for August 2001, up from 16 million in December 1995. (Nielsen NetRatings, 2002, while in rough accord with these figures puts the number of [undefined] "active users" at 260,112,760.) The users comprise 181 million from the US and Canada (35 percent), 155 million from Europe (30 percent) and 144 million from Asia/Pacific (28 percent).

Nua's compilation of Internet use data (table I.3) shows that 166 million Americans have Internet access, 60 percent of the population. Somewhat earlier reports show 55 percent online on a typical day (Howard, Rainie, and Jones), and 55,000 new users each day (UCLA CCP, 2000); 65 percent of US households have a computer, 43 percent with access to the Internet, and 55 percent of Americans with access to the Internet from home or elsewhere (Nie and Erbring, 2000). Canadians have similar profiles: 14 million use the Internet, 46 percent of the population. Somewhat earlier data showed 4.9 million Canadian households with an individual who used the Internet from any location (42 percent of all households in 1999, compared to 29 percent in 1997), and 3.4 million households (29 percent) with use at home (compared to 16 percent in 1997; Statistics Canada, 2000).

The United States does not dominate Internet use nearly as much as it used to, with at least 64 percent of Internet users living elsewhere (Nua, 2001b). Other developed countries now also have high rates of use (table I.3): Sweden is the only country showing a higher percentage of users than the US: 64 percent of the Swedish population (5.6 million) are Internet users, followed by 55 percent in Denmark, 55 percent in Hong Kong, and 52 percent in Australia (note that the list is indicative, not comprehensive). In the United Kingdom (Britain), 33

Table 1.3 Number of people and % of population using the Internet, 1999 and 2001, selected countries

Country	Number of people using the Internet in 2001 (month)[b]	% of population using the Internet in 2001[b]	% of population using the Internet in 1999[a]
Argentina	3.88 m (July)	10.38	3
Australia	10.06 m (Aug.)	52.49	32
Brazil	11.94 m (July)	6.84	2
Bulgaria	585,000 (April)	7.59	2.57[b]
Canada	14.44 m (July)	45.71	36
China	26.50 m (July)	2.08	0.56[b]
Denmark	2.93 m (July)	54.74	28
Egypt	560,000 (Mar.)	0.81	0.6[b]
Finland	2.27[c] m (Aug.)	43.93[c]	33
France	11.70 m (Aug.)	19.65	10
Germany	28.64 m (Aug.)	34.49	19
Hong Kong	3.93 m (July)	54.5	25
India	5.00 m (Dec.)	0.49	0.2
Iran	250,000[c] (Dec.)	0.38[c]	0.15[b]
Iraq	125,000[c] (Dec.)	0.05[c]	NA
Israel	1.94 m (July)	17.12	16
Japan	47.08[c] m (Dec.)	37.2[c]	15
Kenya	200,000[c] (Dec.)	0.66[c]	0.16[b]
Mexico	3.42 m (July)	3.36	3
Norway	2.45 m (July)	54.4	45
Russia	9.20[c] m (Aug.)	6.3[c]	3.69[b]
Saudi Arabia	570,000 (Mar.)	2.5	0.52[b]
South Africa	2.40[c] m (Dec.)	5.53[c]	3.74[b]
South Korea	22.23 m (July)	46.4	21.33
Spain	7.38 m (July)	18.43	7
Sweden	5.64 m[c] (July)	63.55[c]	41
UK	33.00 m (June)	55.32	21
US	166.14 m (Aug.)	59.75	40

Source: [a] World Employment Report 2001: *Life at Work in the Information Economy*. International Labor Office, Geneva, Switzerland, 2001.
[b] Nua, http://www.nua.ie/surveys/how_many_online/. [c] Data available for 2000 only.

million people have access (Nua, 2002), comprising 55 percent of the population. Somewhat earlier data shows 20.5 million UK adults with home access in 2000, 80 percent of whom had accessed the Internet in the last month (National Statistics Omnibus, 2000), three times the number of households connected in 1998. And, although some still consider South Korea to be a developing country, its Internet use is developed, with its 22 million users comprising 46 percent of the population.

The situation is more complex for developing countries (table I.3). Populous China and India show the danger of confusing percentages and absolute numbers: China has only 2 percent of the population online, but these total more than 26 million users. India's 0.5 percent of the population online nevertheless comprise 5 million users, almost the same number as Sweden. Brazil (7.6 percent, 11.9 million) and South Africa (5.5 percent; 2.4 million) have relatively high penetration rates. To be sure, some countries have tiny percentages and numbers of Internet users: Of the counties summarized in table I.3, Egypt, Iran, Iraq, Saudi Arabia, online users in each comprise less than 1 percent of the population and less than 1 million people.

Differences in use

Great though the percentages and numbers are in developed countries, they indicate that even in such countries a large proportion of people are not connected to the Internet, do not know about it, have no interest in using it, have no affordable access to it, or have poor infrastructural support for it. The large social phenomenon of the Internet is passing some by, and for better or worse, that sector is failing to gain access to the resources available to those with access to the Internet (Katz and Rice).

In the US, differences in access show rural and poor populations to be under represented in Internet access and use. This difference between the haves and have nots in Internet access has become known as the "digital divide" (see the Falling Through the Net series by the US National Telecommunications and Information Administration (NTIA), 2000, 2002; see also Sawney, 2000; Strover, forthcoming; Birdsall, 2000; Reddick, 2001; Wellman, Wilkes, Fong, and Kew, 2003).

The term has also been applied more globally to consider differences between the have and have not nations, or members of those nations (see Chen, Boase, and Wellman; Hargittai and Centeno, 2001). For example, Davidson, Sooryamoorthy and Shrum evocatively describe what it is like to use the Internet in Kerala, India, where a research center's phone connection may be two miles away, and where connectivity may be only "theoretical," e.g., a planned connection that is not yet available, an established connection that is not in working order, or a connection with a speed too slow for practical use. The arguments about the role of the Internet in developing countries that they describe may as easily be applied to any country. Is the Internet an "elixir" (an opportunity), or an "affliction" (an "engine of global inequality"), or is it merely suffering from "teething troubles" on its way to integration in everyday life (see Davidson, Sooryamoorthy, and Shrum)?

Although there is evidence that the digital divide in developed countries is shrinking (Chen, Boase, and Wellman; Wellman, Wilkes, Fong, and Kew, 2002), not all studies concur. Nie and Erbring (2000) find difference in access and use particularly pronounced across education and age, as do Wagner, Pischner, and Haisken-DeNew in Germany. Katz and Rice find that differences still persist across gender, age, household income, education and race, although these differences disappear after controlling for awareness of the Internet. They also find that for recent cohorts of adopters, differences across gender and race also disappear.

Moreover, the divide is not one line splitting people into two distinct groups, and is not bridged by one program or policy decision. Marginalized community members, whether marginalized by income, gender, race, or sexual orientation, have different needs with respect to the Internet. There is a need for an action research perspective to understand and ameliorate the needs of marginalized users and guide them through their own "teething troubles" (Mehra, Merkel, and Bishop, 2002; Pinkett, 2001).

Who is online?

Of those who have *access* to the Internet, US and Canadian users are almost evenly split between men and women, but with higher numbers of younger users, whites, urban, higher incomes, higher education levels, and more years of access (Howard, Rainie, and Jones; Kavanaugh and Patterson; Nie, Hillygus, and Erbring; Quan-Haase and Wellman; UCLA CCP, 2000; Nielsen NetRatings quoted in Nua, 2001a). Previously in North America – and currently in the rest of the world – more men than women are likely to use the Internet (Chen, Boase, and Wellman; Katz and Rice; National Statistics Omnibus, 2000).

The greatest change in Internet access over time is observed in the previously under-represented groups: Katz and Rice, comparing across cohorts of users in the US based on the year they began to use the Internet (from 1992 to 2000), find that the percentage of women, users over 40, lower income earners, and non-college graduates has increased most over these years (see also Nua, 2001a). Similarly, Statistics Canada (2000) reports the highest growth rate in Internet use and home connections for 1999 occurred in older age groups: households headed by seniors 65 and over, followed by households headed by individuals 55 to 64. However, their numbers still show fewer regular users in these households compared to younger households (one-tenth of households headed by adults over 65 had a regular Internet user, one-third for the 55–64 year olds, and one-half for younger households). Similarly, Nie and Erbring (2000) find much lower access among those over 65 compared to those under 65.

As statistics on access show a shrinking digital divide, differences in use become more important for understanding overall Internet activity. Howard, Rainie, and Jones show that on any particular day, of those who have access, more of the men, whites, higher income earners, higher educated and more experienced users are likely to be online. For example, 57 percent of men with access will be online compared to 52 percent of the women with access; 56 percent of whites compared to 36 percent of African–Americans, and 49 percent of Hispanics with access (see also Nua, 2001a). Thus, focusing on access alone masks continuing digital divide differences. Similarly, while access as a single measure suggests greater numbers of younger people online, older users are online for more hours. This may be because of use associated with work (UCLA CCP, 2000), and the way work hours have crept into home hours (Nie and Erbring, 2000). Yet, Anderson and Tracey find some British users of retirement age to be heavy users, and Nie and Erbring (2000) also find retired users spend nearly two hours more a week using the Internet than non-retired users.

Across all studies, the largest and most significant differences in access and use are related to years of experience. Those who have been online longer spend more time online each day, and are more likely to be online on any particular day. These *netizens* (Howard, Rainie, and Jones; see also Hauben, 1996; Schuler, 1997) represent the most active and accomplished users. They are the ones who engage in the most kinds of online activities (for specifics on activity differences across demographic characteristics, see the studies in this book; Nie and Erbring, 2000; UCLA CCP, 2000).

As several authors point out, since all users are getting more experience online, these advanced users potentially show the direction in which Internet use is evolving. Thus, they are an important group to watch. However, it is important to note that at this time in Internet history these users still represent early adopters, for even when a majority of the population use the Internet, many do not make skilled or regular use of it. Many studies have shown that behaviors and characteristics of such users differ from those of the later majority of adopters: early adopters are more cosmopolitan, more socially active, and have higher incomes and education (Rogers, 1995; Valente, 1995). Not coincidentally, these are characteristics of longtime Internet users. Indeed several authors point out that the positive social impacts of the Internet may reflect attributes of the users rather than any true impact of the Internet itself (see Nie, 2001; Howard, Rainie, and Jones). Thus, although an important leading group to watch, experienced users' patterns of use may not wholly predict use by later adopters.

Katz and Rice show two other levels at which the digital divide still operates, both of which are consistent with consideration of stages in the adoption of innovations and of adopter characteristics (Rogers, 1995). They describe how the digital divide operates at the level of *awareness* of the Internet. Awareness is the initial stage in individual adoption of an innovation, and thus a prerequisite for adoption. Those Americans more likely to be aware of the Internet are younger, male, higher income earners and white. Once awareness is achieved, Katz and Rice find no divide based on gender or race. Similarly, Nie and Erbring (2000), and Chen, Boase, and Wellman also find that once on the Internet how it is used looks similar across all users, in America and around the world.

The other level at which the digital divide still operates is *discontinuance*, dropping out of the Internet (Rogers, 1995). James Katz and associates present the only statistics we know of about dropouts (Katz and Rice; Katz, Rice, and Aspden, 2001; Katz and Aspden, 1997). They find that 8–11 percent of Internet users drop out each year for reasons such as lost access, insufficient interest, cost, and/or time. These are usually younger, less affluent and less educated users, but not proportionally more women or non-white users. Early discontinuance of an innovation is a characteristic of late adopters, as are lower social connectivity, income, and education levels (Rogers, 1995). These statistics show that considering access as a one-time event fails to capture the churn in Internet access and use, and the behaviors of only partially committed Internet users (Pinkett, 2001).

Churn also brings us back to the issue of the digital divide. Low-income users discontinue most often, and this may be because they lose the infrastructure that supports their use of the Internet, e.g., by losing their job, or by being unable to keep a telephone. As Jorge Schement (1998) notes: "Telephone penetration deserves special attention because it constitutes the access point to many of the new services, such as email and the Internet, associated with the new technologies" (online). Regardless of US federal policy regimes, African–Americans and Latinos have lagged behind whites in telephone penetration, an effect that "holds up even when one examines households within the same income" (Schement, 1998, online).

What are they using the Internet for?

It is clear that *email* and *searching for information* take high priority in Internet time (table I.1; Chen, Boase, and Wellman; Howard, Rainie, and Jones; Katz and Rice; National Statistics Omnibus, 2000; Nie and Erbring, 2000; Nie, Hillygus, and Erbring; Quan-Haase and Wellman; Statistics Canada, 2000; UCLA CCP, 2000). Well over 80 percent of users use the Internet for email, with an estimated 4 trillion email messages exchanged in the US in 1998, and 42 percent of Americans checking their email daily (UCLA CCP, 2000). Users rank email as the number one reason for being online (Katz and Aspden, 1997). The high use of email affirms Michael Strangelove's statement that "The Internet is not about technology, it is not about information, it is about communication – people talking to each other, people exchanging email . . . The Internet is a community of chronic communicators" (quoted in Putnam, 2000, p. 171).

The Internet's other main use is for seeking information, e.g., hobby, medical, sports, travel, news, or product information. Longtime users, new users, non-users and former users all rank this activity as number one or two as a reason for being online (Katz and Aspden, 1997). The UCLA report (UCLA CCP, 2000) found that two-thirds of users consider the Internet an important or extremely important source of information, with 80 percent using the Internet for web surfing and browsing, and with adults spending over a quarter of their time online looking for information.

Smaller, but still large, proportions of Internet users are engaging in e-commerce by shopping and buying products online: from 36 percent (SIQSS study, Nie and Erbring, 2000) to 51 percent (UCLA study) in the US, and 33 percent in Britain (National Statistics Omnibus, 2000). In Canada, 19 percent of households with access had bought goods or services on the Internet in 1999, up from 9 percent two years earlier (Statistics Canada, 2000). Lunn and Suman explore what predicts online shopping behavior. Among the important factors are experience with the Internet, and with remote shopping: already being accustomed to ordering through catalogs or by phone. They find that men spend three times as much as women do online, although they caution that this too may be confounded with experience since men in their study had nearly seven months more experience online than the women.

While some studies find little difference in what people do online once they have access (Nie and Erbring, 2000; Katz and Rice; Chen, Boase, and Wellman; Quan-Haase and Wellman), others find differences by gender, age, and race. The gender differences that are observed do not appear uniformly across studies. The Pew studies (Howard, Rainie, and Jones) find that men are more likely than women to be using the Internet to seek news, product, financial or hobby information, or to do work-related research. The UCLA studies concur that men spend more time on commerce activities such as purchasing, banking, and auctions, but also find that women spend slightly more time on work-related activities (UCLA CCP, 2000; see also Lunn and Suman). The Homenet studies suggest that women carry offline communication behaviors online. They are also more likely to use email for expressive rather than instrumental communication: to exchange small talk and engage in relationship-building communications (Boneva and Kraut).

Women also continue the offline characteristic of being the ones responsible for maintaining ties with kin (Boneva and Kraut; see also Haythornthwaite and Kazmer). Howard, Rainie, and Jones did not find major differences between men and women in use of email, but did find 49 percent of whites send and read email on a typical day compared to 27 percent of African–Americans in their sample. Nie and Erbring (2000) also note that use of anonymous chat rooms is an activity for the young, with usage substantially lower for those older than 25. Chen, Boase, and Wellman sum the situation up well: Although there is an overall similarity in the general nature of what different demographic types do online – most email and web surf, there are important differences in the specifics of what they do.

How much time do they spend online?

All researchers agree that using the Internet takes time, 9.4 hours a week on average in one US estimate (including work; UCLA CCP, 2000). Work-age US users spend the most time online, with those from 19–55 averaging over 9 hours a week, peaking at 11 hours a week among those 25–35 years of age. Younger and older users spend less time online, with 12–15 year olds using the Internet the least at just under 6 hours a week, and those over 65 using it for just under 7 hours a week. In the UK, time online appears to be much lower, at 1 to 3 hours a week across all age groups (Anderson and Tracey).

The number of hours online per week increases sharply with number of years using the Internet: from 6 hours a week for those with less than 1 year of experience, to over 16 hours a week for those with over 4 years experience (UCLA CCP, 2000). Activities and reasons for being online also change with experience. Some users progress from being online "for fun" and playing games to being online for a specific reason, and using it to accomplish personal or professional work (Chen, Boase, and Wellman; Howard, Rainie, and Jones).

Adding Internet based activities to daily life requires a redistribution of limited personal resources of time and effort. Nie and Erbring (2000) find that significant changes in individuals' lives appear when use exceeds 5 hours a week, and this includes approximately 36 percent of Internet users in their sample. To accommodate these hours, other activities are displaced. Time may be "stolen" from local face-to-face exchanges and given to distant friends, "stolen" from the phone and given to email, and "stolen" from now with promise of return later. This change is not without controversy. Spending time communicating via email with distant friends and relatives, takes time from local activity. The controversy is not whether we do take time, but whether taking this time has positive or negative consequences. Expending our social resources on maintaining ties with distant others, or with people we meet only online, may compromise local social relationships, which in turn may compromise individual well-being (Kraut, Patterson, et al., 1998).

The Internet can also affect family relationships as different members of the family change focus or develop expertise. For example, Kraut et al. (1998) found that teenagers in their sample of households used the Internet more than other household members. Their sample consisted of households in their first one to two years of Internet use in households that had not had Internet access before. For the same sample, Kiesler et al. (2000) found teens playing a major role in help seeking and help giving relating to the technical features of the Internet and acting as the technological gurus for the household.

Another possibility is that the Internet may help people make connections to others: gaining another source of companionship, emotional support, help with jobs, and so on, and may fill a void for those who currently operate in an alienating face-to-face environment. Yet another possibility is that the Internet does not embody any dramatic change in behavior, but instead exaggerates what we do already: for example, increasing circles of friends for the outgoing and successful among us, and decreasing social circles for the rest. Indeed, Kraut et al.'s more recent study (Kraut, Kiesler, Boneva, Cummings, Helgeson, and Crawford, 2002) suggests this. Their three-year follow-up of Homenet users found positive effects of using the Internet, but with better outcomes for extroverts than introverts

Sorting out the actual impact of Internet use on social interaction is the second major area addressed in the studies presented here. We turn to this issue next.

Concerns about Social Interaction

We cannot expect to add 16+ hours of Internet time a week to our daily lives (as do users with over four years experience; UCLA CCP, 2000) without changing some patterns of our behavior. As Nie (2001) questions, and as many of the studies in this book examine, when Internet hours are added to already full schedules, what things get dropped? (See Anderson and Tracey; Copher, Kanfer, and Walker; Haythornthwaite and Kazmer; Nie, Hillygus, and Erbring; Robinson, Kestnbaum, Neustadtl, and Alavarez; Salaff.)

One place Internet hours come from is time previously used to watch television: Internet users spend 28 percent less time watching television than non-users, approximately 4.6 hours a week (UCLA CCP, 2000; see also Kraut, Patterson et al., 1998, and Putnam, 2000 for television watching). While UCLA CCP (2000) find that their users reported spending the same amount of time reading books and newspapers, and talking on the phone, Nie and Erbring (2000) find heavy Internet users cut back on use of all traditional media (television, newspapers, phone to friends and family), as well as shopping in stores and commuting in traffic. Looking in more detail, Anderson and Tracey report a long list of activities that are potentially displaced, but found impacts were marginal at best on watching television, gardening, reading newspapers, magazines and books, shopping, telephoning, going to the pub, doing nothing, writing letters, sleeping, playing computer games, and typing on a typewriter. Wagner, Pischner, and Haisken-DeNew find that teenagers' use of the Internet does not take away from the more socially acceptable activities of reading or playing sports. Instead, they find that "computer kids" are less likely to engage in the less socially accepted activities of just hanging around or doing nothing. Similarly, Robinson, Kestnbaum, Neustadtl, and Alavarez find that Internet users show a more active lifestyle than non-users, including less sleep, and more social contact with friends and co-workers (although less time with their children).

A slightly different view can be found when looking at the Internet entering the home for a major undertaking, such as studying or working online. Haythornthwaite and Kazmer, and Salaff both discuss how people manage this type of undertaking. Haythornthwaite and Kazmer find that as time becomes constrained, online learners drop some activities first, while preserving others. First to go are relatively solitary activities such as television, reading for pleasure, needlework, and gardening; next are leisure activities with friends and work for volunteer groups; then work, sleep, and eating are compromised. Kept to the end are time with family (particularly children), and work for the educational program itself. Both Haythornthwaite and Kazmer, and Salaff find that managing the Internet at home requires defining boundaries – both temporal and spatial – so that users – and their work or learning activities – can be cordoned off from the activities and presence of others. Learners and workers at home actively construct a barrier to social interaction because it is not obvious to others that the individual is "at work."

Although all studies report decreased time watching television, Internet users usually are more media connected than non-users. They are ahead in all categories except the percent using the television (tied at 97 percent of both users and non-users). Books are used by 12 percent more Internet users than non-users; video games, 15 percent;

recorded music, 22 percent; newspapers, 6 percent (note also that 57 percent of Internet users report reading news online as a key activity so this figure may under-represent overall use of newspapers); radio, 9 percent; and phone, 3 percent (UCLA CCP, 2000; see also Chen, Boase, and Wellman; Quan-Haase and Wellman). This may be a reflection of the higher education and income of Internet users, and it may also again indicate characteristics of the earlier adopters. Their pre-existing inclination to use media of all types, combined with familiarity and ease with these media, may have made it easier and less complex for them to adopt computing and the Internet (see Rogers, 1995). It may also have exposed them to information about the Internet earlier than others, positively enhancing their awareness of the Internet and precipitating earlier adoption.

One concern regarding all this time spent online is that the possibly solitary activity engendered by the Internet may displace time formerly spent on local social relations and have an adverse effect on individual well-being (Kraut et al., 1998; Nie, 2001). At another level of analysis, there is concern for the well-being of geographically defined communities when individuals spend their time on individual activities, or on interactions with people outside the area (Hampton and Wellman; Wellman, 1999). This concern has been cast in terms of the *social capital* that accrues to different communities according to the contributions from people who belong to the community, and is now best known through Robert Putnam's (2000) work *Bowling Alone*. Communities with high social capital, demonstrated and built through vibrant, face-to-face interaction in voluntary associations, provide a higher quality of life for their members (Kavanaugh and Patterson; Quan-Haase and Wellman).

Thus, there are questions about whether the Internet has a positive or negative effect on individual well-being, relations with others, and social capital building within communities (Hampton and Wellman; Katz and Rice; Kavanaugh and Patterson; Quan-Haase and Wellman). At present, the statistics do not provide a clear position, and can be interpreted to support or refute the claim that the Internet is a solitary activity, harmful to social relations with others. To make sense of this, it is necessary to find out about many aspects of individuals' behavior in regard to the Internet, including answers to questions such as:

- *Does being on the Internet mean being alone?* Does time online actually interfere with time with others or does it replace time spent in otherwise solitary or low-interaction activities? Do user's perceptions of the impact of their time on the Internet on interpersonal relations concur with that of their friends and family members?

- *What is the Internet's impact on friendships?* Are local friendships traded for distant ones or are distant ones added? Are strong, face-to-face interpersonal ties traded for weak, computer-mediated ones (Hampton and Wellman; Kraut et al., 1998; Wellman et al., 1996)?
- *Do the dynamics of social interactions on the Internet add to or detract from individual well-being?* Do they add to or detract from commitment to and participation in local community activities (Hampton and Wellman, 2000; Kavanaugh and Patterson; Putnam, 2000)? Do they increase, decrease or supplement social capital and commitment to community (Chen, Boase, and Wellman; Kraut et al., 1998; Quan-Haase and Wellman)?
- *Does the Internet perpetuate or exaggerate existing offline behavior,* such as increasing connectedness only for those with initially larger networks and better resources (Nie, 2001), increasing communication only among natural communicators (Boneva and Kraut)?
- *Should Internet behavior be considered separately from other aspects of individuals' lives* (all chapters)?

Some brief and initial answers to these questions follow, largely drawn from the studies presented in this book.

Does using the Internet mean being alone?

Being alone may mean sitting at a computer on your own and/or pursuing individual pursuits on the Internet. Yet, using the Internet generally means communicating with others, largely through email, so a good proportion of the time online is social. The UCLA study also suggests that Internet use may not always mean being alone at the computer: 47 percent of users report spending "at least some time each week using the Internet with other household members" (UCLA CCP, 2000, p. 29).

Being alone may also mean abandoning ties with those physically nearby. Individuals may feel this loss, as may the individuals with whom they no longer spend time. Most Internet users do not feel they are reducing time with others. Katz and Rice report that 88 percent of users consider the Internet to have had little impact on time with friends and family. Howard, Rainie, and Jones find that over half the users say they now have more communication with family (59 percent), and with their primary friend (60 percent), as well as nearly a third now having communication with a family member they did not previously contact often (31 percent). Quan-Haase and Wellman find no negative effects of frequent Internet use on an overall sense of community. Moreover, this study, as well as the global study by Chen, Boase, and Wellman, finds that frequent users add a heightened sense of online community to their existing overall sense of community. In the UCLA study, most users (92 percent) connected to the Internet at home say they spend the same amount or more time together with household members.

Being alone can also mean not having others to turn to in times of need. Yet, the Internet is also used to enhance social relations, both near and far. A number of studies point to increased contact with distant friends and relatives (Boneva and Kraut; Hampton and Wellman; Haythornthwaite and Kazmer; Kavanaugh and Patterson; Kraut et al., 1998; Miyata). Several studies also show how the Internet buffers stress for those who move away from family or friends, e.g., college students (LaRose, Eastin, and Gregg, 2001), or those who have moved to new homes (Hampton and Wellman). Online support groups also provide much needed support. For example, Miyata finds social support from membership and participation in online support groups for mothers decreases depression and increases well-being for both active participants and lurkers, although more so for those who are active.

By contrast, other results point to a decrease in sociability. Nie and Erbring (2000) find that the more time people spend online, the greater the percentage of individuals reporting decreased time spent with family and friends: from 4 percent with 1 hour of Internet use per week to 15 percent with more than 10 hours use. Nie, Hillygus, and Erbring estimate that each minute spent on the Internet during the last 24 hours corresponds to a reduction in time with family members of one-third of a minute. Similarly, the more time people spend online, the greater the percentage of individuals reporting decreased time talking on the phone with friends and family: from 9 percent with 1 hour of use to 27 percent with over 10 hours use (Nie and Erbring, 2000). No statistics are available on whether this is a switch from phone to email or a loss of contact altogether.

Also, although the UCLA study participants felt they spent the same or more time with others, Internet users socialize less with household members than do non-users, by close to 4 hours a week

(UCLA CCP, 2000; see also Nie, 2001, for some further discussion). Perhaps Internet users in the UCLA study were already low socializers, and adding Internet use interfered less with their socializing than it might for others. Perhaps the impact is only felt when people use the Internet a lot, e.g., over the 5 hours-a-week level at which Nie and Erbring (2000) find that behavior changes markedly. Other results suggest this may be the case: like the studies by Nie and associates, Kraut, Patterson, et al. (1998) also found that greater use of the Internet was associated with a decline in family communication.

Being alone may also be a judgment made by those who are abandoned while the Internet user spends time online. How do others view Internet user's time with them? The UCLA study found that 75 percent say they do *not* feel ignored by other household members spending too much time online (18 percent *do* sometimes feel ignored; 6 percent often ignored). This appears to be less isolating than television for which 63 percent report *not* feeling ignored by others' television habits (28 percent *do* sometimes feel ignored; 9 percent often ignored). However, we should take with a grain of salt a positive statement about one potentially isolating medium when it is compared to another medium that is also potentially isolating. After all, nearly one-quarter of those asked *do* feel ignored by their Internet-using household members. And, if we compare the numbers given above to those here, we find a disparity between user's perceptions of time spent with others and other's perceptions of being ignored: 92 percent of the users say they are not ignoring others, whereas only 75 percent of others do not feel ignored. Research has yet to explore fully what these sorts of numbers mean in people's lives.

What is the impact on contact with others, friendships, and civic engagement?

Being alone may mean not communicating with anyone, or not having friends and strong interpersonal relationships (Kraut et al., 1998). It may mean living your life almost totally online, having the Internet depress your relations with others, or having the Internet add to, and even multiply your relations with others through opportunities for new contacts or by bolstering existing ties.

Users in the UCLA study reported moderately increased contact with family and friends (as do Howard, Rainie, and Jones's users), and with professional colleagues; a small positive impact on contact with people who share their hobby or recreational activity; and negative impacts for contact with people who share their religion, or share their political beliefs (UCLA CCP, 2000).

Three chapters note that distance still matters, with more contact occurring with those close to home than far away (Hampton and Wellman; Quan-Haase and Wellman; Chen, Boase, and Wellman). These studies find that Internet contact neither increases nor decreases contact with people in person or on the telephone. It adds on to it, so that the more people use the Internet, the more overall contact they have with friends and relatives (see also Copher, Kanfer, and Walker's study of heavy versus light email users). Remarkably, this happens in developing countries, with their poor transportation infrastructures, as well as in developed countries (Chen, Boase, and Wellman). In North America, there are local benefits: Blacksburg Internet users report increased communication with members of formal social groups and with local friends (Kavanaugh and Patterson). Similarly, in Netville, those with high-speed Internet connections had much more informal contact with neighbors than did the non-wired; wired residents knew the names of 25 neighbors compared to 8 for the non-wired, and they made 50 percent more home visits (Hampton, 2001; Hampton and Wellman, 2002).

Being alone locally may be countered by new and enhanced social relations with others expressed via the Internet, and carried from the Internet to offline, face-to-face relationships. Many report high levels of contact with distant friends and relatives that seem attributable to the Internet (Boneva and Kraut; Chen, Boase, and Wellman; Hampton and Wellman; Haythornthwaite and Kazmer; Kavanaugh and Patterson; Kraut et al., 1998; Quan-Haase and Wellman). In the UCLA study, 26 percent of users say they have online friends they have not met in person; and 12 percent have met in person someone they first met online (UCLA CCP, 2000). In 1995, Katz and Rice found 12 percent of users had established friendships via the Internet, and 17 percent had met face-to-face at least once with someone they first met online; in 2000, 14 percent reported online friendships, and 10 percent had met someone offline. Yet such long-distance connectivity did not start with the Internet. Wellman's research group has been pointing out since 1979 that most strong ties with friends and relatives stretch beyond the neighborhood (Wellman, 1979, 1999; Wellman and Tindall, 1993; Wellman and Wortley, 1989, 1990).

It is also evident that connectivity seems to go to the connected: greater social benefit from the Internet accrues to those already well situated socially. As Nie (2001) points out, connectivity already goes to those with higher levels of income and education, and the greater connectivity seen in comparisons of Internet users to non-users may result from the pre-existing high connectivity levels of such people. Other studies also suggest that adding a new medium to communication repertoires is more likely when the relationship is already strong (Haythornthwaite, 2000; Haythornthwaite and Wellman, 1998; Koku, Nazer, and Wellman, 2001; Koku and Wellman, 2002). Frequent contact via the Internet is also associated with frequent contact via other means (Chen, Boase, and Wellman; Katz and Aspden, 1997; Quan-Haase and Wellman; Robinson, Kestnbaum, Neustadtl, and Alvarez). These studies show that the closer the work and/or friendship relationship, the more media people use to communicate. Thus, those who are highly socially connected, and likely within that set of connections to maintain higher numbers of stronger ties, are also more likely to be the ones adopting and using the Internet for communication and connectivity.

Existing connectivity levels may also have an impact on the success of more community-wide Internet initiatives. Quan-Haase and Wellman suggest that civic engagement via the Internet may be positively associated with higher levels of other forms of civic involvement. In a more focused study, Kavanaugh and Patterson find that high levels of community involvement are associated with more use of the Internet for interpersonal and group communication activities. In summarizing their results, they concur with an observation by Putnam that the success of their community network, the Blacksburg Electronic Village, may have been because it was established in an environment that already had high levels of connectivity, and that social capital may be a prerequisite rather than a consequence of effective computer-mediated communication (Kavanaugh and Patterson, citing Putnam, 2000).

Local connectivity – along with gender and Internet experience – affects who becomes more connected online. The chances of making a friend online increase substantially with increased belonging to a neighborhood, and with knowing a neighbor well enough to talk about a personal matter (Hampton and Wellman, 2002; Matei and Ball-Rokeach). Women, who traditionally maintain family ties, are more likely than men to maintain email connections with distant friends and relatives and to maintain larger networks of distant contacts (Boneva and Kraut). Experience also makes a difference. Those more familiar with Internet technologies are also more likely to make social connections. Using the Internet to communicate with others increases with years of use of the Internet (Chen, Boase, and Wellman; Kavanaugh and Patterson; Quan-Haase and Wellman) and increased confidence with the technologies (Haythornthwaite and Kazmer). Connecting with others may even include giving technical help to get distant relatives online so that contact can happen via email (Haythornthwaite and Kazmer).

Key to concerns about people's solitary and social behaviors is the well-supported finding that social contact, and its attendant access to emotional and material support resources, engenders personal well-being (see Kavanaugh and Patterson; Hampton and Wellman; Miyata; Kraut, Patterson et al., 1998). Does use of the Internet decrease personal well-being? The Kraut, Patterson, et al. study (1998) sounded an alarm about this problem. They found a clear association between higher Internet use and increases in depression. These authors cautioned that this result must be interpreted in the light of the age of participants (teenagers being higher Internet users in their study), and with attention to the direction of causation (were more depressed individuals using the Internet more because they were depressed or did the greater use make them depressed). Their results clearly indicate that concern for individual well-being and Internet use has a real foundation. Whether causal or correlational, this needs to be investigated further.

Just such an investigation has been done by LaRose, Eastin, and Gregg (2001). Results from a sample of college students, a mobile population less likely to have local social support, showed that Internet use was positively associated with receiving email from known others, which was in turn associated with greater social support. This support then had a mitigating effect on general stress and on depression. They also found a significant difference in "Internet self-efficacy" (the belief in one's ability to use the Internet successfully) between new and experienced users (less than two years experience and over two years). Those with more self-efficacy experienced less Internet stress (for example, stress associated with technical aspects of Internet use), a contributing factor to depression in their study.

Hampton and Wellman report that another mobile population, new home owners, fared better in maintaining social contacts when connected to the Internet at home than when not: those who were connected reported almost no change in social contact compared to a year before their move, while the non-connected experience a drop in contact. Such social contact will generate social support, easing the transition to a new neighborhood. Both of these studies show how the

Internet may help reduce depression for specific kinds of population, and suggest again the need for exploring Internet use in conjunction with people's lifestage, and not separate from it.

Finally, the most recent study of Homenet users (Kraut et al., 2002), who are now more experienced than when first studied, shows lower depression with higher Internet use, and no significant association with loneliness. They suggest, along with many authors in this book, that the integration of Internet use with everyday life – and the concomitant development of synergies between online and offline life – may provide beneficial outcomes.

Bringing It All Together

Dovetailing with everyday life

Much of the discussion of Internet use considers it as separate from people's lives, an add-on that interferes with "real-life" activity. How separate are Internet activities from other aspects of people's lives? Is it a stand-alone activity, or does it become no more separate than picking up the phone is separate from talking to family?

In considering the integration of the Internet into our daily lives, we need to remember that the Internet is a new social phenomenon, its current version in place now only since the 1990s. Even in this short period, Internet experience and time online changes behavior. We are watching an emerging phenomenon, not a mature one. At present, we see that types of use, time spent online, and connectivity to others all increase with the amount of time people have had access to and used Internet applications. We also find more synergies between different spheres of activity with increased years of experience. Kavanaugh and Patterson note an increase is "social capital building activities" with more years of access, including communication with close and distant friend, relatives, co-workers, and volunteer groups. Howard, Rainie, and Jones distinguish the more experienced "netizens" from others in the way they incorporate the Internet into both home and work life, and their comfort level in spending and managing their money online, and using email to enhance social relationships. Quan-Haase and Wellman show that the more time people spend online, the more they are involved with organizations and politics, offline as well as online, and find longer-term users have a higher sense of online community. And both Salaff, and Haythornthwaite and Kazmer describe how synergy between individuals' work, home, and school worlds develops with experience in an online environment, with more experienced users seeking ways to integrate Internet applications such as email into their personal, work, and volunteer environments.

Access to the Internet also dovetails with daily life. For better or worse, work creeps into home hours as computers and the Internet reach the home (Kraut et al., 1998; Nie and Erbring, 2000; Salaff). Education also enters this overfilled home as adult students engage in Internet-based courses in the midst of domestic and work responsibilities (Haythornthwaite and Kazmer). These crossovers also precipitate greater access. For example, the UCLA study finds that women's access to the Internet (but not men's) is markedly higher when there are children in the household (70 percent versus 57 percent). Computing and the Internet also enter local communities through community network initiatives, as in Blacksburg, Virginia (Kavanaugh and Patterson) and Netville, the "wired suburb" near Toronto, Ontario (Hampton and Wellman). Thus, influences from outside the home – work, school, networking initiatives – precipitate access and use in the home. Yet, this then precipitates use from home to elsewhere, as *netizens* connect from their homes to the homes of others, and bring voluntary groups online.

The Internet and the rise of networked individualism

This book focuses on the relationship between the Internet and both individual behavior and interpersonal relations. The research presented in this book also suggests that the Internet has accentuated a change towards a networked society that had already been underway. Even before the advent of the Internet, there has been a move from all-encompassing, socially controlling communities to individualized, fragmented personal communities. Most friends and relatives with whom we maintain socially close ties are not physically close. These ties are spread throughout metropolitan areas, and often on the other side of countries or seas. Mail, the telephone, cars, airplanes, and now email and the Internet sustain these ties. Most people do not live lives bound in one community. Instead, they maneuver through multiple, specialized partial communities, giving limited commitment to each. Their life is "glocalized" (Hampton and Wellman, 2002): combining long-distance ties with continuing involvements in households, neighborhoods, and worksites (Fischer, 1982; Wellman, 1999, 2001).

Table I.4 Some signs of networked individualism

Groups	→	Networks
Each in its place	→	Mobility of people and goods

United family	→	Serial marriage, mixed custody
Shared community	→	Multiple, partial personal networks
Neighborhoods	→	Dispersed networks
Voluntary organizations	→	Informal leisure
Face-to-face	→	Computer-mediated communication
Public spaces	→	Private spaces
Focused work unit	→	Networked organizations
Job in a company	→	Career in a profession
Autarky	→	Outsourcing
Office, factory	→	Airplane, Internet, mobile phone
Ascription	→	Achievement
Hierarchies	→	Matrix management
Conglomerates	→	Virtual organizations/alliances
Cold war blocs	→	Fluid, transitory alliances
Collective security	→	Civil liberties

Some or all of these arrows may be reversed if security concerns dominate.
Source: See Wellman (2002) for an earlier version of this table

The Internet has continued this turn towards living in networks, rather than in groups. In such networked societies, boundaries are more permeable, interactions are with diverse others, linkages switch between multiple networks, and hierarchies are flatter and more recursive (Castells, 2000; Wellman, 1997, 1999). Hence, many people and organizations communicate with others in ways that ramify across group boundaries. Rather than relating to one group, they cycle through interactions with a variety of others, at work or in the community. Their work and community networks are diffuse and sparsely knit, with vague, overlapping, social and spatial boundaries. Their computer-mediated communication has become part of their everyday lives, rather than being a separate set of relationships. The security and social control of all-encompassing communities had given way to the opportunity and vulnerability of networked individualism. People now go through the day, week, and month in a variety of narrowly defined relationships with changing sets of network members (table I.4).

Hence, the Internet reflects, facilitates, and foretells a transition away from door-to-door group interactions in neighborhoods and even place-to-place interactions where people traveled or communicated with each other's homes even as they passed quickly through the intervening space. Households, not individuals, were often the basis for supportive relationships. But, with mobile phones and wireless Internet access, physical location is becoming less important. Families eat together less often and are less prone to act as solidary units. Although the switch from door-to-door to place-to-place community has enabled communities of choice that were less constrained by distance, place-to-place community has preserved some sense of social context. The shift from place-to-place to person-to-person community reduces this contextual sense, with individualized interpersonal ties replacing place-based, inter-household ties (Rheingold, 2002; Wellman, 2001).

The personalization, portability, ubiquitous connectivity, and imminent wireless mobility of the Internet all facilitate networked individualism as the basis of community. It is the individual, and neither the household nor the group that is becoming the primary unit of connectivity: gleaning support, sociability, information, and a sense of belonging. Because connections are to people and not to places, the technology affords shifting of work and community ties from linking people-in-places to linking people at any place. Computer-supported communication is everywhere, but is situated nowhere in symbolic space. It is I-alone that is reachable wherever I am: at a house, hotel, office, highway, or shopping center. The person has become the portal.

The technological development of computer-communications networks and the societal flourishing of social networks are now affording the rise of networked individualism in a positive feedback loop. Just as the flexibility of less-bounded, spatially dispersed, social networks creates demand for collaborative communication and information sharing, the rapid development of computer-communications networks nourishes societal transitions from little boxes to social networks (Castells, 2000). Where high-speed place-to-place communication supports the dispersal and fragmentation of organizations and community, high-speed person-to-person communication supports the dispersal and role-fragmentation of workgroups and households. Each person is a switchboard, between ties and networks. People remain connected, but as individuals rather than being rooted in the home bases of work unit and household. Individuals switch rapidly between their social networks. Each person separately operates his networks to obtain information, collaboration, orders, support, sociability, and a sense of belonging.

Next Steps for Thinking about the Internet in Everyday Life

It is time for further analyses on the Internet in everyday life. Future analyses need to examine in more detail the effects of the Internet, focus on the types of activities performed online, and explore how these fit into the complexity of everyday life (see also Neustadtl, Robinson, and Kestnbaum; Jones 1999). Explaining Internet behavior entails understanding that "the Internet" is not a separate entity, but instead a complement to ongoing activity. We cannot understand its seemingly contradictory trends without considering a more integrated view of people's lives. We cannot analyze it without considering the specifics of peoples' lives, including "lifestage and lifestyle" (Anderson and Tracey), needs in a mobile world (Putnam, 2000; Wellman, 2001; Rheingold, 2002), multiple world obligations (Haythornthwaite and Kazmer), strong and weak ties (Haythornthwaite, 2002; Kraut et al., 1998; Wellman, 2001), and user and non-user demographics (Nie, 2001; and others). We cannot understand the relations of two people – or a small group – online without considering the broader social networks in which they are connected, offline as well as online.

The studies presented here begin these tasks of broadening our focus from the Internet to the social worlds in which it is embedded. There is more to be done, but here we join others in beginning the large task of understanding the major social phenomenon that is the Internet.

References

Anderson, B. and Tracey, K. (this book). Digital living: the impact (or otherwise) of the Internet in everyday British life.

Barlow, J. P. (1995). Is there a there in cyberspace? *Utne Reader*, 50–6.

Birdsall, W. S. (2000). The digital divide in a liberal state: a Canadian perspective. *First Monday*. Available online at:
http://www.firstmonday.dk/issues/issue5_12/birdsall/

Boneva, B. and Kraut, R. (this book). Email, gender, and personal relationships.

Castells, M. (2000). *The rise of the network society* (2nd edn). Malden, MA: Blackwell.

Chen, W., Boase, J., and Wellman, B. (this book). The global villagers: comparing Internet users and uses around the world.

Copher, J., Kanfer, A., and Walker, M. B. (this book). Everyday communication patterns of heavy and light email users.

Davidson, T., Sooryamoorthy, R., and Shrum, W. (this book). Kerala connections: will the Internet affect science in developing areas?

Dibbell, J. (1993; 1996). Taboo, consensus, and the challenge of democracy in an electronic forum. In R. Kling (ed.), *Computerization and controversy* (pp. 553–68). San Diego, CA: Academic Press. (Originally appeared as "A rape in cyberspace: or, how an evil clown, a Haitian trickster spirit, two wizards, and a cast of dozens turned a database into a society." *The Village Voice*, December 21, 1993, pp. 36–42.)

DiMaggio, P., Hargittai, E., Neuman, W. R., and Robinson, J. P. (2001). Social implications of the Internet: the Internet's effect on society. *Annual Review of Sociology*, 27, 307–36.

Fernández-Maldonado, A. M. (2001, April). *Patterns of social diffusion and use of new information and communication technologies in Lima*. Paper presented at the International Research Seminar on the Social Sustainability of Technological Networks, New York, NY. Available online at: http://www.bk.tudelft.nl/users/fernande/internet/NewYork.pdf

Fischer, C. (1982). *To dwell among friends*. Berkeley: University of California Press.

Gibson, W. (1984). *Neuromancer*. New York: Ace Science Fiction.

Hampton, K. N. (2001). Broadband neighborhoods connected communities. In K. Inkpen and J. Vanderdonckt (eds), *CHI 2001 Extended Abstracts*. ACM Press.

Hampton, K. N. and Wellman, B. (2000). Examining community in the digital neighbourhood: Early results from Canada's wired suburb. In T. Ishida and K. Isbister (eds), *Digital cities: technologies, experiences, and future perspectives* (pp. 475–92). Berlin: Springer-Verlag.

Hampton, K. N. and Wellman, B. (2002). Neighboring in Netville: how the Internet supports glocalized community, social support and social capital in a wired suburb. *City and Community*, 1(4) (forthcoming)

Hampton, K. and Wellman, B. (this book). The not so global village of Netville.

Hargittai, E. and Centeno, M. A. (eds) (2001). Mapping globalization. *American Behavioral Scientist*, 44(10), whole issue.

Hauben, M. (1996). *The net and the netizens: the impact the net has on people's lives*. New York: Columbia University.

Haythornthwaite, C. (2000). Online personal networks: size, composition and media use among distance learners. *New Media and Society*, 2(2), 195–226.

Haythornthwaite, C. (2001). Exploring multiplexity: social network structures in a computer-supported distance learning class. *The Information Society*, 17(3), 211–26.

Haythornthwaite, C. (2002). Strong, weak and latent ties and the impact of new media. *The Information Society* (forthcoming).

Haythornthwaite, C. and Wellman, B. (1998). Work, friendship and media use for information exchange in a networked organization. *Journal of the American Society for Information Science*, 46(12), 1101–14.

Haythornthwaite, C. and Kazmer, M. M. (this book). Bringing the Internet home: adult distance learners and their Internet, home and work worlds.

Haythornthwaite, C., Wellman, B., and Garton, L. (1998). Work and community via computer-mediated communication. In J. Gackenbach (ed.), *Psychology and the Internet* (pp. 199–226). San Diego, CA: Academic Press.

Horrigan, J. and Rainie, L. (2002). *Getting serious online*. Washington: Pew Internet Project. March 3. http://www.pewinternet.org/reports/index.asp

Howard, P. E. N., Rainie, L., and Jones, S. (this book). Days and nights on the Internet.

ITU (International Telecommunication Union) (2001). ITU Internet Reports: IP Telephony. Sept 18.
http://www.itu.int/ITU-D/ict/publications/inet/2000/flyer/flyer.html

Jones, S. G. (ed.) (1998). *CyberSociety 2.0: revisiting computer-mediated communication and community*. Thousand Oaks, CA: Sage.

Jones, S. G. (ed.) (1999). *Doing Internet research*. Thousand Oaks, CA: Sage.

Jones, S. G. (ed.) (1995). *CyberSociety: computer-mediated communication and community*. Thousand Oaks, CA: Sage.

Katz, J. E., Rice, R. E., and Aspden, P. (2001). The Internet, 1995–2000: access, civic involvement, and social interaction. *American Behavioral Scientist*, 45(3), 405–19.

Katz, J. E. and Aspden, P. (1997). A nation of strangers? *Communications of the ACM*, 40(12), 81–6.

Katz, J. E. and Rice, R. E. (this book). Syntopia: access, civic involvement and social interaction on the net.

Kavanaugh, A. L. and Patterson, S. J. (this book). The impact of community computer networks on social capital and community involvement in Blacksburg.

Kiesler, S. (ed.) (1997). *Culture of the Internet*. Mahwah, NJ: Lawrence Erlbaum.

Kiesler, S., Lundmark, V., Zdaniuk, B., and Kraut, R. (2000). Troubles with the Internet: the dynamics of help at home. *Human Computer Interaction*, 15(4), 223–352.

Koku, E. and Wellman, B. (2002). Scholarly networks as learning communities: the case of Technet. In S. Barab, R. Kling, and J. Gray (eds), *Building online communities in the service of learning*. Cambridge: Cambridge University Press (forthcoming).

Koku, E., Nazer, N., and Wellman, B. (2001). Netting scholars: online and offline. *American Behavioral Scientist*, 44(10), 1752–74.

Kraut, R., Kiesler, S., Boneva, B., Cummings, J., Helgeson A. (2002). Internet paradox revisited. *Journal of Social Is

Kraut, R., Kiesler, S., Mukhopadhyay, T., Scherlis, W., and I Social impact of the Internet: what does it mean? *C ACM*, 41(12), 21–2.

Kraut, R., Patterson, M., Lundmark, V., Kiesler, S., Mukhopadhyay, T., and Scherlis, W. (1998). Internet paradox: a social technology that reduces social involvement and psychological well-being? *American Psychologist*, 53(9), 1017–31.

LaRose, R., Eastin, M. S., and Gregg, J. (2001). Reformulating the Internet paradox: social cognitive explanations of Internet use and depression. *Journal of Online Behavior*, 1(2). Available online at: http://www.behavior.net/JOB/v1n2/paradox.html

Lievrouw, L., Bucy, E., Finn, A. T., Frindte, W., Gershon, R., Haythornthwaite, C., Kohler, T., Metz, J. M., and Sundar, S. S. (2001). Current new media research: an overview of communication and technology. *Communication Yearbook*, 24, 271–95.

Lunn, R. J. and Suman, M. W. (this book). Experience and trust in online shopping.

Macaluso, N. (2001). Nearly 60% of homes are online. E-*Commerce Times*, Aug. 13.

Matei, S. and Ball-Rokeach, S. J. (this book). Belonging in geographic, ethnic and Internet spaces.

McLuhan, M. (1962). *The Gutenberg galaxy: the making of typographic man.* Toronto: University of Toronto Press.

Mehra, B., Merkel, C., and Bishop, A. P. (2002). *The Internet for empowerment of minority and marginalized users.* Working Paper, Graduate School of Library and Information Science, University of Illinois, Champaign.

Miyata, K. (this book). Social support for Japanese mothers online and offline.

National Statistics Omnibus (2000). *Internet access.* Available online at: www.statistics.gov.uk

Neustadtl, A., Robinson, J. P., and Kestnbaum, M. (this book). Doing social science research online.

Nie, N. H. (2001). Sociability, interpersonal relations, and the Internet: reconciling conflicting findings. *American Behavioral Scientist*, 45(3), 420–35.

Nie, N. H. and Erbring, L. (February 17, 2000). *Internet and society: a preliminary report.* Stanford Institute for the Quantitative Study of Society (SIQSS), Stanford University, and InterSurvey. Available online at http://www.stanford.edu/group/siqss/

Nie, N. H., Hillygus, D. S., and Erbring, L. (this book). Internet use interpersonal relations and sociability: a time diary study.

Nielsen NetRatings (February, 2002). *Global Internet index average usage.* Report. Available online at: http://www.nielsennetratings.com/hot_off_the_net.jsp

NTIA (National Telecommunications and Information Administration) (2000). *Falling through the net: toward digital inclusion.* US Commerce Department. Available online at: http://www.ntia.doc.gov/ntiahome/digitaldivide/

NTIA (2002). *A nation online.* Washington: National Telecommunications and Information Agency. Available online at http://www.ntia.doc.gov/ntiahome/dn/index.html

Nua.com (2001a). *US no longer dominates the net*. Available online at: http://www.nua.ie/surveys/index.cgi?f=VSandart_id=905356771andrel= true

Nua.com (2001b). *Women outnumber men online in US*. Available online at: http://www.nua.ie/surveys/index.cgi?f=VS&art_id=905356873&rel= true

Nua.com (2002). *How many online?* Available online at: http://www.nua.ie/surveys/how_many_online/world.html

Pastore, M. (2002). U.S. e-commerce spikes in Q4 2001. *CyberAtlas*. Feb. 10. Available online at: http://cyberatlas.internet.com/markets/retailing/article/0,,6061_977751,00.html

Pinkett, R. D. (2001). *The camfield estates-MIT creating community connections project: strategies for active participation in a low-to-moderate-income community*. Digital Cities Conference, Kyoto, October.

Putnam, R. D. (2000). *Bowling alone: the collapse and revival of American community*. NY: Simon and Schuster.

Quan-Haase, A. and Wellman, B. (this book). Capitalizing on the net: social contact, civic engagement, and sense of community.

Reddick, A., Boucher, C., and Groseillers, M. (2000). *The dual digital divide: the Information highway in Canada*. Ottawa: Public Interest Advocacy Centre.

Rheingold, H. (1993). *The virtual community: homesteading on the electronic frontier*. Reading, MA: Addison-Wesley.

Rheingold, H. (2002). *Smart mobs*. Reading, MA: Perseus Books.

Robinson, J. P., Kestnbaum, M., Neustadtl, A., and Alvarez, A. S. (this book). The Internet and other uses of time.

Rogers, E. M. (1995). *Diffusion of innovations*. 4th edn. NY: The Free Press.

Salaff, J. W. (this book). Where home is the office: the new form of flexible work.

Sawhney, H. (ed.) (2000). Universal service. *The Information Society*, 16(2), whole issue.

Scabner, D. (2001). Downturn or not: Americans spend more hours on the job than anyone. ABCNews.com. May 7. http://abcnews.go.com/sections/us/DailyNews/work_howmuch_dayone.html

Schement, J. R. (1998). Thorough Americans: minorities and the new media. Available online at: http://www.benton.org/Policy/Schement/Minorities/

Schuler, D. (1997). Community networks: building a new participatory medium. In P. Agre and D. Schuler (eds), *Reinventing technology, rediscovering community* (pp. 191–218). Greenwich, CT: Ablex.

Smith, M. A. (1999). Invisible crowds in cyberspace: mapping the social structure of the Usenet. In M. A. Smith and P. Kollock (eds), *Communities in cyberspace* (pp. 195–219). London: Routledge.

Smith, M. A. and Kollock, P. (eds) (1999). *Communities in cyberspace*. London: Routledge.

Southwick, S. (1996). *Liszt: searchable directory of email discussion groups* http://www.liszt.com. BlueMarble Information Services.

Statistics Canada (2000). Plugging in: household Internet use. *The Daily.* Monday, December 4, 2000. Available online at: http://www.statcan.ca/Daily/English/001204/d001204a.htm

Sterling, B. (1996). Greetings from Burning Man! *Wired*, 4(11). Available online at: http://www.wired.com/wired/archive/4.11/burningman_pr.html

Strover, S. (forthcoming). The digital divide: exploring equity and politics. *The Information Society*, whole issue.

Turkle, S. (1984). *The second self: computers and the human spirit.* New York: Simon & Schuster.

UCLA Center for Communication Policy (2000). *The UCLA Internet report: "Surveying the digital future."* Available online at: www.ccp.ucla.edu

Valente, T. (1995). *Network models of the diffusion of innovations.* Cresskill, NJ: Hampton Press.

Van Gelder, L. (1985; 1996). The strange case of the electronic lover. In R. Kling (1996), (ed.), *Computerization and Controversy*, 2nd edn (pp. 533–46). San Diego, CA: Academic Press. (Originally appeared in *Ms. Magazine*, 14(4), October 1985, pp. 94, 99, 101–4, 123, 124.)

Wagner, G. G., Pischner, R., and Haisken-DeNew, J. P. (this book). The changing digital divide in Germany.

Webb, S. (2001). Avatar culture: narrative, power and identity in virtual world environments. *Information, Communication & Society*, 4(4): 560–94.

Wellman, B. (1979). The community question. *American Journal of Sociology*, 84, 1201–31.

Wellman, B. (1997). An electronic group is virtually a social network. In S. Kiesler (ed.), *Cultures of the Internet* (pp.179–205). Mahwah, NJ: Lawrence Erlbaum.

Wellman, B. (1999). The network community. In B. Wellman (ed.), *Networks in the global village* (pp. 1–48). Boulder, CO: Westview.

Wellman, B. (2001). Physical place and cyber place: the rise of personalized networking. *International Journal of Urban and Regional Research*, 25(2), 227–52.

Wellman, B. (2002). Little boxes, glocalization, and networked individualism. In M. Tanabe, P. van den Besselaar, and T. Ishida (eds), *Digital Cities II: Computational and Sociological Approaches.* Berlin: Springer-Verlag.

Wellman, B. and Gulia, M. (1999). Net surfers don't ride alone: virtual communities as communities. In M. A. Smith and P. Kollock (eds), *Communities in cyberspace* (pp. 167–94). London: Routledge.

Wellman, B. and Tindall, D. (1993). Reach out and touch some bodies: how telephone networks connect social networks. *Progress in Communication Science*, 12, 63–94.

Wellman, B. and Wortley, S. (1989). Brothers' keepers: situating kinship relations in broader networks of social support. *Sociological Perspectives*, 32, 273–306.

Wellman, B. and Wortley, S. (1990). Different strokes from different folks: community ties and social support. *American Journal of Sociology*, 96, 558–88.

Wellman, B., Salaff, J., Dimitrova, D., Garton, L., Gulia, M., and Haythornthwaite, C. (1996). Computer networks as social networks: collaborative work, telework, and virtual community. *Annual Review of Sociology*, 22, 213–38.

Wellman, B., Fong, E., Kew, M., and Wilkes, R. (2002). Fathoming the digital divide. *Studies in Internet Communication: Theory and Practice*, 19 (forthcoming).

Part II

The Place of the Internet in Everyday Life

I

Days and Nights on the Internet

Philip E. N. Howard, Lee Rainie, and Steve Jones

Abstract

For a growing cohort of Americans Internet tools have become a significant conduit of their social life and work life. The surveys of the Pew Internet and American Life Project track the diffusion of Internet technologies, revealing significant differences in use between men and women, young and old, those of different races and ethnic groups, and those of different socio-economic status. A user typology can be built around two variables: the length of time a person has used the Internet and the frequency with which she or he logs on from home. We contend that use of email helps people build their social networks by extending and maintaining friend and family relationships.

Authors' Note

The authors wish to thank Lisa Amoroso, Scott Campbell, Greg Flemming, and James Witte for assistance and comments in preparation of this chapter.

Introduction

The Internet is widely diffusing into American society. Some people do not use it and never will, some people cannot afford it, and some people do not use it well. But for a rapidly growing number of people the Internet is a useful communication and information-gathering tool and for others it is a vital part of their lives. The rate of Internet diffusion since the creation of the worldwide web surpasses that of other communication technologies, and since the social impact of newspapers, radio, and television has been significant, we set out to understand the role of the Internet in the daily life of users.

As of October 2001 the phone surveys by the Pew Internet and American Life Project show that 106 million American – some 56 percent of American adults – have Internet access and 56 percent of those who have access go online during a typical day. Additionally, 76 percent of youth aged 12–17 have access. The overall population is evenly split between men and women. Proportionally more whites have Internet access than African–Americans or Hispanics. This online population is still somewhat weighted towards the young, towards those with college or graduate degrees, those in relatively well-off households (those who live in households with incomes over $75,000). However, there has been a sharp increase in access to the Internet among those with less than college educations, those from households with middle- and working-class incomes, and, especially, among African–Americans and Hispanics.[1] The overall online population is looking more and more like the population of the country. Our surveys suggest that the next wave of those getting access to the Internet will contain proportionally more minorities, more of those with lower incomes, and more of those with lesser educations. The remaining demographic gaps in access will be defined by income differences and age differences – the poor, especially in rural areas, will continue to lag behind others in getting access, as will the elderly.

When web activities are analyzed from the perspective of the many things users might have done online (we ask survey respondents to tell us the things they have *ever done* online), three major patterns emerge. First, gender gaps become evident in some places. Women are more likely than men to seek health information, get religious information, research new jobs, and play games online. Men are more likely to use the web to get news, shop, seek financial information and do online stock trading, participate in online auctions, access government web sites, and search for sports news.

At the same time, there is a striking amount of online behavior that is similar between men and women. For some Internet activities, the usage story is a generational one, and that is the second major pattern in our exploration of how Americans use the Internet. Younger Internet users of both sexes are more likely than older Americans to have used the Internet for "fun" communications via instant messages or chat rooms, to have gone to the web to browse for fun, to have done

1 We are comparing the Pew Internet Project findings in 2000 with those of the Pew Research Center for The People and The Press in 1996 (see http://www.people-press.org/tec96sum.htm) and 1998 (see http://www.people-press.org/tech98sum.htm).

school- or work-related research, to have accessed popular culture by downloading music or getting information about movies, books and other leisure activities, and to have performed convenience activities online such as banking and arranging travel.

Finally, our surveys show that variations in online behavior are also rooted in users' differing levels of experience with the Internet. Veteran users, those who have at least three years experience online, are more likely than newcomers to have done most Internet activities. The Internet has become an important job-related tool for those with several years' experience. They are much more likely to have done job-related research and use email in job-connected communications than newcomers. In addition, veterans are more likely than newcomers to have performed transactions or managed their money online. These users are disproportionately from higher socioeconomic groups, so education level and household income also show up as important indicators of the things users have done on the Internet.

In short, online life is not monochromatic. Tens of millions of Americans are online every day and they are doing a variety of things. The Internet has become a part of everyday life, rather than a separate place to be.

The Internet's Place in American Life

Ray Oldenburg has described how people use "third places" such as coffee shops, community centers, beauty parlors, general stores, bars, and other hangouts to help them get through the day (Oldenburg, 1991). These places were distinct from home and distinct from work, but were integral parts of social life. As scholars began to look at typical uses of the Internet, many adopted an analytical frame that the Internet was like one of these third places – a growing sphere of social interaction where people played games and socialized. They studied how individuals and small groups behaved within MUDs, MOOs and other specific environments (Sudweeks, 1998).

Internet tools have diffused with such speed and depth that many important forms of social organization – news agencies, business enterprises, charities, and the government – take care to manage their identity on the Internet, and some have been fundamentally altered by the organizational opportunities and stresses provided by such technologies. The Internet is no longer just a third place where people go to escape and play with games and identities. Today, many of the common forms of daily social interaction can be conducted online, from checking the news and sports scores to researching and booking travel reservations. However, there is little consensus about whether the ability of users to conduct personal and professional life through Internet technologies is ultimately good or bad for society at large, local communities, or individual well-being (Wellman and Gulia, 1999).

Those who argue that Internet tools have an ill effect make the case that Internet tools promote the growth of pseudo rather than real communities (Beniger, 1987), breed a new kind of radical individualism (Borsook, 2000), replicate traditional elites, ideologies and American cultural hegemony (Carmel, 1997), facilitate the violation of privacy (Bennett and Grant, 2000), abet sound-bite culture (Willock, 1998), and clutter modern life with useless data and cumbersome technologies (Rochlin, 1998; Shenk, 1997). Others have argued that the Internet shears social networks and lets individuals disconnect from their families and friends, becoming loners, if not Internet addicts (Nie and Erbring, 2000).

In the other camp are those who contend that Internet tools are good for society. One argument is that the Internet allows ideas to circulate to a wide audience and thus helps entrepreneurs with good ideas find capital and bring expertise to bear on marketable products and services (Cairncross, 1997). Others make the case that Internet technologies may help flatten hierarchies (Sproull and Kiesler, 1992), dilute power from traditional elites who monopolize information (Moore, 1987), permit new and interesting forms of community (Etzioni, 1997), make citizen activism easier and more effective (Schwartz, 1996), and encourage a generally self-reflective society (Dizard, 1997; Fishkin, 1992).

Even though Internet use has spread quickly and widely, it is still too early to make conclusions about the long-term social role of the Internet. Most of the ideas about how the Internet may be good or bad for society are, at best, hypotheses, and it may be the case that many or all of them are true. It is certain, though, that the Internet is not a separate and distinct social sphere that can be studied in isolation. Thus, our research is focused on answering more basic sets of questions. First, who goes online on an average day and what do they do? Second, what are the most sensible ways of generalizing about what happens online? Finally, what are the social implications of adding the Internet to a person's repertoire of communication tools?

Method

The research reported here is built on an innovative tracking survey of Internet activities in America. Running almost continuously between March 1 and August 20, 2000, the survey has been completed by over twelve thousand American adults (18 years old and older).[2] From a total sample of 12,638 respondents, the median age was 42 years. The population was 79 percent white, 12 percent African–American, and 46 percent male. In terms of education, 42 percent had high school or less, 29 percent had some post-secondary, 18 percent had a bachelor's degree, and 10 percent had a graduate degree. The raw data file is available at www.pewinternet.org. The 6,413 respondents who said

2   The survey was conducted using a rolling daily sample, with a target of completing 75–80 interviews each day of a survey period. For results based on the total sample, one can say with 95 percent confidence that the error attributable to sampling and other random effects is plus or minus 2.5 percentage points. A basic set of questions about Internet use and respondent demographics were asked of all respondents, and additional more detailed sets of questions were given to different respondents over the six-month survey period. For those additional results, the sampling error is plus or minus 3 percentage points. In addition to sampling error, question wording, and practical difficulties in conducting telephone surveys may introduce some error or bias into the findings of opinion polls.

The sample for this survey is a random digit sample of telephone numbers selected from telephone exchanges in the continental United States. During a survey period, a new sample was released daily and was kept in the field for at least five days. This insures that the complete call procedures are followed for the entire sample. Additionally, the sample was released in replicates to insure that the telephone numbers called are distributed appropriately across regions of the country. At least ten attempts were made to complete an interview at every household in the sample. The calls were staggered over times of day and days of the week to maximize the chances of making contact with a potential respondent. Interview refusals were re-contacted at least once in order to try again to complete an interview. All interviews completed on any given day were considered to be the final sample for that day. When enough respondents had completed the survey to provide statistically significant results, we were able to adapt the questionnaire to address current events and new research interests.

Non-response in telephone interviews produces some known biases in survey-derived estimates because participation tends to vary for different subgroups of the population, and these subgroups are likely to vary also on questions of substantive interest. In order to compensate for these known biases, the sample data are weighted in some analysis. The demographic weighting parameters were derived from a special analysis of the most recently available Census Bureau's Current Population Survey (March, 1999).

they had Internet access were asked a battery of questions about what they had ever done online. If they said they had logged onto the Internet the previous day, they were asked questions about what they did during those online sessions "yesterday," where yesterday includes both week days and weekends. Some 3,506 had been online "yesterday" and their responses allow us to examine a "typical day" on the Internet. Of those respondents, 2,535 were asked about their behavior on weekdays and 971 were asked about their behavior on weekend days. This approach measures day-to-day online life more accurately than conventional surveys because it focuses on activities that are fresh in respondents' minds and because it has examined behavior on various days over an extended period. Although new kinds of web-based survey instruments can overcome some of these difficulties, telephone-based sampling remains the best way to reach Americans who do not have easy Internet access (Witte et al., 2000).

A Typical Day's Activities Online

Every day 55 percent of the American adults who have Internet access (55 percent of the sample of 6,413), around 52 million people, go online and pursue a wide range of activities. During this average day, 48 million Americans are using the Internet's prime communications feature – email. An equal number do something on the web, either seeking information or completing a transaction. The composition of the online population on this average day reflects the profile of those who are the heaviest users of the Internet – and in many cases that means those who have had Internet access for the longest time. This, in turns, raises the possibility that growing familiarity with the Internet increases the likelihood that a user will be a frequent user.

The daily US Internet population contains more men than women and relatively high levels of those from upper socioeconomic groups. It also contains a relatively high proportion of those who have the greatest amount of online experience. Some 57 percent of the men with Internet access are online during this typical day, compared to 52 percent of women with Internet access. About 56 percent of whites who have Internet access are online during a typical day, while only 36 percent of African–Americans and 49 percent of Hispanics with Internet access log on during this prototypical day. Of those with Internet access, 46 percent of those with a high school diploma or less are online during the typical day, compared to 62 percent of those with college or graduate degrees. Similarly, 50 percent of those with Internet access living in households with less than $30,000 are online during this typical day, while 61 percent of those with Internet access in households earning more than $75,000 log on during this typical day. Finally, 68 percent of those who have been online for three or more years log on to the Internet during the typical day, compared to just 41 percent of those who got Internet access within the past six months.

The vast majority of those who are online during a typical day read and send email (see table 1.1). Many of these same people also do other things online and we have classified these activities in four broad groups: 29 percent of Internet users said they also did fun things (e.g. browse for fun, send instant messages, play games, get hobby information), a third said they also used the Internet as an information utility (e.g. to get news, financial information, product or travel information), about a fifth said they did important life activities online (e.g. get health information, do work- or school-related research, find leads about new jobs) and one-tenth said they made some kind of financial transaction (e.g. buy a product, buy or sell stocks and bonds, make a travel reservation).

Some clear differences among groups emerge in our activities-classification scheme for the full sample of 6,413. Young adults who use the Internet are more likely to do fun things like gaming and downloading music compared to older respondents. Of those who went online "yesterday," substantially more men than women used the Internet as an information utility. The most experienced online Americans are relatively heavy users of the Internet as an information utility and proportionally more of them do research for major life activities online than other groups.

Inside each of our broad categories, there are interesting things to note. The gender differences in the daily online world are not very dramatic in some major activities such as using email and browsing for fun (more men do this than women on a typical day), searching for health information (more women do this than men), buying products and making travel reservations (online men and women are doing this in roughly similar proportions). But a gap is evident in some other Internet activities. More online men than women are consuming news online: on a typical day 26 percent of men with Internet access are doing this, compared to 15 percent of online women. A comparable pattern applies to the act of seeking product information: 16 percent of online men are doing this on a typical day, compared to 9 percent

Table 1.1 Daily Internet activities

March–August compiled, weighted		Email %	Online activity[a] % Fun[b]	Information utility[c]	Major life activities[d]	Transactions[e]	Email and online n	%
Gender	Women	88	11	14	12	3	3,197	47
	Men	86	14	21	14	4	3,583	53
Race	White	88	13	17	13	4	5,954	88
	Black	75	15	16	16	4	362	5
	Asian	84	16	21	17	7	133	2
	Hispanic/Latino	86	15	19	15	5	395	6
Age group	18–24	87	20	15	14	4	989	15
	25–34	88	14	18	16	4	1,719	25
	35–44	86	12	19	14	4	1,743	26
	45–54	87	10	18	13	3	1,280	19
	55–64	90	9	18	10	3	616	9
	65 or older	85	8	15	6	2	328	5
Education	Bachelors or more	89	11	19	15	4	1,760	26
Income	20 k or less	87	15	14	15	3	513	9
	20 k–40 k	87	16	17	12	3	1,435	21
	40 k–75 k	86	14	17	13	4	2,010	30
	75 k+	89	11	21	16	5	1,689	25

							N	%
Place of connection[a]	Home	88	14	18	12	4	5,185	76
	Work	90	12	21	20	4	2,725	40
When came online	This year	82	13	14	9	3	1,902	28
	Between 1 and 3 years	88	13	17	13	4	2,229	33
	More than 3 years ago	90	13	21	17	5	2,641	29
Duration of use	At least an hour	85	10	14	10	3	4,150	62
	Between 1 and 3 hours	89	17	21	16	5	1,436	21
	More than 3 hours	94	21	27	22	7	1,140	17
All users[a]	N	5,914	1,987	2,257	1,406	621	6,780	
	%	87	29	33	21	9	100	100

[a] Online activities and home/work access were not exclusive categories, so these row and column totals will not sum to 100% like the other variables.

[b] "Fun" activities are checking sports information, sending/receiving instant messages, seeking information about hobbies, browsing for fun, playing a game, watching video clips, listening to audio clips, listening to music or downloading it, and participating in chat rooms.

[c] "Information utility" activities are getting news, news specifically about politics, financial information, product information, travel information, religious and spiritual information, information from a government website, and checking the weather.

[d] "Major life activities" are seeking information about healthcare, jobs, housing, doing job-related research, and research for school or job training.

[e] "Transactions" activities are buying products, making travel reservations, doing online banking, participating in an online auction, trading stocks/bonds/mutual fund shares, gambling.

of online women. When it comes to seeking financial information such as stock quotes or mortgage interest rates, 18 percent of online men are doing this on a typical day, compared to 8 percent of online women. Men with Internet access use the Internet for work related research more than women; 18 percent of men with access do this on a typical day, compared to 12 percent of women. Similarly, many of those who seek hobby information on a typical day are men: 21 percent of men with Internet access are doing this during the average day, compared to 14 percent of online women.

We have noted that African–Americans with Internet access are proportionally much less likely than whites with Internet access to log on during the typical day. This relationship also applies to the most common Internet activities. For instance, on a typical day, 49 percent of whites with Internet access are sending and reading email, while only 27 percent of African–Americans with Internet access are working with email. In addition, 21 percent of online whites are getting news on that average day, compared to 12 percent of online African–Americans. Some 20 percent of online whites are browsing for fun on an average day, compared to 14 percent of online African–Americans. A final example: 13 percent of online whites are getting product information, compared to 8 percent of online African–Americans.

A Predictive Model of Who Does What

We found some striking variance in the use of the web when we asked respondents what they have *ever done* online. Table 1.2 presents the results of a logistic regression for 29 dependent variables measuring different Internet activities, and modeled with the independent variables age, gender, race, educational background, and income. The logistic regression reveals the comparative effect of different demographic factors in predicting whether a user actually did that particular activity. Although it is common to report the coefficients from the logistic regression of independent variables onto a dependent variables, the exponentiated coefficients are the more intuitive "odds ratios." The odds ratio is the probability that one variable, controlling for all the other factors in a model, will correctly predict a person's response to a question. For example, all other things being equal, the odds that an Internet-using woman has ever sent or read email are 25.6 percent greater $((1.256–1) \times 100)$ than the odds that a man would have used email. Furthermore, the odds that someone with a bachelors degree or more would have ever used email are 92.2 percent greater than those of someone without such a degree.

Table 1.2 helps predict the probability that an individual has done a particular Internet activity. For example, the odds that an Internet-using woman, 25 years old, with a bachelors degree, who self-identifies as Anglo-American and not Hispanic, has used email are 506 to 1. In contrast, the odds that an Internet-using woman, 25 years old, with a bachelors degree who self-identifies as African–American and not Hispanic, has used email are 319 to 1.[3] This model shows that gender accounts for some of the differences in the ways people use the Internet. Female Internet users are more likely than male users to have ever used email. At the same time, online women are less likely than online men to have accessed 15 kinds of web activities. When it comes to checking for news or sports scores, watching or downloading a video or audio clip, or doing most financial transactions, online men are much more likely to have logged on to enjoy those activities than women. However, women are twice as likely as men to look for health information online. Interestingly, women seem to be most taken by researching travel plans and playing games.

Age is significantly associated with the performance of some Internet activities. Younger online Americans are more likely to use the web for fun, to gather most kinds of information, and to perform financial transactions online.

There are large, significant differences in the daily activities of people with different racial backgrounds. Compared to white respondents, Asian–Americans are less likely to research hobbies online and more likely to research politics and travel plans. Asian–Americans are also more likely to have bought or sold stocks, bonds or mutual fund shares online, and to have made travel plans. Although there are few statistically significant odds ratios for African–American respondents, they are much less likely than others to have used email. Online African–Americans are most likely to have done fun things on the web like checking the sports scores and playing games. Interestingly, they are 31 percent as likely as whites, controlling for other variables, to

---

3   In the first example, the odds = $8.373 \times 1.002(\text{Age}) \times 1.256(\text{Female}) \times 1.922(\text{BA}) \times 0.652(\text{Hispanic}) \times 0.868 \text{ (Asian)} \times 0.631(\text{Black}) \times 0.786(\text{Other})$, and since $e^{(0)} = 1$, the odds = $8.373 \times 1.002(25) \times 1.256(1) \times 1.922(1) \times 1 \times 1 \times 1 \times 1 = 506.33$. In the second example the only difference is that the case self-identifies as African–American, so the odds = $8.373 \times 1.002(25) \times 1.256(1) \times 1.922(1) \times 1 \times 1 \times 0.631(1) \times 1 = 319.49$.

Table 1.2 Logistic regression results: odds (e^B) of doing particular Internet activities, modeled with age, gender, education, and race

					Fun					March–August compiled, unweighted N	
	Checked sports scores	Sent instant message	Sought info. about a hobby	Browsed just for fun	Played a game	Learn about movies, books, or music	Watched a video clip or listened to audio clip	Took part in a chat room	Listened to or downloaded music	Unweighted N	%
Baseline odds (Constant)	0.704[a]	1.038	2.409[a]	4.370[a]	0.477[a]	0.606[a]	0.721[a]	1.188	0.605[a]	6,270	100
Age	0.988[a]	0.983[a]	0.989[a]	0.980[a]	0.988[a]	0.968[a]	0.980[a]	0.965[a]	0.977[a]	6,270	100
Female	0.340[a]	0.981	0.789[a]	0.924	1.170[b]	1.059	0.747[a]	0.777[a]	0.779[a]	3,162	50
BA or more	1.124	0.747[a]	0.991	0.614[a]	0.566[a]	1.054	1.072	0.577[a]	0.772[a]	2,579	41
Hispanic or Latino	1.096	1.067	0.862	1.215	1.105	1.291	0.943	0.877	1.057	395	
Race (white as reference)											
Asian	1.013	1.135	0.688[b]	0.914	0.769	0.961	0.964	1.193	1.044	154	
Black	1.347[a]	1.051	0.739[a]	1.476[a]	1.499[a]	1.122	1.174	1.442[a]	1.193	586	
Other	1.068	1.161	0.942	1.081	0.214	1.094	1.067	1.539[a]	1.241	314	

	Email	Information utility						
	Got financial info	Check weather	Got news	Research travel plans	Looked for info. about a product	Sought news about politics	Sought religious info.	Sought info. from government website
Baseline odds (Constant)	8.373[a]	0.647[a]	1.654[a]	1.878[a]	3.048[a]	0.484[a]	0.055[a]	0.622[a]
Age	1.002	1.002	0.999	0.994[a]	0.987[a]	1.000	0.997	1.002[a]
Female	1.256[b]	0.924	0.673[a]	1.118[b]	0.657[a]	0.747[a]	1.165	0.731[a]
BA or more	1.922[a]	1.097	1.445[a]	1.685[a]	1.231[a]	1.537[a]	0.963	1.799
Hispanic or Latino	0.652[a]	0.922[b]	1.036	0.942	0.895	1.085	0.935	0.872
Race (white as reference)								
Asian	0.868	0.671[b]	1.311	1.641[b]	0.889	1.758[a]	0.784	0.891
Black	0.631[a]	0.780[a]	1.127	0.984	0.854	1.079	1.685[a]	0.868
Other	0.786	1.057	1.064	0.769[b]	0.820	1.388[a]	1.346	0.836

Table 1.2 Continued

	Major life activities							Transactions			
	Looked for place to live	Sought info. about a job	Sought health info.	Did work online	Did research for school or got training	Bank online	Participated in online auction	Bought a product	Bought/sold stocks, bonds, mutual fund shares	Made travel reservation	Gambled online
Baseline odds (Constant)	0.164[a]	0.276[a]	0.629[a]	0.966	1.197[b]	0.127[a]	0.316[a]	1.211[b]	0.112[a]	0.444[a]	0.027[a]
Age	0.975[a]	0.971[a]	1.006[a]	0.991[a]	0.972[a]	0.988[a]	0.987[a]	0.990[a]	0.998	0.994[a]	1.002
Female	1.063	1.166	2.039[a]	0.798[a]	1.070	0.853	0.575[a]	0.891[b]	0.482[a]	0.864[a]	0.889
BA or more	1.350[a]	1.198[b]	1.294[a]	3.005[a]	1.319[a]	1.729[a]	1.103	1.721[a]	2.047[a]	1.888[a]	0.614[b]
Hispanic or Latino	1.115	1.055	0.855	1.127	0.979	1.061	0.577[a]	0.835	0.644[b]	0.963	0.974
Race (white as reference)											
Asian	1.192	1.111	0.768	1.361	1.069	1.393	0.865	1.134	2.435[a]	1.367	0.940
Black	1.237	1.316[b]	0.955	1.019	1.099	1.132	0.402[a]	0.592[a]	0.911	0.970	0.804
Other	0.732	1.048	1.060	1.088	1.026	1.405	0.946	0.822	0.992	0.986	1.130

In most models the amount of explained variation is less than 10 percent, though the models still make statistically significant improvements to the predictive power of base line odds alone.

[a] Significant at 0.01.
[b] Significant at 0.05.

have looked for job information online and 68 percent more likely to look for religious or spiritual content online.

The relationship between education and conduct online is straight-forward. The more education a person has the greater the odds that he will be interested in using the Internet for particular activities. On the whole, people with at least a bachelors degree are more likely to have used email and to have been in search of information. A person's level of education strongly predicts the probability that he or she will use the Internet for financial, political, or government information. More-educated people also seem more confident about performing online banking and carrying out other financial transactions online.

A User Typology

A typology can be built around respondents' answers to two questions: how long have you had Internet access? And, how frequently do you log on from home? We tested several other variables – demo-graphic traits and responses to other questions about use of the Internet – and found that responses to questions about experience levels and frequency of home use yield the most robust typology.

One major advantage of focusing on these questions is that they give insights into users' willingness to be innovative, which appears to be more important than demographic characteristics in predicting how people use and feel about the Internet. As characterized by Everett Rogers, "innovativeness [is] the degree to which an individual or other unit of adoption is relatively earlier in adopting new ideas than other members of a social system" (Rogers, 1995, p. 261). By focusing on the moment in time that people began using the Internet, we get a measure of their position relative to others in the social system. Furthermore, their interest in using the Internet from their homes gives a measure of the degree to which they have embraced Internet tools above and beyond the interest they would be compelled to have if they have access to the Internet at work. Those who arranged for Internet access at home have made a decision to seek information and indulge in leisure activities beyond the things that would be necessary at the workplace. Home access and frequent home use are measures, then, of "overt behavioral change" that is the hallmark of people's willingness to be innovative (Rogers, 1995, p. 252). As is the case with Rogers's adopter categories (innovator, early adopter, early majority, late majority, laggard) our typology is intended to produce "ideal types based on abstractions from empirical investigations" (Rogers, 1995, p. 263).

Four broad categories of Internet users can be identified based on the length of their Internet experience and the frequency with which they say they log on from home. We have labeled them this way:

Netizens comprise 16 percent of the adult Internet population and 8 percent of the adult US population, as of September, 2000. They started going online more than three years ago *and* go online from home every day. They have incorporated the Internet into their work lives and home lives; are relatively comfortable spending money online; use the Internet to help manage their personal finances; use email to enhance their social relationships; and are the most avid participants on most web activities on an average day.

Utilitarians comprise about 28 percent of the adult Internet population and 14 percent of the US adult population. They started going online more than three years ago *or* got access two or three years ago but also log on from home every day. Compared to netizens, members of this group are less intense in their use of the Internet, express less appreciation for what the Internet contributes to their lives, are less likely to spend and manage their money online, and are less active in accessing the web's content. At the same time, they exploit the Internet for many tasks in their lives and have a quite functional approach to web use. The Internet is a tool for them, although, as a group, they tend to see it as less useful and entertaining than netizens do.

There are slightly fewer *experimenters* than utilitarians. Experimenters comprise 26 percent of the adult Internet population and 13 percent of the US adult population. They started going online two to three years ago *or* started about a year ago and go online from home every day. Relatively speaking, they have ventured beyond the fun activities that Internet novices enjoy and are interested in using the Internet as an information retrieval utility.

The fourth user type is *newcomers*. They comprise 30 percent of the adult Internet population and 15 percent of the US adult population. They started going online about a year ago or more recently than that. This group shows many of the characteristics of apprentices. They are learning their way around. But even without a great deal of experience, they enjoy many of the fun aspects of the Internet at levels similar to the overall average of the Internet population. That would include playing games, browsing for fun, participating in chat rooms, getting information about hobbies, and listening to and downloading

Table 1.3 Demographic attributes of Internet users

March–June compiled, weighted		User type (%)			
		Newcomers	Experimenters	Utilitarians	Netizens
Gender	Men	44	46	54	62
	Women	56	54	46	38
Race	White	82	86	86	88
	Black	12	8	7	4
	Hispanic	8	7	5	5
Age cohort	18–24	15	17	18	19
	25–9	11	13	12	14
	30–9	28	27	25	24
	40–9	23	22	21	21
	50–64	17	15	18	16
	65+	5	3	5	5
Education	High school diploma or less	45	31	25	18
	Some college	30	32	30	33
	Bachelor's degree +	24	37	45	49
Income	Under $30,000	27	22	20	17
	$30 k–$50 k	32	29	25	22
	$50 k–$75 k	22	23	22	22
	$75,000+	18	26	32	38
Parental status	Parent of child under 18	46	45	38	36
	Not a parent	54	55	62	64
Access	Home only	36	26	25	14
	Work only	43	35	22	—
	Both home/work	15	22	36	28
Weighted N		3,028	2,644	2,909	1,671
%		30	26	28	16

music. More than other groups, newcomers are likely to have access in only one place – either at work or at home (table 1.3).

The most innovative and aggressive users of the Internet are netizens. The composition of this group is heavily weighted towards men, the well educated, the relatively well to do, and whites. Though netizens comprise 16 percent of the overall Internet population in America, they make up a far greater proportion of daily users of the Internet (table 1.4). On a typical day, netizens make up 25 percent of the traffic online. Their role in daily traffic swells even more on weekend days, when they become 29 percent of users. They are also 39 percent of those who spend more than two hours online on a typical day.

Table 1.4 A typology of users by online activity

March–June compiled, weighted Activities "ever"	All users	Newcomers	User type (%) Experimenters	Utilitarians	Netizens
Email	92	84	92	96	97
Fun					
Sought information about a hobby	75	66	76	78	85
Watched video clip, listened to audio clip	48	36	45	53	70
Browsed just for fun	61	60	60	62	66
Sent instant messages	45	35	43	48	59
Listened to or downloaded music	37	32	33	39	47
Checked sports scores	36	29	36	39	46
Played a game	33	35	31	33	36
Taken part in a chat room	24	22	24	24	27
Information utility					
Sought information about product/service	73	63	73	76	86
Got information about travel	65	52	66	69	80
Got news	60	47	56	67	78
Checked weather	62	50	60	68	77

Got financial information such as stock prices	44	32	41	50	63
Sought information from government website	40	29	39	47	51
Got news about politics	34	23	31	41	49
Sought religious information	21	18	20	24	25
Major life activities					
Done work online for your job	50	36	47	58	66
Sought health information	55	48	55	56	64
Research for school or job training	55	47	55	61	64
Sought information about a job	38	26	40	45	46
Sought information on place to live	27	15	26	33	43
Joined online support group	24	15	23	25	31
Transactions					
Bought a product online	47	28	45	54	71
Made a travel reservation online	29	20	29	31	40
Bank online	18	8	14	22	32
Participated in online auction	12	7	11	13	24
Bought or sold stocks, bonds	9	6	7	11	18
Weighted N	10,252	3,028	2,644	2,909	1,671
%	100	30	26	28	16

The differences in Internet use between netizens and other US Internet users are pronounced on that typical day. Netizens are 45 percent of those buying or selling stocks, bonds, and mutual fund shares; 44 percent of those doing online banking; 40 percent of those participating in online auctions; 34 percent of those getting financial information such as stock prices or mortgage rates; 33 percent of those doing work or research for their jobs; 32 percent of those getting news; 32 percent of those getting information about products and services and 29 percent of those buying books, music, toys, or clothing; 32 percent of those doing school research or getting job training.

The degree to which the Internet has become integral to netizens' jobs is highlighted by the gap between them and other Internet users in their use of the web for research related to work. In addition, netizens are conspicuously more likely than other Internet users to do school work and get job training online. Beyond that, netizens are twice as likely as other Internet users to be taking advantage of the web as an information utility on a given day. Still, netizens enjoy the fun features of the Internet that newcomers and less-experienced users enjoy. A two-to-one gap between netizens and the rest of the Internet population generally holds up for most of the fun features of the Web.

Like netizens, utilitarians are also veteran Internet users. But they stand apart from netizens in their lesser involvement. They are mostly average in their embrace and use of the Internet. Behaviorally, they do many things at rates slightly above the norm among the entire Internet population, but nothing about them or their use of the Internet is exceptional. They tend to have a functional, task-oriented approach to their use of the Internet and are much less likely than netizens to use the Internet at home and for fun activities. They spend less time online than netizens and they log on less frequently. They are also less likely than netizens to have oriented their financial affairs around the Internet. If there is a pattern to experimenters' small areas of difference with average Internet users, it is that they have used the Internet more than average for practical and serious reasons.

Unlike netizens and utilitarians, experimenters are a group where women outnumber men. They have ventured beyond games and fun activities on the Internet. They use the web as an information utility and resource to consult on life-changing moves such as finding new housing or job opportunities. Utilitarians show slightly higher-than-average use of the web for certain activities, especially the   most serious and consequential activities. In comparison, experimenters show slightly below average use of the web on those kinds of activities.

Internet Newcomers differ markedly from the other, more experienced types. For one thing, women make up 56 percent of the group. Almost half of all the African–Americans with Internet access (43 percent) are newcomers; they comprise 12 percent of the newcomer class. More than two-thirds of newcomers (69 percent) live in households that earn less than $50,000. Almost half (45 percent) ended their schooling with a high school or trade school diploma.

These newcomers are not nearly as intense in Internet usage as are more experienced users, but they are drawn to the Internet for fun activities, such as chat rooms and instant messaging. What separates newcomers dramatically from veteran users is their relative unwillingness to conduct financial or commercial transactions online. Use of the Internet is a home-based activity for newcomers; they are more likely to log on from home, and less likely to log on from work than more experienced types of users.

Newcomers have not integrated the Internet into their lives to the same extent as more experienced users. Although they constitute 30 percent of overall Internet population, Newcomers are only 19 percent of the Internet population on a typical day. The modest use of the Internet by newcomers is reflected in the fact that they are involved at about half the rate as the Internet population's average with almost every web activity we measure.

Rhythms of Internet Use

In most respects, the rhythms of Internet use follow familiar cadences in everyday life.[4] There is heavier use of the Internet during a typical weekday, when on average 60 percent of Internet users log on, than during a weekend day, when on average 45 percent of Internet users go online. That makes sense because workplace use of computers and

---

4 The continuous tracking survey allows us to examine some of the basic patterns of use of the Internet during different blocks of time during the day, different days of the week, and different seasons of the year. The results presented here come from surveys taken during 122 consecutive nights (March 1–June 30), followed by a three-week break and then another 27 straight nights of polling from July 24 through August 20. The method of asking Internet users about the things they did "yesterday" permits for fresh recall on the part of respondents and for the collection of data about the time of day users logged on.

Table 1.5 Weekdays and weekends online

March–June compiled, weighted Activities "yesterday"	Average daily use by Americans with Internet access (%)		
	Weekday	Weekend day	% change
Go online	60	45	−25
Seek information from a government website	5	2	−60
Do work research	18	8	−56
Get financial information	16	8	−50
Listen to/download music	6	3	−50
Do research for school	13	8	−39
Watch a video clip	8	5	−38
Seek information about a product	14	9	−36
Look for medical information	6	4	−33
Look for information about a hobby	19	13	−32
Send or read email	53	37	−30
Check weather reports	18	13	−28
Get news online	22	16	−27
Browse for fun	20	15	−25
Check sports scores	9	9	0
Participate in an online auction	2	2	0
Buy a product online	4	4	0
Take part in "chat rooms"	3	3	0
Work access only	26	7	−73
Both home and work access	22	11	−48
Home access only	50	79	57
Weighted N	4,422	1,283	
%	78	22	

the Internet is relatively high during days of the week when most people are at their jobs. Even the most popular Internet activities are practiced less often during weekend days than on weekdays: Email use drops 30 percent during the weekend and the seeking of hobby information drops by 32 percent. On weekend days workplace use of the Internet plummets by 62 percent. It is not surprising, then, to see that participation in some of the most serious web activities also falls. On an average weekday, 18 percent of Internet users are doing work-related research, compared to 8 percent who are doing such research on a typical weekend day (table 1.5).

Our surveys have produced data that supports the idea that the boundary between work and home is blurring. There is evidence that

Table 1.6 Mixing home life and work life

March–June compiled, weighted	Activities (%)	
	"Ever"	"Yesterday"
Internet users who have online access *only at work* who do these things on the web		
Seek information about product or service	63	6
Look for hobby information	59	6
Get information about travel	53	7
Browse the net for fun	48	11
Look for medical information	44	3
Get financial information	39	8
Check sports scores and information	36	5
Buy travel services	22	2
Listen to music or download it	26	2
Internet users who have online access *only at home* who do these things on the web		
Do research for school or training	51	8
Do work or research for their jobs	26	5
Weighted N	10,281	5,312
%	100	56

the changes between what is done at work and at home flow in both directions: People use the Internet to do non-work activities while on the job; and people use the Internet to do work-related activities at home. On a typical day, at least a tenth of Internet users who only have access to it on the job use the Internet to do something that is unrelated to work. More than two-thirds of Internet users with work-only access have acknowledged ever doing something extracurricular on the web while on the job. More than half of Internet users who only have access at home have done something related to work and a healthy number are doing "work" at home on a typical day (table 1.6).

Email Enhances the Social World of Internet Users

As daily activity on the Internet grows, there has been considerable interest in the question of whether Internet use encourages social connectedness or social isolation. Respondents tell us that the Internet allows people to stay in touch with both family and friends and, in many cases, extend their social networks. A sizeable majority of those who email relatives say it increases the level of communication between family members. Some 59 percent of those who use email to communicate with their families communicate more often now with their primary family contact, and 60 percent of those who email friends say the same thing about increased communication with their primary friend contact. About 31 percent of family emailers have started communicating with a family member that they had not contacted much before.

Still, the question remains: Does going online divert users from social interactions? These survey results suggest online tools are more likely to extend social contact, rather than detract from it. American Internet users as a group are more socially active than non-users and that might be explained in part because these Internet users are disproportionately from higher socio-economic groups. However, we have found that Internet use is positively associated with social activity. Table 1.7 identifies the odds ratios for predicting someone's response to questions about social networks. For example, the odds that a 25-year old, Anglo-American male without a BA who has never gone online feels that they can turn to many people for support are almost 18 to 1. If this person had ever gone online, the odds would improve to 22 to 1. In another hypothetical case, the odds that a 25-year old, African-American male without a BA who does not go online feels they can turn to many people for support are only 8 to 1. If this person had ever gone online, the odds improve 24 percent to 10 to 1. Thus, controlling for other important variables, those who have ever gone online are 24 percent more likely than those who have never gone online to say they can turn to many people for support. In parallel, those who have ever gone online are 40 percent less likely than those who have never gone online to say they can turn to hardly anybody for support. Moreover, with other variables held constant, people who have ever gone online are 46 percent more likely to have called a friend or relative just to talk on the previous day. This contradicts the assertion by some that the Internet detracts from other forms of socialization (Nie and Erbring, 2000), while supporting the claims of others that the Internet may increase socialization (Wellman and Hampton, 1999).

Many users feel that using Internet tools has improved the way they do their hobbies, manage finances, get information about healthcare, shop, and generally learn about new things. More experienced users are much more likely than new users to be excited about using the Internet for personal hobbies, health or finances because some of that excitement also drives people to explore ever-more Internet resources.

Table 1.7(a) Logistic regression results: odds (e^B) of particular responses to questions about social and personal life, modeled with age, gender, education, Internet use, and race

	Thinking about your personal life, when you need help would you say you can turn to...			Yesterday, did you....					March 2000 iteration Unweighted N	%
	...many people for support?	...just a few people for support?	...hardly any people for support?	...visit with family or friends?	...call a friend or relative just to talk?	...read a newspaper?	...watch an hour or more TV news?	...watch an hour or more TV?		
Baseline odds (constant)	0.721[a]	0.783[b]	1.142[a]	1.407[a]	0.303[a]	0.150[a]	0.100[a]	1.145	3,445	100
Age	0.994[a]	0.999	1.005	0.990[a]	0.968[a]	1.032[a]	1.025[a]	1.005	3,445	100
Female	1.695[a]	0.794[a]	0.691[a]	2.511[a]	1.357[a]	0.734[a]	1.034	0.947	1,829	53
BA or more	1.168	1.101	0.515[a]	0.976	0.960	1.559[a]	1.013	0.680[a]	915	27
Ever online	1.243[b]	1.062	0.593[a]	1.031	1.458[a]	1.391[a]	0.860	0.872	1,647	48
Online yesterday	1.112	0.904	0.977	1.125	0.813	1.255[b]	1.218	0.928	985	29
Race (white as reference)										
Asian	0.327[a]	2.438[a]	1.243	0.583[b]	0.351[a]	0.659	1.070	0.537	70	2
Black	0.450[a]	1.338[a]	2.257[a]	1.403[a]	0.502[a]	0.619[a]	1.282[b]	0.939	417	12
Other	0.890	0.798	1.625[b]	0.853	0.835	0.610[a]	1.052	1.153	185	5

Table 1.7(b) Logistic regression results: odds (e^B) of particular responses to questions about how the Internet has improved social and personal life, modeled with age, gender, education, and connectedness

	Has the Internet affected your social life by improving . . .			Has the Internet affected you personal life by improving . . .				March–August 2000, complied Unweighted	
	. . . connections to your friends?	. . . connections to members of your family?	. . . the way you learn about hobbies?	. . . your ability to learn about new things?	. . . the way you manage your personal finances?	. . . the way you get information about healthcare?	. . . your ability to shop?	N	%
Baseline odds (Constant)	0.974	0.434[a]	0.626[a]	3.853[a]	0.252[a]	0.365[a]	0.581[a]	1,932	100
Age	0.992[a]	1.003[b]	0.994[b]	0.998[a]	0.997	0.999	0.986[a]	1,932	100
Female	1.545[a]	1.815[a]	0.754[a]	0.981	0.764[b]	1.590[a]	0.849	947	49
BA or more	1.066	1.057	0.809[b]	1.030	1.412[a]	1.075	1.200	787	41
Connectedness (new user as reference)									
Average	1.472[a]	1.288[b]	1.094	1.692[a]	1.155	1.012	1.260	463	24
Heavy	2.602[a]	2.046[a]	1.678[a]	2.370[a]	1.892[a]	1.327[b]	1.842	573	30
Daily and experienced	5.164[a]	3.285[a]	2.256[a]	4.042[a]	3.599[a]	1.828[a]	3.245[a]	322	17

In most models the amount of explained variation is less than 10 percent, though the models still make statistically significant improvements to the predictive power of base line odds alone.

[a] Significant at 0.01.
[b] Significant at 0.05.

The magnitude of the effect is surprising – experienced users are two, three, or four times more confident than new users to declare that their online access has improved different aspects of their personal lives.

Conclusion

Many Americans are incorporating Internet tools into their daily lives, and this is reflected in the kinds of activities they pursue online. Many Americans report substantial benefits from being connected. Well over half of all Internet users say the Internet has improved their connection to the family and friends. Three-quarters of them say Internet use has improved their ability to learn about new things. Half say the Internet improves the way they pursue their hobbies; 37 percent say it improves the way they do their jobs; 35 percent say the Internet has improved the way they get information about healthcare; 34 percent say the Internet improves their ability to shop; and 26 percent say it has improved the way they manage their personal finances.

There are a variety of demographic factors that affect people's use of the Internet, including gender, age, education, income, race, and ethnicity. But the most useful predictors of the activities that users enjoy online are their length of experience with the Internet and their frequency of logging on from home. We constructed a typology using these two variables that establishes four categories of Internet users in America: netizens are the heaviest and most enthusiastic Internet users; utilitarians have a more functional approach to the Internet use; experimenters have ventured into various information spheres online; and newcomers are beginning to enjoy the fun features of the Web.

As the Internet becomes a common communication tool, familiar patterns of social interaction appear online. Americans' use of the Internet tracks with the rhythms of their lives at work and at home.

Although results from our surveys have yielded interesting data about people's activities online, more research should be done into the different degrees of effect for people who occasionally log on and those who go online daily. Another important research question is whether today's newcomers will "grow up" after they become comfortable and familiar with the web to behave like today's "netizens" or whether they will chart a different course online because today's novices are so demographically different from Internet veterans.

References

Beniger, J. (1987). Personalization of mass media and the growth of pseudo-community. *Communication Research*, 14, 352–71.

Bennett, C. and Grant, R. (2000). *Visions of privacy: policy choices for the digital age*. Toronto: University of Toronto Press.

Borsook, P. (2000). *Cyberselfish: a critical romp through the terribly libertarian culture of high tech*. New York: Public Affairs.

Cairncross, I. (1997). *The death of distance: how the communications revolution will change our lives*. Cambridge MA: Harvard Business School Press.

Carmel, E. (1997). American hegemony in packaged software trade and the "Culture of Software." *The Information Society*, 13, 125–42.

Dizard, W. (1997). *MegaNet: how the global communications network will connect everyone on earth*. Boulder, CO: Westview Press.

Etzioni, A. (1997). Communities: virtual vs. real. *Science*, 277(n5324), 295.

Fishkin, J. (1992). *The dialogue of justice: toward a self-reflective society*. New Haven, CT: Yale University Press.

Moore, D. (1987). Political campaigns and the knowledge-gap hypothesis. *Public Opinion Quarterly*, 51(2), 186–200.

Nie, N. H. and Erbring, L. (2000). Internet and society: a preliminary report. Available online at: http://www.stanford.edu/group/siqss/

Oldenburg, R. (1991). *The great good place: cafes, coffee shops, community centers, beauty parlors, general stores, bars, hangouts, and how they get you through the day*. New York: Marlowe & Co.

Rochlin, G. (1998). *Trapped in the Net: the unanticipated consequences of computerization*. Princeton, NJ: Princeton University Press.

Rogers, E. (1995). *Diffusion of innovations*. New York: The Free Press.

Schwartz, E. (1996). *Netactivism: how citizens use the Internet*. Sebastopol, CA: Songline Studies.

Shenk, D. (1997). *Data smog: surviving the information glut*. San Francisco, CA: Harper Edge.

Sproull, L. and Kiesler, S. (1992). *Connections: new ways of working in the networked organization*. Cambridge, MA: MIT Press.

Sudweeks, F. (1998). *Network and netplay: virtual groups on the Internet*. Cambridge, MA: MIT Press.

Wellman, B. (1999). The network community: an introduction to networks in the global village. In B. Wellman (ed.), *Networks in the global village* (pp. 1–47). Boulder, CO: Westview Press.

Wellman, B. and Gulia, M. (1999). Net surfers don't ride alone: virtual communities as communities. In B. Wellman (ed.), *Networks in the global village* (pp. 331–67) Boulder, CO: Westview Press.

Wellman, B. and Hampton, K. (1999). Living networked on and offline. *Contemporary Sociology*, 28(6), 648–54.

Willock, R. (1998). *Soundbite culture: the death of discourse in a wired world.* Thousand Oaks, CA: Sage.

Witte, J., Amoroso, L., and Howard, P. (2000). Method and representation in Internet-based survey tools: mobility, community, and cultural identity in Survey2000. *Social Science Computer Review*, 18(2), 179–95.

2

The Global Villagers

Comparing Internet Users and Uses Around the World

Wenhong Chen, Jeffrey Boase, and Barry Wellman

Abstract

As the Internet evolves, its users and uses grow and diversify globally. Data from a National Geographic web survey enables us to compare how people in different parts of the world use the Internet. The widest digital divide is between North America and the rest of the world, and secondarily between other developed countries and developing countries. Substantial differences exist between who uses the Internet and how long they have been using it. The lower the percentage of people using the Internet in a region, the more elite the people using the Internet. However, newcomers to the Internet throughout the world are less likely to be elite and are more likely to resemble the diverse nature of North American Internet users. By contrast to regional differences in the characteristics of users, the Internet is used in similar ways worldwide. Throughout the world, frequent users tend to use the Internet in multiple ways – socially, instrumentally, and recreationally – and to combine it with face-to-face and telephone contact. Moreover, frequent users of the Internet have a more positive sense of online community with friends and family.

Authors' note

We thank Xingshan Cao, Keith Hampton, Eszter Hargittai, Hao Li, Caroline Haythornthwaite, Melissa Kew, Valerie May, Anabel Quan-Haase, and Beverly Wellman for their advice. We are especially grateful to James Witte for organizing Survey 2000 and to Uzma Jalaluddin, Monica Prijatelj, and Uyen Quach for help in preparing the tables and references. Our compatriots at the University of Toronto's NetLab, Centre for Urban and Community Studies, Department of Sociology, and the Knowledge Media Design

Institute have created stimulating milieus for thinking about the Internet in society. Our research has been supported by the IBM Institute of Knowledge Management, the National Geographic Society, the (US) National Science Foundation, and the Social Science and Humanities Research Council of Canada. We dedicate this chapter to Manuel Castells, a shining star of the Internet galaxy.

Exploring the Internet Globally

Uncharted and uneven terrain

As the Internet evolves, its users and uses grow and diversify globally.[1] Social research about the Internet has followed the spread of the Internet itself. With the Internet born and raised in the USA, most research has been American. With Internet use increasing in other developed countries, research about their situations has been on the rise (for example, see the chapters by Anderson and Tracy; Hampton and Wellman; Miyata; Wagner, Pischner, and Haisken-DeNew). However, there has been little research about how Internet use fits into the everyday life of developing countries (see Davidson, Sooryamoorthy, and Shrum's chapter). Furthermore, international comparisons are almost non-existent. Those comparative studies that do exist have focused on the size of the population using the Internet ("penetration rate") and market potential rather than on social characteristics associated with Internet use. These studies have had to rely on statistics gathered with different methods in each country. The result has been uneven data and conflicting results (Jordan, 2001; Norris, 2001).

Two projects have been addressing the need for systematic comparative data. One, the UCLA World Internet Project is an international undertaking to study changes associated with the Internet. Researchers in 24 countries administer a standard set of 30 questions (plus additional modules reflecting local and national interests) in an annual longitudinal study.[2]

We are part of the second project which uses data from *Survey 2000*, gathered at the National Geographic Society website. We draw on the

1 There are no reliable estimates of the number of worldwide Internet users. Some plausibly indicative ones report 900,000 in 1993 (ACNielsen, 2001); 25 million in 1995 (Pew Research Center for People and the Press, 1995); 83 million in 1999 (Intelli-Quest, 1999 as cited in DiMaggio, Hargittai, Neuman, and Robinson, 2001) and 429 million in 2001 (ACNielsen, 2001).
2 For details, see Cole et al. 2001. Lunn and Suman's chapter (19) provides American data from an early survey.

happy circumstance that Survey 2000 attracted respondents from 178 countries to report on who they are and how they use the Internet. Although the nature of the sample limits generality, it is truly global. Moreover, we believe that this is the first scholarly study to compare systematically worldwide data about the users and uses of the Internet.

We use the data to address five questions about the worldwide users of the Internet and the uses they make of it. Our principal comparison is between North America, other economically developed countries in the Organization for Economic Cooperation and Development (OECD), and other, often developing, countries. We also compare seven geographically defined regions. We ask:

1 What are the profiles of users? What is the nature of the global digital divide?
2 How long have people been using the Internet? Is there a temporal digital divide in the length of people's Internet experience?
3 What do people do online? To what extent is their activity instrumental, recreational, and social?
4 Does Internet affect people's sense of online community with friends and family? Are they enthusiastic or alienated?
5 Where in the world are the widest digital divides? Are other economically developed countries more similar in their Internet users and uses to North America or to developing countries?

The global digital divide

The worldwide debate about the Internet's impact on both societies and individuals is not only a scholarly matter. Policymakers see the Internet as a catalyst for broad socioeconomic development, while corporations see the Internet as a profit source. Those accessing the Internet use different levels of technology and make different uses of it. Comparing Internet users and their Internet use inevitably directs attention to the global digital divide at the intersection of international and intra-national differences: socioeconomic, linguistic, and technological (OECD, 2001; Jordan, 2001).

The "digital divide" originally denoted unequal access to the Internet because of characteristics such as gender, age, race, ethnicity, education, income, geographic location, English-language ability, and physical and cognitive disability (NTIA, 1995). Early studies found that users were disproportionately young, white, university-educated, English-speaking, middle/upper-class, male North Americans. By the end of 2001, more than half of the North American population had come online, and gaps of gender, age, and geographic location have decreased. The socioeconomic threshold of Internet access continues to sink with the influx to cyberspace of newcomers from less-privileged social groups (see the chapters by Katz and Rice; Howard, Rainie, and Jones; see also Fong, Wellman, Wilkes, and Kew, 2001).

The expansion of the term "digital divide" to "global digital divide" points to differences in Internet access and use between countries, as well as within countries. Such inequalities have led to "a substantial asymmetry in the distribution and effective use of information and communication resources between two or more populations" (Wilson, 2000). As Manuel Castells notes, "Differences in Internet access between countries and regions in the planet at large are so considerable that they actually modify the meaning of the digital divide, and the kind of issue to be discussed" (2001, p. 248).

There are substantial differences in Internet use within countries as well as between them. For instance, China has a relatively large number of Internet users, 22.5 million, but they are less than 3 percent of its population. Almost 7 out of 10 Chinese users are men, 6 out of 10 are under 30 years old, about two-thirds are single, and 93 percent have been educated beyond high school in a country where only a minority have post-high school education (CNNIC, 2001). As in many developing countries, the bulk of Internet users are located in large urban centers: Beijing, Shanghai, and Guangdong account for more than 30 percent of Chinese Internet users, with 23 percent of the homes in these cities connected to the Internet. The distribution of Internet users is so urban-centric that only 0.8 percent of the users in this largely agrarian country are farmers (CNNIC, 2001). Similarly, 35 percent of Russian Internet users are located in Moscow and St Petersburg, cities containing only 12 percent of the Russian population (Varoli, 2001).

The global digital divide reflects the broader context of international social and economic relations. The between-countries divide represents a center–periphery order marked by North American dominance. Although 5 percent of the world's population is online, more than 60 percent of the online population is North American (ACNielsen, 2001). Other developed countries vary in the percentage of their populations using the Internet, with their penetration rates ranging widely from as high as those in North America to substantially lower. The percentage of Internet users in developing countries is far lower than in developed countries. Hence, developing countries account for 85 percent of the world's population, but only 20 percent of Internet users (*Economist*, 2000). For instance, while the total African online population is no greater than the online population of New York or Tokyo (ABC News, 2000), Africa probably has fewer email addresses allocated to it than the Massachusetts Institute of Technology (McTaggart, 2002).

Issues

A social divide

International differences in the Internet's development are social as well as technological and commercial. The digital divide is not just a matter of differences in access to Internet service providers, broadband, and reliable electric and communication systems. It is a matter of who is going to use the Internet, for what purposes, under what circumstances, and how this use affects other social and economic activities. There are international variations in physical, financial, cognitive, content, and political access (Wilson, 2000). In particular, developing countries have large segments of the population whose poverty and lack of literacy make Internet access unthinkable, and where even those who want to go online live in rural or impoverished urban areas without useful electrical and communication systems.

Use, not just access

Internet use is not just a simple matter of Internet access, although marketers often report only the number of people who have access to the Internet and what they are likely to buy online. Yet, Internet use is not as simple as a binary yes/no access question. "What is at stake is not access to ICT in the narrow sense of having a computer on the premises, but rather in a wider sense of being able to use ICT for personally or socially meaningful ends" (Warschauer, 2003, chapter 2, paragraph 6).

The issue is not if people have ever glanced at a monitor or put their hands on a keyboard; it is if they regularly use the Internet and for what purpose. Having access to the Internet and having the ability to use the Internet effectively are two very different aspects of the digital divide (see also Jung, Qiu, and Kim 2001).

While academic, government, and commercial research have focused on the issues of access, we know less about the effects of the Internet on people in different corners of the global village. Essential elements include price, quality, bandwidth, computer skills, and online content. Cost is more salient outside North America because Internet connection charges, even in developed countries, are more expensive. In the developing world, nearly half of the 228 Internet service providers in Africa are connected via satellite, making the access cost almost prohibitive for most people living in this continent. For example, the cost in some African countries is US$60 for 5 hours a month plus telephone connection charges (United States Internet Council and ITTA, 2001).

Content barriers affect how the Internet is used, for example, English-language dominance and the lack of local information and culturally appropriate material. As Anatoly Voronov, the director of the Russian Internet service provider, Glasnet, exclaims:

> It is just incredible when I hear people talking about how open the Web is. It is the ultimate intellectual colonialism. The product comes from America so we either must adapt to English or stop using it . . . This just makes the world into new sorts of haves and have-nots. (quoted in Crystal, 1997, p. 108)

Most Internet content targets well-off, well-educated, English-speaking users. An estimated 78 percent of all websites are in the English language, even though just over 50 percent of Internet users are native English speakers, and only 10 percent of the world population use English as a first language. Indeed, the predominant standard for computer characters has difficultly using non-English characters: ASCII (the *American* Standard Code for Information Interchange). So far, English-language dominance of the Internet has not been extensively challenged by the worldwide growth of Internet users who natively read other languages (Jordan, 2001). Yet, lack of appropriate content is a reason why the digital divide looms in both developed and developing countries.

The growth of the Internet may even exacerbate existing knowledge disparities and lead to the further social exclusion of disadvantaged groups. DiMaggio, et al. (2001) identify five dimensions of digital inequality: equipment, autonomy of use (location of use), skill, social support, and the purposes of using the Internet. Indeed, access does not always mean continued use. Some Internet users drop out because of frustration with cost, content, or technology (see Katz and Rice, chapter 3).

Newbies and veterans

Most research has focused on comparing users and non-users. Less attention has been paid to comparing different types of users, especially the ways in which newcomers to the Internet ("newbies") and veteran users differ from each other and how those differences might mediate the impact of the Internet. Yet, the length of Internet experience may play a critical role in users' online behavior and their evaluation of the Internet (see the chapter by Quan-Haase and Wellman). For instance, Pittsburgh newbies became alienated and less sociable when they first went online. Yet these negative effects disappeared by their third year online, as they gained more experience and the world became more Internet-literate. Extroverts especially flourish online. (Compare Kraut, Patterson, Lundmark, Kiesler, Mukhopadhyay, and Scherlis, 1998 with Kraut, Kiesler, Boneva, Cummings, Helgeson, and Crawford, 2002; see also LaRose, Eastin, and Gregg, 2001).

The widening and deepening digital divide

The digital divide may be wider and deeper within developing countries than within developed countries: wider in the sense that few people actively use the Internet and deeper in the sense that the consequences for not being online may be greater when moving beyond a subsistence level. In developed countries, people are rapidly becoming newbies, and newbies are becoming veterans. The Internet has become an integral part of everyday life for a great many who use the Internet as a medium to communicate and pursue personal interests. Because the technology has become so pervasive, low costs, training and mentoring afford users the time and experience needed to use the Internet effectively. Non-users can usually find a friend, neighbor, or child to work the Internet for them.

By contrast, high costs in developing countries may mean that users have less of the experience needed to use the technology to their advantage. They are less likely to find help locally in dealing with the online world. If pre-existing inequalities deter people in developing countries from using the Internet, these inequalities may increase as the Internet becomes more central to global life: from keeping in contact with migrant kin, to acquiring information, to engaging in farm-to-market commerce. Hence, rather than socially including marginal people and countries, the embedding of the Internet in everyday life can enhance and deepen power relations underlying existing inequalities.

Research Questions

Who is using the global Internet?

Is the profile of international users recapitulating the socio-demographic development of North American users? If so, would the recent bulk of global Internet users represent the same male, urban, educated, and upper/middle-class profile that was prevalent until recently in North America?

A second possibility is that users outside North America are even more of an elite than the early North American adopters of the Internet were. The preponderance of elite users is because of the high level of poverty in most developing countries and the higher cost of Internet use in almost all countries except for North America. The global digital divide would be widest within those developing countries with much socioeconomic inequity and poverty. This possibility suggests the importance of the digital divide, both culturally and economically, within countries as well as between countries.

A third possibility is that Internet use has become so globally popular that a wide range of people are flocking to use it as needed, including women, rural folks, and those with low socioeconomic status. They overcome their poverty by using facilities in community centers or storefront cybercafes.

Who are the newbies?

If the social demographic profile of users in the global village provides a picture of the spatial divergence of Internet access, the characteristics of newbies should illustrate the temporal dimension of Internet diffusion across countries. A higher percentage of Internet users outside North America are newbies due to the recency of Internet deployment there. Hence, current newbies will be the predominant international Internet users of the near future. To know the current characteristics of newbies is to peek into the future characteristics of many Internet users. Are newbies the same or different around the world, in their characteristics, enthusiasms, and Internet uses?

Do different parts of the world vary in their uses
of the Internet in everyday life?

When users start using the Internet comfortably, they move from being toddlers making their first online keystrokes to being walkers and runners in the global village. What Internet uses are common or different around the world? What social characteristics are associated with different uses? Are differences only temporal, in that it takes time for newbies to become old hands? We know a good deal about how North Americans use the Internet, but do users in other developed and developing countries use it in similar ways?

Does the Internet build sociability and a sense of community?

How does the Internet affect community, in general and online? Although there have been concerns for more than a century about the possible decline of community, the rise of the Internet has increased these fears as well as created new hopes for increased community (reviewed in Wellman, 1999; Wellman and Gulia, 1999; Quan-Haase and Wellman, chapter 10). The debate about the Internet's impact on community has been fierce, with scholars suggesting that Internet use increases, decreases, or transforms community (Quan-Haase and Wellman's chapter (10) sets forth the debate). Evidence from many studies in this book suggests that the Internet may be modestly increasing interaction with friends and relatives at a distance, has mixed local effects, and may be diverting people from household interactions. The Internet can be leading people away from in-person and telephone encounters, and it can substitute for them. It can even increase other forms of contact by intensifying relationships and facilitating meeting arrangements. We examine here the relationship between Internet use, having a sense of online community, and the frequency of social contact – both face-to-face and by telephone.

Surveying the Global Village

The virtual expedition

The *National Geographic* magazine and society publicized Survey 2000 worldwide and featured it on their popular website, September to November 1998. Visitors to the site were encouraged to answer the

survey on the spot. The survey collected data from Internet users in
178 countries about activities they carried out both online and offline.[3]

Twenty thousand (20,282) adults (18+ years) completed all the questions that are of interest to us. The ten largest sources of survey respondents include four predominantly English-speaking countries: United
States (67.4 percent), Canada (9.5 percent), Australia (3.4 percent),
and United Kingdom (3.1 percent), each with populations with high
Internet use (from 40 percent for the United States to 21 percent for
the United Kingdom; figures from 1999). The next six largest sources
are Mexico, New Zealand, Germany, Hungary, South Africa, and
Italy, but numbers in the sample drop markedly with Mexico comprising 1.1 percent of the sample, and Italy, 0.7 percent of the sample
(table 2.1).

The web-based data collection method for Survey 2000 was innovative, convenient, cost-effective, wide-ranging, and produced a
large sample. Yet, it was not based on random sampling that permits researchers to generalize reliably to the characteristics of Internet
users around the world. As the *National Geographic* appeals to a
literate, family-oriented readership, it is probable that the survey
over-sampled well-educated and well-off respondents. However, it is
precisely the well-educated who are apt to use the Internet, especially
in less-developed countries. Hence, there are discrepancies between
the percentage of each country's population using the Internet and the
percentage of the sample coming from each country.

National representation in the sample roughly reflects a complex
combination of population size, Internet penetration rate, English-
language use, and interest in the US-oriented content dominating the
web. There are also some unusual over- and under-representations.
For example, active recruiting led Hungary to be the third most represented European country, after the United Kingdom and Germany
and ahead of Italy, Spain, the Netherlands, and France (in that order).
Hungary accounts for half (52 percent) of the small East Europe
sample, India accounts for 87 percent of the South Asia sample, while

3 Details of Survey 2000 are at http://survey2000.nationalgeographic.com.
Witte, Amoroso, and Howard (2000) discuss the development and administration
of the survey. May (1999) presents preliminary results to the general public. See
Quan-Haase and Wellman's chapter (10) for more detailed analyses of the North
American data obtained from this survey. Although the magazine itself is published in many languages, Survey 2000 was only available in English. Data from
the newer, multilingual Survey 2001 are not yet available. Survey 2001 itself is at
http://survey2001.nationalgeographic.com/ngm/servlet/Page1

Table 2.1 Country ranking, grouping, number of respondents, and Internet penetration rate, 1999

Country	Category	No. of respondents	% of sample	% population using Internet in 1999[a]
US	North America	13,665	67.4	40
Canada	North America	1,934	9.5	36
Australia	Other OECD	690	3.4	32
UK	Other OECD	619	3.1	21
Mexico	Other OECD	221	1.1	3
New Zealand	Other OECD	190	0.9	18
Germany	Other OECD	181	0.9	19
Hungary	Other OECD	158	0.8	6
South Africa	Non-OECD	155	0.8	N/A
Italy	Other OECD	134	0.7	9
Singapore	Non-OECD	134	0.7	29
Spain	Other OECD	129	0.6	7
Netherlands	Other OECD	113	0.6	19
France	Other OECD	112	0.6	10
Greece	Other OECD	106	0.5	N/A
Malaysia	Non-OECD	100	0.5	7
Israel	Non-OECD	93	0.5	16
Argentina	Non-OECD	84	0.4	3
Sweden	Other OECD	82	0.4	41
Ireland	Other OECD	79	0.4	12
India	Non-OECD	77	0.4	0.2
Hong Kong	Non-OECD	72	0.4	25
Belgium	Other OECD	70	0.3	14
Japan	Other OECD	67	0.3	15
Norway	Other OECD	65	0.3	45
Brazil	Non-OECD	60	0.3	2
Switzerland	Other OECD	59	0.3	25
Finland	Other OECD	53	0.3	33
Portugal	Other OECD	48	0.2	7
Colombia	Non-OECD	41	0.2	1
Denmark	Other OECD	38	0.2	28
Puerto Rico	Non-OECD	35	0.2	N/A
Croatia	Non-OECD	34	0.2	N/A
Venezuela	Non-OECD	34	0.2	2
Philippines	Non-OECD	32	0.2	1
Chile	Non-OECD	31	0.2	4
Austria	Other OECD	27	0.1	10

[a] *Source*: World Employment Report 2001. *Life at Work in the Information Economy*. International Labor Office, Geneva, Switzerland, 2001.

South Africa dominates the African sample (87 percent), and Australia comprises 77 percent of Oceania. East Asian respondents are from relatively developed countries, with Japan, Singapore, and Hong Kong accounting for 57 percent of the sample. By contrast, only 11 respondents from China are in the final sample. Clearly, the National Geographic survey's map of the online world does not look like a map of the world's population.

Despite its limitations, Survey 2000 provides useful signposts alerting us to the nature of Internet users and uses worldwide at a time when there is a paucity of survey research analyzing the global diversity of Internet users. Even with sample discrepancies, these data are congruent with the globally uneven access to the Internet. In fall 1998, the Internet was still North American centric. More than three-quarters of the respondents lived either in the US or in Canada, and less than 10 percent lived in non-OECD countries that usually have lower levels of economic development.

Mapping the Global Internet

Grouping the global villagers

In what follows, we examine how the nature of Internet users and uses is related to a variety of social and individual characteristics, including gender, age, language spoken at home, education, marital status, household size, employment status, use of more conventional media (e.g. newspapers/magazines, and television), and the place of Internet access. We examine these variations worldwide, and also compare three categories of countries that differ in Internet centrality and economic development:

1   As *North America* has been the prime source of Internet technology and use, to capture the effects of early adoption, we compare North American respondents (77 percent of sample) with other "international" respondents. We operationalize "North America" as only the United States and Canada because of Mexico's lower Internet involvement and economic development.

2   To explore the importance of economic development on Internet use and access, membership in the Organization for Economic Cooperation and Development (OECD) is a useful indicator to distinguish developed countries from developing ones, although the typology

leaves out some relatively developed countries such as Singapore. Nevertheless, this typology is useful for this first report. Hence, the economically developed countries that are members of the OECD are classified into one group, excluding the U.S and Canada (listed in appendix 2.1). This *other OECD* group represents 15 percent of the sample.

3   All other countries are grouped into the category of *non-OECD* countries (8 percent of the sample).

In each section, we first present findings for the total global sample, and then compare the similarities and differences of the three categorical divisions. As North America comprises the great majority of the sample, its statistics are similar to the overall sample. However, they provide interesting comparisons with the other OECD and non-OECD countries. To see if geographical regions vary in different ways than the aforementioned economic development groupings, in each section we also compare seven geopolitical regions: North America, Latin America, European Union, (the formerly socialist) East European countries, Asia, Africa, and Oceania. As the sample size is so large, statistical significance does not mean substantive significance. Hence, our analysis focuses on the strongest findings, and we only flag in the tables those few associations between variables that do not reach statistical significance.

Inhabitants of the Internet

Who in the world is using the Internet?

The overall demographic profile (table 2.2) of *National Geographic* survey respondents on the Internet shows that they are predominantly male (54 percent), over 30 (mean = 37 years), speak English at home (75 percent), and usually access the Internet from home (63 percent). The respondents have at least an undergraduate university education (58 percent), a full-time job (59 percent), often read newspapers and magazines (88 percent), and often watch television (67 percent).[4]

The lower the percentage of Internet users in a region, the more elite the respondents. A higher percentage of international respondents have a graduate education and work full-time than do North

4   Respondents were asked how often they read newspapers and magazines, and watch TV: "never," "sometimes," and "often."

Table 2.2 Social profile of Internet users in different national categories (%)

	World	North America	Other OECD	Non-OECD
Women	46	50	34	37
Age (mean)	37	38	33	33
Single	39	37	46	52
English not spoken at home	26	14	60	75
Education				
High school or less	11	9	17	17
Some college	31	33	26	23
Undergraduate	32	34	24	29
Graduate school	26	24	33	31
Employment				
Full-time	59	59	62	62
Part-time	6	6	6	5
Unemployment	8	8	5	6
Retired	5	6	2	2
Student	22	21	25	26
Traditional media use				
Frequent print media user (newspaper, magazine)	88	87	89	90
Frequent TV watcher	67	66	71	72
Place of access				
Home	63	66	53	59
Workplace	29	27	36	33
School	5	5	7	5
Community centers, etc.	3	3	3	3
Newbie (<1 year Internet experience)	19	18	23	22
Internet activity				
Number of Internet activities (mean)	6	6	6	6
Instrumental Internet use scale (mean)	16	16	15	15
Recreational Internet use scale (mean)	2	2	1	2
Sense of online community	22	22	23	24
Sense of online kinship	8	8	7	8
Weekly + contact with kin within 50 km				
Personal visit	33	32	37	35
Telephone	43	42	47	46
Email	16	16	12	14
Weekly + contact with friends within 50 km				
Personal visit	61	60	64	60
Telephone	70	69	74	72
Email	48	49	44	48
Weekly + contact with kin beyond 50 km				
Personal visit	4	3	4	5
Telephone	44	46	42	31
Email	37	40	25	31
Weekly + contact with friends beyond 50 km				
Personal visit	4	4	5	5
Telephone	17	17	18	16
Email	39	40	35	40
Number of survey respondents	20,282	15,599	3,079	1,604

Americans (table 2.2). There is an ordered set of differences between North American, other OECD, and non-OECD respondents. The percentage of male, young, better-educated, multilingual,[5] single, and full-time working respondents is generally highest for the non-OECD respondents and lowest for the North Americans with the other OECD respondents somewhere in between. The data provide information about six socio-demographic dimensions of differences in who uses the Internet. Taken separately and together, they help map the terrain of the digital divide between North America, other OECD, and non-OECD countries.

Gender

The proportion of female respondents outside North America is much lower than the approximately equal gender balance of the North Americans. Only 34 percent of users in other OECD countries and 37 percent in non-OECD countries are women. The gender gap is especially marked in South Asia, Latin America, and East Europe where less than 30 percent of the respondents are women. However, even in the developed European Union, only 34 percent of the respondents are women.

Age

With a mean age of 38, North American respondents are the oldest, while respondents from both other OECD and non-OECD countries have a mean age of 33. A 5-year difference means that while the age gap between younger and older users is diminishing in North America, younger users predominate elsewhere. East European and South Asian respondents have the youngest mean age (28), 10 years younger than the North Americans.

Marital status

The proportion of singles is higher outside North America than in North America. While 37 percent North American users are single, 46 percent of respondents from other OECD countries, and 52 percent from non-OECD countries are single.

---

5   As the survey was in English, we crudely classify respondents as "multilingual" if they report speaking a language other than English at home.

Multilingualism: language used at home

Not surprisingly, the proportion of users who use English at home is much less higher in North America (86 percent) than elsewhere. Forty percent of the respondents from other OECD countries and 25 percent from non-OECD countries primarily use English at home. Only a small percentage of those respondents living in some regions primarily use English at home: Latin America (8 percent), Eastern Europe (14 percent), and Asia (6 to 14 percent). African respondents, of whom 87 percent were from South Africa, are likely to use English at home (44 percent).

Socioeconomic status (education)

Education is the only indicator of socioeconomic status available in Survey 2000. The respondents are well educated: 58 percent worldwide have at least an undergraduate (first) university degree. Internet respondents outside North America tend to have more education: 33 percent of respondents from other OECD countries and 31 percent from non-OECD countries have a postgraduate (master's or doctorate) degree, compared with 24 percent of the North Americans. By region, at least one-third of those outside North America have a postgraduate degree (except for the regions of Eastern Asia, 23 percent, and Oceania, 21 percent). Those with the highest level of education are African: 47 percent have a postgraduate degree, while only 9 percent have less than a high school education.

Employment

A majority of the respondents, almost six out of ten respondents (59 percent) work full-time, while another 22 percent are students. The proportion of unemployed or retired respondents is low around the world. Outside North America, Internet use is strongly associated with working full time or being a student. There is an increase in the share of full-time workers and students from North America (80 percent) to other OECD countries (87 percent) and non-OECD countries (88 percent). To put it another way, one-fifth of North Americans get online without the economic advantage of being able to use the Internet while studying or working full time.

There are some regional variations in this. Almost half (47 percent) of East European respondents are students. East Europe also has the lowest percentage of respondents employed full time (50 percent). East Asian respondents tend to be employed full time (60 percent) or students (31 percent). Only a small minority of respondents is neither a student nor employed full-time. Africa has the highest percentage of full-time workers (78 percent) and the lowest percentage of students (13 percent). This is probably the result of low income, low percentage of the population attending university, and the possible lack of Internet connectivity at schools and universities.

Place of use

Around the world, nearly two-thirds (63 percent) of the respondents primarily use the Internet at home. This compares with 29 percent from their workplace and only 8 percent from community centers, cyber cafés, and other locales. Sixty-six percent of North American respondents primarily use the Internet at home. By contrast, only 53 percent from other OECD countries and 59 percent from non-OECD countries do so.

There are marked regional variations in these global tendencies. Middle Easterners (71 percent) and Oceanians (70 percent) primarily use the Internet from home. East Europeans are the least likely to use the Internet from home (only 30 percent do so), followed by South Asians (42 percent) and Africans (44 percent). A relatively high 15 percent of East Europeans and 13 percent of South Asians are principally connected to the Internet at school.

The temporal digital divide

How long have people in different parts of the world been using the Internet?

Not only do a lower percentage of the population use the Internet outside North America, a somewhat higher percentage of the non-North American respondents in this survey are "newbies," defined here as people using the Internet one year or less. While 18 percent of North American respondents are newbies, 23 percent of the respondents from other OECD countries and 22 percent from non-OECD countries are newbies. Compared with North American users, respondents from other OECD and from non-OECD countries are 1.3 times as likely to be newbies (table 2.3, model 2). However, there are regional variations. There are high percentages of newbies in Oceania

Table 2.3 Who are the newbies? (logistic regression)

Independent variables	Global (model 1) B	SE	Exp. (B)	Global with regional controls (model 2) B	SE	Exp. (B)	North America (model 3) B	SE	Exp. (B)	Other OECD (model 4) B	SE	Exp. (B)	Non-OECD (model 5) B	SE	Exp. (B)
Gender (male = 1)	-0.422	0.039	0.656	-0.460	0.039	0.631	-0.496	0.046	0.609	-0.457	0.095	0.633	-0.172[a]	0.13	0.842
Age (reference = older than 65)															
18–29	-0.730	0.139	0.482	-0.819	0.140	0.441	-0.973	0.150	0.378	0.506[a]	0.723	1.658	-0.047[a]	0.636	0.954
30–9	-0.297	0.135	0.743	-0.350	0.136	0.705	-0.415	0.144	0.660	0.816[a]	0.722	2.261	0.085[a]	0.632	1.089
40–9	-0.199[a]	0.135	0.819	-0.220[a]	0.136	0.803	-0.301	0.143	0.740	0.943[a]	0.725	2.567	0.319[a]	0.636	1.376
50–65	-0.117[a]	0.128	0.890	-0.134[a]	0.128	0.874	-0.192[a]	0.135	0.825	0.953[a]	0.713	2.592	0.274[a]	0.621	1.315
English not spoken at home	0.204	0.045	1.226	-0.073[a]	0.051	0.930	-0.092[a]	0.069	0.912	-0.098[a]	0.093	0.906	-0.007[a]	0.144	0.993
Education (reference = high school or less)															
Some college	-0.404	0.057	0.668	-0.342	0.058	0.711	-0.470	0.069	0.625	-0.060[a]	0.130	0.941	-0.048[a]	0.196	0.953
Undergraduate degree	-0.900	0.061	0.407	-0.835	0.061	0.434	-1.019	0.073	0.361	-0.424	0.139	0.655	-0.223[a]	0.199	0.800
Postgraduate	-1.167	0.066	0.311	-1.139	0.066	0.320	-1.309	0.080	0.270	-0.870	0.143	0.419	-0.505	0.210	0.604
Single	-0.028[a]	0.044	0.972	-0.048[a]	0.044	0.953	0.019[a]	0.053	1.019	-0.197	0.105	0.821	-0.388	0.157	0.678
Household size	0.043	0.011	1.044	0.034	0.011	1.035	0.043	0.015	1.044	0.007[a]	0.024	1.007	0.038[a]	0.024	1.039
Employment status (reference = retired)															
Working full-time	-0.174	0.097	0.840	-0.204	0.098	0.816	-0.193	0.104	0.825	-0.077[a]	0.366	0.926	-0.035[a]	0.523	0.965
Working part-time	-0.087[a]	0.113	0.916	-0.138[a]	0.114	0.871	-0.158[a]	0.124	0.854	0.113[a]	0.390	1.119	-0.031[a]	0.573	0.970
Unemployment	-0.160[a]	0.111	0.853	-0.164[a]	0.112	0.849	-0.217	0.120	0.805	0.277[a]	0.401	1.319	0.055[a]	0.570	1.057
Student	-0.673	0.111	0.510	-0.682	0.111	0.506	-0.733	0.123	0.480	-0.409[a]	0.382	0.664	-0.100[a]	0.547	0.905
Traditional media use															
Heavy print media use	0.035[a]	0.057	1.036	0.010[a]	0.057	1.010	-0.002[a]	0.066	0.998	0.055[a]	0.143	1.056	0.003[a]	0.210	1.003
Heavy TV watcher	0.028[a]	0.040	1.028	0[a]	0.040	1	-0.037[a]	0.046	0.964	0.065[a]	0.099	1.068	0.214[a]	0.142	1.238
Place of access (reference = Community center, etc.)															
Home	-0.089[a]	0.103	0.914	-0.084[a]	0.104	0.919	-0.056[a]	0.124	0.946	-0.086[a]	0.243	0.917	-0.292[a]	0.332	0.747
Workplace	-0.689	0.110	0.502	-0.713	0.111	0.490	-0.730	0.132	0.482	-0.638	0.256	0.528	-0.815	0.353	0.443
School	-0.223[a]	0.141	0.800	-0.206[a]	0.142	0.814	-0.247[a]	0.178	0.781	-0.142[a]	0.297	0.868	-0.127[a]	0.425	0.881
National groups (reference = North America)															
Other OECD				0.655	0.055	1.926									
Non-OECD				0.603	0.074	1.828									
Constant	0.085[a]	0.169	1.089	0.114[a]	0.170	1.120	0.332	0.192	1.394	-0.835[a]	0.724	0.434	-0.618[a]	0.707	0.539
Cox and Snell R²	0.055			0.063			0.067			0.061			0.033		

[a] Not significant because $p > 0.10$.

(29 percent of Oceanian respondents), South Asia (28 percent), and the Middle East (26 percent). The low percentages of newbies are in East Asia (13 percent), East Europe (15 percent), and North America (18 percent).

Who are more likely to be newbies?

Newbies are on the wrong side of the temporal digital divide. They are people who have used the Internet for a short time and often are less comfortable with it (Kraut et al., 1998). After a year, they either join the main body of veteran users or stop using the Internet. Hence, when newbies comprise a sizeable portion of users, their characteristics are leading indicators of how the nature of Internet users is changing. In addition to differences between countries and regions, personal characteristics such as gender, age, and education may affect the likelihood of respondents being newbies. A series of logistic regressions show that education, the place of Internet use, and age are associated worldwide with respondents being newbies or veterans (see table 2.3, model 1):

- Respondents with less *education* are more likely to be newbies. Compared with those with a postgraduate degree, respondents with high school or less are twice as likely to be newbies, those with some college education 1.7 times, and those with a university degree 1.2 times.
- *Older* respondents are more likely to be newbies. For instance, those who are more than 65 years old are 1.5 times as likely to be newbies as those who are younger than 30.
- People who use the Internet primarily at *community centers* or similar public places are 1.5 times as likely to be newbies as those who use it at their workplace. Such community centers appear to serve as initiating points to Internet use.

The characteristics of newbies are not the same around the world. In North America, the influential characteristics are education and age (model 3): e.g., respondents with a high school education or less are 2.2 times as likely to be newbies, compared with those with a postgraduate degree. They are 1.7 times as likely to be newbies, compared with those with a university degree. Respondents more than 65 years old are 1.7 times as likely to be newbies, as compared with those younger than 30 years.

As in North America, education is also a predictor of being a newbie in other OECD countries (model 4) and non-OECD counties (model 5). However, age is not a strong predictor while workplace use is. In other OECD countries, respondents with a high school education or less are twice as likely to be newbies as those with a postgraduate degree and 1.4 times as likely as those with a first university degree. The effect of education on the likelihood of being newbies is real, but smaller, in non-OECD countries, where respondents with a high school degree or less are 1.4 times as likely to be newbies than those with a postgraduate degree.

The importance of Internet use at work increases from North America to other OECD countries to non-OECD countries. Compared with those who primarily use the Internet at work, North American respondents using the Internet from community centers or other public places are 1.5 times as likely to be newbies, respondents from other OECD countries are 1.6 times as likely, and those from non-OECD countries are 1.8 times as likely.

Using the Internet around the World

No Internet user is an island. But, how is their online connectivity related to use of other means of communication? We examine here the frequency with which the respondents report keeping in touch with their relatives and friends by using three different kinds of media: face to face, telephone, and email. We ask separately about contact within and beyond 50 kilometers (30 miles): a crude measure of "nearby" and "far-away" (see table 2.2).

Contact with kin within 50 kilometers

Worldwide, email is used less often than face-to-face and telephone to communicate with nearby relatives, even among this sample of Internet users. Only 16 percent of all respondents communicate with nearby kin at least weekly, with slightly lower percentages in other OECD countries (12 percent) and non-OECD countries (14 percent) than North America. The telephone is the most-used medium for contact with nearby kin: 43 percent worldwide have at least a weekly phone conversation. Face-to-face contact is the second most used medium: 33 percent worldwide meet a nearby relative at least once per week. Belying fears that high email use will be associated with less contact by other means, the frequency of email contact is positively correlated with the frequency of both face-to-face contact (r = 0.31) and telephone contact (r = 0.38). By contrast to North Americans' slightly greater use of email, respondents in other OECD and non-OECD countries are slightly more likely to have weekly phone or face-to-face contacts with nearby kin.

Contact with friends within 50 kilometers

Compared with social contact with nearby kin, a much higher percentage of respondents worldwide use email for weekly contact with nearby friends: 48 percent vs. 16 percent. As is the case for nearby relatives, a slightly higher percentage of North Americans email at least weekly (49 percent) than other OECD (44 percent) and non-OECD respondents (48 percent).

Despite the high percentage of respondents who email nearby friends weekly, an even higher percentage (70 percent) telephone weekly. Weekly telephone contact with friends is slightly more common than email contact in other OECD countries (74 percent) and non-OECD countries (72 percent) than in North America (69 percent). The percentage of people having weekly face-to-face contact with their friends is the highest for other OECD respondents (64 percent), and slightly lower for North American and non-OECD respondents (60 percent).

In short, the telephone > face-to-face > email ordering holds for weekly contact with nearby friends and relatives in all parts of the world. The communication patterns of North American, other OECD, and non-OECD respondents are similar despite differences in socio-demographic characteristics, email access, transportation facilities, and population density.

Contact with kin beyond 50 kilometers

More than twice as many respondents worldwide use email at least weekly to contact relatives living more than 50 kilometers away (37 percent) than relatives living within 50 kilometers (16 percent). There are marked differences between the percentage of North American respondents having weekly contact with far-away kin (40 percent) and the percentage of other OECD (25 percent) and non-OECD respondents (31 percent). This may reflect the higher Internet use by North Americans (more far-away kin are online) and the greater distances separating North American kin.

The telephone remains important in all three categories of countries. It is used somewhat more than email by North Americans (46 versus 40 percent), appreciably more by other OECD respondents (42 versus 25 percent) and by the same percentage of non-OECD respondents (31 percent). Only a small percentage of respondents anywhere (3–5 percent) have weekly face-to-face visits with far-away kin.

Contact with friends beyond 50 kilometers

Compared with contact with far-away relatives, far-away friends predominantly use email to communicate. Worldwide, 39 percent of the respondents are in frequent contact with far-away friends. Email is much more popular than telephone (17 percent) or face-to-face interaction (4 percent). The patterns are similar in North America, other OECD, and non-OECD countries.

Communicating online and offline

These data do not support contentions that frequent email contact is associated with less frequent face-to-face and telephone contact. To the contrary, the positive correlations suggest that those who frequently use one means of communication also use the others frequently (see also Quan-Haase and Wellman's chapter (10); Katz and Aspden, 1997). These positive correlations appear for all three categories of countries, for contact with kin and with friends, and for relationships that are nearby or more than 50 kilometers away. Surprisingly, distance does not appear to weaken the association between frequent face-to-face and email contact (see table A2.1).

To be sure, the strongest correlations are between face-to-face and telephone contact (Pearson's r coefficients range from 0.50 to 0.77). However, the worldwide correlations between face-to-face and email contact are positive (ranging between 0.23 and 0.32), while the correlations between telephone and email contact are even stronger (ranging between 0.31 to 0.44). Throughout the world, the correlations are strongest between the frequency of face-to-face and telephone contact and are weakest between the frequency of face-to-face and email contact. The three means of communication are most closely associated in North America. By contrast, the weakest (but still significant) correlations are between face-to-face and email contact for other OECD countries (ranging between 0.18 to 0.28) and non-OECD countries (ranging from 0.10 to 0.20).

In sum, the telephone continues to be the medium most used to contact friends and relatives, except for far-away friends where email predominates. Email is used more to contact friends than relatives, regardless of distance. These data suggest that the norms, demands, and joys of kinship interaction are more apt than friendship to call forth the greater social presence of face-to-face or telephone conversations. Moreover, because people have many more friends than relatives, email enables them to keep in contact with a number of them at a distance (see also Hampton and Wellman's chapter). Yet, wherever they live, sociable people use all three means to communicate.

Instrumental and recreational use

What do people from different parts of the world do online? To what extent is instrumental and recreational use of the Internet related to demographic, social and media-use characteristics? A more complex picture of the global digital divide emerges if we look beyond the basic matter of Internet access to the more differentiated matter of Internet use.

Ten questions in Survey 2000 asked how often respondents carry out different types of activity online. Exploratory factor analysis revealed two distinct sets of activities. Seven items form a scale, ranging from 0 to 35, indicating the extent of using different *instrumental activities* on the Internet to obtain information, goods and services. Based on these seven items, the mean amount of instrumental use for all respondents appears as 16 points, indicating an appreciable instrumental use of the Internet. Three items form a scale, ranging from 0 to 15, indicating the extent of different *recreational activities* on the Internet. Based on these two items, the mean amount of recreational use for all respondents is only 2 points, indicating that few respondents make much recreational use of the Internet (other than web-surfing and email socializing).[6]

6   We use principal axis factor analysis with quartimax orthogonal rotation. Each activity item is coded "0, never," "1, rarely," "2, about monthly," "3, about weekly," "4, a few times a week" to "5, daily." The *instrumental activity* items are: sending / receiving email, participating in mailing lists, using online libraries and other sources of information, taking online courses, online shopping, surfing websites, and participating in Usenet newsgroups. Scores could range from 0 to a maximum of 35 (5 × 7). The *recreational activity* items are: chatting, collective role-playing ("MUDs," etc.), and playing multi-user online games. Scores could range from 0 to a maximum of 15 (5 × 3).

Instrumental use

North American respondents use the Internet slightly more for instrumental reasons (mean score = 16) than those from other OECD and non-OECD countries (mean score = 15; see also table 2.4, model 2). When other variables are controlled in a multiple regression, the data show that respondents in the developing non-OECD countries tend to use the Internet more instrumentally than those in the developed other OECD countries do (see table 2.4, model 2).

- Multiple regression shows that three variables are substantially associated with extensive instrumental use: the strongest association is that the more that people use the Internet *recreationally*, the more they use it instrumentally (table 2.4, model 1). Active users of the Internet use it both instrumentally and recreationally. Perhaps, the two forms of Internet uses reinforce one other.
- The *place of Internet use* is also associated with the extent of instrumental use. Not surprisingly, respondents who use the Internet at their workplaces, use it the most for instrumental reasons (3.9 points higher than community centers), followed by those who use it at home (2.5 points higher) and at school (1.7 points higher).
- *Veteran users* (those who have been on the Internet for at least one year) report nearly 4 points more instrumental use than newbies.

Instrumental use is strongly associated in all three country categories with the recreational use of the Internet, the place of Internet use, and the length of Internet experience (table 2.4, models 3, 4, and 5). The main differences are that age and gender are more strongly associated with instrumental use outside North America. Although age plays a marginal role in North America, there is a clear age divide outside North America. Middle-aged users make more instrumental use in other OECD countries, while instrumental use increases with age (up until 65) in non-OECD countries. Men make comparatively more instrumental use of the Internet in other OECD countries and even more so in non-OECD countries.

Recreational use

North American respondents make slightly more recreational use of the Internet than non-OECD respondents, while other OECD respondents make the least (table 2.5, model 2). There are also regional variations, with East Asians, South Asians, and Latin Americans

Table 2.4 Demographic variables and instrumental Internet usage (multiple regression)

Independent variables	Global (model 1) B	Beta	Global with regional controls (model 2) B	Beta	North America (model 3) B	Beta	Other OECD (model 4) B	Beta	Non-OECD (model 5) B	Beta
Gender (male = 1)	1.196	0.102	1.260	0.107	1.141	0.097	1.640	0.133	1.748	0.154
Age (reference = older >65)										
18–29	0.333[a]	0.027	0.476[a]	0.038	0.261[a]	0.020	2.448	0.208	2.247	0.205
30–9	0.904	0.069	0.996	0.076	0.882	0.066	2.667	0.209	2.307	0.188
40–9	1.076	0.076	1.113	0.078	0.939	0.068	3.061	0.190	2.410	0.155
50–65	0.882	0.055	0.910	0.056	0.765	0.050	2.503	0.125	2.428	0.121
English not spoken at home	−5.37E−02[a]	−0.004	0.390	0.029	0.446	0.026	0.231[a]	0.019	0.284[a]	0.022
Education (reference = high school or less)										
Some college	1.156	0.091	1.047	0.083	1.181	0.094	0.553	0.042	0.972	0.075
Undergraduate degree	1.485	0.118	1.363	0.109	1.494	0.120	0.637	0.046	1.607	0.133
Postgraduate	1.983	0.149	1.927	0.145	2.066	0.151	1.245	0.100	2.223	0.188
Single	−7.99E−02[a]	−0.007	−4.06E−02[a]	−0.003	1.47E−02[a]	0.001	−0.333[a]	−0.028	−0.182[a]	−0.017
Household size	−0.230	−0.065	−0.215	−0.061	−0.230	−0.059	−0.211	−0.065	−0.155	−0.066
Employment status (reference = retired)										
Working full-time	−0.126[a]	−0.011	−8.47E−02[a]	−0.007	4.82E−02[a]	0.004	−1.447	−0.120	−0.899[a]	−0.080
Working part-time	−0.518	−0.021	−0.439	−0.018	−0.337[a]	−0.014	−1.743	−0.073	−0.988[a]	−0.039
Unemployment	−2.39E−02[a]	−0.001	−1.34E−02[a]	−0.001	0.168[a]	0.008	−1.521	−0.056	−1.526[a]	−0.064
Student	0.545	0.038	0.548	0.039	0.752	0.052	−0.785[a]	−0.059	−1.002[a]	−0.081
Traditional media use										
Heavy print media use	0.958	0.054	0.995	0.056	1.039	0.060	0.854	0.046	0.697	0.038
Heavy TV watcher	−4.39E−03[a]	0	3.96E−02[a]	0.003	0.131[a]	0.011	−0.175[a]	−0.014	−0.435	−0.036
Place of access (reference = community Center, etc.)										
Home	2.479	0.205	2.474	0.204	2.450	0.199	2.868	0.245	1.944	0.175
Work	3.955	0.306	3.990	0.309	3.867	0.292	4.690	0.386	3.605	0.310
School	1.671	0.063	1.653	0.062	1.413	0.051	1.803	0.080	3.753	0.145
Newbies	−3.822	−0.257	−3.740	−0.251	−3.813	−0.249	−3.744	−0.271	−3.108	−0.236
Internet recreational use	0.871	0.350	0.861	0.346	0.843	0.343	0.982	0.361	0.855	0.362
National groups (reference = North America)										
Other OECD			−1.089	−0.067						
Non-OECD			−0.923	−0.043						
(Constant)	9.413		9.353		9.324		7.890		8.226	
Adjusted R^2	0.262		0.266		0.253		0.322		0.288	

[a] Not significant because $p > 0.10$.

Table 2.5 Demographic variables and recreational Internet usage (multiple regression)

Independent variables	Global (model 1) B	Beta	Global with regional controls (model 2) B	Beta	North America (model 3) B	Beta	Other OECD (model 4) B	Beta	Non-OECD (model 5) B	Beta
Gender (male = 1)	0.154	0.033	0.167	0.035	0.157	0.033	0.213	0.047	0.152[a]	0.032
Age (reference = older >65)										
18–29	0.713	0.143	0.740	0.149	0.773	0.148	0.403[a]	0.093	9.70E–02[a]	0.021
30–9	0.292	0.055	0.313	0.059	0.36	0.066	–1.45E–02[a]	–0.003	–0.493[a]	–0.095
40–9	8.60E–03[a]	0.002	2.08E–02[a]	0.004	6.50E–02[a]	0.012	–0.331[a]	–0.056	–0.674[a]	–0.103
50–65	–7.34E–02[a]	–0.011	–6.41E–02[a]	–0.010	–1.91E–02[a]	–0.003	–0.356[a]	–0.048	–0.868[a]	–0.102
English not spoken at home	8.07E–02	0.015	0.140	0.026	0.118	0.017	0.108[a]	0.025	0.266	0.049
Education (reference = high school or less)										
Some college	–0.384	–0.076	–0.400	–0.079	–0.480	–0.094	–0.295	–0.060	–0.304	–0.055
Undergraduate degree	–0.979	–0.194	–0.999	–0.198	–1.150	–0.228	–0.558	–0.111	–0.581	–0.114
Postgraduate	–1.119	–0.209	–1.126	–0.210	–1.297	–0.232	–0.705	–0.154	–0.722	–0.144
Single	0.313	0.065	0.315	0.065	0.313	0.063	0.328	0.076	0.240	0.052
Household size	5.11E–02	0.036	5.09E–02	0.036	5.48E–02	0.035	3.51E–02	0.030	3.76E–02	0.038
Employment status (reference = retired)										
Working full-time	–1.02E–03[a]	0	4.57E–03[a]	0.001	1.10E–02[a]	0.002	–2.56E–03[a]	–0.001	0.226[a]	0.047
Working part-time	9.58E–02[a]	0.010	0.110[a]	0.011	0.103[a]	0.010	0.314[a]	0.036	–0.101[a]	–0.010
Unemployment	0.132[a]	0.015	0.134[a]	0.015	0.102[a]	0.012	0.341[a]	0.034	0.264[a]	0.026
Student	1.87E–02[a]	0.003	2.01E–02[a]	0.004	–5.27E–02[a]	–0.009	0.208[a]	0.042	0.665[a]	0.126
Traditional media use										
Heavy print media use	–0.222	–0.031	–0.215	–0.030	–0.194	–0.027	–0.315	–0.046	–0.203[a]	–0.026
Heavy TV watcher	0.137	0.027	0.143	0.029	0.142	0.028	9.94E–02[a]	0.021	0.229	0.044
Place of access (reference = community center, etc.)										
Home	8.62E–02[a]	0.018	8.65E–02[a]	0.018	0.173	0.034	0.113[a]	0.026	–0.771	–0.164
Work	–0.524	–0.101	–0.513	–0.099	–0.432	–0.080	–0.435	–0.097	–1.430	–0.291
School	–0.405	–0.038	–0.400	–0.037	–0.181[a]	–0.016	–0.516	–0.062	–2.084	–0.190
Newbies	0.114	0.019	0.123	0.021	8.77E–02	0.014	0.177	0.035	0.226	0.041
Instrumental Internet use	0.151	0.376	0.150	0.373	0.149	0.366	0.151	0.410	0.161	0.381
National groups (reference = North America)										
Other OECD			–0.219	–0.033						
Non-OECD			–3.14E–02[a]	–0.004						
(Constant)	–0.565		–0.560		–0.551		–0.697[a]		0.162[a]	
Adjusted R²	0.207		0.208		0.203		0.225		0.239	

[a] Not significant because p > 0.10.

making the greatest recreational use of the Internet. Multiple regression shows four variables to be substantially associated with extensive recreational use:

- High involvement in online *instrumental* activities is the most strongly related variable to high recreational use (table 2.5, model 1), revealing again the interplay between recreational and instrumental use.
- *Educational attainment* is negatively associated with recreational use (opposite to that for instrumental use). For example, respondents with a postgraduate degree are the lowest recreational users of the Internet, scoring 1 point lower than those who have high school or less education.
- *Age* is associated with recreational use of the Internet. For example, respondents younger than 30 years old make the most recreational use (0.3 points).
- Using the Internet at *workplaces* (–0.5 points) or at *schools* (–0.4 points) is associated with low recreational use of the Internet. Community centers are the places where the most recreational use takes place.

To summarize, respondents with higher educational attainment make the most instrumental use of the Internet while those with less education make the most recreational use. Not surprisingly, people make the most instrumental use from their workplaces and the most recreational use from their homes and community centers. North American respondents use the Internet more for both instrumental and recreational reasons than users in other parts of the world. However, there is no simple rank order of use by economic development and Internet penetration. Respondents in the non-OECD countries make more instrumental and recreational use than those living in the other OECD countries.

The digital dividend: sense of community online

How does the Internet affect people's sense of online community? Do the diverse community, kinship, transportation, and communication arrangements in North America, other OECD countries, and non-OECD countries have different impacts on people's sense of online community? To ascertain this, we asked respondents to report if they agreed or disagreed with ten statements about the impact of the Internet on their social life (see appendix 2.2). Exploratory factor analysis of these statements suggested two scales based on two distinct sets of items: a six-item online community scale and a two-item online kinship scale. Each item in these scales has Likert-type scoring, with values ranging from 1 (for highly negative responses) to 7 for highly positive responses. See also Quan-Haase and Wellman's chapter (10) for additional analysis of the North American data.

Sense of online community

The sense of online community scale contains items such as "we feel a sense of community with the people we've met on the Internet." Scores range from 6 to 42, with a worldwide mean of 22 indicating a moderate sense of online community. Lower economic development is slightly associated with a higher sense of online community. Respondents from non-OECD countries have the strongest sense of online community (mean score = 24). Respondents from other OECD countries feel slightly less sense of online community (23), followed by North American respondents (22; see also table 2.6, model 2). Regional-level comparison also confirms that respondents in East Europe, East Asia, and Oceania report a greater sense of online community than their North American counterparts.

The more involved people are with the Internet, the greater their sense of online community. Multiple regression shows that three linked measures of Internet involvement – the *amount of overall, instrumental, and recreational Internet use* – are the most strongly associated variables worldwide with having a sense of online community (table 2.6, model 1). The more people use the Internet, the stronger their sense of online community. For instance, a one-point increase in *instrumental* use means almost a half-point increase in a positive sense of online community, while a one-point increase in *recreational* use of the Internet means almost a one-point increase in a sense of online community. In addition, the more *diversified* the Internet activities engaged in, the greater the sense of online community. An increase of one type of Internet activity is associated with a nearly one-point increase in the sense of online community index.

Educational attainment is negatively associated with a sense of online community. For example, respondents who have a high school or less education score almost 2 points higher on the sense of online community scale than those with a postgraduate degree. This suggests that the Internet can empower the disadvantaged by increasing their sense of community.

Table 2.6 Demographic variables, Internet use, and online sense of community (multiple regression)

Independent variables	Global (model 1) B	Beta	Global with controls (model 2) B	Beta	North America (model 3) B	Beta	Other OECD (model 4) B	Beta	Non-OECD (model 5) B	Beta
Gender (male = 1)	0.241	0.013	0.123ª	0.007	0.096ª	0.005	0.223ª	0.012	0.563ª	0.033
Age (reference = older >65)										
18–29	-1.549	-0.080	-1.792	-0.093	-1.918	-0.094	-3.807	-0.220	2.019ª	0.124
30–9	-0.949	-0.046	-1.102	-0.054	-1.084	-0.051	-3.750	-0.200	2.403ª	0.133
40–9	-0.685ª	-0.031	-0.740ª	-0.033	-0.701ª	-0.032	-3.617	-0.152	2.541ª	0.111
50–65	-0.060ª	-0.002	-0.102ª	-0.004	-0.151ª	-0.006	-2.336ª	-0.079	3.032ª	0.102
English not spoken at home	1.244	0.059	0.401	0.019	0.406	0.015	0.015ª	0.001	1.366	0.073
Education (reference = high school or less)										
Some college	-0.568	-0.029	-0.383	-0.019	-0.563	-0.028	0.226ª	0.011	-0.141ª	-0.007
Undergraduate degree	-1.688	-0.086	-1.491	-0.076	-1.677	-0.085	-0.988	-0.049	-1.114	-0.062
Postgraduate	-1.884	-0.091	-1.806	-0.087	-2.063	-0.095	-1.164	-0.064	-0.833ª	-0.048
Single	0.897	0.048	0.811	0.043	0.809	0.042	0.560	0.032	0.598ª	0.037
Household size	-0.013ª	-0.002	-0.045ª	-0.008	-0.121	-0.020	0.054ª	0.011	0.077ª	0.022
Employment status (reference = retired)										
Working full-time	-0.554	-0.030	-0.629	-0.034	-0.693	-0.037	-0.070ª	-0.004	0.152ª	0.009
Working part-time	0.371	0.010	0.240ª	0.006	0.336ª	0.009	0.450ª	0.013	0.092ª	0.002
Unemployment	1.215	0.035	1.197	0.035	1.345	0.040	0.798ª	0.020	0.543ª	0.015
Student	-1.637	-0.074	-1.644	-0.074	-1.732	-0.075	-0.875ª	-0.044	-0.870ª	-0.047
Traditional media use										
Heavy print media use	-0.955	-0.035	-1.033	-0.037	-1.069	-0.039	-0.756	-0.027	-1.287	-0.048
Heavy TV watcher	0.152ª	0.008	0.070ª	0.004	-0.128ª	-0.007	0.870	0.046	0.424ª	0.023
Place of access (reference = community center, etc.)										
Home	0.683	0.036	0.664	0.035	0.781	0.040	0.696ª	0.040	-1.029ª	-0.062
Workplace	-0.101ª	-0.005	-0.201ª	-0.010	-0.077ª	-0.004	-0.582ª	-0.033	-1.141ª	-0.066
School	-0.146ª	-0.004	-0.106ª	-0.003	0.013ª	0	-0.150ª	-0.005	-1.373ª	-0.036
Newbie (<1 year Internet use)	0.391	0.017	0.279	0.012	0.301	0.012	0.021ª	0.001	0.272ª	0.014
Number of Internet activities	0.995	0.256	1.005	0.259	1.025	0.263	1.007	0.252	0.795	0.227
Instrumental Internet use	0.441	0.283	0.452	0.290	0.467	0.294	0.446	0.303	0.301	0.203
Recreational Internet use	0.995	0.256	1.005	0.259	1.025	0.263	1.007	0.252	0.795	0.227
National groups (reference = North America)										
Other OECD			1.797	0.071						
Non-OECD			2.111	0.062						
Constant	13.522		13.573		13.817		16.524		13.338	
Adjusted R²	0.283		0.288		0.294		0.284		0.208	

ª Not significant because p > 0.10.

It is not only the disadvantaged who are more apt to find community online. *Men*, and people who primarily *use the Internet at home*,
have a stronger sense of community online. For example, people who
use the Internet from their homes score 0.7 points higher than those
who use it from community centers.

The pattern that Internet involvement and lower educational attainment are the most closely associated with a sense of online
community is common to all three categories of countries (table 2.6,
models 3, 4, and 5). Respondents who do not use English at home also
feel a stronger sense of online community in all three categories of
countries, although most markedly in non-OECD countries. In North
America and Other OECD countries, older respondents tend to have
a greater sense of online community. However, this age effect is not
apparent in non-OECD countries.

Sense of online connection with kin

Having a sense of online connection with kin is another important
dimension of the Internet's relationship to feelings of community. As
kinship ties are more apt to be active despite physical separation
(Wellman and Tindall, 1993), this reflects the potential of the Internet
for linking kin wherever they may live.

The index of the Internet's effects on a sense of online kinship connection consists of two items, each using a 1–7 point Likert scale (see
appendix 2.2). The index of online kinship ranges from a minimum of
2 to a maximum of 14, with a mean of 8. Overall, there is a moderate
sense of online connection with kin around the world, although
respondents from other OECD countries (mean = 7) have slightly less
sense of online kinship than those from non-OECD countries and
North America (8).

Analysis at the global level (table 2.7, model 1) shows that:

- The more *instrumental use*, the more positive the sense of online
  kinship connectivity. A one-point increase in the instrumental use
  index means a 0.1-point increase in the online kinship index.
- *Older* people report a higher sense of online kinship connectivity than younger adults. Respondents older than 65 score
  1.3 points higher in the online kinship index than those younger
  than 30.
- *Women*, historically the kin-keepers (Wellman and Wortley, 1989),
  report a stronger sense of online kinship connectivity than men.

Table 2.7 Demographic variables, Internet use and sense of online connection with kin (multiple regression)

Independent variables	Global (model 1) B	Beta	Global with controls (model 2) B	Beta	North America (model 3) B	Beta	Other OECD (model 4) B	Beta	Non-OECD (model 5) B	Beta
Gender (male = 1)	-0.943	-0.118	-0.880	-0.110	-0.868	-0.111	-1.005	-0.120	-0.776	-0.094
Age (reference = older >65)										
18–29	-1.290	-0.153	-1.156	-0.137	-1.182	-0.138	-0.368[a]	-0.046	-0.563[a]	-0.071
30–9	-1.274	-0.142	-1.169	-0.130	-1.166	-0.131	-0.524[a]	-0.061	-0.622[a]	-0.070
40–9	-1.180	-0.122	-1.116	-0.116	-1.155	-0.125	-0.330[a]	-0.030	-0.420[a]	-0.037
50–65	-0.587	-0.054	-0.540	-0.049	-0.659	-0.064	0.663[a]	0.049	0.535[a]	0.037
English not spoken at home	-0.389	-0.043	-0.131	-0.014	-0.086[a]	-0.008	-0.045[a]	-0.006	-0.479	-0.052
Education (reference = high school or less)										
Some college	0.343	0.040	0.267	0.031	0.324	0.039	0.369	0.041	-0.260[a]	-0.027
Undergraduate degree	0.760	0.089	0.658	0.077	0.707	0.085	0.752	0.081	0.285[a]	0.032
Postgraduate	0.536	0.059	0.496	0.055	0.584	0.064	0.458	0.054	0.131[a]	0.015
Single	-0.565	-0.069	-0.561	-0.069	-0.537	-0.066	-0.613	-0.077	-0.819	-0.103
Household size	-0.064	-0.027	-0.068	-0.028	-0.087	-0.034	-0.012[a]	-0.005	-0.048[a]	-0.028
Employment Status (reference = retired)										
Working full-time	-0.418	-0.051	-0.393	-0.048	-0.372	-0.047	-0.712[a]	-0.087	-0.329[a]	-0.040
Working part-time	-0.323	-0.020	-0.256[a]	-0.015	-0.255	-0.016	-0.694[a]	-0.043	0.406[a]	0.022
Unemployment	0[a]	0	0.010[a]	0.001	-0.044[a]	-0.003	0.059[a]	0.003	0.546[a]	0.032
Student	-0.569	-0.059	-0.562	-0.058	-0.701	-0.072	-0.179[a]	-0.020	-0.369[a]	-0.041
Traditional media use										
Heavy print media use	0.043[a]	0.004	0.069[a]	0.006	0.070[a]	0.006	0.030[a]	0.002	0.058[a]	0.004
Heavy TV watcher	-0.128	-0.015	-0.101	-0.012	-0.066[a]	-0.008	-0.210[a]	-0.024	-0.392	-0.044
Place of access (reference = community center, etc.)										
Home	0.624	0.076	0.624	0.076	0.687	0.083	0.562[a]	0.071	0.515[a]	0.064
Workplace	-0.062[a]	-0.007	-0.017[a]	-0.002	0.008[a]	0.001	0.087[a]	0.011	0.082	0.010
School	0.543	0.030	0.574	0.032	0.743	0.040	0.179[a]	0.012	0.028[a]	0.001
Newbie (<1 year Internet use)	-0.313	-0.031	-0.270	-0.027	-0.249	-0.024	-0.318	-0.034	-0.331[a]	-0.035
Number of Internet activities	0.132	0.065	0.132	0.065	0.157	0.078	0.110	0.055	0.006[a]	0.003
Instrumental Internet use	0.111	0.163	0.107	0.157	0.107	0.160	0.084	0.125	0.133	0.184
Recreational Internet use	0.037[a]	0.022	0.031	0.018	0.032	0.020	0.023[a]	0.012	0.026[a]	0.002
National groups (reference = North America)										
Other OECD			-1.073	-0.097						
Non-OECD			0.023[a]	0.002						
Constant	7.207		7.238		7.037		5.988		7.769	
Adjusted R²	0.089		0.097		0.081		0.056		0.064	

[a] Not significant because p > 0.10.

- Women score almost 1 point higher than men in having a positive sense of online kinship.
- *Higher educational attainment* is associated with a stronger sense of online kinship connectivity. For instance, those who have a university degree score 0.7 points higher than those with a high school education or less.

Comparing the three categories of countries reveals common patterns worldwide (models 3, 4, and 5). First, greater *instrumental* use of the Internet is associated with a stronger sense of online family ties. This association is strongest in non-OECD countries. Second, *women* everywhere have a stronger sense of online connection with kin. However, different dynamics do affect the sense of online kinship in the three settings. Although older people tend to feel more the positive effect of the Internet on bringing family ties closer than young people in North America, age does not play a significant role outside North America. Furthermore, the positive relation between educational attainment and a sense of online kinship is significant in North American and other OECD countries. By contrast, marital status in non-OECD countries plays a more important role. Although the general trend is that singles feel less of a sense of online kinship than couples, this is especially the case for singles from non-OECD countries.

To summarize, high Internet users have a strong sense of online community in general and with kin. Better-educated respondents have a strong sense of online kinship, while less-educated respondents have a strong sense of online community. North Americans have the strongest sense of online kinship, while other OECD respondents have the least. By contrast, OECD respondents have the strongest sense of online community, while North Americans have the least. Perhaps the more veteran, heavier-using North Americans are more inclined to see the Internet as just a routine part of everyday life and not as a special universe.

Scouting Report on the Global Village

Summary

The primary goal in this chapter has been to examine the profiles of Internet users around the world and to ascertain the ways in which they use the Internet. While many digital divide studies look only at the dichotomy of access/non-access, we have had the privilege of working with an international survey that provides information about behavior online and offline. We have found both noteworthy similarities and differences in the characteristics of the respondents from North America, other OECD countries, and non-OECD countries.

At the time of the 1998 data collection, North American domination of the Internet was reflected in the preponderance of North American residents in the *National Geographic* sample. Moreover, North Americans generally have been online longer, use the Internet more frequently, and do more kinds of activities online. North America has continued to be the "primate region" of the Internet whose influence and activity outweighs the rest of the world combined.

Ontogeny is recapitulating phylogeny. The profile of respondents outside North America looks similar to that of North American Internet users a half-decade earlier. They are apt to be male, well-educated, and younger adults. Where North American Internet use has become broadly based, international use is more restricted to elites, especially in the developing countries.

There are substantial differences between the characteristics of North American respondents and those from other OECD and non-OECD countries. North American respondents are more likely to be veteran users, women, older, married, less educated, use English at home, and to use the Internet from their homes. Except for multilingualism, these characteristics of North American respondents are more similar to those of the world population than to those of other OECD and non-OECD respondents. This suggests that as the penetration rate of the Internet increases outside North America, the characteristics of Internet users will more closely resemble the characteristics of the population itself.

Respondent profiles show a gradient reflecting years of active Internet experience: North America is greater than other-OECD, which is greater than non-OECD. This is not always a smooth gradient because in a number of situations the characteristics of other-OECD respondents are more similar to those of non-OECD respondents than they are to North American respondents. This occurs for gender, educational attainment, and being a newbie. The lower the percentage of people using the Internet in a region, the more elite the population using the Internet.

Newbies use a smaller range of Internet services and may not have the experience to integrate it into their everyday lives. The likelihood of being a newbie is almost the same for other OECD and non-OECD respondents, indicating that the widest digital divide exists between North America and other parts of the world.

In terms of personal characteristics, older adults are more apt to be newbies and to use the Internet to contact friends and family. Married folks, with more kin to contact, especially value the Internet for maintaining kinship ties. The place of use is related to role: newbies are more likely to use community centers, people making extensive instrumental use of the Internet are more likely to access it from workplaces, and those with a strong sense of community and kinship online are more likely to access the Internet from their homes.

Community centers introduce some newbies to the Internet. This is especially true outside North America and crucially true in the developing non-OECD countries (Servon and Nelson, 2001). Community centers are the bases for young adults and recreational users of the Internet.

Newbies' personal characteristics are different from pioneering Internet users in North America and veteran users in other OECD and non-OECD countries. Newbies are more apt to be women, older, less educated, not using English at home, and neither employed full-time nor students. Thus, newbies around the world are less likely to be elite and are more likely to resemble the diverse nature of North American Internet users. This recapitulates what has happened in North America, and suggests that the profile of Internet users outside North America will become more similar to the broader population.

At the time of data collection in 1998, the Internet was important for social communication, yet it was not the dominant way in which respondents communicated with friends and relatives, both near and far. Telephone contact was more frequent than Internet contact. In addition, there was appreciable face-to-face contact with nearby friends and family. Email predominated only for contact with far-away friends. As many of the chapters in this book detail, the frequency of email contact has increased since then, but often as a complement to – not a substitute for – telephone and face-to-face contact.

The proliferation of the Internet means that people communicate more, not less. Internet use does not replace other forms of contact: the more people have telephone and face-to-face contact, the more they have email contact.

Just as one form of contact is associated with other forms of contact, one form of use is associated with another form of use. The more people use the Internet instrumentally, the more they use it recreationally.

Moreover, people who make much instrumental use of the Internet have a greater sense of online community and online connectivity with kin. Productive use is associated with positive sentiments. There are gender differences. Men tend to feel a greater online sense of community, while women, the kin-keepers, tend to feel a greater sense of online connectivity with relatives. North Americans are less apt to perceive a positive impact of the Internet on their sense of online community.

Internet use is a positive social experience. People who use the Internet a good deal use it for a wide range of activities, both instrumental and recreational. Rather than turning away from their friends and relatives, they combine their Internet use with face-to-face and telephone contact, and they have a greater sense of online community.

Although respondents in the North American, other OECD, and non-OECD categories have somewhat different personal characteristics, there are many similarities in the ways in which they use the Internet and in the characteristics associated with such use. The characteristics that are consistently associated with Internet use are: education, gender, age, being a newbie, and place of use. By contrast, some characteristics are not as widely associated with Internet use: marital status, employment status, newspaper/magazine reading, television watching, and using English at home.

The penetration rate of a region is related to how the Internet is used in the region. The lower the penetration rate, the more likely respondents are to be newbies, have strong instrumental use of the Internet, and have a more positive sense of online relationships with community and family. Yet, the differences between North America, other economically developed countries, and developing countries are greater for the users of the Internet than for the uses they make of it. Once people become veteran Internet users, they tend to behave similarly around the world.

Conclusions

In 1998, the world of the Internet continued to be bipolar: North America and everywhere else. International respondents were more likely to be younger, better educated, and male. Why this North American exceptionalism? Not only has the Internet been in North America longer than any other part of the world, the percentage of the population who used the Internet at the time of the study was appreciably higher in North America.

Countries outside North America have wider inequality in access to the Internet and deep inequality in the way the Internet is used. This is not necessarily the only possible outcome when only a small percentage of a population in such countries engages in a skilled activity. For example, professional athletes come from both elite and non-elite backgrounds.

The more economically developed a region, the more developed the Internet in that region and the more experienced its users. North America, the original and continuing home of the Internet, remains ahead of other regions. Developed (other OECD) regions adopted the Internet earlier than developing (non-OECD) regions. Yet, elites in developing countries have long had the capacity and knowledge to go online. That so many of the respondents in developing countries are newbies reveals that such elites are not acting as small quasi-priestly castes of Internet adepts, reserving their skills for themselves. Rather, the Internet is becoming a popular affair in both senses of the word: widespread, and being used by a broad range of people.

These dynamics suggest continued growth in the percentage of the population going online. New users will eventually stop being newbies, just as most people in developed countries now use telephones much more casually than a generation ago. Moreover, the Internet is still diffusing in the developed world, which means that less privileged people in these countries are now adopting the technology.

The Internet is not only a resource to consume, but also a means to access and use opportunities. It can be a gateway to informational, economic, cultural, and social advancement. When elites outside North America disproportionately use the Internet, the socioeconomic digital divide widens worldwide. However, the more demographically representative characteristics of international newbies suggest that in time the Internet may facilitate the narrowing of this divide.

Experience and these data suggest that Internet use worldwide will follow the North American developmental path. In part, this is an outgrowth of North American cultural domination of the content and tools of the Internet. But, it is also a consequence of the clear international trend to have more people – and a greater variety of people – using the Internet. The many international similarities in the uses of the Internet suggest that users behave in similar ways wherever they may live and log on.

Table A2.1 Correlations between the frequencies of face-to-face, telephone, and email contact

	F2F-phone	F2F-email	Phone-email
Worldwide			
Kin within 50 km	0.76	0.23	0.31
Friends within 50 km	0.69	0.31	0.38
Kin beyond 50 km	0.52	0.21	0.39
Friends beyond 50 km	0.63	0.32	0.44
North America			
Kin within 50 km	0.77	0.25	0.32
Friends within 50 km	0.70	0.33	0.39
Kin beyond 50 km	0.50	0.23	0.41
Friends beyond 50 km	0.62	0.38	0.48
Other OECD			
Kin within 50 km	0.71	0.18	0.27
Friends within 50 km	0.66	0.28	0.34
Kin beyond 50 km	0.57	0.16	0.34
Friends beyond 50 km	0.65	0.24	0.37
Non-OECD			
Kin within 50 km	0.73	0.19	0.29
Friends within 50 km	0.63	0.20	0.32
Kin beyond 50 km	0.56	0.10	0.33
Friends beyond 50 km	0.66	0.19	0.30

F2F = Face to Face Communication.

With the spread of the Internet throughout the world, future research should reveal different patterns from those described here. This will stem from the broader diffusion of Internet technologies and practices, the interaction between technology and societies, and the ways in which the impact of new technologies on people's lives is conditioned by social and cultural contexts.

Appendix 2.1

Members of the organization for economic cooperation and development

The 29 members of the OECD are: Australia, Austria, Belgium, Canada, Czech Republic, Denmark, Finland, France, Germany, Greece, Hungary, Iceland, Ireland, Italy, Japan, Korea, Luxembourg, Mexico, the Netherlands, New Zealand, Norway, Poland, Portugal, Slovakia,

Spain, Sweden, Switzerland, Turkey, the United Kingdom, and the United States.

Appendix 2.2

Items for the online sense of community scales

Online sense of community items are: (1) I feel a sense of community with the people I've met on the Internet. (2) I have made new friends by meeting people on the Internet. (3) Talking with people on the Internet is as safe as communicating with people in other ways. (4) The Internet has allowed me to communicate with all kinds of interesting people I otherwise would never have interacted with. (5) I feel I belong to an online community on the Internet. (6) I can find people who share my exact interests more easily on the Internet than I can in my daily life.

Online sense of kinship connectivity items are: (1) The Internet has brought my immediate family closer together; (2) The Internet has brought my extended family closer together.

Each item in these scales has Likert-type scoring, with values ranging from 1 (for highly negative responses) to 7 (for highly positive responses). (See also Quan-Haase and Wellman, chapter 10).

References

ABC News (2000). *What is the digital divide?* Available online at:
http://abcnews.go.com/sections/us/dailynews/digitaldivide000722.html

ACNielsen (2001). *429 Million people worldwide have Internet access, according to Nielsen//netratings*. Available online at:
http://www.eratings.com/news/20010611.htm

Castells, M. (2001). *The Internet galaxy: reflections on the Internet, business, and society*. Oxford, UK: Oxford University Press.

CNNIC (China Internet Network Information Center). (2001). *Semiannual survey report on the development of China's Internet*. Available online at:
http://www.cnnic.org.cn/

Cole, J., Suman, M., Schramm, P., Lunn, R., Coget, J.-F., Firth, D., Fortier, D., Hanson, K., Jiang, Q., Singh, R., Yamauchi, Y., Aquino, J.-S., and Lebo, H. (2001). *The UCLA Internet report 2000: surveying the digital future, year two*. Los Angeles: Center for Communications Policy, University of California Los Angeles. Available online at:
http://www.ccp.ucla.edu/pages/internet-report.asp

Crystal, D. (1997). *English as a global language*. Cambridge, UK: Cambridge University Press.

DiMaggio, P., Hargittai, E., Neuman, R. W., and Robinson, J. P. (2001). The Internet's implications for society. *Annual Review of Sociology*, 27, 307–36.

Economist (2000). *Falling through the net*. (Sept., 23), S34–9. Available online at: http://www.economist.com/printerfriendly.cfm?story_ID=375645

Fong, E., Wellman, B., Wilkes, R., and Kew, M. (2001). *Correlates of the digital divide: individual, household and spatial variation*. Ottawa, Canada: Office of Learning Technologies, Human Resources Development Canada.

Jordan, T. (2001). Measuring the Internet: host counts versus business plans. *Information, Communication and Society*, 4(1), 34–53.

Jung, J.-Y., Qiu, J. L., and Kim, Y.-C. (2001). Internet connectedness and inequality: beyond the "divide." *Communication Research*, 28(4), 507–35.

Katz, J. and Aspden, P. (1997). A nation of strangers? Friendship patterns and community involvement of Internet users. *Communications of the ACM*, 40(12), 81–6.

Kraut, R., Patterson, M., Lundmark, V., Kiesler, S., Mukhopadhyay, T., and Scherlis, W. (1998). Internet paradox: a social technology that reduces social involvement and psychological well-being? *American Psychologist*, 53(9), 1017–31.

Kraut, R., Kiesler, S., Boneva, B., Cummings, J., Helgeson, V., and Crawford, A. (2002). The internet paradox revisited. *Journal of Social Issues*, 58(1), 49–74.

LaRose, R., Eastin, M. S., and Gregg, J. (2001). Reformulating the Internet paradox: social cognitive explanations of Internet use and depression. *Journal of Online Behavior*, 1(2). Available online at: http://www.behavior.net/job/v1n2/paradox.html

May, V. (1999). Survey 2000: Charting communities and change. *National Geographic* December, 130–3.

McTaggart, C. (2002). Tensions in the development of the Internet. *University of Toronto Centre for Innovation Law and Policy Newsletter*, 2(1), 8–12.

Norris, P. (2001). *Digital divide? Civic engagement, information poverty and the Internet in democratic societies*. Cambridge, UK: Cambridge University Press.

NTIA (National Telecommunications and Information Administration) (1995). *Falling through the net: a survey of the "have nots" in rural and urban America*. Washington, DC: US Department of Commerce.

OECD (Organization for Economic Co-operation and Development) (2001). *Understanding the digital divide*. Paris: OECD Publications.

Pew Center for the People and the Press (1995). *Americans going online . . . explosive growth, uncertain destinations: technology in the American household*. Washington, DC. http://people-press.org/reports/display.php3?ReportID=136

Servon, L. J., and Nelson, M. K. (2001). Community technology centers: narrowing the digital divide in low-income, urban communities. *Journal of Urban Affairs*, 23(3–4), 279–90.

UCLA Center for Communication Policy. (2001). *The UCLA Internet report: surveying the digital future*. Available online at: http://www.ccp.ucla.edu

United States Internet Council and ITTA. (2001). *State of the Internet 2000*. Available online at: http://www.usic.org/

Varoli, J. (2001). Russia tries to catch up. *New York Times* (July, 16), 5.

Warschauer, M. (2003). Technology and social inclusion: rethinking the digital divide. Cambridge, MA: MIT Press.

Wellman, B. (1999). The Network community. In B. Wellman (ed.), *Networks in the global village* (pp. 1–48). Boulder, CO: Westview.

Wellman, B. and Gulia, M. (1999). Net surfers don't ride alone: virtual communities as communities. In B. Wellman (ed.), *Networks in the global village* (pp. 331–66). Boulder, CO: Westview.

Wellman, B. and Tindall, D. (1993). Reach out and touch some bodies: how telephone networks connect social networks. *Progress in Communication Science*, 12, 63–94.

Wellman, B. and Wortley, S. (1989). Brothers' keepers: situating kinship relations in broader networks of social support. *Sociological Perspectives*, 32, 273–306.

Whitaker, R. (1999). *The end of privacy*. New York: The New Press.

Wilson III, E. (2000). *Closing the digital divide: an initial review*. Internet policy Institute. Available online at:
http://www.Internetpolicy.org/briefing/ErnestWilson0700.html

Witte, J. C., Amoroso, L. M, and Howard, P. N. (2000). Method and representation in Internet-based survey tools: mobility, community, and cultural identity in Survey 2000. *Social Science and Computing Review*, 18(2), 179–85.

3

Syntopia

Access, Civic Involvement, and Social Interaction on the Net

James E. Katz and Ronald E. Rice

Abstract

Our research, which began fielding surveys in 1995, and thereafter with variation in 1996, 1997, and 2000, was apparently the first to use national random telephone survey methods to track social and community aspects of Internet use, and to compare users and non-users. Our program has explored the Internet in terms of trends in access, political and civic involvement, and social interaction. We uncovered serendipitously what we have coined the "Internet dropout" phenomenon (Katz and Aspden, 1998). Our findings have found a decline in some aspects of the digital divide, especially once awareness has been achieved and when year of adoption is considered. Contrary to the pessimistic assertions of many, no loss was discerned in terms of our indicators of political or community involvement. In fact, our findings support a more positive interpretation of the Internet's impact, at least in terms of interpersonal communication, where Internet use was associated with greater levels of telephone use (though not of correspondence by mail) and social interaction (though this was more widely dispersed). It also led to many face-to-face friendships that were judged by respondents as a positive experience. Thus, some of the earliest research on the social consequences of the Internet, confirmed over a half-decade of additional surveys, finds a decreasing but still significant digital divide, few negative effects on civic involvement and social interaction, and some positive consequences.

Authors' note

The authors thank Philip Aspden for his vital help over a period of years with the research reported herein.

First National Random Study of the Internet's Social Consequences

The diminutive computer mouse has roared, changing the temporal patterns of millions of people. Due to the networked PC, billions of dollars and hours are now spent differently. However, as this edited book attests, social scientists are only now beginning to be able to identify what have been the consequences for American society in this sea change in communication patterns. This chapter sketches our answer to the question of the Internet's social consequences in three domains of human communication endeavors: access to Internet technology, involvement with groups and communities through the Internet, and use of the Internet for social interaction and expression.

We believe we have the earliest comparative national survey data on the social consequences of the Internet. Having a nationally representative quantitative snapshot of Americans' use (and non-use) of the Internet has shed new light on important questions. By starting our analysis with data from 1995, we have been able to create an evolving picture of the situation. We have been pleased that a model of this kind has been subsequently adopted by many other social science research projects.

We published our initial reports (Katz and Aspden, 1997b, 1997c) in 1997, which found that the Internet did not increase social isolation. Rather, it was a source of civic organizational involvement and new personal friendships. A 1998 press release and subsequent study of users in Pittsburgh, which suggested that heavy Internet use might lead to depression and isolation, received national attention from the media (Kraut, Patterson, Lundmark, Kiesler, Mukhopadhyay, and Scherlis, 1998). In their article, Kraut et al., expressed numerous reservations about our findings. The controversy surrounding these competing views helped highlight and call attention to our earlier work. Understandably, though, sharp questions were raised as to which view was correct. The situation became even cloudier when Nie (2001) also concluded that the Internet harms social cohesion and interaction. However, in 2000 the UCLA and the Pew Internet and American Life Project (Howard et al., chapter 1), seemed to confirm our 1995 findings. When in 2001 the Carnegie-Mellon team in Pittsburgh was not able to find further evidence of the so-called Internet paradox (that is, a social technology that made people lonely), we were pleased to have our original conclusions sustained. While science and knowledge are always subject to challenge and change, we were gratified that our national studies appear to have been borne out even by our severest critics.

We can also point with pride to the discovery of what was thought to be a virtually non-existent group (excuse the pun), namely "Internet dropouts." (This was our name for people who at one time had Internet access, but currently did not have any access.) When our research first uncovered the fact that this group was actually a substantial number of people, we were greeted with intense skepticism. Critics thought that even if such a group existed, it would be invisibly small. We too were surprised at the size of this group, having included it partly to ensure conceptual completeness, but our subsequent surveys, as well as surveys by the Pew Internet and American Life project have confirmed that Internet dropouts are no *rara avis*.

What Hath the Mouse Wrought?

Part of the reason we have undertaken our research is that we have seen many arguments that the Internet is harmful, or that it has unleashed a revolutionary liberating force. We are concerned first about the accuracy of both of these dystopian and the utopian views, and second about the consequences of accepting an overly negative or positive view of the Internet if indeed those views are wrong.

The dystopian view is that the consequences have been bleak and the future trend is more dismal still. Commercial and technological forces are gaining control of the Internet, individual users are prey to misinformation, deception, hucksters. The Internet exposes users, and especially children, to violence, pornography, and hate groups. Lonely and outcast people are wasting their time in unreal relationships. Pessimistic or ironic interpretative stories concerning good human intentions going awry have inherent appeal to journalists and academics (including ourselves), and seemingly to the general public as well.

So we have looked for evidence as to whether, as dystopians say, the "social technology" known as the Internet decreases interpersonal connection or if virtual involvement in a cause leads to less real-world participation. We found, contrary to some other analysts, use of the Internet in general has not led to a mass wave of despair and loneliness, nor has it released upon the world armies of disembodied multiple selves acting apolitically. It has not destroyed ordinary social intercourse, nor turned us into puppets of global corporate capitalism.

We have also looked at the utopian view, which is that the Internet provides an overwhelming potential for the development of liberating communities, exponential increases in human and social capital, and the achievement of each individual's full democratic participation in every policy decision. In essence, utopians maintain that the Internet is revolutionary, freeing people and groups to achieve finally an egalitarian, multi-media information society.

Just as we do not agree in the main with the dystopian view, we also do not see that the Internet has ushered in an era of Woodstock-like "peace and love." It has not, nor will it, lift from mankind the blight of hate, prejudice, vindictiveness, poverty, and disease. We may have passed into a completely new millennium, but the Internet is no Second Coming.

Our view is that neither perspective is correct. The little computer mouse, hooked to a keyboard and CPU, and linked with vast networks, servers, and other infrastructure, has acted to weave a rich tapestry of friendship, personal information, and community among people of all nations, orientations, ethnic groups, and classes. In a manner not unlike that of Adam Smith's invisible hand of the marketplace, the sum of the mouse movements and keyboard clicks (and increasingly voice and video streams) has allowed individuals and small groups to find common interests, engage in various types of exchange and create bonds of concern, support, and affection that can unite them. The "invisible mouse tracks" have led around the world, creating electronic and emotional strands among people and their software representations. The result is an intricate tapestry of individuals engaging in what they already do in other arenas, for good or bad, while expanding possibilities for new kinds of thought, interaction, and action.

In this chapter, we analyze these perspectives in more detail, and look at empirical data to probe the Internet's consequences. We explore the consequences for American society in three domains:

1 access;
2 civic and community involvement; and
3 social interaction and expression.

To support our arguments, we have relied on national survey data, much of which we ourselves have collected. These findings are drawn from our book-length treatment, which was published by MIT Press in 2002. Its tentative title is "Social Consequences of the Internet."

Through our efforts, we seek not only to evaluate the answers suggested by a variety of commentators, researchers, policy advocates, and industry proponents. We also wish to propose our own unique take as well. We refer to this view as "Syntopia," and thus the name of our initiative is "The Syntopia Project."

The Syntopia Project

It is worth taking a moment to say a few words about the origin and evolution of the activity reported herein. The work itself is from a larger project, which we now call the Syntopia Project. James Katz and Philip Aspden originally headed the Syntopia Project team; Ron Rice joined as a co-principal in 1999 and has contributed mightily to the project since then. Our joint aim has been to create through a series of national random telephone surveys a multi-year program charting social aspects of American's behavior on- and offline. We began work in 1994, and fielded our first surveys in 1995. We have had the good fortune to be able to conduct surveys again, with variation, in 1996, 1997, and 2000. We reiterate here, to help establish our priority, that our surveys seem to have been the first to:

- use national random telephone survey methods to track social and community aspects of Internet use;
- compare users and non-users, to identify and analyze Internet dropouts; and
- identify and analyze those still unaware of the Internet as opposed to aware non-users.

We chose the name "Syntopia" for our project for several reasons. First, we have been looking at a wide array of emerging communication technologies, including not only the Internet but also the mobile phone and related technologies. Although we focus heavily on the Internet, it bears stressing that the Internet is just one of many tools people use to communicate. Throughout our analysis, we touch on technologies such as newspapers and magazines, TV, and the telephone. Thus, an important aspect of the Syntopia concept is that the Internet is part of a much larger fabric of communication and social interaction. Second, in this connection, an exclusive focus on the online world can be misleading. People do have a physical embodiment, and their physical and social situation and history influence their actions online. Likewise, what they learn and do online spills over to their real-world experiences. By formulating the neologism Syntopia, we deliberately seek to underscore this synergy across media and between mediated and unmediated activities.

Third, the term "Syntopia" draws together the words "syn" and "utopia." Derived from ancient Greek, the word means literally "together place," which is how we see the Internet and associated mobile communication and its interaction with unmediated interpersonal and community relations. The term Syntopia invokes both utopian and dystopian visions of what the Internet does and could mean. At the same time, it brings these two visions together symbolically and, perhaps not so subtly, also alludes to the Internet's dark side in the homophone "sin." Other nominal connections are "synthetic" and "syntheses" all of which are appropriately evocative, and also fit with our project results to date. The Internet is a place for people to interact, express themselves, emote and find new friends. It is also a place in which people seek to hurt, cheat, and exploit others. The Syntopia Project aims to identify what these activities mean for issues ranging from social and community involvement to friendship formation and webcams.

In the Syntopia Project, we have relied heavily on quantitative survey data. This helps provide a rigorous base upon which to build insights and understand the broad flow of social change. But we also draw upon an array of ethnographic observations, case histories, and concrete examples since this allows us to have a nuanced and detailed understanding of peoples' uses of and reactions to the Internet, and more broadly, interpersonal communication technologies (ICTs). ICTs, which is the term of art in Europe, encompass the full array of networked and mobile technologies, including personal digital assistants (PDAs), mobile phones, computer kiosks, and of course the Internet.

Shocking events can cast a stark new perspective on ordinary lived experience. Before delving into the details of our quantitative findings, it is worth noting the use of the Syntopian realm in response to the tragedy surrounding the September 11, 2001 assaults on the United States. In this attack, civilian airliners were hijacked and rammed into the World Trade Center and the Pentagon, killing thousands of Americans and scores of people from other countries; many of the victims were burned alive. This book is about the Internet in everyday life, but both the Internet and everyday life exist within a context that is both contiguous with other technology, in this case other ICTs, and other types of life, here involving extraordinary and tragic events.

Syntopia and Life beyond the Everyday

The major constituents of Syntopia, the mobile phone and the Internet, were understandably central to people's communication activities as the plot unfolded.

Mobile phones, which we see as part of Syntopia, were used to relay what was happening aboard the hijacked airliners. These communications appear to have been instrumental in alerting passengers on one flight (UA Flight 93) of the hijackers' intended suicide mission. By having these mobile phone communications, the passengers on that flight, at the cost of their own lives, were apparently able to thwart the hijackers, bringing the plane down on a southwestern Pennsylvania field rather than a Washington, DC, landmark. Mobile phones were also used to call for help and to let friends and relatives know what was happening as the disaster unfolded. Emergency workers, victims and families coordinated and updated themselves. The voice networks were heavily overloaded due to the spike in use, but two-way pagers, such as the Blackberry, and data networks, were able to keep up with the demand. Mobile phones clearly saved lives as they were used to tell people in the stricken buildings to evacuate immediately. (Some victims initially thought their tower had been bombed and decided to await rescue, unaware that suicide squads had steered fuel-laden passenger jets into the towers: Adam Mayblum, personal communication, September 26, 2001).

In a sick hoax, though, some people used their mobile phone to call emergency services pretending to be trapped. These calls were taken seriously, of course, which led to the distracting and endangering of the rescuers. Phones, both mobile and stationary, were also used to make false bomb threats to federal buildings, synagogues, and mosques. In several of these cases, caller-ID technology was used to catch perpetrators, allowing authorities to relieve fears (Case, 2000; Harden, 2001; Katz, 1999).

The Internet was used to find out information about the attacks and to seek reassurances that loved ones were safe. But the Internet was also used to show the solidarity of the American people as various online sites were established to handle charitable contributions,

Table 3.1   Online resources for responding to September 11, 2001, attacks on World Trade Center and Pentagon

- The *American Red Cross* created websites for those who wished to contribute to disaster relief. They also provide online guidance about how to donate blood. They also established a *Family Registration Web*, to help those searching for information on family members affected by the disaster. Those from the disaster areas could register at the site to help Red Cross workers provide information to family members and loved ones.
- *United Way* and *The New York Community* Trust have established *The September 11th Fund*. Contributions will be used for immediate and longer-term needs of the victims, their families, and communities affected by the events of September 11.
- The *New York State World Trade Center Fund* supports the emergency response and victim support efforts in New York.
- Contributions to the *Salvation Army* go towards the physical, emotional, and spiritual needs of families, individuals, and emergency personnel involved in the disasters. Aid is given to those affected both directly and indirectly by this tragedy.
- The non-profit organization *FireDonations* has established an online contribution site for their *New York Firefighter 9-11 Disaster Relief Fund*. It aids families of the firefighters who died in their attempts to assist others during the World Trade Center tragedy.
- *Mercy Corps* supports organizations that provide counseling for survivors, emergency personnel, and families of the victims. They also support organizations that provide scholarship funds for children who lost parents in the attacks.

provide psychological support services, and communicate emotional succor and concern. Examples of the scores of such sites are given in table 3.1.

One of the authors of this chapter received email messages of concern and condolence from around the world. Many sites were established to allow people to give expression to their feelings. For instance, the *Washington Post* has one at http://www.washington-post.com/wp-srv/metro/daily/sept01/0911react.html

At the same time, the Internet was used to spread a variety of false stories. One was that the US Central Intelligence Agency and Mossad (Israel's intelligence service) had mounted these attacks as a provocation. Another false message concerned the origin of videotapes showing Palestinians celebrating the September 11 attacks. A graduate student in Brazil sent a message to a highly regarded news group accusing CNN of misidentifying the tapes as from another, earlier event. This accusation was found to be in error, and the Brazilian student sent out email retracting his statement. Yet the false challenge continued to circulate and multiply, even becoming transmogrified into an identically phrased letter purporting to be from the head of Internal Communication at the BBC in London. The BBC of course disavowed the forgery (Barringer, 2001). Thus, Syntopian technologies are plastic in that they can be employed for help or harm, information or disinformation, as the person propagating the communication sees fit. They were used in the war to overthrow the Taliban. US Special Forces on the ground in Afghanistan reported that they used laptop computers for email to communicate with their partners, the Northern Alliance fighters. The US troops coordinated with the fighters, and worked to get them what they requested, namely equipment ranging from 9 mm tracer rounds to Oakley sunglasses.

Themes

The rise of the Internet has brought with it some important questions about how this new form of communication might be affecting society. We consider fundamental tensions or opposed positions about the consequences of the Internet in three areas: the digital divide, community and political involvement, and social interaction. Since 1995, we have been examining these three themes through a series of national random telephone surveys.

The first fundamental concern is access, including who has/does not have access to the Internet; what motivates people to use the Internet; what barriers there are to usage; and what characterizes those who stop using the Internet (Katz and Aspden, 1997a, 1997b, 1997c). Access is the major public policy area for those who see the Internet as a universal service and for issues related to political and economic equity (McCreadie and Rice, 1999a, 1999b). Most studies report, for example, that Internet users are more likely to be male, younger, better educated, more affluent, white, and urban (Hoffman, 1998; Katz and Aspden, 1997a, 1997c), although admittedly this is a moving target as the population constantly changes. The usual term for this differential access to and use of the Internet according to gender, income, race and location is "the digital divide."

The second fundamental tension is whether the Internet will decrease community involvement, political participation, social interaction, and integration (Kraut, Lundmark, Patterson, Kiesler,

Mukhopadhyay, and Scherlis, 1998; Selnow, 1994), or whether it will foster diverse mediated communities with greater social capital. Concerns about the decline of community expressed two hundred years ago (by, for example, Benjamin Franklin, Thomas Jefferson, and John Quincy Adams) often seem little different than those expressed continually since World War II (Merton, 1957, p. 356; Putnam, 1996). A major component of this lively debate has been the question of the impact of communication technology on these processes. Analysis and criticism started earnestly shortly after the telegraph was invented, and was reinvigorated and intensified as each new communication technology became popular: the telephone, radio, movies, and, most profoundly, the TV (c.f., Fischer, 1993; Schiffer, 1991).

We discern two broad but conflicting views on social communities in cyberspace. The first general view is pessimistic. Cyberspace cannot be a source of real community, or it detracts from meaningful real-world communities (Baudrillard, 1983; Gergen, 1991; Kiesler, Siegel, and McGuire, 1984; Numes, 1995; Stoll, 1995; Turkle, 1996). There has been concern about a possible reduction in the objectivity of traditional media if these media were to lose their status and impact as a result of the growth of Internet usage (Symposium, 1995; Van Alstyne, 1995). A related concern is that lack of access to Internet resources by various groups in society, relative to traditional outlets such as newspapers, radio, and TV, would translate into a narrowing of the basis of political participation and legitimacy of government (White, 1997). Others argue that the Internet could weaken the legitimacy of the governing process, by encouraging the spread of small, "net-savvy" special interest communities who could pursue their own narrow agenda at the cost of the public commonweal (Starobin, 1996). The quality and validity of material reported on the Internet is also increasingly problematical, leading to concerns about the corruption or debasement of elections, and a consequent reduction in political participation. As noted above, some theorists have argued that the Internet is destroying community groups and voluntary associations that are necessary for the democratic process to succeed (Putnam, 1996; Turkle, 1996). Other critics fear that the Internet will absorb and dissipate the energy of the citizenry away from traditional political processes (Carpini, 1996; Rash, 1997).

The second general view is optimistic. Cyberspace involvement can create alternative communities that are as valuable and useful as our familiar, physically located communities (Poole, 1983; Rheingold, 1993). The Internet may very well foster political involvement: "Life in cyberspace seems to be shaping up exactly like Thomas Jefferson would have wanted: founded on the primacy of individual liberty and a commitment to pluralism, diversity, and community" (Kapor, 1993, p. 53).

The third concern is whether the Internet will hinder expression, or will foster new forms of identity and social interaction (Baron, 1984; Gergen, 1991; Hiltz and Turoff, 1995; Parks and Floyd, 1996; Turkle, 1996; Wynn and Katz, 1997). Can online social activity and creativity translate into meaningful friendships and relationships? The first school of thought holds that computer-mediated communication technology is too inherently antithetical to the nature of human life for meaningful relationships to form (Stoll, 1995). To type is not to be human, to be in cyberspace is not to be real; all is pretense and alienation, a poor substitute for the real thing. Thus, cyberspace cannot be a source of meaningful friendships (Baudrillard, 1983; Numes, 1995). Further, the technology is too limited to provide a useful basis for relationship formation. Hence, CMC inherently leads to "experimentation" (that is lying to others who cannot immediately know what the truth is) about one's identity and qualities. Such an atmosphere can be dominated by trickery, lechery, manipulation, and emotional swindles. So much posturing, "gender-switching" and faking of identities can take place that it is extremely difficult for any real relationships to be created and maintained (Turkle, 1996).

However, a second school of thought increasingly sees the Internet as a medium for social interaction (Rice, 1987a). Numerous case studies of CMC have shown that "the social" is an important glue that binds together the task-oriented aspects of CMC, and in some cases even supplants them (Rice, 1987b). This work has been complemented by research on the functioning of medical discussion lists and newsgroups, health and psychological support groups, Internet relay chats, multi-user dungeons, object-oriented MUDs, and even online dating services, all of which are essentially social and "affect" (as opposed to task) oriented (Rice, 2001). A good proportion of those searching and participating in health information sites and discussion groups do so as "third party" intermediaries, seeking information and support for their significant others, for themselves to help them deal with illnesses of significant others, or to bring information from the Internet to stimulate, challenge, or engage their health care providers (Aspden and Katz, 2001). The growth and persistence of web-based chat rooms and "instant messaging" offering "community" would seem to provide additional evidence refuting the "non-social" nature of CMC. Baym summarizes a decade of research as revealing "the ways in which people have appropriated the commercial and non-commercial networks demonstrate that CMC not only lends itself to social uses but is, in fact, a site for an unusual amount of social creativity" (Baym, 1995, p. 160); Rice (1987a) argued that fundamental aspects of social groups and communities may well be supported, even extended, through online communities, though the boundaries and permanence of such groups might be quite different.

Data Sources

The data summarized here, as well as detailed in various reports from the overall programmatic research, came from a series of national probability telephone surveys, all designed by us but administered by commercial survey firms. These surveys follow rigorous sampling protocols, and use random-digit dialing, to produce statistically representative samples of the adult US population. Figure 3.1 provides summary details on nonusers, users, former users, and sample sizes.

Access to the Internet

During each of the national surveys we asked users the year they started using the Internet (referred to in the surveys as "the Internet, also known as the Information or Electronic Superhighway"). This enabled us to establish cohorts of users based on the year they started using the Internet – those starting in 1992 or before, and those starting in 1993, 1994, 1995, 1996, 1997, 1998, and 1999/2000. We report usage by demographic measures, both for the various cohorts, and for the survey years (1995, 1996, 1997, 2000). Table 3.2 provides the percentages.

Gender

Across the cohorts of users (1992 to 2000), the proportion of female users increases. New Internet users are proportionally more female than are reported in surveys that only indicate usage as of the year of the survey; in recent years females are even more frequent users than are males.

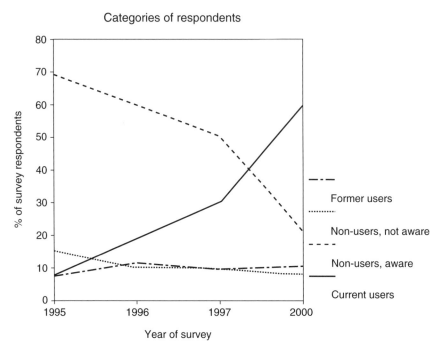

Figure 3.1 Percent of survey samples who are users, former users, aware non-users, and not-aware non-users

Age

Despite the increases in the proportion of users aged 40 and over, this proportion is still well below the proportion aged 40 and over in the general population (approximately 55 percent). Again, new Internet users are older than the average age of users reported in surveys that only indicate usage as of the year of the survey. However, the percentage of those 65 years and older who are using the Internet is still quite small.

Income

The proportion of Internet users with a household less than $35,000 is increasing, with a more even growth across cohort years than is indicated by the data reported by survey year only (as opposed to usage by cohorts).

Table 3.2 All Internet users, by cohort year and by survey year, belonging to each of several demographic categories (%)

Demographic	1992	1993	1994	1995	1996	1997	1998	1999/ 2000	Census (1998/ 2000)
Gender: female	29.3	36.7	38.5	47.0	47.3	56.6	51.9	54.5	51.0
				37.5	46.4	45.0		50.6	
Age: >40 yrs	38.4	38.9	30.5	41.8	43.3	42.0	45.0	48.9	55.0
				34.8	37.7	42.2		44.4	
Age: >65 yrs				0.6	2.9	2.4		5.2	
Income: <$35k	23.3	23.1	31.7	23.5	26.9	23.7	26.5	28.1	44.6
				30.7	37.2	21.2		23.0	
Education: <college	30.2	37.5	47.5	47.6	56.0	65.1	62.8	67.0	71.9
				48.0	52.4	51.2		56.0	
Race: African– American	9.0	2.3	4.7	5.6	9.3	9.4	7.9	8.9	12.7
				6.0	5.1	7.5		9.1	

Each demographic represents one of the dichotomized categories of the full demographic (i.e., gender, income, education, race). The top row of percentages for each demographic variable is the percent of users who belong to that demographic category in each *cohort* year (that is, the year in which the respondent began using the Internet), while the bottom row is the percent of users who belong to that demographic category in each *survey* year (that is, the year in which the survey was conducted), except for age of 65 and older, which is for survey year only. Census figures are from the online Statistical Abstracts of the US, either 1998 counts or July 1, 2000 estimates: www.census.gov/prod/www/statistcal-abstract-us.html (January 1, 2001). Note that the overall percent of African–Americans in the survey samples were 9.3% in 1995, 7.3% in 1996, 11% in 1997, and 11% in 2000, while the percent of African Americans in the Census data is 12.7%. This indicates that at least the 2000 survey, and probably all the surveys, slightly underestimates the percentage of African–Americans in the population. This may mean that the surveys slightly underrepresent the percent of Internet users who are African–American; however, if those African–Americans who are underrepresented in national probability samples are especially poor or less educated, then they are also less likely to know about or use the Internet, so these percentages may be slight overestimates.

Education

For those users who started in 1992 or before, the proportion of non-college graduates was 28 percent, rising to 67 percent for the 1999/2000 cohort. Over the years the surveys were administered, the percentage rose from 48 percent to 56 percent.

Race

The proportion of African-Americans using the Internet rose and then declined a bit over both the cohort and survey years. The difference in percentage of users and non-users between African-Americans and White non-Hispanics was significant only in 1996.

Motivations for Use

Regarding motivations for Internet use, two points stand out (Katz and Aspden, 1997a, 1997c). Users in the 1995 and 2000 survey rated sending/receiving email as a significantly better reason someone might be interested in becoming an Internet user than did non-users (in this analysis, we include former users, or "dropouts", as non-users). There was no significant difference between users and non-users, in both 1995 and 2000, as to the extent that they rated having contact with new people as a motivation for usage. While in 1995 users and non-users did not significant differ in the extent to which they believed that people might be interested in becoming an Internet user "because it's a good thing to do," in 2000 users were more likely to feel this way.

Awareness

Our research identified a second digital divide, relating to *awareness of the existence of the Internet* (defined by the question "Have you heard of the Internet or the Information Highway?"). We looked at the percentages of each binary category of gender (male/female), age (under or over 40), income (less or more than $35k), education (less or more than college), and race (African–American or White non-Hispanic). Of those that were aware of the Internet, the percentage of women rose from 45.5 percent in 1995 to 53.3 percent in 2000; the percentage of those over 40 rose from 47.9 percent to 50.2 percent; the percentage of those earning under $35k fell from 52.1 percent to 33.5 percent; the percentage of those with less than a college education dropped from 70.6 percent to 64.9 percent; and the percentage of those who were African–American rose from 7.2 percent to 10.5 percent. Thus the awareness divide seems to have pretty much disappeared according to gender, age and race, but seems to be increasing by income and education.

Combined influences on usage and awareness

Summary logistic regressions were run to predict awareness (vs. never heard), and to predict usage (vs. non-users; here former users/dropouts were not considered) from the same demographic variables.

In 1995, significant predictors of being *aware* of the Internet were: younger, greater income, greater education, white American (14 percent of variance explained, 86 percent of the 1814 cases correctly predicted. Significant predictors of being an Internet *user* were: male, younger, greater income, and higher education (16 percent, 91 percent of the 1676 cases correctly predicted). In 2000, significant predictors of *awareness* of the Internet were the same as in 1995: male, younger, greater income, and white American (9 percent variance, 93 percent of the 1037 cases correctly predicted). Significant predictors of *usage* were: younger, greater income, and greater education (45 percent, 80.2 percent of 924 cases correctly predicted). Note that, once awareness is achieved, in the multivariate analyses there is no digital divide – differences between non-users and users – on the basis of gender or race in 2000.

Dropouts

Internet dropouts – people who have used the Internet, but no longer do so – are usually overlooked in discussions about cyberspace (Katz and Aspden, 1998). Approximately 8 percent of respondents were dropouts in 1995, 11 percent in the 1996, 10 percent in 1997 and 11.5 percent in 2000. In 1995, 1996, 1997, and 2000, dropouts were significantly younger, less affluent, and less well educated than users – but not more likely to be female or African-American. In 1995, dropouts over 20 years old, compared to current users over 20 years old, were more likely to have been taught to use the Internet by friends (42 percent compared to 19 percent for current users), less likely to have learned at work (18 percent compared to 35 percent), and less likely to have been self-taught (15 percent compared to 25 percent). Of those who dropped out, the following percentage of respondents (averaged across the 1995, 1996 and 1997 surveys) indicated agreement with these three reasons for ceasing to use the Internet were: they lost access to the Internet (23 percent), generally due to losing a job or leaving college; the Internet was not sufficiently interesting (12 percent); connection and/or usage bills were too high (15.7 percent); and it takes too much time (7.5 percent).

Community and Political Involvement

To see whether Internet usage is associated with community and political involvement (or social capital), we analyzed five categories of respondents to the 1995 survey (long-time users, those who started using the Internet before the survey year of 1995, and recent Internet users, those who started during the survey year of 1995, former users, non-users who have heard of the Internet, and non-users who have not heard of the Internet) (Katz and Aspden, 1997b), and the more parsimonious categories of current users versus non/former users for 1995 and 2000.

Participation in organizations

There was no difference between Internet users and non-users in rate of membership in religious organizations, in either 1995 (about 63 percent) or 2000 (about 56 percent). However, in 2000, users who spent more hours online per week were slightly more likely to belong to more religious organizations ($r + 0.07$, $p < 0.01$). Current users were significantly more likely to belong to any leisure organizations than were non-users (60.1 percent compared to 49.4 percent) in 1995, but not differently in 2000 (93.4 percent for both). Users were significantly more likely to belong to at least one community organization than non-users in both 1995 (40.8 percent vs. 37.1 percent) and 2000 (28 percent vs. 15.4 percent). In 2000, for users, spending more hours online was not significantly correlated with membership in more leisure or community organizations.

Political involvement

We identified four dimensions of *offline* political activity: (1) *political activities* such as attending rallies, making phone calls on behalf of candidates, and giving money to political causes, (2) *reading* and the importance of magazines and newspapers, (3) the importance of national and local *TV* shows and interviews in the 96 campaign, and

(4) *voting* in the 1996 election were all greater for Internet users than for non-users. There was no difference in real-world political activity, including voting, between heavy and light users, and long-term and short-term users (Katz, Aspden, and Reich, 1997).

There seem to be two kinds of *online* political activity. *Browsing* was a composite of: reading bulletin boards/discussion groups; visiting websites with political information; following part of the election but reading online news; following election day coverage by computer; and viewing information via the computer after the election. In our sample of Internet users, 46 percent participated in at least one of these. *Interaction* consisted of four activities: participating in electronic discussions with people about the election; receiving emails about the campaign/election; sending/receiving emails to/from government official; and sending emails to others regarding the campaign/election. In this 1996 sample, 28 percent of the Internet users participated in at least one of the four activities.

Communication by letter and telephone

Respondents were asked how often in the week prior to the interview they communicated with other people by letter, or by phone. In 1995, usage of both increased from non-users who had not heard of the Internet (letters, 37 percent reported sending at least one letter; phone, 41 percent reported making 11 or more calls) up through current users (letters, 56 percent; phone, 72 percent). For letter contact, there was no difference between users and non-users, after controlling for significant influences of gender and education. For phone contact, Internet usage was still associated with increased phone contact after controlling for significant influences of education and age. In 2000, two-thirds of Internet users had written no letters in the prior week, while 60.4 percent had made more than 10 telephone calls.

Social interaction

We first explored the extent that respondents met with friends. In the week prior to the 1995 survey, 38 percent of long-time users met 1–3 times with friends and 54 percent met 4 or more times. Of recent users, 40 percent met 1–3 times with friends and 48 percent met 4 or more times. Former users met with friends somewhat less often – 48 percent met 1–3 times with friends and 44 percent met 4 or more times. Of non-users who had heard of the Internet, 48 percent met 1–3 times with friends and 40 percent met 4 or more times. Non-users who had not heard of the Internet reported meeting with friends less – 43 percent reported meeting 1–3 times with friends and 39 percent meeting 4 or more times in the week prior to the survey. In other words, those who had been using the Internet the longest also were the most likely to have met with 4 or more friends, while those who were not even aware of the Internet were least likely to have met with 4 or more friends in the prior week. Clearly long-term Internet usage is associated with more, not less, frequent sociability. These differences between non-users and users, in getting together with friends, remained after controlling for employment status (full-time, part-time, retired, unemployed).

We asked respondents the extent they agreed with the question, "In your social life are you frequently away from home?" The aggregate responses to this question were similar to the above but the differences were more marked with users (current and former) more strongly agreeing to the statement than non-users. Fifty-nine percent of long-time users, 56 percent of recent users and 57 percent of former users agreed or strongly agreed with the statement. By contrast, only 37 percent of non-users who had heard of the Internet and 34 percent of non-users who had not heard of the Internet agreed or strongly agreed with the statement. Differences in being frequently away from home remained for non-users versus users after controlling for significant influences of educational achievement and marital status.

Finally, we asked participants in the survey how many of the 10 people living closest to their home they knew. Of non-users who had not heard of the Internet, 37 percent reported knowing the 10 closest people and 31 percent knowing 4–9 of the 10 closest people. Similarly, of non-users who had heard of the Internet, 33 percent reported knowing the 10 closest people and 36 percent knowing 4–9 of the 10 closest people. Former users reported knowing slightly fewer neighbors – 28 percent reported knowing the 10 closest people and 42 percent knowing 4–9 of the 10 closest people, followed by long-time users – 28 percent reported knowing the 10 closest people and 37 percent knowing 4–9 of the 10 closest people. Recent users reported knowing the fewest neighbors – 21 percent reported knowing the 10 closest people and 43 percent knowing 4–9 of the 10 closest people. So there is evidence that long-term and recent Internet users are more likely to meet with friends in the past week, but also more likely to be away from home and to know fewer neighbors. This implies that users' social communities are more physically dispersed than non-users'. However, there was no significant difference between categories of users and non-users in this knowledge of the 10 closest neighbors after controlling for significant influences of employment status and age, implying that the use of the Internet, per se, is not associated with different levels of awareness of one's neighbors.

In the 1995 survey, 42 percent of users reported contacting family members through the Internet at least once or twice. Long-time users reported contacting family members more often than did recent adopters. In the 2000 survey, 21.8 percent of the users reported contacting family members online at least several times a year.

Other possible indicators of home and social activity include having any children, work situation (full-time, part-time, retired, unemployed, or student), owning one's home, and number of years living in the same home. In 1995, users were more likely than non-users to work full-time (69.5 percent vs. 54 percent for non-users) or be a student (13.5 percent vs. 5.9 percent), and have lived for fewer years in their current house (6.4 years vs. 10.5). The same differences existed in 1996, except that users were also more likely to own their own home. In 2000, users were significantly more likely to have children, work full-time (62.7 percent vs. 44.2 percent) or be a student (8.8 percent vs. 2.1 percent), and have lived for fewer years in their current house.

Finally, respondents' sense of overload (rushed, too much to do) was significantly higher for users than non-users in 1995, but not in 2000, and reported satisfaction (overall, and with communication with friends, family and work colleagues) was significantly greater for users than non-users in 2000, but not in 1995.

New Forms of Expression

In the 1995 survey, 25.5 percent of users reported being a member of an Internet community. Thirty-one percent of long-time users and 17 percent of recent adopters reported participating in Internet communities; 23 percent participated in 3 or 4 communities, and 27 percent participated in five or more communities. For the vast majority of both long-time and recent users, use of the Internet does not appear to have much impact on the time spent with friends and family. The two groups' views were not statistically different. Eighty-eight percent of users reported that the time spent with friends and family face-to-face or by phone had not changed since they started using Internet. The same proportion of users (6 percent) reported they spent more time with friends and family face-to-face or by phone, as reported they spent less time. In 2000, 10.4 percent reported being a member of at least one online community.

In 1995, 11.5 percent, and in 2000, 13.8 percent, of users who responded to the question had established friendships via the Internet. Those reporting a higher number of Internet friends in 1995 were more likely to have met at least one of them. In 1995 17 percent of users who responded to the question reported that they had met face-to-face at least one person they had first encountered online (not necessarily one of those online friends), and in 2000 10.1 percent of users did so. There were only weak or in most cases non-existent statistical relationships of this Internet-based friendship formation with demographic variables, traditional forms of interaction, or personality attributes.

Summary

This chapter summarizes some of the major results from one of the earliest and most comprehensive survey approaches to:

- understand the societal and individual consequences of the Internet;
- consider issues of awareness and dropouts; and
- study the Internet in a way that compares users to non-users and that also controls statistically for their demographic differences.

Concerning access, on all the dimensions considered here – gender, age, household income, education, and race – the digital divide is shrinking. Nevertheless, all the differences within the demographic variables, based on the years of the survey, were significant. Further, for some dimensions of the digital divide there is still a long way to go before the digital divide disappears. Public policy initiatives aimed at extending Internet usage could most usefully focus on low income families, the elderly and African-Americans. The inequities of awareness and use will become increasingly urgent as more job-related services (postings of job opportunities, training), government functions and public service information (health, education, insurance, financial support) become available via the Internet.

Concerning community and political involvement, the results show that Internet users were more likely than non-users to engage in traditional political activity in the 1996 general election, including voting, controlling for demographic differences, and the Internet provided a platform for a significant amount of additional forms of political activity. Users tend to communicate with others through other media (especially telephone) more than do non-users, meet more with their friends, and interact more with others in general, although in a more widely dispersed physical environment. Users were more likely to work, have children and own their home, than were non-users, but had lived in their homes for fewer years. Users experienced greater overload (in 1995) but also greater satisfaction with their communication (in 2000).

Finally, concerning new forms of social interaction, somewhat more than one in ten of users have become friends with others online, have met a notable percentage of them, and belong to online communities.

Our conclusions do not in the main support arguments about pervasive negative or paradoxical effects of the Internet, certainly with respect to involvement or expression, and to some aspects of access, which have generally been based on case studies and samples that were neither random nor representative. Rather, the findings support perspectives maintaining that this new social technology has substantial benefits to society. Let us be clear, however: our survey results do *not* conclude that there are *no* negative aspects or consequences of the Internet. However, the nature of survey research precludes studying particular kinds of negative consequences or detailed aspects of especially damaging, pathological, criminal, or chronic uses. Nonetheless, we find that Internet usage (1) is becoming more equally accessible and widely used, (2) is associated with increased community and political involvement, and (3) is associated with significant and increased online and offline social interactions. Hence, we view the Internet as an important and multiplicative social capital resource for US society.

References

Aspden, P. and Katz, J. E. (2001). Assessments of quality of health care information and referrals to physicians: a nationwide survey. In R. E. Rice and J. E. Katz (eds), *The Internet and health communication* (pp. 107–19). Thousand Oaks, CA: Sage.

Baron, N. S. (1984). Computer-mediated communication as a force in language change. *Visible Language*, 18(2), 118–41.

Barringer, F. (2001, September 24). A false challenge to news photos takes root on the web. *New York Times*, C-9.

Baudrillard, J. (1983). *Simulations*. Translated by Paul Foss, Paul Patton, and Philip Beitchman. New York: Semiotext(e).

Baym, N. K. (1995). The emergence of community in computer-mediated communication. In S. G. Jones (ed.), *Cybersociety: computer-mediated communication and community* (pp. 138–63). Thousand Oaks, CA: Sage.

Carpini, M. X. D. (1996). Voters, candidates, and campaigns in the new information age: An overview and assessment. *Harvard International Journal of Press/Politics*, 1, 36–56.

Case, D. O. Stalking, monitoring and profiling: a typology and case studies of harmful uses of caller ID. *New Media and Society*, 2(1), 67–84.

Fischer, C. L. (1993). *America calling: a social history of the telephone to 1940*. Berkeley, CA: University of California Press.

Gergen, K. (1991). *The saturated self: dilemmas of identity in contemporary life*. New York: HarperCollins.

Harden, B. (2001, September 27). Bomb threats flood in after terrorist attacks. *New York Times*. Available online at:
http://www.nytimes.com/2001/09/27/national/27SCAR.html

Hiltz, S. R. and Turoff, M. (1995). *Network nation* (revised edn). Cambridge, MA: MIT Press.

Hoffman, N. (1998). Bridging the racial divide on the Internet. *Science*, 280, 390–1.

Kapor, M. (1993). Where is the digital highway really heading? *Wired*, July–August, 53–9, 94.

Katz, J. E. (1999). *Connections: social and cultural studies of the telephone in American life*. New Brunswick, NJ: Transaction Publishers.

Katz, J. E. and Aspden, P. (1997a). Motives, hurdles, and dropouts: who is on and off the Internet and why. *Communications of the ACM*, 40(4), 97–102.

Katz, J. E. and Aspden, P. (1997b). A nation of strangers. *Communications of the ACM*, 40(12), 81–6.

Katz, J. E. and Aspden, P. (1997c). Motivations for and barriers to Internet usage: results of a national public opinion survey. *Internet Research: electronic Networking Applications and Policy*, 7(3), 170–88.

Katz, J. E. and Aspden, P. (1998). Internet dropouts in the USA. *Telecommunications Policy*, 22(4/5), 327–39.

Katz, J. E. and Ronald E. Rice. (2002). *Social consequences of the Internet*. Cambridge: MIT Press.

Katz, J. E., Aspden, P., and Reich, W. (1997). *Elections and electrons: a national public opinion survey on the role of Cyberspace and mass media in political opinion formation during the 1996 election*. A paper presented at the 25th Annual

Telecommunications Policy Research Conference, Crystal City (Arlington, VA), September.

Kiesler, S., Siegel, H., and McGuire, T. W. (1984). Social psychological aspects of computer-mediated communication. *American Psychologist*, 39(10), 1,123–34.

Kraut, R., Patterson, M., Lundmark, V., Kiesler, S., Mukhopadhyay, T., and Scherlis, W. (1998). Internet paradox: a social technology that reduces social involvement and psychological well-being? *American Psychologist*, 53, 1,017–31.

McCreadie, M. and Rice, R. E. (1999a). Trends in analyzing access to information, part I: Cross-disciplinary conceptualizations. *Information Processing and Management*, 35(1), 45–76.

McCreadie, M. and Rice, R. E. (1999b). Trends in analyzing access to information, part II: unique and integrating conceptualizations. *Information Processing and Management*, 35(1), 77–99.

Merton, R. K. (1957). *Social theory and social structure* (2nd edn). New York: Free Press.

Nie, N. H. (2001). Sociability, interpersonal relations, and the Internet: reconciling conflicting findings. *American Behavioral Scientist*, 45(3), 420–35.

Numes, M. (1995). Jean Baudrillard in cyberspace: Internet, virtuality, and postmodernity. *Style*, 29(2), 314–27.

Parks, M. R. and Floyd, K. (1996). Making friends in cyberspace. *Journal of Communication*, 46, 80–97.

Poole, I. de Sola. (1983). *Technologies of freedom*. Cambridge, MA: Belknap Press.

Putnam, R. D. (1996). The strange disappearance of civic life in America. *The American Prospect*, 24, 34–46.

Rash, W. (1997). *Politics on the nets: wiring the political process*. New York: Freeman.

Rheingold, H. (1993). *The virtual community: homesteading on the electronic frontier*. Reading, MA: Addison-Wesley.

Rice, R. E. (1987a). New patterns of social structure in an information society. In J. Schement and L. Lievrouw (eds), *Competing visions, complex realities: social aspects of the information society* (pp. 107–20). Norwood, NJ: Ablex.

Rice, R. E. (1987b). Computer-mediated communication and organizational innovation. *Journal of Communication*, 37, 65–94.

Rice, R. E. (2001). The Internet and health communication: a framework of experiences. In R. E. Rice and J. E. Katz (eds), *The Internet and health communication: experiences and expectations* (pp. 5–46). Thousand Oaks, CA: Sage.

Schiffer, M. B. (1991). *The portable radio in American life*. Tucson, AZ: University of Arizona Press.

Selnow, G. W. (1994). *High-tech campaigns: computer technology in political communication*. New York: Praeger.

Starobin, P. (1996). On the square. *National Journal*, June 25, 1145–9.

Stoll, C. (1995). *Silicon snake oil*. New York: Doubleday.

Symposium (1995). Emerging media technology and the First Amendment. *Yale Law Journal*, 104, 1613–850.

Turkle, S. (1996). Virtuality and its discontents: searching for community in cyberspace. *The American Prospect*, 24, 50–7.

Van Alstyne, W. W. (1995). *First Amendment: cases and materials* (2nd edn). Westbury, NY: Foundation Press

White, C. S. (1997). Citizen participation and the Internet: prospects for civic deliberation in the information age. *Social Studies*, 88, 23–8.

Wynn, E. and Katz, J. E. (1997). Hyperbole over cyberspace: self-presentation and social boundaries in Internet home pages and discourse. *The Information Society*, 13(4), 297–329.

4

Digital Living

The Impact (or Otherwise) of the Internet on Everyday British Life

Ben Anderson and Karina Tracey

Abstract

This chapter examines the "impact" of the Internet on the everyday lives of UK citizens through the integration of quantitative longitudinal time-use data and qualitative interviews. It shows that there is little significant change in people's time use that can be associated with their acquisition of an Internet connection and so demonstrates the over-simplicity of the 'impact' model for understanding the role of the Internet in everyday life. Instead, it suggests that lifestyle and/or lifestage transitions may trigger adoption of the Internet and, simultaneously, changes in domestic time-use. It also demonstrates that 'Internet usage' is too coarse a unit for sensible analysis. Rather, researchers need to consider the patterns of usage of the various applications or services that the Internet delivers.

Authors' note

The authors gratefully acknowledge the support of the BT Group Technology Programme and of all the researchers both in BTexact and the Institute for Social and Economic Research at the University of Essex who are involved in the Digital Living research programme. This chapter has been improved by comments from several colleagues including Malcolm Brynin, Leslie Haddon, John Seton, and the editors of this book. We also thank the members of EURESCOM's "P903-ICT Uses in Everyday Life" project for permission to reproduce two of their figures. As usual any remaining errors are our own.

Introduction

The domestic telecommunications market is changing radically and rapidly from one dominated by plain old voice telephony to one where voice is just one of myriad Internet protocol services and applications available from a socket in the wall or a gadget in the hand. In this climate of technological flux there is considerable public debate about the merits, dangers, and opportunities associated with the perceived shift towards a digitally mediated society. This debate is mirrored in the commercial context by an equally passionate argument about the commercial opportunities that may follow from the digital and Internet revolutions. While a review of these arguments and the literature in which they are found is outside the scope of this paper (for reviews see CACM, 1998; Kraut, Patterson, Lundmark, Kiesler, Mukhopadhyay, and Scherlis, 1998), it is worth noting that these debates are nothing new in sociological terms. For example, Gershuny (1983) argues that a consideration of how households achieve their various 'wants or needs' using the social and technological structures at their disposal can help to understand the social significances of technological innovations. Thus where once remote relatives could only be contacted by letter, then telegram, then telephone, they can now be contacted by email. Thus the "mode of provision" has changed although the end goal (interpersonal social communication) has not. Such changes, according to Gershuny, are indicative of socio-technical change or social innovation in his terms and he specifically looks towards (then) future telecommunications infrastructures as the context for such changes.

In an effort to unravel these changing patterns of social innovation and to understand some of the policy and commercial opportunities they present through disciplined social scientific enquiry, we have created a research programme known as Digital Living which centers on the longitudinal study of some 2,600 individuals living in 1,000 UK households (Anderson, McWilliam, Lacohee, Clucas, and Gershuny, 1999; Lacohee and Anderson, 2001). The individuals in this panel are being studied using a range of methods including questionnaires, time-use diaries, call records, Internet usage logs and qualitative interviews. This triangulation of data sources on the same individuals over time enables us not only to build a rich picture of their everyday lives, but also to study the causal relationships between their acquisition and use of new Information and Communications Technologies (ICTs) and changes in their behavior and their social, symbolic, and economic capital in a way that repeated cross-sectional surveys cannot.

Explicit in this approach is a commitment to people-focused rather than an ICT-focused research because it is apparent from even cursory fieldwork in domestic contexts that the acquisition and use of particular ICTs cannot be meaningfully separated from the acquisition and use of others. As a result it makes little sense to try to understand the acquisition and use of mobile telephones, personal computers or "the Internet" in isolation from one another (Silverstone and Haddon, 1996). Instead we choose to build understandings of people's activities and the ways in which they use a dynamic range of ICTs to achieve them.

The simplest analytic model one can adopt when considering ICTs and societal change is that technologies 'impact' upon social life. In this view the uptake and usage of information and communication technologies can be seen as a condition variable and any changes in the lives of the people under study can be attributed, in some unproblematic way, to the introduction of ICTs (see, for example, Nie and Erbring, 2000; Kraut et al., 1998; the discussions in Smith and Marx, 1994; and Edwards, 1994; and similar points made in the organizational context by Kling, 2000).

According to this model we might hypothesize that gaining or losing access to the Internet might reduce or increase the time spent on a number of activities such as:

- using existing media such as TV, video, radio, newspapers, books, cinema, theatre;
- existing communication practices such as making/receiving phone calls and visiting/being visited by friends or relatives;
- other informational practices such as learning/education inside and outside the home.

This chapter uses data drawn from the Digital Living study to test these hypotheses. As this analysis unfolds, the limitations of the impact model for understanding the dynamics of the uptake and usage of the Internet in the UK becomes clear. By integrating quantitative and qualitative data the chapter points the way towards a more nuanced analysis which contributes to the understanding of the socially shaped nature of Internet use (Mansel and Silverstone, 1996). This analysis may lead us to suggest that applications and services delivered via the Internet are not changing the way people live their lives in a simple straightforward manner, but are supporting and enhancing their existing lifestyles, whatever those lifestyles might be, through changes in what Gershuny would term their mode of provision.

Table 4.1 Number of respondents in waves 1 and 2 of the digital living panel

	Wave 1	Wave 2
Survey and time-use diary completed	999	682
Repeated survey and time-use diary (i.e. longitudinal sample)	—	472
Individual survey only	740	947
Time use diary only	17	37
Repeated individual survey only (i.e. longitudinal sample)	—	547

The Digital Living Panel Study

The panel was initiated in July 1998 as a collaboration with the Institute for Social and Economic Research (ISER) at the University of Essex, UK. The longitudinal panel was established and the first wave of survey fieldwork was completed by March 1999. The sample was randomly selected according to UK postal code and in the first wave selection was carried out to ensure that all households had fixed line telephones and 50 percent had computers at home. The second wave of quantitative panel fieldwork was completed in April 2000 and wave 3 was completed in April 2001. The final sample sizes for waves 1 and 2 are shown in table 4.1. The recruitment of the sample and the research instruments used are described in detail in Anderson et al. (1999) and Lacohee and Anderson (2001). The research instruments of relevance to this article are discussed briefly below.

Survey data

This data collection takes the form of a survey and time-use diary for completion by all individuals aged 16 and over which is repeated on a 12-month cycle. A second time-use diary designed explicitly for younger household members is for completion by all individuals aged 9–15. Two questionnaires were used. A household questionnaire was completed by the head of household and individual questionnaires were completed by all individuals over the age of 16. In brief the questionnaires covered ownership of households goods and services, ownership of ICT and socioeconomic data, personal usage of ICT, personal consumption and communication behavior, the extent, nature, and geography of family and other social relationships (social networks), attitudes and socioeconomic data.

The diary splits each day into 96 distinct 15-minute segments and invites panelists to record which of a range of predefined activities they were doing during each 15-minute segment for one week. Respondents were asked to report the main activity they were engaged in (primary activity) and also any other (secondary) activity that they were doing at the same time. Thus respondents could report using the telephone (secondary) at the same time as preparing a meal (primary) or vice versa if appropriate. Younger members of the household (9–15) were asked to complete a similar but differently presented time-use diary.

The quantitative data reported in this chapter were collected during the first and second waves of this panel survey in early 1999 and early 2000 (table 4.1) and derives from two sources:

- the adult (16+) time-use diaries;
- the adult (16+) survey questions related to socioeconomic variables, e.g. age, employment status.

Qualitative interview data

Following the first wave of quantitative survey fieldwork a selection of households were approached for qualitative study. These studies include both structured and unstructured interviews, photo records and prompt-based discussions and repeat visits in what has become a "long conversation" between the qualitative researchers and the selected households (Silverstone et al., 1991).

Altogether the qualitative data is drawn from 104 individual interviews in 70 separate households carried out between December 1998 and October 2000. Ages of participants range from 13 to 67. Of the 104 participants, 55 were male and 49 were female. Forty-three interviews were carried out with individuals from the longitudinal panel; 16 of these focused specifically on the role of the social network in Internet adoption and usage and 27 were more general interviews. These interviewees were selected according to their lifestage, the technology they owned and the technology that they reported they were likely to purchase in the near future. The general interviews covered areas such as the social network members, usage of ICT, lifestyle and usage of time and money. General interviews of this nature were also carried out with 14 individuals who were recruited separately from the panel.

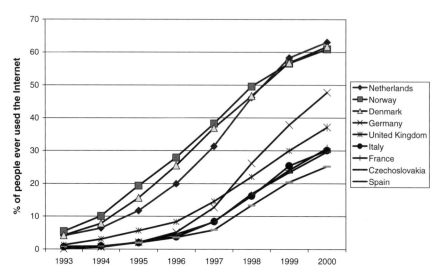

Figure 4.1 Percent of European adults (16+) "who have ever accessed the worldwide web at home or elsewhere"
Source: Mante-Meijer et al. (2001). Used with permission

In addition, similar interviews were conducted with 11 individuals in 8 households who have subscribed to BT's broadband Internet service in London; 6 interviews were carried out as part of a study of 35 students on their experiences of living in shared accommodation; and 30 interviews of a similar nature to those described above have been carried out under the umbrella of a study of the effects of telework on the quality of life of workers and their households (Akelson et al., 2000).

The State of the Internet in Europe

Before discussing detailed research findings it is worth sketching the current state of Internet access and usage in Europe to provide a context to the chapter. By 2000 about 40 percent of all Europeans aged 16 and over had used the Internet at some time (Mante-Meijer et al., 2001) although of these some 5 percent were no longer users. As with other areas of the world where market forces play some role in Internet access, this penetration is extremely uneven whether considered by gross geography or age as figures 4.1 and 4.2 demonstrate. Among

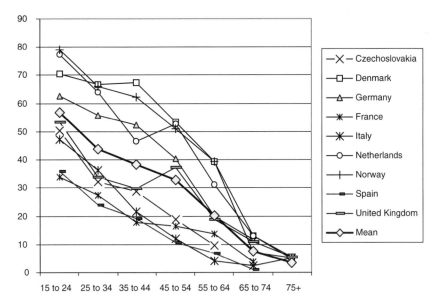

Figure 4.2 Percent of each age group who have ever used the Internet
Source: Mante-Meijer et al. (2001). Used with permission

the UK population views about the Internet vary considerably, from the converts who feel that they now couldn't live without it: "I love the Internet, I'm a great believer in technology I'm a great believer in the democratising nature of the Internet" (DC), to those who have, at best, hazy knowledge about it: "it made me think of a fax machine, is it something like a fax?" (GE).

Overall, there is the impression that despite all attempts by policy-makers and the IT industries, many in the European population remain cautious about the Internet for reasons that include the security of credit card details, the assumed prevalence of pornography, cost, lack of computer skills and lack of time or interest.

It is in the context of these uneven growth patterns that the debates about exclusion and inclusion, whether by age, economic capital or geography, take place (see for example Patterson and Wilson, 2000). Figures 4.1 and 4.2 demonstrate obvious differences in Internet access for different groups of European citizens and similar patterns exist for socioeconomic status (wealthier people are more likely to have access) and educational level (better-educated people are more likely to have access). Even though the emphasis on *access* is simplistic (there are many who have access to ICTs who do not or cannot *use* them), there are now significant efforts being made to combat perceived "exclusion" from access at the European level. These efforts include a number of public-policy initiatives based on the notion of an "Information Society For All" or E-Europe.[1] It is interesting to note in this context that many of those who had not yet acquired Internet access in December 2000 saw no reason to do so and most were not considering it (Mante-Meijer et al., 2001). In a similar study an estimated 54 percent of the UK population did not have Internet access and did not want it whilst 16 percent said they did not have it because they could not afford it (JRF, 2000). Thus for the majority of current non-users, the Internet has no obvious place in their lives and is not likely to have in the foreseeable future. If this is true then massive public investment to "overcome" their "economic exclusion" through reductions in the financial cost of access may be open to question. While it is tempting to reify these debates in socioeconomic terms, to do so overlooks the importance of social and cultural capital, and, increasingly, fashion and identity in individual and household level decisions about ICT acquisition (e.g. Silva, 2000; Nafus and Tracey, 2002).

Applications usage

Access to the Internet is, of course, not even half of the picture. What people do with the Internet once they have access (if they do) must also be considered. When considering patterns of usage it rapidly becomes clear that the Internet is not a single entity that can be analysed as such. One reason for this confusion may be the continuing conflation of "the Internet" with "the worldwide web." Rather, it is a delivery mechanism for a range of services which are continually evolving and which are used differentially by different people.

For example, figure 4.3 shows that average weekly usage of the web or email for the wave-2 diary respondents was not particularly high (between 1 and 3 hours per week). However, while email usage showed no clear pattern with age, usage of the web appeared to be highest in the younger age groups and lowest in the oldest. The youngest group spent less time using email than the web, indeed they spent less time using email than both the 25–34 and 55+ groups.

---

1   See http://europa.eu.int/information_society/eeurope/index_en.htm

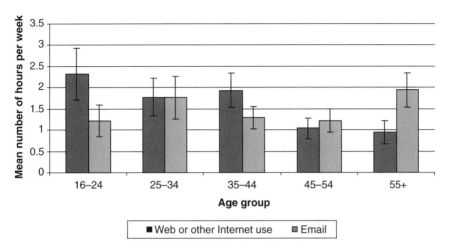

Figure 4.3 Mean number of hours per week spent on "email" or "web browsing or other Internet use" by diary respondents at wave 2 (2000) who reported any Internet use 27 ≤ n ≤ 38 for all cells. Error bars are +/−1 standard error of the mean

However this pattern is almost exactly reversed in the oldest group (55+) who used email more than the web. In addition, figure 4.4 shows that there were some people who used the web but not email and some who used email but not the web. While, interestingly, the heaviest web users are the women who hardly use email, the mean hours per week spent emailing by women was 1.72 while for men it was 2.13. However, these differences were not statistically significant (t = 1.069, df = 117, p = 0.287). Mean hours spent using the web were more comparable at 2.39 for men and 2.65 for women and again the difference was not statistically significant (t = −0.512, df = 99, p = 0.610).[2]

There may be several reasons why some users only use email or the worldwide web. The interviews suggest that some people use the Internet in a very repeated way – they get shown how to use one application and never move on to anything else. Quite often email is perceived as easier to use than searching for information, so some of the users don't move past the email application: "I don't use [WWW], they [son and daughter] use it or if there's anything I want then I tell them

2 Note that all means in this paragraph are calculated for those individuals who recorded this activity in their time-use diary. They are therefore "usage means" rather than "population means."

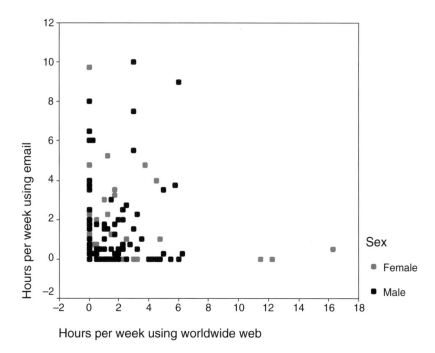

Figure 4.4 Scattergraph of mean hours per week spent on email or web browsing by diary respondents at wave 2 (2000) by sex

to do it for me. I haven't got the confidence to do it. I've used the email so I find that easier" (MC).

Others only perceive a need for one of the applications and so will rarely, if ever, try different things. In the interviews people who had predominantly local social networks tended to perceive less need for email: "it just comes out black and white on a piece of paper and yes it is impersonal . . . I've never asked for her [local friend] email address, we speak quite regularly on the phone so what would be the point of emailing" (JB).

It should therefore be clear that "Internet usage" cannot be conceived of as a simple unitary activity. People are not simply "Internet users." Different kinds of people make differing uses of the range of applications and services that the Internet supports and probably for differing reasons. Thus "the average Internet user" simply does not exist and until a more nuanced understanding of the reasons for different usage patterns, which can do justice to lifestage and lifestyle differences is developed any explanation or forecasting of future change is likely to be extremely unreliable.

The Impact of the Internet on Everyday Life in the UK

As noted above an ongoing research debate is the extent to which the Internet is changing people's lives. One way of addressing this question is to look at how or if people's use of time changes when they acquire access to, and start to use the Internet. In the qualitative interviews with Internet users one topic of discussion was the extent to which the Internet had an impact on the way interviewees spent their time and to what extent Internet use displaced other activities. Although this might appear a relatively straightforward question, informants found it extremely difficult to pin down any clear or explicit changes: "It's difficult to say if it [the Internet] displaces one activity or another" (SC).

The range of activities which were reported as possibly being displaced included watching television, spending time in the garden, reading newspapers, magazines and books, going to the supermarket, making telephone calls, going to the pub, doing nothing, writing letters, sleeping, playing computer games and typing on a typewriter. However, no one activity was mentioned by more than a handful of informants and even the heaviest of users felt that any displacement was marginal at best. One possible reason for this may have been the relatively low level of daily or weekly usage in the UK (as mentioned earlier between 1 and 3 hours per week on average) compared to the USA, although even those who spent as much as six hours per week using the Internet in the evenings (such as SC above) couldn't pinpoint any major displacements. The informants' time use appeared to evolve and change continuously, so rather than a straight substitution effect, it appeared that a range of activities were adjusted or multitasked to enable Internet use to fit in. In addition, other factors have a significant influence on patterns of time-use. For example, during the summer months one respondent's television viewing, game playing and Internet usage were all displaced by spending time in the garden when the weather was good.

Therefore it might be expected that changes in time use would not be significantly associated with a simple transition such as acquiring Internet access. It might also be expected that an analysis of patterns of changing time use would show that the acquisition of Internet access is having relatively little immediate impact on people's lives. If so we can conclude that conceptualizing the relationship between technological change and social change in terms of "impact" or time-use "substitution" may be over simplistic.

The two waves of quantitative time-use diary data that are currently available from the Digital Living panel can be used to explore this issue in a relatively straightforward manner because it enables the comparison of time spent on activities before and after an individual may have acquired Internet access. The remainder of this chapter does exactly this.

Data and Analysis Methods

The time-use diaries record the total amount of time an individual spends doing activity X during the week-long self-reporting period. Two totals can be derived for each time-use category, one for that category as a primary activity, and one for the category as a secondary activity. The analysis described below examined changes in time-use for all categories of activities (see table 4.2) but this chapter only reports statistically significant results.

Individuals were allocated to four groups using data from the wave-1 and wave-2 surveys. The four conditions were:

- No_net: no Internet connection in household at either wave.
- New_net: no Internet connection in household at wave 1, but had Internet connection in household at wave 2 and used it.
- Net_both: had Internet connection in household at wave 1 and wave 2 and used it at both.
- Net_dropout: had Internet connection in household at wave 1 and used it, but no Internet connection in household at wave 2.

The sizes of these groups are shown in table 4.3 while the age distributions are given in figure 4.5. The actual size of n for each subsequent analysis varies because not all of these individuals completed time-use diaries in each wave of data collection.

We use simple paired sample t tests to compare the mean hours per week spent on each of the time-use categories by the groups in wave 1 and wave 2. Our Net_both group acts as a control because they did not acquire Internet access and thus any changes in time use in this group must be due to other factors. This method allows us to

Table 4.2 Time-use categories

1	Sleeping, resting	19	Sports participation, keeping fit
2	Washing, dressing	20	Hobbies, games, musical instruments
3	Eating at home	21	Watching TV/cable/satellite TV
4	Cooking and food preparation	22	Watching videos/laser disks
5	Care of own children or other adults in the home	23	Listening to radio, CD, cassette
6	Cleaning house, tidying, clothes washing, ironing, and sewing	24	Reading newspapers, books, magazines
7	Maintenance, odd jobs, DIY, gardening, pet care	25	Being visited by friends, relatives in own home
8	Travel (to and from work, shops, school, cinema, station, etc.)	26	Receiving phone calls
9	Paid work at workplace	27	Making phone calls
10	Paid work at home (not using PC)	28	Playing PC games/games console
11	Study at home (not using PC)	29	Reading/writing email
12	Courses and education outside the home	30	Browsing web, or other Internet use
13	Voluntary work, church, helping people (not in own home)	31	Study at home (using PC)
14	Shopping, appointment (hairdressers /doctors, etc.)	32	Paid work at home (using PC)
		33	Other PC use
15	Going to concerts, theatre, cinema, clubs, sporting events	34	Doing nothing (including illness)
		35	Other (please write in)
16	Walks, outings, etc.		
17	Eating out, drinking (pubs, restaurants)		
18	Visiting or meeting friends or relatives		

Table 4.3 Number of individuals in each transition group

	Internet connection			
Label	Wave 1	Wave 2	N	% of longitudinal sample
No_net	No	No	462	43.0
New_net	No	Yes	220	20.5
Net_both	Yes	Yes	333	31.0
Net_dropout	Yes	No	60	5.6
			1,075	100.0

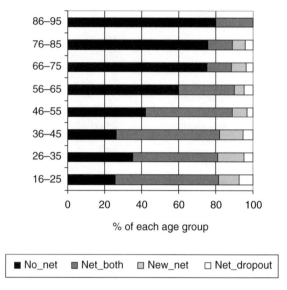

Figure 4.5   Age distribution of transition groups

determine which, if any, changes in time use can be associated with getting and using or losing Internet access in the home.

Analysis and Results

The results suggest that very few of the changes in time spent on primary and secondary activities can be significantly associated with gaining or losing Internet access at home. Table 4.4 shows all the significant results for primary activities. Clearly in most cases (table 4.2) there is no significant change. Our control group (No_net) throws up two interesting results. For reasons that are not clear, it would appear that the population as a whole is spending less time on shopping and appointments and roughly the same amount or more traveling.

The Net_dropout group spent significantly less time eating at home as a primary activity at wave 2. Given that 55 percent of Net_dropout were in paid work at wave 1 it may be that changes in their employment situations (i.e. lifestyle changes) could have led to changes in the amount of time they spent on cooking and food preparation. Simultaneously these lifestyle changes may also have resulted in loss or gain of Internet access.

Table 4.4 Results of paired sample t tests for primary activities

Time-use category	No_net	Net_dropout	New_net	Net_both
Shopping, appointment (hairdressers/ doctors, etc.)	−0.626*			−0.702***
Sports participation, keeping fit				0.418*
Reading/writing email			0.534***	0.224*
Browsing web, or other Internet use			0.755***	0.178*
Doing nothing (including illness)				−0.509**
Eating at home		−1.114*		
Hobbies, games, musical instruments			−1.029*	
Study at home (using PC)			0.363*	
Travel (to and from work, shops, school, cinema, station, etc.)	0.643*			

Empty cells signify non-significant results. * $p \leq 0.05$, ** $p \leq 0.01$, *** $p \leq 0.005$

For example one interviewee who moved from employment with Internet access to a period of unemployment said:

> when I moved here I didn't bother until I left my job in May '98. It was probably only then, yes it would have been only then I took out ... because I had email at work and I had a laptop I could bring home ... Then I thought while I'm not working, while I'm deciding what I'm going to do ... So then I took a subscription to AOL ... then more and more people I knew started to be on it and I was emailing lots people by then and so it became sort of indispensable. (CF)

This quote, and the one below, also shows the extent to which the maintenance of social networks via email can effectively "lock people in" to Internet access as a key social tool. This implies that a policy that focuses simply on supporting initial uptake is not sufficient. There may well be severe social implications of enforced "Internet drop out" whether through financial or other reasons.

It is plausible that a considerable number of individuals might have changed their educational circumstances during 1999. This may affect both their patterns of time use and their access to the Internet at the same time. For example, school leavers may have moved away from the parental home to a residence without access to the Internet. University leavers who had Internet access during their time spent at university may not feel the need to carry this on post-university, perhaps because they now had Internet access in their place of work. However, regardless of the changes in their circumstances once the person had begun to use the Internet as part of their daily life, few seemed willing to give up access completely. Students who currently have access on campus may get access at home post-university if the Internet was not accessible at their place of work and it is interesting to note that 13 percent of Net_dropouts had been students in 1999. A student about to leave university said:

> I've thought about doing it [getting Internet access] but I just haven't got around to it yet. There's things that I subscribe to that I wouldn't want to lose when I finish at university, things that would be useful for me professionally so I ought to get on with it really . . . I'd have to have access at home if I didn't have it at work because I've got so many friends that I wouldn't be able to contact otherwise. (DW)

Interestingly the results do not suggest that Net_dropouts spend significantly less time either emailing or using the Internet in general. This implies that whilst they may no longer have access at home, they may still have access elsewhere such as at work, at a public access point or some other institution. Clearly, an avenue for future research is more detailed investigation of the transitions undergone by the Net_dropout group.

The New_net group spent significantly less time on hobbies, games, and musical instruments suggesting that those who go online may now be pursuing their hobbies via the Internet because this activity might now be recorded as "using the worldwide web." This suggestion is supported by the some of the qualitative respondents:

> Lets say I'm watching TV and there's an interesting programme on, I'm a bit of a foodie, I love to cook and if you're watching something, say a BBC cooking programme . . . and at the end of the programme they give you the BBC or Delia web page, you think "oh, that looks really cool" . . . and you just go and look up Delia Smith and see what's there. (AS)

However it is also plausible that the kind of household transitions referred to above or to others such as becoming a member of a shared household may be contributory factors. This may offer an explanation for the finding that the New_net group spends more time using a PC at home for study (education) than they did at wave 1.

Again our qualitative data supports this. When LA moved in with his new housemate he serendipitously became an Internet user as his new housemate showed him how to use the Internet and set up his email account. LA then recognized that email could help him manage his recycling business and so he started using email. Prior to this LA had very little interest in technology, but now he feels that, should he move out of the flat, he would find it very difficult to manage his business and his personal life without it.

> I was not interested fundamentally in computers and I disliked anything to do with it so it's only been in the last few years that I've become more aware of it. A it's fashionable, B it's incredibly useful. It's only since moving in with [housemate], otherwise I wouldn't have an email address if I didn't live here . . . One of the things I'll miss most about it if I leave is the fact that I have a technological capability that I never had before. (LA)

Similarly retirement from a job that involved computer or Internet access at the place of work can trigger home computer ownership and subsequently access to the Internet. Indeed in some cases they actually took the PC with them from work.

> I used the Internet at work before I retired, it saved me a lot of time, I could punch in a couple of words and it would throw up any page from the *Economist* circulating then and from the last ten years . . . I wanted the Internet [at home] because it's manifestly useful and the email aspect is very attractive. (KS)

> My other friend was given a computer that the work had finished with, it was a really old thing, an elastic band type of job, black and white screen etc. She was made redundant and then she went on a computer course and she was given this antiquated computer at home. And she's into story writing, she's trying to write a book. But that computer died on her, so this Christmas she treated herself to a new computer. (DR talking about a friend)

Other retirees have acquired Internet access in order to enable them to keep in touch with remote relatives (often grandchildren) on a more regular, but cheaper, basis than the telephone. While this may start as relatively simple email, it often rapidly changes to the exchange of media objects (audio and video clips, photos) of family members. Some of the retirees were relatively unskilled at using the computer, but even if they were not able to scan in or send attachments themselves they were often heavy consumers of material sent by other family members. MC, for example, did not own a scanner and was unaware of how to send attachments, however, she frequently received photos from relatives who lived abroad: "He'll email pictures, photos of his kids and things like that" (MC, talking about her cousin who works from Singapore).

RA on the other hand was teaching himself how to use the PC and one of his favorite activities was working with photos or pictures on the PC. He then sent his pictures to his grandchildren: "because I did some things [on the PC] for the children with their photographs and I did some pictures and I needed to say that I wanted that back again because I had to recreate it because I hadn't saved it. And so I emailed" (RA).

The New_net group spent significantly more time reading and writing email than they had at wave 1. Thus there is, hardly surprisingly, evidence that getting Internet access in the household is associated with spending more time emailing. The New_net group also spent significantly more time web browsing or other Internet use than they had at wave 1.

Finally the Net_both group also show some interesting results. Individuals in this group spent significantly more time using the Internet in general at wave 2 than they had at wave 1. This suggests that Internet usage increases as people gain more experience with it and the data show that the increase is larger for email than for other Internet usage. This may confirm Kraut et al.'s result that email is a key driver of Internet use (Kraut, Mukhopadhyay, Szczypula, Kiesler, and Scherlis, 2000). For reasons that are not clear, this group spent less time shopping (perhaps related to the "control" results for No_net) and doing nothing and more time on outdoor fitness activities at wave 2 compared to wave 1.

Table 4.5 shows all the significant results for secondary activities. Again in most cases (see table 4.2) there is no significant change. Our control group (No_net) now appear to be spending more time on walks and outings and more time receiving phone calls as secondary (that is, background) activities. All groups report spending more time listening to the radio, CD, and so on which suggests a population trend, although it is interesting to note that the largest increase (over three hours per week) is for the Net_dropouts, a group who also spent more time watching videos at wave 2 than at wave 1.

New_net individuals appear to spend *more* time watching TV as a secondary activity (contrary to most suppositions) than they did before they had Internet access at home whilst Net_both individuals also watched more TV suggesting that this effect does not disappear as experience with the Internet increases. New_net individuals also

Table 4.5 Results of paired sample t tests for secondary activities

	No_net	Net_dropout	New_net	Net_both
Walks, outings, etc.	0.126*			
Listening to radio, CD, cassette	1.714***	3.288*	1.331*	1.270***
Receiving phone calls	0.383***			
Watching videos/laser disks		0.258*		
Eating at home			0.297*	
Care of own children or other adults in the home				1.790*
Watching TV/cable/satellite TV			0.929**	0.665*
Reading/writing email			0.098*	
Browsing web, or other Internet use				0.158*

Empty cells signify non-significant results. * p $\leq$ 0.05, ** p $\leq$ 0.01, *** p $\leq$ 0.005

spend more time eating at home as a secondary activity than they did for reasons that are not clear.

Taken together these results suggest that changes to an individual's access to the Internet in their home are having very little immediate and significant impact on the time they spend on other activities. Instead, a plausible explanation for the changes in time use uncovered by this analysis is that alterations in lifestage or lifestyle, such as changing employment or educational circumstances trigger changes in an individual's patterns of time use – a reduction in the time they spend preparing food being one plausible effect. At the same time, those social changes may also trigger changes in their access to, and usage of applications and services delivered via the Internet.

Discussion

In general, what is noticeable about these results is not what has turned out to be significant, but what has not. There is no evidence from this data that individuals who now have Internet access in their household, and who use it, are spending less time watching television, reading books, listening to the radio or engaged in social activities in or outside the household in comparison with individuals who do not (or who no longer) have Internet access in their household. Indeed, in some cases they appear to be doing more of some of these. These results, based on longitudinal data refute those of Nie and Erbring

(2000) which are based solely on cross-sectional data and therefore cannot measure true change before and after a transition. The only time-use changes that can be associated with gaining Internet access are a decrease in time spent on hobbies and an increase in time spent studying at home using a PC, eating at home, watching TV and emailing/web-surfing. The latter of course is a staggeringly obvious result. The only changes which can be associated with losing Internet access are less time eating at home, and more time watching videos.

Interestingly there is no evidence of a decrease in the amount of primary or secondary telephone communication received or initiated by new Internet users (New_net) even though Internet use in these households at this point in time would have used the fixed telephone line and thus prevented simultaneous voice calls.

It is also of note that none of the significant changes for secondary activities were negative. Given that time-use is a zero-sum measure (there are only 24 hours in everyone's day) this implies that the activities which increased "stole" time from a range of other activities rather than one or two in particular. This resonates with our earlier point that interviewees could not really say where their Internet time had come from.

These findings suggest that changes in individual's time use cannot be attributed solely to the change in access to the Internet. As the sections above were careful to state, the significant results can only associate changes in time-use with changes in Internet access because a great deal of other significant events could have taken place in the lives of these individuals between waves 1 and 2. Further analysis is needed to unravel these effects using suitable regression models. It should also be noted that the data analyzed here represent just two points in time separated by one year and major changes in most people's time-use are very unlikely to occur over those time periods unless they undergo a significant life transition. In itself, getting or losing access to the Internet does not appear to be such a transition.

This implies that the simple impact model of Internet access and usage is not a useful explanatory tool. Not only have few significant effects been found but a range of confounding processes and triggers may make this kind of analysis over simplistic. As a result, the impact model does not enable much purchase on the problem of how to understand and explain the place of the Internet in everyday life. As this chapter has tried to demonstrate, this can only come from a deeper understanding of the triggers for and processes of its domestication, and a more detailed examination of how individuals and households are making sense of and integrating its applications and services into their lives.

As has been suggested above, the qualitative data in the Digital Living study has started to draw out the complex relationship between Internet uptake and usage and an individual's changing personal circumstances in just this way. At the micro-level certain conditions and transitions in an individual's life may be significant triggers of Internet uptake or usage and, simultaneously, causes of change on patterns of time use.

Work-related transitions such as shifting from home-based to office-based work, or the reverse in the case of new teleworkers or new self-employment seem to affect both access to and the style of Internet usage (see also Akselsen et al., 2000). Changes within employment can also trigger Internet adoption through an explicitly or implicitly recognized need to improve work skills or competencies. Retirement also appears to be a significant trigger for household Internet adoption, particularly for those with distributed social networks and for those who have computer or Internet skills that they have learned in their workplace. Other household related transitions that need to be considered are the departure of household members, perhaps to distant universities, to start employment or to set up independent households because they have an impact on both the communication needs of the leaver and those left behind which Internet applications can meet. There is also some evidence from our qualitative data that household formation transitions such as couples forming cohabiting partnerships or the birth of a child also trigger Internet acquisition (or loss of access) and changes in the style of use.

It should be clear that these effects are extremely important in any attempt to understand the role and place of Internet applications and services in people's lives. In particular, it shows that analysis of these sorts of transitions needs to be taken into account when conducting any kind of analysis of the change in people's patterns of activities that may be associated with the adoption of a particular technology.

Conclusion

This chapter has described and analyzed some of the patterns of domestic Internet acquisition and use in the UK at the end of the twentieth century, with a particular focus on how individuals' patterns of time use may or may not change when they acquire or lose Internet

have become clear that the integration of qualitative
e data sources can be an extremely powerful way to
he average or population-level patterns using quanti-
d the processes that generate them using qualitative
ot sufficient without the other. This is perhaps most
clearly visible in the quantitative analysis of changes in time use
reported which tests the hypothesis that changes in individuals' time
use can be attributed to acquiring Interent access and using it. Without
the subsequent integration of qualitative data on educational and
employment transitions the patterns of changes in time use do not
make much sense. With the qualitative findings taken into account a
plausible explanation emerges and an important conclusion can be
drawn: acquisition of the Internet and usage of its different applications is not necessarily changing individuals' lives but may be embedded within the normal social change of everyday life. As a result, it
seems clear that simple replacement effects are unlikely because other
significant events are ongoing in individuals' lives.

By conducting analysis in this integrated and iterative manner, the
chapter has started to tease out some of the motivations and triggers
for Internet acquisition and usage, such as the role of lifestyle and
lifestage related transitions, which to date have largely been ignored.
A primary avenue for future research must be the further exploration
of these factors.

Finally, it could be argued that people are not doing anything particularly new, they are doing old things in new ways and finding that
some of those new ways suit their lifestyles better. Thus, as Kling
(2000) argues so clearly in the area of organizational information
systems, technological change does not have a simple impact on a
society. Rather, the opportunities for individual and household social
innovation in the domestic arena are bound up with the possibilities
the technology affords, the individual's value systems and goals, and
the varying rates and degrees of change in their everyday lives. In the
household context, this suggests that a second avenue for future
research must be to integrate the insights from longitudinal qualitative research with longitudinal quantitative analysis to build on
Gershuny's model of social innovation to encompass emotional
(e.g. communicative, relationships) and symbolic (e.g. fashion,
identity) as well as functional needs.

To conclude, the place of Internet applications and services in
people's lives appears to be richly varied but by triangulating data

sources some of the patterns and processes that shape this role start to emerge. Given that this role seems to be context dependent and highly variable within and between households, patterns of participation in "the information society" are not necessarily as simple as might be thought and dot.coms of the future may make money, but at the individual customer level they may never know why.

Appendix 4.1

Respondent profiles

DC: male, single, a graphic designer in his thirties. He used to run his own Internet start-up company and now works in a small design company. He has broadband access to the Internet in his home.

GE: housewife, with 5-year-old daughter, living in central England. She is in her late thirties and is married to KE who is an engineer. The family had neither a PC nor Internet access in the home, though KE uses the Internet at work and they thought they would probably get access at home for their daughter in the future.

MC: female, sixties, retired widow, lives alone, two children away at university. Has had Internet access for some time but only really used it since children left home.

JB: male, twenties, lived with parents. Worked in supermarket but about to start a locally based course. Did not have Internet access at home but used it in his local library (5 minutes walk). Did not use email at all.

SC: male, mid-forties. He is married to MC and works in broadcasting. He was trying to set up his own webpage design company at the time of interview and has broadband access in his home.

CF: female, 45 years. She lives alone and works from home as a management consultant. She has been working for herself for 18 months and has broadband access at home.

DW: male, thirties, lives with girlfriend, social science student in an urban university about to complete a Ph.D.

AS: male, mid-thirties and lives in central London. He works in marketing for an advertising agency, and previously ran his own consultancy business from home for 2 years. He is married and has broadband Internet access at home. Delia Smith is a well-known UK TV cook.

LA: Actor and runs small recycling business. Housemate owns PC and ADSL connection which LA uses during the day as he works mainly in the evenings. LA hadn't used PCs or Internet much if at all before moving in. Now uses it extensively for recycling business.

KS: male, sixties, semi-retired, writes for *The Economist*, married with two children who have left home. Has Internet access but a very slow modem.

DR: female, sixties, retired. Married, two children living away from home. Had Internet access for 3 years, son was a computer science student at university.

RA: male, early retiree, used to be an electronic engineer. Married with children and grandchildren. Had Internet access for less than 6 months and was not a confident user. Used PC/Internet heavily for involvement in civic, council, and local charity activities.

References

Akselsen, S., Gunnarsdóttir, S., Jones, M., Julsrud, T., Marion, R., Martins, M. P., and Yttri, B. (2000). *The impacts of telework on quality of life: preliminary results from the EURESCOM Project 904*. Paper presented at 2000 and beyond: teleworking and the future of (tele)work?, Stockholm, Sweden.

Anderson, B., McWilliam, A., Lacohee, H., Clucas, E., and Gershuny, J. (1999). Family life in the digital home: domestic telecommunications at the end of the 20th century. *BT Technology Journal*, 17(1), 85–97.

Edwards, P. (1994). From "impact" to social process: computers in society and culture. In S. Jasanoffet, G. E. Markle, J. C. Petersen, and T. Pinch (eds), *Handbook of Science and Technology Studies* (pp. 257–85). Beverley Hills, CA: Sage Publications.

Gershuny, J. (1983). *Social innovation and the division of labour*. Oxford: Oxford University Press.

Joseph Rowntree Foundation (JRF) (2000). *Poverty and social exclusion in Britain*. Available online at:
http://www.jrf.org.uk/knowledge/findings/socialpolicy/930.asp

Kling, R. (2000). Learning about information technologies and social change: the contribution of social informatics. *The Information Society*, 16(3), 217–32.

Kraut, R. (1996). The Internet @ Home. *Communications of the ACM*, 39(12), 32–35.

Kraut, R., Mukhopadhyay, T., Szczypula, J., Kiesler, S., and Scherlis, B. (2000). Information and communication: alternative uses of the Internet in households. *Information Systems Research*, 10, 287–303.

Kraut, R., Patterson, M., Lundmark, V., Kiesler, S., Mukhopadhyay, T., and Scherlis, W. (1998). Internet paradox: a social technology that reduces social involvement and psychological well-being? *American Psychologist*, 53(9), 1,017–31.

Lacohee, H., and Anderson, B. (2001). Interacting with the telephone. *International Journal of Human-Computer Studies*, 54(5), 665–99.

Mansell, R., and Silverstone, R. (eds) (1996). *Communication by design: the politics of information and communication technologies*. London: Oxford University Press.

Mante-Meijer, E., Haddon, L., Concejero, P., Klamer, L., Heres, J., Ling, R., Thomas, F., Smoreda, Z., and Vrieling, I. (2001). ICT uses in everyday life: checking it out with the people – ICT markets and users in Europe. *Confidential EURESCOM P903 Project Report, EDIN 0161–0903*. Available online at:
http://www.eurescom.de/public/projects/P900-series/p903/default.asp

Nafus, D., and Tracey, K. (2002). The more things change: mobile phone consumption and concepts of personhood. In J. Katz, and M. Aarhus (eds), *Perpetual contact*. Cambridge: Cambridge University Press.

Nie, N. H., and Erbring, L. (2000). *Internet and society: a preliminary report*. Stanford Institute for the Quantitative Study of Society. Available online at: http://www.stanford.edu/group/siqss/Press_Release/
Preliminary_Report.pdf

Office for National Statistics (2001). *Results from the April 2001 National Statistics Omnibus Survey*. UK Office for National Statistics. Available online at: http://www.statistics.gov.uk/pdfdir/int0601.pdf

Patterson, R., and Wilson, E. J. III (2000). New IT and social inequality: resetting the research and policy agenda. *The Information Society*, 16(1), 77–86.

Silva, E. B. (2000). The politics of consumption @ home: practices and dispositions in the uses of technologies. *Pavis Papers in Social and Cultural Research*, Pavis Centre for Social and Cultural Research. Milton Keynes, UK: The Open University.

Silverstone, R., and Haddon, L. (1996). Design and the domestication of information and communication technologies: technical change and everyday life. In R. Mansell, and R. Silverstone (eds), *Communication by design* (pp. 44–74). London: Oxford University Press.

Silverstone, R., Hirsch, E., and Morley, D. (1991). Listening to a long conversation: an ethnographic approach to the study of information and communication technologies in the home. *Cultural Studies*, 5(2), 204–27.

Smith, M., and Marx, L. (eds) (1994). *Does technology drive history? The dilemma of technological determinism*. Cambridge, MA: MIT Press.

5

The Changing Digital Divide in Germany

Gert G. Wagner, Rainer Pischner, and John P. Haisken-DeNew

Abstract

The German Socioeconomic Panel Study (GSOEP) allows a detailed analysis of PC ownership and Internet use by means of 12,000 households which were surveyed in 2000 (in 1998 and 1999 about 7,000 households were surveyed). Private Internet use in Germany is spread across all social strata, however, there are substantial differences with respect to the level of education and age. Use of the PC and the Internet at home and in the workplace is more prevalent in West Germany than in East Germany and Germans also use computers more than foreigners living in Germany. There appears to be strong evidence for the hypothesis that teens who use a PC and/or the Internet do not do so at the expense of what most would consider desirable "leisure activities" such as reading or playing sports.

Introduction

With the ever-growing importance of the computer at home and the workplace, there are emerging concerns of a stratification of the population by a new "digital divide." The case of Germany is of interest in several respects. First, it is an open question whether there is indeed a "digital divide" along social strata in Germany. Given that around 1990 Germany had higher rates of immigration influx than the USA, it is especially of interest to know whether there are identifiable effects for the huge immigrant population in Germany. Second, German data allow one to analyze whether Internet use discourages other leisure activities, which belong to the "social capital" of a society. Using a large German household panel data set, one is able to describe not only recent trends in computer and Internet usage, but also the dynamics since PCs were introduced in the 1980s.

Data and History

Although a large number of surveys have been conducted (see, for example, van Einerem et al., 2001), primarily for marketing purposes, on the use of computers and the Internet, their results do not permit highly differentiated analyses of the socioeconomic aspects of these new technologies in Germany. The German Socio-economic Panel (GSOEP) (see Wagner et al., 1993) provides samples for 1998, 1999, and 2000 that encompass for the year 2000 12,500 households and permit a detailed analysis of Internet use. Within the surveyed households, all 16-year and older household members are interviewed. Thus information for about 24,000 persons is available for 2000. In the years before, the sample sizes were about half as much, but still large enough for in-depth analyses.

By means of a retrospective question, the GSOEP provides unique information about PC use for the past. As current and past PC usage at the workplace was only first asked in 1997, we are at least able to identify usage information directly for those individuals who were in the panel up to that time.[1] Thus the GSOEP clearly provides a unique data set to study PC dissemination, with the complete household context since PCs became widely available in the early 1980s with MS-DOS as a standard operating system.

Examining the absolute levels of PC usage rates at the workplace between 1984 and 1997, Haisken-DeNew and Schmidt (2001) conclude that highly educated employees at all time periods dominate all others, as shown in figure 5.1. Further, usage growth over time is also dominated by the highly educated. Thus, there seems to be the prevalence of complementarity between high levels of education (perhaps computer skills) and computer usage. These developments are further pushed by the steady movement of the economy into services, where PCs are an integral part of the office production function, and away from manufacturing. This leads to an ordering of usage,

1 In addition, using standard matching techniques, such as regression-based, "hotdeck" and "nearest neighbor" methods, usage information was imputed for those respondents exiting the panel before 1997.

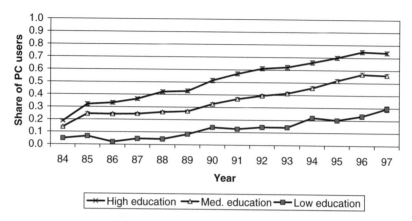

Figure 5.1   Dissemination of PCs at the workplace
Source: GSOEP (Haisken-DeNew and Schmidt, 2001)

increasing by job status and educational background: blue collar–low skill, blue collar–high skill, white collar–low skill, white collar–high skill.

"Digital Divides"

PC ownership in private households

In spring 2000, about 43 percent of the households (17 million) in Germany had at least one PC with Internet access at home (see table 5.1). This has increased since 1998, when 35 percent had private access (see Haisken-DeNew et al., 2000).

Examining the population in Germany according to various social indicators reveals several aspects of a "digital divide" between certain segments of the population, including differences between east and west Germany, between German nationals versus non-nationals, by income level, and presence of children in the household.

East–west differences

Due to the economic and social problems which came with German unification for people in east Germany – the former socialist GDR – as

Table 5.1 % of private households in Germany with personal computers, spring 2000 (N = 12,024)

	Total		West Germany		East Germany	
	PC ownership	PC with Internet connections	PC ownership	PC with Internet connections	PC ownership	PC with Internet connections
Total	43	23	45	25	38	17
Nationality bracket						
German household	44	24	48	27	38	17
Foreigner household	38	20	38	20	.	.
Income bracket						
Social benefit recipient	26	11	25	11	30	9
Low-income household[a]	35	15	35	17	34	12
Middle-income household[a]	41	21	42	22	37	17
High-income household[a]	61	37	61	38	66	34
Household type						
One-person household	30	19	31	20	22	13
(Married) couple without children	38	21	40	23	27	12
Single-parent household	47	21	46	22	51	17
(Married) couple with oldest child younger than 16	68	34	69	36	65	26
(Married) couple with youngest child older than 16	61	28	60	29	64	28
(Married) couple with children in both age groups	76	36	75	36	80	33
Multi-generation household	53	20	75	18	54	25

[a] Low-income households are classified as those with less than half of average equivalent income. High income households are those whose income is more than 150% of the average. The remainder are considered as middle-income households.

Source: GSOEP 2000

outlined in Schwarze and Wagner (2001), east–west differences are of special interest in Germany. The 1998 and 2000 SOEP surveys show significant differences between eastern and western Germany in both computer ownership and Internet access. In 2000, 48 percent of west German households had at least one PC, whereas in east Germany only 38 percent were equipped with a computer. This is a true east–west differential, not primarily an income effect.[2] Beyond these numbers there is no apparent reason for the east–west difference – perhaps there is still an "echo effect" of the socialist economy which was far less modern than the western economies.

German nationals versus non-nationals

As west Germany has a large migrant community,[3] differences in the lifestyles of Germans and immigrants are of interest. This is especially true because, due to German citizenship laws, most of those immigrants still hold their foreign citizenship (normally for a foreigner to become German, he must relinquish his foreign citizenship, which often proves to be a difficult hurdle for many foreigners). Compared to German households in west Germany (with east Germany having historically almost no guest-workers) far fewer households of foreigners own PCs (38 percent ownership by foreigners vs. 48 percent by German households) and fewer have private Internet access (20 percent vs. 28 percent). However the foreign community in west Germany has about the same level of PC ownership as compared to the east Germans. Furthermore, private access to the Internet is slightly better for foreigners than for East Germans. Multivariate analysis shows that the lower ownership rates and access rates are not due to education and income only, but that there is a true immigration effect, although it would go beyond the scope of this survey to clarify this in detail here. We believe that this differential effect might be due to cultural preferences of foreigners. (See table A5.1 and table A5.2, column 1.)

2 For results of multiple regression analysis see for example table A5.2.
3 Due to the immigration of the so-called guest-workers from Mediterranean countries in the 1960's (see Reitz et al., 1999) who along with their children still to a large extent stay in Germany.

Income

Differentiation by household income[4] reveals that PC ownership in low-income households[5] is lower at 35 percent compared to the average household at 41 percent, whereas computer ownership by wealthy households[6] is far above the average at 61 percent. Households which receive (means tested) social assistance have by far the lowest ownership rate (26 percent). In 2000, one out of six households in western Germany was classified as wealthy, whereas in eastern Germany, only one out of twenty belonged to this group.

Looking at private access to the Internet reveals even larger differences by income. The gap between wealthy households (at 37 percent) and those on social assistance (11 percent) and low-income households in general (15 percent) is huge. This is true for west as well as east Germany.

Children

Households with children have an above average rate of PC ownership and private access to the Internet. These shares among single-parent households are, however, relatively low, although higher than the overall average, with 47 percent owning a PC, and 21 percent with Internet access. In this sense, the children of single parents are at a disadvantage compared to children in two-parent households.

Personal use of the computer and the Internet

Table 5.2 provides information about the use of the PC and the Internet on a personal level. Here we see substantial differences between men and women. On average, 39 percent of men living in Germany use a PC in their leisure time, whereas only 26 percent of women. The difference between men and women is in fact larger in west Germany (41 percent vs. 26 percent), whereas in east Germany the difference is not nearly so pronounced (34 percent vs. 26 percent).

4   A needs-weighted income is calculated. This "equivalence income" takes account of the size and structure of households rather than per capita income.
5   A household is classified as "poor" if it has less than half of the average equivalence income at its disposal.
6   A household is classified as "wealthy" if it has at least 150 percent of the average equivalence income at its disposal.

Table 5.2 % using computers for leisure, 2000 (N = 22,414)

	Total		Men		Women		Foreigners	
	PC use, total	With Internet access	PC use, total	With Internet access	PC use, total	With Internet access	PC use, total	With Internet access
Total	32	16	39	20	26	11	23	10
Region								
West Germany	33	17	41	22	26	12	22	10
East Germany	30	11	34	13	26	9	—	—
Age								
16–29 years	50	26	56	29	45	23	28	10
30–44 years	48	24	53	30	42	18	30	15
45–59 years	32	15	39	19	25	10	13	5
60 years and older	8	3	13	4	5	2	12	—
School-leaving certificate								
Minimum school-leaving certificate	16	6	22	9	11	3	14	3
Lower secondary	39	16	45	21	34	13	26	10
Technical college	52	27	59	32	41	20	39	23
University entrance certificate	60	38	67	44	52	31	61	34
Occupational status								
Full-time	45	23	48	25	38	18	27	12
Regular part-time	42	20	58	48	39	16	31	14
Marginal part-time	41	21	49	32	39	17	32	—
In training	49	19	53	21	43	16	44	—
Unemployed	18	8	22	10	16	6	15	6

—: not displayed due to small number of cases.
Source: GSOEP 2000

Table 5.3   % of young people aged 16 and 17 using the Internet, 2000 (N = 226)

(Intended) school-leaving certificate	Internet use (% share)			Internet users' average weekly use in hours		
	Total	Male	Female	Total	Male	Female
Minimum leaving certificate	45	60	25	4	4	5
Lower secondary	67	74	59	10	13	4
University entrance ("prep schools")	75	77	72	9	14	6
Total	68	73	63	9	12	5

Source: GSOEP 2000 (youth questionnaire)

As found in other studies, there are stronger computer preferences for males under 45 than for females of the same age group. Foreigners do use the computer and the Internet less frequently than the average person living in Germany (compare column "foreigners" with column "total" in table 5.2). This holds true for all breakdowns of the population.

Corroborating the evidence found in Haisken-DeNew and Schmidt (2001) for PC usage at work, PC leisure usage increases with educational level (see table 5.2). In 2000 some 60 percent of those with the highest level of high school use a PC during leisure, compared to only 16 percent who have only the mandatory minimum high school level. Although German men who work full time have almost double the PC usage rates as compared to foreigners (48 percent vs. 27 percent), at least for those German men and foreigners who are currently in vocational training, the 5 percent differential is almost negligible. This at least shows some "catch up" in the younger cohorts of foreigners.

In the 2000 GSOEP, a detailed in-depth survey of 226 teenagers, aged 16 and 17 was made by means of a special questionnaire (see table 5.3) which clearly shows that two-thirds of this age group make use of the Internet. Here too, there are substantial differences between those with different levels of education, which prove significant, although the sample size is small. Only 60 percent of the young men and as few as 25 percent of young women either holding or about to receive the minimum school-leaving certificate use the

Internet. Use rates are highest among advanced level high school (grammar school and sixth form college pupils), 75 percent of whom are Internet users.

In terms of the intensity of use, there are significant gender-specific differences. At 12 hours per week on average, young men who surf on the Internet, do so for approximately twice as long as young women. Within the group of Internet users, the education-specific differences are not especially pronounced. Only young men with the minimum school-leaving certificate, at 4 hours per week, spend significantly less time on the web than those with a higher level of education.

Computers and Internet use at work

According to table 5.4, in 2000 around one-half of those in employment use a computer at work; a little bit more than one in five also has access to the Internet. The use of a computer is not different for female and male workers, but Internet access by women is 18 percent, compared to 26 percent of men). This seems to be due to the lower *level* of jobs (compared to men) in which women work (distribution of job levels is not displayed in the table).

As is the case with computer use for leisure, the level of educational attainment is an important determinant of use at work. Some 78 percent of workers with an upper-secondary school-leaving certificate used a computer at work, compared with only just 27 percent of those with the minimum leaving certificate. (This is corroborated in table A5.3 with binary logit estimation, which is explained in the note of the table). The influence of education is even more evident if employees are classified according to the requirements of their work. Occupations demanding a university degree also require, in more than 81 percent of cases, the use of a computer. On the other hand, less than 24 percent of those with no training required need a computer for their job.

Given that experience using modern information technology is expected to become increasingly important, it is interesting to look more closely at the use of the Internet by employees aged less than 30. In 2000 in Germany around one in two workers aged less than 30 used a computer at work.

The differences due to educational level are no less pronounced among younger workers than among the working population as a whole (see last column of table 5.4). Whereas only 30 percent of those

Table 5.4 % using computers at work, 2000 (N = 13,811)

	Men		Women		Foreigners		Workers under 30 years	
	PC use, total	With Internet access	PC use, total	With Internet access	PC use, total	With Internet access	PC use, total	With Internet access
Total	49	26	49	18	22	15	50	25
Region								
West Germany	51	22	49	19	22	15	51	26
East Germany	39	18	50	15	—	—	45	20
Age								
16–29 years	45	25	55	25	24	19	50	25
30–44 years	53	29	54	19	26	16	N/A	N/A
45–59 years	47	24	43	13	14	7	N/A	N/A
60 years and older	39	19	27	—	—	—	N/A	N/A
School-leaving certificate								
Minimum school-leaving certificate	27	9	27	6	9	4	21	7
Lower secondary	50	23	54	17	36	20	51	21
Technical college entrance certificate	70	43	56	20	35	30	64	28
University entrance certificate	81	56	74	37	58	48	82	54

Table 5.4 Continued

	Men		Women		Foreigners		Workers under 30 years	
	PC use, total	With Internet access	PC use, total	With Internet access	PC use, total	With Internet access	PC use, total	With Internet access
Required qualification for task performed								
No training	25	13	22	8	8	4	36	22
Vocational training	46	20	56	17	31	18	51	21
Technical college	84	49	69	29	—	—	89	58
University	83	60	78	44	—	—	90	66
Enterprise size								
Fewer than 5 workers	45	27	45	16	36	—	40	24
5 to 20 workers	37	21	42	15	13	7	42	19
20 to 100 workers	41	22	45	17	13	8	45	22
100 to 200 workers	44	21	48	16	20	—	48	23
200 to 2000 workers	52	28	57	18	21	14	54	26
More than 2000 workers	63	32	61	25	33	23	63	32
Self-employed	68	44	38	19	—	—	—	—
Occupational status								
Full-time	50	26	58	23	22	15	52	25
Part-time	45	27	41	11	23	—	49	32
In training	40	17	46	13	—	—	43	15
In marginal employment	40	28	29	12	—	—	54	43

—: not displayed due to small number of cases.

Source: GSOEP 2000

young workers with minimum school qualifications require computer knowledge for their work, the figure for those with university entrance school qualifications is 80 percent.

Less use of computers is made in small enterprises. In plants with fewer than 5 workers, 54 percent have nothing to do with computers, and a similar figure (58 percent) applies to enterprises with between 5 and 20 workers. In large firms, by contrast, the proportion of non-users is much lower (34 percent in firms with 200–1,999 workers and 40 percent in those with 2,000 or more).

Competition between Internet Use and Social Capital

The world over, there is a discussion whether heavy Internet use "discourages" other activities, especially those which are part of the most important "social capital" (Nie, Hillygus, and Erbring, this volume; Kraut, Patterson, Lundmark, Kiesler, Mukhopadhyay, and Scherlis, 1998). In particular, there are objections about the use of Internet by teenagers who are in the process of accumulating social capital, and thus a lack of this kind of capital could have a negative impact on there future life. Table 5.5 shows differences in leisure activities by age groups. All in all, we did not find any evidence for the discouragement hypothesis, but we can conclude that those who use a PC and the Internet are more active in cultural activities.

The GSOEP data also show that use of the Internet does not prevent 16- and 17-year olds from engaging in activities in other areas. Table 5.6 illustrates that, for example, teenage Internet users have similar reading habits to non-users. For both groups, "playing a musical instrument" is of equal importance. It might be a surprise for many readers that active sport has a larger importance for Internet users than for other teenagers, although Internet users are typically thought to be "stay-at-homes." However, due to the fact that the Internet is used more heavily by teenagers in prep-school, who have more time for active sports than other teenagers, this effect of a positive correlation between Internet use and active sport is not surprising. An ordered logit analysis (see top row of table A5.5) reveals that there is no negative partial effect of Internet use on how *important* teens *consider* sport activities to be. (Here we use standard controls for gender, nationality, born abroad, education status, along with Internet usage. As the dependent variable is defined in *decreasing* levels of importance, negative coefficients indicate an increase in importance.) However, adults

Table 5.5 Private PC and Internet use and other leisure activities by sex and age (% who perform named activity at least once a month) (N = 12,403)

Visits to cultural events, e.g., concerts, theatre, presentations	Total		Male		Female	
	Using PC or Internet	Not Using PC or Internet	Using PC or Internet	Not Using PC or Internet	Using PC or Internet	Not Using PC or Internet
Age 16–29	24	15	21	17	28	12
30–44	16	10	17	7	16	12
45–59	20	12	15	9	27	14
60 and older	32	13	24	12	46	14
Total	20	12	18	11	23	13
Active sport						
Age 16–29	62	45	63	53	61	38
30–44	48	35	49	36	48	34
45–59	40	22	35	20	48	23
60 and older	32	16	35	17	27	15
Total	48	25	47	27	50	23
Participation in public initiatives, in political parties, local government						
Age 16–29	2	1	3	1	2	1
30–44	2	1	3	1	2	1
45–59	6	3	8	3	3	2
60 and older	9	2	10	4	7	1
Total	3	2	4	3	2	1
Church-going, visits to religious events						
Age 16–29	9	13	10	9	8	16
30–44	12	14	11	13	16	15
45–59	22	20	23	14	22	24
60 and older	26	28	25	24	29	30
Total	15	21	15	17	15	24

Source: GSOEP 2000

Table 5.6 Importance of activities to 16 and 17 year olds in 2000 (% responding about each category among PC/Internet users and non-users) (N = 226)

	Not using a PC / Internet			Using a PC / Internet		
	Very important/ Important	Less important	Not important	Very important/ Important	Less important	Not important
Watching TV /Videos	52	43	5	53	45	2
Playing computer games	10	45	44	41	43	16
Listening to music	96	4	0	88	12	—
Playing a musical instrument	16	21	63	17	19	64
Playing sports	65	26	9	75	18	7
Being with boy/girl friend	91	7	3	92	7	2
Being with friends	78	9	13	70	17	14
Reading	31	47	22	39	38	22
Doing nothing, hanging around	45	42	12	37	40	22

—: not displayed due to small number of cases.
Source: GSOEP 2000 (youth questionnaire)

Table 5.7 Use of the PC/Internet and other activities by young people aged 16 and 17, spring 2000 (n = 226)

There are many different ways of being active at school in addition to actual classes. Are you or have you ever been involved in one or more of the following areas?	Those not using PC or Internet (%)	Those using PC or Internet (%)
Yes, I was:		
• class representative to the student council	21	29
• student body president / president of the student council	6	2
• involved in the school newspaper	2	9
• involved in a school theater or dance group	4	21
• involved in a school orchestra, chorus or other type of music group	18	26
• involved in a sports group at school	18	40
• involved in some other type of group	13	19
No, none of these	49	33

Source: GSOEP 2000 (youth questionnaire)

(and also teens specifically) who use the Internet or a computer at home play sports more often, go more often to cultural events and are more active in politics as shown at the bottom of table A5.4. (Here the model with controls for demographics, household composition, income explains intensity of doing a particular activity, and similarly the dependent variable is coded in *decreasing* intensity, such that *negative* coefficients indicate *increasing* intensity.)

There is no negative impact of Internet use on extra-curricular activities in school (table 5.7). As many Internet users are "class presidents" as non-users; Internet users are involved more heavily in school theater or dance groups than other pupils. The same is true for playing music in the school orchestra or exercising sports in special groups. However, again this is not a pure effect of Internet use, but an effect of differences in the composition of users and non-users. Although the Internet does not facilitate or encourage more leisure activities which accumulate social capital, it does not discourage either. For 16- and 17-year-old teenagers in Germany there is, on average, no danger of acquiring insufficient amounts of "social capital" due to the emergence of the Internet and its heavy use by teenagers.

Conclusions

Private Internet use in Germany is spread across all social strata. However, there are substantial differences with respect to the level of education and age. As might be expected, the Internet has so far bypassed most older people. In the spring of 2000, among the top age group (60 and older), the user share was only at a significant level among the relatively small circle of those with a high educational level.

Wealthy parents are far more likely to place a computer at their children's disposal and thus a regular Internet connection than those on lower incomes. Private computer access is particularly relatively low in single-parent households, most of which are on low incomes. Thus schools should have the capacity to offer *all children*, irrespective of their social background, access to computers and the Internet. That implies not only a better endowment with hardware and software, but also funding for maintenance and providing teachers with the required skills.

The lack of experience with the use of computers could exacerbate the difficulties on the labor market already experienced by those with only a minimum school-leaving certificate. Given the discussion in the economic literature concerning "skill-biased technological change," and the resulting increasing skill premium awarded to highly educated employees, getting school children "computer trained" before they go onto the job market could prove to be a crucial career path step.

Use of the PC and the Internet at home and in the workplace is more prevalent in west Germany than in east Germany. Germans also use computers more than foreigners living in Germany. Considering the fact that many foreigners have been living in Germany for generations, one might think of them as being effectively German. However, the multivariate results show clear cultural differences. Further research should analyze the impact of the numbers of years living in the country (degree of cultural assimilation).

There appears to be strong evidence for the hypothesis that teens who use a PC and/or the Internet do *not* do so at the expense of what most would consider desirable leisure activities such as reading or playing sports. Indeed, such "computer kids" are indeed *less likely* to just "hang around" and "do nothing."

Appendices

Table A5.1   Binary logit estimation: PC-Internet-access ownership of households, 2000

	(1) PC, no Internet access	(2) PC and Internet access
Household in West Germany	0.108	0.296
	(0.049)*	(0.058)*
German nationality	0.934	0.663
	(0.077)*	(0.095)*
Equivalence household income	0.000	0.000
	(0.000)*	(0.000)*
Size of household	0.184	0.026
	(0.039)*	(0.041)
Gets social assistance	−0.642	−0.483
	(0.132)*	(0.178)*
Married couple without children	0.168	0.180
	(0.068)*	(0.078)*
Single-parent household	1.087	0.485
	(0.107)*	(0.127)*
Married couple with oldest child younger than 16 years	1.525	1.048
	(0.123)*	(0.131)*
Married couple with oldest child older than 16 years	1.240	0.853
	(0.119)*	(0.128)*
Married couple with children in both age groups	1.835	1.164
	(0.175)*	(0.180)*
Multi-generation household	0.933	0.556
	(0.231)*	(0.265)*
Other combinations	0.392	0.142
	(0.183)*	(0.231)
Constant	−3.256	−3.462
	(0.117)*	(0.134)*
Observations	12,024	12,024
Pseudo R^2	0.1279	0.0583

(Standard errors in parentheses, * = significant at the 10% level). The binary dependent variable is coded as (0) No, (1) Yes. Therefore, larger positive coefficents indicate a higher probability of a particular activity!

Table A5.2 Binary logit estimation: Internet access of adults at home, 2000

	(1) Home PC / Internet	(2) Home PC	(3) Home Internet
Men	0.380	0.632	0.689
	(0.039)*	(0.037)*	(0.046)*
Household in West Germany	0.206	0.137	0.362
	(0.043)*	(0.041)*	(0.053)*
German nationality	1.237	1.082	0.866
	(0.061)*	(0.063)*	(0.087)*
Equivalence household income	0.000	0.000	0.000
	(0.000)*	(0.000)*	(0.000)*
Size of household	0.118	0.170	0.090
	(0.015)*	(0.014)*	(0.017)*
Age of employee (16 years and older)	0.023	0.049	0.052
	(0.008)*	(0.008)*	(0.011)*
Age * age	−0.001	−0.001	−0.001
	(0.000)*	(0.000)*	(0.000)*
Part-time	−0.089	0.156	0.031
	(0.061)	(0.059)*	(0.076)
In training	−0.287	−0.081	−0.380
	(0.105)*	(0.097)	(0.123)*
In marginal employment	−0.194	0.360	0.330
	(0.095)*	(0.091)*	(0.109)*
Minimum school-leaving certificate	−0.436	−0.353	−0.467
	(0.069)*	(0.069)*	(0.096)*
Lower secondary certificate	0.519	0.367	0.284
	(0.069)*	(0.069)*	(0.092)*
Technical college entrance certificate	1.030	0.881	0.840
	(0.096)*	(0.090)*	(0.109)*
University entrance certificate	1.575	1.083	1.161
	(0.079)*	(0.073)*	(0.092)*
Constant	−1.933	−3.277	−4.345
	(0.187)*	(0.183)*	(0.243)*
Observations	22,313	22,414	22,414
Pseudo R²	0.3249	0.2160	0.1976

(Standard errors in parentheses, * = significant at the 10% level). The binary dependent variable is coded as (0) No, (1) Yes. *Therefore, larger positive coefficents indicate a higher probability of a particular activity!*

Table A5.3 Binary logit estimation: Internet use at work, 2000

	(1) Work PC	(2) Work Internet
Men	−0.134	0.449
	(0.043)*	(0.052)*
Household in West Germany	0.601	0.689
	(0.047)*	(0.059)*
German nationality	1.207	0.748
	(0.079)*	(0.101)*
Age of employee (16 years and	0.048	0.028
older)	(0.012)*	(0.014)*
Age * age	−0.001	−0.001
	(0.000)*	(0.000)*
Full-time (reference)	—	—
Part-time	−0.561	−0.560
	(0.059)*	(0.077)*
In training	−0.200	−0.461
	(0.105)*	(0.133)*
In marginal employment	−0.945	−0.321
	(0.092)*	(0.110)*
No certificate (reference)	—	—
Minimum school-leaving	−0.074	−0.211
certificate	(0.104)	(0.152)
Lower secondary certificate	1.079	0.851
	(0.104)*	(0.148)*
Technical college entrance	1.670	1.486
certificate	(0.122)*	(0.159)*
University entrance certificate	2.309	2.163
	(0.109)*	(0.148)*
Constant	−3.168	−3.944
	(0.267)*	(0.332)*
Observations	13,811	13,811
Pseudo R^2	0.1528	0.1473

(Standard errors in parentheses, * = significant at the 10% level). The binary dependent variable is coded as (0) No, (1) Yes. *Therefore, larger positive coefficents indicate a higher probability of a particular activity!*

Table A5.4 Ordered logit estimation: effects of PC or Internet use (2000) on leisure activities of adults, 1998 (16 years and older)

	(1) Cultural events	(2) Active in sports	(3) Active in politics	(4) Active in church
Men	0.1924	−0.2914	−0.4209	0.2603
	(0.037)*	(0.037)*	(0.065)*	(0.037)*
Household in West Germany	−0.1087	−0.5827	−0.0509	−1.3757
	(0.043)*	(0.045)*	(0.075)	(0.048)*
German nationality	−0.6217	−0.5298	−0.6833	0.2185
	(0.063)*	(0.063)*	(0.141)*	(0.058)*
Equivalence household income	−0.0003	−0.0002	−0.0001	0.0000
	(0.000)*	(0.000)*	(0.000)*	(0.000)
Size of household	0.0332	0.0383	−0.1645	−0.2610
	(0.016)*	(0.016)*	(0.028)*	(0.016)*
Age of employee (16 years and older)	−0.0122	0.0355	−0.0707	−0.0123
	(0.006)*	(0.006)*	(0.012)*	(0.006)*
Age * age	0.0002	0.0001	0.0005	−0.0001
	(0.000)*	(0.000)	(0.000)*	(0.000)*
Minimum school-leaving certificate	−0.2303	0.0744	−0.0921	−0.0520
	(0.075)*	(0.077)	(0.158)	(0.071)
Lower secondary certificate	−0.7385	−0.3940	−0.3494	−0.0157
	(0.080)*	(0.080)*	(0.163)*	(0.077)
Technical college entrance certificate	−1.0452	−0.3706	−0.5363	−0.1555
	(0.111)*	(0.107)*	(0.199)*	(0.105)
University entrance certificate	−1.5973	−0.7886	−0.8264	−0.2754
	(0.088)*	(0.086)*	(0.167)*	(0.084)*
Using a personal computer or Internet at home	−0.3524	−0.3578	−0.3599	0.0656
	(0.043)*	(0.041)*	(0.074)*	(0.044)
Observations	12,403	11,982	12,006	12,043
Pseudo R²	0.0848	0.1016	0.0401	0.0626

(Standard errors in parentheses, * = significant at the 10% level). The ordered dependent variable is coded as (1) Every week, (2) Every month, (3) Less than once a month and (4) Never. *Therefore, negative coefficents indicate more of a particular activity!*

Table A5.5 Binary logit estimation: effects of Internet use on importance of other activities, 2000 (16 and 17 year olds)

	(1) Watch TV	(2) Play computer Games	(3) Listen to music	(4) Play musical instrument	(5) Play sports	(6) Boy/girl friend	(7) Being with friends	(8) Reading	(9) Doing nothing
Using a personal computer or Internet	0.106 (0.268)	-1.592 (0.288)*	0.063 (0.275)	-0.002 (0.292)	-0.162 (0.257)	-0.446 (0.282)	-0.129 (0.259)	-0.249 (0.262)	0.486 (0.263)*
Men	-0.540 (0.267)*	-1.944 (0.295)*	0.658 (0.277)*	-0.139 (0.292)	-0.458 (0.260)*	1.217 (0.287)*	0.785 (0.259)*	1.255 (0.273)*	0.631 (0.262)*
German nationality	-0.393 (0.415)	-0.665 (0.435)	-0.281 (0.427)	-0.025 (0.461)	-0.170 (0.404)	0.131 (0.438)	-0.269 (0.385)	1.324 (0.419)*	-0.384 (0.412)
Born in Germany	0.461 (0.710)	0.261 (0.716)	0.024 (0.668)	1.269 (0.734)*	0.639 (0.638)	-0.422 (0.656)	-0.120 (0.634)	-0.852 (0.624)	-0.067 (0.660)
Minimum leaving certificate (Hauptschule)	-1.233 (1.182)	-1.649 (1.199)	-1.931 (1.115)*	0.568 (1.278)	2.490 (1.265)*	-1.701 (1.049)	1.192 (1.082)	0.837 (1.213)	-1.043 (1.155)
Lower secondary certificate	-0.815 (1.142)	-1.068 (1.155)	-0.818 (1.053)	0.069 (1.200)	1.799 (1.225)	-0.952 (0.980)	0.711 (1.017)	0.242 (1.156)	-0.567 (1.111)
School for technical college entrance certificate	-0.278 (1.171)	-1.269 (1.181)	-0.484 (1.089)	0.085 (1.239)	1.731 (1.253)	-1.195 (1.026)	0.430 (1.051)	0.081 (1.186)	-0.095 (1.147)
School for university entrance certificate	-0.725 (1.147)	-1.109 (1.158)	-0.660 (1.062)	-1.116 (1.203)	1.454 (1.233)	-0.646 (0.987)	0.905 (1.029)	-0.714 (1.165)	-0.849 (1.119)
Other school	-1.474 (1.479)	-1.321 (1.518)	1.327 (1.605)	—	2.918 (1.506)*	-1.364 (1.406)	3.659 (1.520)*	-0.277 (1.473)	-2.278 (1.518)
Observations	227	224	226	221	225	222	226	226	225
Pseudo R^2	0.0224	0.1668	0.0432	0.0507	0.0243	0.0512	0.0401	0.0884	0.0374

(Standard errors in parentheses, * = significant at the 10% level) In model (4), there were no teens with "Other certificate." The ordered dependent variable is coded as (1) very important, (2) important, (3) less important and (4) completely unimportant. Therefore, negative coefficents indicate increasing importance of a particular activity!

References

Haisken-DeNew, J. P. and Schmidt, C. M. (2001). Brothers in RAMS: diffusion of the PC and the new economy. DIW Berlin, Working Paper.

Haisken-DeNew, J. P., Pischner, R., and Wagner, G. G. (2000). Use of computers and the Internet depends heavily on income and level of education. *Economic Bulletin*, 37, 369–74.

Kraut, R., Patterson, M., Lundmark, V., Kiesler, S., Mukhopadhyay, T., and Scherlis, W. (1998). Internet paradox: a social technology that reduces social involvement and psychological well-being? *American Psychologist*, 53(9), 1017–31.

Nie, N., Hillygus, S., and Erbring, L. (this book). Internet use, interpersonal relations and sociability: findings from a detailed time diary study.

Reitz, J. G., Calabrese, T., Frick, J. R., and Wagner, G. G. (1999). The institutional framework of ethnic employment disadvantage: a comparison of Germany and Canada. *Journal of Ethnic and Migration Studies*, 25, 397–444.

Schwarze, J. and Wagner, G. G. (2001). Earning dynamics in the East German transition process. In R. T. Riphahn et al. (eds), *Employment policy in transition* (pp. 125–39), Heidelberg, Germany.

Van Einerem, B., Gerhard, H., and Frees, B. (2001). ARD/ZDF-Online-Studie 2001: Internetnutzung stark zweckgebunden. *Media Perspektiven*, 8, 382–6.

Wagner, G. G., Burkhausen, R. V., and Behringer, F. (1993). The English language public use file of the German socio-economic panel study. *Journal of Human Resources*, 28, 429-33.

6

Doing Social Science Research Online

Alan Neustadtl, John P. Robinson, and Meyer Kestnbaum

Abstract

The Internet has been described as the world's largest library, albeit a library of inert, already-analyzed information. Recent Internet developments extend that function to provide users with tools to *produce* new information or to do things – like shopping, managing finances, and even doing original research. In this chapter we discuss several kinds of online tools now available to social science researchers who study Internet life online. Many of these are available on our website, www.webuse.umd.edu, which has been designed to be a portal for Internet researchers. We anticipate that WebUse could be used as a model for other portals that could be dedicated to other research topics (e.g. stratification, inequality, community studies, and so on).

The major statistical tool on WebUse is the Survey and Data Analysis (SDA) software developed at the University of California at Berkeley. In addition to SDA, other types of resources have been incorporated on our WebUse site: (1) original survey data collections and analysis tools; (2) an annotated bibliography on Internet research; (3) research materials from our initial year 2001 "WebShop" (e.g. abstracts and papers); and (4) a new online journal and other publication opportunities.

Authors' note

Grateful acknowledgement is given to the National Science Foundation, Office of Science and Technology for support through grants NSF01523184 and NSF0086143. Please direct all correspondence to Dr Alan Neustadtl (aneustadtl@socy.umd.edu).

Introduction

The Internet means many things to many people – it can be a source of entertainment, information, companionship, and education, to name a few uses. The technology developed around the growth of the Internet has had the effect of dropping a rock into water, sending ripples through many segments in society. Economies, governments, businesses, and social relationships have all been touched in some way.

Whether the rock was large and the lake small is yet to be seen. However, using the Internet for information, fun, and business is a relatively common experience for people in North America and certain northern European countries, where over half the population use the Internet. Further, the Internet is making inroads in developing nations as well.

The comparison of the diffusion of earlier technologies like television to the diffusion of information technologies (IT) has not been lost on social scientists. While the terrain is constantly shifting, we know a lot about what the Internet is, who uses the Internet, and the ways in which Internet use affects people's lives. In the academic community there is tremendous variety in the kinds of questions posed. For example, many people have studied how technology can be used to facilitate distance education. Is the quality of distance education as good as or better than face-to-face based pedagogy? Can the logistical problems associated with geographically dispersed students be overcome? At traditional colleges and universities, others study how technology can be used to enhance the educational experiences of students. Does word processing make writing easier? Better? Does access to the Internet provide research resources to enhance student work?

On the horizon, not clearly seen by many, are other interesting developments in using technology for educational purposes. The focus of this chapter is to discuss the development of one educational web portal – a web portal dedicated to Internet research – as a way to provide sophisticated research tools, data, and other resources to a wide range of people.

Our WebUse portal (www.webuse.umd.edu) is hosted by the University of Maryland with financial support from the National Science Foundation. The purpose of WebUse is to provide research tools, data, and resources to anyone interested in understanding how the Internet, and technology in general, is affecting society. More specifically, the resources on WebUse are structured to facilitate studying the behavioral aspects of Internet technologies and use. Furthermore, like other specialized portals, it need not only be used by specialists. It is organized to be easy to use, and flexible – subject to change and growth as a community of interested people participates in its development. There are four distinct types of research resources on WebUse: (1) survey and secondary data on Internet use and methodological tools; (2) other social science methods; (3) bibliographical resources; (4) *WebShop* materials; and (5) current research and a new online journal.

Data Sets Concerning the Internet

There are numerous data collection efforts underway around the world to help researchers study and understand the impact of the Internet. Perhaps the most well known is the "digital divide" data collected by the US. Bureau of Census for the National Telecommunications and Information Agency (NTIA), as a supplement to the Current Population Survey (CPS). The NTIA/CPS data, with over 120,000 respondents per survey, were the basis for several NTIA and Census reports on the digital divide. Data were collected in 1984, 1989, 1993, 1997, and 2000. While the data collection methodology is state-of-the-art and the sample size is substantial, the imagination of the survey questions leaves much to be desired. For example, all of the questions concerning the availability of Internet access are binary – a household either does or does not have a computer, a household member does or does not use the Internet for educational purposes.

There are no questions in this survey on the extent of Internet usage, or the purposes for which the Internet is used. This is an interesting result of the NTIA's simple historical mission of assessing "universal access" to telephony, with no attention to other aspects of digital inequality (DiMaggio and Hargittai, 2001). Nonetheless, these data are *the benchmark data* collected by the United States government, and so provide a critical link between what we think we know about Internet access and public policy.

Additional data collection efforts have been undertaken by researchers at Carnegie Mellon University (Kraut et al., www-2.cs.cmu.edu/afs/cs.cmu.edu/user/kraut/www/kraut.html), the University of California at Los Angeles (Cole et al., www.ccp.ucla.edu/pages/internet-report.asp), Stanford University (Nie, et al., www.stanford.edu/group/siqss/), the University of Toronto (Wellman et al., www.chass.utoronto.ca/~wellman/), and the University of Maryland (Robinson et al., www.webuse.umd.edu). This list is not exhaustive (a more exhaustive list appears in table 6.1), but illustrative of the distinct strands of research on the Internet.

Challenges in using current datasets

A significant challenge of engaging in any quantitative research endeavor is data management and analysis. Consider the NTIA/CPS data, which are publicly available for downloading on the US Census Bureau's web page. There are several barriers to gaining access to, let alone using, these data. First, one must *find* the data on the Census Bureau web page, sometimes a daunting task. Then, users must complete several forms requesting the variables to be included in the downloadable dataset. In early attempts to download these data, the Census Bureau server would not allow downloading of the entire dataset because it was too large! Sometimes the codebook was generated by the Census server, sometimes it was not. While these problems occur less frequently now, the request forms remain confusing for many users. Second, the August 2000 dataset, for example, is large and requires substantial hard drive space since the data file is 272 megabytes (as a SAS system file). With the falling price of storage, this may be a less critical issue than in the past if one buys new equipment. Third, a high-speed Internet connection is required to move a file of this size from the Census Bureau server to a personal computer.

Once the data have been downloaded, the next problem is how to manage and analyze the data. Experienced social scientists are often comfortable with application packages like SAS, SPSS, and STATA. Undergraduate students as well as new graduate students may have considerable difficulty using these applications to produce accurate and consistent results. Alternatively, many Windows and Macintosh users have a spreadsheet application for numerical analysis. For users with Excel for Windows, for example, the current number of available rows for data is 65,536, slightly less than half of the required 134,986 rows needed to store the NTIA data. With nearly 500 variables, the NTIA data also exceeds the capabilities of Excel. For data management and rudimentary analysis, one could use Microsoft Access, but that also has limitations, notably speed and ease of use. Plus, few statistical routines are provided, and those that are (mean, standard deviation, etc.) do not handle missing data well. In short, it requires significant effort to download and analyze these data.

Table 6.1   Listing of major datasets and data collection efforts regarding Internet use, September 2000

Surveys
American data
[a]National Telecommunications and Information Administration: 1989, 1993, 1997, and 2000
[a]General Social Survey, Internet Module: 2000
[a]Pew Internet and American Life: 2000, ongoing
[a]Pew News Surveys: 1995, 1998, 2000
[a]University of Maryland Time Diary Studies: 1995, 1998
[a]Survey of Public Participation in the Arts
[a]University of California Santa Barbara: Political Uses of the Internet
National Geographic: 1998, 2000
National Election Study: 1998, 2000
Rutgers University: 1995, ongoing
Carnegie Mellon University
Stanford Institute of Quantitative Social Science
University of California Los Angeles: 2001, 2000
University of Toronto: 1995, ongoing
Kennedy School Survey: 1999
Markle Foundation Survey: 2001

International data (surveys using the UCLA questions)
China
France
Germany
Hong Kong
Hungary
India
Italy
Japan
Korea
Singapore
Sweden
Taiwan

Non-survey data
IIQ macro comparative data: 2001
University of Maryland Internet user profiles: 2001

[a] Data set is currently available online at www.webuse.umd.edu

Survey and Data Analysis application software

To reduce the barriers to using data like those provided by the NTIA, researchers at the University of California at Berkeley have developed

	Advantages	*Disadvantages*
Consumers	Easy to use. Extremely fast even with large datasets. Available anywhere the user has access to an Internet connection and web browser.	Cannot create new variables (e.g. v1+v2). Cannot use statistical software that people are already familiar with (e.g. SAS, SPSS, STATA, etc.). Output is in html format and may be difficult to import into other application software. Inability to save recodes and previous data queries.
Producers	Makes data publicly and easily available at low cost.	Requires data management using other application software (e.g. SAS or SPSS). Requires access to a web server to run the SDA application. Significant time required to create online codebook. Significant resources are needed to provide additional functionality (e.g. saving recodes, downloading data, etc.).

Figure 6.1 The advantages and disadvantages of SDA for data consumers and producers

a web-based data analysis application called *S*urvey and *D*ata *A*nalysis, or SDA. SDA is easy to use and fast. Additionally, since it is web based, it is available anywhere a person has access to the Internet and a web browser. The advantages and disadvantages of using SDA are summarized in figure 6.1. In short, the major disadvantages are the inability to create new measures and to save past data recodings and queries. However, in many cases, the advantages outweigh the disadvantages, particularly in the ease of use and speed.

While SDA is easy to use, it does help to have basic data analysis skills like understanding how to regroup values of variables into meaningful groups. Regardless, SDA works by filling out a relatively uncomplicated form, with contextually specific hyperlinks to online help and examples. Figure 6.2 shows an example of an SDA form, using the CPS data and figure 6.3 shows a partial listing of the results. In this example, we are comparing the extent to which black and white households have used a personal computer at home. Respondents were asked, "Has anyone in this household ever used a computer at home?" (Note that out-of-the-universe respondents were excluded.)

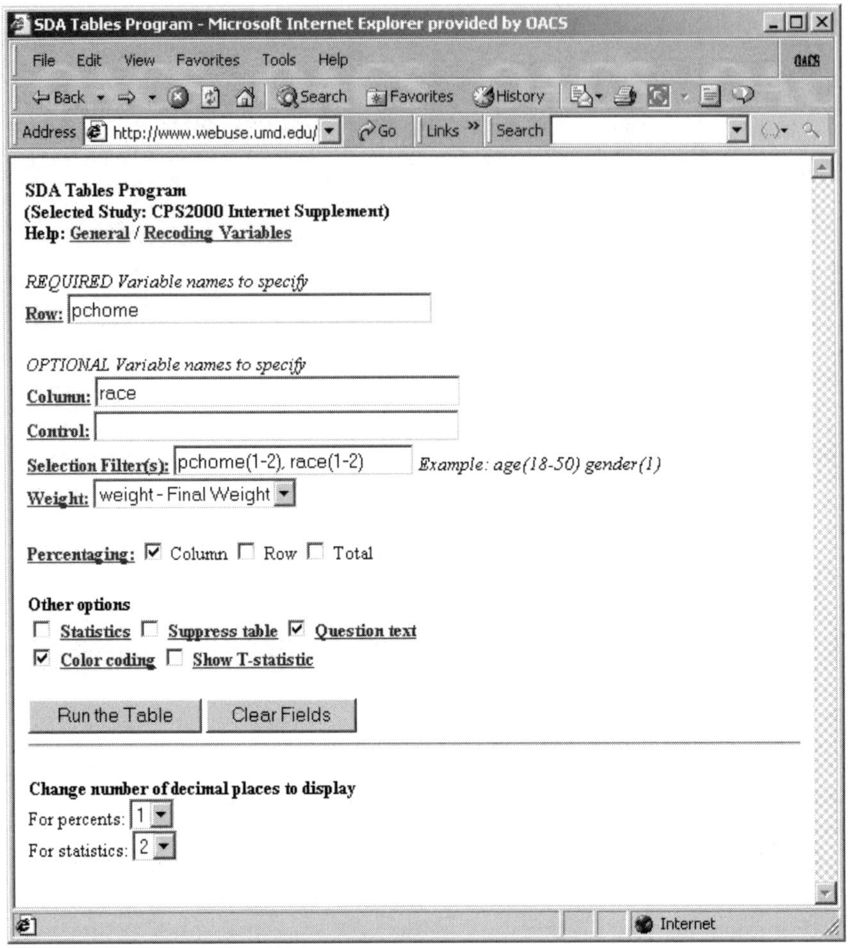

Figure 6.2 Example of using SDA for the analysis of the 2000 CPS (digital divide) data

Respondents were asked to self-identify their race with the following question: "What is your race? Are you white, black, American Indian, Aleut or Eskimo, Asian or Pacific Islander or something else?" Only white and black respondents are included in this analysis. These results indicate a difference of only 2.7 percentage points between white and black households ever using a computer at home. (Note that while the sample size of the 2000 CPS data is 134,986, we used a census

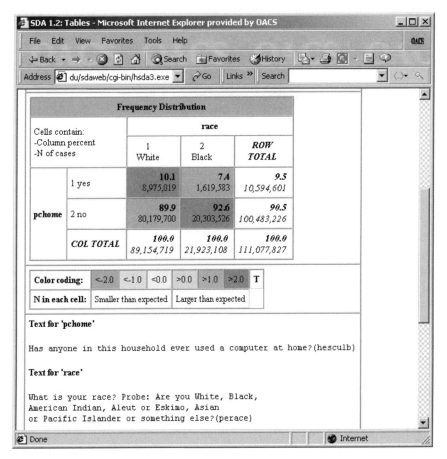

Figure 6.3 Partial results of using SDA for the analysis of the 2000 CPS (digital divide) data

supplied weight that projected a weighted sample size of over 100 million.)

Other Social Science Methods on and about the Internet

Many researchers are interested in how the introduction of the Internet into daily life may have changed individual behaviors. But it may also change how social scientists conduct research – the kind and way that data are collected and analyzed. Shortly, we will be developing a new segment of the WebUse web page to discuss developments in data collection and analysis.

Qualitative/observational data

In-depth interviews

All of the data discussed above are survey data and reflect either the opinions and experiences of individuals or households, but are intended to be used for aggregate comparisons such as what percentage of African–Americans have access to the Internet compared to white Americans. Other kinds of data can supplement and extend these survey data.

For example, a small part of our NSF grant provided resources to begin a series of personal in-depth interviews with computer users selected at random. One respondent, Beth, shared her Internet use habits and demographic information with an interviewer.

> Beth is a 32-year-old married white female who lives with her husband and her three children (ages 12, 8, and 5). They live in a single family home she owns in an all-white, middle-class neighborhood in Conshohocken, PA. Beth is a paralegal employed 40 hours a week for a Center City Philadelphia law firm. Her husband is employed full-time as a maintenance technician with Amtrak. She and her husband have also recently started an Internet retail distribution company of their own. Thus, she uses the Internet in her job, her own business, and at home.

Among the interesting aspects of Beth's use of the Internet, we find that:

> Beth reports a modest social network including approximately 10 people. She reports staying in contact with almost all of them on a regular basis by seeing them socially, while maintaining contact with approximately one-half of them by email or talking on the telephone. Email has increased the number and quality of her contacts. Beth prefers email to the telephone,
> "I've never been much of a phone person. With email you can control the conversation better and not get stuck trying to figure out how to get off the phone."

To date, 23 such in-depth Internet user profiles are available on the WebUse webpage. The richness of these qualitative data will be enhanced as we expand collecting and disseminating these kinds of data from representative samples around the country.

Princeton University user observational laboratory

Further and more detailed observational study is currently underway at a Princeton University observational laboratory, at which community residents are invited to a specialized computer facility to be observed as they complete a series of standardized Internet tasks. These tasks involve using the web to search for and find specialized information on health (e.g. medical advice for a particular ailment) or politics (e.g. a political candidate's stand on particular issues). Notes are taken as these tasks are performed on the efficiency and sophistication of the Internet search strategies that are used. Directly observing these tasks allows the researcher to ask participants further specialized questions about knowledge of alternative strategies and their normal experience of using the Internet at home or work.

An important accomplishment of this project is that those who have been observed represent over 60 percent of the respondents randomly sampled in the community, which ensures far more generalizability of results than found in typical observational studies. By the time the project is complete, it is hoped that more than 100 respondents will be observed from urban, suburban, and rural communities. Methods and procedures on the study itself will be available on the Internet for researchers interested in extending the research into other regions of the country or into other countries. More information is available on their web page (www.webuse.org).

Time diaries

A combination of qualitative and quantitative methods of special relevance to studying the impact of the Internet is the time diary. In distinction to the usual survey estimate questions that ask "How many hours a week do you (activity X)?" or "How often do you do (X)?", the time diary approach involves people completing activity logs for a particular day or series of days (Robinson and Godbey, 1999).

Most recent diary studies are qualitative in that they ask respondents to describe activities in their own words. These textual data are then coded into predefined categories like "house cleaning" or "reading" for quantitative analysis. It is now possible for respondents or researchers to record such activities at 15-minute intervals throughout a day or other longer period of time at WebUse. The resulting totals can then be compared to two national datasets archived on WebUse. A more ambitious approach to collecting diary data from a cross-sectional sample using the Internet via WebTV is described at knowledgenetworks.com.

Archival document data and analysis

Content analysis tools

Researchers at Harvard University and the University of New South Wales have developed a web-based content analysis package, the "General Inquirer," based on earlier personal computer-based software (Stone, Dunphy, Smith, and Ogilvie, 1966; Kelly and Stone, 1975). Many of the advantages and disadvantages associated with SDA apply here as well. For instance, all a researcher needs is an Internet connection, not a particularly fast one, and a browser. The work is done on the server with the application software. The web browser interface lends itself to cutting and pasting content from web resources directly into the General Inquirer facilitating content analyses of web content.

Figure 6.4 shows the kind of output associated with the application of the software to political speeches made by the presidential candidates during the year 2000 campaign. The two charts below are typical examples of one-way ANOVA comparisons. They show the percentage of positive words and the percentage of negative words for the campaign-related speeches of each of the five American presidential candidates (in the presidential primaries as of December, 1999), as gleaned from their web sites.

The dots for each candidate show the spread of scores for his speeches. The width of each diamond shows that candidate's proportion of the total data, with Gore and McCain having respectively 55 and 39 speeches, considerably more than the others. The height of each diamond indicates a 95 percent confidence interval. If two diamonds do not overlap, such as those of McCain and Bradley on both charts, they are considered significantly different. The charts show McCain is higher on the use of both positive and negative words than, for example, Gore. Bradley is low in the use of either positive or negative words. Bush has positive words dominating over negative ones, while Buchanan is more negative than positive.

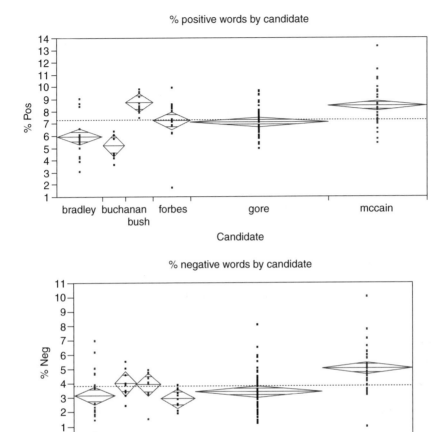

Figure 6.4 Examples of ANOVA analysis based on the *General Inquirer* content analysis tool
Source: www.wjh.harvard.edu~inquirer/, Welcome to the *General Inquirer* Home Page

Stone (www.wjh.harvard.edu/~inquirer/, 2001) and his colleagues have used the Inquirer program to differentiate the content of appeals made on various "protest" websites and the editorial outlooks contained in different college student newspapers. Thus, researchers interested in the structure of political appeals, speeches, and documents will find this tool of special interest.

Macro-comparative data

In addition to textual materials, document analysis can be extended to collections of official government and industry data. Overcoming the paucity of macro-comparative secondary cross-national data, the Information Intelligence Quotient (IIQ) project at Northwestern University (Arquette, 2001) has made an early attempt to collect and assemble standardized cross-national data from more than 180 countries around the world, both their technology infrastructure and use. One project goal is to develop a composite index of information and communication system (ICS) development comprised of three dimensions – infrastructure, access, and use.

Using sources like the United Nations Development Program (UNDP), World Bank Development Indicators, International Telecommunication Union Database, and the United Nations Statistical Database, approximately eighty measures have been collected in this preliminary dataset. Data are available, for example for information and communications technology network infrastructure, technology flow infrastructure, labor force infrastructure, power infrastructure. The measures include items like expenditures on communications and technology infrastructure, Internet hosts per 1,000, personal computers per 1,000, technology exports, research and development investments, and many others.

Data collection is ongoing and is expected to grow to more than 400 such measures in the future. The most current data will be available on the WebUse webpage.

Experimental studies

Laboratory studies

Laboratory-like studies utilizing the Internet have been set up by several social scientists across the country. Perhaps the most innovative and engaging has been the site, pcl.Stanford.edu (Political Communication Laboratory), established by Professor Shanto Iyengar at Stanford University. For example, visitors to this site can engage in the "Whack-A-Pol" experiment based on the popular carnival game "Whack-a-mole." The stated purpose of this game "is to see how computer interfaces affect the way people make evaluations of different individuals" (pcl.stanford.edu/exp/whack/polh/consent.html).

After a short series of demographic questions participants are presented with a series of pictures of various national and world political leaders that pop up like Fidel Castro, Winston Churchill, John F. Kennedy, and others. The player is asked to "whack" the picture. As the speed of the game increases, the player cannot whack every picture and must make decisions, allowing the researcher to analyze their decisions and actions. At the conclusion, players are asked to recall which people popped up and which leader they thought they whacked the most.

Another study conducted by the Political Communication Lab at Stanford University uses the Internet to present a brief video discussing a current political issue and then fill out an opinion survey.

Field experiments

The most thorough, well-known, and sophisticated field experimental studies have been conducted by Robert Kraut and his associates at Carnegie Mellon University. Kraut's studies have been carefully conducted with small samples of residents of the Pittsburgh, PA, area assigned to different experimental conditions as they begin to use the Internet. Kraut's methods provide an ideal model for other researchers who wish to replicate his work in other communities. Particularly of interest is his use of Palm Pilots and other new technologies to collect data on Internet users' day-to-day activities and experiences – all embedded in complex experimental designs.

Social networks

Social network analysis has a rich tradition in the social sciences and focuses on relationships between social entities. These entities can be things like organizations, corporations, states, or individuals. The relationships can be things like transfers of resources (e.g. information or money), or communications. The regular patterns of behavior evident in the relationships between entities reveal what social network analysts call *structure*. The growth of the Internet as a communication medium has increased the opportunities for data collection of social network data. Three research efforts, with different emphases, are underway and illustrative of the kind of network analyses that will be used to study the Internet: Sack uses the content of Usenet exchanges to develop both social and thematic networks; Smith attempts to reveal hidden aspects of online communities using Usenet data; Kim uses traditional network analysis techniques to examine the "structuration of the Internet space."

Analyzing the social networks of very large-scale conversations

Sack notes that:

> On the Internet there are now very large-scale conversations (VLSCs) in which hundreds, even thousands, of people exchange messages. These messages are exchanged daily – and even more frequently – across international borders. Unlike older, one-to-many media (for example, television or radio) where a small group of people broadcast to a larger number of people, VLSCs are a many-to-many communications medium. Also, unlike older, one-to-one media (e.g., the telephone), the people engaged in VLSCs do not necessarily know the electronic addresses of the other participants before the start of the conversation. For these reasons, VLSCs are creating new connections between people who might otherwise not even have imagined the other's existence. (Sack, 2001, www.media.mit.edu/~wsack/CM/index.html)

Many interesting analytic questions can be addressed with data like these, but there are unique problems associated with both the content as well as the amount of data available. Sack has developed a tool that uses network principles to organize Usenet messages by a set of:

- social networks detailing who is responding to and/or citing whom in the newsgroup;
- discussion themes that are frequently used in the newsgroup archive; and,
- semantic networks that represent the main terms under discussion and some of their relationships to one another.

Figure 6.5 shows a screen shot taken from Sack's web page (www.media.mit.edu/~wsack/CM/index.html), where detailed information on the uses of this type of network analysis, as well as numerous examples are available. Significant customization and manipulation of the output are possible.

Understanding the structure of Usenet news: Netscan

Marc Smith is a network analyst who is interested in online communities and provides tools for understanding these communities using

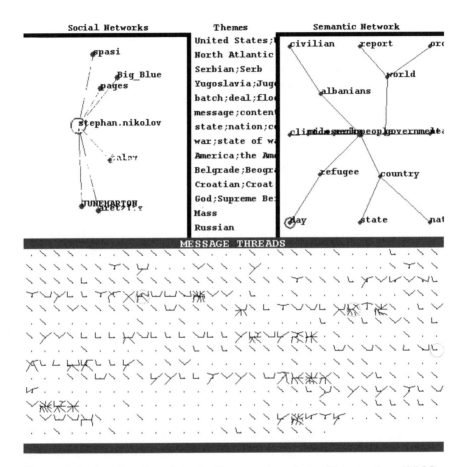

Figure 6.5 Sample output from Sack's network analysis of Internet-based VLSCs
Source: web.media.mit.edu/~wsack/CM/index.html

data from Usenet exchanges (Smith, 1997). The software tool that he has developed is called Netscan that connects to a Usenet News server that carries nearly 15,000 newsgroups and collects all the messages in all the newsgroups. All of these messages are read and selected information is drawn from message headers.

Netscan then constructs and maintains a database of this information that can be analyzed, generating reports of selected news groups over selected periods of time. Three useful tools are available: (1) the news group tracker; (2) crosspost visualization; and (3) tree maps of news groups. The crosspost and tree-map tools are both graphically based. Smith states that his "ultimate goal is to shed light on the vast invisible continent of social cyberspace and to see the crowds that are gathered there" (netscan.research.microsoft.com/).

Using the news group tracker, and selecting the rec.music domain for July 7, 2001, one can discover that there are 125 discussion groups beneath rec.music, starting with rec.music.beatles. Further, there were a total of 11,424 posts made during the requested time period and that 899 individuals made at least one posting. Other information is also presented.

Netscan also allows the analysis of crossposting. Selecting the rec.music domain again, produces the crossposting output shown in figure 6.6: Using an interactive slider bar at the bottom of the screen allows the analysts to filter the groups by the amount of crossposting. The bottom of figure 6.6 shows the same information as in the top graphic, but dropping out groups with little crossposting using the slider bar.

The structuration of Internet space

Kim (2001) is interested in how the worldwide web is used – how people browse or surf the web – and how this creates "spaces" on the web. Using network analysis concepts and measurements, Kim attempts to determine if there is a regularized pattern of "traffic flow" between websites, and if so, if there is a core and periphery of websites. Building on this, he asks what types of sites move to the center in the network traffic and what are the characteristics of sites that attract more visitors? After collecting and analyzing the web-surfing "click" data from Korean users in May and August 2000, Kim finds that in May, the traffic patterns between Web sites is distributed in a more or less random fashion (see figure 6.7a.). Three months later, a very different and well defined pattern or structure emerges (see figure 6.7b). In short, if a web surfer visits a certain website, there is an increased probability that they will surf to another particular website. The network centralization in May was 0.74, but corresponding to the more centralized emerging structure was nearly 14 in August.

This emergent structure, then, may constrain or facilitate the web-browsing habits of people, influencing where they surf. This finding leads to the question of inequality between websites in terms of the number of unique visitors they have. Kim examines this using the gini index, and discovers that the bottom 50 percent of the top 100

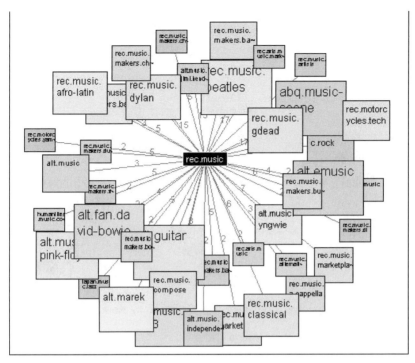

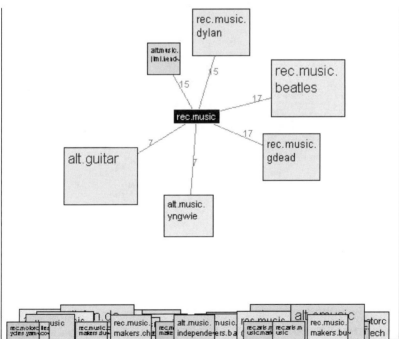

Figure 6.6 Examining the rec.music crossposting for 7/1/01; lower representation filters out weak crosspostings
Source: netscan.research.Microsoft.com

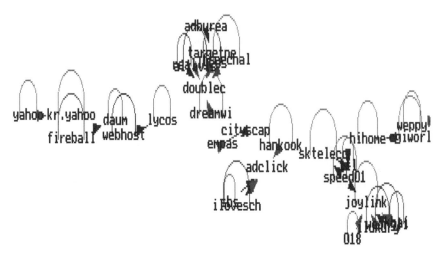

Figure 6.7(a) The structuration of Internet space by Korean web-surfers, May 2000
Source: Kim, personal communication

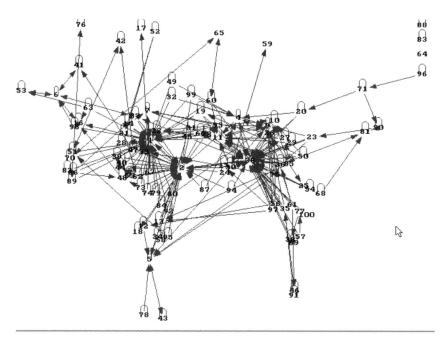

Figure 6.7(b) The structuration of Internet space by Korean web-surfers, August 2000
Source: Kim, personal communication

Table 6.2   Major categories for the webuse annotated bibliography

Consumption patterns	Online communities
Economics	Policy issues
Historical perspectives	Politics
Human computer interaction	Privacy
Inequality and digital divide	Public access and usage
International differences	Qualitative studies
Internet survey analysis/methodology	Social capital implications
Macro/structure issues	Social networks
Multivariate analysis	Time/activity displacement
Navigational skills	Theory

websites visited attracted 7 percent of the web-surfers, confirming his network analysis.

This line of research can be extended in numerous ways such as cross-national comparisons, longer longitudinal series, and analyzing the hyperlinks embedded in web sites.

Other Resources: Annotated Bibliography

Another resource available on WebUse is an annotated bibliography. While there are many sources of excellent articles on Internet research, there are few, if any, collections of articles by topic, and that have an abstract or annotation indicating their substance. Currently, WebUse has a listing of approximately 400 articles, with over 300 annotated and with links, where available and appropriate. Initially, the bibliography was constructed around approximately twenty topics, shown in table 6.2:

While this provided structure to the search for articles and books, it is constraining since there is no logical reason that these resources be mutually exclusive, and clearly not exhaustive. The next stage in the development of the bibliography, besides making additions and corrections, is to (1) add a dynamic query capability, and (2) provide a way for others to make contributions. Providing a searchable database diminishes the need to construct categories *a priori*, and places few constraints on use. For example, it will be possible to search for all articles by a particular author, by keywords in the title or annotation, or a logical combination (AND, OR, NOT, etc.) of any of these fields.

This resource could be a first stop for someone who wants to get a quick overview of research in a specific area, or could be a source of data for meta-analyses – for example, what is the direction of Internet research, or for content analysis (cut and paste into the *General Inquirer!*).

Resources from the Annual WebShop

As part of the National Science Foundation grant, the Sociology and Computer Science Departments and the College of Behavioral and Social Sciences at the University of Maryland in June 2001 hosted the first annual WebShop, with two more planned for the summers of 2002 and 2003. The WebShop is a workshop about Internet research for graduate students and over sixty students came to Maryland in the first year to hear presentations from more than forty speakers – research experts on a wide range of Internet and related technology issues and research.

The WebShop provided these graduate students with the opportunity to listen to and work with leading experts, to receive guidance on their own research, and to live and interact with other students interested in similar topics.

Equally unique, but from the other side of the podium, the presenters had the opportunity to share their ideas and research with the next generation of Internet research scholars. The WebShop was three weeks long (two weeks at Maryland and one week at University of California at Berkeley) and covered the wide range of topics and speakers summarized in table 6.3. Speakers were given the task to present and lead a discussion about the major issues and research problems within each topic area. Each day between three and five speakers made presentations. Several methods were used to capture the content of the presentations and discussions including (1) speaker abstracts, (2) video and audio recordings of the presentations, and (3) a written report of the presentations prepared by the students themselves.

Speaker abstracts

Each presenter wrote a short abstract about his or her presentation that is available on the WebUse webpage. On the first day of the WebShop,

Table 6.3 List of topics and speakers at the first annual WebShop, University of Maryland, June 10–23, 2001

Topics	Speakers
Background/history	DiMaggio, Irving, Kestnbaum
Navigational skills	Hargittai, Shneiderman, Stone
Online communities	Kling, Preece, Silver, Sproull
Digital divide	McConnahey, Neuman, Rice, Robinson
Social capital	Rice, Ritzer, Uslaner
Policy	DiMaggio, Fountain, Galston, Kahin
Organizations	Cramton, Howard, Kiesler, Stark
Social networks	Kraut, Neustadtl, Marsden, Rainie/Howard
Commerce	Cole, McCready, Stipp, Weiss
International	Cole, Hargittai, Wilson, Manchin
Economics	Gey, Varian
SDA	Piazza, Shanks, Robinson
Methods	Iyengar, Nie/Rivers, Reeves
Politics	Bimber, Brady, Lupia, Wolfinger
Future	Miller

for example, Professor Meyer Kestnbaum, Larry Irving, former head of the National Telecommunications and Information Agency (NTIA), and Professor Paul DiMaggio spoke on history and the digital divide. Professor Kestnbaum spoke about one technical antecedent to the Internet – the light telegraph – and how that technology formed the essential basis of point-to-point communication networks currently embodied in the Internet. Larry Irving presented his views on the rights of citizens to access communication media including the Internet, concluding that citizenship requires access to as many possible sources of information as available – creating an institutional structure of haves and have-nots exacerbates many social problems in America. As an aside, Irving noted how he coined the term *digital divide*, less to represent the range of policy concerns now considered to be digital divides, than to engage the media, in order to "sell" the general concept of digital inequality to more reporters. Finally, Professor DiMaggio spoke of the need to move forward from the Census Bureau definition of "digital divide" – the simple percentage of households with access to a computer or the number of households with access to the Internet – to a more refined understanding of the inequalities that exist in people's abilities to *use* the Internet across demographic groups. While a significant percentage of the population may have access to the Internet, they may not all use the Internet effectively – a neglected aspect of the digital divide in terms of how people can use Internet technologies to solve everyday problems.

Video and audio recording of the presentations

While the abstracts speak to the intentions of the presenters, what they hoped to convey to the students, audio and videotape were used to record every presentation. These recordings retrospectively allow one to understand what was actually presented, and more importantly, to observe the interaction with the students, many of whom challenged the speakers' research. While these recordings are not currently available on WebUse, we hope to overcome the technical barriers and to find appropriate search engines for audio and video as they become available. Resources like this will be invaluable for capturing and preserving this kind of information. Currently, these recordings can be made available by contacting the WebShop program coordinator.

Written reporting of the WebShop presentations

Finally, to engage the students and provide an accurate reporting of the speakers' presentations, WebShop students were assigned a note-taking task for each speaker. Each day a different group of student participants, under the guidance of a WebShop research assistant, took careful notes on each speaker's presentation and the subsequent question and answer period. All of these notes were then organized and rewritten to have a common format and to synthesize the major points made by the day's speakers. These individual speaker documents were then edited to a uniform style and format with transitions from section to section. In short, the resulting document provides a comprehensive, yet accessible version of the major intellectual work at the WebShop. This document, currently in draft format, is available at the WebUse webpage.

New Journal: IT@SOCIETY

Another resource being developed on the WebUse web page is a refereed online journal titled *IT@SOCIETY*. The purpose of this journal is to routinely publish articles that are timely, and contain the latest social science research on specific research themes. Upcoming issues will be on:

- *Issue 1*: sociability
- *Issue 2*: time/media displacement
- *Issue 3*: inequality
- *Issue 4*: policy research
- *Issue 5*: Internet research methods

To reduce the time to publication to a minimum, the articles will be read and evaluated by a small editorial board. Further, without page or printing limitations, there is no necessity to delay publication of articles due to space constraints. No subscription is necessary, and anyone may read or download the articles.

Because of the timeliness, it is anticipated that other versions, longer and better conceptualized, would later be published in more traditional journals, and that this journal would fill the need for the most current research.

Working papers

WebUse will also sponsor a working paper section dedicated to promoting collaboration of research in progress. The intention of this area of the webpage is to allow people to publish articles in "prepublication" format seeking comments from interested readers. These articles could be complete articles not yet under review or pieces of research – a developing theory, an interesting research question, or other parts of a research puzzle – that would benefit from the comments of others.

We anticipate that this will require registration. Research on online communities indicates that the quality of the community contributions increases substantially using a registration process as a filter, allowing the most interested and committed access to content (Preece, 2001).

Overall Conclusions

We have discussed a number of tools and resources available on the Internet to study the types and consequence of Internet use interactively. We have also provided a preview of what should be possible in the years ahead as new Internet technologies become available. The basic development of most of these tools was accomplished without large government or foundation development grants, although they would not have been possible without earlier support grants on related topics. Nevertheless, one goal of our present NSF grant is to provide tutorials and other outreach programs (like the summer WebShop) to make the general social scientists community aware and appreciative of the ability of these Internet tools to facilitate and enrich the conduct of current social research.

Not the least of these outreach efforts involves the teaching of undergraduate and graduate methods courses. It is not necessary for students to attend our *WebShop* to learn and appreciate these tools. For example, we have found that statistical analysis techniques that usually take many weeks to be able to teach and perform (e.g. cross-tabulation or correlation/regression) can now be accomplished in as short as a single class session using SDA. Covering those analytic basics in a shorter period of time should empower the next generation of students to become far more technologically and methodologically proficient. This will allow them to concentrate on exploring more interesting questions – particularly as they can establish relationships with students and faculty at other universities using widely available tools such as electronic mail, web boards, chat rooms, and other web communication tools.

References

Arquette, T. (2001). *The information intelligence quotient*™ *(IIQ*™*): assessing global information and communication systems development*. Northwestern University Center for Comparative and International Studies. Available online at: www.northwestern.edu/cics/digitaldivide/

DiMaggio, P. and Hargittai, E. (2001). From the "digital divide" to "digital inequality": studying Internet use as penetration increases. Unpublished paper. Princeton University, Department of Sociology.

Kelly, E. and Stone, P. J. (1975). *Computer recognition of English word senses*. Amsterdam: North Holland Press; New York: Elsevier.

Kim, Y. H. (2001). Personal communication.

Preece, J. (2000). *Online communities: designing usability, supporting sociability*. New York: John Wiley and Sons, Ltd.

Robinson, J. P. and Godbey, G. (1999). *Time for life: the surprising ways Americans use their time*. University Park, PA: Pennsylvania State University Press.

Sack, W. (2001). Conversation map version 0.01 An Interface for Very Large-Scale Conversations. Available online at:
web.media.mit.edu/~wsack/CM/index.html

Smith, M. (1997). Netscan: a tool for measuring and mapping social cyber-spaces. Available online at: netscan.research.microsoft.com

Stone, P. J. (2001). *The General Inquirer* home page,
www.wjh.harvard.edu/~inquirer/

Stone, P. J., Dunphy, D. C., Smith, M. S., and Ogilvie, D. M. (1966). *The general inquirer: a computer approach to content analysis*. Cambridge, MA: MIT Press.

Part III

Finding Time for the Internet

7

Internet Use, Interpersonal Relations, and Sociability

A Time Diary Study

Norman H. Nie, D. Sunshine Hillygus, and Lutz Erbring

Abstract

Using exciting new time diary data, we explore the complex ways in which the Internet affects interpersonal communication and sociability. Rather than dwelling on the increasingly stale debate about whether the Internet is good or bad for sociability, we analyze when and where Internet use impacts face-to-face interactions. Internet use at home has a strong negative impact on time spent with friends and family, while Internet use at work is strongly related to decreased time with colleagues (but has little effect on social time with friends and family). Similarly, Internet use during the weekends is more strongly related to decreased time spent with friends and family than Internet use during weekdays. Our findings offer support for a "displacement" or "hydraulic" theory of Internet use – time online is largely an asocial activity that competes with, rather than complements, face-to-face social time – but it is the location and timing of Internet use that determines which interpersonal relationships are affected.

Authors' Note

We would like to thank John Robinson for his contributions to the survey design and to this article. We would also like to thank the outstanding team of graduate assistants at SIQSS who aided us at every stage in the preparation of this chapter: Sunny Niu, Hahrie Han, Heili Pals, and Shawn Treier. This chapter would not have been possible without their assistance.

Introduction

Few would dispute the idea that the Internet has transformed economic and social life. At the same time, however, the Internet's impact on interpersonal communication and sociability remains a source of heated debate. One group of researchers conclude that the Internet leads to more and better social relationships by creating an additional medium of communication with friends and family, and by enabling the creation of new relationships through Internet interactions. In contrast, other researchers find Internet use to be socially isolating, because time on the Internet replaces other social activities and face-to-face interaction. In this chapter, we try to move the debate beyond this dichotomous view and delineate more specific contours of the relationship between time spent on the Internet and time spent in face-to-face interaction with people. Using a new dataset that relies on more detailed and definitive time diary information than the data available in previous studies, we are better able to explain the complex ways in which the Internet affects interpersonal communication and sociability.

The debate about the impact of Internet use on the quantity and quality of interpersonal communication and sociability has focused on four different academic surveys conducted in 2000. Most of the findings in these surveys have been concurrent with one another. All four studies show similar Internet connection rates – more than half of American households are connected to the Internet. All describe similar patterns of Internet use among those connected: sending and receiving email is ubiquitous; searching for products, news, weather, stock quotes, and entertainment is frequent. All four studies find evidence of a digital divide cut by education, wealth, and generation. The studies diverge, however, in their conclusions regarding the social repercussions of Internet use. At the heart of this debate is whether Internet use is a potentially isolating activity, or one that leads to more communication among people and thus enhances human connectivity and sociability.

Two theoretical paradigms dominate the debate. Franzen (2000) argue that the Internet has made everything – including socializing – more efficient. The efficiency hypothesis holds that the Internet offers an additional technology for engaging in social interaction and coordinating social activities. Additionally, the Internet may make other activities more efficient, freeing up additional leisure time. For instance, if an individual shops online, this may free up time to spend with friends. The alternative theoretical perspective is a displacement hypothesis, or "hydraulic" model – time on one activity cannot be spent on another activity. Time is a zero-sum phenomenon, like a hydraulic system – it can be reshaped and redistributed like a fluid, but it cannot be expanded like a gas. Thus, because there are only 24 hours in a day, time spent on one activity must be traded off against time spent on other activities. Time online, thus, is an asocial activity that competes with, rather than complements, social time.

A third paradigm sometimes discussed in connection with the Internet and its social consequences may be called the communitarian hypothesis. It has to do with the quality, rather than the quantity, of time associated with Internet use and its effects. This view focuses on the unique ability of the Internet to eliminate physical distance and to establish and maintain linkages between individuals on the basis of almost any conceivable shared interest (or even a rediscovery of extended family ties with distant relatives, or a revival of contacts among long-lost friends and neighbors) – thereby creating virtual "communities" of social exchange and support as social networks that extend well beyond the reach (and the need?) for face-to-face contact. In effect, this view seeks to turn the possible loss of real interpersonal interactions displaced by time spent on the Internet into an advantage – not unlike the debate over the alleged compensatory benefits of limited amounts of "quality time" spent by working mothers with children in day care.

The distinction between virtual and real communities, or between real and mediated social interaction, raises the question of what exactly is meant by such categories as sociability and social or personal interaction. If it is true that man is a social animal (such that, e.g., exile or pillory were considered some of the most severe forms of punishment in ancient times), then clearly it is the need for the presence of others in one's everyday life (not always pleasant and rewarding) which is an essential ingredient of human existence – i.e., the physical proximity of people both as individuals and in the form of social groups and institutions. Therefore, in examining the social consequences of the Internet, we focus on the primary social environment, without thereby denying the novel possibilities of global social networks or "communities."

Previous Research

Existing empirical research provides support for both views. One of the earliest surveys examining the social consequences of the Internet was the "Internet and Society" study we conducted through the Stanford Institute for the Quantitative Study of Society (SIQSS) in February 2000 (Nie and Erbring, 2000). This nationally representative study revealed that Internet users (especially heavy Internet users) report spending *less* time with friends and family, shopping in stores, reading newspapers, and watching television – and *more* time working for their employers at home (without cutting back on hours in the office).[1] Our finding concerning the quantity and quality of interpersonal communications and sociability quickly became the focus of further scholarly attention and controversy.

Following our study, three other groups conducted nationally representative surveys on the implications of increased Internet use: Pew, UCLA, and NPR/Kaiser/Harvard's Kennedy School. Like the SIQSS study, the NPR/Kaiser/Kennedy School Study finds an inverse relationship between computer use and sociability. They report that "58% of all adult Americans reported that computers led people to spend less time with friends and family . . . furthermore, the study found that slightly fewer than half of Americans, 46 percent, say that computers have given people less free time," while only 24 percent believe the contrary (National Public Radio, Kaiser Family Foundation and Kennedy School of Government, 2000). In contrast to this finding, as well as our findings at SIQSS, both the Pew and UCLA studies conclude exactly the opposite. The UCLA study concludes: "concerns that the Internet reduces household time together appear nearly groundless" (2000: 7).

There are three main criticisms of the existing research, however. First, most of these studies ignore the *amount* of Internet use.[2] They simply divided the population into users and non-users, and then made comparisons of sociability along these lines. It seems grossly inappropriate to assume that "users" spending one hour per week on the Internet are equivalent to those spending 20 hours on the Internet. As a result, any effects of Internet use are likely to be concealed or diluted.

A second criticism of these studies is that they are largely limited to bivariate analyses, ignoring the importance of controlling for demographic factors such as education, age, marital status, or work status.

---

1   An Internet user was defined as a respondent with Internet access, either inside the home, or at work, at school, or another location. A "heavy" Internet user was one who spent at least 5 hours per week on the Internet.
2   There are some exceptions in this regard (Nie and Erbring, 2000; Wellman et al., 2001).

As argued in Nie (2001), analyses regarding the relationship between Internet use and sociability must include multivariate controls. Bivariate analyses ignore the possibility of spurious correlations between Internet use and sociability. A simple bivariate analysis, for example, could not elucidate whether Internet users have more social contacts because of the Internet, or because they are more highly educated (given that more highly educated individuals tend to have more social contacts *and* are more likely to be Internet users).

Finally, previous research has not done an adequate job of measuring Internet use. Previous studies have relied on respondent estimates of daily or weekly Internet use, but such estimates are undoubtedly fraught with error. Respondent time estimates may be problematic because individuals do not keep a running tally of the number of minutes or hours spent on particular activities, and certainly not for the specific periods (day/week/month) requested by the researcher (Franzen, 2000). Respondents may give their best guess, but in addition to errors of judgment, such estimates are prone to distortion by social desirability concerns (e.g., individuals might not want to admit watching too much TV, or they might want to overestimate time spent on charitable and civic causes).

The analysis reported in this chapter builds on a new dataset that overcomes most of these problems by measuring time and Internet use more directly, and thus may help to reconcile the competing hypotheses by identifying the specific conditions under which Internet use affects sociability.

Research Design

Our research design addresses the problems discussed above through an improved survey instrument and a more complete analysis. We use multivariate analyses to clarify the relationships between time spent online and time spent socializing. And we have developed a novel survey methodology that allows us to differentiate amount, location and type of Internet use, and to generate more accurate measurements of respondents' time use.

The survey is based on a time diary approach. Robinson et al. (2001) argued that a judiciously administered time diary study is necessary to measure time spent on various activities accurately. The diary procedure avoids the problems of a "time estimate" approach by preventing "guesstimate" errors, and by helping to prevent respondents from purposefully distorting activity estimates. Respondents can no longer easily manipulate survey responses to portray themselves in a particular light (for example, as only moderate TV viewers, or as being particularly socially active). With a time diary approach, respondents would have to manipulate their entire diary, not just one report of time spent on a particular activity.

However, there are limitations to a traditional diary approach. Perhaps the principal shortcoming of diary studies is the exhaustive toll they take on respondents. Most diary studies require respondents to report every activity they engaged in for 24 hours. In the traditional 24-hour design, just a few hours into the day, respondents may stop giving details about their activities because they know they still have so many hours to go before the survey is over! The typical phone-implemented time diary places the highest burden on respondents and thus severely limits the number of follow-up questions that can be asked for each activity. In these studies, fatigue and sheer repetition lower the quality of data.[3] Moreover, the phone is an extremely awkward and blunt instrument for constructing detailed activity diaries; phone-implemented surveys do not provide the respondent with any memory recall assistance, such as a diary form or a checklist of secondary or parallel (multi-tasking) activities.[4]

For all these reasons, SIQSS, in consultation with time diary expert John Robinson, developed a research design that combines the best of both worlds – the superior time use estimates of the diary approach without the respondent burden of a 24-hour diary. While closely following the basic methodology of phone implemented diary studies, we adapted these techniques to take advantage of the superior methods of Knowledge Networks' survey instrument for online survey administration, conducted via the Microsoft Web-TV set-top box. In May 2001, Knowledge Networks fielded the SIQSS Time Diary

---

3   This is particularly evident by the low level of feedback received from the question "were you doing anything else at the same time?" While previous time diary surveys conducted by phone have found only a handful of secondary activities during the day, we find 1.7 secondary activities *per main activity*.

4   Mailout, paper diary designs also have numerous limitations, including lack of investigator control, low response rate resulting in biased data, long turnaround time, and high expenses related to data entry and follow-up. Such a design also results in lower quality time diary data because the survey must be simplistic, and it is not possible to ask for clarification or probe to ensure accurate data.

Study to a representative sample of approximately 6,000 Americans between the ages of 18 and 64.[5]

The SIQSS modified time diary study asked respondents about their activities yesterday during six randomly selected hours of the day – one in each of six time blocks (strata): night, early morning, late morning, afternoon, early evening, and late evening. We structured the sampling design to collect an even distribution of days of the week for the total sample, and of hours over the course of the day for each respondent.[6] With a 6-hour design, and an average interview length of about 15 minutes, the survey is much less tortuous and burdensome for respondents than a complete 24-hour diary. Thus, we were able to go into great detail about the social context of each activity without exhausting respondents. We were also able to engage a much larger sample so that we have high-quality comparable data for each hour of the day. This also permits more follow-up questions, including information on social context and interaction for each and every primary activity.[7] In other words, we not only get higher-quality data, we also obtain more detailed data about each specific activity, developing a more fine-grained picture of time use that becomes the backbone of this study.

The Data

This survey design allows us to probe the fundamental questions of how varying amounts of Internet use relate to time spent in interpersonal, face-to-face relationships with family, friends, or colleagues. We have collected data that allow us to compare Internet use

5 Respondents in the Knowledge Networks (KN) panel are randomly selected through Random Digit Dial (RDD) sampling methods on a quarterly-updated sample frame consisting of the entire US telephone population. All telephone numbers have an equal probability of selection, and sampling is done without replacement. Detailed information on the Knowledge Networks methodology can be found at www.knowledgenetworks.com. Though surveys are conducted over the Internet, respondents are a random probability sample of the United States population, in households provided with Internet terminals by Knowledge Networks for that purpose.

6 The sampling time blocks were hour 1: midnight–5am; hour 2: 6–9am; hour 3: 10am–1pm; hour 4: 2–5pm; hour 5: 6–8pm; hour 6: 9–11pm

7 We asked how long the activity lasted, where the activity took place, who was with the respondent, if the respondent was doing anything else at the same time. See appendix 7.1 for more detailed description.

- at home versus at work;
- in the evening versus other times of the day;
- on weekends versus weekdays;
- for work or for leisure.

At the same time, we can control for various demographic background factors, such as education, age, work hours, or household composition, and for other key activities that might affect the relationship between time online and time with people. Finally, we have collected information on email use both for work and for personal matters, to allow us to begin analyzing the potential social benefits of email. Given the magnitude of this rich and detailed survey, however, we can only begin to touch on some of the resulting insights in this chapter. We focus here on the relationship between Internet use and measures of sociability; we do not explore a number of other interesting items in the data – such as the incidence of multi-tasking, gender differences in time utilization, tradeoffs between work and social time, and the fascinating role that sleep plays in shaping the amount of time and the number of daily activities.

We have been careful to improve on previous measures of our main independent variable, time spent on the Internet. We compute Internet use by summing the number of minutes spent on Internet/email *as a main activity* across the 6 diary hours.[8] Based on our diary measures, we find that the average American spends nearly 25 minutes per day on Internet and email. Thirteen percent of the sample report using Internet/email as a main activity yesterday. This percentage is larger than the 8 percent reported by the Robinson study, but it is much less than the 50 percent that report having used the Internet/email at some point yesterday in the usual recall studies.[9] This may be because,

---

8   For ease of interpretation, all diary measures have been expanded to 24-hour estimates from the 6-hour data. As this is almost a linear transformation of the variables, all regression results are nearly identical – only the context of interpretation has changed. The only (slight) departure from perfect linearity is due to the differing lengths (and hence weights) of the six daily time blocks (strata). Such an expansion does not change the relationships, but does assume that the sampled hour is representative of the entire time block.

9   We have a couple of different hypotheses about the differences in the measures. First, the follow-up measure relies on summary recall and thus is susceptible to all of the estimation problems, such as over reporting, that we have already mentioned. At the same time, however, we believe that our diary measure may underestimate time spent on the Internet because respondents choose main activ-

unfortunately, the way we compute our time estimate omits Internet/email use that occurs incidentally, and therefore is coded as a *secondary activity*. We miss, for instance, the individual who reported talking on the phone as a main activity, but who checked his/her email briefly at the same time. We may be able ultimately to account for some of the apparent under-estimation by examining the secondary activities in our data – but that is a substantial task that will take us some time to accomplish.

Given the rich and fine-grained nature of the data, there are a variety of different ways to measure sociability. For ease of exposition, we measure sociability as the number of minutes spent actively engaging or participating in an activity with friends, with family, or with colleagues. We have replicated our analysis on other measures of sociability (e.g., time spent on social activities such as movies, parties, and so on) with identical results, but feel our active engagement measure is the most general and complete definition of interpersonal interaction. These active interpersonal interaction measures serve as the main dependent variables in our analysis of the relationship between Internet use and sociability. For comparison, we also construct a measure of the number of minutes spent alone – defined as the time in which the respondent is *not* actively engaged in an activity with another person.

Table 7.1 presents the basic distributional characteristics of our independent variable (time spent using the Internet) and our four main dependent variables (time spent on social activities). For each measure, we present the mean, median, percent at "zero" (i.e., the percentage never engaging in a given type of activity), and the standard deviation of the extrapolated minutes spent on each activity during 24 hours.

Preliminary Analysis of Data

Before moving to a more detailed analysis of the relationship between Internet use and sociability, we provide a brief analysis of the baseline relationship between our social activity measures and total time spent

ity by substance rather than by mode. In other words, our current research design requires that an individual who was, say, doing research on the Internet must choose between reporting their activity as research or reporting it as Internet, not both. We have improved our estimate of such Internet use in subsequent surveys.

Table 7.1   Descriptives of time-use variables (in minutes)

	Mean	Median	Std deviation	N	% at 0
Estimated total time spent using the Internet yesterday	25.0	0	75.6	6,146	87.0
Estimated active time with family yesterday	272.9	180.0	279.3	6,146	29.7
Estimated active time with friends yesterday	89.5	0.0	184.6	6,146	72.2
Estimated active time with business associates yesterday	124.8	0.0	228.5	6,146	69.7
Estimated time alone yesterday	465.6	480.0	322.1	6,146	12.1

on the Internet. Table 7.2 presents the results of the regression of sociability on Internet use, with Internet use based on the respondents' diary responses. At the same time, we must control for basic demographic characteristics which might be related to both Internet use and sociability and thus distort the relationship between time online and time with others. Our baseline regression models, therefore, control for marital status, gender, age, education, race/ethnicity, single parenthood, and living alone.

The baseline relationship between time on the Internet and time actively spent in activities with friends, family, and colleagues is negative (See table 7.2). For each minute spent on the Internet during the last 24 hours there is a reduction of approximately one-third of a minute spent with family members. The effect is strong and highly significant. With a mean Internet use for the whole adult population (18–64) of about 25 minutes a day, or almost 3 hours a week, the average reduction in time spent with family members approaches 1 hour per week.

The patterns for time spent with friends and colleagues at work are parallel, but not as dramatic. For every minute spent on the Internet, the average person spends about 7 seconds less with friends and 11 seconds less with colleagues. Thus, Internet use subtracts an additional 18 minutes a day, or almost an hour a week, in active participation with others at both work and play. There is, of course, a complementary impact on the other side. For every minute spent on the Internet, there is an additional 45 seconds of time spent alone (measured as the total number of minutes a day spent actively engaged with no one else).[10] Over a week of Internet use, this amounts to about 2 hours and 20 minutes of additional time spent alone. These findings concur with the earlier findings of the SIQSS and the Kennedy School studies. However, they are now based on more detailed and robust data.

The results in table 7.2 also verify that the statistical controls, while predictable and interesting in their own right, do not eliminate the underlying "hydraulic" relationships between amount of Internet use yesterday and the amount of active face-to-face time. As might be expected, we find that men are significantly less likely to spend time with family than women (and more time with friends, colleagues, or alone); that married people and single parents spend more time with family, while those living alone spend less time with family or friends (an average of 1 hour and 23 minutes a day less!); and that age, even well before 65, begins to reduce face-to-face interactions with family members, and even more so with friends, though not with colleagues. Looking at the complementary time alone regressions, only very few demographic variables have any statistically significant impact on time spent alone. Marriage is, of course, related to less time alone, and most notably, living alone has a very large positive effect on time spent without active interaction with others. Turning to the other time controls, we find, as expected, that sleep has a negative relationship with all measures of sociability. Work has a negative relationship with family and friends, and a positive effect with colleagues and time spent alone.[11]

In short, no matter how time online is measured, and no matter which type of social activity is considered, time spent on the Internet reduces time spent in face-to-face relationships, and concomitantly

10 The small difference between the cumulative 0.64 minute decrease in social time (0.34 + 0.11 + 0.19) and the 0.75 minute increase in time alone (for each minute of Internet use) can likely be attributed to our exclusion of "active interaction" with strangers and "others" (user-defined) as dependent variables.

11 For comparison, we also repeated the analysis using recall estimates from our follow-up questions (see appendix 7.1) as an alternative measure of Internet use. This is equivalent to measures used in previous works and is simply the response to the question: "How much time did you spend on the Internet/email yesterday?" Even with this cruder measure, we find that the baseline results are the same – the more time spent on the Internet, the less time spent with family, friends, or colleagues.

Table 7.2 Analysis of diary minutes

| | Active time with … | | | | | | | |
| | Family | | Friends | | Colleagues | | Time alone | |
	β	t	β	t	β	t	β	t
(Constant)	298.83	7.24***	235.45	8.58***	12.52	0.36	267.13	5.56***
Education	2.29	1.69	1.39	1.54	-0.10	-0.09	-2.81	-1.77
Male	-72.40	-10.22***	3.76	0.80	57.93	9.64***	19.56	2.37*
Married	106.84	10.51***	-29.05	-4.30***	-17.19	-1.99*	-39.50	-3.34***
African–American	-17.36	-1.50	5.34	0.69	22.18	2.26*	-1.55	-0.12
Hispanic	0.19	0.02	-4.24	-0.51	9.51	0.89	2.92	0.20
Asian and other	-18.20	-1.11	-7.04	-0.65	24.06	1.73	10.12	0.53
Age	-3.36	-1.65	-6.61	-4.90***	7.32	4.26***	7.44	3.15**
Age-squared	0.04	1.71	0.07	4.24***	-0.11	-5.34***	-0.05	-1.74
Live alone	-86.45	-7.15***	-16.60	-2.07*	-6.72	-0.66	91.98	6.53***
Single parent	49.70	3.62***	-4.60	-0.50	-18.59	-1.60	-15.75	-0.99
Total time online	-0.34	-7.35***	-0.11	-3.55***	-0.19	-4.95***	0.75	13.96***
Adjusted R-square	0.09		0.02		0.03		0.07	
F	54.20		9.64		18.70		41.26	
N	5,737		5,737		5,737		5,737	

* $p < 0.05$, ** $p < 0.01$, *** $p < 0.001$.

increases time spent alone. With the exception of some potentially small overlap between friends and colleagues, all of this time above is strictly additive. Time can be reallocated – from time spent with friends, family, or colleagues to time spent on the Internet – but not expanded; it is indeed like a hydraulic system, where increases in activity in one area reduce time available for other activities.

Context of Internet Use

To advance an understanding of the complex effects of the Internet on sociability, we must move beyond simple analyses of total Internet time. It is overly simplistic to look for *one* effect for *all* Internet use. Where and when an individual uses the Internet is as important as how much he or she uses it. Moreover, differentiating Internet use by location and time should sharpen the results of our analysis and test the validity of our assumptions. For instance, we would expect that Internet use at work has little effect on time spent with family members. And while the *displacement* hypothesis predicts that Internet use at home has a negative effect on social time with friends and family, the *efficiency* hypothesis, predicts no relationship, or even a positive relationship between Internet use and sociability, regardless of time or location. The following multivariate regression analysis will help us to identify which hypothesis, on average, more closely reflects the observed relationships between Internet use and sociability.

Time Constraints

Significant portions of daily life cannot be traded because they are devoted to necessary life activities, like earning a living, taking care of the home, sleeping, and eating. As a result, we expect that Internet use (particularly at home) does not affect time spent on these "fixed" activities but comes disproportionately at the expense of discretionary time that could otherwise be spent in face-to-face social engagement. Thus, we include two controls: time spent on sleep and time spent on work. Time spent on sleep is important because it defines the length of the conscious day. In terms of our "hydraulic" model, time on sleep reduces the denominator of time available. Sleep is like an accounting variable, in that the more of it you do, the less you are able to engage in any other activities. It is the only activity that behaves in this manner, and is unique in the way it expands or contracts the day.

Second, work time is an important control because of the potential spurious relationship between time spent working and sociability. For instance, we would expect that individuals who work more are likely to spend more time on the Internet (at work). We would also expect that those who work more spend less time with their friends and family. Thus, work hours should be included in the regression model so we can identify the direct effect of Internet use on sociability, independent of time spent working.

Third, we include time spent watching TV in the regression model as an interesting comparison. The comparison with time spent on TV viewing is particularly intriguing because Internet and TV use have often been thought of as equivalent or substitutable uses of time. All previous studies have found a negative relationship between TV time and Internet time (which we also find – correlation of –0.27). This, in and of itself, casts some doubt on the efficiency hypothesis. If Internet use has the effect of giving us *more* leisure time (to spend with friends and family, the argument goes), then we would also expect that it would give us more time to watch TV – the number one leisure activity of Americans. A further discussion of the effects of TV versus the Internet is included below.[12]

In the following sections, we present the results of our expanded regression models.

Home versus Work Use

Does it matter where Internet use takes place? Does, for example, time spent using the Internet at home have a greater impact on face-to-face time with family members than time spent on the Internet at work? Table 7.3 presents the findings from the multivariate regression analysis of effect of Internet use, differentiated by use at home and use at work, on active time spent with friends, family, colleagues, and time spent alone.

---

12   The tradeoff with TV time and Internet time is likely to be exaggerated in our data due to the hardware constraints of our online data collection technology: in households without prior Internet connection, where the TV set-top box installed for online survey administration serves as the only Internet access, simultaneous Internet and TV use is difficult or impractical.

Table 7.3 Home versus work Internet use

| | Active time with … | | | | | | | |
| | Family | | Friends | | Colleagues | | Time alone | |
	β	t	β	t	β	t	β	t
(Constant)	532.73	13.83***	381.20	13.58***	116.55	3.62***	457.94	9.45***
Education	1.24	1.03	0.20	0.23	-0.18	-0.18	-1.01	-0.67
Male	-30.26	-4.75***	19.56	4.21***	16.75	3.14**	-1.93	-0.24
Married	100.29	11.21***	-35.06	-5.38***	-13.09	-1.75	-34.94	-3.10**
African–American	-18.17	-1.78	6.64	0.89	13.65	1.60	-10.31	-0.80
Hispanic	-5.44	-0.49	-7.78	-0.97	5.28	0.57	1.48	0.11
Asian and other	-19.35	-1.35	-5.88	-0.56	21.44	1.78	6.30	0.35
Age	3.08	1.71	-5.02	-3.83***	-1.54	-1.02	1.61	-0.71
Age-squared	-0.05	-2.34*	0.05	3.06**	0.01	0.29	0.01	0.38
Weekday	-94.36	-13.13***	-38.01	-7.26***	5.67	0.94	82.78	9.16***
Live alone	-84.57	-7.96***	-18.00	-2.33*	-12.91	-1.45	89.86	6.72***
Single parent	35.74	2.96**	-12.79	-1.45	-11.33	-1.12	-14.78	-0.97
TV time	-0.01	-0.58	-0.18	-11.99***	-0.05	-3.00**	-0.22	8.32***
Sleep time	-0.33	-18.77***	-0.17	-13.09***	-0.08	-5.59***	-0.40	-18.00***
Work time	-0.38	-31.84***	-0.12	-13.54***	0.37	36.68***	0.08	5.58***
Time online at home	-0.50	-10.49***	-0.16	-4.60***	-0.07	-1.75	0.66	11.05***
Time online at work	0.00	0.01	-0.07	-0.89	-0.47	-5.58***	0.60	4.72***
Adjusted R-square	0.30		0.09		0.28		0.17	
F	154.73		35.87		136.95		71.68	
N	5,738		5,738		5,738		5,738	

* p < 0.05, ** p < 0.01, *** p < 0.001.

Table 7.3 shows that distinguishing Internet use by location makes the statistical relationships stronger and clearer. As the displacement model predicts, Internet activity appears to come directly out of time spent actively engaging with others. Home use comes out of time with family and friends, and office use comes from time with co-workers. As is immediately apparent in the first equation, *only* time spent on the Internet "at home" has any impact on time spent with family. Once the number of hours spent at work (for pay) has been taken into account, the amount of Internet use at work has absolutely no impact on time spent face-to-face with family members. This is consistent with the displacement hypothesis. Home is the critical environment where users face the direct tradeoff between Internet/email use and actually "being with" with family. The relationship is identical, though substantively weaker, for time spent with friends.

For the relationship between location of Internet use and time spent with co-workers, the dynamics are different, though entirely equivalent. As shown in table 7.3, the amount of Internet use at work affects *only* the amount of time spent with colleagues. When work time is in the equation, the amount of time spent on the Internet at work has a major negative impact on time spent face-to-face with colleagues. The individual who works 40 hours a week with one hour of Internet use each day can expect to spend 2.5 additional hours a week in isolation from fellow workers. Internet and email clearly deliver a superior and more efficient communication medium for business, but human interactions in the office – whether gossiping, deliberating, or mentoring – may concurrently be sacrificed.

Time spent using Internet/email both at home and at work also plays a substantial role in increasing time spent alone, the complement of social time. The last equation in table 7.3 demonstrates that for every minute spent on the Internet at home, time spent alone increases by 40 seconds (35 seconds for Internet use at work). These findings are all the more impressive because we simultaneously control for marital status, living totally alone, amount of TV viewing, and hours spent at work yesterday. Additionally, time on Internet/email is more highly correlated with time spent alone than either work or TV time. Internet use, more than almost any other activity, isolates people from simultaneous active engagement with others. One simply cannot be engaged with others while being engaged on the Internet.

Interestingly, time on TV is related positively and significantly to time spent alone. Given the frequent comparisons between the

Internet and TV with regard to tradeoffs in time, we detour slightly to compare this particular relationship.

Internet versus TV

Many have written about the deleterious effects of television on sociability inside and outside the home (Robinson and Godbey, 1997; Putnam, 1995). We believe that the Internet has much more isolating potential than TV. Television is fundamentally different from Internet use in that the TV can easily retreat from the foreground of attention to background noise. Activities, even interpersonal ones, can occur while the television is on. In many homes, the TV is always on and may shift from the foreground to the background while other activities take place.

The Internet, on the other hand, is an interactive device and is, therefore, a more demanding activity. Unlike TV, the Internet is necessarily user-driven. While interruptions can certainly still occur, it is much more difficult for the Internet to become a background activity. Furthermore, TV sets are often in central locations in the home – living rooms or family rooms, for example – while computers are often in more private spaces where interruptions are less likely to occur. It also seems much less likely for Internet use to be a group activity, while TV, at the very least, invites several family members to watch together.

Figure 7.1 shows evidence of the uniquely isolating effects of the Internet. It presents a bar chart comparing those who watched TV yesterday to those who used the Internet yesterday. It shows the percentages, within each group, of people who report that at least some of each activity was done alone, with others passively present, or actively engaging in the activity with others. We can clearly see the fundamental difference between TV viewing and Internet/email as primary activities. Of those people who watched TV yesterday, only 39 percent watched TV alone at some point. Of those who used the Internet yesterday, by contrast, 64 percent used the Internet alone at some point. At the opposite end of the spectrum, we see that a full 59 percent of those who watched some television report that they watched some of it actively with others, while only 10 percent of Internet users report that any of their Internet use on the previous day was done actively with others.

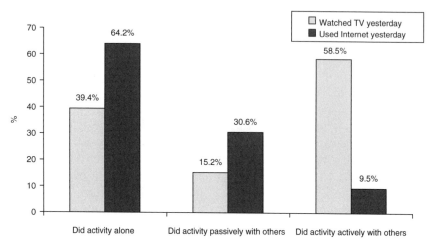

Figure 7.1   Sociability of Internet versus TV
Note: For those who spent time on TV, N = 3,304. For those who spent time online, N = 757. Percentages can sum to greater than 100% because categories are not mutually exclusive.

Internet Use and Leisure: Weekdays versus Weekends

For most people, the weekend presents at least a partial respite from work and household duties. The weekend typically holds many more discretionary moments in the day, in which individuals can choose how they wish to spend their time and with whom they wish to spend it. Certainly not all weekend time is leisure time because of certain chores, family, and social obligations, and even an occasional work deadline, but most people have many more opportunities to spend time with friends and family during the weekends than during the weekdays. If our hydraulic model is correct, the amount of home use of the Internet should have its strongest impact on time spent with both friends and family on weekends, when people have more freedom to choose what they wish to do and with whom, if anyone, they wish to spend their time.[13]

13   It should be remembered that weekday vs. weekend was used as a dichotomous variable in our prior analyses so as not to distort or bias the results. But using a dummy variable as a control averages out its impact across the sample. Here we are looking for structural changes in the strength of the relationship by splitting the sample into weekday vs. weekend.

The relationship between time spent on Internet/email at home on the weekend and time spent with family is the strongest we have yet observed: the coefficient is 0.755 (see table 7.4). This means that for every minute spent online, there is a corresponding 0.48 seconds less spent with family members. Given that the average American spends 14.3 minutes on the Internet over the weekend, there is a 26 percent, or 11-minute, average loss of time spent with family on Saturdays and Sundays. The weekday regressions, too, find that time spent on the Internet at home has a strong, significant, negative influence on time spent with family members, but the strength of the relationship is only about half of what it is on weekends, once again offering support for the hydraulic hypothesis.[14]

Email and Sociability: A Closer Look

Many believe email to be the most important breakthrough in human communication since the invention of the telephone. From the perspective of businesses, email may be responsible for much of the reported growth in productivity that accompanied the last decade of rapid economic expansion, and organizational intranets are perhaps the most important set of advancements in business communication since the introduction of the telegraph and telephone. There is also robust evidence that many people use and enjoy email. The UCLA study, for instance, reports that 76 percent of email users report checking their email at least once each day. The Pew study finds that 49 percent of Internet users report exchanging email with family members at least once per week, and that 49 percent of email users report that they would "miss it a lot" if they no longer had email available to them. Email reduces the personal costs and risks of written communications: less committal than a letter and less personal than a telephone conversation. Exchanging greetings and information by email rather than by phone is also much easier when many time zones separate the correspondents and make synchronous communication difficult. There also appears to be a greater motivation to send email, knowing that it will be received in a matter of minutes, rather than days.

14   Similarly, we replicated the analysis for time of day (evening Internet use vs. daytime Internet use). We find that primetime (6–8pm) Internet use has a much stronger effect than Internet use during the rest of the day.

Table 7.4 Weekend versus weekday Internet use

	Active time with							
	Family		Friends		Colleagues		Time alone	
	β	t	β	t	β	t	β	t
Weekend regressions								
(Constant)	660.28	8.43***	523.23	8.39***	-16.25	-0.36	390.45	4.50***
Education	-1.00	-0.38	1.81	0.87	1.94	1.27	-2.31	-0.80
Male	-40.71	-3.04**	27.23	2.55*	10.95	1.40	18.98	1.28
Married	124.95	6.56***	-54.42	-3.58***	-13.94	-1.25	-34.55	-1.64
African–American	-27.19	-1.36	10.45	0.66	-5.45	-0.47	6.15	0.28
Hispanic	4.85	0.22	-12.45	-0.71	9.33	0.73	9.69	0.40
Asian and other	-12.94	-0.42	10.51	0.43	24.38	1.36	-8.42	-0.25
Age	4.32	1.17	-9.56	-3.25**	1.92	0.89	0.79	0.19
Age-squared	-0.07	-1.50	0.10	2.77**	-0.02	-0.98	0.01	0.29
Live alone	-101.14	-4.35***	-35.74	-1.93*	-5.03	-0.37	105.10	4.08***
Single parent	20.30	0.82	-34.23	-1.73	-6.57	-0.45	15.26	0.56
TV time	-0.19	-4.56***	-0.22	-6.67***	-0.04	-1.66	0.33	7.08***
Sleep time	-0.46	-13.36***	-0.24	-8.79***	-0.04	-1.97*	-0.30	-7.70***
Work time	-0.62	-23.28***	-0.20	-9.43***	0.37	24.16***	0.26	8.81***
Time online at home	-0.75	-6.59***	-0.36	-3.94***	-0.11	-1.65	0.96	7.60***
Time online at work	0.17	0.39	-0.03	-0.09	-0.42	-1.65	0.51	1.07
Adjusted R-square	0.35		0.11		0.31		0.19	
F	58.17		13.49		47.85		25.49	
N	1,645		1,645		1,645		1,645	

Weekday regressions

(Constant)	387.33	9.15***	281.97	9.53***	181.25	4.41***	565.72	9.85***
Education	1.60	1.23	−0.47	−0.52	−0.98	−0.78	−0.31	−0.18
Male	−29.51	−4.21***	15.09	3.08**	20.01	2.94**	−8.27	−0.87
Married	90.41	9.268**	−28.92	−4.23***	−11.14	−1.17	−36.11	−2.72**
African–American	−15.46	−1.34	6.18	0.76	23.14	2.06*	−19.48	−1.24
Hispanic	−10.12	−0.82	−5.98	−0.69	2.63	0.22	−1.44	−0.09
Asian and other	−20.21	−1.29	−11.18	−1.02	20.44	1.34	11.03	0.52
Age	1.71	0.86	−3.38	−2.43*	−3.23	−1.67	2.86	1.06
Age-squared	−0.03	−1.43	0.03	1.84	0.02	0.88	0.00	−0.04
Live alone	−78.38	−6.84***	−11.97	−1.49	−16.52	−1.48	84.74	5.45***
Single parent	43.11	3.23**	−6.04	−0.65	−11.59	−0.89	−28.23	−1.56
TV time	0.09	3.82***	−0.16	−9.66***	−0.06	−2.50*	0.15	4.75***
Sleep time	−0.26	−13.14***	−0.13	−9.45***	−0.10	−5.28***	−0.45	−16.76***
Work time	−0.29	−22.52***	−0.09	−9.59***	0.37	28.93***	0.02	1.02
Time online at home	−0.39	−7.89***	−0.09	−2.66**	−0.06	−1.23	0.55	8.17***
Time online at work	−0.04	−0.46	−0.07	−1.03	−0.48	−5.07***	0.63	4.81***
Adjusted R-square	0.22		0.06		0.25		0.14	
F	78.02		16.72		92.06		44.09	
N	4,091		4,091		4,091		4,091	

$* \ p < 0.05$, $** \ p < 0.01$, $*** \ p < 0.001$.

Despite these tremendous social benefits there remains an empirical question as to the effect of personal email on the amount of time spent face-to-face with friends and family. Are those who communicate via email more gregarious people? Are they generally better communicators across all media, and with richer social lives in every sphere, as some of the prior literature suggests? Is personal email activity positively associated with spending more time with friends and family as the UCLA and Pew studies suggest? Or is time spent on email, even personal email, subject to the same "hydraulic" constraints as other types of time spent on the Internet? Table 7.5 provides some of the answers.

The results of our now familiar equations in table 7.5, instead of examining time spent online as the main independent variable, initially examine the impact of the number of work versus personal emails (sent and received) on time spent in active face-to-face interactions.[15] Within each column of our dependent variables – time spent with family, with friends, with business associates, and alone – we then estimate a second regression by adding total Internet time to the equations in order to identify any remaining effects of email beyond being a simple surrogate measure for time spent online.

The number of work-related emails has no significant impact on the amount of time people spend with their family members (nor should it). However, for each personal email message sent or received, there is almost a 1-minute drop in the amount of time spent with family. With a mean of 13 personal emails sent and received, that amounts to about 13 minutes less of family time a day, or about 1.5 hours a week. The results in the right panel of each dependent variable column suggests, however, that the separate analysis of email provides no new information. Once we control for total time on the Internet, the effect of email becomes statistically insignificant and the coefficient for total time on the Internet is unaltered from prior equations. When time online is included in the regression, number of personal emails likewise has no significant effect on the amount of time spent with friends, colleagues, or time alone. In other words, these email measures do indeed appear to be simple proxies of time spent online.

As we have demonstrated repeatedly, Internet use is time spent alone, and personal emails too are fundamentally time spent online.

---

15   If the respondent reported more than 100 emails, their number was truncated to 100 to control for outlier influence on the regression coefficients.

Table 7.5 Email analysis by content

	Active time with . . .							
	Family		Friends		Colleagues		Time alone	
	β	β	β	β	β	β	β	β
Constant	524.81***	538.55***	361.99***	365.77***	70.76*	75.24*	510.84***	490.74***
Education	1.66	1.76	1.46	1.48	0.61	0.64	-2.52	-2.66
Male	-38.96***	-34.03***	17.22***	18.57***	13.86*	15.47**	8.21	1.01
Married	106.46***	101.95***	-35.06***	-36.30***	-16.02*	-17.50*	-33.34**	-26.74*
African–American	-20.34	-22.31*	8.30	7.75	19.76*	19.11*	-12.65	-9.76
Hispanic	-12.25	-7.15	-10.09	-8.69	12.70	14.36	7.89	0.44
Asian and other	-19.50	-16.07	-9.44	-8.49	26.70*	27.82*	3.89	-1.13
Age	3.17	3.08	-4.67**	-4.70**	-0.13	-0.16	-0.46	-0.32
Age-squared	-0.05*	-0.05*	0.04*	0.04*	-0.01	-0.01	0.04	0.03
Weekday	-96.90***	-92.22***	-38.22***	-36.93***	3.80	5.32	85.80***	78.95***
Live alone	-83.96***	-82.96***	-19.11*	-18.83*	-21.38*	-21.06*	95.59***	94.13***
Single parent	29.63*	28.73*	-14.48	-14.73	-21.15*	-21.45*	-3.24	-1.92
TV time	0.00	-0.01	-0.19***	-0.19***	-0.05*	-0.05*	0.21***	0.23***
Sleep time	-0.33***	-0.34***	-0.17***	-0.18***	-0.07***	-0.07***	-0.41***	-0.38***
Work time	-0.37***	-0.38***	-0.11***	-0.11***	0.37***	0.37***	0.07***	0.09***
Work emails	-0.50	-0.27	-0.62***	-0.56**	-0.19	-0.11	1.11***	0.77*
Personal emails	-0.98***	-0.30	-0.31	-0.12	0.02	0.24	1.33***	0.33
Time online		-0.44***		-0.12***		-0.14***		0.64***
Adjusted R-square	0.29	0.30	0.09	0.09	0.27	0.28	0.15	0.17
F	129.65	128.58	31.53	30.39	117.49	111.53	55.53	59.76
N	4,960	4,960	4,960	4,960	4,960	4,960	4,960	4,960

* $p < 0.05$, ** $p < 0.01$, *** $p < 0.001$.

The benefit of email in helping individuals stay in touch people whom they would otherwise not contact is a benefit in its own right, separate from the face-to-face interactions considered here – but it comes at the expense of some of those "real" personal interactions. We do not mean to trivialize the importance of having another means of reaching out to individuals; users who spend their days online or check email very frequently certainly do have a new supplemental way to reach out. This social benefit of email, however, does not mean that these individuals' social interactions and relationships on email are the same as traditional personal interactions. Nor does it mean that email will have effects comparable to traditional social activity.

While email may promote a sort of "contact" with friends and family, that virtual contact may be more superficial than that which occurs in more personal settings. Interpersonal communications have a purpose far different from the instant, asynchronous control and coordination purposes of email in the business world. Face-to-face and even telephone communication among friends, family, and colleagues, are as much about affect as information. Although empathy, tenderness, reassurance, flirtation, sadness or happiness can be written into email messages, email misses the eye contact, body language, facial expressions, vocalization, hugs, tears, embraces, and giggles that are the fundamentals of our socio-emotional evolution. Email thus appears to imply an obvious tradeoff between quantity and quality of social interaction. Similarly, even the most gratifying telephone calls cannot replace a personal visit. To be sure, writing letters, too, is an activity between self and mind, all the while imagining the recipient and his or her reactions. Email, in this regard, is more like letter writing, as we have understood it through the ages – but in a more casual mode, with less emotional involvement or exposure.

Unquestionably, more detailed analysis of the context of email communication is something to consider as we continue to pursue the manner in which Internet use affects sociability.

Conclusion

We find that the results from our recent time diary survey offer strong support for the "hydraulic" or displacement hypothesis – and no evidence to support the efficiency hypothesis. On average, the more time spent on the Internet, the less time spent with friends, family, and colleagues. Alternatively, the more time spent on the Internet, the more time spent alone. Even more compelling, perhaps, are our findings regarding location of Internet use. Internet use at home has a strong negative impact on time spent with friends and family, while Internet use at work is strongly related to decreased time with colleagues (but has little effect on social time with friends and family). Similarly, Internet use during the weekends is more strongly related to decreased time spent with friends and family than Internet use during weekdays, for it is during these hours – evenings and weekends – that time on Internet and email competes most directly with time spent in face-to-face interactions with others. And while email undeniably brings some social benefits, time on the Internet – email or otherwise – is fundamentally time spent alone.

It is always difficult in an empirical work, primarily designed to test competing hypotheses, to stand back and rise above the specific findings to consider the larger social implications. The concerns we raised in this chapter, and with the original SIQSS study about the potential social consequences of the Internet in reducing the density and heterogeneity of face-to-face social relationships, were not predicated on the Internet as a single social invention, but rather, as part of on ongoing sociological trend. Much of the social history of the nineteenth and twentieth centuries is a story about the dissolution of community and family connections – the social support networks that linked individuals to one another and to their communities. It is a central theme among those who study modernity. Moreover, much of this decline in face-to-face social connectedness has arisen from one technological change after another. The mobility made possible by the railroad and automobile also made possible sub-urbanization and the atomistic bedroom community. Likewise, airplanes, highway systems, and the telephone made it feasible for the modern corporation to exist in many places at once, and, consequently, made it necessary to move its managers (if not its workforce) from one city or country to another. In stark contrast with just a generation or two ago, it is common for people to be born and raised in one community but live their adult lives in another (or a series of several others). All of these innovations have had unintended negative effects on lifelong family, extended family, and friendship ties. Siblings, parents, children, aunts, cousins, grade school and high school friends are no longer present daily, and they no longer form the lifelong support and friendship groups they once did.

To be clear – we are not offering a doomsday warning about any immediate threat of extinction of face-to-face interpersonal relationships. Rather, we want to emphasize that Internet use – whatever its possible benefits to virtual communities – involves a time tradeoff in which time on the Internet at home and (to a lesser extent) at work displaces face-to-face social interactions. We do believe that it is particularly important to be conscious and aware of this tradeoff because Internet use in American society continues to grow as bandwidths and connection speeds increase. Moreover, in a world of DSL and beyond, increasing commuting times, and ever more expensive office space, workers may increasingly be telecommuting from home – and yet another rich source of human interactions will have slipped away. Coupled with the fact that single member households are the fastest growing type of American household, it seems possible that a growing portion of the population may soon live as well as work alone. Within such a context, the unintended social consequences of the Internet become more pervasive.

The human psyche evolved under a much richer and enduring social world – kith, kin, and community were both daily and enduring interactions of life. The Internet is not, by any means, itself responsible for the transformation to a world in which people spend more of their waking hours alone than with others. But, the Internet follows a long string of technological innovations that each have had the unintended consequence of reducing the number and meaningfulness of emotionally gratifying face-to-face human interactions.

Appendix 7.1

Respondents were asked about their *main* activities during six randomly selected hours, distributed over the course of the previous day ("yesterday"). Respondents could select from a list of 13 main activities, or enter one of their own:

Main activity	Definition
Work (for pay)	Any work or business activity
Education	In class, doing homework, other school activities
Housework	Cleaning, chores, cooking, home finances
Childcare	Feeding, clothing, playing with children
Errands/shop	Groceries, appointments, offices
TV/Internet/ media	Watch TV, Internet/email, read
Social outing	Socializing, parties, events, movies

Recreation/ hobby	Sports, fitness, outdoors, hobbies, games
Organizations	Church, volunteer, or club activities
Travel	All traveling and commuting (including walking)
Eat	Meals or snacks
Dress/wash	Dress, shower, bathe, groom
Sleep	Sleep, nap, or doze
Other	*User defined*

Respondents were then asked to identify their *specific* activity categorized under the main activity they selected. For instance, if they selected housework as their main activity the were asked to select among the following specific activities: cooking, kitchen cleanup, laundry, repairs, yard work, internet/email, telephone calls, plant/pet care, paperwork, organize/unpack, other (*user defined*).

For each of the main activities, Internet/email, telephone, computer work was included as an option. Thus, we are able to pick up Internet use whether that use was, say, educational, professional, or simply recreational use. The respondents were then asked *how long* the activity lasted (10 mins to 1 hour+), *where* the activity took place (home, other's home, office/factory, vehicle, store, outdoors/park, school, restaurant/bar, theatre/stadium, other), and *with whom* the activity was performed (whether alone, with other people present but not participating, or with others participating – and in addition, the specific individuals participating: spouse, children, other family, roommates, friends, business associates, strangers, or other).

Respondents were finally asked if they did *anything else* at the same time as this (*primary*) activity. Respondents were provided with a checklist of 21 (*secondary*) activities (including user defined other) and were asked to identify any or all that they did at the same time as the main activity. After each sampled hour, respondents were shown a diary form that was filled out and completed based on their answers, to facilitate orientation.

After finishing these questions for each of the activities recorded in each of their six randomly selected hours, respondents were then asked a series of follow-up questions including estimates of the amount of Internet use, content and number of emails (personal vs. work related), type of Internet use (for example, type of websites browsed), amount of TV watching, sleep, and social interactions. Besides providing supplemental information, these follow-up questions provided an additional measure of our independent and dependent variables (and analyses were replicated using these measures with identical results) as well as an accuracy checking mechanism for the time diary estimates.

References

Franzen, A. (2000). Does the Internet make us lonely? *European Sociological Review*, 16(4), 427–38.

Hafner, K. (2000). Working at home today? *New York Times*, November 2. Available online at:
http://www.nytimes.com/2000/11/02/technology/02TELE.html

National Public Radio, Kaiser Family Foundation and Kennedy School of Government (2000). Survey shows widespread enthusiasm for high technology. *NPR Online Report*, 3.

Nie, N. H. (1999). Tracking our techno future, *American Demographics*, 21(7), 50–2.

Nie N. H. (2001). Sociability, interpersonal relations, and the Internet: reconciling conflicting findings. *American Behavioral Scientist*, 45(3), 420–35.

Nie, N. H. and Erbring, L. (2000). *Internet and society: a preliminary report.* Stanford, CA: Stanford Institute for the Quantitative Study of Society.

Nie, N. H. and Sackman, H. (1970). *The information utility and social choice.* Montvale, NJ: AFIPS.

Pew Internet and American Life Project (2000). Tracking online life: how women use the Internet to cultivate relationships with family and friends, *Online Internet Life Report*, 10 May.

Putnam, R. (1995). Bowling alone: America's declining social capital, *Journal of Democracy*, 6, 65–78.

Putnam, R. (2000). *Bowling alone: the collapse and revival of American community.* NY: Simon and Schuster.

Robinson, J. and Godbey, G. (1997). *Time for life: the surprising ways Americans use their time* (2nd edn). University Park, PA: Pennsylvania State University Press.

Robinson, John P., Kestnbaum, M., Neustadtl, A., and Alvarez, A. (2001). *Information technology, the Internet and time displacement.* Revision of paper presented at the Annual Meetings of the American Association of Public Opinion Research in Portland, OR, May 2000.

Salaff, J., Wellman, B., and Dimitrova, D. (1998). There is a time and place for teleworking. In R. Suomi, P. Jackson, L. Hollmén and M. Aspnäs (eds), *Teleworking Environments: Proceedings of the Third International Workshop on Telework* (pp. 11–31). Turku, Finland: Turku Center for Computer Science General Publication No. 8.

Steiner, G. A. (1963). *The people look at television: a study of audience attitudes.* New York, NY: Knopf.

UCLA Center for Communication Policy (2000). *The UCLA Internet report: "Surveying the digital future."* Available online at: www.ccp.ucla.edu

Wellman, B., Quan Haase, A., Witte, J., and Hampton, K. (2001). Does the Internet increase, decrease, or supplement social capital? Social networks, participation, and community commitment. *American Behavioral Scientist,* 45(3), 436–55.

8

The Internet and Other Uses of Time

John P. Robinson, Meyer Kestnbaum, Alan Neustadtl, and Anthony S. Alvarez

Abstract

The Internet represents a departure from previous communication technologies, combining features of interpersonal and mass communication. The "functional equivalence" argument in media studies predicts decreases in both types of communication activities as Internet use increases. A 1998–9 national sample of 948 individuals aged 18–64 who completed 24-hour time diaries of all daily activities is used to test this hypothesis.

Few differences in either interpersonal or mass communication activities are found across Internet users and non-users. Nor are there significant decreases in other free-time activities. As has been the case of television, certain personal care and other non-free time activities are most different. This raises questions about whether the Internet acts more to enhance communication behaviors rather than to displace behavior (which has been the case for television).

Authors' Note

Grateful acknowledgement is given to the National Science Foundation, Office of Science and Technology for support through grants NSF01523184, NSF0086143, and SBR-9602058 and the Alfred P. Sloan Foundation's Working Families Program. This chapter is a revision of a paper presented at the Annual Meetings of the American Association of Public Opinion Research in Portland, OR, May 2000. Please direct all correspondence to Dr John P. Robinson (robinson@socy.umd.edu).

The Internet and Other Uses of Time

Modern IT has not arrived in a social vacuum, so it is instructive to see how the technologies that preceded it played a role in changing communication and other behavior patterns. When television first appeared in the US, it significantly affected other mass media. Audiences abandoned their radio sets, movie theaters closed, and magazines that featured the type of content now prevalent on television (such as the light fiction in *Colliers* or the *Saturday Evening Post*) ceased publication. The general explanation offered for these effects was in terms of the *functional equivalence* of television content to alternative media outlets, in which television provided their functions (and maybe others) more efficiently for its audiences (Weiss, 1970).

When full-time diary data covering all daily activity became available in the 1965 Multinational Time-Budget Research Project, it was clear that television's apparent impact did show declines in the most functionally equivalent activities (Szalai, 1972). Thus, radio listening was about 60 percent lower, movie attendance 50 percent lower, and book and magazine reading 40 percent lower among television owners compared to non-owners (Robinson, 1972). Probably because of television's inability to provide newspaper-like content in its early stages (especially at the local, community level), it is important to note that newspaper reading was virtually the same among television owners and non-owners.

Of more direct sociological concern, however, was the difference in the social lives of individuals and families after acquiring a television: the out-of-home socializing of television owners (compared to non-owners) was lower by 34 percent and conversation in the home lower by 26 percent, with the combined average 1.6 hours per week of lower social life in these two activities being almost as large as the average 2.2 hour decline in other mass media use. Applying the functional equivalence argument, this suggests that television was performing some of the functions of social life.

Perhaps surprisingly, but notably, "other" free-time activities were not as significantly different between television owners and non-owners. That provides further support for the functional equivalence argument – that those displaced activities are the ones for which the technology offers a functionally equivalent alternative.

Arguing against the hypothesis, on the other hand, were the differences in time use that extended beyond these free-time activities. This is particularly the case for the personal care activity of sleep, which was on average 1.4 hours per week lower among television owners (Robinson, 1972). The extent to which viewers were in a sleep-like condition while watching could have been a factor here, along with the sheer novelty that kept one up after bedtime – to this day, television is often equated with rest and relaxation, activities associated on the continuum from sleep to fully awake activity.

Even larger differences were found for *secondary* activities reported in the diaries: there was a 22-minute decline in secondary radio listening, offset by an almost equivalent *rise* in secondary television viewing. Television owners also spent 10–30 minutes less time alone, and 20 minutes more time with their spouses and children (thus perhaps inadvertently promoting a new form of family life, as described in Robinson, 1990). In line with the declines in socializing with friends and relatives, contact time with friends and neighbors was also lower for television owners. Equally impressive differences were found by location, with television owners spending more than half an hour more time at home indoors than non-owners, mainly at the expense of spending time in one's yard, in other people's homes, and on the streets. Television did bring people home, but indoors rather than outdoors.

While many of the activity differences in the 1965 study do not fit under the functional-equivalence umbrella, most of the changes predicted by it are found. Time spent on both personal and mass media activities were lower among television owners. The question, then, is whether the present data on the Internet will continue to show the same patterns of change.

Previous Studies of the Impact of the Internet

Speculation and publications on the impact of the Internet have tended to focus on social life, personal communication, and mass communication. Again, the content of communication in both types of channels can be seen to be equivalent, and more effectively or attractively conveyed by the Internet, so that we should expect to find the same sorts of changes as found for television. Specifically, we should find declines in both print and broadcast media usage among Internet users, along with declines in visiting and socializing both at home with one's family and in the homes of others.

Two widely publicized studies of early Internet impact reported results consistent with that hypothesis. Both Kraut et al. (1998) and Nie and Erbring (2000) suggest declines in some aspects of social life. Kraut et al. (1998), for example, found:

> Greater use of the Internet was associated with small, but statistically significant declines in social involvement as measured by communication within the family and the size of people's local social networks, and with increases in loneliness, a psychological state associated with social involvement. Greater use of the Internet was also associated with increases in depression. Other effects on the size of the distant social circle, social support, and stress did not reach standard significance levels but were consistently negative. (1998, p. 1017)

The samples used in both studies are quite different and each had its strengths and weaknesses. The Kraut et al. (1998) study followed a panel of 73 families (169 individuals) from eight neighborhoods of Pittsburgh, Pennsylvania, across a one- to two-year period. These longitudinal data were used to examine causal relationships, in this case causal relationships between "social involvement, and certain likely psychological consequences of social involvement."

The Nie–Erbring sample, on the other hand, was drawn from a national panel sample of approximately 4,113 respondents in 2,689 households. While exploring causal relationships is more difficult with these data since they come from only one point in time, they were not limited to any single geographic area and the sampling error, given the large sample size, is relatively small (±2.5 percent). These data, then allow greater generalization than the Kraut et al. data.

However, studies that have used a less ambitious set of questions and research designs have produced somewhat different results. For example, the Pew Center for Public Opinion Research has been conducting national surveys related to the public's use of IT since 1995, with periodic updates on certain questions on almost a monthly basis. Its most complete surveys were conducted in 1995 and 1998 with samples of more than 3,600 respondents. One value of the Pew data is that they asked intensive questions about media and social activity "yesterday" (as well as more generally), which allows respondents to report on a time period which is most recent in memory, as well as clearly defined in temporal terms.

Based on the 1995 Pew data, Robinson, Barth, and Kohut (1997) found that 1995 Internet and IT users were significantly *more* likely to use print media, radio newscasts, and movies than non-users, and not significantly less likely to be television viewers of either entertainment or news content. These results are robust, remaining after statistical controls for gender, age, education, income, race and marital status were introduced to the analyses.

Moreover, these results were largely replicated by Robinson and Kestnbaum's (1999) analysis of the 1997 SPPA national data, which asked about weekly computer use for hobbies or recreational uses, rather than about news media use. Again, the self-described general IT users were significantly more likely to read books and literature and to use the media for arts content, even after control for other factors. Users were also more likely to attend arts events, and to participate in a wide variety of other free-time activities, like attending sports events or movies, playing sports, and doing home improvements. They were no more likely to do gardening or to watch less television.

In their examination of the more recent 1998 Pew data, Robinson et al. (2000) showed that the proportion of Internet users had grown in the interim since 1995, and with somewhat different results. Print media use, while still greater, was no longer significantly greater among Internet users. Television use was lower among users, but it was not significantly lower after introducing multivariate controls.

Overall, then, these analyses provide little support for time displacement following the functional equivalence argument and the earlier results for television.

These re-analyses of large national survey data, then, provide little support for Internet users being any less active in their usage of other news or entertainment media, or for their being less social either in their behavior or their attitudes toward others. However, these results are based on single-time surveys that have limited capacity to identify causal processes or to monitor dynamic relations between IT use and other activity, as the Kraut et al. study did.

Data, Measures, and Methods

The time-use evidence in the present chapter is based on a comprehensive set of diary data on how people spend their time, as reported by a 1998–9 national probability survey of 948 respondents aged 18 to 64 in the form of 24-hour recalled time diaries. These diary data, which have been collected on irregular bases in more than twenty western countries since 1965 (with some measurements extending back to the 1920s) provide unique insights into how daily life is structured and has been changing (Robinson and Godbey, 1999).

In these diary accounts, cross-section samples of the public (such as in 1998–9) provide complete accounts of what they do on a particular day – and for the full 24 hours of that day. Respondents in these surveys take the analyst step-by-step through their day, by describing when they went to bed, when they got up and started a new day, and all the things they did throughout the day until midnight of that day. In the 1998–9 accounts, the people also reveal where they spent their day, who they were with, and the other activities they were doing. Because they represent complete accounts of daily activity, diary data collected from cross-section samples allow one to generate estimates of how much time is spent on the complete range of human behavior – from work to free time, from travel to time spent at home.

Target respondents in this national random digit dial survey were selected using the "next birthday" method between March 1998 and March 1999, with all days of the week and all seasons of the year equivalently covered. All sampled numbers were called at least twenty times. Respondents who refused were recontacted by specialized interviewers, who obtained conversion for about a fifth of such respondents. Overall, 56 percent of eligible respondents completed a diary account of their previous day's activities. The data were weighted to 1998 Census Bureau distributions on gender, age, race, education and region and to adjust for the small differences by day of the week. For each activity in the diary, the respondent reported the start and end time, a description of the activity, the secondary activity, the location of the activity and the persons present during the activity. Further details of the diary method used are shown in appendix 8.1.

New activity codes 56 (Internet use), 57 (computer games) and 58 (other computer use) were developed for this study and, like other activities, coded in minutes per day. They were then converted into hours per week after weighting the data to ensure that all days of the week were equally represented. Thus, the sampling units involved are in terms of person-days rather than persons, since the latter were only interviewed about a single day. The data are weighted by demographic variables to match 1998 US Census Bureau characteristics (for example, gender, age, education, income, and employment status).

Multivariate controls for demographic differences were introduced by using Multiple Classification Analysis or MCA (Andrews, Morgan, and Sonquist, 1973). MCA is a multiple regression based statistical technique implemented in SPSS that provides differences in categorical predictor variables that make the statistical effects of other predictors equal. Its value in the present analysis is that it allows one to show comparable differences across different categories of each independent measure.

Internet/IT use, the major independent measure, was operational-ized in two different ways to capture both single-day and longer-term use. First, a single-day ("yesterday") measure was developed from the time diary, defined by whether respondents explicitly mentioned Internet or IT usage as either a primary or secondary activity in the diary for the previous day. The longer-term (general) measure was developed from responses to a questionnaire item asking how many hours a week they generally used the Internet. While 39 percent (of the 984) respondents said they used the Internet during a typical week, only 8 percent reported such usage "yesterday" in the diary.

Results

Comparison of the daily diary activities of Internet users vs. non-users is shown in table 8.1 for the yesterday IT users ($n = 77$) and in table 8.2 for general Internet users ($n = 381$). Even though the time-diaries are only for a single day, data are shown in extrapolated weekly hours that add to 168 hours per week to aid in interpretation. Statistically significant bivariate differences ($\alpha < 0.05$) were then subjected to MCA adjustment for the demographic control factors and these results are shown in the final columns of tables 8.1 and 8.2.

Turning first to comparisons for free-time activities in table 8.1, it can be seen that, consistent with earlier Internet studies, "yesterday" Internet users reported reading more than non-users (books, maga-zines, and newspapers). While their television viewing is lower, it is not significantly lower. "Yesterday" Internet users socialize and visit with people outside the home for two hours less than non-users on average; however, their conversation inside the home (with family and by phone) is an hour greater on average. After MCA adjustment, neither difference is statistically significant, thus not supporting the functional equivalence argument.

What differences are found? To which activities do Internet users devote less time to offset the average of 10.8 hours they spend on the Internet? Once that nearly 11 hours of weekly extrapolated Internet use is taken into account, it can be seen that the total amount of *free time* is about 8 hours greater for Internet users than non-users. Moreover, there are hardly any differences in specific activities like religion, organizations, fitness activity, and hobbies. None are statisti-cally significant, except for the greater amount of time Internet users spend attending events.

Table 8.1 Differences between IT users and non-users on a "yesterday" basis (hours per week)[a]

Non-free time activities	Non-IT (n = 852)	IT (n = 77)	IT difference	After MCA adjustment[b]	Free time activities	Non-IT (n = 852)	IT (n = 77)	IT difference	After MCA adjustment[b]
Work	29.9	31.4	1.5		Religion	0.8	1.4	0.6	
Commute	3.6	4.4	0.8		Organizations	1.0	0.9	-0.1	
Total work	33.5	35.8	2.3		Attend events	1.2	1.4	0.2	
					Social/visit	5.6	3.4	-2.2	
Housework	13.0	10.0	-3.0	-1.0[c]	Fitness	2.5	2.6	0.1	
Childcare	5.4	3.6	-1.8		Hobby	1.9	1.6	-0.3	
Shopping	6.3	4.7	-1.6						
Total family care	24.7	18.3	-6.4	-3.0[c]	Television	12.2	10.4	-1.8	
					Read	2.1	2.4	0.3	
Eat	7.7	7.3	-0.4		Stereo	0.2	0.0	-0.2	
Sleep	56.0	53.0	-3.0	-2.2[c]					
Personal grooming	9.7	8.3	-1.4		Conversation	5.7	6.4	0.7	
Total personal care	73.4	68.6	-4.8	-3.4[c]	Computer/Internet	0.0	10.8	10.8	10.0[c]
					Other	1.6	0.4	-1.2	
Education	1.6	4.1	2.5	-1.1[c]					
					Total free time	34.8	41.7	6.9	7.0[c]
Total non-free time	133.2	126.8	-6.4	-7.0[c]	**Total time**	168.0	168.0	0	
					Total travel	11.6	10.3	-1.3	

[a] Defined as use of IT on the diary day. [b] Controls for gender, age, education, employment status, and marital status. [c] Indicates the difference is statistically significant, p < 0.05.

Table 8.2 Differences between Internet users and non-users on a "general" basis (hours per week)[a]

Non-free time activities	Non-Internet (n = 552)	Internet (n = 381)	Internet difference	After MCA adjustment[b]
Work	30.2	33.2	3.0	
Commute	3.3	4.2	0.9[c]	0.5
Total work	33.5	37.4	3.9[c]	2.1
Housework	13.7	11.3	−2.4[c]	−0.5
Childcare	5.6	4.7	−0.9	
Shopping	6.3	5.7	−0.6	
Total family care	25.6	21.7	−3.9[c]	−1.3
Eat	7.2	8.2	1.0[c]	0.8[c]
Sleep	57.0	53.8	−3.2[c]	−3.0[c]
Personal grooming	9.4	9.7	0.3	
Total personal care	73.6	71.7	−1.9	
Education	1.0	3.2	2.2[c]	1.5
Total non-free time	133.7	134.0	0.3	

Free time activities	Non-Internet (n = 552)	Internet (n = 381)	Internet difference	After MCA adjustment[b]
Religion	0.9	0.7	−0.2	
Organizations	1.1	0.9	−0.2	
Attend events	0.7	2.0	1.3	0.9[c]
Social/visit	5.6	5.2	−0.4	
Fitness	2.3	2.9	0.6	
Hobbies	2.2	1.4	−0.8	−1.0[c]
Television	13.4	10.0	−3.4	−2.3[c]
Read	1.7	2.7	1.0	1.0[c]
Stereo	0.2	0.2	0.0	
Conversation	5.5	4.9	−0.6	
Computer/Internet	0.4	3.2	2.8	2.6[c]
Other	0.3	0.0	−0.3	
Total free time	34.3	34.1	−0.2	
Total time	168.0	168.1	0.0	
Total travel	10.9	12.3	1.4	0.5

[a] Defined as an Internet user by self-report. [b] Controls for gender, age, education, employment status, and marital status. [c] Significant at $p < 0.05$ level.

Within *non-free-time* activities, the situation is reversed with "yesterday" Internet users spending about 8 hours on average less than non-Internet users on such necessary activities. Which of the non-free activities differ? First, the paid work hours of Internet users and non-users are basically the same. The groups do differ, however, in the amount of time spent on family care and personal care activities, with Internet users spending less time on both of them. In the case of family care, the largest difference is found for core housework activities, like cleaning and cooking, which is the only difference that is statistically significantly lower for Internet users. Nonetheless, childcare and shopping are both almost two hours lower among Internet users as well. That adds to almost seven hours weekly less overall family care. After MCA adjustment for family and other demographic background factors, however, that figure declines to three hours and is not statistically significant.

In the case of total personal care, Internet users spend about 5 hours less time per week than non-users. The biggest difference is the three hours less sleep reported by Internet users and this difference is still significant after MCA adjustment. Parallels to earlier results with television are thus apparent, with certain family and personal care activities being lower among Internet users.

Similar patterns are found in the comparisons of longer-term "general" Internet users and non-users shown in table 8.2. Perhaps because of the larger sample qualifying as users in this table, more comparisons are found to be statistically significant. Turning first to the mass media, it can be seen that the number of hours of reading is actually *higher* among Internet users and here significantly so. The three-plus hours lower average television viewing, drops to approximately two hours less after MCA adjustment, and that difference is also significant. However, when reading and television are combined, the overall media differences are less than an hour a week.

In terms of social life, both in-home and away socializing are lower for "general" Internet users, but by less than an hour a week – hardly evidence of a serious decline in social life. Differences in religious, organizational, and fitness activity are not significant. However, "general" Internet users spent almost three times more time attending social events. In contrast to table 8.1, the total free time hours of users and non-users are identical, even taking the greater IT use of Internet users into account.

In terms of *non-free* activities, the work hour differences between longer-term general users and non-users are again not statistically significant. Internet users again report less housework/family care and less sleep. As in table 8.1, the housework hour differences are not statistically significant after MCA adjustment. However, the three hours less sleep of Internet users here *is* statistically significant after MCA control, and is about the same magnitude and direction as shown in table 8.1.

In terms of overall mobility, "general" Internet users (long-term) spend more time traveling, but not significantly so. In, table 8.1 "yesterday" users also reported less travel.

Secondary activities

The diary method also records multi-tasking or "secondary" activities, activities that are done to the accompaniment of primary activities – such as watching television or talking while having a meal. Table 8.3 shows the six main secondary activities reported in the diaries, along with the total minutes of secondary activity (i.e., for these six as well as for all other secondary activities). Separate differences are shown for "yesterday" users on the left side of table 8.3 and for "general" users on the right side.

It can be seen that by far the most commonly reported secondary activity in table 8.3 is conversation – more than 5 hours per day on average. On the left-hand side of table 8.3, "yesterday" IT users reported talking only slightly more if examined on the basis of the daily diary. However, on the right-hand side, "general" Internet users reported significantly more conversation than non-users, a difference that was actually *larger* after MCA adjustment.

The next most frequent secondary activity was listening to radio, and here again, Internet users listened more than non-users. This difference was statistically significant after MCA adjustment for "general" users; but the reported difference was only slightly higher for "yesterday" users. For the other two secondary media activities – television and reading – there were no statistically significant differences either for "yesterday" or "general" users. Nor was there a significant difference for secondary activity childcare. On the final secondary activity, eating meals and snacks, the significantly greater meal time of ("general") Internet users was reduced and not statistically significant after MCA adjustment, much as was found for "yesterday" users.

Table 8.3 Internet usage differences in secondary activities, social company, and location (hours per week)

	Daily				General Internet			
	Non-IT users (n = 842)	IT users (n = 77)	Differences	MCA Adj.	Non-Internet (n = 522)	Internet users (n = 371)	Differences	MCA Adj.
Secondary activities								
Conversation	35.5	35.9	0.4		34.0	37.8	3.8[a]	4.2[a]
Radio	10.2	10.5	0.3		9.2	11.7	2.5[a]	2.0[a]
TV	5.4	5.8	0.4		5.7	4.8	-0.9	
Reading	2.2	2.2	0.0		2.1	2.6	0.5	
Child Care	2.2	2.7	0.5		2.5	2.1	-0.4	
Eating	5.7	6.0	0.3		5.0	6.8	1.8[a]	-0.9
Total (all)	61.2	63.1	1.9		58.5	65.7	7.2[a]	8.8[a]
Social company								
Time alone (while awake)	37.9	42.7	4.8		37.3	39.9	2.6	
Spouse	15.7	15.0	-0.7		15.2	16.4	1.2	
Children	18.3	11.0	-7.3[a]	-3.4	19.4	15.1	-4.3[a]	-1.3
Co-workers	21.8	24.0	2.2[a]	-1.5	8.5	12.8	4.3[a]	4.0[a]
Friends	9.8	9.2	-0.6		8.8	11.3	2.5[a]	0.3
Relatives	7.6	8.1	0.5		8.6	6.2	-2.4[a]	-1.2
Other	3.7	5.5	1.8		3.6	4.4	0.8	
Location								
At home	104.2	107.9	3.7		107.1	100.1	-7	4.2
Others' home	7.6	4.4	-3.2		7.2	7.5	0.3	

[a] Significant at $p < 0.05$ level.

The final entry in the first part of table 8.3 is for *all* secondary activities, that is, for the six activities just reviewed plus all other secondary activities. It can be seen that the overall multi-tasking time spent is greater for ("general") Internet users, and it is statistically significant after MCA adjustment. It is also statistically significant if all secondary activity except conversations is tabulated separately (not shown). While the differences are not as large for "yesterday" users, they are in the same direction. This suggests that Internet users are more involved in multi-tasking in general, perhaps a reflection of their busier lifestyles.

The second set of entries in table 8.3 shows time spent with different social partners. The first entry is for time spent alone while awake (thus excluding time spent at sleep). "Yesterday" Internet users reported spending about one-half hour more weekly time alone on average, on the diary day (not statistically significant before or after MCA adjustment). Moreover, "general" Internet users also spent about 3.8 hours more weekly time alone, a difference that is statistically significant.

Time spent with one's spouse and children is also lower, but again, not significantly so after MCA control for such factors as marital status and presence of children are introduced. Time spent with co-workers and with friends tends to be higher for "general" Internet users, although neither difference is statistically significant after MCA adjustment. There are no differences for time spent with others. In contrast, time with relatives is lower (for "general" users), but not after the introduction of statistical controls.

In general, then, despite their 20 to 40 minutes more time alone, there are few statistically significant "social contact" differences between Internet users and non-users after MCA adjustment. Part of this greater time alone may be due to their lower sleep time. Thus, there is no consistent evidence in these data that Internet users have impoverished social contacts relative to people who do not use the Internet. The slightly lower average times with children and relatives are offset by slightly greater average times with co-workers and friends.

The third and final set of entries in table 8.3 describe the average *total* time that the respondents spent at home and in others' homes. While "yesterday" Internet users spend more time at their own home and about one-half hour less time in others' homes, these differences are not significant. Moreover, the pattern is reversed when looking at the "general" Internet users. Thus again, no consistent patterns emerge from these results.

Summary

In this analysis of recent differences between the daily activities of IT users and non-users, little clear evidence of a pattern consistent with functional equivalence was found to parallel the 1965 comparisons between owners and non-owners of television. There was no evidence of IT users either making less use of the printed media or listening less to the radio. Indeed, if anything they made more use of these traditional media. There was evidence of less television usage, but this did not hold up in certain multivariate comparisons, nor for viewing as a secondary activity.

Nor did the other ways of using free time consistently and statistically differ across samples (for example, there was greater attendance at entertainment and cultural events). Internet users did not spend notably less time in social contact, and they were slightly more active in family or home communication and home phone calls. Overall, Internet users spent more time in conversation, significantly more in the context of general long-term Internet activity.

More consistent differences, surprisingly, were found for non-free time activities, like lower family care and personal care times among IT users. While some of these differences disappeared or were reduced significantly after adjustment for demographic predictors, some notable ones remained after these adjustments. In particular, the lower average sleep times of IT users is a robust finding. This would seem to be a difference not easily captured in terms of the functional equivalence argument.

The more active lifestyles of IT users are further suggested by their higher reporting of all secondary activities, and by their higher reports of social contacts with friends and co-workers. At the same time, IT users reported somewhat more time alone and less time with their children – but more time with friends and co-workers.

In terms of the historical and theoretical issues raised at the outset of this article, then, IT in its initial stages seems to depart from the massive displacement effects found with television and perhaps earlier media. Outside of displacing modest amounts of television or sleep time, Internet use seems more a "time enhancer"; people do not seem to be forced to give up other activities to accommodate it. Indeed, it may function like many home appliances and especially like the telephone in allowing one to be more productive in use of time, using print media for affirming information, or enriching old social networks with new or newly resurrected social contacts. Such differences, of course, could easily change as people increasingly accommodate to new technologies.

Appendix 8.1 Features of the Time Diary and a Sample Diary

The measurement logic behind the time diary approach follows from that employed in the most extensive and well known of diary studies – the Multinational Time Budget Study of Szalai et al. (1972). In that study, roughly 2,000 respondents from each of twelve different countries kept a diary account of a single day. The same diary procedures and activity codes were employed in each country in 1965. Respondents were chosen in such a way that each day of the week was equally represented (although only in the fall and spring seasons). In subsequent studies, all seasons of the year were represented.

Table A8.1 shows the diary filled out by one (non-Internet) respondent in the study. This respondent was watching television at midnight as the new day began and that she went to pick up her daughter between 12:15 and 12:30 a.m. She then got ready for bed and got to sleep at 12:50. She then woke up to make breakfast and lunches for her son and husband from 4 to 4:30 a.m. She then got ready for work and left at 4:55 a.m., arriving at 5:00 a.m. She took a work break at 8:00 for fifteen minutes with a friend who worked nearby. She returned to work and took fifteen minutes to eat lunch and then continued to work until 1:30 p.m., at which time she drove home, arriving home at 1:35. Here, she visited with a neighbor in the back yard for twenty-five minutes, before doing a marathon three and one-half hour house clean. She then went out to pick up her daughter from school, returning home to serve and eat supper until 8:00 p.m. and spent the next hour washing dishes and doing laundry. She watched television for seventy-five minutes and then went out to pick up her daughter from work. Returning at 10:30 p.m. she got ready for bed and was asleep by 10:45 p.m.

The task of keeping the diary may have some recall difficulties, but it is fundamentally different from that of making time estimates. The diary keeper's task is to recall all of the day's activities in sequence. This is likely to be similar to the way the day was structured chronologically for the respondent and to the way most people store their activities in memory. Rather than having to consider a long time period, the respondent need only focus attention on a single day

Table A8.1 Sample of completed time diary: female, cook, age 40, married with two children, Friday

What did you do?	Time began	Time ended	Where?	With whom?	Doing anything else?	Coded Prim'Sec'Min'With'Loc
Watch TV	12:00	12:15	Home	—	No	91'00'015'00'0
Went after daughter at work	12:15	12:30	Transit	Daughter	No	49'00'015'30'4
Got ready for bed	12:30	12:50	Home	—	No	40'00'020'00'0
Sleep	12:50	4:00	Home	—	No	45'00'190'00'0
Got up, made lunches for husband and son and also breakfast	4:00	4:43	Home	—	No	10'00'030'00'0
Got ready for work	4:30	4:55	Transit	—	No	40'00'025'00'0
Left for work (car)	4:55	5:00	Transit	—	No	09'00'005'00'4
Work	5:00	8:00	Restaurant	Employees	No	00'00'225'50'1
Coffee break	8:00	8:15	Restaurant	Friend	Talked	08'96'015'50'1
Work	8:15	12:00	Restaurant	Employees	No	01'00'225'50'1
Ate lunch	12:00	12:15	Restaurant	Employees	Talked	06'96'015'50'1
Work	12:15	1:30	Restaurant	Employees	No	00'00'075'50'1
Off work, drove home	1:30	1:35	Transit	—	No	09'00'005'00'4
Visited with neighbor	1:35	2:00	Yard	Neighbor	Talked	75'96'025'70'2
Cleaned house	2:00	5:15	Home	—	Radio	12'90'195'00'0
Went after daughter at school	5:15	5:45	Transit	Daughter	No	12'90'195'00'0
Took shower	5:45	6:00	Home	—	No	40'00'015'00'0
Made supper	6:00	6:25	Home	—	No	10'00'015'12'0
Ate supper	7:15	8:00	Home	Family	Talked	11'96'030'20'0
Did dishes	8:00	8:30	Home	Daughter	Talked	11'96'030'20'0
Washed clothes	8:30	9:00	Home	—	No	14'00'030'00'0
Sat down and watched TV	9:00	10:15	Home	Family	No	91'00'075'12'0
Went after daughter at work	10:15	10:30	Transit	Daughter	No	29'00'015'30'4
Got ready for bed	10:30	10:45	Home	—	No	40'00'015'00'0
Went to bed, sleep	10:45	12:00	Home	—	No	45'00'075'00'0

Table A8.2   Basic two-digit activity code

00–59 Non-free time

00–09 Paid work
- 00 (Not Used)
- 01 Main job
- 02 Unemployment
- 03 Work travel
- 04 (Not used)
- 05 Second job
- 06 (Not used)
- 07 (Not used)
- 08 Breaks
- 09 Travel to/from work

10–19 Household work
- 10 Food preparation
- 11 Meal cleanup
- 12 Cleaning house
- 13 Outdoor cleaning
- 14 Clothes care
- 15 Car repair
- 16 Other repair
- 17 Plant/garden care
- 18 Pet care
- 19 Other household

20–29 Childcare
- 20 Baby care
- 21 Child care
- 22 Helping/teaching
- 23 Talking/reading
- 24 Indoor playing
- 25 Outdoor playing
- 26 Medical care-child
- 27 Other child care
- 28 Dry clean
- 29 Travel/child care

30–39 Obtaining goods/services
- 30 Everyday shopping
- 31 Durable/house shop
- 32 Personal services
- 33 Medical appointments
- 34 Govt./financial services
- 35 Repair services
- 36 Other services
- 37 Other shopping
- 38 Errands
- 39 Travel/goods, services

40–49 Personal needs and care
- 40 Washing, hygiene, etc.
- 41 Medical care
- 42 Help and care
- 43 Eating
- 44 Personal care
- 45 Night sleep
- 46 (Not used)
- 47 Dressing
- 48 NA activities
- 49 Travel/personal care

50–59 Educational
- 50 Attend classes
- 51 Other classes
- 52 (Not used)
- 53 (Not used)
- 54 Homework
- 59 Travel/education

55–99 Free time

55–58 IT/library
- 55 Using library
- 56 Using the Internet
- 57 Playing games on a PC
- 58 Other PC use

60–69 Organizational
- 60 Professional/union
- 61 Special interest
- 62 Political/civic
- 63 Volunteer helping
- 64 Religious groups
- 65 Religious practice
- 66 Fraternal
- 67 Child/youth/family
- 68 Other organizations
- 69 Travel/organizational

70–79 Entertainment/social
- 70 Sports events
- 71 Entertainment
- 72 Movies
- 73 Theater
- 74 Museums
- 75 Visiting
- 76 Parties
- 77 Bars/lounges
- 78 Other social
- 79 Travel/social

80–89 Recreation
- 80 Active sports
- 81 Outdoor
- 82 Exercise
- 83 Hobbies
- 84 Domestic crafts
- 85 Art
- 86 Music/drama/dance
- 87 Games
- 88 Computer use games
- 89 Travel/recreation

90–99 Communications
- 90 Radio
- 91 Television
- 92 Records/tapes
- 93 Read Books
- 94 Magazines/etc.
- 95 Reading newspaper
- 96 Conversations
- 97 Writing
- 98 Think/relax
- 99 Travel/communication

(yesterday). Rather than working from some list of activities whose meanings vary from respondent to respondent, the diary keepers simply report their day's activities in their own words.

Automatic procedures were built into the diary recording procedures that are now conducted by Computer Assisted Telephone Interviewing (CATI) to ensure accurate reporting. Whenever respondents report consecutive activities that involve different locations, they are reminded that there needs to be some travel episode to connect them. Activity periods that last more than two hours automatically involve the probe, "Were you doing anything else during that time, or were you (activity) for the entire time?" As is apparent in table A8.1, all periods across the day must be accounted for in order that the diary account total to 1,440 minutes (or 24 hours).

As in earlier diary surveys, these largely open-ended diary reports are then coded using the basic activity-coding scheme developed for the 1965 Multinational Time Budget Research Project (as described in Szalai, 1972). As shown in outline form in table A8.2, the Szalai code first divides activities into non-free time activities (codes 00–54, 59) and free time activities (codes 55–8, 60–99); non-free activities are further subdivided into paid work, family care and personal care, and free time activities are further subdivided under the five general headings of computer usage, organizational activity, social life, recreation and communication. This division refers to the *usual* nature of different activities, even though *all* social life or media use may not be freely chosen by the individual, or that *no* work or housework has a leisurely component.

References

Andrews, F., Morgan, J., and Sonquist, J. (1973). *Multiple classification analysis.* Ann Arbor, MI: Institute for Social Research.

Kraut, R., Patterson, M., Lundmark, V., Kiesler, S., Mukhopadhyay, T., and Scherlis, W. (1998). *American Psychologist*, 53(9), 1017–31.

Nie, N. H. and Erbring, L. (2000). *Internet and society: a preliminary report.* February 17, 2000 report. Stanford Institute for the Quantitative Study of Society.

Robinson, J. P. (1972). Television's impact on everyday life: some cross-national evidence. In E. Rubinstein et al., *Television and social behavior* (pp. 410–31). Washington, DC: Government Printing Office.

Robinson, J. P. and Godbey, G. (1999). *Time for life: the surprising ways Americans use their time.* University Park: Pennsylvania State University Press.

Robinson, J. P., Barth, K., and Kohut, A. (1997). Personal computers, mass media, and use of time. *Social Science Computer Review*, 15, 65–82.

Robinson, J. P., Kestnbaum, M., Neustadtl, A., and Alvarez, A. (2000). Mass media use and social life among Internet users. *Social Science Computer Review*, 18(4), 490–501.

Robinson, J. P. and Kestnbaum, M. (1999). The personal computer, culture and other uses of free time. *Social Science Computer Review*, summer, 209–16.

Szalai, A. (ed.) (1972). *The use of time: daily activities of urban and suburban populations in twelve countries*. In collaboration with P. E. Converse, P. Feldheim, E. K. Scheuch, and P. J. Stone. The Hague: Mouton.

Weiss, R. (1970). Effects of mass media of communication. In G. Lindzey and E. Aronson (eds), *Handbook of social psychology*, vol. 5 (pp. 77–195). Reading, MA: Addison-Wesley.

9

Everyday Communication Patterns of Heavy and Light Email Users

Janell I. Copher, Alaina G. Kanfer, and Mary Bea Walker

Abstract

Detailed 7-day, 24-hour-a-day communication diaries completed by leaders of a midwestern community were used to compare the communications of 23 heavy (35 or more messages a week) and 22 light (7 or fewer messages a week) email users. Email use supplemented communication beyond the level of the other media, especially for work communication. Heavy email users communicated more frequently to more people, although they neither spent more time communicating (except for work communication) nor communicated with more unique others than light email users. Heavy email use altered overall communication style across both work and non-work content (smaller percentages for several other media across several variables), and a slight displacement of phone contacts was noted in the "personal" and "other business" communication of heavy email users. Results suggest that email finds a niche in everyday communication but also support perceptions of e-stress associated with heavy email use.

Authors' note

This project was funded by Nortel. We would like to express our sincere appreciation to Joel Riphagen, Aileen Kelly Schwab, and Lecheng Li for their research assistance; to Caroline Haythornthwaite for her many helpful comments and suggestions on earlier versions of this manuscript; and to Uzma Jalaluddin, Uyen Quach, and Barry Wellman for editorial assistance.

Email is speedier than postal mail, more convenient than telephone tag, and more efficient than other means of group coordination (see Sproull and Kiesler, 1991), and it is largely because of these advantages that email is becoming a fixture of everyday life, with almost half (42 percent) of Americans now reading email daily (UCLA CCP, 2000).

Despite all this, references to this "killer application" (Choney, 2000), to a people "decidedly short on time" (Weil and Rosen, 1997), and to "e-stress" (Pitney Bowes Inc., 2002) abound, hinting at a dark side to this relatively recent technology. Is email a blessing or a curse?

This study attempts to clarify the impact of email on communication and everyday life through 7-day, 24-hour-a-day examination of communication behavior. Communication diaries were kept for one week by a group of community leaders. Results are compared for those for whom email use was a significant feature of daily life (35 or more emails a week) and those for whom it was not (7 or fewer emails a week). Although previous investigations give insight into email use, this study crosses both communication contexts (work, home, and community) and contents (work, personal, and non-work-related business) and provides a unique opportunity for looking at the impact of email technology on everyday communication.

Impact of email use on communication

Are heavy email users, whether due to personal choice or circumstance, simply heavier communicators than others – or is heavy reliance on email associated with decreased use of other communication media? Although previous research generally suggests that heavy email use has been associated with a higher overall communication rate (for example, Rice and Shook, 1988), the precise relationship between email use and employment of other communication media remains an enigma.

Some studies have found heavy email use to be associated with heavy use of all communication media. For example, Kraut and Attewell (1997) found that bank employees who used any one communication medium heavily also tended to use others heavily and that relationships among individual media were positive though weak. Similarly Bikson and Eveland's (1990) computer-using volunteer task force had a greater number of communications of all types (except unscheduled meetings) than their non-electronic task force. Based on studies of a university research group and distance learners, Haythornthwaite and Wellman (1998) and Haythornthwaite (2000, 2001) found communication pairs to add communication media as they communicated more heavily, starting with unscheduled face-to-face, adding on scheduled face-to-face, and then adding on email (see also chapters by Quan-Haase and Wellman, and Chen, Boase, and Wellman). Communicators with closer work or social ties communicated more often and used more media to communicate.

However, other studies have suggested that, instead of increasing all forms of communication, email displaces the use of other media. In Finholt, Sproull, and Kiesler's (1990) laboratory study, groups using more computer-mediated communication used other media (face-to-face, phone, and memo) less. Nyce and Groppa's (1983) bank employees claimed email replaced the phone and, to a lesser extent, memos, Rice and Case's (1983) managers stated that it reduced phone calls more than paper communication, and Rice and Shook's (1988) aerospace employees reported use of email to slightly decrease initiation of paper, letters, and phone calls.

The results at home parallel the inconsistency of those in the workplace. For example, 83 percent of those surveyed by Katz and Aspden (1997) stated that time spent with friends and family face-to-face and by phone had not changed since they began using the Internet (which would include email) while 6 percent claimed that such time had increased and 6 percent claimed that such time had decreased. However, 48 percent of Dimmick, Kline, and Stafford's (2000) sample of Columbus residents claimed that they used the phone less since adopting email, while 49 percent noted little to no change, and 3 percent claimed to use the phone more.

So what can one conclude? Certainly, it seems that email use is associated with a higher rate of communication in general. However, the precise impact of email on the frequency with which other communication media are employed may vary with communication content and context as well as the strength of the relationships among the communicators (see Haythornthwaite, 2001, 2002). Moreover, most of this evidence is based upon self-reports a long time after the reported events (and sometimes even estimates of relationships between behaviors such as current email use and past telephone use), and these may simply be inaccurate (see Bernard, Kilworth, and Sailer, 1981; Bernard, Kilworth, Kronenfeld, and Sailer, 1984). This study not only includes all communication contexts and contents but also avoids recall issues by capturing use as it occurs by using communication diaries.

Patterns of media use

A similar issue in communication media use relates to the proportionate use of the various media: that is, communication patterns.[1]

1   We exclude from this review the multitude of investigations that have studied solely "media perceptions" and/or "media choice," with no consideration of actual communication media use, to avoid confusion of attitudes and intentions with communication behavior.

How often are the various communication media used and where does email sit in the communication patterns of everyday users?

Both Zack's (1994) 18-member newspaper editorial staff and Haythornthwaite and Wellman's (1998) university research group used mainly email and face-to-face meetings to communicate. The editorial staff also used occasional telephone conversations and rare memos. The university research group also used occasional phone, fax, and videoconferencing contacts. Wijayanayake and Higa (1999) found that members of distributed work groups used email and telephone for about 96 percent of their job-related communications, and fax, audioconferencing and videoconferencing for the remaining 4 percent of their communications (face-to-face and paper communications were not mentioned).

However, once again, other studies show a different profile. Dobos's (1992) key informants from for-profit organizations reported media use to include 44.3 percent face-to-face communications, 17.4 percent written memos, and 38.3 percent communication technologies. Of the latter 45.6 percent were audioconferencing, 40.2 percent fax, 3.7 percent phone, and a mere 5.4 percent email. Zeffane and Cheek's (1995) telecommunications employees also reported more frequent use of verbal communication rather than written or computer-based communications, with computers being the least used medium (no percentages given).

Although these results vary greatly in the proportion of communications via different media, particularly email (with content and context variation in the communications and self-report data once again likely factors for the variation), they are consistent in that all but one indicate face-to-face communication to be most frequent. This study seeks to expand upon these results, again through examination of actual communications across contexts and contents.

Email use in life context

Although face-to-face communications have been seen to be the predominant mode of communication, we also see in several studies a high use of email, a trend that is increasing with the spread of Internet access. As email use becomes more common, a consideration of importance in the conceptualization and study of this mode of communication is whether communicators are more appropriately characterized as intrinsically email users versus non-users – or simply as those who have encountered and adopted a lifestyle that includes email versus those who have not (as yet). Therefore, we consider what it is that leads individuals to use email.

Research has shown computer training, age, ethnicity, income, and "technophobia" to be related to use of technological devices (Rosen and Weil, 1995) and education and income to be associated with the decision to use (or not to use) the Internet (GVU, 1998; Miller and Clemente, 1997). Predictors of actual email use have been limited to skill (Trevino, Webster, and Stein, 2000) and experience (see studies in this volume), favoring the second hypothesis – that heavy email use is more a situational than personal issue.

On an organizational level, we find that the decision to use (or not to use) email has been shown to be influenced by group, organizational, social, and transnational structures (Contractor and Eisenberg, 1990; Poole and DeSanctis, 1990; Rice, 1994). Factors affecting use have included use by relevant co-workers (Steinfield, 1986; Schmitz, 1987), attitudes of supervisors toward email (Trevino et al., 2000), use by supervisors (Schmitz and Fulk, 1991), attitudes of co-workers toward the usefulness of email (Schmitz and Fulk, 1991; Trevino et al., 2000), managerial encouragement of email use (Markus, 1994; Shin, Higa, Sheng, and Ide, 1999; Wijayanayake and Higa, 1999), and classroom norms (Haythornthwaite, 2000). Additionally, email use has been found to be related to job type, whether secretarial, analyst, or director (Sullivan, 1995) or director versus manager (Carlson and Davis, 1998; Rice and Shook, 1990). Communication tasks and group use have been found to account for significant portions of the variance in number of emails sent (tasks explained 18 percent of the variance, and group use 10 percent; Soe and Markus, 1993).

While these results correspond well with the social network analyst's view of "structured social relationships" as "a more powerful source of sociological explanation than personal attributes of system members" (Wellman, 1988, p. 31), we find that we cannot ignore individual variables in our efforts to unravel the factors in email use (or non-use). Such elements are needed to explain Eveland and Bikson's (1987) findings that department, program, and professional group membership did not significantly predict messaging behavior and that there were individual differences not explained by whether others in the individual's communication network used email. They postulated that use by such individuals might be explained by media style preferences. Fulk and Boyd (1991) concurred with this notion, stating that organizational culture, policies, and resource constraints as well as rational and social influence factors and individual media style need to be considered in media choice.

The important point to draw from all this is that although individuals may come to a given communication situation with some definite preferences, they are also embedded in a local context in which they may find themselves swept up in prevailing usage norms and situational media availability to such an extent that their own media preferences come to represent only a small, but noticeable, influence on their actual media use. Not so strangely, this notion of the individual being swept up into email use by their social network is in keeping with expectations and results based on diffusion of innovations research (Rogers, 1995; see also Haythornthwaite and Wellman in the introduction to this volume).

Although the phenomenon of heavy versus light email use is in itself worthy of comparison, it also appears that we may consider a group of light email users as a rather fair representation of heavy email users if they had not become involved in their current, heavily email using social networks. Our approach, then, is, first, to explore whether the two groups (heavy and light email users) are comparable to the heavy and light email users of former investigations and, second, to compare the communication patterns of our heavy and light email users. The latter comparison is achieved through addressing the following specific questions:

1　How does heavy email use affect frequency of use of other media? Do heavy and light email users differ in frequency of communication, time spent in communication, and number of communication partners across: (a) all communications, (b) all non-email communications, (c) individual communication media (face-to-face, phone)?

2　How does heavy email use affect proportionate use of other media? Considering only non-email communications, do heavy and light email users differ in the percentage of communications they conduct, percentage of time spent communicating, and/or percentage of communication partners communicated with (a) face-to-face, (b) by phone, etc.?

3　How does heavy email use affect communication style? Considering all communications, do heavy and light email users differ in the percentage of communications they conduct, percentage of time spent communicating, and/or percentage of communication partners communicated with (a) via email, (b) face-to-face, (c) by phone, etc.?

4   Does frequency of use (see 1), proportionate use (see 2), and/or communication style (see 3) of heavy and light email users differ for (a) work, (b) "business" other than work, and (c) personal communications?

Participants, Data Collection, and Analysis

Participants

Study participants were recruited from a mailing list of 424 community leaders obtained from a county chamber of commerce in a small midwestern American city in spring 1997.[2] This population was selected to increase similarity of participants in educational and income levels, two factors on which Internet users differ from others (see GVU, 1998; Clemente, 1998). To increase homogeneity regarding length of email usage, all university personnel (who would have had earlier access to email and the Internet) were excluded a priori from the study. The remaining names were randomly ordered, and contacted by telephone. In this initial call, participants were asked to estimate separately the number of email messages they sent and received on an average weekday and sent and received on an average weekend day. They were also asked if they would be willing to participate in a more detailed data collection effort. The total number of reported emails per week ranged from 0 to 2,130 messages. Phone calls continued until 30 heavy email users (over 100 reported per week) and 30 light email users (under 10 reported per week) agreed to participate in the study. A total of 117 subjects completed this initial phone survey, yielding 60 study recruits.

Though recruits were offered both a cash stipend and a personalized communication report in exchange for study participation, participants reported the latter as the greater incentive, increasing our confidence in the accuracy of their communication diaries. Participants were guaranteed confidentiality and signed informed

2   An earlier investigation of these data is reported in Kanfer (2000). Though the earlier report considered some social issues not addressed in this study, it did not provide the comprehensive comparison of media use and examination of interrelationships among media attempted here.

consent forms in accordance with the university's Institutional Review Board.

Of the 60 study recruits, 5 dropped out before data collection was completed. Following data collection, the data were reviewed to compare diary reported email use to that reported during the initial phone contact. Because of inconsistencies in these two reports, heavy and light email use was redefined and only study participants whose phone and diary reports matched in terms of "heavy" versus "light" classification were retained for the current study.

The resulting group of heavy email users consists of 23 community leaders who used email 35 or more times per week and 22 light email users who used email 7 or fewer times a week. The "heavy" email users reported an average of 7.61 years of email use before this study; of the "light" email users, 15 had never used email (and did not use it during the study week), and 7 reported using email for an average of 2.0 years before this study.

Data collection

Data were collected in three parts: (1) a weeklong communication diary, (2) a follow-up social network survey about the participants' communication partners, and (3) a face-to-face interview to collect demographic and other information.

Diaries were used to obtain a record of all communications (Conrath, Higgins, and McClean 1983). Study participants were asked to record "all communications involving the transmission of information beyond a simple greeting" with the sole exception of broadcast communications such as presentations, lectures, and concerts. Email broadcasts were included in the diaries, but are excluded from the current analyses because comparable data are not available for other media.[3]

For each communication, study participants recorded the approximate length of the communication; whether the content of the communication was primarily "business," "personal," or "other business"; and the communication medium used (face-to-face, phone, phone

---

3   Broadcast communications were defined as "any information transmitted to a group of people, at least one of whom you do not know, without intention of initiating a two-way conversation."

message, fax, paper, and email).[4] "Work" content was defined as "all communication which relates to your job in any manner." "Other business" was defined as all communications relating to the conduct of business which is not connected to your job (such as communication with cashiers, waiters, bank tellers, doctors, and so forth as well as communication with family members regarding this personal business). "Personal" content included "all non-work, non-business communication."

Communications recorded in the diaries included those inside and outside the work environment as well as both weekday and weekend communications, 24 hours a day for one full week. Participants recorded as many as possible of the names of people involved in all one-to-one communications, all group real-time communications, and delayed group communications in which they were the sender of the communication. When they did not know a name, they were asked to use descriptive words that would help them remember the person involved. If they were the recipient of a delayed group communication, they were to record only the sender's name.

Study participants were given the choice of recording communication data in a paper diary or in a hand-held personal digital assistant (PalmPilot™ by US Robotics). Thirty of the participants used the Palmpilot to enter data for at least part of the week, and one participant, who had a physical impairment, used a cassette recorder to enter data. The remaining 24 participants recorded all their communication data in a paper diary.

Following the week of recording details of each communication, participants were given a self-administered survey about each of their communication partners or *alters*. For each alter, they recorded the type(s) of relationship(s) they had with that alter, when they had first become acquainted, and the relative location of their home to that of the alter (same town, same state, and so on). A final phase of data collection included a face-to-face interview in which demographic and other data on the participants were recorded. In addition, each participant completed a personality assessment (EASI-11, Buss, and Plomin, 1975) that included five questions for each of three components of temperament: activity, sociability, and impulsivity.

---

4   Participants also recorded online real-time communications. However, these are excluded here because they comprised only about 0.1 percent of the recorded, non-broadcast communications.

Analyses

T-tests[5] were used to compare heavy email users to light email users across all communications, all non-email communications, and for each of six media (face-to-face, phone, phone message, fax, paper, and email) for five measures: (1) number of communications; (2) time spent communicating; (3) number of named and unnamed communication alters (including duplicates, that is, alters were counted each time the participant communicated with them); (4) number of named communication alters, including duplicates; and (5) number of unique, named alters (each alter counted once and only once).

Next, percentages were calculated for communication media use as measured by each of the five variables for each of the six communication media across (1) all non-email communications (to examine the impact of heavy email use upon proportionate use of other communication media) and then (2) all communications (to examine the impact of heavy email use upon overall communication style). T-tests comparisons were also run on these percentages.

Finally, these analyses were re-run for each of the three content areas separately: work, other business, and personal communications.

Results

Participant characteristics and overall communication behavior

Were our study participants and their communication behavior comparable to those of previous investigations? Several preliminary analyses were run to make this determination.

Whereas previous studies found 39 percent of bank employees' (Kraut and Attewell, 1997) and about 75 percent of managers' (Mintzberg, 1973; Rice and Shook, 1990) workdays spent on communication, our participants averaged 21.2 hours on work-related communication (53 percent of an 8-hour workday). Given that 60 percent

5   Initially, correlations were calculated among the six media for the five media use variables. Based on low correlations in both this study and Kraut and Attewell's earlier (1997) study (as well as the sometimes negative relationships in our own study and some other studies), we decided that a series of t-test analyses, reflective of the relative independence of the six types of media use, would best serve the purposes of this study.

of these participants were managers, this figure seems in line with communication patterns found in previous studies. Moreover, our participants were comparable to those of other studies in that they reported more communications face-to-face than for any other media (see patterns of media use) and our heavy email users communicated more frequently than our light email users (see impact of email use).

As noted earlier, previous investigations also suggest that heavy and light email users differ in job variables and may, based on studies of technology and Internet use, differ in age and education (see email use in life context). In this study, heavy email users did tend to work in different places (X^2 (3) = 21.899, p < 0.05) as well as to have different sorts of positions (X^2 (2) = 14.422, p < 0.05) than light email users. Heavy email users worked more often than light email users in education and information related industries (65 percent versus 9 percent, X^2 (1) = 15.069, p < 0.01) and less often in government and law offices (4 percent versus 41 percent, X^2 (1) = 8.696, p < 0.01) or in small business (13 percent versus 46 percent, X^2 (1) = 5.750, p < 0.05). There was no difference in proportions working in the banking industry. Heavy email users were more often in information technician and research positions (35 percent versus 0 percent, X^2 (1) = 9.307, p < 0.01) and less often in public service positions (4 percent versus 41 percent, X^2 (1) = 8.696, p < 0.01). There was no difference in the proportions in management positions.

As might be expected, heavy email users tended to be younger (means of 41 versus 52, t(43) = 4.252, p < 0.01) and more educated (65 percent versus 27 percent having a masters degree, X^2 (1) = 6.505, p < 0.05) than light email users. The two groups did not differ in gender or marital status. Only one of the three personality variables (impulsivity) even approached significance, with heavy email users scoring a mean of 13.4 on a scale of 5 to 25 (based on 5 items scored from 1 [defined as "a little"] to 5 [defined as "a lot"]) compared to 11.4 for light email users (t(43) = −1.833, p < 0.10).

In summary, these results confirm an equivalence between our study participants and their communication behaviors and that of previous investigations.

Email use

All but one comparison of email use between heavy and light email users showed significant differences between the groups. Heavy users had greater numbers and percentages of communications, time spent communicating, and alters than light email users (all comparisons significant at $p < 0.05$) for all communication types except the total number of "other business" alters (which yielded $p < 0.10$).[6]

Media use for all communications

Heavy email users differed from light email users not only in email use but also in having significantly higher numbers of communications and numbers of alters (both total and named; see table 9.1).[7] Daily communications averaged 400 versus 275 for heavy versus light email users ($t(43) = -2.843$, $p < 0.05$). These communications involved an average of 692 total alters for heavy email users versus 411 for light users ($t(43) = -3.637$, $p < 0.05$) and 493 versus 341 named alters ($t(43) = -2.827$, $p < 0.05$) for heavy versus light email users.

Heavy email use had little impact on the proportionate use of other communication media (percentages excluding email), with the only difference between heavy and light email users that approached significance being a slightly greater percentage of phone communications for light email users than for heavy email users (24 percent versus 19 percent, $t(43) = 1.745$, $p < 0.10$). However, heavy email use had several effects on overall communication style (percentages including email). Light email users had significantly greater percentages of face-to-face (64 percent versus 52 percent, $t(43) = 2.994$, $p < 0.05$) and phone (24 percent versus 14 percent, $t = (43)$ 3.769, $p < 0.05$) communications as well as a greater percentage of fax communications at near significance (0.0128 percent versus 0.0069 percent, $t(43) = 1.809$, $p < 0.10$). Light email users also had significantly greater percentages of total alters with whom they communicated via these three means of communication than did heavy email users (73 percent versus 55 percent

6 Sample size in all cases for both these and the following analyses was 45 except for those analyses involving percentages of "other business" communications. In these cases three study participants were dropped from the analyses because percentages could not be calculated since they had reported no "other business" communications for the study week.

7 Numbers in tables do not always sum precisely due to rounding as well as because of a small number of communications for which no mode was recorded. Additionally, the percentages of unique alters for the individual media total greater than 100 percent because alters could and often were contacted via more than one medium.

Table 9.1 Communication media usage by heavy versus light email users across all communications

Email use	No. of communications		Communication time		No. of alters		No. of named alters		No. of unique alters	
	Light	Heavy	Light	Heavy	Light	Heavy	Light	Heavy	Light	Heavy
Mean										
All media	275 (141)	400 (152)[a]	3,183 (947)	3,504 (928)	411 (165)	692 (331)[a]	341 (162)	493 (197)[a]	160 (61)	179 (67)
Non-email media	275 (141)	303 (137)	3,182 (947)	3,286 (938)	410 (164)	484 (209)	340 (161)	374 (172)	160 (60)	142 (67)
Face-to-face	177 (104)	214 (115)	2,722 (819)	2,879 (805)	292 (112)	362 (165)	240 (122)	282 (157)	88 (31)	81 (50)
Phone	64 (40)	53 (27)	352 (313)	291 (172)	65 (42)	55 (29)	65 (42)	54 (28)	45 (28)	34 (16)
Phone message	15 (19)	18 (17)	22 (29)	29 (29)	16 (19)	19 (19)	15 (19)	18 (17)	11 (12)	11 (9)
Fax	4 (4)	3 (3)	10 (11)	13 (21)	4 (4)	3 (3)	4 (4)	3 (3)	3 (4)	2 (2)
Paper (excl. fax)	13 (13)	13 (14)	58 (54)	67 (117)	31 (70)	43 (82)	14 (15)	15 (16)	12 (11)	11 (10)
Email	0 (1)	96 (47)[a]	1 (2)	218 (138)[a]	0 (1)	208 (219)[a]	0 (1)	119 (71)[a]	0 (1)	37 (12)[a]
Mean %: all communications										
All media	100	100	100	100	100	100	100	100	100	100
Face-to-face	64 (13)	52 (13)[a]	86 (08)	82 (07)	73 (12)	55 (17)[a]	70 (12)	56 (14)[a]	69 (12)	59 (13)[a]
Phone	24 (12)	14 (06)[a]	11 (07)	08 (03)	16 (08)	09 (05)[a]	20 (10)	12 (05)[a]	33 (13)	27 (09)[b]
Phone message	05 (04)	04 (03)	01 (01)	01 (01)	04 (04)	03 (03)	04 (04)	04 (03)	08 (07)	09 (07)
Fax	01 (01)	01 (01)[b]	00 (01)	00 (00)	01 (01)	00 (01)[a]	01 (01)	01 (01)	02 (03)	02 (02)
Paper (excl. fax)	05 (04)	03 (03)	02 (02)	02 (03)	06 (10)	05 (06)	04 (03)	03 (03)	08 (07)	08 (07)
Email	00 (00)	25 (11)[a]	00 (00)	07 (04)[a]	00 (00)	27 (17)[a]	00 (00)	25 (12)[a]	00 (00)	31 (12)[a]
Mean %: non-email communications										
Non-email media	100	100	100	100	100	100	100	100	100	100
Face-to-face	64 (13)	69 (13)	86 (08)	88 (06)	73 (12)	75 (13)	70 (12)	74 (13)	69 (12)	70 (11)
Phone	24 (12)	19 (08)[b]	11 (07)	09 (03)	16 (08)	13 (08)	20 (10)	16 (07)	33 (13)	32 (12)
Phone message	05 (04)	06 (04)	01 (01)	01 (01)	04 (04)	04 (04)	04 (04)	05 (04)	08 (07)	11 (09)
Fax	01 (01)	01 (01)	00 (00)	00 (00)	01 (01)	01 (01)	01 (01)	01 (01)	02 (03)	02 (02)
Paper (excl. fax)	05 (04)	04 (03)	02 (03)	02 (03)	06 (10)	07 (09)	04 (03)	04 (03)	08 (07)	10 (08)

Standard deviations are in parentheses. [a] $p < 0.05$, two-tailed; [b] $p < 0.10$, two-tailed.

for face-to-face, 16 percent versus 9 percent for phone, and 0.0094 percent versus 0.0044 percent for fax, $t(43) = 4.015$, 3.501, and 2.136, respectively, $p < 0.05$). Finally, light email users had greater percentages of named alters and unique, named alters with whom they communicated face-to-face (70 percent versus 56 percent for named and 69 percent versus 59 percent for unique alters, $t(43) = 3.654$ and 2.659, respectively, $p < 0.05$) and by phone (20 percent versus 12 percent for named and 33 percent versus 27 percent for unique, $t(43) = 3.599$, $p < 0.05$, and 2.024, $p < 0.10$, respectively) but not by fax. Heavy email users, as expected, had greater percentages of email communications, time spent communicating, and alters (all three measures of alters).

Media use for "work" communications

Comparing the means for work communications showed much the same pattern as had the comparisons for "all" communications. However, in addition to having significantly more work communications, total alters, and named alters, heavy email users spent somewhat more time in work communications than light email users (table 9.2). Daily work communications averaged 234 versus 150 for heavy versus light email users ($t(43) = -2.645$, $p < 0.05$). These communications involved an average of 435 versus 219 total alters, and 281 versus 180 named alters for heavy versus light email users ($t(43) = -3.294$ and $t(43) = -2.643$, respectively, $p < 0.05$). Heavy email users spent 1,437 minutes in these communications compared to 1,100 minutes for light email users ($t(43) = -1.768$, $p < 0.10$).

Though heavy email use had no impact on the proportionate use of other media for work-related communications (percentages excluding email), the results for communication style (percentages including email) were very similar to those across all communication contents. Light email users had greater percentages of face-to-face (57 percent versus 43 percent, $t(43) = 2.901$, $p < 0.05$), phone (27 percent versus 15 percent, $t(43) = 3.292$, $p < 0.05$), and fax communications (0.0195 percent versus 0.0098 percent, $t(43) = 1.754$, $p < 0.10$) as well as greater percentages of total number of alters with whom they communicated via these means (66 percent versus 48 percent for face-to-face, 18 percent versus 10 percent for phone, and 0.0150 percent versus 0.0064 percent for fax, $t(43) = 3.349$, 2.756, and 1.997, respectively, $p < 0.05$ in the first two cases and $p < 0.10$ in the third) than did

Table 9.2 Communication media usage by heavy versus light email users across "work" communications

Email use	No. of communications		Communication time		No. of alters		No. of named alters		No. of unique alters	
	Light	Heavy	Light	Heavy	Light	Heavy	Light	Heavy	Light	Heavy
Mean										
All media	150 (104)	234 (109)[a]	1,100 (690)	1,437 (587)[b]	219 (137)	435 (283)[a]	180 (120)	281 (135)[a]	96 (57)	118 (61)
Non-email media	150 (104)	167 (98)	1,100 (690)	1,276 (550)	218 (137)	285 (174)	180 (120)	195 (107)	96 (56)	89 (59)
Face-to-face	84 (66)	101 (63)	809 (557)	992 (421)	133 (78)	186 (127)	112 (79)	125 (73)	44 (27)	43 (39)
Phone	41 (37)	38 (29)	210 (248)	186 (157)	42 (37)	39 (30)	42 (37)	38 (29)	31 (25)	25 (17)
Phone message	10 (13)	13 (15)	15 (18)	22 (26)	11 (13)	14 (16)	11 (13)	14 (15)	8 (9)	9 (9)
Fax	3 (4)	2 (3)	9 (11)	12 (21)	3 (4)	3 (3)	3 (4)	2 (3)	3 (4)	2 (2)
Paper (excl. fax)	11 (12)	11 (14)	51 (51)	61 (112)	28 (70)	41 (83)	11 (13)	13 (16)	9 (9)	9 (9)
Email	0 (1)	67 (40)[a]	0 (1)	161 (153)[a]	0 (1)	151 (198)[a]	0 (1)	86 (71)[a]	0 (1)	28 (15)[a]
Mean %: all communications										
All media	100	100	100	100	100	100	100	100	100	100
Face-to-face	57 (16)	43 (17)[a]	74 (15)	70 (14)	66 (16)	48 (20)[a]	64 (15)	46 (18)[a]	61 (15)	51 (16)[a]
Phone	27 (15)	15 (07)[a]	17 (12)	12 (07)[b]	18 (11)	10 (07)[a]	22 (13)	13 (7)[a]	36 (15)	30 (13)
Phone message	06 (06)	05 (04)	01 (02)	01 (01)	05 (05)	04 (04)	06 (05)	04 (4)	10 (09)	11 (10)
Fax	02 (02)	01 (01)[b]	01 (02)	01 (02)	02 (02)	01 (01)[b]	02 (2)	01 (1)	03 (04)	02 (02)
Paper (excl. fax)	07 (07)	04 (04)	06 (07)	05 (10)	09 (14)	07 (10)	06 (5)	04 (4)	12 (11)	12 (10)
Email	00 (00)	31 (16)[a]	00 (00)	11 (09)[a]	00 (00)	30 (19)[a]	00 (0)	31 (18)[a]	00 (00)	39 (17)[a]
Mean %: non-email communications										
Non-email media	100	100	100	100	100	100	100	100	100	100
Face-to-face	58 (16)	61 (17)	74 (15)	79 (13)	66 (16)	68 (19)	64 (15)	65 (15)	61 (15)	62 (14)
Phone	27 (15)	23 (12)	17 (12)	13 (07)	18 (11)	15 (12)	22 (13)	20 (13)	36 (15)	37 (16)
Phone message	06 (06)	08 (06)	01 (02)	02 (02)	05 (05)	05 (05)	05 (05)	07 (05)	10 (09)	14 (11)
Fax	02 (02)	02 (02)	01 (02)	01 (02)	02 (02)	01 (01)	02 (02)	01 (02)	03 (04)	03 (03)
Paper (excl. fax)	07 (07)	06 (07)	06 (07)	05 (11)	09 (13)	11 (14)	06 (05)	06 (05)	12 (11)	14 (12)

Standard deviations are in parentheses. [a] $p < 0.05$, two-tailed; [b] $p < 0.10$, two-tailed.

heavy email users. Light email users also had significantly greater percentages of named alters with whom they communicated face-to-face (64 percent versus 46 percent) and by phone (22 percent versus 13 percent) ($t(43) = 3.681$ and 3.039, respectively, $p < 0.05$), but not by fax. Heavy email users had greater percentages of email communications, time spent communicating via email, and email alters (all three measures of alters).

Unlike the analyses across all communication contents, light email users only had a significantly greater percentage of unique alters with whom they communicated face-to-face about work (61 percent versus 51 percent, $t(43) = 2.237$, $p < 0.05$). Moreover, the difference in percentage of time spent in work-related communication on the phone by light versus heavy email users (17 versus 12 percent, respectively) approached significance ($t(43) = 1.864$, $p < 0.10$). None of the comparisons of percentages across content had yielded significant results for the amount of time spent communicating.

Media use for "other business" communications

Results for comparisons of means for "other business" communications were somewhat different from those for the all-content and work content analyses (table 9.3). Although heavy email users still differed from light email users in email use for all five variables, the comparisons for all media combined were not significant as they had been for the two previous sets of analyses. Moreover, the difference in unique phone alters between light and heavy email users (7 versus 4, respectively) approached significance for this analysis ($t(43) = 1.815$, $p < 0.10$). This is the only raw number analysis for any of the content areas for which the comparison of heavy and light email users on any medium other than email attained even near-significant results.

The impact of heavy email use on phone use for "other business" communication was even more salient when impact on proportionate use (percentages excluding email) was considered: that is, light email users had greater percentages of phone communications (27 percent versus 18 percent, $t(40) = 2.026$, $p < 0.10$), total phone alters (20 percent versus 12 percent, $t(40) = 1.768$, $p < 0.10$), and named phone alters (24 percent versus 16 percent, $t = 1.756$, $p < 0.10$) than did heavy email users. This finding contrasts with the absence of any impact of heavy email use on the proportionate use of other media for work communications.

Table 9.3 Communication media usage by heavy versus light email users across "other business" communications

Email use	No. of communications		Communication time		No. of alters		No. of named alters		No. of unique alters	
	Light	Heavy	Light	Heavy	Light	Heavy	Light	Heavy	Light	Heavy
Mean										
All media	31 (24)	36 (36)	350 (368)	324 (386)	45 (34)	76 (108)	36 (28)	43 (42)	27 (19)	27 (21)
Non-email media	30 (24)	28 (30)	350 (368)	308 (378)	44 (33)	44 (46)	36 (28)	33 (36)	26 (19)	21 (18)
Face-to-face	19 (19)	20 (24)	296 (330)	271 (350)	33 (29)	37 (41)	25 (23)	26 (30)	17 (14)	15 (14)
Phone	8 (9)	5 (6)	47 (74)	27 (43)	8 (9)	5 (6)	8 (9)	5 (6)	7 (7)	4 (3)[b]
Phone message	2 (4)	2 (3)	2 (4)	3 (4)	2 (3)	2 (3)	2 (4)	2 (3)	1 (3)	1 (2)
Fax	0 (1)	0 (0)	0 (2)	1 (2)	0 (1)	0 (0)	0 (1)	0 (0)	0 (0)	0 (0)
Paper (excl. fax)	1 (2)	1 (1)	4 (11)	4 (7)	1 (3)	1 (1)	1 (2)	1 (1)	1 (2)	1 (1)
Email	0 (1)	8 (10)[a]	0 (1)	16 (21)[a]	0 (1)	31 (76)[b]	0 (1)	10 (13)[a]	0 (0)	5 (6)[a]
Mean %: all communications										
All media	100		100		100		100		100	
Face-to-face	63 (21)	59 (23)	80 (20)	78 (21)	71 (23)	62 (27)	67 (22)	61 (24)	70 (20)	62 (22)
Phone	27 (14)	14 (11)[a]	17 (17)	11 (14)	20 (13)	09 (09)[a]	24 (14)	12 (11)[a]	27 (15)	16 (15)[a]
Phone message	06 (10)	05 (05)	02 (04)	02 (02)	05 (10)	03 (04)	06 (10)	04 (05)	07 (11)	06 (07)
Fax	00 (01)	01 (01)	00 (01)	00 (02)	00 (01)	00 (00)	00 (01)	00 (01)	01 (02)	01 (01)
Paper (excl. fax)	02 (04)	03 (04)	01 (03)	01 (02)	02 (04)	02 (03)	02 (03)	02 (04)	03 (06)	04 (05)
Email	00 (01)	19 (20)[a]	00 (00)	08 (11)[a]	00 (01)	24 (28)[a]	00 (01)	20 (22)	00 (01)	21 (22)[a]
Mean %: non-email communications										
Non-email media	100		100		100		100		100	
Face-to-face	63 (22)	72 (19)	80 (20)	83 (20)	72 (23)	80 (18)	67 (22)	74 (19)	70 (20)	74 (19)
Phone	27 (14)	18 (15)[b]	17 (17)	13 (19)	20 (13)	12 (14)[b]	24 (14)	16 (15)[b]	28 (15)	20 (19)
Phone message	06 (10)	06 (07)	02 (04)	02 (03)	05 (10)	04 (06)	06 (10)	05 (06)	07 (11)	07 (08)
Fax	00 (01)	01 (02)	00 (01)	00 (02)	00 (01)	00 (01)	00 (01)	00 (01)	01 (02)	01 (02)
Paper (excl. fax)	02 (04)	04 (06)	01 (03)	02 (03)	02 (04)	02 (03)	02 (03)	03 (05)	03 (06)	05 (08)

Standard deviations are in parentheses. [a] $p < 0.05$, two-tailed; [b] $p < 0.10$, two-tailed.

Comparing communication style (percentages including all media), "other business" patterns were again different from those across contents and for work content, the only significant differences (other than email use) being total phone communications and phone alters (and not for face-to-face and fax). Light email users had significantly more phone communications and alters (on all three alter measures) than did heavy email users. More specifically, 27 percent of light email users used the phone compared to 14 percent of heavy email users (t(40) = 3.360, p < 0.05), and light email users compared to heavy email users contacted 20 versus 9 percent of their total alters, 24 versus 12 percent of their named alters, and 27 percent versus 16 percent of their unique alters via phone (t(40) = 3.198, 3.069, and 2.388; p < 0.05).

Media use for "personal" communications

Comparisons of heavy and light email users' mean media use for personal communications showed a difference only in the number of communications (other than the comparisons of email use which, of course, yielded significant differences). Heavy email users (table 9.4) had 128 personal communications compared to 93 for light email users (t(43) = −1.725, p < 0.10).

In comparing proportionate media use of heavy and light email users for "personal" communications (percentages excluding email), the only differences that approached significance were the greater percentage of face-to-face and lower percentage of phone communications for heavy versus light email users. Heavy email users communicated face-to-face 84 percent of the time as compared to 79 percent of the time for light email users (t(43) = −1.779, p < 0.10). Light email users, on the other hand, communicated via phone 17 percent of the time, compared to 12 percent of the time for heavy email users (t(43) = 1.800, p < 0.10).

Comparing communication style (percentages including all media), "personal" content communications resemble those across contents and for work content, but with some reversal of significant results for face-to-face and phone communications and no significant differences for fax. Light email users had a significantly greater percentage of phone communications (17 versus 10 percent, t(43) = 2.792, p < 0.05), total face-to-face (86 versus 76 percent) and total phone (11 versus 7 percent) alters (t(43) = 2.093 and 2.067, p < 0.05), named phone alters (14 versus 8 percent, t(43) = 2.656, p < 0.05), and a nearly significantly

Table 9.4 Communication media usage by heavy versus light email users across "personal" communications

Email use	No. of communications		Communication time		No. of alters		No. of named alters		No. of unique alters	
	Light	Heavy	Light	Heavy	Light	Heavy	Light	Heavy	Light	Heavy
Mean										
All media	93 (52)	128 (81)[b]	1,718 (834)	1,723 (615)	146 (75)	179 (126)	123 (70)	167 (127)	49 (29)	49 (28)
Non-email media	93 (52)	107 (74)	1,717 (834)	1,682 (608)	146 (75)	154 (117)	122 (70)	145 (119)	49 (29)	43 (24)
Face-to-face	74 (43)	93 (73)	1,611 (781)	1,598 (598)	126 (68)	138 (115)	102 (61)	130 (117)	37 (22)	33 (20)
Phone	15 (11)	10 (6)	95 (118)	77 (82)	15 (12)	11 (7)	15 (12)	11 (7)	9 (6)	7 (5)
Phone message	3 (5)	3 (4)	5 (8)	4 (6)	3 (5)	4 (6)	3 (5)	3 (4)	2 (3)	2 (2)
Fax	0 (1)	0 (0)	0 (2)	0 (1)	0 (1)	0 (0)	0 (1)	0 (0)	0 (0)	0 (0)
Paper (excl. fax)	1 (2)	1 (1)	4 (9)	2 (3)	2 (4)	1 (1)	2 (4)	1 (1)	2 (3)	1 (1)
Email	0 (0)	21 (37)[a]	0 (1)	41 (64)[a]	0 (0)	25 (39)[a]	0 (0)	22 (38)[a]	0 (0)	6 (6)[a]
Mean %: all communications										
All media	100		100		100		100		100	
Face-to-face	79 (12)	73 (19)	94 (06)	93 (06)	86 (09)	76 (19)[a]	82 (11)	77 (19)	85 (10)	79 (12)[b]
Phone	17 (11)	09 (06)[a]	06 (06)	05 (05)	11 (08)	07 (05)[a]	14 (09)	08 (05)[a]	22 (13)	17 (09)
Phone message	03 (03)	02 (04)	00 (00)	00 (00)	02 (02)	02 (04)	02 (03)	02 (03)	04 (05)	04 (04)
Fax	00 (00)	00 (00)	00 (00)	00 (00)	00 (00)	00 (00)	00 (00)	00 (00)	00 (01)	00 (01)
Paper (excl. fax)	01 (02)	01 (01)	00 (00)	00 (00)	01 (02)	00 (01)	01 (02)	00 (01)	03 (05)	02 (03)
Email	00 (00)	14 (18)[a]	00 (00)	02 (04)[a]	00 (00)	14 (18)[a]	00 (00)	12 (18)[a]	00 (01)	14 (13)[a]
Mean %: non-email communications										
Non-email media	100		100		100		100		100	
Face-to-face	79 (12)	84 (09)[b]	94 (06)	95 (05)	86 (09)	87 (08)	82 (11)	87 (08)	85 (10)	87 (08)
Phone	17 (11)	12 (08)[b]	06 (06)	05 (05)	11 (08)	09 (07)	14 (09)	10 (07)	22 (13)	20 (10)
Phone message	03 (03)	03 (04)	00 (00)	00 (00)	02 (02)	03 (05)	02 (03)	02 (03)	04 (05)	05 (04)
Fax	00 (00)	00 (00)	00 (00)	00 (00)	00 (00)	00 (00)	00 (00)	00 (00)	00 (01)	00 (01)
Paper (excl. fax)	01 (02)	01 (01)	00 (00)	00 (00)	01 (02)	01 (01)	01 (02)	01 (01)	03 (05)	02 (04)

Standard deviations are in parentheses. [a] $p < 0.05$, two-tailed; [b] $p < 0.10$, two-tailed.

greater percentage of unique, named face-to-face alters (85 percent versus 79 percent, $t(43) = 2.047$, $p < 0.10$) than did heavy email users.

Discussion

The results concur with those of previous investigations in several ways: participants spent about half their workday in work-related communication, communications were most often face-to-face, and heavy email users communicated more frequently than did light email users. This study *adds* to our understanding of the impact of heavy email use on communication by delineating differences in actual media use of heavy and light email users across communication content, context, and media for five communication variables.

One of the most interesting findings of the raw number analyses is the lack of significant differences between heavy and light email users for all analyses where non-email media were combined. This similarity of the two group profiles (minus email) suggests that one impact of heavy email use is simply to supplement communication via other media.

A second point of interest for these analyses is the greater density of communication for heavy email users. In the analysis of all communications, heavy email users communicated more often and to more people (both total and named only, counting duplicates, but not unique) than did light email users, but they did not spend more time communicating. Not only were all of these differences primarily driven by differences in work communication but the separate analysis for work communication indicated that, even though they spent more time on work communication, the heavy email users' schedule of work communication was still denser than that of the light email users: that is, 10 communications and 18 alters versus 8 communications and 12 alters per communication hour. These findings confirm many email users' perceptions of communication overload, particularly for work communication.

To further explore these data we looked at percentages of media use by participants. This had the effect of removing some of the tremendous variation among study participants – a variation that may have contributed in some cases to lack of statistical significance despite large differences in the raw numbers.

For the first set of percentage analyses we excluded email, thus leveling the number of communications across heavy and light email users, to determine the impact of email on proportionate use of other media. Based on these data, heavy email users had a slightly lower percentage of phone communication than light email users. However, unlike the preceding differences between the two groups, this result was driven more by "other business" and "personal" than by "work" communications. There might be some justification, perhaps, in portraying this as a slight but noticeable trend toward displacement or substitution of phone by email communication, and certainly this is worth examining further through additional research.

Another point of interest for this analysis is that heavy email users had a greater percentage of face-to-face personal communications than light email users, a difference that may or may not relate to job type: for example, heavy email users may have jobs involving both heavy email use and a greater percentage of unscheduled face-to-face communications among non-email communications. In any event, this finding points to a need to examine media use by relationship as well as content to differentiate where personal encounters are occurring (e.g., co-workers, neighbors, co-participants in social organizations, etc.).

The second set of percentage analyses concerned overall communication style and included all communication media. Based on these, heavy email users showed smaller percentages of communications across several of the five communication variables for face-to-face, phone, and fax communication than light email users, and this appeared to be driven mostly by work communications. For "personal" communications, heavy email users had smaller percentages of only face-to-face and phone communications, but, again, this was true across several variables; for "other business" communications, heavy email users had smaller percentages of only phone communications, but this held for all variables except time spent communicating.

Clearly, then, heavy use of email (which comprised 25 percent of our heavy email user's communications) did have an impact on communication style that transcended the boundaries of work communication. Although these heavy and light email users engaged in different types of jobs, presumably with different communication demands, the differences in non-work communications suggest a generalization of communication style to other contexts – a style that included more email and relied less on other media. However, in none of these cases can we say that email displaced or substituted for phone, face-to-face, and fax communication. Rather, where email communication was included in an analysis, it added communications over and beyond those carried by other modes.

This second percentage analysis also revealed a smaller percentage of face-to-face alters for heavy (versus light) email users for personal communications – seeming to suggest that the heavy email user is losing touch with humanity. Only 76 percent (versus 86 percent) of personal communication alters were communicated with face-to-face while 14 percent (versus 0 percent) were communicated with via email for heavy versus light email users. However, it is important to note that the first percentage analysis proclaims precisely the opposite relation between heavy email use and face-to-face personal communication and that only that analysis relates to displacement or substitution whereas this second percentage analysis only considers overall communication style.

This study has shed light on some perplexing questions: how does heavy email use impact use of other communication media? How does it affect communication style? How can users of this new, efficient technology be so overwhelmed? However, in answering these questions others remain unanswered. Additional research is needed to sort out effects due to the types of settings, participants, and measures, and the relationships between participants and their communication partners. Will these results apply equally to university researchers, bank managers, long distance learners, and so forth? Will the results of this investigation apply equally across work, family, and social relationships; co-worker/fellow student versus supervisor/instructor relations; and nameable versus unnameable others? Finally, how are different measures of communication (for example, perceived versus actual use and sent versus received messages) related, and how do these interact with perceptions of stress and communication overload?

In summary, this investigation was initiated to clarify the impact of heavy email use upon communication – to consider whether email is a blessing or curse. We find it to be a bit of both. It enables participants to communicate more, in less time, but it is also likely to increase stress levels, particularly for work communication. Moreover, we find that heavy email use, perhaps begun through work obligations, can lead to a more general communication style that relies more on email and less on other media, extends beyond work to include personal communications and business outside of work, and possibly includes some substitution of email for phone for non-work communication. While this research has clarified some of the findings of previous studies, our results suggest that further exploration of variations in settings, participants, relationships, and communication measures is needed.

References

Bernard, H. R., Kilworth, P., and Sailer, L. (1981). Summary of research on informant accuracy in network data and the reverse small world problem. *Connections*, 42(2), 11–25.

Bernard, H. R., Kilworth, P., Kronenfeld, D., and Sailer, L. (1984). The problem of informant accuracy: the validity of retrospective data. *Annual Review of Anthropology*, 13, 495–517.

Bikson, T. K. and Eveland, J. D. (1990). The interplay of work group structures and computer support. In J. Galegher, R. E. Kraut, and C. Egido (eds), *Intellectual teamwork: social and technological foundations of cooperative work* (pp. 245–90). Hillsdale, NJ: Lawrence Erlbaum Associates.

Buss, A. and Plomin, R. (1975). *A temperament theory of personality development*. New York: Wiley.

Carlson, P. J. and Davis, G. B. (1998). An investigation of media selection among directors and managers: from "self" to "other" orientation. *MIS Quarterly*, 22(3), 335–62.

Choney, S. (2000). Once status symbol, e-mail now staggering. Available online at:
http://at.uniontrib.com/index.html

Clemente, P. C. (1998). *The state of the net: the new frontier*. New York: McGraw Hill.

Conrath, D. W., Higgins, C. A., and McCLean, R. J. (1983). A comparison of the reliability of questionnaire versus diary data. *Social Networks*, 5, 315–22.

Contractor, N. S. and Eisenberg, E. M. (1990). Communication networks and new media in organizations. In J. Fulk and C. Steinfield (eds), *Organizations and communication technology* (pp. 143–72). Newbury Park: Sage.

Dimmick, J., Kline, S., and Stafford, L. (2000). The gratification niches of personal email and the telephone: competition, displacement, and compatibility. *Communication Research*, 27(2), 227–48.

Dobos, J. (1992). Gratification models of satisfaction and choice of communication channels in organizations. *Communication Research*, 19(1), 29–51.

Eveland, J. D. and Bikson, T. K. (1987). Evolving electronic communication networks: an empirical assessment. *Office: Technology and People*, 3, 103–28.

Finholt, T., Sproull, L., and Kiesler, S. (1990). Communication and performance in ad hoc task groups. In J. Galegher, R. E. Kraut, and C. Egido (eds), *Intellectual teamwork: social and technological foundations of cooperative work* (pp. 291–326). Hillsdale, NJ: Lawrence Erlbaum Associates.

Fulk, J. and Boyd, B. (1991). Emerging theories of communication in organizations. *Journal of Management*, 17(2), 407–46.

GVU (1998). GVUs WWW users surveys. Available online at:
http://www.cc.gatech.edu/gvu/user_surveys/User_Survey_Home.html

Haythornthwaite, C. (2000). Online personal networks: size, composition and media use among distance learners. *New Media and Society*, 2(2), 195–226.

Haythornthwaite, C. (2001). Exploring multiplexity: social network structures in a computer-supported distance learning class. *The Information Society*, 17(3), 211–26.

Haythornthwaite, C. (2002). Strong, weak and latent ties and the impact of new media. *The Information Society* (forthcoming).

Haythornthwaite, C. and Wellman, B. (1998). Work, friendship, and media use for information exchange in a networked organization. *Journal of the American Society for Information Science*, 46(12), 1,101–14.

Hovland, C. I., Janis, I. L., and Kelley, H. H. (1953). *Communication and persuasion: psychological studies of opinion change*. New Haven: Yale University Press.

Kanfer, A. G. (2000). *It's a thin world: the association between email use and patterns of communication and relationships*. Available online at: http://www.ncsa.uiuc.edu/edu/trg/info_society.html

Katz, J. E. and Aspden, P. (1997). A nation of strangers? *Communications of the ACM*, 40(12), 81–6.

Kraut, R. E. and Attewell, P. (1997). Media use in a global corporation: electronic mail and organizational knowledge. In S. Kiesler (ed.) *Culture of the Internet* (pp. 323–42). Mahwah, NJ: Erlbaum.

Markus, M. L. (1994). Electronic mail as the medium of managerial choice. *Organization Science*, 5(4), 502–27.

Mintzberg, H. (1973). *The nature of managerial work*. New York: Harper and Row.

Nyce, H. E. and Groppa, R. (1983). Electronic mail at MHT. *Management Technology*, 23, 65–72.

Pitney Bowes Inc. (2002). E-mail or e-stress?

Poole, M. S. and DeSanctis, G. (1990). Understanding the use of group decision support systems: the theory of adaptive structuration. In J. Fulk and C. Steinfield (eds), *Organizations and communication technology* (pp. 173–93). Newbury Park, CA: Sage.

Rice, R. E. (1994). Network analysis and computer-mediated communication systems. In S. Wasserman and J. Galaskiewicz (eds), *Advances in Social Network Analysis* (pp. 167–203). Newbury Park, CA: Sage.

Rice, R. E. and Case, D. (1983). Electronic message systems in the university: a description of use and utility. *Journal of Communication*, 33(1), 131–52.

Rice, R. E. and Shook, D. E. (1988). Access to, usage of, and outcomes from an electronic messaging system. *ACM Transactions on Office Information Systems*, 6(3), 255–76.

Rice, R. E. and Shook, D. E. (1990). Relationships of job categories and orga-nizational levels to use of communication channels, including electronic mail: a meta-analysis and extension. *Journal of Management Studies*, 27(2), 195–229.

Rogers, E. M. (1995). *Diffusion of innovations*. 4th edn. NY: The Free Press.

Rosen, L. D. and Weil, M. M. (1995). Adult and teenage use of consumer, busi-ness, and entertainment technology: potholes on the information super-highway? *Journal of Consumer Affairs*, 29(1), 55–84.

Schmitz, J. (1987). *Electronic messaging: system use in local governments*. Paper presented at the International Communication Association, Montreal, Canada.

Schmitz, J. and Fulk, J. (1991). Organizational colleagues, media richness, and electronic mail: a test of the social influence model of technology use. *Communication Research*, 18(4), 487–523.

Shin, B., Higa, K., Sheng, O. R. L., and Ide, T. (1999). Analyzing the media usage behavior of telework groups: a contingency approach. *IEEE Transac-tions on Systems, Man, and Cybernetics – Part C: Applications and Reviews*, 29(1), 127–39.

Soe, L. L. and Markus, M. L. (1993). Technology or social utility? Unraveling explanations of email, vmail, and fax use. *The Information Society*, 9(3), 213–36.

Sproull, L. and Kiesler, S. (1991). *Connections: new ways of working in the networked organization*. Cambridge, MA: The MIT Press.

Steinfield, C. W. (1986). Computer-mediated communication in an organi-zational setting: explaining task-related and socioemotional uses. In M. McLaughlin (ed.), *Communication Yearbook 9* (pp. 777–804). Beverly Hills, CA: Sage.

Sullivan, C. B. (1995). Preferences for electronic mail in organizational com-munication tasks. *The Journal of Business Communication*, 32(1), 49–64.

Trevino, L. K., Webster, J., and Stein, E. W. (2000). Making connections: com-plementary influences on communication media choices, attitudes, and use. *Organization Science*, 11(2), 163–82.

UCLA Center for Communication Policy (2000). *The UCLA Internet report: "surveying the digital future."* Available online at: www.ccp.ucla.edu

Weil, M. M. and Rosen, L. D. (1997). *Technostress: coping with technology @work @home @play*. New York: John Wiley.

Wellman, B. (1988). Structural analysis: from method and metaphor to theory and substance. In B. Wellman and S. D. Berkowitz (eds), *Social structures: a network approach* (pp. 19–61). Cambridge: Cambridge Univer-sity Press.

Wijayanayake, J. and Higa, K. (1999). Communication media choice by workers in a distributed environment. *Information & Management*, 36(6), 329–38.

Zack, M. H. (1994). Electronic messaging and communication effectiveness in an ongoing work group. *Information & Management*, 26(4), 231–41.

Zeffane, R. and Cheek, B. (1995). The differential use of written, computer-based, and verbal information in an organizational context – an empirical exploration. *Information & Management*, 28(2), 107–21.

Part IV

The Internet in the Community

10

Capitalizing on the Net

Social Contact, Civic Engagement, and Sense of Community

Anabel Quan-Haase and Barry Wellman, with James C. Witte and Keith N. Hampton

Abstract

How does the Internet affect social capital in terms of social contact, civic engagement, and a sense of community? Does online involvement increase, decrease, or supplement the ways in which people engage? Our evidence comes from a 1998 survey of North American visitors to the National Geographic Society website, one of the first large-scale web surveys of the general public. We find that online social contact supplements the frequency of face-to-face and telephone contact. Online activity also supplements participation in voluntary organizations and politics. Frequent email users have a greater sense of online community, although their overall sense of community is similar to that of infrequent email users. The evidence suggests that as the Internet is incorporated into the routine practices of everyday life, social capital is becoming augmented and more geographically dispersed.

Authors' note

This chapter has benefited from the advice and assistance of Wenhong Chen, Caroline Haythornthwaite, Philip Howard, Kristine Klement, Uzma Jalaluddin, Gad-Quentin Jones, Uyen Quach, Ann Sorenson, and Beverly Wellman. We especially acknowledge the help of Monica Prijatelj in preparing the tables and figures. Our compatriots at the University of Toronto's NetLab, Centre for Urban and Community Studies, Department of Sociology, Faculty of Information Studies, Knowledge Media Design Institute, and Bell University Laboratories have created stimulating milieux for thinking about the Internet in society. Research underlying this chapter has been supported by Communication and Information Technology Ontario, the IBM Institute of Knowledge Management, Mitel

Networks, the National Geographic Society, and the Social Science and Humanities Research Council of Canada. This chapter is dedicated to S. Roxanne Hiltz and Murray Turoff, early explorers of "the network nation" (1978).

Debating the Internet's Effects on Social Capital

How the Internet affects social capital is neither a trivial nor an obscure question. Scholars, pundits, and policy-makers have long worried that the Industrial Revolution – and more recently, the Information Revolution – have led to the decline of community (Wellman, 1999). Although different analysts focus on different causes – from industrialization and bureaucratization in the 1800s to television and the Internet – they all have feared:

(1) *The weakening of private community*: social contact with kin, friends, workmates, and neighbors.
(2) *The decline of public community*: gatherings in public places, involvement in voluntary organizations, civic concerns, and commitment to community.
(3) *The disengagement from community*: positive attitudes towards community life and willingness to contribute to the well-being of the community.

Recently, Robert Putnam (1996, 2000) documented a decline since the 1960s in American private and public community. But what if Putnam is only measuring old forms of community and participation, while new forms of communication and organization underneath his radar are connecting people? Some evidence suggests that the observed decline has not led to social isolation, but to community becoming embedded in social networks rather than groups, and a movement of community relationships from easily observed public spaces to less-accessible private homes (Wuthnow, 1991, 1998; Guest and Wierzbicki, 1999; Wellman, 1999, 2001; Fischer, 2001; Lin, 2001). If people are tucked away in their homes rather than conversing in cafes, then they may be going online: chatting online one-to-one; exchanging email in duets or small groups; or schmoozing, ranting, and organizing in discussion groups such as "list serves" or "newsgroups" (Smith, 1999; Kraut, Patterson, Lundmark, Kiesler, Mukhopadhyay, and Scherlis, 1998; Matei and Ball-Rokeach, 2001).

The rapidly expanding Internet has infiltrated North American life. More than half of the North American population has been online, e-commerce is growing, and both the mass and the scholarly media are fascinated with the technological and social wiring of society (Horrigan, Lenard, and McGonegal, 2001). The Internet's ubiquity has raised questions about whether its use is increasing or decreasing social capital. Utopians claim that the Internet is providing new and better ways of engaging in community and finding information (e.g., De Kerckhove, 1997; Lévy, 1997). However, dystopians argue that the Internet lures people away from their in-person communities and informed discussions (e.g., Slouka, 1995; Stoll, 1995).

While the debate surrounding the influence of the Internet on social capital has been ongoing, systematic data has only recently come to replace hype, hopes, and fears. (In addition to the chapters in this book, see also the reviews in Wellman and Gulia, 1999; DiMaggio, Hargittai, Neumann, and Robinson, 2001; Flanagan and Metzger, 2001). Analysts have moved from seeing the Internet as an external world to seeing how it becomes integrated into the complexity of everyday life (for example, compare the first and second editions of Rheingold, 1993, 2000).

We contribute to the debate by asking if the Internet increases, decreases, or supplements social capital? We examine people's use of the Internet within the broader context of their offline social interactions – face-to-face and by telephone – as well as their information-seeking habits – reading newspapers and going to libraries. We look at three forms of social capital:

1 *Network capital:* the frequency of social contact with friends, relatives, and workmates. This is the private side of community.
2 *Civic engagement:* participation in voluntary organizations and political activities affords opportunities for people to bond, create joint accomplishments, and collectively articulate their demands (Curtis, Baer, and Grabb, 2001; Eckstein, 2001; Schofer and Fourcade-Gourinchas, 2001; Tilly, 1984). Such civic engagement is the public side of community, enshrined in the American heritage by Tocqueville (1835) and given fresh life by Putnam (2000).
3 *Sense of community:* social capital consists of more than interpersonal interaction and civic engagement. When people have a strong attitude toward community – a motivated and responsible sense of belonging – they should mobilize their social capital more willingly and effectively (Tilly, 1984; Diani and McAdam, 2002). This is the attitudinal side of community.

The evidence for our analysis comes from a large web survey of North American visitors to the National Geographic Society website in the fall of 1998. This chapter builds on an earlier, preliminary analysis of these same data (Wellman, Quan-Haase, Witte, and Hampton, 2001). We expand the preliminary analysis in several ways by: describing in more detail the users of the Internet; using more specific measures of email and web use; comparing online and offline contact; including information seeking in our analyses; and providing corrected and revised analyses of having a sense of community.

Does the Internet increase social capital?

Early – and continuing – excitement about the Internet saw it as stimulating positive change in people's lives by creating new forms of online interaction and enhancing offline relationships. The Internet would restore community by providing a meeting space for people with shared interests that would overcome the limitations of space and time (Sproull and Kiesler, 1991; Baym, 1997; Wellman, 2001). Online communities would promote open, democratic discourse (Sproull and Kiesler, 1991), allow for multiple perspectives (Kapor, 1993), and mobilize collective action (Schwartz, 1996; Tarrow, 1999).

Although early accounts focused on the formation of online "virtual" communities (e.g., Rheingold, 1993), it has become clear that most relationships formed in cyberspace continue in physical space, leading to new forms of community characterized by a mixture of online and offline interactions (e.g., Rheingold, 2000; Müller, 1999; Matei and Ball-Rokeach, 2001). Online interactions fill communication gaps between face-to-face meetings and make non-local ties more viable. Non-local community has been flourishing well before the advent of the Internet as people move frequently and sometimes far away. Cars, planes, trains, and phones maintain ties with family and friends; former neighbors and workmates become separated; immigrants keep contact with friends and relatives in their homelands (Wellman, 1999).

The possibilities of the Internet lie beyond their facilitation of interaction, for one of its most used features is the provision of information: easily, wide-ranging, up-to-date, and at low cost. Public debate becomes more broadly accessible as the digital divide narrows and most North Americans have some Internet access (Katz and Rice, this volume; NTIA, 2000; Reddick, 2000; Fong et al., 2001). Governmental, non-governmental, and corporate organizations have made it their mandate to have a strong web presence that informs Internet users of their agendas (DiMaggio et al., 2001). People can have a public voice by creating a website, discussing current issues on list serves, and expressing opinions through polls (Sunstein, 2001).

Putnam (2000) argues that the decline in social capital has not been a general decline in the American population as a whole but is a decline specific to younger generations. Yet, it is younger generations who have been the most active on the Internet even as they have eschewed traditional forms of community. They have gone online at a younger age, may have more years of experience than older generations, and are often savvier. Hence, the Internet has the potential to reverse the decline in social capital by providing a medium for younger generations to increase their social contacts, civic engagement, and sense of community. *If the Internet increases social capital, high Internet use should be accompanied by more offline social contact, civic engagement, and sense of community.*

Does the Internet decrease social capital?

Dystopians argue that the Internet is fostering a decline in social capital and an increase in interpersonal alienation. For example, a longitudinal study of "newbies" (newcomers) to the Internet found that high Internet use was associated with lower social contact offline, and higher depression and loneliness. Although the Internet enhanced weak online ties, it simultaneously decreased stronger offline interactions (Kraut, Patterson, Lundmark, Kiesler, Mukopadhyay, and Scherlis, 1998; but see LaRose, Eastin, and Gregg, 2001).

The Internet may compete with other activities for time in an inelastic 24-hour day. There are discrepant findings about whether or not online time-sinks pull people away from other interactions inside and outside the household (Nie, 2001; Nie, Hillygus, and Erbring this volume say they do; Gershuny, 2001; Anderson and Tracy, this volume say they do not). Some researchers see a parallel in the impact of the Internet with the way that television has had an absorptive effect that reduced social interaction in the home (Steiner, 1963; Nie and Sackman, 1970; Wei and Leung, 2001). Yet, one-way broadcast television is quite different from socially interactive email and chatting online.

The Internet may foster contact with weak ties of acquaintanceship at the expense of socially close ties. Weak ties provide new information and access to diverse networks while strong ties provide commitment, friendship, and supportiveness (Granovetter, 1973; Wellman and Wortley, 1990). However, not all uses of the Internet are social; much activity is *a*social, such as seeking information or engaging in solitary recreations. Obtaining political and organizational information from the Internet is affordable and convenient. Nevertheless, such Internet features as customization and personalization can narrow the spectrum of information obtained online (Sunstein, 2001). This can decrease the potential for serendipitous information retrieval, limit multiple perspectives, and create a false sense of unanimity. *If the Internet decreases social capital, high Internet use should be accompanied by less offline social contact, civic engagement, and sense of community.*

Does the Internet supplement social capital?

Where the increase and decrease arguments privilege the Internet by seeing it as radically changing how people interact offline, the supplement argument gives this new technology less of a central role in shaping social trends. It treats the Internet as integrated into rhythms of daily life, with life online being an extension of offline activities. This suggests that the Internet's effects on society will be similar to the telephone: important and pervasive but evolutionary (Pool, 1977; Fischer, 1992). For example, British time-use data suggests that the Internet both helps arrange get-togethers and replaces them. There is a small positive association between increased Internet use and going out to socialize, but also a smaller negative association between Internet use and private socializing (Gershuny, 2001).

The Internet may be more useful for maintaining existing ties than for creating new ones (Koku, Nazer, and Wellman, 2001; Koku and Wellman, 2003). It provides a convenient, affordable, and powerful supplement to telephone and face-to-face contact. For example, one study finds the Internet to be "a multidimensional technology used in a manner similar to other, more traditional technologies" (Flanagan and Metzger, 2001, p. 153). Face-to-face and telephone contact continue, complemented by the Internet's ease in connecting geographically dispersed people and organizations who are bonded by shared interests.[1]

1   Our data and others (e.g., Wellman, Carrington, and Hall, 1988) show that other than ritual greeting cards, people rarely send letters through the traditional post any more, even as the Internet itself boosts the sheer volume of written communication. It would be interesting to compare the effects of the Internet to that

The Internet may also provide a supplementary source of information for those interested in public affairs and governmental decision-making (Horrigan, Lenard, and McGonegal, 2001). Yet, no radical shift of a person's habits may accompany Internet use (Howcroft, 1999). Nor might the Internet lead to organizational and political participation if users have no interest in such matters. Some evidence shows that it is the politically involved that use the Internet for enhanced political participation (Johnson and Kaye, 2000). For example, wiring Blacksburg Electronic Village did not produce major changes in interpersonal contact and community involvement (Kavanaugh and Patterson, this volume; see also Uslaner, 2000). Similarly, organizations have often absorbed new information and communication systems without marked changes in their organizational communication structures and other forms of behavior (Orlikowski and Barley, 2001). *If the Internet supplements social capital, Internet use should add on to social contact, not affect civic engagement, and increase a sense of community. Thus, the level of Internet involvement will not be associated with either more or less offline activity.*

An Expedition to Study Users of the Internet

The National Geographic "Survey 2000"

The National Geographic Society "Survey 2000"[2] was available to visitors to the society's website, September–November 1998. It was publicized through the widely distributed, monthly *National Geographic* magazine, a prominent notice on the Society's homepage, and multiple public information sources. Although people around the world participated in the web survey, we focus on the 20,075 North American adult participants who completed all of the questions we analyze here: 17,711 Americans (88 percent) and 2,364 Canadians

of the introduction of the telephone as a complement to and replacement for face-to-face and postal communication. For the beginnings of such analysis, see Fischer (1992); Wellman and Tindall (1993).

2 "Survey2000" is available at http://survey2000.nationalgeographic.com. The community section was a module not presented to all respondents, thereby reducing our sample size. As we are interested in Internet users, and not of the general population, we do not report on 365 extreme newbies who encountered the Internet for the first time when completing the survey. The questions on personal visits with friends were given only to a sub-sample of 12,490 respondents (62 percent of the total sample). Our research group collaborated in preparing the survey. We realize that the large sample size and non-random sample selection methods pre-

(12 percent). Even though we do not have a random sample of the North American Internet-using population, comparisons with the 1993 and 1996 US General Social Surveys suggest that self-selection bias does not greatly distort estimates. However, the 1998 date of data collection calls for some caution in making inferences to current situations, for the percentage of North American adults has grown since 1998 and its demographic characteristics have changed.

National Geographic survey participants are rarely newbies. At the time of the survey, they have been on the Internet for a median of 36 months since fall 1995. More than three-quarters (81 percent) had been online for at least one year when they took the survey, while only 10 percent had been online for 6 months or less.

Survey participants report that the Internet is an important, but not dominant, means of communication for contact with socially close friends and relatives. They use the telephone most often (an estimated 41 percent of all communications), followed by email (33 percent), face-to-face visits (22 percent), and more rarely, postal letter writing and greetings cards (4 percent).[3] Even among relatively heavy email users, those using it daily, email comprises less than half of their contacts with friends and kin (39 percent). Compared to the pre-Internet situation of thirty years ago, telephone use is higher now and face-to-face contact lower. As in pre-Internet days, people communicate almost as much with socially close kin (45 percent of all reported informal communications) as they do with socially close friends (55 percent), even though they have fewer kin in their lives than friends

clude any discussion of statistical significance. Nevertheless, we flag significant coefficients in the tables to provide a rough indicator of the magnitude of observed effects relative to variance found in our sample. Supplementary tables are available at www.chass.utoronto.ca/~wellman/publications For other descriptions of these data, Witte, Amoroso, and Howard (2000); Chmielewski and Wellman (1999); Wellman, et al. (2001). Chen, Boase, and Wellman (chapter 2) analyze the worldwide sample.

3 Survey participants were asked: "How often do you have social contact with friends [relatives] who live more [less] than 30 miles (50 kilometers)" via four types of media (face-to-face contact, telephone, letter writing, and email). For each item, participants could answer: "never," "rarely," "several times a year," "about monthly," "about weekly," and "daily." We recoded these responses into days/year equivalents. Overall sociability was obtained by adding all 16 items and counting each person's reported contact with friends and kin, within and beyond 30 miles (50 km), and doing this separately for face-to-face, telephone, letter, and email contact. In some analyses, we combine face-to-face, phone and letter contact into a single "offline communication" variable.

and acquaintances (Wellman, 1979; Fischer, 1982; Wellman, Carrington, and Hall, 1988).

What do Internet users do online?

Although dystopians fear the Internet will be socially alienating, the most frequent Internet activity is socially integrating: sending and receiving emails. National Geographic participants exchange emails more than five days per week, a mean rate of 278 days per year. Web surfing (163 days/year) is the second most frequent activity. As email and web surfing are by far the predominant activities on the Internet, this chapter focuses on them. However, Internet users engage in other activities on the Internet including:

- *Real-time chatting* without a time delay, such as Internet Relay Chat (IRC) or instant messaging (mean rate = 25 days/year);
- *Playing multi-user online games*, such as Doom and Quake (11 days/year);
- *Visiting MUDs* (multi-user dimensions), MOOs (multi-user object oriented environments), or other online role-playing environments (7 days/year).

Email is more widely used than chatting. It is longer established, and people can communicate without being online simultaneously. Game playing and participating in multi-user environments are immersive activities, appealing to specialized tastes and requiring more time and involvement than emailing, web-surfing, and chatting.

Email

The most popular Internet activity, email, does not require much technical skill and fills communication gaps (Sproull and Kiesler, 1991; Wellman, 2001). Survey participants report that their email comprises 28 percent of their contacts with relatives and 37 percent of their contacts with friends. This compares with telephoning – 46 percent of their contacts with relatives and 35 percent of their contacts with friends – and face-to-face encounters – 21 percent of their contacts with relatives and 24 percent of their contacts with friends. Email has multiplier effects that telephone calls and face-to-face contacts rarely have: broadcasting the same message to many people increases traffic

Table 10.1   Effects of demographic characteristics on Internet activities

	Email[a]	Surf web[a]	Chat, IM[a]	Multiuser environment[a]	Online games[a]
Gender (male = 1)	−0.022	0.196	0.060	0.073	0.046
Age (reference = 30–9)					
18–29	−0.035	−0.011[b]	0.027	0.030	0.045
40–9	−0.008[b]	−0.055	−0.024	−0.022	−0.058
50–65	0.027	−0.120	−0.059	−0.038	−0.067
66+	0.011[b]	−0.088	−0.049	−0.031	−0.008[b]
Race (reference = white)					
Asian	0.013[b]	0.008[b]	0.007[b]	−0.003[b]	−0.004[b]
Black	0.000[b]	0.012[b]	0.013[b]	0.015	0.031
Other	−0.012[b]	−0.004[b]	0.024	0.018	0.002[b]
Education (reference = undergraduate degree)					
High school or less	−0.022	0.005[b]	0.052	0.015[b]	0.045
Undergraduate degree	0.034	−0.049	−0.149	−0.070	−0.098
Graduate degree	0.057	−0.094	−0.151	−0.069	−0.114
Marital status (reference = married)					
Single	0.032	0.043	0.082	0.029	0.028
Living non-maritally with Partner	0.016	0.040	0.053	0.018	0.029
Employment (employed = 1)	0.015	−0.017	−0.047	−0.005[b]	−0.017
Time online	0.340	0.177	0.104	0.104	0.052
Adjusted R²	0.129	0.106	0.076	0.031	0.044

[a] Standardized beta coefficient. [b] Indicates non-significant coefficients ($p > 0.05$).

because it often leads to multiple replies that spark responses back. Use leads to more use, although at some point, the sheer volume of traffic overloads the length (and probably the thoughtfulness) of messages (Jones, Ravid, and Rafaeili, 2002).

The number of months that people have been using the Internet is a strong – and the only meaningful – predictor of the amount of email they send and receive ($\beta = 0.34$; table 10.1; see also in this volume: Howard, Rainie, and Jones; Kavanaugh and Patterson). The

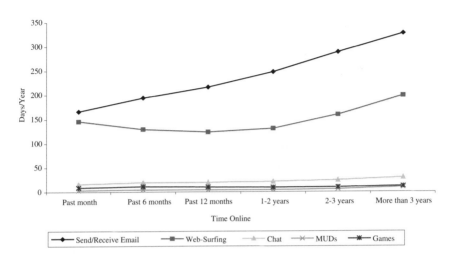

Figure 10.1 Length of time online by frequency of Internet use

relationship is positive and linear (figure 10.1), with email use increasing 13 percent for every year online. By contrast, demographic characteristics, such as age and education, are not appreciably associated with the frequency of email contact (although other studies show that socioeconomic status continues to predict to whether people use the Internet at all, see Fong et al., 2001; DiMaggio et al., 2001; see Chen, Boase, and Wellman's chapter).

At least three reasons account for the association between the number of months online and the frequency of Internet use:

- Those who have been online for a long time may be more likely to be Internet enthusiasts. Veteran users are not only more likely to be online on a typical day, but to engage in a greater variety of Internet activities (see the chapters in this volume by Howard et al.; Nie et al.).
- Experience makes veteran Internet users more savvy and more likely to use the technology to communicate.
- Veteran Internet users are more apt to have friends who are also active Internet users and hence, available to exchange email messages, play online games, and chat. As the Internet is a social technology, there is a network effect: The more people available for online interaction, the more the Internet is used (Rogers, 1995; Valente, 1995; Shapiro and Varian, 1998).

Web-surfing

Web-surfing is the only Internet activity with appreciable differences. Men surf more frequently ($\beta = 0.20$): a mean of 190 days per year as contrasted with women's 137 (see also Singh, 2001). As is the case with email, no other personal characteristic is appreciably associated with the frequency of surfing the web.

As with email, the number of months using the Internet is associated with the frequency of web surfing ($\beta = 0.18$). However, the relationship between the number of months online and web surfing is different from email. It is weaker and, based on the descriptive results in figure 10.1, is probably less linear. Web use is one of the first things that most people do. Newbies use it as often as email (figure 10.1). Unlike email, web use does not increase with more Internet experience until people have been online for two years (see also Howard et al., this volume). The cross-sectional nature of the data do not allow us to investigate whether the relationship between the number of months online and web use is because (1) early adopters are a special population who surf the web often, or (2) more online experience leads to more web-surfing. Experience may make people more curious and adept at finding information online.

Chat, games, and role-playing

Neither demographic characteristics nor the number of months online is associated with how often people engage in other social Internet activities: chats, online games, and multi-user role-playing environments. The only exception is that those without a university degree are more likely to engage in chat and play multi-user games (see also the chapters by Katz and Rice; Howard et al.).

Network Capital

Communication with far away kin and friends

Email is useful for communicating with people who are far away because its costs do not increase with distance and its asynchronousness makes it easy to contact people living in other time zones. Do these characteristics enable the Internet to fulfill the utopian dream of compressing the map of the world so that communication with those who are far away is as frequent as with those who are nearby? The more refined sample and measures used here to answer these questions differ to some extent from the preliminary analysis reported in Wellman et al. (2001) which suggested that the frequency of email contact is independent of the frequency of face-to-face and phone contact.

Even in the Internet era, distance still constrains communication (see also Hampton and Wellman, this volume). Only a minority of contact (30 percent) is with friends and relatives living "far-away": beyond 30 miles/50 kilometers. Email is the most frequently used communication medium for distant relationships. It is used for 59 percent of all distant social contacts: in particular, 49 percent of all social contact with far-away kin and 62 percent of all social contact with far-away friends (figure 10.2). The telephone is the second most used communication medium for distant social contact (24 percent), used for 35 percent of all social contacts with far-away kin and 22 percent with far-away friends. Face-to-face contact is rare (9 percent): 8 percent of all social contact with far-away kin and 9 percent with far-away friends.

Communication with nearby kin and friends

Is email only used for communicating with the distant reaches of the global village and not for local contact? The evidence is mixed. Unlike the situation for distant friends and relatives, the telephone (45 per cent) – and not email (24 per cent) – is the most used medium for contact with network members living "nearby": within 30 miles/50 kilometers. The telephone is used for 53 percent of all contact with nearby kin and 39 percent for all contact with nearby friends (figure 10.2).

On the other hand, email is widely used for nearby contact. Email comprises 29 percent of all contact with nearby friends while face-to-face encounters comprise a similar 29 percent. Email comprises 17 percent of all contact with nearby kin while face-to-face encounters comprise 27 percent. Nearby friends are contacted three times as often as those further away (ratio = 2.9); nearby kin are contacted twice as often as those further away (ratio = 1.9).[4]

4 We produced these ratios by calculating the proportion of frequency of one relationship by another. Thus, the ratio "nearby friend /distant friend" for contact via email is 86/62 days per year = 1.39:1. In this example, the mean annual communication via email with nearby friends is divided by the mean annual communication with distant friends.

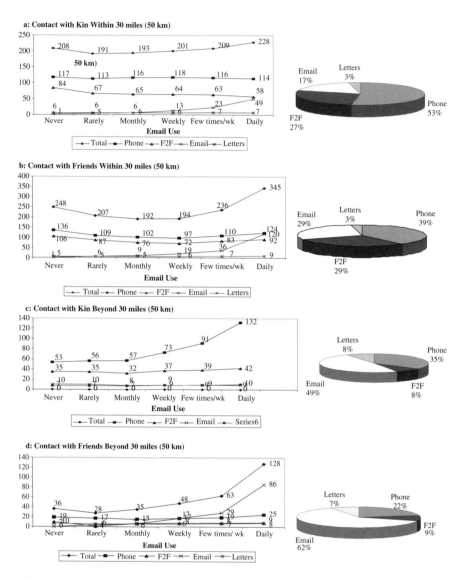

Figure 10.2 Social contact with kin and friends living far away and nearby by medium used and frequency of email use

People have more email contact with nearby friends (58 per cent) than with distant ones (42 per cent) because people have more friends living nearby than far away. By contrast, they have less email contact with nearby relatives (40 per cent) than with distant relatives (60 per cent). Daily users of email use the medium most frequently to communicate with nearby friends (120 days per year), followed by distant friends (86 days per year), distant kin (71 days per year), and the less numerous nearby kin (49 days per year). For daily users of email, three-fifths (58 percent) of their email contact with friends is with those living nearby, as is two-fifths (41 percent) of their email contact with kin (figure 10.2).

More friendship contact than kinship contact is local. Personal visits occur 9.8 times more often with nearby friends than with distant ones, and telephone contact occurs 5.2 times more often with nearby friends than with distant ones. Kinship relations are less local, with the ratios between distant and nearby social contacts with kin smaller: personal visits occur 6.7 times more often with nearby kin than with distant ones, and telephone contact occurs only 2.9 times more often with nearby kin than with distant kin. As kinship relations are usually more densely knit than friendship, kinship systems are better at fostering frequent contact than are friendship ties. Hence, distance does not reduce social contact to the extent it does in friendship relations.

Who uses the Internet for social contact?

The number of months that people have been online is related to their overall use of the Internet (Wellman et al., 2001). As email is the most common Internet activity, it is not surprising that the longer people have been online, the more they use email to communicate with friends far away ($\beta = 0.11$) and nearby ($\beta = 0.15$; table 10.2). However, the number of months people have been online is only slightly related to email communication with kin, both far away ($\beta = 0.07$) and nearby ($\beta = 0.06$). This suggests the possibility that kinship continues to be the relatively stable core of people's personal communities (as Wellman and Wortley showed for pre-Internet days, 1989, 1990), while online contact with friends increases over time.

As friends are more numerous than kin and more variable in their contact, email is especially useful for increasing network capital. However, the lack of associations between the number of months people have been online and the extent of their face-to-face and telephone social contact suggests that the Internet neither increases nor decreases other forms of social contact.

The data give some hope that higher Internet use by younger generations may eventually bolster community. Younger adults (18–29)

Table 10.2 Effects of demographic characteristics, seeking information, and time online on online and offline social contact

	Overall social contact[a]	Relatives				Friends			
		Email		Offline		Email		Offline	
		Far[a]	Near[a]	Far[a]	Near[a]	Far[a]	Near[a]	Far[a]	Near[a]
Gender (male = 1)	−0.045	−0.083	−0.050	0.051	−0.055	−0.024	−0.019	−0.004[b]	0.017
Age (reference = 30–9)									
18–29	0.102	0.025	0.000[b]	0.042	0.000[b]	0.076	0.060	0.052	0.101
40–49	−0.059	−0.012[b]	−0.022	−0.027	−0.032	−0.033	−0.048	−0.014[b]	−0.040
50–65	−0.009[b]	0.043	0.055	0.007[b]	0.037	−0.032	−0.038	0.003[b]	−0.026
66+	0.015[b]	0.024	0.046	0.007[b]	0.037	−0.024	−0.010[b]	−0.012[b]	0.009[b]
Race (reference = white)									
Asian	−0.019	−0.008[b]	0.007[b]	−0.015	−0.017	−0.007[b]	0.006[b]	0.006[b]	−0.029
Black	0.007[b]	−0.010[b]	0.004[b]	0.016	0.032	−0.002[b]	−0.004[b]	0.016	−0.006[b]
Other	0.011[b]	−0.010[b]	0.015[b]	0.004[b]	0.017[b]	0.005[b]	0.001[b]	0.023	0.005[b]
Education (reference = some college)									
High school or less	0.001[b]	−0.007[b]	0.009[b]	−0.022	−0.015[b]	0.001[b]	0.008[b]	0.012[b]	0.009[b]
Undergraduate degree	−0.027	0.016[b]	−0.035	0.024	−0.050	0.005[b]	0.014[b]	0.001[b]	−0.043
Graduate degree	0.003[b]	0.022	−0.040	0.046	−0.056	0.037	0.030	0.023	−0.013[b]
Marital status (reference = married)									
Single	0.129	−0.018		−0.043	−0.078	0.129	0.138	0.105	0.165
Living non-maritally									
With partner	0.001[b]	−0.019	0.003[b]	−0.026	−0.061	0.026	0.045	0.011[b]	0.012[b]
Employment (reference = unemployed)									
Employed	−0.054	−0.064	−0.008[b]	−0.048	−0.031	−0.070	0.011[b]	−0.026	−0.026
Watch TV	−0.024	−0.014	−0.004[b]	0.005[b]	0.009[b]	−0.030	−0.021	−0.023	−0.020
Seeking information	0.068	0.032	0.014[b]	0.038	0.029	0.033	0.028	0.015	0.070
Time online	0.080	0.072	0.064	0.003[b]	−0.030	0.111	0.148	0.016	0.004[b]
Adjusted R²	0.069	0.022	0.011	0.013	0.024	0.060	0.069	0.021	0.065

[a] Standardized beta coefficient. [b] Indicates non-significant coefficients ($p > 0.05$).

have higher levels of social contact ($\beta = 0.10$). Single participants socialize more with friends, both by email and offline, in comparison with married participants and those living non-maritally with a partner.

Online and offline contact

Does email increase, decrease, or supplement in-person and telephone interactions? In the information age, where speed plays a crucial role, email could become the communication medium of choice. Not only does it overcome time and space constraints, email is cheap, ubiquitous, and convenient. On the other hand, email's lack of social presence may hinder rich, fulfilling interactions (Daft and Lengel, 1986).

The data are complex, showing that, depending on the circumstances, email use increases, supplements, and decreases offline social contact.[5] The positive regression coefficients in the first column of table 10.3 support the increase argument. The strongest beta coefficients in the regressions are for the interplay between the frequency of email and offline contact for specific combinations of distance and role relations:

- The frequency of emailing nearby relatives is associated with the frequency of telephone ($\beta = 0.19$) and face-to-face contact ($\beta = 0.10$) with them.
- The frequency of emailing nearby friends is associated with the frequency of telephone ($\beta = 0.31$) and face-to-face contact ($\beta = 0.24$) with them.
- The frequency of emailing far-away relatives is associated with the frequency of telephone ($\beta = 0.20$) and face-to-face contact ($\beta = 0.11$) with them.
- The frequency of emailing far-away friends is associated with the frequency of telephone ($\beta = 0.26$) and face-to-face contact ($\beta = 0.16$) with them.

5   Overall offline social contact was calculated by adding all reported face-to-face, telephone and letter contact with kin and friends within and beyond 30 miles (50 km) in days per year. Note that the results in this section are somewhat different from those initially reported in Wellman et al. (2001) because of changes in the sample size and more precise measurement of contact.

In each situation, the association between the frequency of email and telephone contact is stronger than the association between the frequency of email and face-to-face contact.[6] This suggests that the processes leading to email and telephone contact are more similar than those leading to face-to-face contact. Although face-to-face contact often happens through the unplanned juxtaposition of people in a physical space, telephone calls and email messages are more voluntary. The especially strong associations between emailing nearby friends, phoning them, and seeing them highlights the importance of email as an important, complementary component of voluntary local interaction (Hampton, 2001; Hampton and Wellman, 2002).

Email increases the overall amount of social contact with friends and relatives, living nearby and far away. (We caution that unlike the regression coefficients in table 10.3, the trend lines in figure 10.2 do not control for the effects of other variables.) The total lines in figure 10.2 show that overall contact (including email) is markedly higher for daily email users than for those who never use email: +255 percent for far-away friends (figure 10.2d); +149 percent for far-away kin (figure 10.2c); +40 percent for nearby friends (figure 10.2b); although only +10 percent for the smaller number of nearby kin (figure 10.2a). People rarely communicate by traditional post.

For distant relationships, high email use increases phone contact and supplements face-to-face contact. Daily email users have higher phone contact than those who never email with friends (+32 percent; figure 10.2d) and relatives (+20 percent; figure 10.2c). Face-to-face contact, rare among such physically distant relationships, is essentially unchanged. It is not possible to tell with these data if email use is actually fostering more offline contact, or if gregarious people are taking advantage of an additional communications medium to supplement their social contact.

The situation is different for nearby relationships where high email use is associated with slightly lower telephone and face-to-face contact. Daily users have 9 percent less telephone contact with nearby friends than those who never email and 3 percent less telephone contact with nearby kin (figures 10.2a and 10.2b). The decrease is similar for face-to-face contact with nearby friends (−13 percent) but more marked for face-to-face contact with nearby kin (−31 percent; figures 10.2a and 10.2b). However, when email is taken into account,

---

6 Unstandardized regression coefficients not shown here, were also used for this analysis.

Table 10.3 Effects of email contact and seeking information on offline social contact

				Relatives				Friends			
				Visits		Telephone		Visits		Telephone	
	Offline social contact[a]	Social contact with relatives offline[a]	Social contact with friends offline[a]	Far[a]	Near[a]	Far[a]	Near[a]	Far[a]	Near[a]	Far[a]	Near[a]
Gender (male = 1)	-0.049	-0.048	0.030	0.009[b]	0.000[b]	-0.024	-0.066	0.003[b]	0.064	0.009[b]	0.002[b]
Age (reference = 30–9)											
18–29	0.075	0.010[b]	0.088	0.016[b]	0.008[b]	0.028	-0.004[b]	0.008[b]	0.088	0.018[b]	0.073
40–9	-0.054	-0.034	-0.028	-0.011[b]	-0.027	-0.012[b]	-0.028	0.018	-0.023	-0.018[b]	-0.031
50–65	0.013[b]	0.023	-0.014[b]	0.011[b]	0.010[b]	0.025	0.014[b]	0.021[b]	-0.007[b]	0.002[b]	-0.029
66+	0.043	0.019[b]	0.007[b]	0.016[b]	0.019[b]	0.003[b]	0.010[b]	0.010[b]	0.018[b]	-0.013[b]	-0.008[b]
Race (reference = white)											
Asian	-0.039	-0.024	-0.025	-0.015[b]	-0.017	-0.008[b]	-0.021	0.017[b]	-0.026	0.008[b]	-0.034
Black	0.009[b]	0.035	0.011[b]	0.027	0.024	0.011[b]	0.028	0.011[b]	-0.011[b]	0.014[b]	0.018
Other	0.006[b]	0.017[b]	0.013[b]	0.029	0.014[b]	0.014	0.005[b]	0.031	0.010[b]	0.007[b]	-0.002[b]
Education (reference = some college)											
High school or less	-0.027	-0.019[b]	0.021	-0.016[b]	-0.015[b]	-0.016[b]	-0.013[b]	0.014[b]	0.022	0.019	0.003[b]
Undergraduate degree	0.045	-0.035	-0.050	-0.008[b]	-0.041	0.020[b]	-0.035	-0.015[b]	-0.060	-0.002[b]	-0.036
Graduate degree	0.050	-0.032	-0.011[b]	-0.002[b]	-0.037	0.034	-0.039	0.004[b]	-0.029	0.013[b]	-0.007[b]
Marital status (reference = married)											
Single	-0.096	-0.094	0.117	-0.027	-0.028	-0.060	-0.097	0.020[b]	0.104	0.066	0.090
Living non-maritally with partner	-0.064	-0.065	0.004[b]	-0.024	-0.046	-0.019	-0.057	0.011[b]	-0.005[b]	0.004[b]	0.012[b]
Employment (reference = unemployed)											
Employed	-0.013	-0.040	-0.013	-0.022	-0.028	-0.022	-0.024	0.002[b]	0.002[b]	-0.011[b]	-0.020
Watch television	-0.029	0.014[b]	-0.014[b]	0.005[b]	0.004[b]	0.013[b]	0.016[b]	-0.019	-0.011[b]	-0.004[b]	-0.009[b]
Seeking information	0.110	0.033	0.065	0.017[b]	0.009[b]	0.028	0.023	0.008[b]	0.068	0.003[b]	0.047
Time online	-0.025	-0.041	-0.032	-0.014[b]	-0.030	-0.011[b]	-0.034	0.005[b]	-0.015[b]	-0.006[b]	-0.041
Email with relatives close	0.096	0.171	-0.020	0.018[b]	0.096	-0.005[b]	0.188	0.024	-0.034	-0.021	-0.028
Email with friends close	0.141	-0.009[b]	0.296	-0.002[b]	-0.027	0.001[b]	-0.003[b]	0.011[b]	0.238	-0.004[b]	0.307
Email with relatives far	0.095	0.085	0.027	0.107	0.014[b]	0.200	0.009[b]	-0.013[b]	0.028	-0.010[b]	0.023
Email with friends far	0.121	0.021	0.098	0.034	0.015[b]	0.034	0.000[b]	0.162	0.015[b]	0.261	0.023
Adjusted R²	0.135	0.074	0.182	0.019	0.019	0.054	0.060	0.031	0.111	0.082	0.142

[a] Standardized beta coefficient. [b] Indicates non-significant coefficients ($p > 0.05$).

total contact is higher for daily email users as compared to those never using it: +40 percent for contact with nearby friends and +10 percent for contact with nearby kin.

Civic Engagement

Organizational involvement

The Internet supplements other forms of organizational involvement, rather than increasing or decreasing them. Neither long-term Internet use nor frequent current use are related to the extent of organizational involvement (table 10.4).[7] The only noteworthy association is that frequent visitors to multi-user environments such as MUDs ($\beta = 0.10$) are slightly more likely to participate in organizations. Multi-user environments, with their structured role-playing and social controls, are in some sense, a type of organization. However, few survey participants are involved in multi-user environments.

Traditional communication media continue to be important: The more often people contact friends offline ($\beta = 0.14$), the more they are involved with organizations. By contrast, frequent social contact using email is not associated with organizational involvement. It could be that the persuasive power of face-to-face and telephone contact is more powerful than email in drawing people into participating in organizations. However, it could also be that organizational participation increases face-to-face and phone contact through group meetings and interpersonal follow-up.

Education is the strongest predictor of organizational participation (see also Putnam, 1996, 2000). The most highly educated, the 23 percent of the survey participants with a graduate degree ($\beta = 0.18$), are the most organizationally involved. Unlike the situation for network capital (social contact), the frequency of Internet use and the

---

7 Twenty items asking about organizational participation measured organizational involvement. Survey participants were asked to indicate the extent to which they were involved in different organizations. The options were "not at all," "am a member," and "am an active member." From the 20 items, a scale measuring the degree of organizational involvement for each participant was constructed by summing the number of memberships for each item, with membership including both members and active members. Thus, for each participant a score was obtained that reflected the sum of all the activities engaged. Similar regression results were found for a scale measuring active membership only.

Table 10.4 Effects of email contact and seeking information on civic engagement

	Political participation[a]	Organizational participation[a]
Gender *(male = 1)*	0.062	−0.002[b]
Age *(reference = 30–9)*		
18–29	−0.042	−0.011[b]
40–9	0.119	0.086
50–65	0.139	0.083
66+	0.064	0.060
Race *(reference = white)*		
Asian	−0.009[b]	0.012[b]
Black	0.001[b]	0.016
Other	0.043	0.043
Education *(reference = undergraduate degree)*		
High school or less	−0.036	−0.047
Undergraduate degree	0.035	0.078
Graduate degree	0.109	0.175
Marital status *(reference = married)*		
Single	−0.048	−0.044
Living non-maritally with partner	0.000[b]	−0.042
Employment *(reference = unemployed)*		
Employed	0.002[b]	−0.009[b]
Social contact with friends offline	0.122	0.141
Social contact with relatives offline	0.032	0.033
Social contact with friends online	0.090	0.061
Social contact with relatives online	0.015	0.002[b]
Watch TV	−0.071	−0.062
Seeking information	0.137	0.138
Time online	0.048	0.032
Surf web for recreational purposes	−0.026	−0.056
Engage in chats, instant messaging	0.074	0.033
Visit MUDs, MOOs, other multiuser Environments	0.078	0.099
Play multiuser online games	−0.012[b]	0.005[b]
Adjusted R^2	0.139	0.135

[a] Standardized beta coefficients. [b] Indicates non-significant coefficients ($p > 0.05$).

number of months using the Internet are not related to organizational participation.

People who frequently seek information participate more in organizations (β = 0.14).[8] By contrast, frequent television watching is not associated with organizational participation. Seeking information is an active behavior performed by those who have an interest in such things as news, cultural events, or sports. Watching television for entertainment is more passive. The active information seekers are involved in organizations and not the passive television watchers.

Political participation

Does the Internet affect people's political participation by providing a new platform for debate and engagement, as Castells (1996) and others have suggested? The results show that the Internet supplements political activities but does not change people's levels of involvement (see table 10.4).[9] Political participation is a social activity, with network members involving each other (Tilly, 1984; Tindall, 1994; Diani and McAdam, 2002). More politically active survey participants have more social contact with friends, both offline (β = 0.12) and by email (β = 0.09). Newbies are as likely as veterans to participate.

More education means more political participation. The most highly educated, with a graduate degree, are the more politically engaged (β = 0.11). By contrast with organizational participation, those with an undergraduate degree do not participate more in politics. Political participation is also more strongly associated with age than is organizational participation, with those between 40–65 being the most engaged.

The results support Putnam's (1993, 2000) argument that being informed is positively associated with political participation (β = 0.14). Educated information seekers – usually more interested in public

8 Three items measured seeking information: reading books, reading newspapers and magazines, and going to libraries. Participants were asked to indicate if they did each activity "often," "seldom," or "never." We use here a 0–3 scale counting if participants "often" use each of these three means of seeking information.

9 The 13-item political participation scale is based on the participatory acts and political protest scale designed by the Roper Centre for Public Opinion Research (2001). One item was added: political participation on the Internet. For our study, we created a scale summarizing the number of activities in which a person is involved, with scores ranging from 0 (no participation) to 13.

debate, governmental decision-making, and political changes – are more likely to be politically active. By contrast, watching television has a slight negative association with political participation (β = –0.07). Television is a solitary activity that decreases social involvement (Wei and Leung report similar results, 2001).

Sense of Community

General sense of community

If high use of the Internet supplements face-to-face and telephone contact, and if it affords greater political participation, then both network capital and political participation should foster a greater sense of community. This is not the case. There is no association between how long people have been on the Internet, the extent of their Internet use, and their general sense of community in everyday life (table 10.5).[10] Veteran Internet users have about the same sense of community as newbies. The only association is with participation and offline social contact. Those who participate more in organizations (β = 0.18) and politics (β = 0.12) have a greater sense of community. Social contact offline with friends (but not with relatives) is associated with a slightly higher general sense of community (β = 0.10).

Sense of online community

Although people who have been on the Internet a long time have no greater general sense of community, they do have a greater sense of online community than those who have only been online for a short

10 Responses to 15 items were summarized into an overall sense of community scale. In addition, two measures of a sense of community online were guided by factor analysis (principal components analysis with orthogonal varimax rotation): a scale measuring a general sense of online community, and a scale measuring sense of community with kin online. Cronbach's alpha, measuring scale reliability, is 0.77 for the overall sense of community scale, 0.86 for the sense of community online scale, and 0.76 for the sense of online kinship scale. The results reported here correct a coding problem that distorted the preliminary findings in Wellman et al. (2001). Note that in contrast to the findings here, Matei and Ball-Rokeach (2001; this volume chapter 14) report a small positive association between Internet connectivity, participation in community organizations, and a general sense of community.

Table 10.5 Effects of social contact, seeking information, civic engagement, and Internet use on sense of community

	Overall sense of community offline[a]	General sense of community online[a]	Sense of community online with kin[a]
Gender (man = 1)	0.029	−0.019	−0.085
Age (reference = 30–9)			
18–29	−0.008[b]	−0.085	−0.035
40–9	0.015[b]	0.024	0.012[b]
50–65	0.026	0.051	0.058
66+	0.015	0.036	0.053
Race (reference = white)			
Asian	−0.010[b]	−0.009[b]	0.002[b]
Black	0.000[b]	−0.011[b]	−0.056
Other	−0.006[b]	0.002[b]	−0.021
Education			
(reference = undergraduate degree)			
High school or less	−0.032	0.005[b]	−0.024
Undergraduate degree	0.055	−0.063	0.021
Graduate degree	0.069	−0.074	−0.007[b]
Marital status			
(reference = married)			
Single	−0.063	0.039	−0.065
Living non-maritally with partner	−0.031	0.024	−0.011[b]
Employment			
(reference = unemployed)			
Employed	0.041	−0.031	−0.023
Social contact with friends offline	0.104	−0.083	−0.031
Social contact with relatives offline	0.029	−0.018	−0.010[b]
Social contact with friends online	−0.002[b]	0.107	0.060
Social contact with relatives online	0.019	−0.006[b]	0.263
Watch TV	−0.020	0.004[b] ·	0.004[b]
Seeking information	0.047	−0.018	0.011[b]
Political participation	0.122	0.054	0.033
Organizational participation	0.178	0.032	0.064
Time online	0.024	0.074	0.064
Surf web for recreational purpose	−0.018	0.140	0.066
Engage in chats, instant messaging	−0.023	0.361	0.042
Visit MUDs, MOOs, MUSHs, other Multiuser environments	−0.014[b]	0.072	0.019
Play multiuser online games	−0.009[b]	0.028	0.015
Adjusted R²	0.136	0.279	0.145

[a] Standardized beta-coefficients. [b] Indicates non-significant coefficients ($p > 0.05$).

time (table 10.5). People who exchange many emails with friends have a greater sense of general community online (β = 0.11), and people who exchange many emails with kin have a greater sense of community online with kin (β = 0.26).

By contrast, frequent "real time" chatting online (using instant messaging, etc.) is strongly associated with a general sense of online community (β = 0.36) although not with a more focused sense of online community with kin (β = 0.04). Online chatting is principally an environment for socializing, where friends meet to schmooze, form new bonds, and have serendipitous interactions. By contrast, kin are more apt to exchange email messages at their convenience, perhaps because communication in their long-established relationships does not have as frequent a need for instant contact. Surfing the web for recreational purposes also is associated with a general sense of online community (β = 0.14). Thus, exposure to the Internet leads towards perceiving online space as a positive medium for creating and sustaining community.

Social Capital in the Internet Era

The users of the Internet

The general lack of relationship between demographic characteristics and Internet activities fit recent findings that the digital divide has been narrowing (see also DiMaggio et al., 2001; Fong et al., 2001; Wellman et al., 2002; Katz, this volume; NTIA, 2000; Reddick, 2000). Affluent, university educated, white men no longer predominate. Internet use is associated more with behavior than with social status. People who have been on the Internet longer, and thus are likely to be more familiar with the technology, engage in more types of Internet activities more frequently (see also Howard et al., this volume).

Internet use is not a uniform activity: People engage in both social and asocial activities when online. On the one hand, the Internet is a tool for solitary activities that keep people from engaging with their communities. On the other hand, not all online activities compete with offline interactions. The time people save because they shop online may be spent in socializing offline with family and friends.

The earlier people began using the Internet, the more they use it. We wonder if a plateau will eventually be reached where longer experience online will no longer be associated with more use of the

Internet. Heavy email and chat traffic, or finding 1,000+ results on a search engine, can overload users (Brown and Duguid, 2000; Jones, Ravid, and Rafaeili, 2002; Thorngate, 1990). Time is inelastic (even with multi-tasking), and at some point, Internet use should plateau (see the chapters by Nie, Hillygus, and Erbring, Neustadtl, Robinson, and Kestnbaum; Robinson, Kestnbaum, Neustadtl, and Alvarez).

Network capital

How does the Internet affect social capital in terms of social contact, civic engagement, and sense of community? In terms of social contact (network capital), it is clear that using the Internet frequently does not substantially decrease using other communication media for contact with far-away friends and relatives. Telephone contact continues to be frequent with those living both nearby and far away. Frequent email use is not appreciably associated with (already-rare) face-to-face contact with friends and relatives who live far away. These rare, often ceremonial, events happen as frequently for heavy and light email users. However, frequent email use is associated with lower amounts of face-to-face contact with friends and, especially, relatives living nearby. Although the trend lines in figures 10.2a and 10.2b show these slight negative relationships, the trend lines do not take into account the effects of other variables. Indeed, the regression coefficients in table 10.3 do not show any association – negative or positive – between the frequency of offline and online contact. The absence of any association in the regressions suggests that other factors besides email use may be responsible for the slightly lower offline contact of frequent email users.

The data also suggest that about a third of all contact is with distant network members, those living more than 30 miles away. We suspect that active contact with distant friends is higher than has normally been the case: email, along with the telephone and long-distance means of transportation (from freeways to airways) is supporting the maintenance of active relationships with a sizeable number of distant friends and relatives. The proportion of distant ties in personal networks is high, as is the frequency of contact with them.

Our cross-sectional data cannot accurately show if email use actually increases or decreases face-to-face and telephone contact, or if other factors may be operating. For example, gregarious people may seize upon email as a welcome additional means to communicate with distant friends and relatives. In this case, email use supplements high levels of face-to-face and telephone contact, but does not "cause" these levels.

Most Internet contact is with people who live within 30 miles/50 kilometers. Within 30 miles, the Internet is important but trails face-to-face and telephone contact in the frequency of interactions with friends and relatives. Beyond 30 miles, people have less overall contact but rely on email proportionately more. Email joins the telephone as the everyday means for keeping long-distance ties connected.

Email use increases network capital by supplementing existing levels of face-to-face and telephone contact. For all forms of relationship – kin and friend, near and far – email increases the total volume of social contact by adding its connectivity to continuing levels of face-to-face and telephone contact. Thus, the overall volume of communication is higher with high Internet use. People continue to visit and phone, but they also email. Email adds on to face-to-face and telephone contact as one more medium to communicate with friends and relatives.

The continued use of face-to-face and telephone contacts suggests that they provide unique ways of communicating for which the Internet cannot substitute. Among friends, frequent use of the Internet is associated with frequent offline contact. The data show that people continue socializing via different media. Thus, the Internet is a new and viable form of managing social life.

Our research does not support assertions that the Internet has markedly changed people's patterns of interaction or is socially alienating. The overall volume of communication goes up with frequent email use even when telephone and face-to-face contact is a bit lower. The lower rate of face-to-face and telephone contact with nearby friends and relatives would be cause for alarm only if email was seen as an inadequate form of social contact, yet it is abundantly clear that email provides a wide range of sociability and support (Wellman and Gulia, 1999). The positive association between email use and a sense of online community suggests that email is valued for communication.

Rather than forming a unique entity, the Internet has become a part of everyday life. Those who have been online longer are especially apt to combine email contact with face-to-face and telephone contact. This suggests that there has been unwarranted fear that the Internet will destroy community.

Civic engagement

Internet use supplements existing offline participation in organizations and politics. We had expected that the possibilities of the Internet would counteract a decrease in civic engagement. However, the data do not support utopian hopes that the Internet draws people to greater civic engagement. On the other hand, the data also do not support dystopian fears that the Internet isolates people and reduces civic engagement. Rather, the Internet provides a new sphere for those already civically involved to pursue their interests in an additional way.

The Internet does not appear to be impelling younger generations to be more politically involved than older generations. Although the Internet provides a viable alternative for acquiring political information and becoming politically active, the youngest and least educated remain the least active. A generational and educational gap still exists, with older generations being more active in politics and the well-educated being more active in voluntary organizations as well as politics.

Sense of community

Frequent use of the Internet turns people on, not off. Involvement in the Internet is the best predictor towards having a positive attitude towards community online. The correlations between active community behavior and a sense of community are specific: frequent online communicators with friends have a positive sense of online community, while frequent online communicators with kin have positive feelings towards the Internet as a facilitator of kinship relations. The positive associations argue against contentions that the Internet is alienating. Our findings suggest that the Internet provides a sphere for social interaction, for people to meet others with similar interests, and for the creation of social cohesion.

Frequent Internet use has a different effect on having a general sense of community than it does on having a sense of *online* community. On the one hand, frequent Internet use is not associated with either an overall sense of community or feeling alienated. It neither turns people on nor turns them off from an overall sense of community. On the other hand, the more people use the Internet, the more positive their sense of online community.

Our findings suggest that the Internet is neither fulfilling the utopians' dreams of greater community euphoria nor evoking the dystopians' nightmares of greater alienation. Those who spend more time online value the Internet for its positive social virtues as a space for supportive social interactions to flourish. Online encounters function as positive feedback, increasing use of the Internet. Using the Internet may also be leading people to realize that complementary and alternative ways of finding community exist online in addition to those available offline.

The Internet and social capital

Taken together, our results suggest that the Internet is increasing social capital, civic engagement, and developing a sense of belonging to online community. We suspect that people not only have more relationships than in pre-Internet times, they are in more frequent contact with their relationships, and the strengthening of the bonds through more frequent contact means that ties can be more readily mobilized for aid. The experiences of frequent Internet users probably provide the best window into the future, as more people come to use the Internet and as more people use it frequently and routinely.

What of the two nagging anomalies with our account? First, while high email use is associated with a greater sense of online community, it is not related to either a higher or a lower sense of overall community. Second, high email use with nearby friends and relatives is related to somewhat less offline contact with friends and relatives. These two findings might signal a slight shift to online relations at the expense of offline relationships. However, the nature of the survey questions about sense of online community suggests that people are expressing the pleasure they feel in increased communication with kin and friends that was not possible before. In perspective, these findings suggest the continuing flourishing of community, the new role of the Internet in maintaining and increasing social capital, but also some shift in emphasis from the local and the proximate to the distant and the ethereal (see also Hampton and Wellman, this volume).

Our research shows no single Internet effect. At a time of spatially dispersed community, the Internet facilitates social contact that supplements face-to-face and telephone contact. At a time of declining civic engagement, the Internet provides tools for those already involved to increase their engagement. At a time of partial identity with multiple personal communities, the Internet provides another means for feeling connected with friends and kin. Rather than weakening other forms of community, those who are more active offline are more active online – and vice versa. In this way, people are incorporating the Internet into their everyday lives even as the Internet is quietly fostering the changing composition of social capital.

References

Baym, N. K. (1997). Interpreting soap operas and creating community. In S. Kiesler (ed.), *Culture of the Internet* (pp. 103–20). Mahwah, NJ: Erlbaum.

Brown, J. S. and Duguid, P. (2000). *The social life of information*. Boston, MA: Harvard Business School Press.

Castells, M. (1996). *The rise of the network society*. Oxford: Blackwell.

Chmielewski, T. and Wellman, B. (1999). Tracking geekus unixus: an explorers' report from the National Geographic website. *SIGGROUP Bulletin*, 20 (December), 26–8.

Curtis, J., Baer, D., and Grabb, E. (2001). Nations of joiners: explaining voluntary association membership in democratic societies. *American Sociological Review*, 66(6), 783–805.

Daft, R. L. and Lengel, R. H. (1986). Organizational information requirements, media richness and structural design. *Management Science*, 32(5), 554–71.

De Kerckhove, D. (1997). *Connected intelligence: the arrival of the web society*. Toronto: Somerville House.

DiMaggio, P., Hargittai, E., Neuman, R. W., and Robinson, J. P. (2001). The Internet's implications for society. *Annual Review of Sociology*, 27, 307–36.

Diani, M. and McAdam, D. (eds) (2002). *Social movement analysis: the network perspective*. Oxford: Oxford University Press.

Eckstein, S. (2001). Community as gift-giving: collectivistic roots of volunteering. *American Sociological Review* 66(6), 829–51.

Fischer, C. (1982). *To dwell among friends*. Berkeley: University of California Press.

Fischer, C. (1992). *America calling: a social history of the telephone to 1940*. Berkeley: University of California Press.

Fischer, C. (2001). *Bowling alone:* What's the score? Paper presented to the American Sociological Association conference, Anaheim, August.

Flanagan, A. and Metzger, M. (2001). Internet use in the contemporary media environment. *Human Computer Research*, 27, 153–81.

Fong, E., Wellman, B., Wilkes, R., and Kew, M. (2001). *The double digital divide*. Ottawa: Office of Learning Technologies.

Gershuny, J. (2001). *Web-use and net-nerds: a neo-functionalist analysis of the impact of information technology in the home*. Institute for Social and Economic Research Working Paper 2001–1. Colchester, UK: University of Essex.

Granovetter, M. S. (1973). The strength of weak ties. *American Journal of Sociology*, 78, 1360–80.

Guest, A. and Wierzbicki, S. (1999). Social ties at the neighborhood level: two decades of GSS evidence. *Urban Affairs Review*, 35, 92–111.

Hampton, K. (2001). Living the wired life in the wired suburb: Netville, glocalization and civil society. Unpublished doctoral dissertation, University of Toronto, Toronto.

Hampton, K. and Wellman, B. (2002). Neighboring in Netville: how the Internet helps connect people in a wired suburb. *City and Community*, 1 (Sept.) in press.

Hiltz, S. R. and Turoff, M. (1978). *The network nation*. Reading, MA: Addison-Wesley.

Horrigan, J. B., Lenard, T. M., and McGonegal, S. (2001). *Cities online: urban development & the Internet*. Washington, DC: The Progress and Freedom Foundation and The PEW Internet and American Life Project.

Howcroft, D. (1999). The hyperbolic age of information: an empirical study of Internet usage. *Information, Communication and Society*, 2(3), 277–99.

Johnson, T. and Kaye, B. (2000). Democracy's rebirth or demise? The influence of the Internet on political attitudes. In D. Schulz (ed.) *It's show time! media, politics and popular culture* (pp. 209–28). New York: Peter Lang.

Jones, Q., Ravid, G., and Rafaeili, S. (2002). *An empirical exploration of mass interaction system dynamics: individual information overload and Usenet discourse*. Proceedings of the Hawaii International Conference on System Sciences, IEEE Press.

Kapor, M. (1993). Where is the digital highway really heading? *Wired* (July), 53–9.

Koku, E. and Wellman, B. (2003). Scholarly networks as learning communities: the case of TechNet. Forthcoming in S. Barab, R. Kling, and J. Gray (eds) *Building online communities in the service of learning*. Cambridge: Cambridge University Press.

Koku, E., Nazer, N., and Wellman, B. (2001). Netting scholars: online and offline. *American Behavioral Scientist*, 44, 1750–72.

Kraut, R., Patterson, M., Lundmark, V., Kiesler, S., Mukhopadhyay, T., and Scherlis, W. (1998). Internet paradox: a social technology that reduces social involvement and psychological well-being? *American Psychologist*, 53(9), 1017–31.

LaRose, R., Eastin, M. S., and Gregg, J. (2001). Reformulating the Internet paradox: social cognitive explanations of Internet use and depression. *Journal of Online Behavior*, 1(2). Available online at:
http://www.behavior.net/JOB/v1n2/paradox.html

Lévy, P. (1997). *Collective intelligence*. New York: Plenum.

Lin, N. (2001). *Social capital*. Cambridge: Cambridge University Press.

Matei, S. and Ball-Rokeach, S. (2001). *The Internet in the communication infrastructure of urban residential communities: macro or meso-linkage?* Paper presented to the Association for Internet Research conference, Minneapolis, October.

Müller, C. (1999). Networks of 'personal communities' and 'group communities' in different online communication services. *Proceedings of the Exploring Cyber Society: social, Political, Economic and Cultural Issues* (pp. 1–14). University of Northumbria, Newcastle, UK.

Nie, N. (2001). Sociability, interpersonal relations, and the Internet. *American Behavioral Scientist*, 45(3), 420–35.

Nie, N. and Sackman, H. (1970). *The information utility and social choice*. Montvale, NJ: AFIPS Press.

NTIA. (2000). *Falling through the net: Toward digital inclusion*, [Report]. National Telecommunications and Information Administration, US Department of Commerce, Economic and Statistics Administration. Available online at: http://www.ntia.doc.gov/ntiahome/digitaldivide/

Orlikowski, W. and Barley, S. (2001). Technology and institutions. *MIS Quarterly*, 25, 145–65.

Pool, I. d. S. (ed.). (1977). *The social impact of the telephone*. Cambridge, MA: MIT Press.

Putnam, R. (1993). *Making democracy work: civic traditions in modern Italy*. Princeton, NJ: Princeton University Press.

Putnam, R. (1996). The strange disappearance of civic America. *The American Prospect*, 24, 34–48.

Putnam, R. (2000). *Bowling alone*. New York: Simon & Schuster.

Reddick, A. (2000). *The dual digital divide: the information highway in Canada*, [Report]. The Public Interest Advocacy Centre, Human Resources Development Canada, Industry Canada. July. Available online at: http://olt-bta.hrdc-drhc.gc.ca/publicat/index.html

Rheingold, H. (1993). *The virtual community*. Reading, MA: Addison-Wesley.

Rheingold, H. (2000). *The virtual community* (revised edn). Cambridge, MA: MIT Press.

Rogers, E. M. (1995). *Diffusion of innovations*. New York: Free Press.

Roper Center for Public Opinion Research. (2001). *Roper social and political trends*, [Online]. Available online at: http://www.ropercenter.uconn.edu.

Schofer, E. and Fourcade-Gourinchas, M. (2001). The structural contexts of civic engagement: voluntary association membership in comparative perspective. *American Sociological Review*, 66(6), 806–28.

Schwartz, E. (1996). *Netactivism: how citizens use the Internet*. Sebastopol, CA: Songline.

Shapiro, C. and Varian, H. R. (1998). *Information rules*. Cambridge, MA: Harvard Business School Press.

Singh, S. (2001). Gender and the use of the Internet at home. *New Media and Society*, 3(4), 395–416.

Slouka, M. (1995). *War of the worlds: cyberspace and the high-tech assault on reality*. New York: Basic Books.

Smith, M. A. (1999). Counting on community. Paper presented to the CHI'99 conference, Pittsburgh, May.

Sproull, L. S. and Kiesler, S. B. (1991). *Connections*. Cambridge, MA: MIT Press.

Steiner, G. A. (1963). *The people look at television*. New York: Knopf.

Stoll, C. (1995). *Silicon snake oil: second thoughts on the information highway*. New York: Doubleday.

Sunstein, C. R. (2001). *Republic.Com*. Princeton, NJ: Princeton University Press.

Tarrow, S. (1999). Fishnets, Internets and catnets: Globalization and transnational collective action. In M. Hanagan, L. Moch, and W. TeBrake (eds), *The past and future of collective action*. New York: Russell Sage Foundation.

Thorngate, W. (1990). Got a minute? Attentional limits revisited. *Canadian Psychology*, 31, 288–91.

Tilly, C. (1984). *Big structures, large processes, huge comparisons*. New York: Russell Sage Foundation.

Tindall, D. (1994). *Collective action in the rainforest*. Unpublished doctoral dissertation, University of Toronto, Toronto.

Tocqueville, A. de. (1835). *Democracy in America*. New York: Knopf.

Uslaner, E. M. (2000). Social capital and the net. *Communications of the ACM*, 43(12), 60–5.

Valente, T. W. (1995). *Network models of the diffusion of innovations*. Cresskill: Hampton Press.

Wei, R. and Leung, L. (2001). *Impact of Internet use on traditional media, leisure and work: a path model approach*. Paper presented to the International Communication Association, Washington, May.

Wellman, B. (1979). The community question. *American Journal of Sociology*, 84, 1201–31.

Wellman, B. (1999). The network community. In B. Wellman (ed.), *Networks in the global village* (pp. 1–48). Boulder, CO: Westview.

Wellman, B. (2001). Physical place and cyber-place. *International Journal for Urban and Regional Research*, 25, 227–52.

Wellman, B., Carrington, P., and Hall, A. (1988). Networks as personal communities. In B. Wellman, and S. D. Berkowitz (eds), *Social structures: a network approach* (pp. 130–84). Cambridge: Cambridge University Press.

Wellman, B. and Gulia, M. (1999). Net surfers don't ride alone. In B. Wellman (ed.), *Networks in the global village* (pp. 72–86). Boulder, CO: Westview.

Wellman, B. and Tindall, D. (1993). Reach out and touch some bodies: how telephone networks connect social networks. *Progress in Communication Science*, 12, 63–94.

Wellman, B. and Wortley, S. (1989). Brothers' keepers. *Sociological Perspectives*, 32, 273–306.

Wellman, B. and Wortley, S. (1990). Different strokes from different folks. *American Journal of Sociology*, 96, 558–88.

Wellman, B., Quan-Haase, A., Witte, J., and Hampton, K. (2001). Does the Internet increase, decrease, or supplement social capital? Social networks, participation, and community commitment. *American Behavioral Scientist*, 45(3), 437–56.

Wellman, B., Wilkes, R., Fong, E., Kew, M., and Chen, W. (2002). Fathoming the digital divide. *Studies in Internet Communication: Theory and Practice*, 19 (forthcoming).

Witte, J., Amoroso, L., and Howard, P. (2000). Method and representation in Internet-based survey tools. *Social Science Computing Review*, 18(2), 179–95.

Wuthnow, R. (1991). *Acts of compassion: caring for others and helping ourselves.* Princeton, NJ: Princeton University Press.

Wuthnow, R. (1998). *Loose connections: joining together in America's fragmented communities.* Cambridge, MA: Harvard University Press.

11

The Impact of Community Computer Networks on Social Capital and Community Involvement in Blacksburg

Andrea L. Kavanaugh
and Scott J. Patterson

Abstract

This chapter adds to the debate over whether easy access to the Internet is the only outcome of community computer network projects or if there are tangible impacts to these initiatives. Building from Putnam's (2000) links between quality of life, community involvement, and social capital the authors provide evidence as to the quality of life implications of the community computer network known as the Blacksburg Electronic Village (BEV). The results of the longitudinal study indicate frequent and increasing use of both the BEV (local online content and services) and the Internet for local, social capital building activities. However, there is no trend toward an increase in community involvement or attachment, except in a subset of the population. This subset is comprised of people who were already more actively involved in the local community, and then began using the Internet to increase their involvement. Early Internet adopters are more likely than later adopters to use the community computer network for purposes of civic engagement or community involvement. The longitudinal data show that while there is an increasing use of the Internet for social networking, there is a leveling off of the proportion of the population that reports increased community involvement since getting on the Net. The results offer Putnam justification for his claims about the Internet's role in social capital formation. Putnam argues that initiatives such as the BEV are an outcome of communities with already high levels of social capital, community involvement, and community attachment. Our results are also consistent with earlier studies regarding early adopters, social status, and civic engagement.

Authors' note

The authors are grateful for support for this research from the National Science Foundation, the US Department of Commerce, the University of Pennsylvania, San Francisco State University, and Virginia Polytechnic Institute and State University. The authors would also like to give special thanks to Armando Borja, Daniel Eno, Robert Noble, Lucinda Willis, and Kimberly Kirn for help in the data analyses for this manuscript. Early versions of this manuscript were presented to the National Communication Association. The authors thank Barry Wellman, Caroline Haythornthwaite, and several anonymous reviewers for their helpful comments. Authorship is listed in alphabetical order.

Let us find ways to ensure that by 2010 the level of civic engagement among Americans then coming of age in all parts of our society will match that of their grandparents when they were that same age.

Robert Putnam

When computer networks link people as well as machines, they become social networks.

Barry Wellman

What are the implications for the quality of life in a geographic community when the communication patterns in that community are bolstered by the addition of a universally available community-based computer network? This becomes a central question for the information society. One significant impact of a community computer network is a decrease in the digital divide and an increase in access to the information society among members of the community (Cohill and Kavanaugh, 1997, 2000; Patterson, 2000; Patterson and Kavanaugh, 2002). This chapter presents an additional picture of the case study developed in Blacksburg, Virginia surrounding the Blacksburg Electronic Village (or "BEV," see www.bev.net for background materials).[1] The BEV community computer network project began in 1993 and in seven years enabled over 80 percent of the community residents to gain access to the Internet and the information society. In this chapter we extend a debate about whether access to the Internet is the only outcome of community computer networking projects or if there are tangible quality of life impacts to these networking initiatives. We

1 For more detail on specific interventions by the BEV to increase social capital in the community please see the BEV website. The fully realized URL for the research pages of the Blacksburg Electronic Village is: http://www.bev.net/project/research/index.html.

begin with a case for the importance of a link between communication and quality of life, follow with evidence from the Blacksburg Electronic Village case, and then finish with a discussion of the role of the Internet in the quality of communal life.

Quality of Life in Communities

One approach to issues surrounding quality of life in our local communities is to focus on the amount and quality of communication that occurs within those communities. This link between communication and quality of life is elegantly postulated by Robert Putnam (1993, 1995a, 1995b, 2000). Putnam (1993) attributes variation in the quality of life among geographic communities to different levels of social capital and corresponding civic engagement within those communities. Putnam defines social capital as the "features of social organization, such as trust, norms and networks, that can improve the efficiency of society by facilitating coordinated actions" (1993, p. 167). Social capital, in part, refers to the amount and quality of communication about a community that takes place among its members within their social networks. One outcome of this participation and talk is the development of social trust that facilitates collective social action toward achieving common social goals (i.e. civic engagement). Thus, civic engagement is a function of communication among members via their social networks and as civic engagement increases so does quality of life in the community. Communities with vibrant communication networks are likely to have a higher quality of life.

Putnam (2000) argues that a variety of macro-level social conditions served to decrease the amount of social capital in US communities during the last century. Primary among these conditions is a "generational shift" that began in the 1960s where individuals no longer devoted time to running the voluntary associations (like the PTA and bowling leagues) necessary to build social capital and its corresponding social networks and social trust. These voluntary organizations gave their members the opportunity to develop self-government skills of organization, teamwork, and relationship building essential to increase the quality of life in their local communities. Putnam's central claim is that communities that exhibit high levels of social capital exhibit a higher quality of life and that quality of life decreases with reductions in social capital. Or stated another way, communities that exhibit high levels of interpersonal, vibrant, face-to-face communication have corresponding high qualities of life (Ryan, 2000). The question for media scholars and especially Internet scholars is what is the role of mediated communication in the quality of life in our local communities?

The claim made in this research is that one effect of community computer networks is to build social capital in the communities that host them. This claim is significant because of the implications drawn between social capital and quality of life in local communities. To summarize our expectations:

H1: As the number of community computer network users increases, the greater the community involvement and attachment within the community.

H2: As the number of community computer network users increases, the greater the use of the network to build social capital by communicating with other community members.

Community Computer Networks and Quality of Life

Research about the role of media in the quality of life of local communities indicates general support for a link between media use and community involvement. While Putnam argues that increased television use is a symptom of decreasing social capital (see Putnam, 1995a, 1995b), others argue that frequent newspaper readers are more attached to their local communities (Stamm, 1985), involved in their local communities (Rothenbuhler, 1991), and exhibit higher levels of social trust (Cappella, Lee, and Southwell, 1997) than infrequent readers. Dimmick, Patterson, and Sikand (1996) argue for the role of the traditional telephone in developing and maintaining strong interpersonal communication patterns in the local community.

Tomita (1980) and Neuman (1991) provide a starting point for the examination of the role of interactive media in building social capital. Tomita, anticipating the advent of email, chat, and so on juxtaposes the variables of audience size and speed of communication, and posits the existence of a "media gap" where no technology exists to facilitate small group communication. We agree with Neuman who posits that the advent of computer networks and applications such as chat and email, could be successful in filling the gap in media communication technologies described by Tomita. Several scholars view the Internet as especially well suited to communication activities that lead to community building, virtual or otherwise (Jones, 1998; Rheingold, 2000; Wellman, 1997; Cohill and Kavanaugh, 1997, 2000).

Some researchers argue that the Internet is a social capital building technology because existing social networks can take advantage of the information distribution aspects of the network to become more effective and connected communicators (Wellman, Carrington, and Hall, 1988; Wellman and Gulia, 1999; Wellman, Salaff, Dimitrova, Garton, Gulia, and Haythornthwaite, 1996). Bonchak (1996) argues that Internet users are active consumers of political information and participate in a variety of online political activities. Kohut (1999) indicates that early adopters of the Internet are more politically active and civic minded than are later adopters. Moreover, while early adopters of the Internet are interested in news and political information, later adopters are more interested in commercial services such as shopping or games (see also Patterson and Kavanaugh, 1994). One important implication of the Kohut finding is that if the critical mass of early Internet adopters are more civic minded and active in communication, they might encourage new adopters to engage in talk about community – a social capital building activity. This conclusion seems confirmed by a study that finds Internet users are vibrant socialites who spend lots of time with family and friends and have a wide range of outside interests (Cole, 2000). Finally, perhaps most convincingly, Hampton and Wellman (1999) find in their study of the Netville community computer network, "online activity led to increased local awareness, high rates of in-person activity, and to rapid political mobilization" (p. 490).

Others paint a bleak picture of the role of the Internet in fostering the communication behaviors that lead to building social capital. Kraut and his colleagues (Kraut, Patterson, Lundmark, Kiesler, Mukhopadhyay, and Scherlis, 1998) find that Internet users tend to become more isolated and depressed over time. Others argue that the Internet use is dysfunctional to traditional interpersonal relations and can lead to an "Internet addiction disorder" (see Walther, 1999). While these authors paint a picture that Internet use is anathema to social relations, Turkle (1997) argues that the communication that occurs on the Internet may be more gratifying for participants than traditional face-to-face communication. Internet users may spend their social capital building energies in developing placeless virtual communities rather than enhancing their local geographic communities. For Turkle, it is sufficient that people use the Internet for social capital building activities whether they are building that capital for offline or online communities.

Respondents were not asked in any of these studies specifically about the role of the Internet in building and maintaining their local communities. One important implication of the emerging literature on community computer networks is that such networks facilitate community development (Cohill and Kavanaugh, 1997, 2000; Acker and McCain, 2000; Patterson, 2000; Schmitz, 2002). One specific purpose of the Blacksburg Electronic Village is to encourage local community organizations (formal and informal) to take advantage of network resources to facilitate information exchange and communication with members or constituents and to mobilize collective action. The basic premise is that the BEV encourages members of the community to become users of the Internet. Further, the BEV provides structures such as listservs, grants for businesses to build online content, server space for local voluntary organizations to create a web presence and help for building that presence, and free high-speed access at public locations throughout the town. These are interventions designed to increase local content, community involvement and attachment, and eventually affect the quality of life in Blacksburg (Cohill and Kavanaugh 2000; Patterson and Kavanaugh, 2001).

More about the Blacksburg Electronic Village

Blacksburg is a university town (population 43,839 in 2000), home of the land grant university Virginia Polytechnic Institute and State University (also known as Virginia Tech). The town lies in the foothills of the Allegheny Mountains in rural southwest Virginia. It is fairly isolated and remote, geographically, about a five-hour drive from Washington, DC. Roughly 85 percent of the town residents are affiliated with the university, as faculty, staff or students. Even controlling for students, the demographics of the population are higher than the national average on measures of education, income and occupation. In both 1996 and 1999 survey rounds, the average level of education was college graduate; median household income was above the national median.

The high proportion of residents with above-average socioeconomic status has given impetus to Internet diffusion from the earliest years of the project (1993-4). As early surveys indicate (Cohill and

Kavanaugh, 1997) about half of the households in Blacksburg had PCs in 1994 (above the national average of about 35 percent at the time). Respondents with higher levels of education and income are more likely to have Internet access in both 1996 and 1999. Nonetheless, the education group with the biggest increase in Internet access is those reporting "some high school or less." The percentage of respondents in this group reporting Internet access jumps from only 13 percent in 1996 to 63 percent in 1999.

The university's leadership in the BEV project has been key in introducing technological options, ensuring project stability, and building a critical mass of users. From the outset of the project in 1993, the predominant task of BEV staff has been education and training, aimed at individuals and organizations in the public, private, and non-profit sectors. The project staff have initiated and sustained these ongoing interventions to attract and support Internet adoption and use among community members and organizations as information producers, as well as consumers. Interventions of the project staff include training and technical support for basic Internet services (email, listserv, web space) packaged at cost recovery rates to serve local non-profit organizations. Organization members or constituents have an ongoing need for exchanging information (meeting agendas, minutes, updates, announcements, newsletters) as well as discussion within the group. Services such as organizational email account, listserv and web site provide additional channels of communication and information exchange. The BEV bundles these basic Internet services in a package for a low annual fee (about $20 per year). It holds monthly support sessions over a brown bag lunch to further facilitate adoption and use by community organizations.

When people discover that their church or their child's teacher, soccer team, or Boy Scout troop is distributing news and inviting discussion via the Internet, they have a direct interest in using that service. Furthermore, as with telephone networks, computer networks provide increased access to members of a person's social circle, including members of the same group or organization. The acceleration of Internet adoption by organizations ratchets up the adoption by members affiliated with those organizations. By fall 2001, over a hundred and twenty non-profit organizations in the community were annual subscribers of these bundled Internet services offered by BEV in 2000.

Many of the interventions by the BEV staff have been supported through outside funding that provided connectivity and training in the public schools and library systems, the town and county govern-ments, and non-profit organizations. As the project established a crit-ical mass of users in the early years of the diffusion process, more organizations, including those in the private sector, began to take on support roles, and to provide ongoing services. The high density of users also fostered numerous new web-based businesses. In many cases, the clients of these new businesses were predominantly other organizations that sought to facilitate or enhance information ex-change with their own clientele, constituency, or organizational mem-bership via the Internet. The town government provided an average of $350 in economic development mini-grants to any local business interested in establishing a web site. The only requirement was that the applicant business commit to covering the long-range costs of maintaining and updating its site (see Kavanaugh and Cohill, 1997). Of the 67 local businesses that applied for mini-grants, 47 received awards. The existing web service companies and several start-up com-panies marketed furiously to offer web publishing to businesses receiving these grants. As each business completed its online pages, usually by contracting services from one of the local publishing com-panies or consultants, it sent a copy of the invoice to BEV, Inc., for reimbursement. The number of online commercial listings more than doubled during the one-year period between 1995 and 1996 (from 100 to over 200). This intervention helped to build critical mass in the com-mercial area of the local Web content, and to add value and attract sub-scribers to the network. By Fall 2001, over 75 percent of local businesses had Web sites, most of which were established and main-tained with their own funds.

Expectations of the Study

It is important to reiterate that the Blacksburg Electronic Village was not initially conceived as a social capital building project (Cohill and Kavanaugh, 2000; Patterson and Kavanaugh, 2001). The initial purpose of the BEV was to increase access to the Internet in the inter-est of overcoming rural isolation or "digital divide" based on geogra-phy. Over time, as critical mass was achieved and near universal access to the Internet emerged among the residents of Blacksburg, the emphasis of network planners shifted from access to use. Once they reach critical mass, community computer networks such as the BEV can become interventions by designers directly targeted at increasing the amount of communication within a community about that community. Whether that communication is an information product (like a web-site) or a discussion forum (like a listserv) the result is to add another means to facilitate exchange among local and distant network members. Indeed, the goal of community computer network designers is not to "replace" existing channels of communication and information exchange, rather to supplement these channels (see Quan-Haase and Wellman, this volume).

Methods

The main source of data for this chapter comes from a 1999 telephone survey of the year-round (non-student) residents (N = 320) of Blacksburg. The survey instrument employed in the 1999 survey was previously used in a 1996 telephone survey of the residents of Montgomery County, in which Blacksburg is located. In 1996, 156 year-round (non-student) residents of Blacksburg were interviewed as part of the larger survey project.

In this chapter we compare the 1999 (N = 320) and the 1996 (N = 156) datasets to address our research claims. For both samples, households were randomly selected using a random digit dialing selection procedure and individual respondents were selected using the most recent birthday technique (Frey, 1989).

The telephone survey instrument operationalized key concepts related to Internet use, community attachment, and community involvement, as well as demographic and media use measures. To measure community involvement we employed the Rothenbuhler (1991) community involvement scale. Community attachment was measured, following Stamm (1985), by a single indicator asking how happy the respondent would be if they had to leave the community. Several other correlates of community involvement and attachment were also measured including home ownership, length of time residing in the community, and mobility. Internet use measures focused on whether or not the respondent had access to the Internet and the extent to which they used the Internet to communicate with a variety of different social network partners. Undergraduate students enrolled in a research methods course administered the 1996 surveys. Students conducted interviews in a telephone survey research facility supervised by the authors. In 1999, a professional telephone survey research firm administered the surveys after initial training by the authors.

Table 11.1 Descriptive statistics and tests for differences over time, demographic variables, 1996 and 1999 samples

Variable name	1996[a]		1999[a]		Significance test[b]
	Mean	SD	Mean	SD	
Freq. read paper	5.33	1.39	5.57	1.41	n.s.
% subscribe cable TV	78.6%		78.5%		n.s.
Education	5.22	1.71	4.95	1.65	n.s.
Age	44.21	17.68	48.28	14.34	n.s.
Income	3.91	3.68	4.87	3.02	$F = 9.84, p < 0.01$

[a] 1996 (N = 156); 1999 (N = 343). [b] ANOVA for time by interval-level data; χ^2 for time by nominal.

Results

The data do not support our expectation that as access to the BEV increased, so would community attachment and involvement. Comparisons between the 1996 and 1999 scores on the community involvement scale and the community attachment indicator are not significantly different.

Yet, the general pattern of our data does point to significant increases in the use of the Internet for social capital building activities during the study period. As we agree with Putnam, among others, that social capital and civic engagement (or community involvement) are linked, we offer two interpretations of the unexpected results. This section first describes the general characteristics of the persons interviewed for this project, then considers the relationship between increasing access to and use of the Internet and community involvement and attachment. The third section of the results focuses on the relationship between the length of time using the net and predisposition to use the network to build social capital.

Neither the 1996 nor the 1999 samples were significantly different from each other in terms of demographic variables (see table 11.1). The majority of people in both samples were college graduates in their mid-forties. Income in the 1999 sample was reported as higher than in the 1996 sample but this difference is not significantly different when we control for inflation. Both samples represent roughly equal amounts of males and females (51.3 percent female in 1996; 53.4 percent female in 1999). Cable television penetration and use of the newspaper were not significantly different.

Table 11.2 Descriptive statistics and tests for differences over time, community involvement and Internet use variables, 1996 and 1999 samples

Variable name	1996[a] Mean	SD	1999[a] Mean	SD	Significance test[b]
Community involvement					
Community involvement scale	2.81	0.68	2.82	0.70	n.s.
Community attachment	3.46	1.09	3.29	1.03	n.s.
Years in community	14.61	16.17	19.54	13.89	$F = 12.20$, $p < 0.001$
No. of times moved	1.05	1.49	0.58	1.03	$F = 16.26$, $p < 0.001$
No. of meetings per week	1.45	0.64	1.32	0.66	$F = 4.24$, $p < 0.05$
% own home	58.4		74.6		$\chi^2 = 20.43$, $p < 0.001$
% church members	50.0		63.1		$\chi^2 = 8.54$, $p < 0.01$
% formal organization members	37.2		26.2		$\chi^2 = 5.81$, $p < 0.05$
% informal organization members	36.5		42.4		n.s.
Internet use					
% with Internet access	69.2%		80.1%		$\chi^2 = 7.14$, $p < 0.01$
Years using net	–	–	3.43	1.18	n.s.
Use the net to communicate with . . .					
Local family	2.20	1.64	2.89	1.67	$F = 13.35$, $p < 0.001$
Non-local family	3.28	1.66	3.48	1.58	n.s.
Local friends	3.27	1.67	3.38	1.60	n.s.
Non-local friends	3.68	1.52	3.58	1.51	n.s.
Co-workers	3.04	1.82	2.97	1.82	n.s.
Church members	1.71	0.80	2.05	1.32	$F = 16.21$, $p < 0.001$
Formal social groups	1.65	1.21	2.01	1.43	n.s.
Informal social groups	2.35	1.23	2.52	1.44	$F = 19.13$, $p < 0.001$

[a] 1996 (N = 156); 1999 (N = 343). [b] ANOVA for time by interval-level data; χ^2 for time by nominal.

There was a significant increase in Internet access (see table 11.2) among the residents of Blacksburg from 1996 to 1999 with over 80 percent of the community reporting access to the Internet in 1999. Also, Patterson (2000) reports that among people with Internet access in Blacksburg, virtually all (98 percent) were aware of the Blacksburg Electronic Village presence as part of the Internet.

While there were not significant differences in community involvement and attachment between 1996 and 1999, there were significant differences on associated measures of involvement and attachment, such as length of residence, home ownership, and number of times moved. Respondents in 1999 were more likely to have lived in the community longer, moved less frequently, and were more likely to own a home than respondents in 1996. While it is difficult to link these activities to use of the Internet, they do provide evidence that the residents of Blacksburg were more predisposed to community involvement and attachment in 1999 than in 1996. However, in 1999 respondents were less likely to attend a meeting of a civic organization and were less likely to belong to formal social organizations such as the PTA or the Lions Club. This lack of participation in social capital building activities should point to a decrease in overall community involvement and attachment, however, there were no differences over time. Perhaps the presence of the Internet and the BEV contributed to social capital formation in new ways?

Residents of Blacksburg were significantly more likely in 1999 to use the Internet to communicate with local family members, church members, and members of informal social groups (such as baby-sitting circles and sports clubs) than in 1996. And although not statistically significant, Internet use also increased for communicating among members of formal social groups (the PTA or service organizations like the Rotary) and with local friends. In the aggregate, while there were no appreciable differences in community involvement and attachment over time, there were significant differences in the use of the Internet for social capital and community building activities.

To investigate this pattern, we examined questions from the 1999 dataset about the length of time (in years) people had been users of the Internet. Table 11.3 presents the correlations between length of Internet use and community involvement, attachment, and social capital variables.

Again, the community involvement and attachment variables are not significantly associated with Internet use. However, the longer people are users of the Internet the more likely they are to use the Internet for a variety of social capital building activities (all but communication with local friends). We also took a cue from the Kohut findings about community involvement and Internet adoption patterns and asked: what is the relationship between community involvement and length of Internet use?

The more the community involvement, the greater the predisposition to use the Internet for social capital building activities (table 11.4). People who used the Internet to communicate with members of formal

Table 11.3 Pearson product moment correlations with length of time using the Internet, 1999

	Length of Internet use
Community involvement scale	0.041
Community attachment	0.051
Years in community	−0.032
No. of times moved	−0.059
No. of meetings a week	0.021
Use the Internet to communicate with . . .	
Local family	0.097
Non-local family	0.199**
Local friends	0.336***
Non-local friends	0.361***
Co-workers	0.410***
Church members	0.140*
Formal social groups	0.192***
Informal social groups	0.195***

* p < 0.05; ** p < 0.01; *** p < 0.001 (two-tailed).

Table 11.4 Pearson product moment correlations for Internet users, community involvement scale by Internet communication activities, 1996 and 1999 samples

	Community involvement scale	
	1996	*1999*
Community attachment	0.135	0.035
Years in community	0.156*	0.103*
No. of times moved	−0.107	−0.073
No. of meetings a week	0.145	0.248***
Use the Internet to communicate with . . .		
Local family	−0.077	0.236***
Non-local family	−0.039	0.139**
Local friends	−0.039	0.233***
Non-local friends	−0.158	0.138*
Co-workers	−0.012	0.095
Church members	0.061	0.198***
Formal social groups	0.334***	0.312***
Informal social groups	0.244**	0.328***

* p < 0.05; ** p < 0.01; *** p < 0.001 (one-tailed).

Table 11.5 Comparison of self-perception of change in involvement by time, 1996 and 1999 samples

Variable name	1996 Mean	SD	1999 Mean	SD	Significance Test
Involved with issues	2.36	0.55	2.26	0.57	n.s.
Connected with people	2.47	0.60	2.18	0.65	$F = 16.06$, $p < 0.001$
Involved with community	2.22	0.55	1.99	0.57	$F = 13.54$, $P < 0.001$
Attended meetings	1.99	0.47	1.91	0.44	n.s.

For the 1999 sample only:
Pearson product moment correlations between length of time using the Internet and self-perception of change in involvement

	Length of Internet use
Involved with issues	0.329***
Connected with people	0.301***
Involved with community	0.181**
Attended meetings	0.062

* $p < 0.05$; ** $p < 0.01$; *** $p < 0.001$ (two-tailed).

and informal social groups were highly involved in their communities. This trend strengthens in 1999: people who had high levels of community involvement used the Internet more for a variety of interpersonal and small-group communication activities.

These results suggest a strong relationship between community involvement and the use of the Internet for social capital building activities. Why then was there no increase in community involvement, attachment, or participation as the number of Internet users in the community increased? In both the 1996 and 1999 surveys respondents were asked whether "Since getting on the net do you think you have:

Become more, equally, or less involved with issues that interest you;
Become more, equally, or less connected with people like you;
Become more, equally, or less involved with the community; and
Attended more, equal, or fewer meetings of local groups."

Table 11.5 presents the means and standard deviations and comparison tests between the 1996 and 1999 groups. Significant differences in the means for self-perceptions of change in involvement (falling between 1996 and 1999) suggest that people feel they have become less involved and attached to the community since beginning to use the

Internet. However, the 1999 data reveal significant positive associations between the length of time people have been using the network and the extent to which they feel more involved and connected to their local communities (see also Quan-Haase and Wellman, chapter 10). The longer people used the network, the more likely they were to use the Internet for social capital building activities that lead to increased community attachment and involvement. One interpretation is that late adopters report equal or less sense of involvement in the local community and over time these late adopters may report a sense of increased involvement as a result of increasing use of the Internet for social capital building activities. Alternatively, the observed 'decreasing involvement' trend may persist among late adopters, despite Internet use over time, as Kohut (1999) suggests. Kohut finds that later adopters are less politically active and civic minded, and that they prefer commercial services such as entertainment and online games to political news and participation.

Discussion

Our general expectation was that over time, the residents of Blacksburg would report higher levels of community involvement and community attachment. Further, these higher levels of community involvement and attachment would be attributable in part to increasing use of the Internet and the local community computer network to facilitate the building of social capital within the community. Evidence from the Blacksburg case supports only the claim that the longer people have been connected to the Internet, the more likely they are to use the network to build social capital, and to increase involvement in local community and issues. One logical extension of this conclusion is that if social capital building activities occur in the community, involvement and attachment should increase and quality of life should improve.

What's not supported is an increasing proportion of the population becoming more involved in the local community. While participation in social groups decreased over time, community involvement and attachment remained unchanged. There are two potential explanations for this finding. First, Putnam (2000) directly confronts the role of the Blacksburg Electronic Village and other community computer networks in building social capital. His claim is that perhaps initiatives such as the BEV are an outcome of communities with already high levels of social capital, community involvement, and community attachment. Specifically, "Experience in Blacksburg suggests that . . . social capital may turn out to be a prerequisite for, rather than a consequence of, effective computer-mediated communication" (Putnam, 2000, p. 177). These results offer Putnam justification for his claims about the relationship between the Internet and the processes of social capital formation.

Putnam has little hope for community computer networks in the building of social capital. It is a basic chicken or egg problem – which comes first the community computer network or high social capital? Community computer networks may just be a "voluntary organization" for the information society. Just as the Lions Club or the PTA served to build social networks and social trust during the last century, it is possible that community computer networks may serve as a modern functional alternative. Perhaps people spent less time involved in traditional face-to-face meetings and more time building the Blacksburg Electronic Village? The conclusion that community computer networks are more likely to succeed in communities with already high levels of social capital needs further research and testing. One means of answering this question would be to compare the Blacksburg experience to experiences in other communities with local computer networks.

There is another approach to explaining the Blacksburg data. It is based on the notion that there is a latent capacity for civic engagement in every community. The demands of modern life compete for people's time and attention. Nonetheless, many community members are interested in local issues, and are predisposed or 'poised' to be more active. They will become involved under certain circumstances (including, basic awareness, and more convenient access to information and communication). For individuals predisposed to become more involved, the Internet and associated community computer networks help to distribute information of interest more widely, more conveniently, and allow for efficient participation in discussion. Thus, the Internet capitalizes on existing social networks while at the same time it reaches people 'predisposed to be more active.' In so doing, it draws additional participants into discussions and decision making. This explanation hinges on the notion that it is easier to reach people on a listserv or via a website than it is to get them to attend a face-to-face meeting or event, or to circulate information widely or efficiently by telephone.

The demographic data show that these additional participants are not individuals who are traditionally disenfranchised or otherwise under-represented in civic and community life. These are individuals of higher social and economic status, with high demands for their time and attention. By reintroducing their voice and attention into community life, computer networking may be helping to restore some of the "eroded" social capital and civic engagement to which Putnam refers.

The significant differences in community involvement between early versus later adopters in the results from the Blacksburg data clearly support the Kohut finding that early adopters of the Internet are more politically interested and civic minded than later adopters. The media, including the Internet, contribute to the political communication process, according to Norris (2000), by a "virtuous circle" of ratcheting up and reinforcing the participation of interested individuals. Over time these people serve as opinion leaders in the diffusion process. The longer people use the community computer network and the Internet, the more they report feeling involved in the local community, feeling connected to people like themselves, and becoming involved with issues that interest them. Is this an "early adopter" phenomenon that will persist, such that even over time later adopters do not become more civic minded or involved in their community? Or is this a temporary lag – a passing phase – in what may be a trend toward increased involvement by the majority of the population (notably, later adopters) over time? In either case there is an overall rising trend in the use of the Internet for social networking and relations (that is, social capital building activities). Further, the longer people are on the Internet, the more likely they are to use the Internet to engage in these social capital building activities.

Perhaps the most encouraging finding about the role of the Internet and community computer networks revolves around evidence indicating that people will use the Internet for social capital building activities. Whether the community computer network is a new kind of voluntary association or an efficient way of extending traditional associations to new audiences, network users are engaging in communication with their community members. It is this talk or social capital building among community members that strengthens social networks and social trust, and helps lead to community involvement and higher quality of life. It would be interesting to explore the extent to which people take community building behaviors learned online into offline community realities. Perhaps, as Turkle suggests, we are capable of existing in multiple realities and each of our realities can learn and benefit from experiences in the others. Learning to build social capital online may transfer to offline social capital building behaviors. There is every reason to believe that the Americans coming of age in the year 2010 will have the opportunities to learn social capital building communication behaviors and that the Internet, especially community computer networks, will play an important role in that process.

References

Acker, S. and McCain, T. (2000). Living in the information age. Unpublished manuscript. Columbus: The Ohio State University.

Bonchak, M. (1996). From broadcast to netcast: the Internet and the flow of political information. Unpublished doctoral dissertation, Harvard University, Cambridge.

Capella, J., Lee, G., and Southwell, B. (1997). The effects of news and entertainment on interpersonal trust: political talk radio, newspapers, and television. Paper presented at the meeting of the International Communication Association, San Francisco, CA.

Cohill, A. and Kavanaugh, A. (1997). *Community networks: lessons from Blacksburg, Virginia* (first edn). Norwood, MA: Artech House.

Cohill, A. and Kavanaugh, A. (2000). *Community networks: lessons from Blacksburg, Virginia* (revised edn). Norwood, MA: Artech House.

Cole, J. (2000). *Surveying the digital future.* Los Angeles: University of California at Los Angeles, Center for Communication Policy. Available online at: http://ccp.ucla.edu/pages/internet-report.asp

Dimmick, J., Patterson, S., and Sikand, J. (1996). Personal telephone networks: a typology and two empirical studies. *Journal of Broadcasting and Electronic Media,* 40 (1, winter), 45–59.

Frey, J. (1989). *Survey research by telephone.* Newbury Park: Sage.

Hampton, K. and Wellman, B. (1999). Netville online and offline: observing and surveying a wired suburb. *American Behavioral Scientist,* 43(3), 475–92.

Jones, S. G. (1995). Understanding community in the information age. In S. G. Jones (ed.), *Cybersociety: computer-mediated communication and community* (pp. 10–35). Thousand Oaks, CA: Sage.

Jones, S. G. (ed.) (1998). *CyberSociety 2.0: revisiting computer-mediated communication and community.* Thousand Oaks, CA: Sage.

Kavanaugh, A., Cohill, A., and Patterson, S. (2000). The use and impact of the Blacksburg Electronic Village. In A. Cohill and A. Kavanaugh (eds), *Com-*

munity networks: lessons from Blacksburg, Virginia (revised edn) (pp. 77–98). Norwood, MA: Artech House.

Kohut, A. (1999). *The Internet news audience goes ordinary.* Washington, DC: The Pew Research Center.

Kraut, R., Patterson, M., Lundmark, V., Kiesler, S., Mukhopadhyay, T., and Scherlis, W. (1998). Internet paradox: a social technology that reduced social involvement and psychological well-being? *American Psychologist,* 53(9), 1,017–31.

Neuman, R. (1991). *The future of the mass audience.* New York: Cambridge University Press.

Norris, P. (2000). *A virtuous circle: political communications in post-industrial democracies.* Cambridge, MA: Harvard University Press.

Patterson, S. (2000). *Comparing users and non-users of community computer networks: implications for the digital divide.* Paper presented at the International Communication Association, Acapulco, Mexico.

Patterson, S. and Kavanaugh, A. (1994). Rural users expectations of the information superhighway. *Media Information Australia,* 74(4), 57–61.

Patterson, S. and Kavanaugh, A. (2002). Building critical mass in community computer networks. *The Electronic Journal of Communication,* 11(2) (forthcoming).

Putnam, R. (1993). *Making democracy work: civic traditions in modern Italy.* Princeton, NJ: Princeton University Press.

Putnam, R. (1995a). Bowling alone: America's declining social capital. *Journal of Democracy,* 6, 67–78.

Putnam, R. (1995b). Tuning in, tuning out: the strange disappearance of social capital in America. *PS: Political Science & Politics,* 28(4), 664–84.

Putnam, R. (2000). *Bowling alone: the collapse and revival of American community.* New York: Simon & Schuster.

Rheingold, H. (2000). *The virtual community: homesteading on the electronic frontier* (revised edn). Cambridge, MA: MIT Press.

Rothenbuhler, E. (1991). The process of community involvement. *Communication Monographs,* 58, 63–78.

Ryan, A. (2000). My way [Review of the book Bowling alone: the collapse and revival of American community]. *The New York Review of Books,* 67(13), 47–50.

Schmitz, J. (2002). Editor's introduction. *The Electronic Journal of Communication* (forthcoming).

Stamm, K. (1985). *Newspaper use and community ties: toward a dynamic theory.* Norwood, NJ: Ablex.

Tomita, T. (1980). The new electronic media and their place in the information market of the future. In A. Smith (ed.) *Newspapers and democracy: international essays on a changing medium* (pp. 49–62). Cambridge, MA: MIT Press.

Turkle, S. (1997). *Life on the screen: identity in the age of the Internet.* New York: Touchstone.

Walther, J. (1999). *Communication addiction disorder: concern over media, behavior and effects*. Paper presented at the American Psychological Association, Boston, MA.

Wellman, B. (1997). An electronic group is virtually a social network. In S. Kiesler (ed.), *Culture of the Internet* (pp. 179–205). Mahwah, NJ: Lawrence Erlbaum.

Wellman, B., Carrington, P., and Hall, A. (1988). Networks as personal communities. In B. Wellman and S. Berkowitz (eds), *Social structures: a network approach* (pp. 130–84). Cambridge: Cambridge University Press.

Wellman, B. and Gulia, M. (1999). Net surfers don't ride alone. In B. Wellman (ed.), *Networks in the Global Village* (pp. 331–66). Boulder, CO: Westview Press.

Wellman, B., Salaff, J., Dimitrova, D., Garton, L., Gulia, M., and Haythornthwaite, C. (1996). Computer networks as social networks: collaborative work, tele-work, and virtual community. *Annual Review of Sociology*, 22, 213–39.

12

The Not So Global Village of Netville

Keith N. Hampton and Barry Wellman

Abstract

We examine the experience of the residents of Netville, a suburban neighborhood with access to some of the most advanced new communication technologies available, and how this technology affected the amount of contact and support exchanged with members of their distant social networks. Focusing exclusively on friends and relatives external to the neighborhood of Netville, "community" is treated as relations that provide a sense of belonging rather than as a group of people living near each other. Computer-mediated communication (CMC) is treated as one of several means of communication used in the maintenance of social networks. Contrary to expectations that the Internet encourages a "global village," those ties that previously were "just out of reach" geographically, experience the greatest increase in contact and support as a result of access to CMC.

Authors' note

This research was supported by the Social Science and Humanities Research Council of Canada, IBM's Institute of Knowledge Management, Mitel Networks, and Communication and Information Technologies Ontario. At the University of Toronto, we have benefitted from our involvement with the NetLab, Centre for Urban and Community Studies, the Department of Sociology, and the Knowledge Media Design Institute. We thank a host of people for their comments, assistance, and support. At the University of Toronto: Dean Behrens, Nadia Bello, Sivan Bomze, Bonnie Erickson, Todd Irvine, Kristine Klement, Emmanuel Koku, Alexandra Marin, Dolly Mehra, Nancy Nazer, Christien Perez, Grace Ramirez, Janet Salaff, Richard Stren, Carlton Thorne, and Jeannette Wright. Others: Ross Barclay, Donald Berkowitz, Damien De Shane-Gill, Jerome Durlak, Herbert Gans, Paul Hoffert, Timothy Hollett, Thomas Jurenka, Marc Smith, Liane Sullivan, and Richard Valentine. Our greatest debt is to the residents of Netville who have given their time and patience, allowing us into their homes and answering many questions. Portions of this work are reprinted from Keith Hampton's doctoral dissertation, and previously published under the title "Long distance community in the network society: contact and support beyond netville," *American Behavioral Scientist* 45(3), 476–95, © Sage Publications, 2001. For more papers on the Netville project please visit www.mysocialnetwork.net and www.chass.utoronto.ca/~wellman

Redefining Community in a Network Society

Early urban ethnographies of the mid-twentieth century played a major role in defining the sociological treatment of "community" (see Anderson, 1978; Whyte, 1943; Clark, 1966; Gans, 1962, 1967). For the most part a "community study" still refers to the study of neighborhoods. Yet most of the social support, and much of the information and resources that people require to function in their day-to-day lives comes from sources outside of the local setting (Fischer, 1982; Wellman, Carrington, and Hall, 1988). Social network analysts and others have long suggested that the *social* aspect of community should be emphasized over the *spatial* (Fischer, 1982; Wellman, 1999). Indeed, "community without propinquity" is hardly a new concept, but it is one that is often neglected (Webber, 1963). Only with recent innovations in communication technology – the growth of the Internet – has there been widespread recognition by the public, the media, and indeed, scholars, that supportive social relations exist at a distance (Rheingold, 2000).

The creation of a whole new type of community, the "virtual community," has done much to highlight the geographic dispersion of social ties. Yet the study of virtual communities has largely maintained the traditional framing of "community" as something that is physically bounded, but by geographies of bits and bytes rather than by streets and alleyways. Online relationships are treated as entities in themselves as if existing social networks and existing means of communication, did not exist (see the review in Wellman and Gulia, 1999).

Community is best seen as a network – not as a local group. We are not members of a society which operates in "little boxes," dealing only with fellow members of the few groups to which we belong: at home, in our neighborhood, workplaces, or in cyberspace (Wellman and Hampton, 1999). Rather, each person has his/her own "personal community" of kinship, friendship, neighboring and workmate ties. People use multiple methods of communication in maintaining ties with community members: direct in-person contact, telephone, postal mail, and more recently fax, email online chats, and email discussion groups. This social definition of "community" emphasizes supportive, sociable, relations that provide a sense of belonging rather than a group of people living near to each other (Wellman, 1999). This approach implies that computer-mediated communication (CMC) has not introduced a new geography to community; it has introduced a new means of social contact with the potential to affect many aspects of personal communities.

This chapter examines the experience of the residents of "Netville,"[1] a suburban neighborhood with access to some of the most advanced new communication technologies available, and how this technology has affected the contact and social support that Netville residents have with friends and relatives living outside of this "wired suburb."

Wired Ties and the Fate of Community

Unlike the almost universal earlier fear that technologies such as the automobile and television would harm community (Stein, 1960), the debate about the Internet comes in two flavors (Wellman and Gulia, 1999). Enthusiasts hail the Internet's potential for making connections without regard to race, creed, gender or geography. As Phil Patton early proclaimed: "Computer-mediated communication . . . will do by way of electronic pathways what cement roads were unable to do, namely connect us rather than atomize us, put us at the controls of a 'vehicle' and yet not detach us from the rest of the world" (1986, p. 20). By contrast, dystopians suggest that the lure of new communication technologies withdraws people from in-person contact and lures them away from their families and communities (Kraut, Patterson, Lundmark, Kiesler, Mukhopadhyay, and Scherlis, 1998; Nie and Erbring, 2000; Nie, Hillygus, and Erbring, 2002). They worry that meaningful contact will wither without the full bandwidth provided by in-person, in-the-flesh contact. As Texas commentator Jim Hightower warned over the ABC radio network: "While all this razzle-dazzle connects us electronically, it disconnects us from each other, having us 'interfacing' more with computers and TV screens than looking in the face of our fellow human beings" (quoted in Fox, 1995, p. 12).

Yet, several scenarios are possible. Indeed, each scenario may happen to different people or to the same person at different times. In

---

1   "Netville" and the "Magenta Consortium" that implemented the project are pseudonyms.

an "information society" where work, leisure, and social ties may all be maintained from a "smart home," people could reject the need for social relationships based on physical location. They might find community online or not at all, rather than on street corners or while visiting friends and relatives. In such a scenario, new communication technologies may advance the home as a center for services that encourage a shift toward greater home-centeredness and privatization. At the same time, the location of the technology inside the home facilitates access to local relationships, suggesting that domestic relations may flourish, possibly at the expense of more distant ties.

Our research has been guided by a desire to integrate the study of community offline and online. We are interested in the totality of relationships in community ties and not just in behavior in one communication medium or locale. In this we differ from studies of "virtual community" that only look at relationships online (e.g. Baym, 1997; O'Brien, 1998) and from traditional sociological studies of in-person, neighborhood-based communities (e.g., Gans, 1967; Whyte, 1943). The former can over-emphasize the importance of computer-only ties, while the latter do not take into account the importance of transportation and communication in connecting community members over a distance. Unlike many studies of CMC that observe undergraduates in laboratory experiments (reviewed in Sproull and Kiesler, 1991; Walther, Anderson, and Park, 1994), we study people in real settings. We focus here on the effect of new communication technologies on the residents of the wired neighborhood of Netville.

The Social Affordances of the Internet[2]

Pre-Internet advances in transportation and communication technology partially emancipated community from its spatial confines. The cost of mobility and of social contact have decreased with the advent of technologies such as the train, automobile, airplane, and telephone (Hawley, 1986). People decentralized their active social ties as the financial and temporal costs of transcending space decreased. CMC – in the form of email, chat groups and instant messaging – introduces

2 "Affordances" is a term used in the study of human computer interaction (Gaver, 1996; Norman, 1999). Erin Bradner (2000), writing for computer scientists, coined the term "social affordances" to emphasize the social as well as individual possibilities of computer networks.

new means of communication with friends and relatives at a distance. The Internet has the capacity to foster global communities in which ties might flourish without the constraints of spatial distance. On the Internet, neighbors across the street are no closer than best friends across the ocean. In practice, the shrinking of the map of the world is unlikely to go so far. Most ties probably function through the interplay of online and offline interactions. Hence, CMC should lessen, but not eliminate, the constraints of distance on maintaining personal communities.

With the telephone, the cost of contact increases with physical distance. By contrast, the cost of contact with CMC does not vary with distance but is based on a flat fee, along with access to a personal computer and the Internet. For most, the decision to purchase a home computer has been based on a desire to expand educational or work opportunities and not directly out of a need to maintain contact with distant network members (Ekos, 1998). As a result, the ability to use CMC as a form of contact is largely a byproduct of a financial investment in other activities.

In addition to reducing the financial cost of social contact, specific forms of CMC, such as email, provide temporal freedom. Asynchronous email means that both parties do not have to be present for contact to take place. Analogous to the traditional paper letter, email can be composed without the immediate participation of the receiving party. Those with free, high-speed, always-on, Internet access, that was available to the residents of Netville are even better situated to experience increased social contact with network members. They can send messages whenever the urge hits them, without waiting to boot up the computer, dial the Internet, or worry about interfering with telephone calls. They can quickly send and receive pictures, audio messages, and email. As temporal flexibility becomes more important with complex, individualized daily lives (Wellman, 2001), CMC should improve the ability of contact to take place for local as well as distant network members.[3]

What kinds of community does this type of technology afford? It is time to move from speculation to evidence. This chapter tests the hypotheses that:

3   As it takes at least two to do high-speed CMC, the contact of Netville residents was limited because many of their friends and relatives who lived elsewhere had much slower and more sporadic connections.

- Living in a wired neighborhood with access to free, high-speed, always-on, Internet access increases social contact with distant network members.
- Those ties located at the greatest distance will experience the greatest increase in contact as a result of Internet access.

Previous studies have demonstrated that CMC can be used for the exchange of non-instrumental support, such as companionship and emotional aid (Haythornthwaite and Wellman, 1998). In this way, CMC is similar to the telephone in its ability to participate in the exchange of social support regardless of physical distance. However, instrumental aid – such as lending household items and providing childcare – relies more on physical access and is more appropriately exchanged with physically available network members (Wellman and Wortley, 1990; Wellman and Frank, 2001). For ties in close proximity, the introduction of CMC may help facilitate the delivery of aid but is likely limited to supplementing existing means of communication. At best, CMC will contribute to a modest increase in support exchanged with nearby ties.[4]

The more physically distant ties are also unlikely to experience a significant increase in the exchange of support as a result of CMC. Regardless of the means of communication, distance between network members makes it difficult to provide many goods and services. Support that depends less on contact to be effective – such as financial aid, companionship, and emotional aid – are more likely to benefit from CMC between distant network members.

When CMC is adopted, it is likely to afford the greatest increase in support among mid-range ties located somewhere between the most distant network members and those who live nearby. CMC, particularly email, should facilitate coordination with mid-range ties, increase awareness of network members' social capital, and increase the amount and breadth of support exchanged. Network members within this mid-range can provide non-instrumental aid that does not rely on in-person contact. With some coordination and effort, they can also provide instrumental aid. The reduced cost and temporal flexibility of email reduces previous barriers to obtaining such support from mid-range network members. We would therefore expect the greatest increase in the exchange of overall support to occur with those who were previously "just out of reach." We hypothesize that:

4 Neighborhood ties are an exception in Netville and are treated as a special case in Hampton, 2001b and Hampton and Wellman, 2002.

- Moving into a wired neighborhood with free, high-speed, always-on, Internet access increases overall levels of support exchanged with network members. In particular, mid-range ties (50–500 km) will experience the greatest increase in the exchange of overall support.

Studying Netville

Netville

The evolving nature of the Internet makes it a moving research target. Almost all research can only describe what has been the situation, rather than what is now or what will soon be. We have been blessed with a window into the future by having spent several years studying "Netville": a leading-edge "wired suburb" filled with a series of new information and communication technologies that are not yet publicly available. The widespread use of such technology in Netville[5] makes it an excellent setting to investigate the effects of future forms of CMC on community.

Netville is a newly built development of approximately 109 medium-priced detached homes in a rapidly growing, outer suburb of Toronto. Most homes have three or four bedrooms plus a study: 2,000 square feet on a 40-foot lot. In its appearance Netville is nearly identical to most other suburban developments in the Toronto area. Its distinguishing feature is that it is one of the few developments in North America where all of the homes were equipped from the start with a series of advanced communication technologies supplied across a broadband, high-speed, local network. Users could reliably expect network speeds of at least 10 Mbps, more than ten times faster than other commercially available "high-speed"[6] Internet systems (that is, telephone DSL and cable modem services), and more than 300 times faster than dial-up telephone connections. For two years, the local network provided residents with high-speed, always-on[6] Internet access (including electronic mail and web-surfing), computer-

5 For more details, see Hampton (2001b), Hampton (2001a), Hampton (1999), and Hampton and Wellman (1999).
6 "Always on" Internet access refers to a property of most high-speed Internet services which allows users to be connected to the Internet whenever the computer is turned on, without performing any special tasks, manually starting any additional programs, or "dialing up" to the Internet.

desktop videophone, an online jukebox, entertainment applications, online health services, and local discussion forums. In exchange for free access to these advanced services, Netville residents agreed to be studied by the corporate and scholarly members of the Magenta Consortium, the organization responsible for developing Netville's local network.[7] Approximately 60 percent of Netville homes participated in the high-bandwidth trial and had access to the network for up to two years. The other 40 percent of households, for various organizational reasons internal to the Magenta Consortium, were never connected to the network despite assurances to residents at the time they purchased their homes that they would be.[8] These households, not connected to the local network, provide a convenient, quasi-random comparison group for studying the effects of computer-mediated communication.

Wired and non-wired Netville residents were similar in terms of age, education and family status (Hampton, 2001b). Residents were largely middle class, English-speaking, and married. More than half of all couples had children living at home when they moved into the community, and as with many new suburbs, a baby boom happened soon after moving in. Although most residents were white, an appreciable minority were racial and ethnic minorities. About half had completed a university degree. Residents worked at such jobs as technician, teacher, and police officer. Their median household income in 1997 was C$75,000 (US$50,000). Netville residents were as likely as other Canadians of similar socioeconomic status to have a televison, a VCR, cable TV, a home computer and home Internet access (Hampton, 2001b). While the decision of some to purchase a home in Netville was motivated by the technology available, only 21 percent of home purchasers identified Netville's "information services" as one of the top three factors in their purchasing decision.

As technology developed and fashions changed, the telecommunications company responsible for Netville's local network decided that the hybrid fiber coaxial technology used in the development was not the future of residential Internet services. They terminated the field trial early in 1999 to the dismay of the residents (Hampton, 2002).

7   This agreement was only lightly enforced and often forgotten by the residents. No resident was ever denied service for refusing to participate, and no data were ever collected without the residents' knowledge and consent.
8   Magenta never clarified why some Netville homes were connected and others were not. The two most likely causes were the consortium's limited access to resources for completing home installations, and miscommunications with the housing developer in identifying homes that had been occupied.

Research design

Our research objectives led us to gather information about residents' community ties online and offline, globally and locally. These included: relations within Netville (see Hampton, 2001b; Hampton and Wellman, 2002), personal networks extending well beyond Netville (the subject of this chapter), civic involvement, and attitudes toward community, technology and society. We used several research methods, principally ethnographic fieldwork and a cross-sectional survey.

Ethnography

In April 1997, one of us, Keith Hampton, began participating in local activities. Hampton moved into Netville in October 1997 (living in a resident's basement apartment), staying until August 1999. Given the widespread public interest in Netville, residents were not surprised about his research activity and incorporated him into the neighborhood. Hampton worked from home, participated in online activities, attended all possible local meetings (formal and informal), walked the neighborhood chatting, and did ethnographic participant-observation. Like other residents, he relied on the high-speed network to maintain contact with social network members living outside of Netville. His daily experiences and observations provided detailed information about how residents used the available technology, their domestic and neighborhood relations, and how they used time and local space. Insights gained through observation and interactions were instrumental in developing the survey and in establishing trust with local residents.

Survey

The survey was first administered to those moving into Netville in April 1998 and was expanded in September 1998 to include existing wired and non-wired residents. The survey obtained information on geographic perception, personal and neighborhood networks, neighboring, community alienation, social trust, work, experience with technology, time-use, and basic demographics. We tried to learn the extent to which Netville residents' personal networks were abundant, strong, solidary, and local. Our attempt to collect detailed information on residents' closest social ties was met with mixed success as a result of Magenta's decision to end the technology trial and problems in our use of computer-assisted interviewing (see Hampton, 1999). As a result, while recognizing that different types of ties (friends, relatives, etc.) and ties of different strength are likely to provide different types of aid and support, this chapter does not include an analysis of specific types of ties or forms of support. Instead we focus exclusively on changes in social contact and exchange of support with friends and relatives at various distances. Noticeably absent from this chapter is a full review of Netville residents' neighborhood ties, explored briefly in the conclusion of this chapter and more extensively in Hampton (2001b), Hampton (2002), and Hampton and Wellman (2002).

Measuring social contact and support

We report here on *change* in contact and support with *non-local* friends and relatives living outside Netville.[9] We asked 18 questions about change in support and contact with network members living at the distances of (1) less than 50 kilometers (excluding neighborhood ties), (2) 50 to 500 km, and (3) greater than 500 km in comparison to one year before their move to Netville. Participants were asked to indicate on a five-point scale from −2 (much less) to +2 (much more) how their overall levels of contact and support exchanged with friends and relatives had changed. The 18 ordinal variables were combined into eight scales that document:[10]

9   Some caution should be taken in the interpretation of this data, Participants were not asked to indicate if they had ties at the specified distances both pre- and post-move. Participants who responded that they did not have social ties at a given distance were coded as having the "same" level of contact or support pre- and post-move. Participants may have experienced no change in contact as a result of not having ties at the specified distance, or report change as a result of not having network members at the specified distance either pre- or post-move. However, there is no indication that this limitation in the data should significantly affect the results as they are presented here.

10   Cronbach's alpha, a measure of internal consistency and reliability among scale items shows that all scales (except one) have a satisfactory alpha above 0.7. The exception, the scale for change in contact with non-neighborhood network members living within 50 km, is retained because the significant correlation of 0.32 between the two variables comprising it validates the underlying consideration in scale construction that participants respond consistently across scale constructs.

1 Change in social contact with all social ties regardless of distance
2 Change in support exchanged with all social ties regardless of distance
3 Change in social contact with ties outside Netville but within 50 km
4 Change in support exchanged with ties outside Netville but within 50 km
5 Change in social contact with mid-range (50–500 km) social ties
6 Change in social support exchanged with mid-range (50–500 km) social ties
7 Change in social contact with ties more than 500 km away
8 Change in support exchanged with ties more than 500 km away.

To test hypotheses of how living "wired" in Netville, with access to the local high-speed network, affects contact and support exchanged with social network members, the distribution and mean scores for wired and non-wired participants are compared for change in social contact and support (1) regardless of distance, and with network members living at (2) less than 50 km (which includes Toronto, but excludes immediate neighbors), (3) 50–500 km, and (4) more than 500 km.

Social contact and support scales are dependent variables in regressions that include the independent variables of wired status (connected or not connected to Netville's high-speed network) and control variables for gender, age, years of education and length of residence (the length of time participants had lived in Netville at the time they were interviewed). The rationale for inclusion of the control variables are:

1 *Gender*: women may be more likely than men to experience a change in social contact or support as a result of their role in maintaining the majority of household ties (Wellman, 1992; Wright, 1989).
2 *Age*: age may contribute to network stability and reduce the likelihood of experiencing change in social contact or support.
3 *Education*: education contributes to greater social and financial capital which may help in the maintenance of social contact and support networks (Putnam, 2000).
4 *Length of residence*: moving may disrupt communication with network members. Length of residence in Netville is included to

control for the possibility that early movers may report a drop in social contact and support in comparison to those who have had time to settle into their new home.

Social Contact and Social Support

Overall changes

Contact

Compared to one year before moving to Netville, 41 percent of Netville residents report a drop in social contact with friends and relatives, 32 percent report no change, and 28 percent report an increase. Yet wired residents have significantly more contact than non-wired: 68 percent of wired residents report that their overall level of social contact either increases or remains the same as compared with only 45 percent of non-wired residents (figure 12.1). On average, non-wired residents report a drop in contact and wired residents report almost no change in social contact compared to a year before their move (table 12.1). Holding other factors constant, the negative intercept coefficient in table 12.2 indicates that Netville residents generally experience a drop in contact as a result of their move. This is consistent with the observations of S. D. Clark (1966) and Herbert Gans (1967) who found a similar loss of social contact among new suburban dwellers.

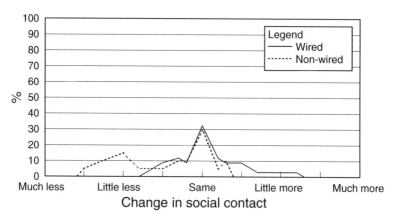

Figure 12.1   Overall change in social contact

Table 12.1 Comparison of wired and non-wired residents by mean change in contact with social ties at various distances (km)[a]

	Overall		Less than 50 km		50–500 km		More than 500 km	
	Non-wired	Wired	Non-wired	Wired	Non-wired	Wired	Non-wired	Wired
Mean	−0.33*	0.03*	−0.28	−0.13	−0.43*	0.03*	−0.30*	0.19*
SD	0.51	0.38	0.73	0.58	0.61	0.56	0.73	0.46
Min.	−1.5	−0.67	−2	−1.5	−1.5	1	−2	−0.5
Max.	0.33	1.17	1	1	0.5	1.5	1	2

[a] Scale for mean score ranges from −2 "lot less" to +2 "lot more"; N = 34 wired, 20 non-wired. Difference between means is significant at [+] $p < 0.05$ * $p < 0.01$ ** $p < 0.001$ (ANOVA).

Table 12.2 Coefficients from the regression of change in social contact on wired status and other independent variables at various distances (km) (N = 54)

Control variables	Overall	Less than 50 km	50–500 km	More than 500 km
Wired[a]	0.25[+]	—	0.45*	0.40[+]
	(0.26)		(0.36)	(0.32)
Female[b]	—	—	—	—
Education	0.06[+]	0.10[+]	—	—
	(0.26)	(0.32)		
Age	0.02[+]	—	—	0.03[+]
	(0.25)			(0.30)
Residency	—	—	—	—
Intercept	−1.73*	−1.74*	−0.43*	−1.16*
R^2	0.26*	0.10[+]	0.13*	0.24**

Numbers in parentheses are standardized coefficients (β). Only those variables that significantly improved on the explained variance (R^2) are included in the final model; [+] $p < 0.05$ * $p < 0.01$ ** $p < 0.001$. [a] Dummy variable for wired status, reference category is wired – access to the high-speed network. [b] Dummy variable for gender, reference category is female.

Although moving to a new suburban neighborhood generally decreased the contact of Netville residents with friends and relatives, access to the high-speed network helped wired residents to maintain contact. Both personal attributes and high-speed access affect contact with social network members. Being wired, better educated, and older positively affect change in overall contact (table 12.2). Being connected to the local network has the same effect on boosting social contact as four more years of education or nearly thirteen years of increased age.

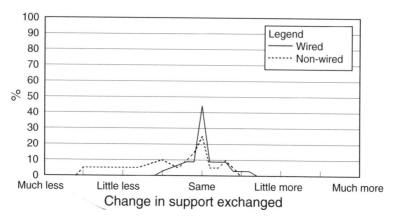

Figure 12.2 Overall change in social support

Table 12.3 Comparison of wired and non-wired residents by mean change in support exchanged with social ties at various distances (km)[a]

| | Overall | | Less than 50 km | | 50–500 km | | More than 500 km | |
	Non-wired	Wired	Non-wired	Wired	Non-wired	Wired	Non-wired	Wired
Mean	−0.24*	0.05*	0.03	0.1	−0.51**	0.04**	−0.24*	0.01*
SD	0.5	0.2	0.72	0.41	0.64	0.21	0.52	0.19
Min.	−1.5	−0.5	−1.5	−1	−2	−0.5	−1.5	−0.5
Max.	0.33	0.58	1	1	0.25	0.75	0.5	1

[a] Scale for mean score ranges from −2 "lot less" to +2 "lot more"; N = 34 wired, 20 non-wired. Difference between means is significant at [+] $p < 0.05$ * $p < 0.01$ ** $p < 0.001$ (ANOVA).

Among younger residents with fewer years of formal education, wired status is particularly important in helping to maintain contact at pre-move levels.

Support

Fully 79 percent of wired Netville residents report the same or more support after moving as compared to only 50 percent of non-wired residents (figure 12.2). As with social contact, wired residents on average have maintained support near pre-move levels while non-wired residents report significantly less support (table 12.3). Control-

Table 12.4 Coefficients from the regression of change in support exchanged on wired status and other independent variables at various distances (km) (N = 54)

Control variables	Overall	Less than 50 km	50–500 km	More than 500 km
Wired[a]	0.29*	—	0.55**	0.25*
	(0.39)		(0.54)	(0.33)
Female[b]	—	—	—	—
Education	—	—	—	—
Age	—	—	—	—
Residency	—	—	—	—
Intercept	−0.24*	—	−0.51**	−0.24*
R^2	0.15*	—	0.29**	0.11*

Numbers in parentheses are standardized coefficients. Only those variables that significantly improved on the explained variance (R^2) are included in the final model; [+] $p < 0.05$ * $p < 0.01$ ** $p < 0.001$. [a] Dummy variable for wired status, reference category is wired − access to the high-speed network. [b] Dummy variable for gender, reference category is female.

ling for other factors, those who moved into Netville report an overall decrease in support exchanged with network members across all distances (figure 12.2). Living in Netville and being connected to the local high-speed network reverses this trend. On average, non-wired residents report a moderate drop in support, while wired residents have been able to maintain support slightly above pre-move levels. Indeed, being wired is the only variable that is significantly associated with changes in the exchange of support (table 12.4).

Ties living within 50 kilometers (excluding neighbors)

Contact

We have hypothesized that as distance to ties increases, access to CMC will facilitate increased contact. At this distance, 65 percent of wired and 55 percent of non-wired residents report either no change or a small increase in contact with nearby ties (figure 12.3). On average, wired and non-wired residents both experienced a minor drop in contact with ties at this distance (table 12.1). While non-wired residents average a slightly greater drop in contact, analysis of variance does not identify a statistically significant difference between the mean scores of wired and non-wired residents. Controlling for gender, age, education and length of residence fails to reveal an effect of wired

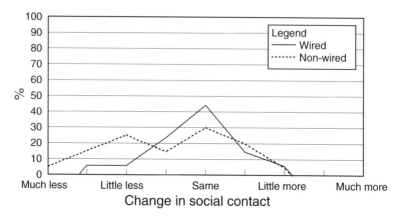

Figure 12.3 Contact with ties within 50 km

status on contact with network members living within 50 km, but not within Netville (table 12.2). Years of education is the only significant variable predicting contact. As in the previous analysis, the act of moving contributed to a loss of contact for all Netville residents. While those with at least seventeen years of education (more than a bachelor's degree) have been able to maintain contact at pre-move levels, all other residents experienced a drop in social contact with non-neighborhood ties living within 50 km compared to a year before their move.

In sum, being wired neither increases nor decreases social contact with non-neighborhood network members living within 50 km. Much contact with these network members continues to use established means of communication, such as the telephone and in-person meetings. Moving to Netville and accessing its high-speed local network does not appreciably change the amount of contact.

Support

Wired residents (82 percent) are more likely than non-wired (75 percent) to report either a small increase or no change in support from nearby network members (figure 12.4). On average, non-wired residents report almost no change in social support while wired residents report a very slight increase compared to a year before their move (table 12.3). The mean scores for wired and non-wired residents are not statistically different (table 12.3), nor does any other variable predict to changes in support with nearby network members (table

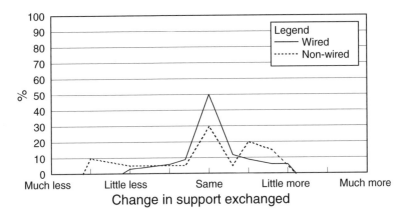

Figure 12.4 Support with ties within 50 km

12.4). As hypothesized, there is no effect of CMC on the exchange of support with non-neighborhood ties living within 50 km.

Mid-range ties (50–500 kilometers away)

Contact

When network members live 50 to 500 km away, they are at a distance where telephone and in-person contact become more costly and difficult, and where less-costly CMC may be used more. Controlling for other factors, Netville residents have less contact with mid-range network members as a result of their move (negative intercept in table 12.2). Unlike nearby ties, wired residents are better able than non-wired residents to maintain contact with mid-range ties (tables 12.1 and 12.2). Indeed, being wired is the only significant variable for change in contact with mid-range ties. The majority (62 percent) of wired residents report no change in contact, 18 percent report a decrease, and 21 percent report an increase. By contrast, although 50 percent of non-wired residents report no change, fully 45 percent report some level of lost contact, and only 5 percent report increased contact (figure 12.5).

Support

Mid-range ties should experience the greatest increase in support as a result of being wired. They are far enough apart that CMC is

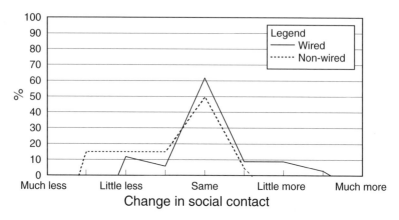

Figure 12.5 Contact with mid-range ties

especially useful for communication, but they are near enough to each other that the delivery of material aid (as well as emotional aid) can be accomplished without great strain. Being wired is the only variable significantly associated with changes in the level of support from mid-range ties (table 12.4).[11] Although mid-range support in Netville does not increase with being wired, being wired has enabled residents to maintain pre-move levels of supportiveness with mid-range ties. By contrast, residents who were not wired exchange significantly less support after moving (tables 12.3 and 12.4). Fully 82 percent of wired residents report no change in support after moving, only 6 percent report a decrease, and 12 percent an increase (figure 12.6). By contrast, only 40 percent of the non-wired residents report no change in support, the majority (55 percent) report a decrease, and only 5 percent an increase.

As with the previous analysis, moving to Netville introduced a barrier to the exchange of support with network members. However, when Netville residents become connected to the local high-speed network, they are able to overcome after-move barriers to the exchange of support with network members living 50 to 500 km away.

11 The lack of variation in the support scale for wired residents suggests that some caution should be taken in interpreting the results of the regression analysis.

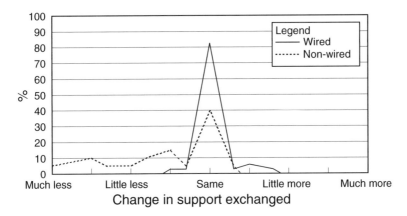

Figure 12.6 Support with mid-range ties

Distant ties (more than 500 kilometers away)

Contact

Social contact by conventional means (for example, telephone, in-person meetings) is more expensive with network members who live more than 500 km away. To support the hypothesis that access to Netville's local network is most successful in increasing contact with the most distant social ties, wired residents should report an increase in contact relative to non-wired residents of greater magnitude than for their mid-range ties.

As expected, wired residents have been better able than the non-wired to maintain contact with network members living far away (table 12.1, figure 12.7). By contrast, non-wired residents have not been able to maintain pre-move levels of contact. This is the only measure of social contact where the wired have not only been able to maintain contact at pre-move levels but on average report an increase over pre-move levels. Being wired and being older both significantly affect contact at this distance (table 12.2).[12] Those over the age of 38 and

12   The small amount of variation in the contact scale for wired residents suggests that some caution should be taken in interpreting the results of the regression analysis. Regression analysis with a dependent variable that is extremely light-tailed, as is the scale for change in support at more than 500 km, violates the assumption of equal variance. The results of the regression reported in table 12.4 for ties at this distance should be interpreted with caution.

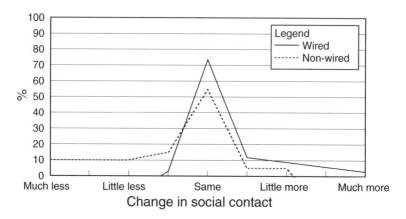

Figure 12.7 Contact with distant ties (500 km+)

non-wired, and those over the age of 25 and wired have been able to maintain contact with distant network members at pre-move levels. Only one wired resident reports a decrease in social contact, while 74 percent report no change and 24 percent report an increase (figure 12.7). By contrast, 35 percent of non-wired residents report a decrease in contact, 55 percent report no change, and only 10 percent an increase. The distribution of the social contact scale follows the trend of the previous two analyses: the greater the distance between Netville and network members, the more likely that Netvillers will not experience any change in social contact.

Support

By contrast to our expectation of increased *contact*, we did not expect that being wired would increase *support* exchanged with the most distant social ties. The lack of easy physical access makes distant network members less suited for exchanging tangible goods and services. Access to new methods of communication, provided through high-speed Internet availability, may at best afford a minor increase in the exchange of intangible, non-material support, such as emotional aid.

In practice, most wired and non-wired residents report no change after moving in the supportiveness of their most distant network members. Yet there are significant differences between the wired and non-wired residents (table 12.3). Once again, the Internet enables

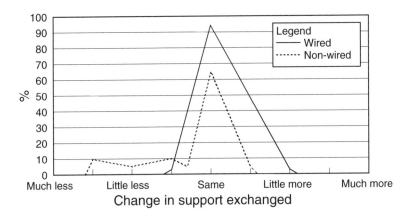

Figure 12.8 Support with distant ties (500 km+)

almost all wired residents (94 percent) to maintain support at pre-move levels (figure 12.8). Only 3 percent have experienced an increase and 3 percent a decrease. By contrast, a significant minority (30 percent) of non-wired residents have experienced a drop in support with their most distant social ties, 65 percent of non-wired residents report no change, and only 5 percent an increase. Being wired is the only variable which affects changes in level of support with distant ties (table 12.4).

Discussion

The not so global village of Netville

Moving to Netville, a new suburban neighborhood, reduced contact and support with friends and relatives. The move to a new home and neighborhood is itself stressful, former neighbors are no longer at hand, and with the move to an outer suburb, distance may play a role in reducing contact and the exchange of support with network members (Gans, 1967; Clark, 1966). Yet Netville residents with access to a free, high-speed, always-on, computer network have been more successful than non-wired residents in maintaining contact and exchanging support with friends and relatives.

Wired residents have maintained higher levels of contact as a result of CMC and have been able to maintain contact at pre-move levels with network members living more than 50 km away. By contrast, non-wired Netville residents experienced a drop in contact with social ties at all distances in comparison to a year before their move.

As hypothesized, living in a wired neighborhood with access to free, high-speed, always-on, Internet access affords more social contact with distant network members. Being wired affords as much contact at mid-range than at long distance. Comparing unstandardized regression coefficients at 50–500 km and 500+ km does not confirm the expectation that as distance increases, CMC facilitates greater contact (table 12.2). Those who are wired have experienced nearly the same change in social contact with ties beyond 500 km as they did with ties between 50–500 km. The slightly smaller regression coefficient for the effect of being wired on contact with ties 500+ km suggests a leveling off or even a slight drop in the effect of CMC on contact as distance increases. The slightly greater effect of being wired on contact with mid-range ties may relate to easier in-person contact and the types of support that are likely to be exchanged with ties at this distance. Frequent contact and the provision of tangible support reinforce each other (Homans, 1961; Wellman and Wortley, 1990; Wellman and Frank, 2001).

If they are not wired, Netville residents have had difficulty in maintaining pre-move levels of support with network members living more than 50 km. Wired residents have maintained support at pre-move levels with ties at all distances, whereas non-wired residents have had decreased support with ties more than 50 km away. Based on a comparison of unstandardized regression coefficients, being connected to Netville's high-speed network has had nearly twice the effect on support with network members at the 50–500 km range as it did with those at more than 500 km (table 12.4). This is consistent with the hypothesis that Netville's free, high-speed, always on, Internet access increases overall levels of support exchanged with network members, but that mid-range ties experience the greatest increase in the exchange of support. Although the move to a new suburb depressed contact and support, Netville's local computer network has helped residents maintain contact and support at pre-move levels.

The increased connectivity of a high-speed network should increase contact and support beyond pre-existing levels in an established neighborhood. It is not that the Internet is special. Rather, the Internet is another means of communication used along with existing media, especially in-person contact and the telephone. When distance makes in-person and telephone communication difficult, CMC has the potential to fill the gap.

Glocalization: CMC fosters contact and support, near and far

What has not been explored in this chapter, but is explored in detail in Hampton (2001b) and Hampton and Wellman (2002), is that in Netville computer-mediated communication reaches across distances both *locally* as well as *globally*. The wired residents of Netville neighbor much more extensively and intensively than their non-wired counterparts. Many local friendships and community activities have developed. Although this is a usual characteristic of moving into a new suburban development (Gans, 1967), wired Netville residents neighbor much more than those who are offline. Wired Netville residents on average know the names of 25 neighbors as compared to 8 for the non-wired, they talk to neighbors twice as often, and they visit in each others' homes 50 percent more often (Hampton, 2001b; Hampton and Wellman, 2002). The social ties of wired Netville residents, in particular weaker social ties, are spread more widely throughout the neighborhood. Instead of knowing just those neighbors in the few homes that surround their own, the wired residents of Netville know people down the street, around the corner and on the other side of the block.

Computer-mediated communication has not replaced existing means of communication, but it has provided a new form of social contact to personal networks. Within Netville, CMC increased social contact by additional means of communication. Wired Netville residents not only email and videophone with their neighbors, but they telephone them much more often (Hampton, 2001a). For neighbors to come together and act collectively often requires motivated individuals to knock on the doors of near strangers in order to generate grassroots support for individual causes. In Netville, CMC, combined with a dense network of local weak ties (Granovetter, 1973), has facilitated collective action (Hampton, 2002). Residents organized to protest perceived housing deficiencies, and when those providing their technology announced that it would be taken away, they again organized collectively (Hampton, 2001b; Hampton, 2002).

On average, most North Americans have few strong ties at the neighborhood level (Wellman, 1979, 1999; Fischer, 1982; Putnam, 2000). Personal communities consist of networks of far-flung kinship, workplace (Wellman, Carrington, and Hall, 1988) and interest group relations. They are not place-based communities of geography. Yet, in Netville, the local computer network facilitated the formation of local social ties of various strengths. While the existence of diverse subcultures in the modern urban environment allows people to place similarity of interest over similarity of setting in selecting social ties (Fischer, 1975, 1982), what may ultimately be lacking is an opportunity to meet and interact locally. Local institutions that do exist to promote local interaction (cafés, bars, community organizations, and so on) are in decline (Putnam, 2000; Oldenburg, [1989] 1999), and often are rare in suburban Netville. *Access* is equally as important as social similarity in determining the likelihood of tie formation (Feld, 1982) for the presence of neighborhood common space increases tie formation, the strength of local ties, and higher levels of community involvement (Brunson, Kuo, and Sullivan, 1996). Computer-mediated communication can foster "glocalization": increased local as well as distant social contact.

Conclusion

The blossoming of the Internet has affected the ways in which people connect with each other, eliminating the financial cost of long-distance communication, reducing the time and psychological cost of contacting near and far away people. Although some community ties function solely online, so-called "virtual communities" (Rheingold, 2000), in practice, most people use whatever means are necessary to stay in contact with community members: in-person, by telephone, as well as the Internet (Quan-Haase and Wellman, chapter 10). Contrary to dystopian predictions, new communication technologies do not disconnect people from communities. Computer-mediated communication reinforces existing communities, establishing contact and encouraging support where none may have existed before.

References

Anderson, E. (1978). *A place on the corner.* Chicago, IL: Chicago University Press.

Baym, N. K. (1997). Interpreting soap operas and creating community: inside an electronic fan culture. In S. Kiesler (ed.), *Culture of the Internet* (pp. 103–20). Mahwah, NJ: Lawrence Erlbaum.

Bradner, E. (2000). *Understanding groupware adoption: the social affordances of computer-mediated communication among distributed groups.* Working Paper, Department of Information and Computer Science, University of California, Irvine, February.

Brunson, L., Frances, E. K., and Sullivan, W. (1996). The use of defensible spaces: implications for safety and community. Paper presented at the 27th Annual Meeting of the Environmental Design Research Association, Salt Lake City, UT. Available online at: http://www.aces.uiuc.edu/~herl/brunson.html.

Clark, S. D. (1966). *The suburban society*. Toronto: University of Toronto Press.

Ekos Research Associates (1998). *Information highway and the Canadian communications household*. Ottawa, Canada: Ekos Research Associates.

Feld, S. (1982). Social structural determinants of similarity among associates. *American Sociological Review*, 47, 797–801.

Fischer, C. (1975). Toward a subcultural theory of urbanism. *American Journal of Sociology*, 80, 1319–41.

Fischer, C. (1982). *To dwell among friends*. Berkeley: University of California Press.

Fischer, C. (1984). *The urban experience*. Orlando: Harcourt Brace Jovanovich.

Fox, R. (1995). Newstrack. *Communications of the ACM*, 38(8), 11–2.

Gans, H. (1962). *The urban villagers*. New York: Free Press.

Gans, H. (1967). *The Levittowners*. New York: Pantheon.

Gaver, W. (1996). Affordances for interaction: the social is material for design. *Ecological Psychology*, 8, 111–29.

Granovetter, M. (1973). The strength of weak ties. *American Journal of Sociology*, 78, 1360–80.

Hampton, K. N. (1999). Computer assisted interviewing: the design and application of survey software to the wired suburb project. *Bulletin de Méthode Sociologique*, 62, 49–68.

Hampton, K. N. (2001a). Broadband neighborhoods connected communities. In J. Jacko and A. Sears (eds), *CHI 2001 extended abstracts*. ACM Press.

Hampton, K. N. (2001b). Living the wired life in the wired suburb: Netville, glocalization and civil society. Doctoral dissertation, Department of Sociology, University of Toronto. Available online at: www.mysocialnetwork.net

Hampton, K. N. (2002). *Grieving for a lost network: Collective action in a wired suburb*. Working Paper, Department of Urban Studies, MIT, February.

Hampton, K. N. and Wellman, B. (1999). Netville online and offline: observing and surveying a wired suburb. *American Behavioral Scientist*, 43(3), 475–92.

Hampton, K. N. and Wellman, B. (2002). Neighboring in Netville: how the Internet supports community, social support and social capital in a wired suburb. *City and Community*, forthcoming.

Hawley, A. (1986). *Human ecology*. Chicago: University of Chicago Press.

Haythornthwaite, C. and Wellman, B. (1998). Work, friendship and media use for information exchange in a networked organization. *Journal of the American Society for Information Science*, 49(12), 1101–14.

Homans, G. (1961). *Social behavior: its elementary forms*. New York: Harcourt Brace Jovanovich.

Kraut, R., Patterson, M., Lundmark, V., Kiesler, S., Mukhopadhyay, T., and Scherlis, W. (1998). Internet paradox: a social technology that reduces social involvement and psychological well-being? *American Psychologist*, 53(9), 1017–31.

Nie. N. (2001). Sociability, interpersonal relations, and the Internet: reconciling conflicting findings. *American Behavioral Scientist*, 45(3), 420–35.

Nie, N. and Erbring, L. (2000). *Internet and society: a preliminary report*. Stanford, CA: Stanford Institute for the Quantitative Study of Society: Stanford University, Stanford, CA.

Nie, N., Hillygus, S., and Erbring, L (2002). Internet use, interpersonal relations and sociability: Findings from a detailed time diary study (this volume).

Norman, D. (1999). Affordance, conventions, and design. *Interactions*, 6(3), 38–44.

O'Brien, J. (1998). Writing in the body: gender (re)production in online interaction. In M. Smith and P. Kollock (eds), *Communities in cyberspace* (pp. 76–104). London: Routledge.

Oldenburg, R. (1999). *The great good places: cafés, coffee shops, book stores, bars, hair salons and other hangouts at the heart of a community*. New York: Marlow.

Patton, P. 1986. *Open road*. New York: Simon and Schuster.

Putnam, R. (2000). *Bowling alone*. New York: Simon and Schuster.

Quan-Haase, A., Wellman, B., with Witte, J. and Hampton, K. (2002). Capitalizing on the net (this volume).

Rheingold, H. (2000). *The virtual community* (revised edn). Cambridge, MA: MIT Press.

Smith, M. and Kollock, P. (eds) (1999). *Communities in cyberspace*. London: Routledge.

Sproull, L. and Kiesler, S. (1991). *Connections*. Cambridge, MA: MIT Press.

Stein, M. (1960). *The eclipse of community*. Princeton, NJ: Princeton University Press.

Walther, J. B., Anderson, J. and Park, D. (1994). Interpersonal effects in computer-mediated interaction: a meta-analysis of social and antisocial communication. *Communication Research*, 21(4), 460–87.

Wellman, B. (1979). The community question. *American Journal of Sociology*, 84, 1201–31.

Wellman, B. (1992). Men in networks: private communities, domestic friendships. In P. Nardi (ed.), *Men's Friendships* (pp. 74–114). Newbury Park, CA; Sage.

Wellman, B. (1997). An electronic group is virtually a social network. In Kiesler, S. (ed.), *Culture of the Internet* (pp. 179–205). Hillsdale, NJ: Lawrence Erlbaum.

Wellman, B. (ed.) (1999). *Networks in the global village*. Boulder, CO: Westview Press.

Wellman, B. (2001). Physical place and cyber place: the rise of ne individualism. *International Journal of Urban and Regional Research*, 52.

Wellman, B. and Frank, K. (2001). Network capital in a multi-level world: getting support in personal communities. In N. Lin, K. Cook, and R. Burt (eds), *Social capital: theory and research* (pp. 233–73). Chicago, IL: Aldine DeGruyter.

Wellman, B. and Gulia, M. (1999). Net surfers don't ride alone: virtual communities as communities. In B. Wellman (ed.), *Networks in the global village* (pp. 331–67). Boulder, CO: Westview Press.

Wellman, B. and Hampton, K. (1999). Living networked on and off line. *Contemporary Sociology*, 28(6), 648–54.

Wellman, B. and Leighton, B. (1979). Networks, neighborhoods and communities. *Urban Affairs Quarterly*, 14, 363–90.

Wellman, B. and Tindall, D. (1993). Reach out and touch some bodies: how telephone networks connect social networks. *Progress in Communication Science*, 12, 63–94.

Wellman, B. and Wortley, S. (1990). Different strokes from different folks: community ties and social support. *American Journal of Sociology*, 96, 558–88.

Wellman, B., Carrington, P., and Hall, A. (1988). Networks as personal communities. In B. Wellman and S. D. Berkowitz (eds) (1988). *Social structures: a network approach* (pp. 130–84) Cambridge: Cambridge University Press.

Wellman, B., Quan-Haase, A., Witte, J., and Hampton, K. N. (2001). Does the Internet increase, decrease, or supplement social capital: social networks, participation, and community commitment. *American Behavioral Scientist*, 45(3), 436–55.

Whyte, W. F. (1943). *Street corner society*. Chicago, IL: University of Chicago Press.

Wright, P. (1989). Gender differences in adults' same and cross-gender friendships. In R. Adams and R. Blieszher (eds), *Older adult friendship* (pp. 197–221). Newbury Park, CA: Sage.

13

Email, Gender, and Personal Relationships

Bonka Boneva and Robert Kraut

Abstract

The current chapter uses both quantitative and qualitative data to examine how women and men use the Internet, and email in particular, to sustain their personal relationships. Socially constructed gender roles, we argue, influence, and in return are further enhanced, by the way the new technology is used for relationship maintenance. Women use email more than men in communicating with family and friends, and women use email more than men to revive family ties. Thus, our study suggests, women are using the new technology more than men in maintaining and even expanding their social networks. But men and women are using it similarly to keep up with their siblings, their parents, and they use email comparably when communicating most often with a friend. The new technology seems to encourage fathers to communicate more regularly with sons and daughters who live away from home and with whom they did not otherwise keep up with very much, while wives fulfill gender role obligations to keep up with the in-laws by using email to revive these relationships. Our study shows that email is having a generally beneficial effect on personal relationships, although more so for women than men.

Authors' note

This research was supported by NSF grants IRI-9408271 and IRI-9900449 and by support from Apple Computer Inc., AT&T Research, Bell Atlantic, Bellcore, CNET, Carnegie Mellon University's Information Networking Institute, Intel Corporation, Interval Research Corporation, Hewlett Packard Corporation, Lotus Development Corporation, the Markle Foundation, The NPD Group, Nippon Telegraph and Telephone Corporation (NTT), Panasonic Technologies, the US Postal Service, and US West Advanced Technologies. We would like to thank the Pew American Life & Internet Project for giving us the opportunity to use their March 12–April 9, 2001 data in this study. Debra Hindus, Scott Mainwaring, Bonnie Johnson, Eric Dishman at Interval Research Corporation, and Jane Manning, Tridas Mukhopadhyay, William Scherlis, Jonathon Cummings, Sara Kiesler, Vicki Lundmark, Bozena Zdaniuk, and Andrea Klein at Carnegie Mellon participated in interviewing. The chapter benefited from discussions with Sara Kiesler, Vicki Helgeson, Anne Crawford, and Jonathon Cummings at Carnegie Mellon University, Irene H. Frieze at the University of Pittsburgh, and colleagues at the Hewlett Packard Laboratories in Bristol, England. This chapter is based on Boneva, Kraut, and Frohlich (2001).

The gender gap in the amount of Internet use has been narrowing, but gender differences in Internet use patterns and application preferences persist. Women, for example, are more likely to search the web for health information and educational purposes, while men are more likely to seek news and entertainment online (Pew Internet & American Life Project, 2000a; Weiser, 2000). The most profound gender difference in the use of the new technology, however, is electronic mail, with women, on average, using email more than men (Pew Internet & American Life Project, 2000a). Both women and men use email mostly to connect with others they already know, predominantly relatives and friends (Kraut, Mukhopadhyay, Szczypula, Kiesler, and Scherlis, 2000; Pew Internet & American Life Project, 2000a; Stafford, Kline, and Dimmick, 1999).

The current chapter examines how women and men use the Internet and email in particular to sustain their personal relationships. Socially constructed gender roles, we argue, influence and in return, are further enhanced by the way the new technology is used for relationship maintenance. Previous research suggests that women are more likely than men to define themselves through their social relations and to act as the communication hub between the household and kin and friends. Women, we argue, have now appropriated the Internet for these purposes. Further, we explore the specific ways in which the new communication technologies influence women's and men's social networks.

Between 1995 and 1998, there was an almost 50 percent growth in the use of email for personal relationships, whereas there was virtually no growth in the work-related use of email (Cummings and Kraut, 2002). However, very few studies have examined how already existing personal relationships are maintained online (Cummings, Butler, and Kraut, 2002; Pew Internet Report, 2000a; Stafford, Kline, and Dimmick, 1999), and even less is known about the impact of gender on relationship maintenance online (e.g., Boneva, Kraut, and Frohlich, 2001; Pew Internet & American Life Project, 2000a).

Gender differences in relating to others

Women and men tend to value relationships differently and to have different styles in sustaining them (e.g., Deaux and Major, 1987; Duck and Wright, 1993; Eagle and Steffen, 1984; Spence and Buckner, 1995). As a result, one would expect to see differences in the way men and women use the Internet for interpersonal communication. Some indications of such differences have started to appear in the research literature (e.g., Kraut, Patterson, Lundmark, Kiesler, Mukhopadhyay, and Scherlis, 1998; Pew Internet & American Life Project, 2000a), but their nature is still not well understood. Many authors have identified differences in the way men and women relate to others and manage their relationships, but these studies have focused on face-to-face communication.

In order to provide a context for examining gender-specific patterns of using the Internet to communicate with family and friends, we first review some of the gender differences in relating to others. Spence and Helmreich (1978) proposed the term *expressiveness* to indicate a set of attitudes and behaviors associated with emotional intimacy and sharing in personal relationships, and the term *instrumentality* to indicate a more "agentic" (interested in making things happen) style of relating to others, oriented around common activities. Even though women and men vary widely from one person to another on these styles, there is evidence that women are, on average, more relationally oriented, more expressive of their feelings and less "agentic" than men (e.g., Deaux and Major, 1987; Eagle and Steffen, 1984). Consequently, women have been found to be more expressive and men to be more instrumental in maintaining their relationships. Women tend to engage in intimate conversation with their good friends, whereas men tend to spend time in common activities with theirs (Caldwell and Peplau, 1982; Davidson and Duberman, 1982; Duck and Wright, 1993; Spence and Buckner, 1995; Twenge, 1997; Walker, 1994; Wright and Scanlon, 1991). It has also been suggested that women are more likely to communicate in order to avoid isolation and gain community, whereas men tend to communicate to gain and keep social position (e.g., Tannen, 1992).

Other authors have emphasized that men and women differ in their conversation styles. Hauser and colleagues (1987), for example, distinguish between a *facilitative* style of communication, when the parties seek continuous dialogue, which helps to 'ramp up' a conversation, and a *restricting* style, characterized by interrupting the communication process at an early stage that tends to dampen the interaction. Women are socialized into using the facilitative style and men the restricting style (Maccoby, 1990).

Since women, on average, invest more in personal relationships, some studies have found that women have more extensive social networks (e.g., Moore, 1990; Walker, 1994; Wellman, 1992). Other studies, however, indicate that men report more same-sex friendships than women, although male friendships tend to be less intimate than female friendships (e.g., Claes, 1992). More specific gender role obligations are consistent with the general tendency of women to connect to others: women are expected to be the maintainers of family ties (Di Leonardo, 1987; Rosenthal, 1985) and of their family's connections to friends (Wellman, 1992).

These gender differences, while first reported in face-to-face behavior, have also been observed in the ways men and women use the telephone (Noble, 1987). Women, for example, are more frequent users of the telephone than men (e.g., Brandon, 1980; Lacohée and Anderson, 2001; Walker, 1994). Men use the phone more instrumentally than women do. Men are more likely than women to consider small talk and emotional sharing to be illegitimate motives to initiate phone contact, and they may not call if they do not have an instrumental reason to do so (Lacohée and Anderson, 2001; Walker, 1994). Because technology makes it easier to share thoughts and feelings at a distance than to engage in or organize common activities at a distance, women use the telephone more often than men to sustain a larger circle of distant friendships (Lacohée and Anderson, 2001; Walker, 1994).

Do these gender differences in communication and relationship styles hold for computer-mediated communication as well? Do women embrace computers more than men as a new means of connecting to others? If so, we may expect more use of the Internet for communication by women than men, and more expressive communication by women, and more instrumental communication by men. On the other hand, the technological features of email may somehow interfere with women's expressive communication style. Some studies indicate that the text-based communication format of email makes it less suitable for maintaining personal relationships than face-to-face communication or the phone (Cummings, Butler, and Kraut, 2002; Walther, 1996). Other studies suggest that email is especially suitable for management and coordination of activities, not for personal relationships (Sproull and Kiesler, 1986). That is, the text-based format of email may facilitate an instrumental communication style more commonly associated with men.

A national survey of Internet use (Pew Internet & American Life Project, 2000a) showed that women use the Internet more for communication than do men. Of those who use email, women are more likely than men to use it to communicate with family and friends. Women, for example, were more likely than men to have sent email to their parents or grandparents and to have reached out electronically to their extended families of aunts, uncles or cousins. Women were more likely than men to use email to sustain distant friendships; 73 percent of women who use email said they had sent email to friends who lived far away, compared to 65 percent of men. More women than men emailers liked email, mostly because they find it more efficient than other forms of communication (Pew Internet & American Life Project, 2000a). Other studies have also suggested quantitative, and possibly qualitative, differences in how men and women use computers to communicate (e.g., Kraut, Patterson et al., 1998).

The current chapter examines in more detail how men and women use email to maintain their personal relationships. Guided by previous findings about gender differences in relational maintenance, we investigate how email use in maintaining certain types of relationships is influenced by gender. In particular, if women tend to be more relationally oriented than men, then it can be predicted that they will utilize email to maintain their larger personal networks more so than men. Gender role expectations of women to maintain relationships with family and relatives and, for married women to maintain relationships with family friends can be expected to result in women using email more often than men as an efficient way to fulfill these gender-role obligations.

In addition, because women tend to use an expressive relationship style – sharing thoughts and feelings – which is easier to accomplish at a distance, while men tend to use an instrumental relationship style – doing things together with others – which is more difficult to accomplish with those living far away, then it can be predicted that women will use email to maintain a larger distant social circle than men. Similarly, it can be expected that women, compared to men, spend longer time using email, since a facilitative communication style – characterized by encouraging dialogue and more typical of women, triggers more intensive email exchange locally as well as at a distance.

And lastly, if email is appropriated by women to maintain their relationships more so than by men, it can be expected that women's attitudes toward email will be more positive than men's, and women will miss email more than men, because they benefit more than men from using email for personal relationships maintenance. We also explore what specific types of relationships are maintained by email most often, what types of dormant relationships are revived by email, and what types of messages are sent by email, and the impact gender may have.

We test our predictions analyzing three sets of data: Pew Internet & American Life Project March 2001 survey data, HomeNet Project 1998–9 survey data and HomeNet Project 1996–9 interview data. We first draw upon the two sets of survey data to set context, and then analyze the interview data in order to provide more detail to our understanding of how email is used by women and men to sustain active or revive dormant relationships.

Method

Quantitative data

The Pew Internet & American Life Project survey

SAMPLE

The Pew Internet & American Life Project 2001 survey (www.pewinternet.org) was a daily tracking survey on the use of the Internet in the United States, conducted in March 12–April 9, 2001. Results are based on data from telephone interviews of 2,135 respondents (48.2 percent men and 51.8 percent women). Because the HomeNet 1998–9 survey sample was predominantly Caucasian and the qualitative data analyses were based only on adults, we selected for Caucasian adults in the Pew Internet & American Life Project data analyses (N = 1,276). Of these, 11.6 percent had less than high school education, 34 percent were high school graduates, 28.4 percent had technical school or some college education, 16.1 percent were college graduates and 9.9 percent had some post-graduate education; 16.8 percent had household income of $30,000 or less, 28.9 percent over $30,000 but under $50,000, 34.5 percent over $50,000 but under $75,000 and 19.8 percent $75,000 or over.

MEASURES

In order to assess types of relationships sustained by email, we first analyzed the following two items: using email to communicate with immediate and extended family ("Do you ever send email to any member of your immediate and extended family?"; measured on a dichotomous scale. The question was asked to only those who started to email family in the last year), and the family member/relative most often contacted by email ("Thinking about both immediate and extended family, which family member do you email *most often?*", with 8 categories: spouse, child, parent, sibling, aunt or uncle, cousin, niece or nephew, in-laws). In addition, using email ever to communicate with friends was assessed by one item ("Do you ever send email to any of your friends?"; measured on a dichotomous scale). Geographic location of a friend most often contacted by email was measured by the item "Which of your friends do you email most often – a friend who lives close by to you or a friend who lives far away?" (measured by a dichotomous scale, 1 = "a friend who lives close by"; 2 = "a friend who lives far away"). Two items were used to test for using email to expand communication with family and friends ("Since you started using email, have you started communicating with a family member that you did not keep up with very much before?" and "Have you used email or the Internet to look for or locate an old friend or family member you had lost touch with?"; both items were measured on a dichotomous scale). In addition, we analyzed three items measuring attitudes about email: "How useful to you is email for communicating with members of your family/with friends?" (both items were measured on a 4-point scale rating from 1 = "very useful" to 4 = "not at all useful") and "How much would you miss using email if you could no longer use it?" (measured on a 4-point scale, from 1 = "a lot" to 4 = "not at all"). For those who reported that they did start communicating with a family member regularly by email, they were also asked to point out which family member that was (using the same 8 categories above).

The HomeNet 1998–1999 survey

SAMPLE

We also draw upon cross-sectional quantitative data from the 1998–9 HomeNet survey (Kraut, Kiesler, Boneva, Cummings, Helgeson, and Crawford, 2002). The HomeNet project is a long-term investigation of how using the Internet at home is influencing the lives of Americans (for more details, see Kraut, Patterson, et al., 1998; Kraut et al., 2002). The 1998–9 HomeNet survey sample consisted of 446 individuals from 237 households in Pittsburgh, Pennsylvania, who had recently purchased either a computer or a television during the spring of 1998. They were followed for one year. Respondents completed the survey questionnaire three times: in the spring of 1998, the fall of 1998, and the spring of 1999. Several measures of communication by email were consistently used in the three questionnaire surveys. Since the HomeNet interview sample that we analyzed included only Caucasian adults, for the purposes of the present report on the HomeNet survey data we selected on Caucasian adults with Internet access (N = 253). Because the first questionnaire was administered before many of the households had Internet access, the analyses here were done only on data from the second and third questionnaires, with scores averaged across the two surveys.

MEASURES

Overall, email was assessed by two measures: an item asking about the time (in minutes) spent on sending email on the most recent weekday, and a four-item index of email use ("I use email frequently," measured on a 5-point scale; average time (in minutes) spent on a weekday using email; frequency of sending email messages from home, measured on a 7-point scale; "I hardly ever use email" reversed item, measured on a 5-point scale. Cronbach's alpha = 0.91; the scale was standardized and centered, with a mean of 0.) Because the distributions of the measures of email use were skewed, we took their log in the analyses that follow. When these measures had outliers, they were truncated. (For details on the measures used in the 1998–9 HomeNet Project survey, see Kraut et al., 2002). Using email to keep in touch with a friend or a relative who lives far away, and with people who live nearby was measured using two items ("In the past six months, how frequently have you used the Internet at home for keeping in touch with someone far away?" and "In the past six months, how frequently have you used the Internet at home for communicating with friends in the Pittsburgh area?"; measured on a 5-point scale, 1 = never; 5 = often).

Another set of questions asked about attitudes toward using computers to communicate with others. Respondents were asked to rate, first, how useful and second, how much fun computers were for a number of behaviors. For the purposes of this study, we analyzed items associated with using the Internet for communication: sending email, keeping up with family and friends, and finding new people to communicate with from all over the world. To put these findings in context, we also analyzed items associated with using the Internet for entertainment: keeping up with music and entertainment, playing computer games and searching the worldwide web for hobby information. All items were measures on a 5-point scale, where one meant not at all useful (or fun) and five meant extremely useful (or fun).

Qualitative data

The present study is also based on analyses of interviews with adult women and men from 41 households in Pittsburgh, Pennsylvania. These interviews were conducted within the HomeNet Project between 1996 and 1999 in four sub-samples: 10 households in 1996, 14 in 1997, 5 in 1998, and 12 in 1999. We selected households where at least one member was in the top quartile (in the HomeNet survey sample as a whole) in time spent online.

All interviewees were Internet neophytes, and included 32 women (mean age 47) and 28 men (mean age 48.8). The sample comprised highly educated and high-income adults, with 77.5 percent having at least some college education and 35.2 percent a graduate degree; 73.1 percent had a household income of more than $35,000. Ninety-eight percent were Caucasian.

Interviews were semi-structured and lasted two to three hours. As a rule, all household members (including children) were interviewed, first as a group around the kitchen or dining room table and then individually in front of the family computer. All interviews were tape recorded and transcribed. The portion in front of the computer was videotaped as well. The analyses of the interviews followed standard guidelines for structured thematic analyses (see, for example, Silverman, 2000), using NUD*IST software (QSR, 1999). Coding was first done for three major types of relationships (relatives, friends, and acquaintances) and for three major Internet applications (email, chat rooms, and instant messaging) separately for the adult men and women in the four interview sub-samples. We analyzed the contents of 18 collections of excerpts from the interview transcripts, nine referring to women's and nine to men's electronic communication with relatives, with friends, and with acquaintances by email, or in chat rooms, or by instant messaging. However, we do not report our findings for each year separately, because, with very few exceptions, we did not identify changes over time in the way men and women were using the Internet to maintain personal relationships.

Does Email Perpetuate Gender Differences In Relational Maintenance?

Quantitative data results

2001 Pew Internet & American Life Project data results

First, logistic regression was conducted to test for gender differences in using email to communicate with immediate and extended family, and to communicate with friends, controlling for age, educational level, family income, and Internet use. Women more often than men reported having sent email to family (β = 1.36; p = 0.002): 78.7 percent of the women but only 68.2 percent of the men who use email had ever sent email to a family member. Similarly, women more often than men reported having sent email to friends (β = 1.42; p < 0.001): 83 percent of the women but only 76.3 percent of the men who use email had ever send email to a friend (see table 13.1).

Because our dependent variable was categorical (with more than two categories), multinominal logistic regression was conducted to test for gender differences in the family members they most often communicated with by email. We controlled for age, educational level, family income, and amount of Internet use. There was a significant gender effect (χ^2 = 41.45; df = 7; p < 0.001). Women reported sending email most often to their sisters and brothers (34 percent), followed by their parents (18.8 percent), their in-laws (14.1 percent), and their daughters and sons (13.6 percent). Men who used email to communicate with family, sent email most often to their sisters and brothers (38 percent), followed by their parents (17.5 percent), their daughters and sons (12 percent) and their cousins (11.4 percent). Unsurprisingly, 14.1 percent of the women but only 3 percent of the men reported an in-law as someone they send email to most often, and 6.6 percent of the men but none of the women reported emailing their spouse (see table 13.1).

To test for gender difference on where a friend they email most often lives – nearby or far away, logistic regression was conducted, controlling for age, educational level, family income and Internet use. There was no significant gender effect on location of friends (β = −0.24; p = 0.28).

Logistic regression was conducted to test for gender differences in reviving family ties by email and using email to locate a friend or a family member, controlling for age, educational level, family income, and Internet use. There was a significant gender effect on reviving

Table 13.1 The effect of gender on email use for different types of relationships

Using email to	Women (%)	Men (%)	beta[a]	s.e.
Email immediate and extended family ever	78.7	68.2	1.36**	0.43
Email friends ever	83.0	76.3	1.42***	0.37
Send email most often to a nearby friend	43.3	45.8	−0.24	0.22
Send email most often to a far away friend	56.7	54.2	−0.24	0.22
Revive family ties	39.1	21.6	1.21***	0.23
Locate a family member or a friend	28.5	28.1	0.25	0.21

Choice of family member in email communication

	Email most often to[b]		Have revived family ties with[c]	
	Women (%)	Men (%)	Women (%)	Men (%)
Spouse	0	6.6	0.5	1.6
Child	13.6	12.0	1.9	8.1
Parent	18.8	17.5	5.7	4.0
Sibling	34.0	38.0	26.5	35.5
Aunt or uncle	5.8	7.8	10.9	7.3
Cousin	9.9	11.4	34.1	30.6
Niece or nephew	3.7	3.6	8.1	8.9
In-laws	14.1	3.0	12.3	4.0

Attitudes toward email[e]

	Women	Men	F[d]
Useful for family communication	1.69 (0.86)	2.06 (0.82)	17.18***
Useful for communication with friends	1.44 (0.63)	1.55 (0.71)	6.56**
Will miss email if no longer uses it	1.42 (0.79)	1.55 (0.96)	4.13*

[a] Values are based on logistic regression described in the text.
[b] Multinominal logistic regression revealed significant gender effect ($\chi^2 = 41.45$; df = 7; $p < 0.001$).
[c] Multinominal logistic regression revealed significant gender effect ($\chi^2 = 17.36$; df = 7; $p < 0.05$).
[d] F-values are based on multivariate analysis of variance.
[e] 1 = very useful/a lot; 4 = not at all. * $p < 0.05$; ** $p < 0.01$; *** $p < 0.001$.
Source: Pew Internet and American Life Project, March 2001 survey data, http://www.pewinternet.org

family ties by email (β = 1.21; p < 0.001), with 39.1 percent of the women and 21.6 percent of the men reporting having started communicating regularly by email with a family member that they did not keep in touch with before. Multinominal logistic regression was conducted to test for which family member they revived communication with by email. Men and women had somewhat different preferences (χ^2 = 17.36; df = 7; p = 0.015). Men revived most often their communication with siblings (35.5 percent, compared to 26.5 percent for women), followed by cousins (30.6 percent) and nieces and nephews (8.9 percent, compared to 8.1 percent for women). Women revived most often their communication with their cousins (34.1 percent), followed by siblings (26.5 percent of the cases for women) and their in-laws (12.3 percent, compared to only 4 percent for men); 8.1 percent of the men but only 1.9 percent of the women reported starting regularly email communication with their sons or daughters with whom they had not kept in touch. However, logistic regression found no significant gender effect on using email to locate a friend or a family member (β = 0.25; p = 0.23).

Since three of the self-report measures of attitudes – usefulness of email for keeping in touch with family/relatives, with friends and importance of email – were theoretically and statistically related, a multivariate analysis of covariance was conducted to test for gender differences, controlling for age, education, household income, and Internet use. There was a significant multivariate (Hotelling's test) gender effect (F(3,327) = 6.41; p < 0.001). The univariate tests showed significant gender effects on usefulness of email in communicating with family (F(1,327) = 17.18; p < 0.001) and with friends (F(1,327) = 6.56; p = 0.01), with women finding email more useful in communicating both with family and with friends than men. In addition, women indicated they would miss email more than men (F(1,327) = 3.02; p = 0.04) (see table 13.1).

By and large, the Pew Internet & American Life Project data results support our predictions. Women use email more than men to communicate with family and with friends. However, women and men both email their immediate family most – siblings, parents, and children. However, men also communicate with their spouses by email, while women communicate with their in-laws. Men and women also differ in frequency of using email to revive family ties, and their patterns of family ties revived online are somewhat different. Women, for example, started communicating with their cousins most often and only second with their parents; men, in contrast, started communicating most often with their parents and then, with their cousin. Interestingly, many more fathers (than mothers) started communicating with their daughters and sons, while, unsurprisingly, more women than men started communicating with their in-laws because of email. Men and women, however, seem equally interested in locating a family member or a friend online.

1998–1999 HomeNet survey data results

We used MANOVA to test for the effect of gender on frequency of email use and on time spent sending email, controlling for educational level, household income, and Internet use. (Since 98 percent of the HomeNet survey sample was Caucasian and we selected on adults, we did not control in these data analyses for race or age.) The overall effect of gender was not significant, although women were marginally more likely than men to report using email ($p = 0.11$).

Further, univariate analysis was conducted to test for gender effects on time spent on a weekday using email, controlling for education, household income and Internet use. There was a significant effect of gender ($F(1,217) = 4.23$; $p = 0.04$), with women spending more time ($M = 30.7$; $SD = 69.25$) than men ($M = 16.66$; $SD = 24.59$) per day sending email. There were no significant interactions, however, in the univariate analysis testing for overall email use (as measured by an index) men and women did not differ significantly ($F(1,218) = 0.77$; $p = 0.38$), although the difference was in the predicted direction (see table 13.2).

MANOVA was conducted to test for gender effects on frequency of email communication with friends in the local area and with people far away, controlling for education, household income and Internet use. The multivariate test was significant for gender ($F(2,239) = 3.31$; $p = 0.038$). There was no significant interaction of gender by geographic distance of the partner. Univariate tests showed no gender differences in frequency of people's use of email to communicate with local friends, but women were more likely than men to use email to keep up with people far away (see table 13.2).

Similarly, we used multivariate analyses to test for gender differences in attitudes about how useful and how much fun it is to use computers for five different activities, controlling for education, household income, and email usage. There was a significant gender effect on the dependent variables measuring how useful computers

Table 13.2 Means and standard deviations for women and men on measures of email use for personal relationships

Overall use of email	Women	Men	F[a]
Using email (minutes)	30.70	16.66	4.23*
	(69.25)	(24.59)	
Frequency of using email	0.25	0.10	0.77[b]
	(0.81)	(0.76)	

Frequency of using the Internet for different purposes[c]

	Women	Men	F
For communicating with friends in the Pittsburgh area	2.48[†]	2.36[†]	2.76[†]
	(1.30)	(1.24)	
For keeping in touch with someone far away	2.98*	2.55*	6.62**
	(1.41)	(1.29)	

Attitudes toward Internet use for specific activities[d]

Software that allows you to . . .	How useful is . . .			How much fun is . . .		
	Women	Men	F	Women	Men	F
Send email	4.17	3.94	0.98	3.98**	3.48**	9.34**
	(1.12)	(1.11)		(1.15)	(1.08)	
Keep in touch with family and friends	4.09**	3.63**	8.95**	4.01**	3.56**	7.66**
	(1.02)	(1.10)		(1.07)	(1.09)	
Find new people to communicate with from all over the world	2.95*	2.53*	6.38**	3.18*	2.78*	4.91**
	(1.21)	(1.02)		(1.21)	(1.06)	
Keep up with music and entertainment	2.76	2.59	0.05	2.99	2.82	0.35
	(1.15)	(1.16)		(1.20)	(1.13)	
Play new computer games	2.59	2.52	0.55	3.07	3.05	0.07
	(1.20)	(1.06)		(1.34)	(1.18)	
Search the Internet or the worldwide web for hobby information	3.82	3.80	0.46	3.80	3.69	0.001
	(1.18)	(1.04)		(1.22)	(0.98)	

[a] F-values are based on the univariate analyses of covariance described in the text. Df for the numerator is 1 and df for the denominator varies between 217 and 240 for different dependent variables.

[b] This variable was centered with a mean of 0.

[c] Measured on a 5-point scale (1 = never and 5 = often).

[d] Measured on a 5-point scale (1 = not at all useful (or fun) and 5 = useful (or fun).

[†] $p < 0.10$; * $p < 0.05$; ** $p < 0.01$; *** $p < 0.001$.

Source: The HomeNet Project, 1998–9 survey data

were $(F_{(6,233)} = 4.12; p = 0.001)$. Univariate tests indicated that women more than men believed the Internet was useful for keeping up with family and friends, and scored higher than men on usefulness of computers in finding communication partners (see table 13.2). In contrast, there were no significant gender differences on non-social items, such as keeping up with music and entertainment, playing computer games, or searching the Internet for hobby information. However, although women scored higher than men on the usefulness of sending email, this difference was not statistically significant.

A comparable pattern was found for the effect of gender on the set of dependent variables measuring how much fun computers were for certain activities. Univariate tests showed that women more than men believed that computers were fun for sending email, for keeping up with family and friends, and for finding communication partners. In contrast, there was no significant effect of gender on the items that were not associated with personal relationships, namely, keeping up with music and entertainment, playing computer games, or searching the Internet for hobby information (see table 13.2).

The HomeNet survey data results support most of our prediction. Overall, women spent more time than men using email per day, although they did not use email more days per week. They used email more frequently than men to communicate with friends far away. Moreover, women more than men found email useful and fun.

By and large, the results of the two data sets analyses suggest a number of consistent patterns of using email to maintain personal relationships. Women, for example, are spending more time than men communicating with family and with friends by email, but both men and women send email most often to their siblings and parents. There are, however, mixed results on whether women and men are using email differently when communicating with people nearby and with people far away. On the other hand, data results show consistently that women think of electronic mail in more positive terms than men.

Qualitative data results

The survey data analyses reveal gender-related patterns of sustaining personal relationships using computers, but they provide no detail about differences in communication between friends and family. They provide no information about the substance of the communication online. To explore these issues, we turn to the interview data.

All interviewees had Internet access, and at least one member in each household was in the top quartile (in the HomeNet survey sample as a whole) in time spent online. In the interviews, more women than men reported using email for personal relationships. Of the 32 women who were interviewed, 29 reported using email at home to communicate with others, whereas of the 28 interviewed men, only 14 used email. Of those who did not use email, all 3 women, but only 2 of the 14 men attributed it to lack of time and/or knowledge about how to use email or to having difficulty typing. None of the women and 5 men in the sample reported lack of interest in using email to communicate with others, illustrated in the following comments of 2 men who did not use email.

JIM:[1]   I utilize the computer for entertainment and information. I don't email or any . . . I don't email at all.

MARC: I don't email friends or relatives . . . I don't know why . . . I'm not one to communicate often with friends, you know, like, I communicate with them once a month and that's fine with me.

In the context of these findings – that 91 percent of the women and only half of the men in our sample use email to communicate with others – we further examine what specific relationships are sustained by this mode of communication.

Types of relationships sustained by email

Communication with family and kin

As in the Pew survey, interviewees conducted little communication within the household by email. Only two families reported using email among themselves. In one case, a family used email to communicate with each other in different parts of the house. In another case, a husband at work exchanged messages with his wife at home – on topics ranging from how their day was going to making shopping lists.

Communication by email with other family and more distant kin perpetuates the gender-role pattern described earlier. One of the female interviewees described explicitly such a gender-related pattern in her family.

---

1   For considerations of confidentiality, we use pseudonyms throughout the text.

BARBARA: In our family . . . I'm much more of the communicator and
my husband is not. It's a typical, I guess, gender division, and it
happens to be true in our case. I'm the one who, you know, talks on
the phone to the other family members and makes social arrangements and all kinds of things like that, and when we got the email,
that trend just stayed. I mean I am the one who emails our son, who's
at college and I email other family members and my husband really
has no interest in email. And he was never one who would talk on
the phone, either. He occasionally has used it [the computer] to
pursue a few of his, you know, hobby interests on the Internet, but
other than that he doesn't use it. So, I don't know, it's not because he's
shy, I just think people who aren't that interested in communicating
they're not going to do it with email either.

The interview data suggest that women in the recent cohort were more
likely to use the Internet to communicate with family and kin than
those in the earlier sub-samples. Only 12 out of 20 women who used
email between 1996 and 1998 reported extensively using it to contact
their family and kin, while all nine women interviewed in 1999 did so.
We did not see similar cohort effects in men's email use.

Women reported communicating by email most frequently with
their siblings and with their parents. Of the 29 women who used email,
10 corresponded with their siblings and 6 with their parents. Communication with family was less common among the 14 men emailers
– only four reported staying in touch with siblings by email, and
none with parents. When women failed to use email with siblings or
parents, their most common explanation was that the relatives did not
have Internet access. Men were less likely to give this explanation.
These findings are consistent with the Pew Internet & American Life
Project data results for women, but not for men. However, the one time
that men reported they chit chat by email was when they emailed to
siblings. For example, in describing what sort of things he used to
write about in email with his brother, one male participant explained:

JERRY: Um, reunion coming; what his life has been . . . You know, his
circumstances, um, what my niece, his daughter is doing . . .

We also found weak evidence that email supplemented women's
telephone conversations with their parents, whereas it substituted
for telephone calls with their siblings. For example, some of the
women who communicated with both elderly parents and siblings

by email explained that they also called their parents as before, but called their brothers and/or sisters less often, since having the email connection.

Ten of the female interviewees (34.5 percent of the email users) and 3 of the male interviewees (21.4 percent) reported communicating by email with other kin – namely, cousins, aunts and uncles, a niece and a nephew, or, with their in-laws, findings very similar to the Pew Internet & American Life Project data results. One case is of particular interest because it presents a non-traditional way of meeting future in-laws. After their wedding date was announced, Jean started communicating with her future in-laws online before she even met them in person. For example, she developed a relationship with her sister-in-law online long before she met her in person on the wedding day.

The interviews do not contain adequate information on email communication between the parents and their children who do not live at home, because adults in the sample were young and the sample contained only four children (two daughters and two sons) away in college. Mothers reported staying in touch with all four by email, whereas only one father reported occasionally corresponding with his son. Three more women, who expected their daughters to be leaving for college soon, expressed enthusiasm about using email in the future to stay in touch with daughters in college. One family kept a common email account that they could use to keep in touch with their son in college, but only the mother regularly checked the account. With one exception (when a son regularly did not answer email), mothers found email connections with their children in college to be useful and satisfying.

As a whole, our qualitative data findings do not indicate that email usage introduced any dramatic changes in the gender-specific pattern of communication with family and kin. There was, however, one case when using email resulted in redefining a traditional communication pattern. One participant, Barbara, took advantage of email to change dramatically her relationships with both her father and her son. From the beginning of her marriage, she had long, weekly phone conversations with her mother; her father would get on the line only briefly to say "hi." She had hardly ever exchanged personal thoughts and emotions with him before he started using email. With email, they started a regular correspondence and her father shared his feelings, thoughts and personal history with her. Still, when Barbara would call home, it would be only her mother, but not her father, who would talk to her. "If it were not for the email, I wouldn't have talked to my father . . ." Barbara also found email communication with her son in college more gratifying than phone communication with him.

> BARBARA: I email him [my son] a lot. And I enjoy that and I feel that we have a much better communication on email than we would on the phone. And if we didn't have email I wonder what our communication would be, because somehow when I call, it's like, you know, he's busy, or he's tired, or he's studying, or whatever.

Such cases suggesting that email is radically changing relationships with friends and kin, however, were exceptions in our data. Despite this, we believe it is important to investigate in depth such cases in the future in order to better understand why this is happening and how gender and other social and personal factors influence this process.

Communication with friends

In our interview sample, women and men differed in the size of the circle of friends they sustained by email. Twenty-three women, or 72 percent of the women interviewed (79 percent of the email users) and 9 men, or 32 percent of the men interviewed (64 percent of the email users) reported staying in touch with friends using email. These findings, again, are comparable to the Pew Internet & American Life Project data results. In addition, the interviews suggest that, like communication with family and kin, women have the responsibility for sustaining relationships with common family friends by email. Irene and Tom, a husband and wife whom we interviewed, described this pattern in their family. It seemed natural to them that Irene was the one who communicated directly with family and common friends by email, thus leaving Tom feeling that he did not need to duplicate the activity.

> IRENE: [talking about relatives and friends] . . . people email me stuff and I'll send it to him [her husband].
>
> TOM: . . . rather than both sending [email] . . . I mean, she talks [by email] to them and then she emails me anything I need to know, so I don't really communicate directly with them, but indirectly, through her routing me the emails.

Communication with local friends

Women and men did not seem to differ much in their use of email to communicate with geographically local friends. Seven men (25 percent of those interviewed and half of the male emailers) and 10 women (31 percent of those interviewed and 34 percent of the female emailers) reported using email to communicate locally with friends. These findings are consistent with the survey results, and support our prediction about local personal email exchange. In the interviews, both men and women emphasized the convenience of email for organizing activities and arranging events with friends and acquaintances in the area. However, the uncertainty of whether the message would be accessed on time was a major reason for not using email even more often for local personal communication.

Neither women nor men seemed to use email just to chat with local friends. There was only one exception – a woman who reported preferring email over phone to "chat" with her closest friend locally.

JANE: I have a friend that lives 10 minutes away and we email back and forth [just to chat] . . . I could pick up the phone and talk, but we don't.

Jane explained that they email instead of talking by phone, because "it is painless," "[i]t's like sending notes in class" – she could do it at the spur of the moment.

Communication with geographically distant friends

In contrast to its restricted use for local relationships, the interviews showed email as more central to distant relationships – be it with friends or with relatives, with women using it more extensively for this purpose than men. The interviews showed that email made it easier for both men and women to sustain personal friendships with people far away in at least three different ways. First, email helped people to retain relationships despite geographic mobility. Several interviewees reported that after moving to a new location or a job, email kept them in touch with people from the old location – former colleagues, friends from college, or neighbors. Hampton and Wellman (2001) report similar findings. While geographic relocation frequently interrupted regular contacts with extended family and non-intimate friends, email countered this disruption with low-cost communication.

SUSAN: [W]e use email to keep in touch with people who live in places where we've lived at various points and you know, who we haven't seen in a long time and who would otherwise be tricky to keep in touch with. So, we email, certainly not on a daily or even . . . well, depending . . . at least weekly or monthly . . . way back and forth.

Second, email provided a low-cost means of reinvigorating previously dormant relationships. The Pew survey data results, for example, showed that about 28 percent of those who use email have tried to locate a family member or a friend online. Similarly, some of the interviewees reported that a combination of email and the worldwide web allowed them to actively search for friends they had lost contact with and to re-initiate contact with them. Thus, through email people intensified their communication with dormant friends and acquaintances. Jill, for example, explained how she was able to keep in touch with some friends, with whom in the past she had only exchanged Christmas cards.

JILL: On Christmas cards I sent out the email address and I did discover I had some surprising contacts . . . I did find again some long lost friends.

Finally, and more rarely, email allowed people to develop relationships with others far away that they would not have maintained otherwise. Irene, for example, described being able to build strong relationships communicating frequently by email.

IRENE: [T]here are people I never talk to, like my friend in Alaska, I never talk to him on the phone, we just email each other. Also, my friend in Ireland, we never talk, we just email, so, that's really nice because . . . My friend in Alaska I've only seen him three times ever and we . . . basically our whole relationship for the three or four years has been over the Internet and emailing, so, that's kind of interesting.

The interviews suggest that email expands the circle of geographically distant friends more for women than for men. Eleven women (38 percent of emailers and 34 percent of all women with Internet access) and 4 men (29 percent of emailers and 14 percent of all men with Internet access) reported keeping in touch with more geographically distant friends because of email. The HomeNet Project survey data also showed that women use email more often to keep in touch with someone far away. However, when it concerns one far away friend to whom they email *most often*, the Pew Internet & American Life Project data results did not show a significant gender difference.

Message types and patterns of message traffic

To better understand how email builds and sustains relationships, we analyzed interviewees' descriptions of their email content and a limited sample of email messages that they made available to us. These data suggest that there are at least three types of email messages: boilerplate messages, messages for coordination, and messages for personal sharing. Each of them plays a different role in developing and sustaining relationships. Because of the small sample of messages, we do not even speculate here on possible gender differences.

Message types

BOILERPLATE MESSAGES

Boilerplate messages include jokes, stories, sayings, greeting cards, pointers to music sites, and other pre-fabricated messages copied by the sender from one source and then forwarded, often to more than one recipient. For example, one of the women in the sample received the following note addressed to her and nine other recipients, most of whom she did not know:

> *Feminist saying*, ca. *1968–72*: "The hand that rocks the cradle can also cradle a rock."

Like conventional greeting cards, these boilerplate messages serve to remind partners of each others' existence and, as such, preserve a relationship as a potential resource for companionship, advice, or social support at some later time. It is also important to emphasize that these are messages often addressed to a group of receivers – the circle of sender's friends and/or relatives. Whether and how this could affect the density of one's social network needs to be studied further.

COORDINATION MESSAGES

A second type is a coordination message. It is used to set up a joint activity or other occasion where the participants share companionship and other social resources. This excerpt from a message of one woman to another illustrates this second type:

> JULIE: I don't know how your plans are working out for tomorrow night, but it's no problem with me if we have to reschedule it for next week or whenever. I will be out of the house most of tomorrow, so you probably won't be able to get me on the phone then anyway.

Other examples of messages for coordination included organizing a group of friends to play golf over the weekend, arranging monthly board-game nights with 20 other family friends, and managing activities of a local community committee on families and education.

MESSAGES FOR PERSONAL SHARING
The third type of messages have personal content that directly supports the relationship. Such messages have an expressive nature, and in themselves provide companionship and social support by allowing communicators to share thoughts and feelings with one another. Contrast, for example, the coordination email from Julie above with the following message Alice sent. Alice's message has substantive content, which enacts the relationship.

> Long time no hear from! How are you? I'm getting by. I'm still working at the law firm as a receptionist but I am bored!!! And I was turned down for two jobs this week. I had second interviews for both. I thought at least one would be good! I really feel like I suck!!! Anyway, I came across your address and thought I'd write you. Hope all is better for you. I'm glad spring is coming!!

Dorothy, a creative writer, exchanges emails with her artist mother, along with regular phone calls and occasional visits. They talk about family gossip and the events of the day, and in particular, what her mother has been working on that day. These messages also serve to enact the relationship, by themselves providing companionship and social support.

> DOROTHY: For her [my mother], talking about work in progress is very interesting to her and can get her going. So, she'll be telling me she's working on something and ask for my ideas on it and I'll send ideas back and so, back and forth, that kind of thing, and then family gossip . . . you know, this sister is coming to dinner, or you know, this nephew said this funny thing. There's a certain amount of family chit chat in there, too.

We have some preliminary evidence that women may not consider email very suitable for sharing of emotions and personal thoughts. Six women reported that they restricted their email contacts to light conversation, reserving deep conversations involving social support for more interactive media – the phone or, in more recent times, instant messaging. Kathleen described media choice when communicating with her daughter this way:

> KATHLEEN: [W]hen times were stressful, she [my daughter] would call up . . . you know, that upset does not necessarily come through on an email. And so, I was there for emotional support . . . So, a lot of it was not conversational . . . While, just here [in her email messages] is some information . . . what are you doing, Mom, and I would write back and you know, those kind of things . . . it's likely to be much longer and in depth if we're on the phone.

However, at least two women judged email more appropriate than the phone for deep, emotionally laden topics with someone far away. In one case, a female family friend was terminally ill and her husband used email to keep friends informed about her physical and emotional state. In another case, email communication supplied indispensable emotional support for two sisters after their mother died.

> CYNTHIA: My Mom had died a while ago and . . . we were talking about that through email and you know, she [my sister] said stuff about my Mom and everything, and . . . the way we were talking, I'm thinking, I probably never would have said that to her.

Although these examples may only be exceptions, they suggest some of the conditions under which email may be preferred over the telephone for sharing deep emotions. Email is more efficient than interactive media for broadcasting messages to a group of recipients. In addition, email is a more reflective medium than the phone or instant messaging, and allows the writer to more carefully choose and review message content before sending it.

Patterns of message traffic

The interviews data suggest two differing styles of email use for maintaining personal relationships: *facilitating dialogue* (enacting the relationship in intense bursts of email communication) and *restricting dialogue* (interrupting the communication at an early stage). Several women emphasized that they emailed others "in spurts," activating a dormant relationship through an intensive communication exchange for a few days, then allowing it to die back. The following excerpt is an example of how initiating communication with another stimulates further communication for women.

> JILL: For a short spurt I'll email her back and we'll email for a couple of days and then we sort of fade out for awhile until the next spurt . . . [Once we get in touch,] I usually get excited about emailing the person, it just makes me want to talk to them more.

In contrast, some of the male interviewees seemed more apt to accept substantial delay between messages. One of the interviewees, Jim described this pattern in some detail. When he would get an email message from a friend, he would almost never respond to it right away. He may or may not get back to him in some future communication session.

> JIM: I don't see much use [in email] unless it's something important. If it's something [important], I'd like to get to it later, like, I won't answer right then. Like, say, if I'm just checking email, but if I really want to write [back] something, I'll leave it [the message] there, so the next time I can come back and write whatever it is.

Another interviewee, Harry emphasized that intensive email message exchange with another person was not something "men do."

> HARRY: For me, it [email] usually has a point of giving him [his friend] information, asking him questions: are you available for that . . . Not back and forth simultaneously in chains. Not for me; maybe for Elizabeth [his daughter].

A wife commenting on her husband's use of email revealed a similar *restricting* email communication style.

> MARY: People generally send him a letter and then a couple of weeks later he sends them three lines. And that's about it . . . You know, he'll have lots of things to say every so often, but then months will go by and he won't be very interested in it.

Our interview data findings also suggest that instant messaging, by facilitating dialogue, may be more appealing to women than to men. Melanie, interviewed in 1999, preferred instant messaging to email for reasons described below.

MELANIE: Well, first of all, an email message . . . it's a one-sided conversation, you have to get a response before you can type anymore, but on instant chat we use a split screen all the time, so you can chat constantly. It's just like talking on the telephone except that you're using a printed word instead, [which is] much better.

However, because instant messaging did not exist when we started to collect interview data, its use is under-represented in our sample.

Both email and instant messaging are text-based communication modalities. Some previous studies have suggested that women express themselves better in words than men, and men tend to be more reluctant to communicate using written text (Maccoby and Jacklin, 1974). In our interviews, four of the women emphasized that they enjoy using email because it is a text-based communication medium, as illustrated below.

JILL: [W]hen you're typing, at least in my own self, I can talk better when I'm typing and I'll type my thoughts better than if I'm saying them on the phone, you know.

IRENE: I say it in email, you know, I write it, 'cause I'm more careful when I write than when I talk. So, if I do not want to give, say, some information that they're not gonna be happy to hear, I will do it very diplomatically [by email].

It is not clear, though, if text per se or the possibility of having more control over the communication process is what may make email or instant messaging more attractive to some people than non-text-based communication modalities.

Discussion and Conclusions

Our study suggests that women use email more often than men to sustain or invigorate their personal relationships. Similar to previous findings (for example, The Pew Internet & American Life Project, 2000a), our analyses of all three datasets show that overall, women use email more than men in communicating with family and friends, and women use email more than men to start communicating regularly with a family member that they did not keep up with very much before. The different role obligations men and women have in personal relationship maintenance and the different value they place on personal relationships may account for these differences in email use.

Thus, our study suggests, women are using the new technology more than men in maintaining and even expanding their social networks. But both men and women are using it intensively to keep up with their siblings and their parents. The new technology seems to encourage men to communicate more regularly with their sons and daughters, while wives are taking advantage of less costly (both in time and money) email to fulfill gender role obligations to communicate with the in-laws. Email is having a generally beneficial effect on personal relationships, although, it seems, more so for women than for men.

Our findings, of course, are conditional on the limitations of our survey and interview samples. Our survey and interview samples are not directly comparable. For example, HomeNet survey data were collected from a relatively small sample only in the city of Pittsburgh. The Pew Internet Project data are more diverse, but still is not representative of the population as a whole. The face-to-face interviews were accumulated gradually between 1995 and 1999, while the survey data reported here were collected in 1999 and 2001 using different methods (mail surveys and phone interviews). While the HomeNet Project data reflects mostly email usage at home, most of the Pew Internet Project data include both home and work email usage. The participants in our samples were predominantly middle aged, middle class, married, white Americans. Men and women who are not middle class and white may have different gender ideologies and different patterns of personal relationship maintenance and styles of relating to others. For example, at least one study (Argyle and Henderson, 1985) found that the number of friends and choice of communication modality vary across social groups. People from higher socioeconomic groups tend to have more friends compared to lower socioeconomic groups, and working-class women tend to communicate more face-to-face than higher socioeconomic group women. Married people, on average, have fewer friends compared to non-married people (Hause, 1995).

Only one author coded the interviews, and our conclusions about message content are based on the text of a small sample of messages as well as on interviewees' comments about their messages. Also, we do not compare email to other modes of communication, nor do we consider the gender of the corresponding partner. Previous studies, for example, show differences in communication patterns between same-gender and different-gender friends (e.g., Parker and de Vries, 1993). We do not control for availability of email for interviewees' relatives and friends.

Despite these limitations, our study shows some patterns across samples. It appears that some pre-existing differences between men and women in their beliefs and behaviors in maintaining personal relationships are being perpetuated in email communication. For example, women in the United States have been traditionally responsible for maintaining relationships among family and friends, and we find that they have appropriated email as a new tool for this traditional role obligation. Women also reported more often than men sending email to extended family, especially cousins and in-laws. These findings of gender differences using email replicate gender differences using the phone, or sending greeting cards, and letters. In all these modes of communication, women do most of the "work of kin" (cf., Di Leonardo, 1987). However, for both women and men, the new technology seems to have stimulated communication with adult siblings and cousins, and between fathers and their children more so than between mothers and their children. Relationships with siblings – for both women and men – outnumbers any other type of relationship maintained by email. Our findings show that, in fact, women and men have quite similar patterns of types of family/kin relationships that they maintain regularly by email, but they differ in frequency of communication with family and kin.

We have mixed results on the role of proximity in email use and how it is influenced by gender. Our study shows that men and women do not differ in using email locally for personal relationship maintenance. Email is useful for setting up joint activities, and both men and women use it for coordinating social activities with local partners. These findings are consistent with recent reports on a tendency for women to become more instrumental in their relationships (Duck and Wright, 1993; Spence and Buckner, 2000; Twenge, 1997; Wright and Scanlon, 1991). In addition, women seem to use email to keep in touch with relatives and friends far more often than men. But women and men do not differ when using email to contact one friend they communicate with most often by email – whether nearby or far away. It could be that women use email more than men to maintain a larger social network at a distance, while email is similarly used when emailing frequently to one friend of choice, independent of where this friend lives – nearby or far away.

Both HomeNet and Pew Internet & American Life survey data show that women have more positive attitudes toward using email as a tool to connect to others. They find sending email to family and friends more useful and more enjoyable than men do. Other studies have come to a similar conclusion – email is more psychologically gratifying to women than to men (see, for example, Pew Internet & American Life Project, 2000a; Stafford, Kline, and Dimmick, 1999). One reason could be that women tend to express themselves better in words than men do (Maccoby and Jacklin, 1974). Also, since using text in an asynchronous mode provides the individual with more control over the conversation (e.g., McKenna and Bargh, 2000), email could be psychologically more advantageous to women than to men. Research findings show that women tend to worry more about their relationships and the impression they make on others in communicating, while men tend to be more relaxed about the state of their personal relationships (Michelson, 1988). Using communication modalities that allow for more control over what they say and when they say it may be more gratifying to women than to men.

We have only weak evidence that gender differences in communication styles show in email communication too. Women, who are more likely to use a facilitative communication style (seeking dialogue), seem to communicate by email "in spurts," enacting their relationships in intense bursts of communication. In contrast men, being more prone to a restricting style of communication, seem to tolerate considerable delays between communication sessions. These findings suggest that instant messaging may differentially appeal to women than men, because it better supports highly interactive communication sessions.

While our study shows that email is appropriated by both men and women to enact already existing patterns of relationship maintenance, we also found some indications that certain types of personal relationships may be changing as a consequence of computer-mediated communication. For example, email seems to intensify communication with siblings, and of fathers with their daughters and sons. Also, our interview data suggest that women are using email to supplement telephone conversations with their parents, whereas they are substituting it for telephone calls with their siblings. Is computer-mediated communication slowly changing relationship dynamics, or is it just shifting communication modalities?

While our study focuses on email, Internet services for real-time communication have been spreading rapidly, especially among the younger population. Future research on the issues of how a variety of new technologies are used to sustain or change personal relationships should include all these modalities, and more diverse demographic groups.

References

Argyle, M. and Henderson, M. (1985). The rules of relationships. In S. Duck and D. Perlman (eds), *Understanding personal relationships: an interdisciplinary approach* (pp. 63–84). London: Sage.

Boneva, B., Kraut, R., and Frohlich, D. (2001). Using e-mail for personal relationships: the difference gender makes. *American Behavioral Scientist*, 45(3), 530–49.

Brandon, B. (1980). *The effects of the demographics of individual households on their telephone usage*. Cambridge, MA: Ballinger.

Caldwell, M. A. and Peplau, L. A. (1982). Sex differences in same-sex friendships. *Sex Roles*, 8, 721–32.

Canary, D. J. and Stafford, L. (1994). Maintaining relationships through strategic and routine interactions. In D. J. Canary and L. Stafford (eds), *Communication and relationship maintenance* (pp. 3–22). New York: Academic Press.

Claes, M. E. (1992). Friendship and personal adjustment during adolescence. *Journal of Adolescence*, 15(1), 39–55.

Cummings, J. N. and Kraut, R. (2002). Domesticating computers and the Internet. *Information Society* (forthcoming).

Cummings, J. N., Butler, B., and Kraut, R. (2002). The quality of online relationships. *Communications of the ACM*, 45(7), 103–8.

Davidson, L. R. and Duberman, L. (1982). Friendship: communication and interactional patterns in same-sex dyads. *Sex Roles*, 8, 809–22.

Deaux, K. and Major, B. (1987). Putting gender into context: an interactive model of gender-related behavior. *Psychological Review*, 94, 369–89.

Di Leonardo, M. (1987). The female world of cards and holidays: women, families and the work of kinship. *Signs: Journal of Women in Culture and Society*, 12, 440–53.

Duck, S. and Wright, P. H. (1993). Reexamining gender differences in friendships: A close look at two kinds of data. *Sex Roles*, 28, 709–27.

Eagle, A. H. and Steffen, V. J. (1984). Gender stereotypes stem from the distribution of women and men into social roles. *Journal of Personality and Social Psychology*, 46, 735–54.

Hampton, K. and Wellman, B. (2001). Long distance community in the network society: contact and support beyond Netville. *American Behavioral Scientist*, 43(3), 476–95.

Hause, K. S. (1995). *Friendship after marriage: can it ever be the same?* Paper presented at the conference of the International Network on Personal Relationships, Williamsburgh, Virginia.

Hauser, S. T., Powers, S. I., Weiss-Perry, B., Follansbee, D. J., Rajapak, D., and Greene, W. M. (1987). The constraining and enabling coding system manual. Unpublished manuscript.

Kraut, R., Mukhopadhyay, T., Szczypula, J., Kiesler, S., and Scherlis, W. (2000).

Communication and information: alternative uses of the Internet in households. *Computer–Human Interaction,* 10, 287–303.

Kraut, R., Patterson, M., Lundmark, V., Kiesler, S., Mukhopadhyay, T., and Scherlis, W. (1998). Internet paradox: a social technology that reduces social involvement and psychological well-being? *American Psychologist,* 53(9), 1017–31.

Kraut, R., Kiesler, S., Boneva, B., Cummings, J., Helgeson, V., and Crawford, A. (2002). Internet paradox revisited. *Journal of Social Issues,* 58, 49–74.

Lacohée, H. and Anderson, B. (2001). Interacting with the telephone. *International Journal of Human–Computer Studies,* 54, 665–99.

Maccoby, E. E. (1990). Gender and relationships: a developmental account. *American Psychologist,* 45(4), 513–20.

Maccoby, E. E. and Jacklin, C. N. (1974). *The psychology of sex differences.* Palo Alto, CA: Stanford University Press.

McKenna, K. Y. A. and Bargh, J. A. (2000). Plan 9 from cyberspace: the implications of the Internet for personality and social psychology. *Personality and Social Psychology Review,* 4, 57–75.

Michelson, W. (1988). Divergent convergence: the daily routines of employed spouses as a public affairs agenda. In C. Andrew and B. M. Milroy (eds), *Life spaces: gender, household, employment* (pp. 81–101). Vancouver: University of British Columbia Press.

Moore, G. (1990). Structural determinants of men's and women's personal networks. *American Sociological Review,* 55, 726–35.

Noble, G. (1987). Individual differences, psychological neighbourhoods and use of the domestic telephone. *Media Information Australia,* 44, 37–41.

Parker, S. and de Vries, B. (1993). Patterns of friendship for women and men in same- and cross-sex relationships. *Journal of Social and Personal Relationships,* 10(4), 617–26.

The Pew Internet & American Life Project (2000a). *Tracking online life: how women use the Internet to cultivate relationships with family and friends.* Available online at http://www.pewinternet.org/reports/

Pew Internet & American Life Project (2000b). *Daily Internet activities.* Available online at: http://www.pewinternet.org/reports/

Rosenthal, C. (1985). Kinkeeping in the familial division of labor. *Journal of Marriage and the Family,* 47, 965–74.

QSR NUD*IST software. (1999). SCILARI. Sage Publications Software.

Silverman, D. (2000). Analyzing talk and text. In N. K. Denzin and Y. S. Lincoln (eds), *Handbook of qualitative research* (pp. 821–34). Thousand Oaks, CA: Sage.

Spence, J. T. and Buckner, C. (1995). Masculinity and femininity: defining the undefinable. In P. J. Kalbfleisch and M. J. Cody (eds), *Gender, power, and com-*

munication in human relationships. (pp. 105–40). Hillsdale, New Jersey: Lawrence Erlbaum Associates.

Spence, J. T. and Buckner, C. E. (2000). Instrumental and expressive traits, trait stereotypes, and sexist attitudes: what do they signify? *Psychology of Women Quarterly*, 24, 44–62.

Spence, J. T. and Helmreich, R. L. (1978). *Masculinity and femininity: their psychological dimensions, correlates, and antecedents*. Austin: University of Texas Press.

Sproull, L. and Kiesler, S. (1986). Reducing social context cues: email in organizational communication. *Management Science*, 32, 1492–512.

Stafford, L. and Canary, D. J. (1991). Maintenance strategies and romantic relationship type, gender and relational characteristics. *Journal of Social and Personal Relationships*, 8, 217–42.

Stafford, L., Kline, S. L., and Dimmick, J. (1999). Home email: relational maintenance and gratification opportunities. *Journal of Broadcasting & Electronic Media*, 43(4), 659–69.

Tannen, D. (1992). *You just don't understand: women and men in conversation*. London: Virago Press.

Twenge, J. M. (1997). Changes in masculine and feminine traits across time: a meta-analysis. *Sex Roles*, 36, 305–27.

Walker, K. (1994). "I'm not friends the way she's friends": ideological and behavioral constructions of masculinity in men's friendships. *Masculinities*, 2, 38–55.

Walther, J. B. (1996). Computer-mediated communication: impersonal, interpersonal, and hyperpersonal Interaction. *Communication Research*, 23(1), 3–43.

Weiser, E. (2000). Gender differences in Internet use patterns and Internet application preferences: a two-sample comparison. *CyberPsychology & Behavior*, 3(2), 167–77.

Wellman, B. (1992). Men in networks: private communities, domestic friendships. In P. M. Nardi (ed.), *Men's friendships* (pp. 74–114). London: Sage.

Wright, P. H. and Scanlon, M. B. (1991). Gender role orientations and friendship: some attenuation but gender differences abound. *Sex Roles*, 24, 551–66.

14

Belonging in Geographic, Ethnic, and Internet Spaces

Sorin Matei and Sandra J. Ball-Rokeach

Abstract

The relationship between online and offline social ties is studied in seven Los Angeles ethnically marked residential areas. Contrary to visions proposing a zero-sum game between the two, we advance a "the more, the more" approach to online social ties. Higher level of belonging to real communities translates into a higher propensity for interaction online. This approach is informed by a social shaping of technology perspective, which proposes that strong anchoring to offline social and cultural groups links, rather than separates, "cyberspace" from people's local communities. Empirical evidence, produced by logistic regression, indicates that the chances of making a friend online increase by 7 percent for each "belonging" index unit and by 32 percent for each neighbor known well enough to talk about a personal problem. "Belonging" is captured through an index measure, combining eight items concerning objective and subjective involvement in residential community. Ethnic differences are less pronounced than expected. However, Asian respondents, particularly those of Korean descent, are more likely to form online ties than "mainstream" white respondents. Focus group data suggest that online ties are established with people of the same ethnicity.

Authors' note

This chapter reports results of an ongoing research project, Metamorphosis, conducted under the auspices of the Communication Technology and Community Program at the Annenberg School for Communication, USC. It is funded by the Annenberg Center and Annenberg School for Communication at the University of Southern California: Sandra J. Ball-Rokeach, Principal Investigator.

The emergence of the Internet as a communication and social interaction tool was initially met with great hopes (Rheingold, 1993) for revitalizing the faltering sense of community afflicting late-modern societies (Giddens, 1991; Sennett, 1998). Although this optimistic perspective is still popular, especially in technophile media circles (Katz, 1997; Meeks, 1997), there are fears that the main asset of Internet interaction – "virtual" social connections between people who never meet in person – could, in fact, become a social liability. The greatest fear is that online social ties will substitute for real social bonds, in a zero-sum game; the more we connect online, the more we will abandon our neighbors and families (Kraut, Patterson, Lundmark, Kielser, Mukhopadhyay, and Scherlis, 1998), preferring online relationships for their greater degree of freedom (Nie, 2001). Some of the fear is that we'll engage online not with people but just with the online environment, that is, not so much a change of venue, but a change from people to technology.

These fears might be just as unsubstantiated as the hopes they try to debunk. Starting with the telephone (Fischer, 1992), communication technology has been used for reinforcing pre-existing social, political, and cultural patterns (Dutton, 1996; Winner, 1977). More recently, empirical studies taking a social shaping of technology perspective (Ball-Rokeach, Gibbs, Jung, Kim, and Qiu, 2000; Hampton and Wellman, 2000; Katz and Aspden, 1997; Rainie and Kohut, 2000) have provided substantial evidence that people who connect to the Internet are more likely to use it for cultivating their social and cultural proclivities (Mansell and Silverstone, 1994; Silverstone and Hirsch, 1997). This perspective proposes that technology is primarily a cultural and social subsystem of society, through which individuals and groups express and try to achieve their constellations of values, social dreams, and so on. Technology is seen not as an autonomous force with a unique capacity to shape social and cultural arrangements, but as a cultural device utilized for achieving various social and cultural goals.

However, the explanatory models offered by this type of research are often insufficiently specified. They only indicate that there is a relationship between being an Internet connector[1] and the likelihood of being involved in the real world. Although useful heuristic tools, these models do not address the core question of if and how *social relationships* in either space (real or virtual) interact. More important, they are rarely concerned with the way in which particular respondent characteristics (social class or status, marital status, ethnic, or cultural

1 We prefer the term connector to "user," more commonly encountered in the literature, trying to point to the fact that social connections online can be and in fact are more than instrumental.

background) mediate the relationship between online and offline social bonds.

The present study seeks to fill this gap with findings from a multi-year study of communication technology and sense of community in real and virtual spaces that is being conducted at the Annenberg School for Communication, University of Southern California. Our research indicates that the best predictor of making friends online is the presence of personal ties in real community. The fact that study samples are drawn from seven different ethnically marked neighborhoods in Los Angeles increases the substantive significance of these findings. The relationship between online and offline ties holds after controlling for socio-demographic characteristics (gender, income, age, education) and, most importantly, for respondent ethnic community/residential area and their generation of immigration to the United States.

Our research also indicates that there are substantial connectivity differences between the Asian study groups and a Caucasian study group closest, in sociocultural terms, to the American mainstream population. The Korean[2] group and, to a lesser extent, the Chinese, included are far more likely to have made a friend online than any of the other groups. We interpret these findings from a sociocultural shaping of technology perspective.

Online Sociability and the "Sociocultural Shaping of Technology" Paradigm

The exponential growth of Internet access since the early 1990s has transformed several means of communication, previously reserved for the corporate and academic elites, into mass consumption goods. This has led some observers to speculate about the capacity of computer communication to generate new social formations, freed from place and traditional institutional constraints (Barlow, 1994; Dyson, 1997; Gates, 1995; Katz, 1997; Meeks, 1997; Mitchell, 1995; Rushkof, 1994; Schuler, 1996; Toffler and Toffler, 1995).

The Internet and its component technologies (for example, email, newsgroups, chat facilities, on-demand media, homepages) were seen

2   Ethnicity is designated in text, for conciseness, by the shortest label available: African–American, Chinese, Korean, Mexican or Central American, and White. Obviously, these names reflect the ethnic or racial origin. Thus they should be read as "Chinese" or "Korean"-origin groups or individuals.

as eminently democratic tools of communication because they were relatively cheap, compared to the costs of traditional media publishing, and they could enlarge freedom of speech and equality of access to public debates (Rheingold, 1993; Schuler, 1996). Moreover, the capacity to participate anonymously in online conversations was seen as an opportunity for encouraging more authentic dialogue between people who otherwise feel constrained by their social, racial or gender background (Poster, 1997; Turkle, 1995). In essence, the new medium was presented as generative of an open communication environment where access and authenticity of feeling are maximized.

One of the central themes of this vision was that Internet communication creates sui-generis social groups, capable of supplementing and, in the long run, replacing interaction in the real world. The thinking was that online social spaces would ease the burden of ascribed identities and allegiances built into our social, ethnic, and physical communities (Poster, 1997; Rheingold, 1993; Watson, 1997). The net effect would be more freedom, more equality and more creativity (Negroponte, 1995; Rheingold, 1993).

Soon, however, a number of academic and non-academic critics started to question this view. To the claims of ease of access were brought counter-claims of a gaping digital divide (Barbrook and Cameron, 1995; Boal, 1995; Castells, 1996; Downey and McGuigan, 1999; McConnaughey, Lader, Chin, and Everette, 1998). Other critics pointed to the fact that identity switching can weaken social responsibility (Seabrook, 1997; Slouka, 1995). Nie and Erbring (2000) concluded that the Internet leads to social atomization, a finding prominently featured in the American media (Markoff, 2000). Learning that people who spend more than five hours a week online report spending less time with friends and family they announced that the Internet replicates the social isolation effects of television and of the automobile (Markoff, 2000; Nie, 2001; Putnam, 1995). Kraut, Patterson, Lundmark, Kielser, Mukhopadhyay, and Scherlis (1998) similarly infer from self-reported psychological data that those who spend more time online become lonelier and more depressed.[3]

Although a useful corrective factor, some of these critiques (Boal, 1995; Kraut et al., 1998; Nie, 2001) presented the negative social effects

---

3 The results were based on a panel study started in 1998. In a more recent working paper the authors, however, report that after one year the effect was in fact reversed (more time spent of the Internet translates into less self-reported loneliness and depression).

of the Internet in no less direct or powerful terms than those of the position they scrutinized (Kraut et al., 1998; Nie, 2001). Both perspectives overestimate the capacity of technology to change deep-seated social and cultural arrangements and proclivities.

An alternative to this Manichean fight in the mirror is the position taken by researchers inspired by a broader sociological perspective. They propose that changes in the web of social and technological connections come from the dynamics of general social and cultural forces (Baym, 1998; Fernback and Thompson, 1995; Jones, 1997). Their social-influence vision offers a much more refined explanatory framework for the role of the Internet in mediating social interaction.

Refusing the legitimacy of the claim that the Internet is a medium that affects (positively or negatively) society from outside, social influence analysts view it as a process involving the interplay of social, cultural, and technological factors (Baym, 1998; Carey, 1988; Contractor and Eisenberg, 1990; Fernback, 1997; Fulk, Schmitz, and Steinfield, 1990; Jones, 1997; Mantovani, 1994; Nye, 1997). This view can be synthesized in the proposition that communication technologies are the product of social choices that predate them (Bijker, Hughes, and Pinch, 1987; Dutton, 1996; MacKenzie and Wajcman, 1985; Williams and Edge, 1996; Winner, 1977). The Internet, like many other modern electronic media, is rooted in social and cultural history, and participation in online groups is linked to powerful socio-cultural forces outside the domain of technology per se (Baym, 1998; Beniger, 1987; Contractor and Eisenberg, 1990; Doheny-Farina, 1996; Fernback, 1997; Fischer, 1992; Fulk et al., 1990; Mantovani, 1994; Matei, 1998; Wellman et al., 1996).

Communication scholars dissatisfied with the ideological poverty of early theorizing on the "social effects" of Internet technologies have tried to offer more dynamic scenarios about the role of computer-mediated communication in society (Ball-Rokeach, Gibbs, Jung, Kim, and Qiu, 2000; Ball-Rokeach and Reardon, 1988; Baym, 1998, 2001; Beniger, 1987; Fernback, 1997; Fernback and Thompson, 1995; Mantovani, 1994; Wellman, 1997, 2001). Some have, even if tacitly, embraced a social shaping of technology perspective, proposing that computer-mediated communication creates social spaces that are quite similar to those we encounter in everyday life (Parks and Floyd, 1996). Others have rejected the idea that online groups, by being "virtual," will also be more open or free (Mantovani, 1994). Computer networks can strengthen human connections when they carry strong communal values, but they can also weaken them when the values transacted are individualistic (Jones, 1997).

This theoretical approach has fueled a number of studies that provide empirical support for the idea that virtual and real spaces are interconnected. Parks and Floyd (1996) have documented the strength and similarity of online and offline personal relationships. The Pew Internet studies suggest that Internet connectors are increasingly using the medium to maintain and reinforce their existing offline social networks (Rainie and Kohut, 2000). Howard, Rainie, and Jones (2001) report that online experience does not replace other forms of social interaction; instead it complements and extends them. Controlling for socio-demographic characteristics, they found that people who have been online at least once are more likely to have called a friend or relative yesterday. Also, they found that people, and especially women, feel that the Internet has improved the way they manage their social lives. Email was found to be an important communication tool for improving intra-family communication.

An early 1995 social effects of the Internet study concluded that experienced Internet users compared to those less experienced maintain stronger connections with their friends and families, and are more likely to be members of community organizations and to be involved in community affairs (Katz and Aspden, 1997). A study conducted in a highly Internet connected exurban Toronto neighborhood found that Internet-access households are more likely to establish both strong and weak (in network analysis terms) social ties in the neighborhood than households unconnected to the Internet. Connected residents know three times as many local residents, talk with twice as many, and are more likely to invite their neighbors to their homes than their non-Internet connected neighbors (Hampton, 2001; Hampton and Wellman, 2000).

Some early "cybertown boosters" now argue that the technical advantages of the medium can be maximized only in social contexts, including geographic communities, which take full advantage of the social commitments of their users (Rheingold, 1998).

These findings should come as no surprise, since studies of "old media," like the telephone, have revealed the localizing effect of telecommunications. A number of important studies (Fischer, 1992; Pool, 1983) conclude that telephone diffusion in the United States did not end up making the distant more familiar, as initially expected, but in strengthening local social ties.

Thus, the social "effects" of Internet technologies should not be seen as a "pure" media problem. Computer-mediated communication and communicators should be researched as part of everyday social life (Ball-Rokeach, Gibbs, Jung, Kim, and Qiu, 2000; Ball-Rokeach, Kim, and Matei, 2001). Forces similar to those operating in non-networked groups – cultural, social, ethnic – will most probably affect online groups as well (Baym, 1998). Visions about, and value-orientations toward, online and offline spaces are, in fact, similar because they originate in people's minds, not in cyberspace itself. They are influenced by all those things that have an impact on the way people think: education, social class or status, gender, ethnic background, residential location, and so on.

The larger theoretical corollary of this proposition is that the social "effects" of the Internet should be placed in the framework of people's socio-structural connections, including cultural, ethnic, social and local-physical circumstances. The methodological implication is that real and virtual space cannot be studied in isolation. Since offline ties and values precede online connections historically – both at a social and at an individual level – the strength of virtual ties can be expected to reflect those of real ones.

Hypothesis and Research Question

The core assumption of this study, that people take with them their social propensities wherever they go – that is, that "belongers" belong everywhere – is explored through one central hypothesis and a related research question. The hypothesis advances the proposition that online and offline social ties are related. The dataset utilized includes a wide array of ethnic groups living in an urban setting. Thus, the present study is also informed by a concern to detect how ethnic specific social and cultural characteristics shape or mediate the link between online and offline social ties. This concern springs not only from the nature of the data but also from the paucity of research on ethnically diverse environments. To our knowledge, this study is the first quantitative assessment of the way in which specific ethnicities (e.g., Chinese or Korean versus "Asian" racial category) incorporate the Internet in their daily lives. Previous studies took an ethnographic, case-study approach (Cisler, 1998; Mitra, 1997; Zurawski, 1996), with rare exceptions taking a comparative approach (Gibbs, Matei, Mandavil, and Yi, 1997).

Off-line social anchoring is considered from a sociological perspective. That is, offline social ties are considered under the rubric of "belonging," a measure that captures two dimensions of community insertion. The first dimension concerns the ties we directly construct with other people in daily communication and interaction. The second and related dimension refers to images and social perceptions that contribute to community cohesion. This "belonging" measure is synthesized into an index score, which incorporates both *subjective appraisals of neighborliness* and *actual interaction* in real communities (see "Method" section).

This measure is central in testing the central assertion of this study, that is, that the likelihood of making social ties online is stronger when people have stronger social ties in physical neighborhoods. This, once again, is based on the assumption that both types of ties are reflections of a more general orientation to social life that predisposes individuals to community involvement. Because this predisposition is acquired and developed in physical communities, we test the hypothesis that belonging to local community is a predictor of social interaction online:

Hypothesis: The higher the level of belonging to local community, the higher the likelihood of making new personal bonds online.

Our multiethnic study samples live in seven distinct urban-residential areas. Differences in social connection on and offline can be influenced by social contexts and by value orientations reflected in ethnic/residential background. Thus, we are able to assess the mediating effect of ethnic background/residential area. Since there is little research or theoretical work on which to base predictions about such inter-ethnic differences, this is formulated as a research question:

Research question: Do residential/ethnic differences mediate the relationships between offline social bonds and online social ties?

Method

Data collection

The data analyzed in this chapter were provided by the "Metamorphosis" project. Individual and group-level information about communication technology and community attachment in a large American city was collected through a multi-method strategy, including telephone and mail surveys, a media census, focus groups, mental mapping and structured interviews. The core of the study is a random telephone survey of selected Los Angeles neighborhoods.[4] The ethnicities represented in the study samples constitute 90 percent of the Los Angeles county population (Matei, Ball-Rokeach, Wilson, Gibbs, and Gutierrez Hoyt, 2001).

The response rate to the telephone survey was low, 31 percent, calculated by dividing the number of completed interviews by the number of *theoretically* eligible phone numbers. Despite the fact that the phone interview was relatively long (40 to 45 minutes) the cooperation rate – percentage of eligible respondents contacted who completed the survey – was relatively high, 62 percent.[5] While there are sample biases due to the response rate, they appear to be within the normal range for a survey of this complexity (Keeter, Kohut, Groves, and Presser, 2000). The sample overrepresents females, higher income earners, those with higher education and older residents (Matei et al., 2001). Our unusual multilingual data collection procedures include non-English-speaking persons often excluded in survey research. Hence, our study has relatively large numbers of ethnic minorities and new immigrants who live in homogeneous residential areas.

Instruments

The bulk of the data presented in this study was collected through the telephone survey, focus groups and the mail survey. They were all

4   Westside, White; Greater Crenshaw, African–American; East Los Angeles, Mexican–American; Pico-Union, Central-American; Koreatown, Korean; South Pasadena, White; Monterey Park, Chinese (Allen and Turner, 1997). From each neighborhood only respondents of the target ethnicity were recruited for the study.
5   The main reason for the low response rate is inability to determine eligibility for 40 percent of the phone numbers introduced in the sampling frame, due to no response, despite five callbacks. These phone numbers had to be kept in the sampling frame, as "theoretically eligible" and were used in determining the final response rate. A full discussion of the response rate can be found in the Metamorphosis study technical report, available at
http://www.metamorph.org/vault/techreport.zip.

made accessible to non-English speakers in their native languages (Chinese – both in the Mandarin and Cantonese dialects, Korean, and Spanish). The telephone interviews include measures of (1) participation and level of social interaction in online groups; (2) a "sense of belonging" to the community or neighborhood, measured by integration with the community or neighborhood; and (3) socio-demographic information (for example, age, education, income, generation in the United States).

In addition to participating in the telephone survey, Internet connected telephone survey respondents and their children were invited to participate in focus groups and a supplementary mail survey ($N = 115$). Focus groups revealed how Internet social relations are integrated into the life of each participant's family and community. The mail survey provided information about the types and scope of social online connections, such as websites most frequently visited and their location (country).

Measures

Social involvement in physical communities was measured through a belonging index specifically developed for this study, building on pre-existing literature (Chavis and Wandersman, 1990; Hui, 1988; McLeod et al., 1996). This eight-item measure captures subjective and objective attachment/involvement with the neighborhood (Chavis and Wandersman, 1990; Hui, 1988; McLeod et al., 1996).

Four items capture the subjective dimension of belonging to the neighborhood: "Do you strongly agree, agree, neither agree, nor disagree, disagree or strongly disagree with the statement(s)": (1) You are interested in knowing what your neighbors are like (55 percent of respondents agree or strongly agree); (2) You enjoy meeting and talking with your neighbors (73 percent of respondents agree or strongly agree); (3) It's easy to become friends with your neighbors (67 percent of respondents agree or strongly agree); (4) Your neighbors always borrow things from you and your family (32 percent of respondents agree or strongly agree).

Four other items capture the objective dimension of belonging, asking: "How many of your neighbors do you know well enough to ask them to" (respondent can specify any number equal to or greater than 0): (1) Keep watch on your house or apartment? (mean = 3.5; standard deviation = 5.8); (2) Ask for a ride? (mean = 3; standard deviation = 5.6); (3) Talk with them about a personal problem? (mean = 1.4; standard deviation = 2.8); (4) Ask for their assistance in making a repair? (mean = 1.9; standard deviation = 3.4).

The "number of neighbors" items were capped at "10 or more," due to skewness. They were further divided by 2, to be brought to the same metric with the "agree/disagree" (subjective) variables. To reduce missing cases in the final belonging index score, all missing cases were replaced with the variable mean. The belonging index was created by summing all eight items. The Cronbach alpha test for the eight-item index scalability is a high 0.78.

South Pasadena/white respondents and Crenshaw/African–Americans had the highest mean level of belonging, 19.5 (standard deviation = 5.81; N = 251) and 20 (standard deviation = 6.5; N = 252), respectively. The lowest scores are for the Greater Monterey Park/Chinese, 15.7 (standard deviation = 3.8; N = 321) and Greater Koreatown/Korean respondents, 16 (standard deviation = 5.4; N = 238). In the rest of the study areas, the mean belonging scores were: East Los Angeles/Hispanic–Mexican, 18.8 (standard deviation = 5.7; N = 250), Westside/white, 17.68 (standard deviation = 5.6; N = 250), and Pico-Union/Hispanic-Central-American 16.6 (standard deviation = 5; N = 250).

Social connectedness online

This was measured by asking if the respondent has "ever met someone online that you consider a personal friend?" Of the 350 respondents eligible to answer this question – that is, those who participate in online activities that include other people – 22.3 percent answered "yes." Raw likelihood of making friends online varies widely across ethnic groups. While 44 percent of the qualified Koreans and 31 percent of Chinese respondents have made a friend online, only 19 percent of the whites from Westside, 16 percent of the African–Americans from Crenshaw, 15 percent of Pico-Union Hispanics, 13 percent of South Pasadena whites, and 7 percent of East Los Angeles Hispanics respondents did the same.

The mail survey provided information about the scope of new media connections. That is, respondents were asked to indicate the five worldwide web sites they visited most frequently. Sites were then categorized according to the location of their main target audience: local (Los Angeles), national-ethnic (country of origin), in the United States, and "placeless" (for example, addressing a world audience, such as Yahoo, or Hotmail).

Analysis

Dataset preparation and statistical models design

Data were first inspected for normality and the "number of friends" variables were recoded to reduce skewness. Analysis was performed by logistic regression due to the categorical nature of the dependent variable, which is a "yes"/"no" response indicating whether or not the respondent has made a friend online. Belonging and residential location are treated as main predictor variables. Community location was operationalized as a series of dummy variables. All locations were compared to South Pasadena study area respondents (middle-class Protestants) as they are considered to be the closest to the American "mainstream." Since only one ethnicity was sampled from each area, the location variable also represents ethnicity.

Age, income, education, gender and generation of immigration to the United States were employed as control variables.

Findings

We hypothesize that attachment to local neighborhood, measured as "level of belonging," positively influences likelihood of making personal bonds online. The expected result is that stronger subjective and objective anchoring to local community increases the likelihood of making friends online. Logistic regression produces a significant relationship. A model predicting chances of having made friends online indicates that firmer anchoring to one's neighborhood (higher "belonging" score) is associated with greater chances of making personal friends in "virtual" (online) environments (see table 14.1). For each unit increase in "belonging" (i.e., number of people known in the neighborhood and assessment of spirit of neighborliness), the chances of making a friend online are augmented by 7 percent ($B = 0.06$, $SE = 0.03$, Wald = 4.66, $p < 0.05$, $\exp(B) = 1.07$).

Thus, the results are consistent with our hypothesis. People's basic community orientation is equally strong on and offline, after controlling for socio-demographic and area characteristics. This finding supports the main point of our study: belongers belong everywhere.

Table 14.1   Variables predicting likelihood of making a personal friend online

Independent variables	B	SE	Wald	P	Exp(B)
Education	0.18	0.12	2.45	0.12	1.20
Age	−0.01	0.01	0.43	0.51	0.99
Income	−0.10	0.09	1.42	0.23	0.90
Gender (male)	0.54	0.30	3.20	0.07	1.71
Immigration generation	−0.14	0.13	1.10	0.29	0.87
Belonging index	0.06	0.03	4.66	0.03	1.07
Koreatown resident	3.21	1.33	5.80	0.01	24.69
Crenshaw resident	0.22	0.57	0.15	0.70	1.25
East LA resident	−1.21	0.89	1.84	0.17	0.30
Monterey Park resident	0.58	0.58	1.00	0.31	1.79
Westside resident	0.13	0.54	0.06	0.80	1.14
Pico Union resident	−0.56	0.82	0.46	0.50	0.57
Interaction Koreatown residency /belonging	−0.12	0.07	3.07	0.08	0.88

Model df = 321, χ^2 = 31.47, $p < 0.01$.

The special case of Korean connections

The model providing this result, however, required us to introduce among the independent variables an interaction term between being Korean and "belonging." This was demanded by the fact that an initial model, using as independent variables only belonging, location and socio-demographics, failed to provide significant results for belonging or for any of the residential areas/ethnic group variables.[6]

Our introduction of an interaction term into the logistic regression equation was directed by the observation that Koreatown respondents who have made a friend online score disproportionately low on the belonging scale. Dividing Koreans into three groups, in terms of belonging "low," "medium," and "high,"[7] indicates that while 56 percent of those in the bottom category have made a friend online, only 44 percent of the top category have done the same. This is even more surprising upon finding that Koreans living in Koreatown have a 25 times greater chance of making a personal friend online than the "mainstream" whites living in South Pasadena (see table 14.1).

6   Belonging B = 0.04, SE = 0.03, Wald = 2.41, p = 0.12, exp(B) = 1.04.
7   The "medium" category includes scores +/− 0.5 deviations from the mean; "low," scores below 0.5 deviations; and "high," scores above 0.5 standard deviations.

Post hoc analysis interpretation

We suspected that Koreans' irregular behavior in terms of belonging and online social ties is due, at least in part, to the characteristics of the area in which they live rather than to individual-level social inclinations. Koreatown is one of the poorest, crime ridden and most ethnically diverse study areas (Ball-Rokeach, Gibbs, Gutierrez Hoyt et al., 2000). Lower level of belonging among Koreatown online interactors was believed to be produced by lower assessment of neighborliness, not by lack of personal ties in neighborhood. To explore this alternative, a post hoc logistic regression model was generated using one of the components of the belonging measure as the main predictor. This is the item that captures the most intimate neighborhood connections: "number of neighbors known with whom a person can talk about a personal problem." This is highly correlated with the whole index ($r = 0.65$, $N = 1,746$). The model includes the same control variables and no interaction term. The rationale behind this model was if number of strong personal ties in the neighborhood predicts, in absence of any interaction terms, likelihood of making online friends, then the problem we faced in Koreatown came from the items left out (weak interpersonal links and strength of neighborliness).

The results indicate that the variable "number of neighbors with whom one can talk about a personal problem" predicts more directly (that is no interaction terms were used) likelihood of making friends online. For each extra person known in this way the chances of making a friend online increase by 32 percent ($B = 0.27$, $SE = 0.13$, Wald $= 4.45$, $p < 0.05$, $\exp(B) = 1.32$, Model $df = 311$, $\chi^2 = 27.19$, $p < 0.01$). Thus, respondents from all groups (including Koreans) are equally likely to form personal ties online, when they know a greater number of people in the neighborhood to talk about a personal problem.

Research question: the role of ethnicity in general

The logistic regression presented in Table 14.1 also provides the data necessary to assess the more general role played by ethnicity in mediating the relationship between online and offline ties. These results were supplemented by information collected through focus group discussions. The findings suggest that the role of ethnicity is weaker than expected. Only for one community, out of the seven studied – that of Koreatown Korean residents – did we detect an effect for ethnicity/residential area above and beyond social connection and control variables.

The data indicate, however, that before controlling for basic socio-demographic variables, not only the Korean but also the Chinese study group displays a higher propensity for forming online ties than the white comparison group. We took the difference between the Asian and the white mainstream group to be phenomenological, that is, to be a key element of what it means to be a Korean or Chinese immigrant in Los Angeles – for example, relatively low income, but higher educational attainment and higher Internet connectivity. In the following discussion we seek a fuller account of these ethnic differences in online connections by examining our qualitative focus group data and data gathered through the mail survey.

Korean and Chinese focus group insights

A consistent theme that emerged during the focus groups was that online connections link our respondents to people or institutions of similar ethnicity or from countries of origin: 36 percent of the websites visited by most of the Koreans and 24 percent by the Chinese focus group and mail survey participants were in Korea or China, respectively. Except for a few (4 percent of total) Central American websites visited by Latino Internet connectors from Pico-Union, no country-of-origin websites were visited by the Mexican, Caucasian, or African-American respondents.

Focus group discussions also reveal that new online social connections are mostly made within the ethnic group. Korean respondents indicate that they have met or know of friends who have met mostly other Koreans online. A Chinese respondent believes that "making friends on the Internet is like making friends in the real world,"[8] the assumption being that ethnicity plays the same important role. During the discussion, a Korean woman said that she found it difficult, when she first came to the United States, to make friends. Email was for her a natural way to contact friends who live far away. In her own words, through email "It seems like they live close to me."

Compared to the white samples, the Asians seem far more cautious when it comes to online interaction. Although expressing their own reservation toward Internet encounters, especially when involving

8   Citations are from the focus group transcripts.

their children, some white respondents from the Westside and South Pasadena do show interest in meeting people online. One respondent from South Pasadena, for example, declares that she loves making friends from other countries online or participating in French chat rooms. Respondents from the Westside seemed to be relatively more open to business virtual relationships. Yet, in general terms, Asian and white respondents converge in using the Internet for reinforcing ethnic ties. For the white respondents this takes a family, rather than an ethnic twist. They indicated that the Internet is a good tool for reconnecting with lost friends and distant relatives.

The budding home-country or US-based ethnic community online environments seem to be two factors that have particular importance in shaping the online experience of our Asian samples. The diffusion of the Internet in South Korea has been rapid and widespread. South Korea is the country with the highest Internet penetration in Asia, the number of Internet users increasing by five times between 1999 and 2000. Three of the top ten most popular sites on the entire worldwide web are Korean (Terazano, 2000). Korean respondents indicated that many of their social connections online are facilitated by the fact that their friends use the Internet and email.

The Chinese respondents seem to be surrounded by a similarly sophisticated socio-technical environment. A Chinese respondent told us that although her computer does not support Chinese characters, her friends in Taiwan have enough technical skill to send their messages as pictures so that she can read them.

Thus, pre-existing social networks organized along ethnic lines support the two Asian groups' propensity for making friends online. These are seen as natural environments for meshing "real" and online social networks. The importance of these pre-existing environments is highlighted by the general apprehension both Chinese and Korean respondents manifest toward making anonymous online relationships. A Chinese respondent told a relevant anecdote: "People may cheat you. In Taiwan there was a woman who cheated lots of guys to mail her money by sending out beautiful pictures. But she's actually ugly and fat." Another Chinese respondent is weary of the licentiousness of some online environments. "People can say everything including shameless stuff. I was in a chat room once. There were some shameless guys there. I felt bad about it and never tried chat rooms again."

The Korean respondents resonate with these opinions. They believe that online relationships outside one's in-group are shallow. One man declared that what turns him away from online relationships with people met randomly on the Internet is that: "people talk about happy things, but not about sad things. Sad stories are not usually shared via Internet." A woman continued his thought: "On-line friends are just for fun, not for serious relationships." In conclusion, focus group information suggests that Asian respondents have an "in-group" social orientation when building ties online. These are seen as a continuation of their offline social networks, created largely through ethnic affiliation.

Discussion and Conclusions

This chapter investigated the relationship between online and offline social ties in an ethnically diverse urban environment. Contrary to visions proposing a zero-sum game, our research advances a "the more, the more" approach to online bonds. Rejecting overly optimistic perspectives (Anderson, Bikson, Law, and Mitchell, 1995; Harasim, 1993; Kiesler and Sproull, 1992; Meeks, 1997; Rheingold, 1993; Sproull and Kiesler, 1991) or those overly pessimistic (Boal, 1995; Kraut et al., 1998; Nie, 2001), we propose that a higher level of belonging to real communities translates into a higher propensity for interaction online. The inclination to form and maintain lasting ties on or offline derives from social and cultural resources and the proclivities of people acting in context of their real communities, rather than from characteristics of the medium, per se.

Our findings support the social shaping of technology perspective in that strong anchoring to offline social and cultural groups links, rather than separates, "cyberspace" from people's local communities. In concrete terms, after controlling for basic socio-demographic characteristics, individuals are more likely to make friends online when they have a relatively high level of "belonging" (i.e., if they know more people in the neighborhood and believe that they live in an area characterized by neighborliness). These findings confirm a growing body of research looking at the online sociability phenomenon (Hampton and Wellman, 2001; Haythornthwaite, 2001a, 2001b; Howard, Rainie, and Jones, 2001; Katz, Rice, and Aspden, 2001; Wellman, 2001).

The present findings are also consistent with parallel research about the role more traditional communication channels (from interpersonal to print and electronic media) play in boosting or hindering belonging in the same seven ethnic neighborhoods of Los Angeles (Ball-Rokeach, Gibbs, Gutierrez Hoyt et al., 2000). In essence, the Internet adds a new layer of communication opportunities and competencies to pre-existing communication environments, shaping our social lives through reinforcement rather than through displacement.

Korean residents of Koreatown, however, present a deviant outcome. Those more likely to make friends online are slightly less, although not statistically significant, likely to belong. Controlling for location and socio-demographics, Koreans are also the ones most likely to have friends in cyberspace. The Chinese respondents are also more likely than non-Asian groups to be connected to other people online. Focus group data indicate that the propensity for online interaction among these Asian groups may represent a tendency to migrate their ethnic social networks online, rather than to create entirely new "cyberspaces." Asian focus group participants seemed to be quite skeptical of random online relationships, seeing them as a form of entertainment rather than as community experience. Nonetheless, the tendency of the two Asian samples to create ethnic patterns of Internet association makes even more intriguing the finding that Korean respondents are less likely to belong to their Los Angeles neighborhood when making online ties.

On the basis of the observed interaction effect between being a Korean Koreatown resident and belonging we suggest that this reflects residential area, not ethnicity characteristics. Koreatown is culturally and socially fragmented. The overall level of belonging for Koreans in Koreatown, both for Internet connectors and non-connectors, is one of the lowest among our study samples. In addition, most middle-class, educated Koreans are spread throughout wealthier Los Angeles suburbs. Relatively educated Internet-connected Koreans residing in Koreatown may feel isolated from their residential environs compensating for the social shortcomings of the area by extending their connections to other Koreans in South Korea.

The particularities of the Korean sample point both to the limitations and the advantages of our research design. Our samples are slices of urban-metropolitan areas defined in terms of ethnically-marked social experiences. This allows, on the one hand, investigation of the particularities of community life in context of associated communication webs. On the other hand, the sensitivity of our strategy to the individuality of each specific place, limits generalizations.

Most generally, our analysis is limited because we surveyed only one ethnicity per study area. Thus, a multilevel analysis procedure, to more clearly distinguish between ethnic-group versus area character-istics effects was not possible. However, post hoc analysis has shown that the density of residential community ties more uniformly predicts the likelihood of making friends online than the complex measure of "belonging" (that is, number of neighbors known and assessment of neighborliness in the community). This circumstantial evidence sug-gests differences between simple ties and complex "belonging" in their effects on online sociability. A more conclusive analysis awaits future research in which we sample multiple ethnicities from the same residential area.

Until then, the potential significance and strength of our findings is in the substantial convergence of these case studies. Across seven dif-ferent neighborhoods, three races and multiple national origins, the best predictor for online ties is the presence of offline personal con-nections or belonging.

This tells us a story about neighborhoods in one American metro-politan environment. Does this account apply nationally, and does it apply to the patterns of social interaction and communication in the home countries of our study samples? These issues are also on our research agenda. We hope, however, that our current results will inform community and communication technology policies of local officials or community organizers in Los Angeles or other metropoli-tan areas populated by similar ethnic groups.

Our findings suggest that technology/community building inter-ventions should be dual track. Efforts to build community locally should have payoffs for Internet community – what we call a "mag-nifying glass" effect. People who contribute social capital to their res-idential places can also be expected to lend their "social capital" to the online groups they inhabit. Put another way, unless social connections online are supported by pre-existing social and cultural networks offline, their long-term prospects are probably not that great. Contin-ued efforts to understand the linkage between the two social spaces can help us to more effectively foster stronger and more viable ties between people in both worlds.

References

Allen, J. P. and Turner, E. (1997). *The ethnic quilt: population diversity in Southern California.* The Center for Geographical Studies. Northridge, CA: California State University.

Anderson, R. H., Bikson, T. K., Law, S. A., and Mitchell, B. M. (1995). *Universal access to email: feasibility and societal implications*. Santa Monica, CA: RAND.

Ball-Rokeach, S. J. and Reardon, K. (1988). Monologue, dialogue and telelog: comparing an emergent form of communication with traditional forms. In R. P. Hawkins, J. M. Weiman, and S. Pingree (eds), *Advancing communication science: merging mass and interpersonal processes* (pp. 135–61). Beverly Hills: Sage.

Ball-Rokeach, S. J., Kim, Y.-C., and Matei, S. (2001). Storytelling neighborhood: paths to belonging in diverse urban environments. *Communication Research*, 28(4), 392–428.

Ball-Rokeach, S. J., Gibbs, J., Jung, J.-Y., Kim, Y.-C., and Qiu, J. (2000). *The globalization of everyday life: visions and reality* (White Paper 2). Los Angeles: Annenberg School for Communication. Metamorphosis Project. Available online at: http://www.metamorph.org/vault/globalization.html

Ball-Rokeach, S. J., Gibbs, J., Gutierrez Hoyt, E., Jung, J.-Y., Kim, Y.-C., Matei, S., Wilson, M., Yuan, Y., and Zhang, L. (2000). The challenge of belonging in the 21st century: the case of Los Angeles (White Paper 1). Los Angeles: Annenberg School for Communication, Metamorphosis Project. Available online at: http://www.metamorph.org/vault/belonging.html

Barbrook, R. and Cameron, A. (1995). *The Californian ideology*. Available online at: http://www.wmin.ac.uk/media/HRC/ci/calif5.html

Barlow, J. P. (1994). *Jack in, young pioneer*. Available online at: http://www.eff.org/pub/Misc/Publications/John_Perry_Barlow/virtual_frontier_barlow_eff.article

Baym, N. (1998). The emergence of online community. In S. Jones (ed.), *Cybersociety 2.0* (pp. 35–68). Thousand Oaks: Sage.

Baym, N. (2001). *Is the Internet really any different?: social interactions across media*. Paper presented at International Commmunication Association Conference. Washington, DC.

Beniger, J. R. (1987). Personalization of the mass media and the growth of pseudo-community. *Communication Research*, 14(3), 352–71.

Bijker, W. E., Hughes, T. P., and Pinch, T. J. (1987). *The social construction of technological systems: new directions in the sociology and history of technology*. Cambridge, MA: MIT Press.

Boal, I. (1995). A flow of monsters: Luddism and virtual technologies. In J. Brook and I. Boal (eds), *Resisting the virtual life: the culture and politics of information*. San Francisco, CA: City Lights.

Carey, J. (1988). The mythos of the electronic revolution. In J. Carey (ed.), *Communication as culture* (pp. 113–41). Boston: Unwin Hyman.

Castells, M. (1996). *The rise of network society*. Cambridge, MA: Blackwell Publishers.

Chavis, D. M. and Wandersman, A. (1990). Sense of community in the urban environment: a catalyst for participation and community development. *American Journal of Community Psychology*, 18(1), 55–79.

Cisler, S. (1998). Introduction: the Internet and indigenous groups. *Cultural Survival Quarterly*, 21(4). Available online at: http://www.cs.org/publications/CSQ/csqInternet.html

Contractor, N. S. and Eisenberg, E. M. (1990). Communication networks and new media in organizations. In J. Fulk and C. W. Steinfield (eds), *Organizations and communication technology* (pp. 143–72). Newbury Park: Sage.

Doheny-Farina, S. (1996). *The wired neighborhood.* New Haven, CT: Yale University Press.

Downey, J. and McGuigan, J. (eds) (1999). *Technocities.* London: Sage.

Dutton, W. H. (ed.) (1996). *Information and communication technologies: visions and realities.* Oxford, UK: Oxford University Press.

Dyson, E. (1997). *Release 2.0: a design for living in the digital age* (1st edn). New York: Broadway Books.

Fernback, J. (1997). The individual within the collective: virtual ideology and the realization of collective principles. In S. Jones (ed.), *Virtual Culture* (pp. 36–54). Thousand Oaks, CA: Sage.

Fernback, J. and Thompson, B. (1995). *Virtual communities: abort, retry, failure?* Available online at: http://www.well.com/user/hlr/texts/VCcivil.html

Fischer, C. (1992). *America calling: a social history of the telephone to 1940.* Berkeley, CA: University of California Press.

Fulk, J., Schmitz, J., and Steinfield, C. W. (1990). A social influence model of technology use. In J. Fulk and C. W. Steinfield (eds), *Organizations and communication technology* (pp. 117–40). Newbury Park: Sage.

Gates, B. (1995). *The road ahead.* New York: Viking.

Gibbs, J., Matei, S., Mandavil, A., and Yi, H. (1997, 10–13 July). *Expression of local/global identity in personal homepages.* Paper presented at the Rochester Institute for Technology Communication, Technology, and Cultural Values Conference, Rochester, NY. Available online at: http://matei.org/natid/natidreport.rtf

Giddens, A. (1991). *Modernity and self-identity: self and society in the late modern age.* Stanford: Stanford University Press.

Hampton, K. (2001). Living the wired life in the wired suburb: Netville, glocalization, and civic society. Unpublished doctoral dissertation, University of Toronto, Toronto.

Hampton, K. and Wellman, B. (2001). Long distance community in the network society: contact and support beyond Netville. *American Behavioral Scientist*, 45(3), 476–95.

Hampton, K. and Wellman, B. (2000). Examining community in the digital neighborhood. Early results from Canada's wired suburb. In T. Ishida and K. Isbister (eds), *Digital cities: technologies, experiences, and future perspectives* (pp. 194–208). Heidelberg, Germany: Springer-Verlag.

Harasim, L. (1993). Networks: networking as social space. In L. Harasim (ed.), *Global networks* (pp. 15–34). Cambridge, MA: MIT Press.

Haythornthwaite, C. (2001a). Introduction: the Internet in everyday life. *American Behavioral Scientist*, 45(3), 363–82.

Haythornthwaite, C. (2001b). Tie strength and the impact of new media. Paper presented at the Hawai'i International Conference on System Sciences, Maui, Hawaii.

Howard, P., Rainie, L., and Jones, S. (2001). Days and nights on the Internet: the impact of a diffusing technology. *American Behavioral Scientist*, 45(3), 383–404.

Hui, C. H. (1988). Measurement of individualism and collectivism. *Journal of Research in Personality*, 22(1), 17–36.

Jones, S. (1997). The Internet and its social landscape. In S. Jones (ed.), *Virtual culture: identity and communication in cybersociety* (pp. 7–35). Thousand Oaks, CA: Sage.

Katz, J. (1997, December). The Netizen – Special report. *Wired*, 5, np. Available online at: http://www.wired.com/wired/archive/5.12/netizen.html

Katz, J. and Aspden, P. (1997). A nation of strangers. *Communications of the ACM*, 40(12), 81–6.

Katz, J., Rice, R. E., and Aspden, P. (2001). The Internet, 1995–2000: access, civic involvement, and social interaction. *American Behavioral Scientist*, 45(3), 405–20.

Keeter, S., Kohut, A., Groves, R. M., and Presser, S. (2000, January). *Consequences of reducing nonresponse in a national telephone survey*. Available online at: http://mason.gmu.edu/~skeeter/nonresponse.zip.

Kiesler, S. and Sproull, L. (1992). Group decision making and communication technology. *Organizational behavior and human decision processes*, 52, 96–123.

Kraut, R., Patterson, M., Lundmark, V., Kielser, S., Mukhopadhyay, T., and Scherlis, W. (1998). Internet paradox: a social technology that produces social involvement and psychological well-being? *American Psychologist*, 53(9), 1017–31.

MacKenzie, D. and Wajcman, J. (1985). *The social shaping of technology: how the refrigerator got its hum*. Philadelphia, PA: Open University Press.

Mansell, R. and Silverstone, R. (1997). *Communication by design: the politics of information and communication technologies*. Oxford, UK: Oxford University Press.

Mantovani, G. (1994). Is computer-mediated communication intrinsically apt to enhance democracy in organizations? *Human Relations*, 47(1), 45–62.

Markoff, J. (2000, February 16). Portrait of a newer, lonelier crowd is captured in an Internet survey. *The New York Times*, np. Available online at: http://www.nytimes.com/library/tech/00/02/biztech/articles/16online.html

Matei, S. (1998). Virtual community as rhetorical vision and its American roots. In M. Prosser and K. S. Sitaram (eds), *Civic discourse: intercultural, international, and global media*. (pp. 45–59). Greenwich, CT: Ablex.

Matei, S., Ball-Rokeach, S. J., Wilson, M., Gibbs, J., and Gutierrez Hoyt,

E. (2001). Metamorphosis: a field research methodology for studying communication technology and community. *The Electronic Journal of Communication / La Revue Electronique de Communication*. Available online at: http://www.cios.org/www/ejc/v11n201.htm

McConnaughey, Lader, W., Chin, R., and Everette, D. (1998). *Falling through the net: defining the digital divide*. Washington, DC: US Department of Commerce. Available online at:
http://www.ntia.doc.gov/ntiahome/fttn99/FTTN.pdf

McLeod, J. M., Daily, K., Guo, Z. S., Eveland Jr, W. P., Bayer, J., Yang, S. C., and Wang, H. (1996). Community integration, local media use, and democratic-processes. *Communication Research*, 23(2), 179–209.

Meeks, B. (1997). Better democracy through technology. The next 50 years: our hopes, our visions, our plans. *Communications of the ACM*, 40(2), 75.

Mitchell, W. J. (1995). *City of bits: space, place, and the infobahn*. Cambridge, MA: MIT Press.

Mitra, A. (1997). Virtual communality: looking for India on the Internet. In S. Jones (ed.), *Virtual culture: identity and communication in cybersociety* (pp. 55–79). Thousand Oaks, CA: Sage.

Negroponte, N. (1995). *Being digital* (1st edn). New York: Knopf.

Nie, N. H. (2001). Sociability, interpersonal relations, and the Internet: reconciling conflicting findings. *American Behavioral Scientist*, 45(3), 420–35.

Nye, D. E. (1997). Shaping communication networks: telegraph, telephone, computer. *Social Research*, 64(3), np. Available online at:
http://proquest.umi.com.

Parks, M. R. and Floyd, K. (1996). Making friends in cyberspace. *Journal of Communication*, 46(1), 80–97.

Pool, I. d. S. (1983). *Forecasting the telephone: a retrospective technology assessment of the telephone*. Norwood, NJ: Ablex.

Poster, M. (1997). Cyberdemocracy: Internet and the public sphere. In D. Porter (ed.), *Internet culture* (pp. 201–18). New York and London: Routledge.

Putnam, R. (1995). Tuning in, tuning out: the strange disappearance of social capital in America. *Political Science and Politics*, 28(4), 664.

Rainie, L. and Kohut, A. (2000). *Tracking online life: how women use the Internet to cultivate relationships with family and friends* (Internet Life Report 1). Washington, DC: Pew Internet and American Life Project. Available online at: http://63.210.24.35/reports/pdfs/Report1.pdf

Rheingold, H. (1993). *The Virtual Community: homesteading on the electronic frontier* (1st HarperPerennial edn). New York, NY: HarperPerennial.

Rheingold, H. (1998). Misunderstanding new media. *Feed Magazine*, September 10. Available online at:
http://www.feedmag.com/essay/es102lofi.html

Rushkof, D. (1994). *Cyberia*. San Francisco, CA: HarperSanFrancisco.

Schuler, D. (1996). *New community networks: wired for change*. Reading, MA: Addison-Wesley.

Seabrook, J. (1997). *Deeper*. New York, NY: Simon and Schuster.

Sennett, R. (1998). *The corrosion of character*. New York City: Norton.

Silverstone, R. and Hirsch, E. (1994). *Consuming technologies: Media and information in domestic spaces*. London: Routledge.

Slouka, M. (1995). *War of the worlds: cyberspace and the high-tech assault on reality*. New York: BasicBooks.

Sproull, L. and Kiesler, S. B. (1991). *Connections: new ways of working in the networked organization*. Cambridge, MA: MIT Press.

Terazano, E. (2000, October 19). South Korea: A regional leader for dotcoms. *Financial Times*, pp. 7. Available online at:
http://www.lexis-nexis.com/universe

Toffler, A. and Toffler, H. (1995). *Creating a new civilization: the politics of the third wave*. Atlanta, GA: Turner Publishing, Inc.

Turkle, S. (1995). *Life on the screen: identity in the age of the Internet*. New York: Simon and Schuster.

Watson, N. (1997). Why we argue about virtual community: a case study of the Phish.net fan community. In S. G. Jones (ed.), *Virtual culture* (pp. 102–32). London, Thousand Oaks, New Delhi: Sage.

Wellman, B. (1997). An electronic group is virtually a social network. In S. Kiesler (ed.), *Culture of the Internet* (pp. 179–205). Mahwah, NJ: Lawrence Erlbaum.

Wellman, B. (2001). Physical place and cyber place: the rise of personalized networks. *International Journal of Urban and Regional Research*, 25(2), 227–52.

Wellman, B., Salaff, J., Dimitrova, D., Garton, L., Gulia, M., and Haythornthwaite, C. (1996). Computer networks as social networks: collaborative work, telework, and virtual community. *Annual Review of Sociology*, 22, 213–39.

Williams, R. and Edge, D. (1996). The social shaping of technology. In W. H. Dutton (ed.), *Information and communication technologies: visions and reality*. Oxford, UK: Oxford University Press.

Winner, L. (1977). *Autonomous technology: technics-out-of-control as a theme in political thought*. Cambridge, MA: MIT Press.

Zurawski, N. (1996, 24–8 June, 1996). *Ethnicity and the Internet in a global society*. Paper presented at the Sixth Annual Conference of the Internet Society, Montreal. Available online at:
http://www.isoc.org/inet96/proceedings/e8/e8_1.htm

Part V

The Internet at School, Work, and Home

15

Bringing the Internet Home

Adult Distance Learners and Their Internet, Home, and Work Worlds

Caroline Haythornthwaite and Michelle M. Kazmer

Abstract

Debate about the role of the Internet in everyday life has raised questions about whether time spent online provides benefits to the individuals who are online and the families and friends around them. While recent surveys provide data on the overall picture of Internet use, here we look at adult users' views of what is gained and lost with the addition of online hours to already full schedules. For one year, we followed seventeen adult students as they engaged in an Internet-based distance degree program. We explored their involvement with the online learning community, how this affected their relationships with family, work, volunteer, and peer groups, and how they managed and juggled their involvement in these multiple social worlds. We find that students' satisfaction with the program increased, and anxiety about operating in the online world decreased, with increased involvement with the learning community. Although this was often realized in the short term at the expense of offline communities and activities, we believe that taking this as a negative effect discounts the very real support that such students were receiving online from other students. Moreover, we find two encouraging effects for local communities: first, that both work and home environments gain benefits from students' online activity as more experienced students find and act on synergies between their online learning and work and home activities, and second that retreat from local community is only temporary as students make up for lost time with others during breaks, and re-engage with their offline life as they near the end of their program.

Authors' note

Our thanks go to the 17 individuals who gave generously of their time for the interviews that provide the data for this chapter, to Jenny Robins and Susan Shoemaker who were active in interviewing and earlier analyses, and to Jeff Boase for helpful comments. This work was supported by a grant from the University of Illinois Campus Research Board.

Introduction

Debate about the role of the Internet in everyday life has raised questions about its impact on the home, friendships, and the social well-being of its users. Researchers agree that we are spending a lot of time online: nine hours a week on average for both work and non-work activities for US users (UCLA CCP, 2000). Disagreement exists on whether all this time spent online is providing benefits to the individuals who are online and the families and friends around them.

While recent surveys provide data on the overall picture of Internet use, here we provide a user's level view of what is gained and lost at home, with friends, and at work with these hours online. The Internet users in this study are not teenagers, nor are they spending their hours in the online games or anonymous chat rooms associated with the darker predictions about the impact of the Internet on "real life." Instead they are mature adults, with responsibilities and obligations to others, living with spouses and children and holding down full-time jobs, who have taken an intense, committed use of the Internet into their homes as part of a distance education degree program. They have made a serious life decision that a higher degree is important to them, and that the Internet option accords best with their ongoing commitments.

This chapter examines how involvement in this Internet-based distance program fit, and sometimes clashed, with the lives of adult distance learning students. These adults represent a new and growing sector of Internet users whose educational experiences will color their future use of computers and the Internet. Moreover, these adults are not without influence on others: bringing the online educational experience into the home has an impact on how children and spouses will use computers; becoming conversant with technology helps them bring others online such as relatives who live at a distance and people reached through volunteer work; and sharing their reports of the pros and cons of their online experiences can affect how others view online education, perhaps affecting also the future success of online programs. Educational programs can thus become a way in which the Internet reaches the home, even for those not directly involved in the program.

These adults are among the early pioneers in online education, and among the first to accommodate this type of experience into their offline lives. They did not know others who had taken a degree or even individual courses online and found that only other members of their program understood their "different kind of world" (a description from one of the students). They represent the beginning of a continuing and growing trend. As the Internet continues its penetration into work and home life, so does its presence as a medium for the delivery of education to students of all ages and walks of life, whether by established institutions of higher education or those in the private sector (Beller and Or, 1998; Gibson, 1998; Rout, 2001). In 1998, 85–90 percent of institutions of higher education with over 3,000 students expected to offer distance education (Gibson, 1998, editor's notes, reporting on a 1997 Chronicle of Higher Education study). The increasing percent of households with computers (65 percent of US households) and Internet access (43 percent with access from home; 55 percent of all Americans with access from home or elsewhere; Nie and Erbring, 2000) increases the potential number of online learners and also the likelihood that individuals will find themselves learning online. Increased home and work access, combined with increased efforts by institutions to offer distance education, increases dramatically the number of individuals who will be bringing an Internet education program home in the near future. Indeed, a *Wall Street Journal* article puts the expected number of US distance learners at 2.2 million for 2002, up dramatically from the 710,000 in 1998 (Grimes, 2001).

While distance education has been in place for a long time, Internet-based education is not a simple reworking of old paradigms. Greater expectations for interpersonal interactivity, collaborative learning, immediacy, "just-in-time" delivery, development of distributed learning communities, and technological competencies, make this a new endeavor for all concerned (Bruffee, 1993; Dede, 1996; Harasim, Hiltz, Teles, and Turoff, 1995; Koschmann, 1996; Renniger and Shumar, 2002). Students entering this domain must learn new norms about communication with instructors and other students. Whereas traditional distance courses consist of exchanges between instructors and students through broadcast and print media, newer online programs require peer-to-peer exchange, with students managing conversations and discussion online through media such as email, bulletin boards, and chat rooms. Using these new forms of communication requires learning new norms for conversation and community. These means of "persistent conversation," i.e., conversations that "may be searched, browsed, replayed, annotated, visualized, restructured, and recontextualized" (Erickson, 1999) leave users unsure of communications norms. Even when familiar with a particular medium, local norms must be discovered and learned before students can feel confident about the online presentation of themselves and their work (Bregman and Haythornthwaite, 2001). New online learners get a dual education, including both the intended educational content of the program and grounding in the use of technologies for work and social interaction (Haythornthwaite et al., 2000).

Controversy about the Internet suggests on the one hand that the Internet reduces involvement with those with whom we share strong, local, interpersonal ties, taking us away from face-to-face involvement and potentially decreasing our overall well-being (Kraut et al., 1998; Nie and Erbring, 2000; Putnam, 2000). On the other hand, the Internet is seen as providing the means for increased contact with others, particularly with distant friends and relatives (Howard, Rainie, and Jones, 2001; Kraut, Kiesler, Boneva, Cummings, Helgeson, and Crawford, 2002; Wellman, Quan Haase, Witte, and Hampton, 2001; and this volume) and those with whom we share common interests (Sproull and Kiesler, 1991; Wellman, Salaff, Dimitrova, Garton, Gulia, and Haythornthwaite, 1996), and for increasing continuity with others as we move about daily, and/or as we move homes (Hampton and Wellman, 2001).

When many hours are taken from local, face-to-face activity and given to an online activity, it can be expected that disruption or displacement will occur. What we set out to explore here is what this disruption means to a set of individuals involved in intensive Internet use that is not shared with local family members. How does their time committed to the online endeavor affect their time with others? Does involvement pull them away from local family, work, or volunteer associations? What is the impact on friendships? Do they lose or gain friends while involved in the distance program? Are online friendships real and enduring, or merely instrumental connections to other students? Do they feel isolated and alone when spending time on the Internet? Is their Internet use and Internet experience a separate part of their life, cordoned off from work and family, or are there synergies between the online and offline worlds?

To explore these questions, we examined in detail the results of longitudinal interviews with 17 students (nearly 70 hours of interviews), and results from a one-time questionnaire given to members of the program in fall 1999. This chapter also draws on our earlier analyses of these interviews that explored the presence and meaning of online community for these students (Haythornthwaite et al., 2000); the management and juggling of the multiple social worlds students cope with, including home, work, and the online education world (Kazmer and Haythornthwaite, 2001); and students' concerns about self presentation through the persistent conversations of email, bulletin boards, and online chat (Bregman and Haythornthwaite, 2003). We begin with a description of the distance, multimedia environment and the data collection, proceeding then to an examination of how students' experiences affect their involvement with others.

Media and Interaction in the Online Environment

The students in this study are enrolled in the distance option of an American university masters degree program. The option, known as LEEP, is given by the Graduate School of Library and Information Science at the University of Illinois.[1] Students complete a masters degree in library and information science (LIS) at a distance through courses conducted via the Internet. The program begins with a two-week intensive on-campus session ("boot camp"). All remaining courses are taken from home via the Internet, with required on-campus sessions once a semester.

Both synchronous and asynchronous media are used to deliver classes and to provide means for student-to-student, and student-instructor interaction. "Live" lectures (given from twice a semester to weekly depending on the course and the instructor's preference) are delivered via RealAudio, with the instructor speaking to the distributed audience. During the lectures, students use Internet Relay Chat (IRC) to pose questions to the instructor that are visible to all students. Both the broadcast lecture and the contents of the main class chat room are recorded and available for review by students. IRC is also used for discussion; students may gather in subgroups outside the main chat room as part of the lecture time. Sessions in these chat rooms are not recorded. Students also make use of IRC's "whisper" facility to pass non-recorded messages to specific, named other students during class sessions.

Along with lectures and synchronous discussion via IRC, courses make use of webboards (web-based bulletin boards) for class discus-

1 For details on the program see http://leep.lis.uiuc.edu.

sions and exercises. Students post comments or homeworks to the webboards where they are visible to other students and the instructor. Other program-wide webboards are used for announcements and discussion. All students have email accounts, and there is a toll-free phone number for calls to campus. Assignments, which may include group projects, are submitted as web pages, webboard postings, or attachments to emails, and less frequently by fax and regular mail. Grading and comments are returned to students via regular mail or email.

Data collection

For one academic year, from fall 1998 to spring 1999, we followed 17 students (13 female (76 percent), 4 male (24 percent))[2] as they progressed through their distance education experience. Hour-long phone interviews were conducted with each student mid-semester and near the end of each semester.[3] Interviews were tape recorded and transcribed; names used below with quotes are pseudonyms reflecting the gender of the interviewee. Interviewees were at various stages in their degree program: three began with the first LEEP cohort in 1996, two began in 1997, and the remainder in 1998. All were new to this type of program and to distance education. Each student worked outside the home (16 full-time; 1 part-time, but full-time by the end of the year), most (12 of the 17, 71 percent) in library or library related endeavors (for example, archives), with 1 to 20 years experience. Students were all mature adults, living in their own accommodations, usually with a spouse or significant other; three had small children, four had grown children; only two lived alone.

Interviews explored students' involvement with the online learning community, and how this affected and was affected by their relationships with family, work, volunteer, and peer groups. Analysis of each

---

2   The students are completing a degree for a profession that is female dominated. Proportions of women and men returning the questionnaire (86 percent female, 14 percent male) suggest that interviews slightly over-represent men for this particular program.

3   One student only participated in the first three interviews; all others participated in all four interviews.

set of interviews was used to formulate hypotheses and areas of questioning for following interviews; analysis follows grounded theory practice and consisted of coding the data for themes in student experiences, comparing for commonalities and differences, and analyzing the themes that emerged (Strauss and Corbin, 1990). Questions focused on social network aspects of social support, such as interactions between the interviewee and people in their personal social network (Wasserman and Faust, 1994; Wellman, 1997). We explored involvement with and obligations toward fellow students, family, friends, parents, co-workers, and so on who provided social, technical, and other support, who helped students manage classwork, childcare, household chores, and so on and what kinds of online and offline activities students engaged in and with whom.

In fall 1999 we gave a questionnaire to each student attending the on-campus mid-semester session. Questionnaires were distributed during class and handed to the researchers as soon as completed. Of the 138 students enrolled in the LEEP email list, 113 returned questionnaires (82 percent response rate). Of these, 97 (86 percent) were female, 16 male (14 percent). Most began their program in 1998 or 1999, with only 1 from the first cohort (1996), and 8 from 1997. Three-quarters (73 percent) worked full-time outside the home (79 outside the home full-time; 1 self-employed full-time; 3 full-time volunteers); 19 (17 percent) worked at home full-time on family related activities. Almost all others (27 percent of respondents) worked part-time (21 outside the home part-time; 9 self-employed part-time). Sometimes overlapping with paid work, 13 worked part-time in volunteer work, and 13 worked at home part-time on family related activities. The majority (81 percent) did or had worked and/or volunteered in a library at some time.

The questionnaire asked about how people got to know each other in LEEP, the number of friends they felt they had made in LEEP, which media were used to maintain contact with them, and which media were best for receiving support from other LEEP students. More general social support was explored by having students rank the importance of different people both inside and outside the program for helping with their educational and professional goals. A final set of questions explored their expectations regarding the mid-semester on-campus session and how well these were met. The results from this questionnaire are used here to situate the interview results against the larger student experience.

Students' Experience of the Online Environment

Our first analysis of the interviews (Haythornthwaite et al., 2000) focused on whether LEEP was perceived by students as a community, and how students defined and maintained this virtual community through the "lean" media (Daft and Lengel, 1986) available for interaction. We did indeed find that students perceived LEEP to be a community, and belonging to it was highly important for their personal well-being.

Interviews also revealed how important it is to take into consideration the amount of time people have been in the program and the way this affects their experiences. It takes time for students to become at ease in this environment with its new technologies (new for almost all students), multiple media, and strange new ways of interacting with others. For some this start-up is especially stressful, combining doubts about being a student with doubts about the ability to work with the technology. Writing publicly through webboard postings combines the agony of self-exposure with the self-doubts of the returning student (Bregman and Haythornthwaite, 2001). However, it is not long (usually no longer than one semester) before students are old hands at online exchanges, carrying on conversations according to the norms of this environment, finding other LEEP students who can help put the program and their experiences into perspective, and providing each other with social support, companionship, major emotional support, and sociability.

These accounts of early stress and later benefit from online contact echo findings reported by Kraut, Kiesler et al. (2002) in their third survey of participants in the Homenet project. While their earlier studies showed loneliness and depression were associated with higher Internet use, the latest survey showed lower depression with higher Internet use, and no significant association with loneliness. As Kraut et al. suggest, and as we will show below, integration of Internet use with daily life, and development of synergies between online and offline life, provide more beneficial outcomes from such use.

Along the way to becoming fluent in the LEEP environment, students develop a strong sense of community with other students in the LEEP program. They find they belong to a "different world" that is only understood and shared by other LEEP students, and this gives them a way of partitioning and naming their experience. In building and perceiving this community, students report that they particularly benefit from and appreciate synchronous interaction, whether during the "live" sessions or on-campus visits (one day per course per semester, with all days taking place within the same week). When off campus, students reinvent physical proximity as virtual proximity, appropriating technology and the opportunities afforded them by class and program structures to socialize and work with people they met on-campus, for example, by engaging in near-synchronous email exchanges. Those who fail to make such connections feel isolated and more stressed than those who are more active in communicating with others.

The initial boot camp, the immediacy of later synchronous sessions, and the on-campus face-to-face sessions help to keep connections current, so students feel they are there with people they know rather than with strangers,

> Even though they would be just a name on the screen in the chat room or on the webboard, you still had the memory of knowing them from boot camp, which was such an intense experience. That gave you a connection. It was almost like they were there. You could imagine them. Since it was just recently, and you had them fresh in your mind, you knew exactly who was saying it and what it sounded like, if they had really said it, and what it would have sounded like. (Alice)

The immediacy of synchronous and on-campus sessions helps to overcome isolation and helps students know they are completing this program with others,

> I seem to get more out of class when we meet live more often . . . It keeps you from feeling isolated . . . The immediacy [is nice], even though you're typing, not speaking to them directly, you're typing with them. (Janet)

While immediacy is important, students also find that they learn about each other from webboard postings, email, and interaction in class chat. While synchronous communication may be perceived as the best, continuous interaction via webboard postings has been described as "butter on toast, real thin but still tasty" (Jerry). The combination of media provides an integrated environment in which there is more than one way to get to know others.

In answer to questions about formation and maintenance of friendships in LEEP, questionnaire respondents ranked the on-campus sessions as the most important for maintaining their circle of LEEP

Table 15.1   Importance of each medium for maintaining a circle of LEEP friends

Medium[a]	Average rank[b]	Number of respondents who provided a rating, this item
On-campus sessions	6.0	86
Email	5.7	85
Live class sessions	5.4	84
Other[c]	4.9	12
Class webboards	4.4	83
Other LEEP webboards	3.1	82
Off-campus face-to-face	2.6	75
Telephone	2.1	77

[a] Media are listed in order from most to least important according to the average of the ranks given by all the respondents. [b] 7 = "very important"; 1 = "not at all important." [c] "Other" includes IRC whispering, and group projects; note that only 12 respondents gave a ranking for this category (n = 113).

friends, followed by email, "live" class sessions, class webboards, other LEEP webboards, other face-to-face contact (for example, among those who live near each other), and the phone (see table 15.1).[4] Although only offered by a few in the "other" category, whispering via IRC and group projects were ranked above class webboards for maintaining these friendships.

Along with the temporal adjustment to activity within LEEP, we also observed that, over time, LEEP work and its environment become less separate from everyday life, and students begin to recognize the overlaps and synergies with other areas of activity (Kazmer and Haythornthwaite, 2001). Janet explains how this is different from experience in other school programs,

> More than being an educational program, it's more a life program. I think in order to be in LEEP [you] have a sense of where you are and where you're going at home and at work and at school. In my past experience in graduate and undergraduate programs when you focus on school it's school and when you focus on home it's home. But here the

4   Students were asked first if they had "found a circle of friends or people you talk to often from among other LEEP students? (answered yes/no)." If they had found friends, they were then asked how many there were in this close circle, how they first got to know these people, and then to rank the importance of each means of communication for maintaining this circle of friends.

lines are all very fuzzy. I didn't anticipate that . . . that the lines would be so fuzzy between work and school and home. (Janet)

Since many of the students are working in organizations appreciative of what they are learning, synergy arises early between work and school for many. Students may be given special opportunities or duties, and access to computers and knowledgeable co-workers. Work environments gain by having employees with special skills, and who are more knowledgeable about workplace practices. For others such synergy never occurred and some changed jobs to gain a better balance.

Involvement in Social Worlds

Involvement in any intensive program can be expected to affect other aspects of students' lives. Yet a program that takes too much from offline life may become unmanageable for students, and eventually lead to the failure of such endeavors. At present the LEEP program has a very high retention and completion rate (97 percent), and so we consider the reports from these students as indication of a manageable load, even if a difficult one and one that requires adjustments to offline commitments.

The first step in understanding the impact of the Internet experience on offline life is to identify students' commitments and obligations. In speaking of these commitments, we find it useful to discuss them in terms of the "social worlds" in which they operate (see Kazmer and Haythornthwaite, 2001). A social world consists of people who share activities, space, and technology, and who communicate with one another (Strauss, 1978). These emerge from the way individuals allocate their time and resources. Each world is coordinated around a primary activity, for example, learning, tending family, earning a living, and is usually associated with one site, such as the university, the home, the workplace. These multiple worlds are not isolated; individuals do not leave all obligations in one world behind as they move to another. Instead, social worlds interact and impinge on each other: we take work home from the office, manage school work while watching children, take family phone calls at the office, and read work-related email at home and on the road. We'll return to discussion of students' social worlds below, but first it is important to consider whether the Internet is a world of its own.

With the advent of the Internet and online communities, we find that social worlds are not confined to offline activity. While many speak of the Internet as if it were a social world of its own – and indeed many examinations of online community speak singularly of the online activity without reference to its place in individual's lives (including our own first analysis of LEEP) – the Internet's communication landscape includes many purposes, and intersection with many worlds. It includes email communications for work, social exchanges with family, searching for community information, buying products for the home, and playing games for personal entertainment alone or with known or unknown others. Treating the Internet as one social world and lumping together "time spent on the Internet" fails to acknowledge the way in which individuals make use of the Internet to serve multiple purposes in support of multiple social worlds. The distance students also did not immediately perceive overlap between their online and offline worlds, but, as explored below, it emerged over time as their newly acquired technical competence allowed them to help children with Internet searching, make and keep connections with travelling and distant friends and relatives, and bring their skills into the workplace.

We see the Internet not as a social world, but as a medium through which we have the opportunity to maintain our multiple social worlds. Recognizing the Internet as a medium rather than as a world comes with accepting the computer "as a medium through which individuals and groups can collaborate with others" (Bannon, 1989, p. 271), with having the technology fade to the background and the information and interpersonal landscape come to the foreground (Bruce and Hogan, 1998). Rene explains how this came about for her when she first began to communicate online after boot camp,

> It was, I think, immediately disconcerting to be back, because as soon as you got back to where you were, meaning like home and work, it felt like boot camp was some other life you had miles and miles away. Then when you started up again it was very easy to fall back into the old rhythms of being with someone in person as you were online. It's like, "Oh, hi . . . How's your little boy. How is he doing." Because you know everything about the person, because you've talked to them. (Rene)

By "wading right in" to online communication, and "taking off as if [the others] were still right next to each other, talking," Rene found that:

> That is really where the technology fades away. It is just the other person
> and some other medium of communicating with them. You don't even
> think about it when you're typing. It is like they are sitting right next to
> you and you are talking to them. (Rene)

While Rene, "waded right in" and accepted immediately that she was
talking with others rather than with the computer, others take longer
to come to see the possibility of continuing the boot camp conversation. For example, Nancy bonded with a set of students at the on-
campus session, yet in the middle of her first semester she felt unsure
about emailing them: "Everybody's working. Everybody . . . well . . . I
just . . . I guess I just was not really sure that I . . . that I really should
[email them]." At this time, she emphasized her preference for the
face-to-face, traditional classroom, and spoke of the pervasiveness of
computers and how we must all interact *with* computers,

> I realize that computers are a part of our lives. No matter what I do . . .
> I'm going to interact with computers at some time or another. I mean
> . . . when I go to the grocery store a lot of you know . . . when I go to
> the ATM . . . you know we do a lot of things I mean with computers
> now. We are on line . . . electronic book stores, buying things. It's just a
> part of our lives. There's no way we can get around not using a com-
> puter. And at work on our jobs . . . just about everybody's job includes
> working on a computer now. I mean it's a fact of life. (Nancy, mid-first
> semester)

None of her rhetoric refers to reaching others via computer, just interacting with the computer. But by the beginning of her second semester she is able to talk of her experiences with more transparency about
computers, focusing instead on chatting, and gathering in groups,
even though all this is computer-mediated,

> the online classes . . . we do, kind of chat, before our class, before [the
> instructor] starts the lecture. And then, you know, we get into small
> groups sometimes, or every week, we get into it because she'll have
> some questions, which she's made up beforehand. She wants us to get
> into these small groups to discuss them, and then we come back
> together. (Nancy, after the beginning of the second semester)

Experience, whether gained intensively by being thrown in the deep
end of a distance learning program, or through longer, less frequent
use of the Internet may be the key to reaching technological trans-

parency and transcendence of individual social worlds. Recent Internet surveys reveal different uses of the Internet by those with more years of experience online that support this view. *Netizens*, as Howard, Rainie, and Jones (2001) refer to them, spend more time online each day, are more likely to be online on any particular day, and engage in the most kinds of online activities (see also Nie and Erbring, 2000; UCLA CCP, 2000; and other chapters in this book). Their extra time online and extra activities suggest that if asked we would also find that they were spending more time online working with different social worlds.[5]

Social Worlds Obligations and Time with Others

To return to one of the key debates about Internet use and benefits we ask: how does time committed to the online endeavor affect students' time with others? We can examine the impact of time with others through students' obligations in their multiple social worlds. Interviewing the students showed that there are three *mandatory* worlds that need to be dealt with on a daily basis: the worlds of LEEP, work, and home. Obligations in these mandatory worlds cannot be shirked (although occasionally they can be deferred, see below). The *LEEP world* consists of instructors, administrators, support staff, and fellow students. Obligations include declaring courses, paying fees, attending classes, getting assignments done, working with other students, and sharing emotional support with other students. Their "world view" of LEEP is largely defined by their student–student relationships and thus this world mainly involves obligations and interactions with other students. The *work world* encompasses where students earn their living, their job, and the people with whom they work (supervisors, co-workers, and others in the same organization). Obligations involve getting the company or institution's work done. Some (but not

---

5 A caveat about this conclusion for general Internet behavior is one well articulated by Nie (2001). Current long-term users are also the early users of this technology and represent a group marked by higher socio-economic status and greater interpersonal connectivity. The connectivity of such people may be due to their personal characteristics as already well-connected people rather than to years of experience on the Internet, i.e., the next generation of new users may not show the same integration of the Internet into all aspects of their lives because their personal characteristics may not lead them to this type of use (see also Haythornthwaite and Wellman, this volume).

all) work environments allowed and indeed encouraged overlap with the LEEP world. Many supervisors and co-workers were supportive and often helpful in gaining entry to the program and being open to discussion in relation to school work. The *Home world* primarily comprises immediate family – spouses, significant others, and children below college age. Young children occupy a central position in this world; they require attention at home, and parental involvement in school and extra-curricular activities. While spouses and significant others are highly important to the LEEP students' home worlds, it is children who take first place in their attention and prioritizing.

Along with the mandatory worlds are *optional* worlds with less pressing obligations. These include, in decreasing order of obligation, other family and close friends, remote family and old friends, and volunteer groups (for example, parent–teacher organizations, church, civic organizations). The professional library and information science world is another optional world. It becomes more significant over time as students increasingly identify with the profession and are identified by co-workers and other librarians as (soon to be) members of the profession.

In much of the examination of the Internet and its impact, concern has been expressed about the loss of time with local family. However, concern is not expressed about time with co-workers or time with members of an online community. However, these students tell us that all three of these represent mandatory worlds for these students, in which obligations must be met and cannot be shirked. Loss in *any* of these three areas can impact negatively on students' lives. Concern has also been expressed about the loss of engagement in volunteer activities (e.g., Putnam, 2000), and as an optional world such activities are vulnerable. While long-term effects may be felt by the community, a student prioritizing their time is not likely to suffer from dropping (temporarily) their volunteer work, and we do see students abandoning these activities early.

Juggling multiple worlds

In managing their multiple worlds, students effect a juggling act – a term a number of them offered to describe their life. Unlike on-campus students, who generally pursue the degree full-time, and pre-plan by leaving work, LEEP students drop very little. They take on the distance option precisely so they do not have to give up work. Most students take two courses a semester and report that it takes them from 10 to 20 hours a week to keep up with readings, webboard postings (1–2 hours a day), being present in live sessions (typically 2 hours a week) and assignments. These hours are added to their already filled schedules of work, family, and friends. No wonder that they speak of "juggling," "handling," "deciding," "rearranging," and "accommodating" LEEP and their other obligations when describing how they manage their schedules!

Juggling requires constant attention, and students must be responsive to changes in each world in order for the next "throw" to be successful. Clarissa, for example, juggles her own activities to accommodate LEEP, but those rearrangements affect: her husband, who has to miss activities to do child care; her work, where she has had to take days to complete LEEP work; and her meeting schedules for other groups. Ted, like many others, is faced with juggling full-time work with family, including young children, and the LEEP program. He applies extra effort to build a schedule that enables him to stay involved with his family and still get some sleep. He has put off tasks, such as gardening, that can be done when he was less busy, and added tasks that support his LEEP work, such as implementing changes to technology at home (for example, adding a telephone line). He prioritizes his children's activities as number one, even if that means missing a LEEP class, or taking a lower grade in a course,

> When it's one of the kids concerts, I'll go and just try to make it up another time. Maybe my grades will suffer, but I felt those were more important. So I would just have to rearrange my time and maybe work late at night. I remember from my first assignment I did an all-nighter, then went to work the next day. At my age I can't do that any more. But when it comes to the kids' activities, I want to be sure that I'm able to go . . . I'm really not concerned with my GPA that much. Maybe I'll find out I should have been. Right now if I just get a B in the class I'm just overjoyed. (Ted)

Beth, in a similar situation, made the decision to take her schooling slowly, taking only one course a semester "because I have to do all the [children's] sports and the academic [work] and maintain my family." Holly, who also has children, chose the distance program deliberately "because my family is my number one priority . . . I didn't want to be traveling." She also prioritized by giving up her volunteer work: "Before I started LEEP I was real involved in [a civic organization] here in my town, and I was on the board and real active, and I pretty much had to just forgo that completely."

Managing multiple obligations

To deal with the simultaneous and competing demands of their multiple social worlds, students *prioritize* by deciding which of their worlds is more important, and then which tasks and relationships are most important within the world. They balance emotional needs (for example, with family and children) with task needs (such as school-work), and managing relationships with inhabitants of their worlds (children, spouses, bosses, co-workers, friends, and family) with accomplishing tasks in these worlds (doing paid work, making dinner, completing homework). They balance what must be done now with what can be done later in a cycle of *neglect and repair*. Within this pri-oritizing and juggling, students also manage multiple obligations by creating *isolation* or *insulation*, carving out time and space to deal with one and only one world for a time (see also Salaff, this volume).

First students prioritize and identify expendable tasks, things that can be dropped outright. As students prioritize they all show a con-sistent hierarchy of dispensing with activities. First to go are *solitary leisure activities* such as television, reading, needlework, gardening, as well as household cleaning chores:

> You know what I've learned? I have learned that you know those little dust bunnies can sit there another day. They're not going anywhere. (Nancy)

Next are *social leisure activities* with friends such as going to the movies or out to dinner. *Volunteer work*, if not dropped before beginning LEEP, is dropped or reduced at this stage. Next, *classes, work, sleep, and even eating*, are compromised. As Putnam (1995) points out, "harried souls do spend less time eating, sleeping, reading books, engaging in hobbies, and just doing nothing" (p. 6).[6] As they get more harried, stu-

---

6   Putnam (1995) goes on to note that such people forgo these activities but still maintain their involvement in volunteer organizational activity. Here we find stu-dents drop volunteer work to maintain engagement in their important organiza-tional activity, that is, LEEP. However, we may also consider this as voluntary work, and perhaps fits the same niche in individuals' lives.

dents may begin to use live class time for other homework, work time for LEEP, and sleep time for anything else – prioritizing has given way to cramming. Last to go are *time with family, particularly children, and schoolwork itself.* But even these can give way: sometimes family has to "understand that [Mommy or Daddy] is doing work now and can't be disturbed," and as Ted noted, expectations for grades can be reduced. This order of dropping activities shows that concerns about loss of time with family are real, but that individuals strive to keep these relationships active. It also implies that harried schedules may be more responsible for loss of family time than time on the Internet.

In the next few sections we rotate through the worlds, examining sequentially the effects in each world of synergies, overlap, and/or collisions between worlds. Although these sections focus on one world at a time, in fact we cannot separate worlds so cleanly and instrumentally; they are intricately connected and should be considered that way.

Interleaving Internet activity and home

In their prioritizing and even with the final desperate cramming, students are choosing which responsibilities can be neglected and set aside for future repair. Relationships with spouses and partners, close and extended family, and friends most often require repair. Students repeatedly mention the need to "say no" to outings with spouses or friends,

> I have had to say no a lot more to different activities, involvement in church, involvement in my kids' school, socially. I feel like I have to say no a lot because I work and because I have a family, I have to look at my time and say oops, I've got a couple hours block on Saturday to do this, I can't plan to do other things. So I've really found over the last year especially that I'd had to be much more of a manager of my time. (Holly, married, school-age children)

Holly's story, while an example of one way that many students prioritize, leaves out the number of students such as Ellen (married, no children) and Sue (married, older children at home) who say flat-out that they do *not* say "no" a lot. They tend to focus more on cramming, or losing sleep, than on saying "no" to activities and relationships around them.

Those who do muster the courage to say "no" depend on semester breaks and summers to nurture interpersonal relations neglected during academic semesters. Alice, for example, maintained close touch with her large family but found involvement in LEEP reduced her visits with friends from once a month to once every two months, and involved shifting visits to the summer when she did not take classes. To stem the potential impact of neglect on interpersonal relationships, some students do frequent "temperature taking," thinking about and discussing how both partners can continue to nurture the relationship. A common solution is to schedule time together, setting up "dates" to watch movies or just "hang out" (Kazmer, 2000).

In keeping with the mandatory and optional worlds, students spend more time managing close personal relationships than those with friends and other relatives. While most have tolerant family members who can wait for future repair, there are also some who report difficulties with the reallocation of priorities. Spouses may have to take on extra duties, and children have to honor the student's work times. It is in these relationships that the involvement in an intense program can have a negative impact on immediate social relationships. Although many cope and accommodate to manage these relationships, live sessions, homework deadlines, and on-campus visits do take time away from these close personal ties. Whether long-term benefits and repair of time together repays the immediate effort is beyond the scope of the data on hand. However, it is important to note that involvement in this program is time limited and thus may differ from involvement in continuous online communities that may not include the breaks that allow for relationship repair.

The cycle of neglect and repair – with loss of time spent together now with promise and/or actual delivery of time together later – suggests that to understand the impact of time spent with others requires an understanding and recognition of this cycle of relationship maintenance. This also suggests that new users of the Internet, such as these students in their first semester of the program, may be seen to neglect and ignore others because no stage of repair has yet been enacted. Once the use of the Internet finds its balance with home life, then feelings of ignoring others or being ignored by others may diminish when viewed from a longer perspective. While the UCLA CCP study tells us that 8 percent of Internet users *do* feel they are ignoring other household members, and 25 percent *do* feel ignored by household members spending too much time online, it would be useful to know further how this plays out with the number of years of use of the Internet to see if more perceptions of neglect are prevalent in new user households.[7]

Another impact is that while the student may be at home, they are not available to others. Even though physically in one world (home), they are mentally in another (LEEP). Students try to carve out time and physical space within the home where they can concentrate on LEEP work. They have mixed success in this. Those who have the greatest success have spouses, partners, and so on, who give them space, both physical and mental, in which to get their work done. Giving space (and time) is a form of social support received from others within the home. Some students gain time and space as spouses take up family and household duties, others enjoy a more intangible support, for example,

> Other people who help me? My boyfriend definitely does because he doesn't come over when I have a class and he doesn't talk to me if he is here and I have a class . . . if he is here, he'll be in a different room if I'm studying or something like that. So he definitely helps. (Alice)

Those who have less success find they cannot clearly delimit their time and space for LEEP. Even in accommodating households, claiming a room and a computer is not always easy, and often students juggle their office space and their time on the computer. Beth found herself moving to various locations in her house as family members needed each workspace for other purposes; Ted tried locations around his house to find a quiet space where he could work.

Even when physical space can be claimed, family members, especially children, often have difficulties accepting these boundaries between worlds as barriers to interaction. Young children don't understand that "If Mommy has the door to her office closed you're not supposed to be bothering her" (Barbara). Clarissa does different kinds of work in her room, some of which is interruptible and some of which is not, and family members can't tell the difference. Though she has talked about and tried several different techniques for reducing interruptions, after one year of distance education, she was still wrestling with creating a private space for herself and her school work. Even when they have claimed space, students still split their attention

---

7   Note also that the Kraut et al. (1998) studies did focus on new user households and found greater neglect of interpersonal relations.

between the LEEP and Home worlds. Local conditions in the Home world can reach levels that put their priority above that of LEEP activities, for example,

> I still have not been able to teach my kids not to disturb me when I'm working. It's hard to do when they come up with a math problem they don't understand or a fight, the youngest ones particularly, they fight like cats and dogs. You have to stop and quell that. (Ted)

To further carve out time and space, more experienced students leverage the benefits of the asynchronous portions of the program. Doris, for example, prefers to work at night; she discovered that she can do LEEP work then, leaving her daytime schedule fairly intact. Other students may not prefer to work at night, but that is the time most open in their schedules, and is therefore when many LEEP tasks get done. Holly leverages the ability to work asynchronously to do her LEEP work in small chunks throughout the day. They learn to interleave and wedge LEEP into times of the day when other worlds are not pressing for attention.

Juggling worlds, maintaining relationships and managing priorities "on-the-fly" are intrinsic parts of multiple world management. We should not see on-the-fly prioritizing as a failure, but rather as the reason for success. As Mark Levine (1998) remarks, reflecting on the skills of juggler Enrico Rastelli:

> It isn't simply that jugglers can do things that other people can't, I thought, but that jugglers are a peculiarly apt embodiment of the human effort to cope gracefully with more demands, from more directions, than one person can reasonably be expected to manage. (Levine, 1998, p. 76)

We note that the ability to "cope gracefully," or even to cope at all, may distinguish these students from others who try to juggle multiple worlds. Both deliberate planning and coping with change are important for balancing worlds. While we believe other populations may also function in this way, it is possible that such coping strategies are a function of the maturity and higher educational attainment of these students. Involvement in online worlds may overwhelm less accomplished managers, creating the kind of withdrawing from "real world" activity observed in other studies.

Synergies between Internet activity and work

While we have concentrated so far on the impact on the home world, obligations in the work world also cannot be ignored. As noted above, many are working in fields related to the nature of the degree, and find both cooperation and appreciation of their work from supervisors and fellow workers. For them the content of their education fits seamlessly with their work environment, and that environment even provides input to their education with help from knowledgeable co-workers. Benefits flow from LEEP to the workplace as students gain course content and technical expertise that they can apply at work. They may be able to assume additional work duties, or do projects for LEEP that can be used in the workplace so that "being involved with the program . . . made something happen that wouldn't have otherwise happened" (Barbara).

Workplaces benefit from students' LEEP involvement and support them in many ways. Often students are given time and access to computers at work for LEEP, allowing them to build a LEEP space within the work world. Even those with offices at home sometimes bring LEEP into work and try to juggle the two worlds simultaneously,

> Every once in a while something will come up at work and I can't get away for the synchronous session at home so I'll be at work so I'll do it at work, but I try to do it at home so I can participate without getting phone calls and interruptions. (Jerry)

Students also bring their work experiences to class, providing a two-way synergy in learning between work and LEEP.

Even with synergy and opportunities, work is still being juggled with responsibilities for LEEP, and the work world may also be treated to a cycle of neglect and repair. For example, Barbara takes a little from work with expectation of repayment in the future,

> I might not be 100% as productive at work [after late night studying], but for me that is a short-term situation. I know that the long-term effect of me being involved in this program and getting the knowledge I think is going to . . . outweigh those drowsy moments. (Barbara)

Where the two worlds are ultimately synergistic, as they are for Barbara, the short-term deficit is easily repaid in the long run. Such is not always the case. Sue, for example, found her work environment unreconcilable with the demands of the education program. She found no alternative but to change work worlds in order to accommodate her LEEP world and her personal goals,

> What I did was quit that job, because the director didn't want to be more flexible with more time off. I didn't want to ask her. I could see that she wasn't going to be flexible with it. So I quit that job and now I have a job with less hours. Now I have more time to do my homework and I did that on purpose, because I don't feel I need that extra stress. (Sue)

Near-term demands of this job were unable to accommodate the "neglect and repair" strategy for managing multiple worlds.

Impacts on the online learning environment

Home and work demands can at times overwhelm involvement in LEEP, subjecting LEEP to the cycle of neglect and repair. Doris, having a difficult semester personally, shared that after the loss of a good friend,

> It just seemed like a monkey wrench kept being thrown into my plan to be methodical about this, so I was kind of proud of myself for getting that assignment out of the way and just begin like, okay, now the crises have all past and I'm going to make more of a plan and stick to it. (Doris)

While this sort of neglect and repair is another example of managing multiple world obligations, neglecting to join the online world has far more negative consequences on students. Those who fail to make connections, particularly those who do not make connections in their first semester, show much greater distress about their LEEP involvement. Here is one student's account of how she felt at the beginning of their first semester:

> I'll have to tell you that it has been one of the most stressful times in my whole life . . . I've had quite a lot of difficulty adjusting to the isolation of being in a non-traditional classroom . . . not being able to talk face to face with the other students . . . I started to have a lot of anxiety . . . just wondering if what I was posting sounded okay or if it sounded so bad . . . Finally I just had to take time off work. (Nancy)

Although the stress experienced by this student represents an extreme case, others also had trouble adjusting to the conditions of a "persistent conversation" (Erickson, 1999) environment, that is, of recorded, visible and enduring texts. While students approach a learning environment bringing with them expectations in line with the traditional classroom, such as how to participate in class, communicate with an instructor, or carry on a discussion with fellow students, they find that what would previously have been an ephemeral conversation is now recorded and preserved for review; previously private exchanges of homework between instructor and student now become public bulletin board documents. Every opinion, however well expressed, every joke and typographical error, leaves a written legacy of an individual's persona and style. They are suddenly exposed in a persistent, public form as never before (see also Bregman and Haythornthwaite, 2003).

It should not be surprising that many feel exposed, and unsure how to communicate. Nancy's feelings of uncertainty are present in others' reports also, particularly in relation to webboard postings. For example,

> At the beginning it was difficult for me because I felt like when I posted something it had to be perfect. All the time all these other people are just talking away . . . I found that difficult to get used to because I felt like I had to be perfect. (Ted)

> When you pretty much communicate with other people through writing I think holy cow these people are so smart. I'll look dumb if I ask them this question. (Alice)

Many students remark that they are not comfortable in LEEP until they get their first grade. Students do not know whether they are doing the right thing until the external confirmation of a grade arrives. Nancy (quoted above) finally telephoned the instructor to find out how she was doing. Making this connection to the faculty member, and other connections with LEEP students, including a strong personal tie that provided her with social support, greatly increased her comfort level in the program.

Social support from within LEEP is extremely important for students to be able to manage their LEEP experience. Many report how meeting students at the first on-campus session after they began the program (approximately two months after their time together in "boot camp," and six weeks into the semester) allowed them to compare notes and find out that their experiences were normal, and par for the course, for example,

> I felt it was individual for me at times, when I thought certain assignments were difficult, but then you talk to other students and they're having the same challenges, same difficulties. (Beth)

Many find their support in close ties formed at boot camp. Of the 113 questionnaire respondents, 81 said they had found a circle of LEEP friends; 74 of those 81 (91 percent) first got to know these people at boot camp. These circles of friends ranged from 1 to 15 others, with mean of 4.5 and median of 4 others in the circle (only 11 claim a circle of over 6 others). These sets of friends find ways to keep together over their time in the program: they try to take the same courses together, stay on campus in the same place, and even visit at each others' homes. Others maintain friendships and gain support through a close friend they "talk" to through email, often finding each other online late at night when assignments are due.

In particular, and perhaps to the chagrin of instructors who are aware of it, students make use of the "whisper" facility of IRC to catch up socially, make jokes, pass information, and concurrently help to explain the content of the lecture. This facility makes it easy for students to ask "dumb questions" of their friends that they do not need to post publicly. It provides another way in which students can become comfortable with their virtual classmates.

However, all the mediated conversations require making the effort to talk and require students to join the LEEP world and stay part of it. When this is accomplished LEEP offers:

> A support system. An emotional support system, an intellectual support system, people you could ask questions, get information from. (Holly)

The online world itself becomes a place where general social support can be gained. Students help each other not just with work, but also with coping with the program, its load in their lives, and events in their offline lives. But it also is a world that students feel requires more effort to belong to than an offline world. "Sometimes it's easier to say 'no' to an online community because it's not right there in front of your face all the time" (Holly). And, as Doris describes it,

> You have to make more of a point to reinforce things because you're not going to bump into people, you have to make a point of nurturing

friendships more so than you do in a neighborhood community or church community or work community where you just bump into people . . . Maybe you do have to work at it more, because it's easier to drop out of it, too . . . you can just kind of fade back if you want and just say, well I'm just going to sit here and do it more like a correspondence course. (Doris)

Much has been made of the lack of personal well-being that can come from the absence of close, local contacts. The LEEP experience also shows that well-being can be compromised by a lack of online contacts. Students will feel alone when online if they have not gone beyond communication with the computer and reached instead communication with others *through* the computer. As students make contacts and form relationships with other LEEP students, and with faculty and staff, they move from a stressful position of isolation to confident membership in the online world. In keeping with results of research on social support in other settings, the more others with whom individuals maintain supportive ties, the more positive the association with happiness, mental health, and well-being (Haines and Hurlbert, 1992; Hammer, 1981; van der Poel, 1993; Walker, Wasserman, and Wellman, 1994; Wellman and Gulia, 1999).

As students gain friendships online, none speak of losing their offline friendships. Instead they seem to have welcomed more people into their social circle, adding a set of virtual, and soon to be professional, friends to their network.[8] This computer-supported social network is already serving people well in the search for new jobs, and in wider searches for difficult to find information. We do not know yet how these friendships and this network will endure past graduation, but given students' ongoing association with the profession, the opportunities to meet at professional conferences, and the enduring online connectivity they will be able to maintain, one can expect these to be as durable as any offline friendships and perhaps more so.

---

8   We note again that these more highly educated users, and early adopters of Internet based distance education may again – as Nie (2001) points out – be more able to add connections because they are better connectors. While this ability may still hold true for later adopters of this program, who will still be more highly educated as they enter this graduate program, this may not hold true for all forms on online education.

Disconnection, connection, and optional worlds

We have already noted where lines between LEEP and work provide opportunities for mutual exchange of resources, information, and know-how. Similarly, the worlds of home, and extended family and friends can also co-exist beneficially with LEEP. These worlds often provide the emotionally supportive interpersonal contact that students say helps keep them going in LEEP.

When asked to rank the importance of people within and outside the program for helping with their educational and professional goals, spouses and partners score well ahead of others (see table 15.2). These are followed by: LEEP class mates; people at work; professors or instructors for classes; personal friends; parents, children or other family members; LEEP technical support personnel; GSLIS and LEEP administrators; LEEP students not in their class(es); members of voluntary organizations (religious groups, social groups, and so on); and non-family household members (e.g., room mates). Listed in the "other category" which ranked between LEEP class mates and people at work, 12 volunteered as significant supporters a variety of people including faculty advisors, non-LEEP professors and technical support, and library personnel (see table 15.2).

Home, work, and friend worlds often provide technical equipment and support and are "repaid" with the technical expertise students gain from LEEP. Students leverage their new comfort with electronic communication to re-establish and strengthen ties with far-away family and friends, and to introduce technologies into their volunteer organizations. Beth found that the expertise with technology she gained in LEEP allowed her to plan her family's vacations using the Internet, help her college-age daughter with information retrieval, and carry out banking, word processing, and scheduling online. Because of her example and her help, more of her geographically remote family has come online and she keeps in touch with friends and family "all over the world." Another student helped establish a used computer distribution program to benefit low-income users, boding well for future payback to volunteer worlds.

Thus, we see increased social contact associated with learning and using online technologies; however, we note that that this effect is not seen until students have gained experience and confidence with the technologies. Along with this confidence comes a recognition of the generalizability of the technology they are using, and the fact that it

Table 15.2 Importance of support providers in students' achieving library and information science educational and professional goals

Support provider[a]	Average rank[b]	Number of respondents who provided a rating, this provider
Spouse/partner	1.6	93
LEEP class mates	2.8	101
Other[c]	3.3	12
People at work (outside the home)	4.1	87
Professors or instructors for class(es)	4.4	99
Personal friends	4.6	82
Parents, children or other family members	4.6	79
LEEP technical support personnel	4.8	90
GSLIS and LEEP administrators	5.3	86
LEEP students not in your class(es)	5.6	61
Members of voluntary organizations	6.8	35
Non-family household members (e.g., room mates)	8.3	21

[a] Providers are listed in order from most to least important according to the average of the ranks given by all the respondents. [b] 1 = "most important"; 12 = "least important." [c] "Other" included faculty advisor, professors from other programs, library directors and administrators, non-LEEP technical personnel, pets, religious figures, and themselves; note that only 12 respondents gave a ranking for this category (n = 113).

can be used for other worlds. Instead of seeing it as a means of communicating with boot camp friends and classmates, they become aware that it can connect them to others – the friend in Europe, the parents a few states away, as well as the larger network of LEEP members and graduates.

Discussion

Bringing the Internet home as part of an intense online educational program can, like any other major challenge we take into our lives, affect our time with others. While much emphasis has been placed on the Internet's impact on time spent with those at home, the LEEP experience shows that for the individuals involved, there are three mandatory worlds to be accommodated: LEEP, home, and work. While concern has been expressed for the impact on face-to-face local contact, we suggest that for success and well-being while participating in an online program, concern must be turned as well to the friendships and support available from members of the online world. Like any other world, it requires community development in order to be a rewarding place to spend time.

Time online does indeed affect time with those nearby. As students merge participation in an online world with the mandatory worlds of home and work they prioritize and schedule involvement with others. Students ration and apportion time with spouses and partners, and make adjustments to work schedules and loads, decrease time spent with family and friends, and drop volunteer work. However, as students gain more experience in the online world, its capabilities and uses leak out into other worlds in various ways. New technology skills transfer to work and home. Synergy develops with people at work, and in the library and information science profession; extended and remote family and friends gain technology support, and email as a communication channel; and volunteer groups reap the benefits of LEEP students' new technical skills and confidence.

Concern that involvement in the online environment will erode friendships seems unfounded with these students. While they may delay and space out face-to-face contact with friends, none report abandoning or losing friendships. Instead, they talk at length about the new friends they have made through the program and the social support they gain from them, ranking them second after spouses and partners in providing support towards their educational and professional goals. Although we do not yet know how enduring these friendships will be once everyone has moved on from LEEP, their common profession and their already established ability to maintain these relationships at a distance suggest they may endure.

Support is found for concerns about individual isolation online and isolation is evident among these students particularly when new to the intense, foreign, and non-physical online world. It takes time to learn communication norms, and it takes more effort to stay in touch and be present with others than in a face-to-face environment. Some find it difficult to overcome their own reticence to contact instructors and other students, and to overcome anxieties about presenting themselves online. Isolation can be overcome by more continued online contact, particularly synchronously, and by becoming aware of themselves as members of a community rather than as isolated individuals communicating with the computer. With experience, the technology and the overhead of communication protocols fade to the background, allowing personal online relationships to move to the foreground, and diminishing feelings of isolation.

We also see that students' ability to cope with this intense online undertaking can depend heavily on the support and cooperation of offline friends and family. As home and work worlds dovetail with LEEP, cooperation from those worlds is as essential for successful completion of the program as is the support from those within the program on how to manage its daily routine. These worlds all co-mingle in the daily responsibilities, obligations, and management of demands achieved by the individual student.

Is there benefit to all this work, to the extra effort needed to get to know online norms, to make and keep connections with others, and to juggle their and others' responsibilities in their multiple worlds? And, indeed, in their first semester, many students may be asking themselves this very question. Our interviews do suggest a number of benefits from taking this education in this way. First, this distance option allows many to fulfill what has been a long-term desire to acquire this degree, one they could not have fulfilled if required to move to the university campus. Students place-bound by jobs, spouses' jobs, and children now have the option of obtaining the degree. Second, the technological proficiency, ease of use, and recognition of opportunities that arise with increased experience in the program provide a variety of benefits. Many receive immediate respect from supervisors, colleagues at work, LIS professionals, and family for taking on this endeavor; they are chosen for opportunities at work as a result of their online involvement; and they become able to take the knowledge they have acquired to work, home, and volunteer organizations. For better or worse they have become part of the new digital revolution rather than watchers from the sidelines, and even those with existing technical and computing skills gain in the continued exposure to working and learning with others online.

References

Bannon, L. (1989). Issues in computer supported collaborative learning. In C. O'Malley (ed.), *Computer supported collaborative learning* (pp. 267–82). Berlin: Springer-Verlag.

Beller, M. and Or, E. (1998). The crossroads between lifelong learning and information technology: a challenge facing leading universities. *JCMC*, 4(2). Available online at:
http://www.ascusc.org/jcmc/vol4/issue2/beller.html

Bregman, A. and Haythornthwaite, C. (2003). Radicals of presentation: visibility, relation, and co-presence in persistent conversation. *New Media and Society* (forthcoming).

Bruce, B. C. and Hogan, M. P. (1998). The disappearance of technology: toward an ecological model of literacy. In D. Reinking, M. McKenna, L. Labbo, and R. Kieffer (eds), *Handbook of literacy and technology: transformations in a post-typographical world* (pp. 269–81). Hillsdale, NJ: Erlbaum.

Bruffee, K. A. (1993). *Collaborative learning: higher education, interdependence, and the authority of knowledge*. Baltimore: Johns Hopkins University Press.

Daft, R. L. and Lengel, R. H. (1986). Organizational information requirements, media richness and structural design. *Management Science*, 32(5), 554–71.

Dede, C. (1996). The evolution of distance education: emerging technologies and distributed learning. *American Journal of Distance Education*, 10(2), 4–36.

Erickson, T. (1999). Persistent conversation: an introduction. *JCMC*, 4(4). Available online at:
http://www.ascusc.org/jcmc/vol4/issue4/ericksonintro.html

Gibson, C. C. (ed.) (1998). *Distance learners in higher education*. Madison, WI: Atwood.

Grimes, A. (Mar. 12, 2001). The hope . . . and the reality: big money is pouring into the business of education but it's too soon to tell whether there will be any payoff. *Wall Street Journal*, p. R6.

Haines, V. and Hurlbert, J. (1992). Network range and health. *Journal of Health and Social Behavior*, 33, 254–66.

Hammer, M. (1981). Social supports, social networks, and schizophrenia. *Schizophrenia Bulletin*, 7, 45–57.

Hampton, K. and Wellman, B. (2001). Long distance community in the network society: looking at contact and support beyond Netville. *American Behavioral Scientist*, 45(3), 476–95.

Harasim, L., Hiltz, S. R., Teles, L., and Turoff, M. (1995). *Learning networks: a field guide to teaching and learning online*. Cambridge, MA: The MIT Press.

Haythornthwaite, C. (2000). Online personal networks: size, composition and media use among distance learners. *New Media and Society*, 2(2), 195–226.

Haythornthwaite, C., Kazmer, M. M., Robins, J., and Shoemaker, S. (2000). Community development among distance learners: temporal and technological dimensions. *JCMC*, 6(1). Available online at:
http://www.ascusc.org/jcmc/vol6/issue1/haythornthwaite.html

Howard, P., Rainie, L., and Jones, S. (2001). Days and nights on the Internet: the impact of a diffusing technology. *American Behavioral Scientist*, 45(3), 383–404(22).

Kazmer, M. M. (2000). Coping in a distance environment: sitcoms, chocolate cake, and dinner with a friend. *First Monday*, 5(9). Available online at:
http://www.firstmonday.dk/issues/issue5_9/kazmer/index.html

Kazmer, M. M. and Haythornthwaite, C. (2001). Juggling multiple social worlds: distance students on and offline. *American Behavioral Scientist*, 45(3), 510–29.

Koschmann, T. (ed.) (1996) *CSCL: theory and practice of an emerging paradigm.* Mahwah, NJ: Lawrence Erlbaum.

Kraut, R., Kiesler, S., Boneva, B., Cummings, J., Helgeson, V., and Crawford, A. (2002). Internet paradox revisited. *Journal of Social Issues*, 58(1), 49–74.

Kraut, R., Patterson, M., Lundmark, V., Kiesler, S., Mukhopadhyay, T., and Scherlis, W. (1998). Internet paradox: a social technology that reduces social involvement and psychological well-being? *American Psychologist*, 53(9), 1017–31.

Levine, M. (1998). The juggler. *The New Yorker*, Dec. 7 and 14, 72–80.

Nie, N. H. (2001). Sociability, interpersonal relations, and the Internet: reconciling conflicting findings. *American Behavioral Scientist*, 45(3), 420–35.

Nie, N. H. and Erbring, L. (Feb. 17, 2000). *Internet and society: a preliminary report.* Stanford Institute for the Quantitative Study of Society (SIQSS), Stanford University, and InterSurvey Inc. Available online at: http://www.stanford.edu/group/siqss/

Putnam, R. D. (1995). Bowling alone: America's declining social capital. *Journal of Democracy*, 6(1), 65–78.

Putnam, R. D. (2000). *Bowling alone: the collapse and revival of American community.* NY: Simon & Schuster.

Renniger, A. and Shumar, W. (eds) (2002). *Building virtual communities: learning and change in cyberspace.* Cambridge, UK: Cambridge University Press.

Rout, L. (ed.) (Mar. 12, 2001) Pass or fail: is there business in online education. *Wall Street Journal*, Section R.

Sproull, L. and Kiesler, S. (1991). *Connections: new ways of working in the networked organization.* Cambridge, MA: The MIT Press.

Strauss, A. L. (1978). A social world perspective. *Studies in Symbolic Interactions*, 1, 119–28.

Strauss, A. L. and Corbin, J. (1990). *Basics of qualitative research: grounded theory procedures and techniques.* Newbury Park, CA: Sage.

UCLA Center for Communication Policy (2000). *The UCLA Internet report: "surveying the digital future."* Available online at: www.ccp.ucla.edu

van der Poel, M. (1993). *Personal networks: a rational-choice explanation of their size and composition.* Lisse, Netherlands: Swets and Zeitlinger.

Walker, J., Wasserman, S., and Wellman, B. (1994). Statistical models for social support networks. In S. Wasserman and J. Galaskiewicz (eds), *Advances in social network analysis* (pp. 53–78). Thousand Oaks, CA: Sage.

Wasserman, S. and Faust, K. (1994). *Social network analysis.* Cambridge, MA: Cambridge University Press.

Wellman, B. and Gulia, M. (1999). The network basis of social support: a network is more than the sum of its ties. In B. Wellman (ed.) *Networks in the global village* (pp. 83–118). Boulder, CO: Westview Press.

Wellman, B. (1997). Structural analysis: from method and metaphor to theory and substance. In B. Wellman and S. D. Berkowitz (eds), *Social structures: a network approach* (updated edition) (pp. 19–61). Greenwich, CT: JAI Press.

Wellman, B., Quan Haase, A., Witte, J. C., and Hampton, K. (2001). Does the Internet increase, decrease, or supplement social capital? Social networks, participation, and community commitment. *American Behavioral Scientist*, 45(3), 436–55.

Wellman, B., Salaff, J., Dimitrova, D., Garton, L., Gulia, M., and Haythornthwaite, C. (1996). Computer networks as social networks: collaborative work, telework, and virtual community. *Annual Review of Sociology*, 22, 213–38.

16

Where Home is the Office

The New Form of Flexible Work

Janet W. Salaff

Abstract

Internet and local computer-based technologies challenge the relation between work and home life. Drawing on advances in technology, many hi-tech firms promote remote forms of work. Teleworkers give up their company office some or all of the time, and work from home. By separating the place of employment from the place where the work is actually carried out, teleworking restructures the relationship between public and private spheres. This paper looks at how, in the mid- to late 1990s, a teleworking sales force organized their work processes after transferring their office to their homes. I describe how employees and their families contribute to the company as they develop ways to manage their home work space and time with the family.

In studying this "boundary work," I look at telework as a form of exchange. I ask whether telework is "post-Fordist," transferring to employees craftsmanlike control over their product, lightening managerial oversight, and providing more family time? If telework enhances worker autonomy and reduces stress, this should be visible in the greater time and place flexibility that employees enjoy. Or is teleworking "neo-Fordist," where the company uses new coordination mechanisms, which maintain control and increase exploitation? I find that teleworkers do hidden work, putting effort into balancing job and family spheres. At the same time, I locate mechanisms through which telework extracts more from employees, their families, and home. I explore how, through telework, capital penetrates the home in new ways, as teleworkers openly contribute money and time to production at home. Through telework, firms relinquish tight hierarchical control while increasing labor extraction.

Author's note

This research was sponsored by a grant from the Social Sciences and Humanities Research Council of Canada; a Research and Development Grant to the University of Toronto (from Bell Canada), and a seed grant from Information Technologies Research Centre and the Telepresence Project (CSRI, University of Toronto). The Centre for Urban and Community Studies at the University of Toronto gave us helpful, on the ground support. An earlier version was written with the assistance of Kathleen Hoski, whom I wish to thank. Dima Dimitrova and Debbie Hardwick also contributed to the original research team. I also wish to thank the firm and their employees that generously shared with us their time. Their open access to information proved invaluable to the work I report upon here. Barry Wellman, Caroline Haythornthwaite, and Arent Greve gave helpful editorial advice.

Introduction

Internet and local computer-based technologies not only change work and home life, but also challenge the relation between them. Drawing on advances in technology, many hi-tech firms promote remote forms of work. Teleworkers give up their company office some or all of the time, and work from home. By separating the place of employment from the place where the work is actually carried out, teleworking restructures the relationship between public and private spheres. Organizations expect to profit from the deep-seated restructuring and decentralization that telework entails. While firms may start teleworking with their budget in mind, however, employees adopt telework to balance their work and family commitments. Indeed, since promoters of telework use different symbols for different groups, goals often come into conflict (Sturesson, 1997). The integration of family and work spheres raises deeper issues than moving data from the center to the periphery, and propels us to understand how employees experience working at home for the firm.

My discussion looks at how, in the mid- to late 1990s, the sales force for the small business market, a subset of a telecommunications firm's teleworking employees, transfer their office to their homes. Using qualitative methods, I join those that take the employees' standpoint (Gurstein, 2001; Mirchandani, 1997; Nippert-Eng, 1996). In the pages that follow, I first examine issues raised in the literature, and define telework. Next, I briefly review the background of the firm and the characteristics of our respondents, then turn to the views of those that I studied who engage in this new form of labor. I describe how employees and their families contribute to the company as they develop ways to manage their home, work, space, and time with the family.

Background: literature, terms, and numbers

Literature

Teleworking entered the North American business parlance in the late 1950s to address problems of daily travel (Mokhtarian, 1997). While urban decentralization and commuting have continued to motivate North American firms to adopt flexible forms of work, in the 1980s larger structural changes contributed to telework. These include the drop in telecommunications costs, greater importance of information processing work in all industrial sectors, the increase in intangible forms of commodities, and creation of large numbers of service sector jobs (Agres, Edberg, and Igbaria, 1998; Ellison, 1999; Mitter and Efendioglu, 1997). These changes have brought about a strategy of "flexible specialization" in the production process to meet diversified markets and reduce production costs, of which telework is a form (Harvey, 1989, 1993; Piore and Sabel, 1984). Manufacturing, telecommunications and other backbone services could decentralize many operations, relying on communications media to link knowledge exchange (Castells, 1989).

Project and contract work is also associated with telework. Firms are less likely to use their employees' time continuously in one locale (Perin, 1996). Teleworking firms can also contract professionals who, as scarce employees, can bargain to work at a distance. Disabled professionals that can telework need not be excluded from their fields. As firms aim to contract labor more flexibly, innovative technology coupled with telework reduces the need for moving employees to a central location. Consultants predict that each full-time teleworker can save firms thousands of dollars per year (Pratt, 1999).

It is the promise of greater control over work conditions that most appeals to professional, technical, and managerial employees like those we study. Employees, increasingly educated, and familiar with computing, try to achieve more control over their product, and this expectation further contributes to the work at home movement.[1] More

---

1 According to a 2001 European survey of teleworkers and non-teleworkers on stress levels in the workplace, 41 percent of workers rate travel as the most annoying aspect of their office job, followed by office politics (37 percent) and constant interruptions (33 percent). One quarter of office workers spend between one and

professional women remain in the labor force throughout their careers, and balance multiple roles. Both parents also wish to share more with their children, but face mounting time pressures as the pace of work accelerates.[2] Home tasks also take time. The physical merging of work and family spheres promises to ease the "time bind." Telework also responds to employees' dissatisfaction with office culture (MORI, 2001). To this, has been added anxiety over working in high rise offices, and away from family and friends.

Urban Canada, and in particular the metropolis of Toronto where our study was conducted, embodies many of these factors that make telework an option. At the time of the study, the large metropolitan area had four million people, who traveled frequently to work. Women's employment in Ontario is higher than in Canada overall, and the majority of married women work, including those with children. The populace is increasingly well educated, and wives want to use their education: 80 percent of Canadian women with university level education surveyed in 1995 felt that "being able to take a paying job is important to happiness." Further, most believe that both the man and the woman should contribute to household income. At the same time, 19 percent of all full-time workers surveyed in 1992, and even more of the full-time women workers, were "time stressed." Although 30 percent of the employed women resolved this with flexible work schedules, nevertheless 18 percent of these still felt highly stressed. Many also believe "most women really want a home and family over a job" and an "employed mother can have as close a relationship with her children as an unemployed mother" (Statistics Canada, 2000: 71–2, 154). These overlapping and contradictory attitudes create role strain. Able to use computers, having them in their homes, people start to move home to work.[3]

---

two hours travelling each day, and 15 percent are late to work between one and three times a week due to travel delays. Not surprisingly, over half of office workers want to work from home because of the freedom it gives them, 42 percent to cut down on commuting time (MORI, 2001).

2   There is some debate over whether work hours have increased in the 1990s (Parcel, 1999). Nevertheless, most people feel they are overworked.

3   There were over 1,437,000 daily inter-regional person trips in 1991 between the downtown and four adjacent parts of the greater Toronto area, a factor convincing firms like ours to reduce travel to the office. Women's employment in Ontario was high (58 percent, 1988), and 66 percent of all husband–wife families (1986) were dual earner families. In 1986, 14 percent of wives in dual-earner families had

There are, however, many problems in implementing telework (Bailey and Kurland, 1999). There are economic barriers to accessing the Internet (Castells, 2001; Mckie and Thompson, 2000: 194; NTIA, 1998; OECD, 2001). Yet since access is broadening, clearly other factors limit telework. Among these are challenges to "deference" and "demeanor," and the difficulties of managing the supervisor/employee relationship remotely. Working parents that try to adopt a firm's "family friendly work policies" are invisible to the office (Hochschild, 1997; Perin, 1991). As teleworkers, they need continuously to do "career identity work," demonstrating their progress to their supervisor, and commitment to the group (Tippin, 1994; Whittle, 2001).

The social organization of work also slows adoption of telework (Olson, 1988). Work processes entail more than capital and routine labor. Before embarking on telework, management may not have thought through the cultural arrangements that work processes involve (Featherstone, 1993). Many employees need collegial support that is hard to get at a distance, which work restructuring may disrupt (Greve, Salaff, Wellman, and Dimitrova, 2002; Krebs, 1996). Management styles may not suit decentralized work (Gainey, Kelley, and Hill, 1999; Hochschild, 1997). As well, when people turn to telework holding high expectations which are not met, many do not continue (Armstrong, 1997; Gurstein, 2001).

The intrusion of companies into family time and space did not start with telework. The family has long done unpaid back-up work for industrial labor, most visible in home-based manufacturing. Workers that do simple manufacturing "putting out work" at home absorb many production costs (Mirchandani, 1998). Large corporations also depend on the unpaid emotional and back-up labor of the wife in supporting the husband's job (Luxton, 1980; Smith, 1973). Hochschild (1997) described the extension of capital into family terrain through overtime and shift work.

university degrees versus 6 percent of wives in traditional families; for husbands: 18 percent in dual-earner families had a university degree, versus 14 percent in traditional families. 57 percent of mothers with children under 6 yrs old were employed (1991). In 1999, 49 percent of Toronto households used the Internet, 35 percent from home. Those with university education, like our sample, (52 percent) were more likely to use computers from home (Dickinson and Jellison, 2000: 10, 13; Mckie and Thompson, 1990: 100, 162, 163, 316; Mckie and Thompson, (1994: 79, 145).

Moving the workspace into the home draws the family even more deeply into the service of the firm. Teleworkers do hidden work, putting effort into balancing work and family spheres. This "boundary work" has become a focus of telework research. Many explore how families handle the ambiguity of laboring in family space. They find that professionals that telework do considerable emotion and cognitive work to handle these dual spheres (Ellison, 1999; Goldman, 2000; Mirchandani, 1997; Nippert-Eng; 1996, 1998; Silver, 1993; Sullivan, 2000).

This chapter takes the "boundary work" teleworkers do one step further. Given the competing goals of telework, I ask whether telework is "post-Fordist," transferring to employees craftsmanlike control over their product, lightening managerial oversight, and providing more family time? Or is teleworking "neo-Fordist," where the company uses new coordination mechanisms, which maintain control and increase exploitation (Prechel, 1994; Sullivan and Lewis, 2001)? To answer these questions, I look at telework as a form of exchange. If telework enhances worker autonomy and reduces stress, this should be visible in the greater time and place flexibility that employees enjoy. At the same time, I locate mechanisms through which telework extracts more from employees, home, and their families. I explore how through telework, capital penetrates the home in new ways, as teleworkers openly contribute money and time to production at home.

Telework's complexity lies in its range of effects. Through telework, firms relinquish tight hierarchical control while increasing labor extraction. In describing how telework as a new form of work reshapes the relation between work and family, I organize the material around the factors of production. (1) Starting with property, capital and space, I discuss the costs to employees when they move their office in their home. (2) Moving on to labor, time, and the family, I describe how employees give more to the company as they develop ways to manage their home work space and time with the family. (3) I then turn to ways teleworkers legitimate giving more to the company.

Terms and numbers

Many forms of telework evolved as firms have adapted telework to their needs. Some classify forms of telework by spatial location. Work carried out away from the employer's premises includes individual home based teleworking and multi-location mobile working, as well as collective forms of teleworking in non-domestic premises controlled by the employer (Huws, 1996). Others define telework by the amount of time people spend away from the office.[4] Lumping these together gives rise to estimates of 10 million European teleworkers in 2000 (IDC, 2001). The proportions vary widely by nations, ranging from, in 1999, media-strong Finland (15 percent) and Sweden (16 percent), to the US (9 percent) and Canada (7 percent), to Spain (4 percent).[5] In Europe, large firms and companies that have installed remote technology are more likely to sponsor telework. Companies that depend on computer based technologies in their own work and as products they engineer and sell most readily shift the location of work and the employees. Over 45 percent of European mobile workers and teleworkers are employed by "large and very large" companies, mostly in the business services, finance and health sectors (Pusceddu and van de Roer, 2001). In addition, firms with multiple sites, and those that use email are more likely to telework (Kordey, 2000).

To understand more fully how the entry of work into family space restructures both work and home, I study only those teleworkers that have given up their office to work full time from home. The current chapter describes the home–work life of mobile workers in the small business sales force who retained their full-time employment contract. They mainly worked from home, and also could book a cubicle, much like booking a hotel room, at company quarters ("hoteling"). These cubicles are not "theirs," however, and employees carry in their own lap top computers and documentation to work every day.

The teleworkers

The history of telework in "Telecom"

The telecommunications provider I study, which I call "Telecom," is a key industry player, with an established history. Telecom had been

---

4   The European Economic Community distinguishes "mobile workers," that spend at least 20 percent of their working hours outside of both their home and office, from "telecommuters" who spend at least one day a week working from home.

5   Extrapolating to 2001, and for all work sectors, the Canadian Telework Association estimates the number of Canadian teleworkers at 1.5 million, a number that includes telework, overtime, or the self-employed. Telecom, the firm I study here, now has approximately five thousand teleworkers, one of the largest Canadian programs. http://www.ivc.ca/part12.html#statcan.

known as a good employer and was a popular job choice for Canadians. Stressing loyalty, company culture, and image, Telecom kept employees on for a lifetime. But in the 1990s, when the telecommunications market was deregulated, the company faced a crisis, and reduced its head count through layoffs and early retirement. Teleworking was a strategy to cut costs further and improve productivity.

In the mid-1990s, the company initiated an experimental pilot project for volunteers to telework, drawing on employees from several departments. The company wanted to see how telework could be practiced, and how they might sell teleworking as a product. In a short period of time, the firm applied this initiative to the business sales force in the belief that sales workers, who traveled daily to clients, needed no fixed office. At the same time, the company increased sales targets. This speed-up that accompanied telework somewhat compromised its meaning. Some felt that telework was part of the effort to boost output at their expense.

Technical changes paved the way. The firm was integrating scattered sales databases to mutual readability and remote accessibility. Sophisticated networks allowed faster data transmission. A mechanization task force upgraded the sales force's PCs. However, at the time, few used advanced technologies. Nor were these supporting technologies fully operative, creating bottlenecks in sales work (Dimitrov and Dimitrova, 1995; Dimitrova and Salaff, 1998).

As a sizeable and old organization, Telecom's employees were diverse. In the small business market, engineering-oriented sales people were keen on trying out all the latest computer based applications from home. The people-oriented sales workers were less enraptured by new technologies. Newcomers that had transferred from other firms and were familiar with ruthless sales approaches, wanted to work "quicker and smarter." In contrast, tenured employees felt that company restructuring hampered their performance. These different orientations were played out in sales people's views towards the tradeoffs in telework.

Our sample

I learned about these teleworkers from on-site observation, focus groups, time budget studies, and in-depth interviews of 94 full-time company employees between 1993 and 1997; 48 are sales workers in the small business market. Twenty-eight salesworkers gave up their office entirely to work at home, the rest had not begun, were trying hoteling, or other alternatives. We located these in a number of ways: some participated in the company's teleworking "trial," others replied to a company survey.[6] Supervisors and colleagues introduced still others. Learning in advance that several offices would shut down, we collected information on some sales workers "before" and "after" this event. Our interview detailed their daily work and family activities in several one to three and a half-hour sessions. Wherever possible, we conducted an interview in the teleworker's home office to understand their work set-up in a family context, speaking with supervisors and spouses as well. We taped interviews, transcribed them verbatim, and analyzed the texts qualitatively for themes.

Most of the sales teleworkers in our sample are mature workers. Their ages ranged from 28 to 46; the modal age is 40. Half are fairly new teleworkers, but almost all have worked at home long enough to settle into their remote location. I have background information for 42 and learned that 19 came to the firm fresh from school, then rose through the ranks to their sales position; 23 transferred from other companies, nearly all from sales. Nearly half the sales workers in our study are women, equally divided between teleworkers and office workers.[7] Twenty-three have young children, which helped us understand how teleworkers combine family chores with work life.

Boundary Issues: Home Space and Work

Information and communications technologies dissolve traditional boundaries in time and space. Telework, which draws on these technologies, is particularly likely to reshape the meaning of work. Essential concepts of workplace, home, and everyday life are deconstructed and reformulated most visibly in the merging of home space and work (Gunnarsson, 1997: 57). But as many have noted, the boundary work is fraught with ambiguity. It is not the technology that creates this con-

---

6   To learn more about the representativeness of our sample, we analyzed survey responses from the firm's middle-level employees. The survey showed that more split their work between their home and the central office. Of the 846 employees that gave their teleworking status in the company survey, 32 percent teleworked fewer than three days a week, while 13 percent worked nearly full time from home.

7   In 1986, 46 percent of the sales workers in Canada were female (Mckie and Thompson, 1990: 54).

fusion, nor will the company's teleworking procedures easily solve it. In many ways, placing corporate work in the home is ill-defined, creating considerable uncertainty and the need for teleworkers to do boundary work.

This uncertainty begins with the costs of working at home. Traditionally, an employer foots all direct production costs. However, teleworkers and their families absorb home office expenses, from rent forgone, to extra maintenance costs, consumer durables and services, and production equipment. Putting out funds on behalf of the company is the ambiguous first step in merging the family and work spheres.

Choice

Given that teleworkers dedicate sizeable amounts of money and energy to this project, we need to ask: was telework required? Many telework studies, including those done by one of Telecom's departments, advocated employee participation in the decision, or what is known as an "RSVP." However, Telecom wished to close entire office floors and consolidate buildings. To do so, it needed complete participation by the sales force. Nevertheless, Telecom did not portray the move home in this manner to its sales force. They were not always clear whether teleworking was compulsory or optional, giving rise to some confusion. Although exemptions were possible, many sales workers surmised that they had to give up their company office. Others bargained or resisted.

Taking the perspective of the company, a radio services salesman, and former real estate salesman, explained why they all had to telework:

> [T]he Company is liquidating their assets. They want to sell their real estate. Real estate is expensive and it costs them money to keep the Scarboro office functioning as it's functioning right now. So they're getting rid of their offices and they're putting us in our home offices. It's part of the three year plan to make them more competitive. (radio services salesman 1)

Others thought they had a choice. One implied that if reducing driving was a goal, Telecom might instead have rearranged sales areas to match the salesperson's home location. Yet in this uncertain atmosphere she complied, seeing the willingness to telework as a test of loyalty.

I mean I have a choice. If I don't like it I can go back to the office, okay? (Q. Do they give you a choice?) Well, they'd like to think they did. But I mean it wouldn't be to my benefit to do that. [B]ecause then I start two hours of commuting a day, okay? And I don't want to do that. It's the opposite way to my customers, the majority of them. See [the office is] in Markham. I live in Oshawa. My customers are in Durham Region. I want to be close to my customers. So I think they could have done a little bit more that way. (equipment saleswoman 1)

Another sales representative with a small apartment objected.

So the company's saving money big time on the real estate because they've reduced their costs and everything. That's great but what about us that have . . . inconvenience from the standpoint from space to accommodate this? . . . Well I think the company should clearly spell out in terms of whether it's something that, you know what I mean, it's kind of like a mandate, that this is what they want or if they're giving you a choice, because it was not clear. It was not clear. It was implied but I think a lot of people thought well, I have to do it. But how can they, you know, if you're living in an apartment and I know this has happened with people who are living in a one bedroom apartment, that isn't exactly fair to them. So what are you saying that if they don't get a bigger apartment or if they don't cut into their living space you're going to what, get rid of them? Demote them? So it was kind of almost like a threat in a sense. (network saleswoman 1)

Others defined the choice as theirs:

We were given a choice. You know I had an extra bedroom so it was fine for me. (equipment salesman1)

Space

Citing business security, Telecom requires teleworkers to have a separate space to work in, usually an office with a door, but does not pay for that space. Many of the 28 teleworking sales people already had a work space at home. Others had to renovate. Those with one bedroom apartments had to put office machinery in the dining room. Many saw the task of turning living space into multiple uses as burdensome.

A saleswoman converted half the family room to office space, from which her family was excluded.

> I have a living room – family room, so I've taken over half of the living room. There's a divider. We don't come in here. There's a chesterfield and chair, and the idea is that if . . . somebody needs to come in to the house to meet me or something then that furniture is there. The living room we weren't really using so that's why I took it over. (equipment saleswoman 2)

Yet another turned an unfinished basement into an office.

> This office was done professionally. I acted as a sub-contractor if you will. I hired all the various trades, electrician, plumber for the bathroom over there, the drywaller, the carpenter . . . I knew I was going to work out of the office, out of the home. I knew [Telecom] was going to go in that direction. So about a year ago my wife and I decided to get this done, so I've been like this now for about a year. It wasn't always in this state. It wasn't as functional. (radio services salesman 1)

He justified the cost and his unpaid labor as upgrading his property. Nearly all paid for added features, light, electricity, and heat to accommodate the new use of their home space.

Several acclimated much more, and moved in order to telework. A salesman sold his suburban home with sizeable landscape, and moved to a smaller place, anticipating that since he would have to work harder as a teleworker, he would have no time to garden. Another pushed forward her marriage and moved to a house to coincide with the closing of her office.

Yet another vacated a rented apartment and bought a new house. Although she had previously complained to her supervisors about the inconvenience of working from her own apartment, her rather costly adjustment to the teleworking deflected her own opposition.

> (Q. How do you like teleworking?) [A] lot better than I did right at the time (I began) because I had all my equipment in my bedroom, and I was having to move into my living room to use my table. So it was not convenient. All the plugs were in different spots. It was just I was in a very small place. (network saleswoman 1)

In addition to their dedicated office space, these teleworkers use different parts of their houses more or less freely for work. They integrate their new time and space schedules with the home use even wider than the office. In good weather, they work on sales proposals in the garden or on their decks.

Employees received used company office furniture and equipment, but this was rarely adequate to the home that had not been built as an office. A young salesman moved plugs, transforming his condominium solarium into an office for the fax, printer, and other substantial machinery. Many objected to the office-grade furniture, and paid for their own.

> It's not fair. I think personally what they should have done when they put us into a teleworking environment, they should have, let's say, said, "okay, I'll allow you up to $2000," . . . like "show me receipts up to and I'll cover . . . ," like I said, $1000 or $2000, whatever that figure be . . . That would have been positive on the company's behalf. But they've done absolutely nothing. (equipment saleswoman 1)

Although the employees are donating part of the house to the firm, they do not get tax benefit. In this firm, sales people earn salaries, and under tax law, since they are not self-employed, they cannot get tax breaks for a home office. At the same time, their home no longer has "use value" alone, but is an integral part of the work process. This increases the ambiguity of the contribution of the family to the company.

Some were unwilling to make the changes to the home. "My home is private. I don't want my business at home" (data salesman 1). Instead, they used the general purpose hoteling facility the company gave the sales unit when they closed office floors. To this they had to carry their own equipment daily.

Spatial boundaries: maintaining a work front from home

Once past the home office door, teleworking draws Telecom's sales employees' families into the work process in other ways. Small business market sales people must represent the company to their customers. To maintain a professional image, sales workers have to monitor their families. Families become complicit to maintaining the work process and the company image.

Spatial segregation

Rules about spatial segregation emerge which restrict the teleworkers' ability to integrate their family with their work lives. Family members can no longer fully use the house as they had before. Identifying personal sounds, such as dogs barking, children playing or crying, grand-father clock chimes, create confusing "noise" for the customer during remote conversations.

Teleworkers train their children to notice new spatial distinctions. Their children learn the difference between a parent that is at home for the family or for work. Clues like a shut door tell children to remain outside. They know not to pick up the business line when it rings, and not to interrupt their parents on the phone. Teleworkers then have to manage the children and others that also use their home.

To handle these constraints on use of home space, many act as if they were in the downtown company office. Still company employees, Telecom expects those with young children to continue their former child care arrangements. None provide day care themselves at home. Some hire nannies. Some have at-home spouses. The rest remove their youngsters from the home during working hours. As before, they have contingency plans for overtime work, out-of-town meetings, ill children, and school days. Neighbors and nearby kin are back-ups, who help them cope with overlaps in the demands of the company and their children's needs.

Many could not segregate their family lives from the work lives when children and workers were under one roof. One salesman with small children at home discussed his problems with merging the two realms. His wife cares for his children at home, and he feels the home environment is distracting as well (like the light bulb that might need to be replaced).

> Well my wife and my two kids are in the house so even though I'm isolated . . . you hear the kids screaming or somebody falls down and starts to cry you know that type of thing. So there are those distractions and they are probably equal to those you would have at work . . . There, you know, there's always somebody popping their head up and saying "hey do you want to go for a coffee?" or "how was your weekend?" Or whatever the case. So in my case [too] because my house is "full" of people.

His resolution is to remove himself from his home office by hoteling. Since he has no fixed locale anymore, he is able to choose among a range of work places to visit, and feels he is not spending company time driving to an office.

> As long as I have a phone and my laptop then I can pretty well work anywhere . . . But usually it's combined. I mean I'm going to have to

make that journey anyway. You know I'm going to go to a customer visit so I'm driving downtown so it's not like I'm going out of my way. I'm not driving downtown just to go to work. (network salesman 2)

An equipment saleswoman maintains strict boundaries between family and work life. During the school year, she requires her 12-year-old son to follow new behavioral and space rules at home. After school,

> my son walks in the door, he sees that I'm on the phone, he comes over, he waves to me, and he goes and does his homework or watches TV in a totally different area of the house . . . He acknowledges that he's home which is great, and then he continues on his way.

But when he is on vacation, she sends him to his grandparents so that he does not have to follow these work imposed rules all day long,

> This March break I sent him away to my mother's. That way I didn't have to worry about him being noisy when I was on the phone and stuff like that. So I'm very cognizant of not having that happening cause this is, after all, a workplace from 8 to 5. (equipment saleswoman 3)

A salesman felt guilty at having to enforce this redefinition.

> It may be cruel, but to get them out of your way until you're finished doing your work, you just send them outside with a snack to tide them over until dinner time, and they play with their friends (radio services salesman 1).

Boundary Issues: Labor and Home Time

Telling time

A poorly defined element of the telework contract, and perhaps its crucial feature, is labor time. The home-based sales worker is obligated to put in the same amount of clock time at work as before, a minimum 37.5 hour week. (This includes time channeled into several Scheduled Days Off ("SDOs") a year that they can take off without penalty.) It is assumed teleworkers will continue to work these hours, but how they do so is not specified. This is part of their new flexible time.

In a classic essay, E. P. Thompson (1967) distinguishes craftsman's from factory workers' time. The craftsman may put in long hours to complete a product, but then delay beginning another. Assembly line "factory time" instilled workers' conformity to fixed production schedules. Teleworking assumes that Fordism has done its job and that workers have an internal clock. Teleworking holds out the humanist premise that, like artisans, employees can gain control over their work time and schedule it in a flexible manner.

Nevertheless, the comparison with craftsmen is only half right. Sales workers do not work for themselves. They are both company and customer driven. First, they often work with others. They must respond when others need their input. Much work is face to face. Managers sometimes set joint client visits, or the sales team may visit a client together. This greatly limits their ability to decide on their own when to work.

Next, office workers are socialized to work company time, without having a supervisor in front of them. The "timing" of office time has themes. Employees can "stay late," "leave early," "work overtime." They also rely on certain props to trigger changes from one timeframe to the other. Some of these props were other people who arrived and left at set times. Other props were commuting trains and ride shares, knowing the "good times" to avoid commuter traffic jams, and quitting work to meet family obligations. In addition to adhering to an internal clock, and external rhythms, there are external sounds. Office workers may not listen to factory bells, but they are trained to jump when the phone rings, and calls stop at the end of the day. They hear elevator bells, and when these stop, it signifies the workday is over.

The initial transformation from an "at home" to an "at work" mentality creates problems when people first start teleworking, which Nippert-Eng (1996) refers to as the "transition ritual" to work. Since their home office is not specialized for work, they have to find new ways to define their time schedule. Hence, they frequently ask themselves: "When does work start?" A sales woman told us for the first few weeks as a teleworker, she dressed, walked out the door, and traversed the block, then re-entered her home in work mode.

Many mimic office hours to handle the ambiguity of sharing family and time with office time. One woman deals with family issues at lunch time or after work in the same manner as if she were in the office. Others do family work during office time, and then will make up by doing office work during family time. This usually ends with increasing company time.

The crucial problem for teleworkers is when to stop (Goldman, 2000). This is as much an issue of their high quotas as of cues and frames. Mandated customer visits, and a sizeable quota of quarterly sales all push them to work hard. Completing one sale does not give them time off from the next. How much they have accomplished and when is a sale final is also ambiguous. Network sales people promote an ongoing service. Their database software cannot always distinguish whether the deal has been struck or is just being discussed. Further, a customer can terminate at any time. Hence managers, who must ensure that their group meets quotas, constantly worry that the teleworker is not putting time into winning a sale. Since managers cannot directly watch or control the worker's output, they develop their own methods to ascertain whether their employees are working (Tippin, 1994). Some hound the teleworkers to remind them of work undone.

While they may feel empowered by working "on their own time," work from home puts teleworkers at the mercy of the project. Disassociating themselves from work is the greatest problem. Teleworkers easily expand their work time to the point of self, and often family, exploitation. No one now compels the employees to start to work, neither will anyone stop them from working.

Nearly all are conscious that they labor longer hours. Many do so willingly. Some believe they owe the company this time, in exchange for reduced commutes to the office. They are grateful for the flexibility of being able to do family and personal affairs during the day. They speak of "splitting" the time they save from not having to commute with the company. By this they mean they divide the time they would have spent on commuting, and devote part of it to their family and then lengthen their working day without "charging" the company. An equipment saleswoman recounted she had deliberately to break her day to get some rest. Although she took breaks for only a few minutes, she returned the gift by giving hours to the company

> So it's becoming more aware of, how do I word this? You've got to become aware that maybe you need to walk away from it for five minutes and things like that. The only issue with teleworking is that you work far harder. You don't walk away from it at like 5:00 at night and go home. It's far easier to come back to it after the kids have gone to bed or whatever is appropriate cause it's all here. So I work far more hours now than I ever did before . . . They probably get eight, ten hours out of me more [a week]. (equipment saleswoman 4)

Many devised ways to solve the problem of overwork. Before tele-working, a network saleswoman anticipated not having enough space to telework. She initially put her office in her bedroom. When she found that she could not separate herself from her work mentally because she was always looking at it, she finished her basement and moved her office there. Recreating the office environment at her own expense was a costly physical way to resolve the temporal boundary issue.

Another reported that she answered the phone at all hours. She worked more hours simply because there was work to be done, and the office phone was in the house and more convenient to get to than if it was located some distance away in the company office.

> Because it's here. So now, like you know before, I may not have left the house until 7:30, quarter to 8 in the morning, [that's when] I'm starting work. [But now] I'm in here at like 7:00 in the morning if not earlier. Okay? If it was 5:00 before, I'd put my phone on call forward and walk out. Now it's like I'm talking as if I was in the office. A customer appoint-ment is a different scenario. But now it's like I may be cooking dinner and I hear the phone ring. Instead of putting it on call forward. And I'll come and I'll answer the phone, and it may be you know, it's 5:30 at night and next thing you know it's 6:30 . . . Well at the beginning it was because the phone was here. I thought I had to answer it all the time. So it was my, that was the wrong thinking on my part, but that's the way I was. And it's because there's work to be done and it's very easy because it's sitting here to do it. Where before [in the office] it wasn't quite so convenient. (equipment saleswoman 5)

One equipment vendor gives equipment sales people prizes and honors if they sell more. These become badges of success. To get these, sales people may double the 37.5 required hours, and telework helps them do so. These folk pass their new-found time and place savings from telework to the work flow. An equipment saleswoman logged so many hours in the office that her husband, fearing for her safety in a darkened high rise office at night, encouraged her to telework. He built a narrow space in the laundry room for her computer equipment and files. She then could work such long hours that she collapsed on the rare family vacation.

Her colleague with a newborn had the same problem of how to protect important family time and keep up with the job simultane-ously. She hired two people – a nanny to care for her child in the day and a housekeeper to clean – and relied on her supportive husband.

Every night, the couple spends three hours with the infant and then the saleswoman returns to her office every evening after her infant goes to sleep. She reported:

> I had to work very hard to get my husband to buy into [telework]. I convinced him, but it was a struggle. Now it is not a struggle. He knows that it's best for [the baby] and me and because you know it's very important, our family life. (equipment saleswoman 6)

For this teleworker, working at home eased in longer hours, while still making it possible for her to maintain family time.

Others' spouses were disappointed in their expectation that they would give them, not the company, more time. A saleswoman's family thought that a working mom at home meant that she would have more time to cook nice dinners, that dinner would be ready at 5:30 and that she would have more time to spend with them.

> [My husband] thought that [teleworking] would mean more time for us when the kids weren't around, and I would take lunches [with him] and I could have more time together. But that didn't work out either. (equipment saleswoman 7)

Time pressures kept her on the road or at her desk, and away from a relaxing lunchtime with her spouse. Her reaction was to deny the family-friendly nature of telework: She sat them down and talked to them,

> I explained what was expected of me. My husband realizes that it's a changing environment out there in the job world, and everybody's trying to keep their job so you do whatever is required to keep your job, and he supports me in that respect.

Family time

Children have schedules of their own. Outside organizations structure many activities. The parent has to handle school, library, club, sports, and medical schedules. Then there is the children's own personal rhythm, their needs, their cares, that they turn to the at-home parent to meet (Hardwick and Salaff, 1998). The most crucial time is just after school when the children return home at 3:30. Another important time is the 5 to 7 dinner time slot. Many try to meet their family's schedules, while not losing any work time. Some use "office time" to be with their children and repay the company in "family time." They may stop the project that they are working on at dinner time.

Trading time often extends their unpaid work for the firm. Grateful for this time they can spend with their children, they may return to work after. Unlike an office worker, who leaves the office for home for good at night, teleworkers can pick up where they left off. They thus face a dilemma. Even though they may have worked their daily allotment, they haven't finished their job. They know they can pick up the work. They thus easily work after dinner, whether feeling refreshed from their family break or guilty at having stopped "early."

A radio waves salesman reported, he made sure he repaid the company for this "right" to participate in family time during "working hours."

> If I'm home [when they return from school], I open the door for them and I sit with them for a little bit. I don't hide that. If I'm at a customer appointment they go to the neighbor's or they go to my mom's house. Again it's all part of working smartly. If I do stop work at 3:30, I don't think I'm cheating the company 'cause there's a lot of times where, for example, [I go out of the way for the company.] Monday night . . . the foreman [had to get these plans] in order to do the job right. I put them through the company mail. They had to go to Barrie. The job was due on Tuesday and the foreman didn't have the plans yet. So I got in my car at 7:30 at night and I delivered them to Newmarket on my own. Now I'm going to submit my mileage because it was my car on my time for company purposes, but still I went out of my way during my family time to go to Barrie. So it's give and take. (radio services salesman 1)

Telework has raised the ante. Now that the norm is working more hours from home, they fear their careers will suffer if they cannot increase their workload at home. A new mother lamented,

> When I go home at night I don't have the same opportunities as everybody else to be able to continue doing my job at home because I have a new job when I get home, taking care of the family and everything else. (network saleswoman 7)

She accepted the need to incorporate her family into her work, even as she bewailed her inability to do so (Mirchandani, 1999).

Family labor time for the company

It is not only that the family must stay out of their way while they work and they must juggle two schedules in the same locale. Family members often treat the home as work place themselves, taking on company roles.

There is continual upkeep, not just for family use. The home office is also a company show case.

> The . . . thing that bothers me is once when I was at home, I quickly realized how much dust, and perhaps 'cause you don't see it during the day and on week ends you're busy, and my house isn't dirty, please don't misinterpret. But you realize [when you are working at home] that that wall's got a couple of marks on it because now you're seeing it in day light. So I ended up wall papering and painting a few rooms, 'cause I all of a sudden realized I wasn't happy with them 'cause I was here all the time. So I guess that was an impact of teleworking . . . [My husband and I did] it together. (equipment saleswoman 2)

New issues like business security permeate the home. One new family-wide obligation is enforcing company privacy:

> (Q. Do you have a lot of stuff to shred?) No, I burn it. My husband burns it. I have two fire places . . . I have a fire every week. And even in the summer . . . 'cause it has all my pricing in it you see. Yes, he cooperates, he's great. I'm very lucky. (equipment saleswoman 8)

No longer able to get a company technician to fix their computers, they involve knowledgeable family members. Another equipment saleswoman reported

> Actually my husband was quite helpful. If I got stuck on the computer or something like that . . . he knew (it) better than I did, so he was able to help me. (equipment saleswoman 7)

Productivity and managing work

Is telework more productive? Many teleworkers feel they produce more work at home. However, remote workers' feeling of more output are not easily documented.[8] Most teleworkers point to time savings.

8   It is difficult to study the productivity of remote workers, apart those that can be closely monitored (Dubrin, 1991). However, one comparative study of IBM marketing and service teleworkers and office workers found that the teleworkers believe they are more productive, but multivariate analyses do not confirm any difference in output (Hill, Miller, Weiner, and Colihan, 1998).

They usually refer to adding more hours to the work week. They also quickly note that being teleworkers means being better organized. They are forced to account for their time and motions; nothing can be taken for granted. They have to do this management work themselves, however, another part of their unpaid work.

> Well you know when you're working in the office you're surrounded by your files, all of your pamphlets, etc. On a way out to a customer you just grab whatever you need and away you go. Whereas now I have to think about what I need to make it through the entire day 'cause once I leave the home I'm not usually going to come back until later that evening so I have to have all the documentation. Whatever I can have electronically I do. So it's probably made me a little bit more productive. (consultant 1)

Others find specific areas where they feel empowered and thus more productive. As a salesperson insists, teleworking removes her from office politics, and thus makes her more productive.

> Actually I believe [telework is] better than being in the office because the relationship is totally different with a customer than it is with people in the office. Because sometimes the office can be quite political . . . And sometimes you find the office, especially with a lot of companies today, the morale can be low. And you can be easily brought into that. So I've always been the type of person that has avoided the lunch room and the break, and I always made sure who I sat with were up-beat people not people who were always complaining. So you know, that can be a down factor as well, being in the office so it depends. (equipment saleswoman 5)

Another equipment saleswoman complained that she gave more to the company, but was not paid for it:

> So I think you know I've helped the company out. They've been getting far more time out of us, okay? So I'm far more productive and I've just proven that in a normal week. (equipment saleswoman 1)

Communication with colleagues

A central issue for most was how to communicate with each other. They worried that they would not find out about issues colleagues are dealing with. They are concerned that now that their peers are dispersed, they cannot get support when they face a difficult problem, cannot rely on the help of a co-worker who may have had a similar situation in the past. They stressed the importance of learning from one another – a process which is not a formalized dimension of the sales process. While working in the office they go for coffee and hang around the water cooler or fax machine, socializing or talking about "non-work" topics. They attend meetings to discuss problems, celebrate awards, retirements, birthdays, join sales rallies.

Now, from their quiet home office, they look back at these informal water cooler chats as "non-productive." Mirchandani (1996) learned that teleworkers consider going to the office as "non-work," especially when their files and materials are at home. They may not see the ways some of these activities contribute to the job. Yet they do notice that teleworking breaks many of the informal social networks that people have built around the work process (Greve et al., 2002). Informal interaction is not institutionalized and they now take extra time to see these peers, to complete the work process.

> Normally if I'm going to meet with my peers I would meet with them after a customer meeting or something like that, and then I would go to lunch or something to share information that way.

Legitimating telework

Telecom's contract specifies teleworkers' rights and obligations on both sides. Past this, teleworkers incur unspecified costs in boundary work. Teleworkers have to manage their image of themselves as working at home instead of the office. They make actual capital expenditures, and put time into managing their office in the home. To "account for" and make sense of these expenses they think in terms of a balance sheet.

They start by an actual account of costs and savings, by which they become aware of some of the hidden costs of work. They posit a balance sheet: the company reduces its overhead through passing on costs of work to them and their families and, in exchange, teleworkers recover other expenses. Apart from driving time, there are other real costs, such as dress codes, parking, lunches, paying for premium time services. They note that working at home reduces some of these common, but usually unacknowledged, costs of work.

Tools of the trade

Getting new technology is a perk of telework. The new computers they were given and the integrated data bases are signs that telework will work. However, it took a year before the technology was in place, and throughout our study, the integrative data bases were ineffective. Nevertheless, the projected plans were enough to legitimate those with an engineering orientation.

Many are eager to uphold the company culture. Since teleworking is mandated, they define the project as ensuring a more competitive product, and job security for themselves. More, many are committed to being in the "modern" world of computer-based telecommunications. They see telework as pushing the company in that direction.

The most enthusiastic fully enjoy the "toys" they are given and are proud of the new equipment. They define themselves as well organized, modern sales people, who get ahead by using all the tools they can get their hands on. They look forward to the "paperless office" and hope to achieve it at home, fully embracing computer-based technologies. Teleworking is just another technique that gives them more of the computerized environment they enjoy. The embracing of technique is a cultural construction, frequently termed a masculine mystique. However, many saleswomen also hold the engineering perspective, proud of being in the forefront of change (Massey, 1996: 114).

A 32-year-old network salesman rattled off what he could do as a teleworker at home. Nevertheless, he and others downplayed the fact that the technology was not fully upgraded. He is taking his accounts and putting them into the data base, winnowing out one piece of paper after another:

> The [computerized data bases]: They need fine tuning, but are very good. You do it daily, [put] all information there. The senior [level] can go into it and get what they need to. Great, get rid of paper files, what you're viewing is there anytime you want. I inherited a bunch of files and looked at them and said 'this stuff is going into the garbage!' . . . [Other equipment]: I have just one business phone line, records 100 phone calls that come in, whether they leave a message or not. Name display, call waiting, call answer. It's a Meridian phone 9417. I can make phone calls from there. With [the spreadsheet] as my base, I can make cold calls, I can fax through the NSL, but if my fax is on no one can call in, but the Micro link solves that problem. So I pretty well can live with what I had if I had to. Res. line and business line. (network salesman 1)

A 40-year-old wireless radio-phone salesman looked forward to being equipped for the job with pride. At the time, however, he had only cast-off company equipment.

> (Q. So you've got a fax machine, two computers, printer what else?) I will be getting laser printers. That printer's very good though. I'll be getting CD ROM on our computers. I'll be getting some kind of a photocopier . . . I have two lines. I have my personal line plus I have a Telecom phone line. And in the near future, I'll be getting Micro link. It's a data line. It processes information much quicker. It's a faster line and they will provide that to us and with that Micro link I will be able to tap into the server at the office. And this will all be taking place, I would imagine, this year some time. (radio services salesman 1)

A saleswoman excused the inability to work at speed at home due to the slow implementation of technology, because the company made amends.

> At the beginning . . . I couldn't get on to the main frame and things like that . . . It wasn't until I got the new Pentium lap top that I could get on to the main frame. And that was a real inconvenience cause any time I wanted to get something off the main frame, I had to go into Toronto. So they created a real issue that way. However, they realized that and they got it corrected . . . They knew they had to with us teleworking. (equipment saleswoman 9)

Given the importance of technology, teleworkers do not stress that the company should "stay out" of their homes. Rather, so long as they are teleworking "at home," the company should truly enter the home. The company should make their equipment work better.

> I think one of my problems with this . . . is that it would have been nice to have, perhaps, a consultant come in for half a day or something cause I've got all this equipment and just to help us in terms of integrating everything together. Because I've heard there's some incompatibilities with some of the lap tops with the ISDN and also when I get Windows and NT I heard that it's not compatible with the Brother unit so these kind of issues I'm fearing because it would have been nice to have somebody come in and say, okay this is how this works and it works with this and so forth. And also to go through the ergonomics of the room as well.

Far from complaining that the company is now in her home, she is frustrated that the company is not doing enough in the house.

So when I plug in my computer I plug in my modem 28-8 to my fax machine, so I'm getting only 28-8 speed. Micro link allows for you to get 2 × 64 so 128. I'm not getting that because they gave us these boxes they don't even sell any more. An NT1 and a terminal adapter from Nortel that just allows us to have these two B channels they're called. So (a) I'm not getting the speed I should be getting; (b) if I'm on Lotus Notes or whatever and I'm hooked up to my LAN I can't receive a fax because it's busy and I can't send a fax. So I have to disconnect my LAN and then go and use my fax machine which is ridiculous. And also I have access to the Internet. The Internet is an extremely competitive tool. It is fantastic to get information to your own customers about your own company and so forth, and I know that I don't utilize it to its capacity because it is so damn slow at 28-8 it's ridiculous. So I have no incentive to go in there unless I have a project to work on. Pulling out that one paragraph per customer of mine that I did on my territory plan took me two hours to cut and paste it because the Internet is so slow. So I've been talking about this and trying to, and I talked about it in our territory plan meeting and said like just like can I buy the box cause you can buy a box for $500 that'll bond the two channels together and give you that speed. And I got good news saying that they're actually looking at buying these other modems that will be able to do a little bit more.

The formal administrative support was inadequate.

I think there should be a teleworker hot line too. [To deal with] technicalities, like equipment not working and so forth. I've got like six different help desk numbers for different applications. I call one and it's like no I'm supposed to call the other, and it's just, I really don't feel confident that everything that I have here is hooked up properly (network saleswoman 4).

They felt slighted that their manager did not pay attention to their new need to bridge office equipment with equipment that was not meant for the office.

I think that if I were a manager, whether they have time to do this is probably unrealistic, but I would have liked to have gone to each of my co-workers' houses. They were actually supposed to do this. And see how they're set up. Find out what, if there are any concerns, whether it's how things are connecting or what have you, you know? And then maybe taken that information back and say you know I need some consulting on this. Like I need some help with this. I remember last year we were given a grid, a floor grid, and we had to put down our addresses and so forth and a manager was supposed to sign it. They were supposed to come to our house and we were supposed to do a floor plan of our office. And that never was done. It wasn't even pushed. (network saleswoman 8)

For those that want to take full advantage of the teleworking arrangement, the available technology is not still enough. They want even more advanced technology to bring back the important "water cooler conversation":

> I would love to see something to bring back that team environment, the water cooler, that's the one thing they haven't replaced with the whole teleworking thing, it's the concept of the water cooler where you talk about your weekend, what happened at your last appointment and all those kind of things; . . . I think they should do it through an Internet site, which is set up for video conferencing . . . It's funny 'cause after our breakfast meetings, you know, you'll find that everyone kind of wants to hang around a little bit you know in the office and just chat about stuff. People are anxious to talk about stuff. (solutions specialist 1)

Sales workers do not want to avoid peer interaction. They want to manage it. Some felt better about teleworking as soon as people got used to communicating remotely. They even wanted their clients to be enmeshed in the newest techniques. At the time, the company did not push Internet communications with customers, yet some sales people pushed their managers to urge their best customers to connect to them through the Internet. They saw this as a means to commit the customers further. Free Internet service was to become a company bonus offered to the committed small business customer.

Others define the "essence" of sales as people work, not paper work. They express the view that they are "people" people. They felt that "whether you're working with support people or with peers, you have a better idea of what each person is doing if you have face-to-face contact." With the remote communications characteristic of home work, "you're just another phone call, another voice mail as opposed to up live and in person." Since they need face-to-face interaction to influence people and to establish strong working relationships to get things done, several think politically. These sales workers use the flexibility of teleworking arrangement to maximize face-to-face interaction with peers. Some spend less time working at home and more in hoteling facilities. There they figure out who they can work near and when. They try to maximize their contact with their supervisors.

Summary

As a humanist ideal embedded in the human relations office, giving up the central office and working at home for the company has caught on among the media and scholars. It was hoped that teleworkers could use their time and space in "new ways" and gain ownership of their time and space, a post-Fordist goal. However, the company held a neo-Fordist perspective, whose agenda was to to increase profits by decentralizing. In the process of meshing these two goals, the sales workers took on more of the costs of their employment, without concrete reimbursement. They assumed more of the burden of property and labor, spending more time at work and incorporating family labor into the work process.

In many ways employees have adopted the company perspective. They take the role of the company in this restructuring, and try to fit their family life to the new company demands and definitions of work. They adopt the slogan, "work smarter and faster." Few see costs as all one way, however. Most see telework as an exchange. The engineering-oriented employees and the more aggressive new hires extol telework as a sign that their company is now moving to the forefront of new technologies. They hope in this way that Telecom will best the competition. Those that competed to win perks also appreciated the ability to work harder. The people-oriented employees, and those who were more tenured feel that the telework does not benefit clients, and is not worth the costs.

Understanding that teleworking entails more issues than saving travel time, sociologists have begun to explore its deeper social structural impacts. The social implications of telework go beyond change of workplace. Looking at the factors of production, I noted how telework further deepens capital penetration in a sacrosanct area, the home as a private space. Through telework, this "last frontier" becomes a factor of production. Teleworking firms openly enter this hitherto unexplored domain to accumulate capital.

References

Agres, C., Edberg, D., and Igbaria, M. (1998). Transformation to virtual societies: forces and issues. *The Information Society*, 14(2), 71–82.

Armstrong, N. J. de F. (1997). Negotiating the boundaries between "home" and "work": a case study of teleworking in New Zealand. In E.

Gunnarsson (ed.), *Virtually free? Gender, work and spatial choice* (pp. 175–200). Stockholm: NUTEK.

Bailey, D. E. and Kurland, N. B. (1999). *New directions for research in telework.* Stanford University, Working Paper.

Castells, M. (1989). *The informational city: information technology, economic restructuring, and the urban-regional process.* Oxford: Blackwell.

Castells, M. (2001). *The Internet galaxy: reflections on the Internet, business, and society.* Oxford: Oxford University Press.

Dickinson, P. and Jellison, J. (2000). *Plugging in: the increase of household Internet use.* Statistics Canada Science, Innovation and Connection Series, Electronic Information Division. Available online at: http://www.statcan.ca/english/IPS/Data/56F0004MIE00001.htm

Dimitrov, S. and Dimitrova, D. (1995). Development, management, and organizational implications: office systems in Bell Canada. Paper presented to Department of Engineering, University of Toronto, Toronto.

Dimitrova, D. and Salaff, J. W. (1998). Telework as social innovation: how remote employees work together. In P. Jackson and J. Van Wielen (eds), *Teleworking: international perspectives: from telecommuting to the virtual organisation* (pp. 261–79). New York: Routledge.

Dubrin, A. (1991). A comparison of the job satisfaction and productivity of telecommuters versus in-house employees: a research note. *Psychological Reports,* 68, 1223–34.

Ellison, N. (1999). Social impacts: new perspectives on telework. *Social Science Computer Review,* 17(3), 338–56.

Featherstone, M. (1993). Global and local cultures. In J. Bird, B. Curtis, T. Putnam, G. Robertson, and L. Tickner (eds), *Mapping the futures: local cultures, global enchange* (pp. 169–87). London: Routledge.

Gainey, T. W., Kelley, D. E., and Hill, J. A. (1999). Telecommuting's impact on corporate culture and individual workers: examining the effect of employee isolation. *SAM Advanced Management Journal,* 64(4), 4–10.

Goldman, D. (2000). Today's work and family issue: curbing abusive overtime. In J. Casner-Lotto (ed.), *Holding a job, having a life: strategies for change* (pp. 175–9). Scarsdale, NY: Work in America Institute, Inc.

Greve, A., Salaff, J., Wellman, B., and Dimitrova, D. (2002). Office workers go virtual: contrasting bureaucracy and network organization (in preparation).

Gunnarsson, E. (ed.) (1997). *Virtually free? Gender, work and spatial choice.* Stockholm: NUTEK (Swedish National Board for Industrial and Technical Development).

Gurstein, P. (2001). *Wired to the world, chained to the home: telework in daily life.* Vancouver: University of British Columbia.

Hardwick, D. and Salaff, J. (1998). *Fragmented lives: how do teleworking parents juggle work and children care?* Paper delivered to the Annual Meeting of the American Sociological Association, Toronto.

Harvey, D. (1989). *The condition of postmodernity.* Oxford: Basil Blackwell.

Harvey, D. (1993). From space to place and back again: reflections on the condition of postmodernity. In J. Bird, B. Curtis, T. Putnam, G. Robertson, and L. Tickner (eds), *Mapping the futures: local cultures, global change* (pp. 3–29). London, Routledge.

Hill, E. J., Miller, B. C., Weiner, S. P., and Colihan, J. (1998). Influences of the virtual office on aspects of work and work/life balance. *Personnel Psychology*, 51(3), 667–83.

Hochschild, A. (1983). *The managed heart: communication of human feeling.* Berkeley: University of California Press.

Hochschild, A. (1989). *The second shift: working parents and the revolution at home.* New York: Viking Penguin.

Hochschild, A. (1997). *The time bind: when work becomes home and home becomes work.* New York: Henry Holt and Co.

Huws, (1996). *Teleworking: an overview of the research.* A Report to the Department of Transport, Department of the Environment, Department of Trade and Industry, and Department for Education and Employment. London: Analytica.

IDC (2001). *Western European teleworking: mobile workers and telecommuters, 2000–2005.* Report. (October) (Summarized at http://www.ivc.ca/studies/European.html.)

Kordey, N. (2000). *Benchmarking telework in Europe (1999). Answers from the general population survey (GPS).* Bonn: Empirica. Gesellschaft für Kommunilkations und Technologieforschung mbH. ECaTT, (2001). Available online at: http://www.ecatt.com/ecatt/surveys/result/nwwg9001.html

Krebs, V. (1996). Visualizing human networks. *Release 1.0*, 2–96. Feb. 12.

Luxton, M. (1980). *More than a labour of love.* Toronto: Women's Educational Press.

Massey, D. (1996). Masculinity, dualisms, and high technology. In N. Duncan (ed.), *Body space: destabilizing geographies of gender and sexuality* (pp. 108–26). London: Routledge.

Mckie, C. and Thompson, K. (1990; 1994; 2000). *Canadian social trends.* Vols, 1, 2, 3. Toronto: Thompson Publishing, Inc.

Mirchandani, K. (1996). Professional telework: the technological diffusion of organization culture into the home. Paper delivered at Annual meeting of Society for the Study of Social Problems.

Mirchandani, K. (1997). Feeling and flexibility: teleworkers' emotion work of linking home and work. In P. Jackson and J. van der Wielen, (eds), *Amsterdam '97 Second International Workshop on Telework*, Vol. II (pp. 414–25).

Mirchandani, K. (1998). Shifting definitions of the public-private dichotomy: legislative inertia on garment homework in Ontario. *Advances in Gender Research*, 3, 47–71

Mirchandani, K. (1999). Legitimizing work: telework and the gendered reification of the work–nonwork dichotomy. *La Revue Canadienne de Sociologie et d'Anthropologie/The Canadian Review of Sociology and Anthropology*, 36(1), 87–107.

Mirchandani, K. (2000). The best of both worlds and cutting my own throat: contradictory images of home-based work. *Qualitative Sociology*, 23(2), 159–82.

Mitter, S. and Efendioglu, U. (1997). Teleworking in a global context. In E. Gunnarsson (ed.), *Virtually free? Gender, work and spatial choice* (pp. 13–20). Stockholm: NUTEK.

Mokhtarian, P. (1997). The transportation impacts of telecommuting: recent empirical findings. In P. Stropher and M. Lee-Gosselin (eds), *Understanding travel behaviour in an era of change* (pp. 91–106). Oxford: Elsevier.

MORI. (2001). British office workers want to work from home. Available online at:
http://www.mori.com/polls/2001/mitel.shtml.

Nippert-Eng, C. (1996). *Home and work: negotiating boundaries through everyday life*. Chicago: University of Chicago Press.

Nippert-Eng, C. (1998). Cited in *IIT Annual Report*. Available online at: www.iit.edu/departments/pr/98annualreport/Improve/Commutwork/commutwork.html+Nippert-Engandhl=en

NTIA (National Telecommunications and Information Administration). (1998). *Falling through the net II: new data on the digital divide*. Washington, DC: US Department of Commerce.

OECD (Organization for Economic Co-operation and Development) (2001). *Understanding the digital divide*. Paris, France: OECD.

Olson, M. H. (1988). Organizational barriers to telework. In W. Korte, S. Robinson, and W. Steinle (eds), *Telework: present situation and future development of a new form of work organization* (pp. 77–100). North Holland: Elsevier Science.

Parcel, T. (1999). Work and family in the 21st century: it's about time. *Work and Occupations*, 26, 264–74.

Perin, C. (1991). The moral fabric of the office: panopticon discourse and schedule flexibilities. *Research in the Sociology of Organizations*, 8, 241–68.

Perin, C. (1996). Project management models as social, cultural, and cognitive systems: relating paid and unpaid work schedules. In *Proceedings of workshop on new international perspectives on telework*. Brunel University, 31 July-2 August, 293–304.

Piore, M. and Sabel, C. (1984). *The second industrial divide: possibilities for prosperity*. New York: Basic Books.

Pratt, J. (1999). *Cost/benefits of teleworking to manage work/life responsibilities*. Telework America National Telework Survey for The International Telework Association and Council.

Pratt, J. (2000). *Telework and society: implications for corporate and societal cultures*. Paper commissioned for the US Department of Labor Symposium on Telework, October 16. Xavier University, New Orleans, LA.

Prechel, H. (1994). Economic crisis and the centralization of control over the managerial process. *American Sociological Review*, 59, 723–45.

Pusceddu, R. and van de Roer, A. (2001). Western European teleworking: mobile workers and telecommuters, 2000–2005. IDC, Report No. W25698 (October, 2001). Available online at: http://www.ivc.ca/European.html (excerpts).

Silver, H. 1993. Homework and domestic work. *Sociological Forum*. 8(2), 181–201.

Smith, D. (1973). Women, the family and corporate capitalism. In M. L. Stephenson (ed.), *Women in Canada*, Toronto: New Press.

Statistics Canada. (2000). *Canadian social trends*. vol. 3. Toronto: Thompson Educational Publishing, Inc.

Sullivan, C. (2000). Space and the intersection of work and family in home-working. *Community, Work and Family*, 3(2), 185–204.

Sullivan, C. and Lewis, S. (2001). Home-based telework, gender, and the synchronization of work and family: perspectives of teleworkers and their co-residents. *Gender, Work and Organization*, 8(2), 123–45.

Sturesson, L. (1997). Telework: symbol of the information society? In E. Gunnarsson (ed.), *Virtually free? Gender, work and spatial choice* (pp. 79–90). Stockholm: NUTEK.

Thompson, E. P. (1967). Time, work-discipline, and industrial capitalism. *Past and Present*, 38.

Tippin, D. (1994). *Control processes in distance work situations: the case of satellite offices*. Paper presented at the Annual Meeting of the Canadian Sociology and Anthropology Association, Calgary, Alberta.

Whittle, A. (2001). *Out of sight, out of mind? A virtual ethnography of teleworking careers*. Paper presented at 6th International ITF Workshop, Working in the New Economy: Work–Family Issues, Amsterdam, Netherlands.

17

Kerala Connections

Will the Internet Affect Science in Developing Areas?

Theresa Davidson, R. Sooryamoorthy,
and Wesley Shrum

Abstract

Three general arguments on the role of the Internet in developing areas have been suggested. The "elixir" argument holds that the Internet does not represent a potential problem but only an opportunity. Information technologies are a developmental tool on a par with educational and agricultural programs. The "affliction" argument holds that Internet diffusion is an engine of global inequality, an insidious form of dependency creating new technology gaps between rich and poor, professionals and laborers, urban and rural dwellers, English and non-English speakers. The third argument holds that there are temporary "teething troubles" that may arise from telecommunications infrastructure or cultural differences that will soon diminish. We describe a project to examine the rapid introduction of the Internet in the south Indian State of Kerala. The "Kerala model" is unique in the developing world owing to its combination of high social development with low economic development. Using qualitative data from interviews with scientists in universities and governmental research institutes, we examine early views of the Internet in an advanced developing area.

Authors' note

Please direct all correspondence to Wesley Shrum, Department of Sociology, Louisiana State University, Baton Rouge, Louisiana 70803. Data were collected under a SGER grant from the US National Science Foundation. Our particular thanks to Alice Leeds, Marjorie Lueck, Rachelle Hollander, Michael Sokal, and William Bainbridge, who made these findings possible. Technical assistance was provided by Sojan Mathew, Binish Augustine, Leona

Coffee, Gerry Boudreaux, Ann Whitmer, Emilio Icaza, Brian Ropers-Huilman, Isaac Traxler, Rick Duque, Vasudeva Bhattathiri, and Suresh Pavithran.

Introduction

Internet technology is a crucial aspect of scientific work. The problems and opportunities afforded by new information and communication technologies were first experienced in the developed world, the US in particular (Abbate, 1999). Modern Internet technology has its origins in the development of means for more efficient scientific communication and holds greater promise of integrating the global research community than any previous technology. Computer mediated communication is a two-way flow that aids scientific researchers by providing (1) access to colleagues, information, and databases for research, and (2) opportunities for sharing findings with the scientific community.

Yet at the turn of the millennium, the digital divide is nowhere more evident than in science itself. Scientists, as part of the professional elite in developing areas, have been projected as early and extensive users of Internet technology, just as in western countries. Yet many scientists in the developing world may be falling behind, without the basic connectivity and certainly without the bandwidth that is taken for granted in the developed countries. For example, during the course of our project, we came across one research station in western Kenya without a phone connection, in which the only way to make contact with the director of the station was to call the district prison located two kilometers away, and request delivery of a message.

In this chapter, we explore the early introduction of the Internet among scientists in universities and governmental research institutes in the south Indian state of Kerala. First, we examine the idea of "isolation" of scientists in developing countries. We go on to review the basic perspectives on the role of information and communication technologies (ICTs) in development, and note the lack of empirical research on the role of ICTs in science in developing areas. Next, the social context of Kerala is described. We then present first results from an ongoing exploration of the opportunities and constraints posed by this new technology for science in developing areas. These results are organized in terms of three general perspectives on the role of the Internet in development: as an "elixir," as an "affliction," and as a technology with potential but subject to "teething troubles." While it is too early to declare clear support for any one of these perspectives, this essay is offered as a "status report" on the introduction of the Internet in an advanced developing area characterized by a high commitment to education and literacy.

Science in developing countries

For decades scientists in developing countries have been viewed as "isolated," a state of affairs with both informational and interpersonal dimensions. While conditions have changed since the colonial era, descriptions of the situation in the mid-1960s remains relevant today (Dedijer, 1963; Salam, 1966). It was obvious to any observer then that access to current scientific information was seriously limited. Articles in scientific journals, books, newsletters, preprints, and manuscripts of current but unpublished work are essential sources of information for active researchers. In developing areas, acquisition costs are prohibitive and scientists are limited by inadequate libraries and documentation centers. Hence, critical deficits were and are faced by knowledge workers in the south in the availability, cost, and timeliness of informational resources.

The second dimension of isolation is interpersonal, involving barriers to contact with active research communities in the west. Access to information is not merely through journals, but can occur through communication with colleagues, whether by mail, telephone, or face-to-face meetings. Less developed areas have smaller research communities, and these few scientists are often dispersed over long distances. When separated geographically, scientists are unable to maintain regular communication with others in their field, nor can they benefit from the intellectual stimulation that accompanies contact. Isolation was said to exist locally as well as internationally. Owing to infrastructural problems with transportation and communication technologies, it was difficult for researchers to communicate with regularity and efficiency even with those in their own city or region. The central assumption is that unless scientists can interact frequently with others in the field, they will remain peripheral to the research community and out of touch with developments in their field.

Although some of these characterizations may well be true, evidence based on empirical studies of scientists in developing areas is extremely limited. Jacques Gaillard (1991) surveyed 489 scientists who received grants from the International Foundation for Science between

1974 and 1984. Gaillard found that scientists in developing areas communicate infrequently with others in their own country. Those who had never studied abroad were less likely to communicate with foreign researchers. Because conferences are often held in industrialized countries, scientists from developing areas find it difficult and costly to attend. Methodological problems make it difficult to generalize these findings. First, Gaillard's sample consisted of a relatively "elite" group of scientists – those who received a grant from an international foundation. Second, these results are based on reported frequency of communication with different categories of scientists at the rate of once a year (1991, pp. 77–8). Without information on specific ties and their organizational locus, it is impossible to draw conclusions about the distribution of professional contacts.

While scientists in developing areas are not "isolates" in the usual network sense of having no ties to other members of their professional community, the thrust of these studies supports the notion of serious constraints on the availability of information and communication. For some locations, in Africa, Asia, and Latin America, communicative and information-search options were not much different in the mid 1990s than they were in the period when Dedijer and Salam wrote. However, with the gradual development of server and routing technology and the rapid diffusion of Web browsers in the mid-1990s, the Internet rapidly became a focus of development agencies and nongovernmental organizations. Was the Internet the solution to the problem of isolation?

Three general viewpoints on the role of the Internet in developing areas have been suggested: the "elixir" argument, the "affliction" argument, and the "teething" argument.[1] These arguments organize our qualitative findings below, representing a view of present and future. We focus on the present, without any summary judgment of overall effects, but as an account of changes now underway. To be sure, it is important to assess the ways that humans employ new information and communication technologies, but the more critical task in developing countries is to understand the ways the Internet affects the everyday life of those that use it and those who observe its use by others.

The "elixir" argument asserts that the Internet does not represent a potential problem but only an opportunity. Information technologies are a developmental tool on a par with educational and agricultural

---

1   We adopt a slightly modified version of Rutger Engelhard's 1999b usage.

programs (De Roy, 1997). Internet connectivity in general and increased bandwidth in particular are inevitable processes that will aid developing countries. In this view, ICTs first introduced in Western nations represent an opportunity for the south to leapfrog into the new economic regime and become true partners in the global scientific enterprise. Technology will allow the repatriation and production of data about developing areas that are now often controlled in research libraries in Northern countries (De Roy, 1998; UNDP, 1999). With respect to educational and research institutions, the Internet will solve the problem of the "isolation" of developing country scientists that has been noted since the 1960s (Dedijer, 1963; Salam, 1966). By allowing scientists in developing regions to keep in touch with current scientific developments, publish and distribute their work, and develop national scientific communities in areas where researchers cannot currently contact each other easily, the Internet will bring researchers into the global system.

The "affliction" perspective views the Internet as an engine of global inequality that creates new technology gaps between rich and poor, urban and rural dwellers, English and non-English speakers. This is so for three reasons. First, the content of the web is dominated by the organizations, languages, and actors where it was first developed. Second, the promotion of ICTs by development agencies removes resources from more important areas like health care and food security, the Internet is a harmful diversion. Finally, and of special importance to research and educational institutions, increasing dependence on the Internet and other communications media may increase inequality between institutions in developing areas and their counterparts in the US and Europe. Although connectivity is being introduced in developing countries, the rate of increase in technology required to use the web is increasing more rapidly than the technologies themselves. The Internet may indeed be a beneficial technology, but one that is not disseminating with sufficient speed. As platforms for the diffusion of information shift to electronic format, the absence of connectivity or low availability of bandwidth leaves researchers with greater constraints than previously.

The "teething" argument falls somewhere between the preceding two arguments. It focuses on temporary "teething troubles" arising in less developed areas (Engelhard, 1999b), suggesting that a net benefit will eventually accrue to developing areas, but not without significant problems in the short term. These can include problems in telecommunications infrastructure as regulations in some areas have yet to liberalize and national telecommunications companies have been slow to privatize, with power outages, surges, and unreliable telephone circuits common. The teething argument is most sensitive to the temporal aspects of technology diffusion but relies, as does the affliction argument, on the observation of lagging development, spawning a large literature on what has become known as the digital divide (Adams, 2000; Arunachalam, 1999; Hindman, 2000). Moreover, the teething argument views cultural differences as crucial. If developing areas emphasize personal, face-to-face relations there is an important adjustment period when communication begins to occur electronically.

Studies of Internet technology in developing areas are badly needed. First, there is tremendous variability in the extent to which the "connectivity" of a country represents actual access for its population. Second, work on ICTs in development is often speculative and lacks a foundation in empirical evidence, either quantitative or qualitative. While research on the role of the Internet and computer-mediated-communication (CMC) in developing areas is sadly lacking, prior research has demonstrated its importance in the developed world (Robbin, 1995; Walsh et al., 2000; Walsh and Bayma, 1996a, 1996b).

One important strand of the literature on technology is based on the concept of diffusion, investigating the factors that influence the use or adoption of information and communication technology in scientific work (Abels et al., 1996; Hurd and Weller, 1997). Hurd and Weller (1997), for example, document the adoption of technological innovations by university faculty. They argue, using Everett Rogers' influential typology (1995), that barriers exist to the adoption of a new technology based on its perceived attributes. These barriers include the relative advantage it provides over other methods, its compatibility with the needs of the adopters, the ability of users to understand the innovation, the ease of adoption of the technology, and the degree to which the results of the innovation are visible to others. However, to the extent that there is a general lack of access to Internet technology in developing countries, it is unclear how perceived attributes could play a significant role – such barriers will become important after it is available.

Abels et al. (1996) examine the adoption and use of electronic networks by science and engineering faculty at small institutions, a context that may have more in common with some developing areas. They find that accessibility and the number of people sharing a workstation are both important attributes that influence use of the network. For those scientists in developing countries, who may not have easy access to computers that are Internet connected, these same factors are likely to inhibit their use of this technology.

Another segment of the literature on computer-mediated communication specifically focuses on the networks that are facilitated by this technology. Haythornthwaite and Wellman (1998), for example, examined the communication patterns of researchers located in the same building. They find that the stronger the work tie, the more frequent the communication, the more varieties of information exchanged, and the more media used (including face-to-face interaction). Of course, the promise of the Internet is in connecting scientists who do not work in the same building, or even the same country.

Walsh and Bayma (1996a, 1996b) examined the use of computer mediated communication technology among scientists in four different fields: mathematics, physics, chemistry, and experimental biology. They found that mathematicians, who have traditionally worked alone, increased remote collaboration through the use of email. For physicists, who have traditionally collaborated with large numbers of other scientists, email was a helpful addition to the face-to-face interaction that is still required. Chemists and biologists reported that email provides more frequent communication than was available previously, resulting in coordinated experiments that are completed sooner. Overall, Walsh and Bayma found that CMC increases collaboration by overcoming geographical barriers, increasing the frequency of communication among those involved in a collaborative research project, and providing opportunities and resources to scientists who are new to the field or located at less prestigious institutions. In a second study Walsh et al. (2000) examined the use of CMC in the fields of experimental biology, mathematics, physics, and sociology. They conclude that email use is important to scientific research, though its use varies by field. Email use is related to frequency of contact among scientists and access to information.

Such work shows the increasing importance of the Internet and computer mediated communication technology in facilitating scientific work in the developed world. However, it does not investigate the use of computer-mediated communication in developing countries where access may be limited or problematic. One study that attempts such an assessment is Jimba and Atinmo's examination of the relationship between accessibility to information technology and research productivity in Nigeria (2000). They find no significant relationship between the accessibility of information resources and self-reported publication measures. The authors observe that much of the information now available to Nigerian and African scientists comes from western countries and may not address the concerns of Nigerian scientists, whose knowledge becomes subordinated and marginalized. However, Jimba and Atinmo include only those scientists who had some access to electronic information resources. Without a comparison to those who do not have access, it is difficult to argue that informational resources have no impact. In general, there remains a severe deficit of sound empirical work on the adoption and consequences of ICTs in developing areas.[2]

The Kerala Model

Our objective in the present work is to explore the present status and meaning of the Internet among scientists for a location in the developing world that is in many respects special. While our larger project includes east and west African locations, this report centers on the state of Kerala in southwestern India, where preliminary data was collected in the summer of 2001. No claim is made that Kerala is representative of developing areas in general. Many scholars would argue precisely the opposite: the idea of a "Kerala model" of development is a clear expression of this sentiment (Jeffrey, 1992; Parayil, 1996). Specifically, Kerala has a combination of features that provide a unique setting for examining the introduction of the Internet.

The central reason analysts have identified a Kerala model is that the level of social development within the state is much higher than one would expect based on its level of economic development. Owing to its reputation for labor militancy, capital investment and economic growth in the state remain low. Economic growth has been only around half the national level for India (Gulati, 1995). Unemployment rates are among the highest in India. In particular there is a problem of unemployment for those with higher degrees (Mathew, 1995; EPW, 1994). From 1985 through 1994 unemployment registration among professional graduates increased nearly 200 percent (Iyer and MacPherson, 2000). Although extreme forms of poverty are rare, the

---

2   One problem when conducting research on communication and information in developing areas is that it is difficult for sociologists in both developed and developing areas to access work that has been done in the region.

proportion living below the poverty line is still high. Certain sectors of the population, such as the tribal people who comprise roughly 1 percent of the state population, remain "backward," and deaths from starvation have recently been reported.

Indicators of social development – including literacy rates, demographic trends, the presence of social programs, and the status of females – paint a far different picture of the state. Most important for the adoption and diffusion of the Internet is the extremely strong emphasis on literacy and education that pervades the state, placing Kerala on a par with most developed countries (Franke and Chasin, 1994; Iyer and MacPherson, 2000). The 91 percent literacy rate is well above the Indian average of 52 percent. The literacy gap between males and females has narrowed in Kerala, counter to the national trend. The emphasis on education in Kerala has resulted in three specific problems for economic development: an increase in labor militancy that has inhibited external investment, increased expectations and decreased job satisfaction among the educated, and greater demand among both men and women for the high quality professional and management positions that remain scarce in the Kerala economy.

Beyond education and literacy, there are numerous and far-reaching social programs and initiatives, including public food distribution, labor market interventions to raise rural and urban wages, health services, and infrastructure that includes schools, hospitals, and dispensaries (Franke and Chasin, 1994; Kannan, 1995). Demographic indicators of their success are low birth and death rates. These have declined so rapidly that Kerala resembles countries that have completed the demographic transition associated with industrialization (Bhat and Rajan, 1990). The Kerala sex ratio of 1036 females to 1000 males is, again, closer to European and North American ratios than those of India as a whole. Though Keralites may prefer sons, the practices of selective abortion, female infanticide, and neglect of females are relatively rare. Recently, there are suggestions of an actual *preference* for daughters over sons among the middle class.

The status of women is relatively high compared with other Indian states. However, there are indicators of a lower than Indian average workforce participation for females in Kerala (Saradomoni, 1994). While lower fertility has increased the number of women in the workforce, there is reduced demand for female labor in agriculture, where food crops are primarily the province of women. In addition, gender relations still display a high degree of inequality. For example, women are still subject to arranged marriages, are nearly invisible in public life, and are largely unable to travel alone even in daylight hours (Saradamoni, 1994; Sooryamoorthy, 1997). Atrocities and crimes against women are increasing, which is evident from the type and number of cases registered with the Kerala State Women's Commission, established to protect the interests of women. The divorce rate has recently increased, and family courts are appearing throughout the state, testifying to the changes in the family life of Keralites.

The diffusion of the Internet in Kerala is likely to be a function of these economic and social conditions. While the level of external investment would predict a reduced rate of diffusion compared with the Indian average, the level of literacy and education would predict a high level of awareness of and interest in telecommunications technology. Currently, Kerala ranks first among Indian states and union territories in the density of telephone connections. Kerala has the third highest rate of mobile phone usage in the country after New Delhi and Mumbai, with over 300,000 users in the state, about seven percent of the Indian total (Parthasarathy, 2001).[3] By late 2000, there were approximately 50,000 Internet connections in the state, ranking it eighth among Indian states.[4]

Before the Internet

Our project began in 1994 – prior to the diffusion of the worldwide web – with a series of 293 personal interviews with scientists in Kerala, Ghana, and Kenya. This broad sample of researchers from universities, state research institutes, and NGOs yielded a picture of professional networks that were primarily local in character (Shrum and Campion, 2000). An inverse relationship obtained between the size of domestic and international personal networks: for government and academic scientists, those with more ties to the developed world had

3   There are approximately two million fixed phones, about 5 percent of the total in India (Parthasarathy, 2001). According to estimates by the cellular operators' association, there are 4.29 million mobile phone users in India. See "Mobile Varikkar Koodunnu," *Malayala Manorama* (Thiruvananthapuram Edition), August 27, 2001, p. 7.

4   The number of Internet connections in the country was approximately two million, led by the state of Maharashtra with 0.619 million, followed by Delhi (0.319 million), Tamil Nadu (0.291 million), Karnataka, West Bengal and Gujarat. See also "Growth in Internet connections lopsided," *The Hindu* (Thiruvananthapuram Edition), December 10, 2000, p. 8.

fewer local ties. Moreover, those that were educated in the developing world did not have more international ties – links to advisors and colleagues were lost owing to the difficulty of communication. In short, we found that local context was more important than the development level of the country in shaping opportunities for professional contacts. Developing countries' scientists are not "isolated," their relationships are simply drawn more from the national than the international arena.

In 1994, only 6 percent of Keralite researchers reported some access to electronic mail systems (Shrum, 1996). During the early 1990s, it would not be an exaggeration to say that modern electronic communication was almost wholly absent from the educational and governmental research sectors. Yet when asked directly about desired facilities, scientists did not consider this absence to be one of the highest priorities in the improvement of the research system. One of the most surprising findings in the 1994 survey was the low priority given to the development of electronic communication networks both domestically and internationally. From a list of twenty items, these networks were rated fifteenth and sixteenth respectively. An item on "creating international electronic communication networks" received the lowest average rating for any of the seven items on communication and networking. One African scientist said it best: "It'll be another white elephant. The donors will come in and try to establish electronic links, then leave and not support the system. It's not that important."

But even then we wondered why ICTs were such a low priority for Kerala scientists, and whether this would soon change. There were several reasons. First, we did not provide any background information about electronic communication or how it operated: the term "worldwide web" was little known in south India in mid-1994. Second, Kerala researchers were more interested in electronic communications than those in Ghana or Kenya, the two African locations in the study. And most significantly, the priority given to *improving various forms of linkages* was much higher than the priority of electronic communication technology, as an end-in-itself. The four highest priorities for scientists were:

1   providing operating funds for field and lab work;
2   expanding and improving libraries;
3   improving communication between researchers and extension;
4   improving links with international research organizations.

Excepting the first, the Internet has a potential impact on each of these. Given the high priority of "libraries," "communication," and "links," one of the central findings of the 1994 study was that the *means* of communication were not viewed as important as the *ends* – information acquisition and networking. Of course, these are the promises of the Internet.

In what follows, we present results from 33 interviews with scientists in educational and research institutions. Our informants were drawn from research institutes and teaching departments of the three universities in the state, including Kerala Agricultural University, Cochin University of Science and Technology, and Calicut University. These institutes and universities are located in nine of the fourteen Kerala districts: Trivandrum, Kottayam, Alappuzha, Ernakulam, Thrissur, Palakkad, Kozhikode, Wayanad and Kasaragod. We interviewed respondents in their respective workplaces during the months of May and June in 2001.[5] About three-quarters of our respondents were men.[6] Nineteen of these scientists were employed in central research institutes (run by the government of India) or in research institutes of the state of Kerala. Fourteen were employed in academic settings. All but four had a Ph.D. as their highest degree, and these four were in various stages of Ph.D. work.[7] Our informants represented a variety of research specialities, though half of them work in the areas of agronomy, horticulture, plant breeding, and plant pathology. Agriculturalists and agronomists in our sample were more likely to be employed by the research institutes.[8]

About one-fifth of the sample has some experience abroad – generally to developed countries – for study, training, or attending conferences, workshops, and seminars. On average, these seven individuals have spent 1.5 years outside India (five of these were from research institutes).[9] Two of our informants had been employed abroad, one in

5 Interviews lasted from one to two hours.
6 We interviewed 26 men and 7 women.
7 A variety of training disciplines are represented, with an emphasis on agriculture (30.4 percent), economics, engineering (12.1 percent each), statistics, horticulture, veterinary and animal science, and zoology (9.1 percent each). We interviewed single individuals in botany, oceanography, and plant breeding.
8 Biotechnology, marine science, microbiology were also represented.
9 Six of the seven were females, which is somewhat surprising in light of findings by Campion and Shrum (forthcoming) that women have fewer opportunities to work abroad.

biotechnology and one in plant pathology. Nearly three-quarters of these individuals (24, or 72.7 percent) did not have a computer in their office for their personal use, but shared computers with others.[10] Using an open-end interview structure, we explored the use and perceptions of the Internet, the opportunities and benefits it implies for their professional lives, and the problems that accompany the introduction of this technology. These views are organized in terms of the elixir, affliction, and teething perspectives reviewed above.

Internet elixir

One point seems clear even from these preliminary interviews: the advent of the Internet has begun to change the way many Kerala scientists think about their work. During a journey away from India, this fisheries scientist realized the importance of email when it was no longer accessible:

> During my recent visit to Vietnam, I felt it very deeply in the sense that there it was very difficult to get email connections. I realized the necessity of email. Whatever things happen here . . . my students used to communicate to me then and there. Even if I am away I get all the information regarding the activities here. But when I could not open my mail in Vietnam, I was a bit tense because I was cut off from the news of my university and activities. I could really feel it.

A marine scientist at Cochin University of Science and Technology was quite as avid as any dot com marketer in the west. For him, the Internet is indeed an elixir for the state of Kerala:

> The facilities of email and Internet are unimaginable. Now the whole world has become small and accessible to everybody. Even if you are away, you don't feel that you are away. We can contact anyone at anytime. The whole world is like a small village.

While many of our informants voiced like sentiments of possibility, we sought evidence that the Internet has begun to generate more specific shifts in the way science is conducted. Most scientists are aware of the large quantity of information available through the web and the

10 Among the nine who have this facility, five were employed by universities and four by research institutes.

opportunities for communication with other scientists through email. Some report specific benefits from both these functions with respect to their ability to gather research resources through the Internet. One agricultural scientist located just outside the capital described the information he is able to obtain:

> Internet is used in reviewing literature to find what are the works already done in the area. Internet has helped in understanding statistical analysis of data in different works. It is used in getting photographs. For example, the first photo of the mite which causes *mandari* disease[11] was from England. We downloaded it from the Internet. And we got about 500 pages of literature on the mite from Internet.

Such testimony bears special significance in light of the high priority given to the improvement of library facilities by our survey of Kerala scientists in 1994.

The "hypothesis of isolation" discussed above (Dedijer, 1963; Salam, 1966) pertained directly to the ideal of a globalized scientific community, with scientists throughout the world communicating about their research goals and problems. Some Kerala scientists spoke directly to these issues of connectivity and currency:

> Yes, I am a member of many groups. It gives a lot of advantages to me. When I have some doubts I post them on the Internet. I receive more than fifty replies [on average] every time. That is a wonderful opportunity now possible through Internet. We have now many an active discussion group, based mainly in the US. They are giving adequate support when we are posting some queries.

It is not truly "global science" but "US science" that is filtered through the groups encountered by this scientist in a college of fisheries. Yet fifty replies to a query, while it may not be typical, give rise to issues that are the polar opposite of isolation, that is, issues of credibility and reliability, and of information sorting and selectivity rather than acquisition. Western scientists are now more likely to complain about volume than deficiency of information.[12]

The issue of information currency is important because there is widespread sentiment among scientists in developing areas that one

---

11   This disease attacked coconut palms throughout the state, causing a significant reduction in yield.
12   We did not hear complaints about excessive volume of information in Kerala.

may be engaged in significant research that has already been done. Kerala scientists often discussed the problem of duplication. Some felt the Internet had brought them the remedy. This environmental chemist felt he now had the ability to remain informed of the latest developments in his field, preventing his research from becoming irrelevant:

> We were feeling that we were getting outdated. We were not informed of what was exactly happening in other parts of the world. Thousands of papers are published every month of which tens of papers will be relevant to what we are doing today. Unless we know what others are doing we will be only duplicating the same thing. People will be working in some area for about four years but after three years you find someone else publishing a paper on the same thing. Then your work becomes irrelevant. Now, with the arrival of the Internet, it does not happen.

What seems novel is the reported sense of gaining the capacity to *know* where one stands with respect to global standards of scientific work. For one scientist, not only is information received more rapidly, but the Internet allows him to keep up with developments in other countries:

> Now I know what is going on in my subject and what is going on in the U.S., Europe, etc. I am aware of what is going on in the world [as far as his subject is concerned]. Earlier, the articles in the journals will take two to three years to reach us . . . Information reached us very late earlier. Now we get everything instantly . . . Now we know what others are doing on our areas in other countries which avoids duplication.

A university scientist directly asserted his scientific work would improve because of this new capacity for global awareness:

> We can converse with the world standards. You know what is happening in different parts of the world. We have access to such type of information and that will improve a lot to develop our side also, because, you know, our type of research will be always in comparison with some set standards. Once we get information from such laboratories, we will also try to improve our activities, on par with those institutions and their standards. So that will improve, that will make a lot of changes in our methodology in our search, topics and everything. Career-wise it will always be a revolutionary change with the introduction of email and Internet facilities.

Information flow is not just unidirectional. A scientist discussed the new capacity to publish gene sequences online and participate in a global scientific endeavor, collecting and disseminating information:

> Once we have a gene, a new gene, we can submit online. So I did that online, once we have found a new gene sequence or new gene, we can submit the data or deposit the data on the day you got it. There is a specific programme for sending and submitting. They will screen it for genuineness and it will be in their web which can be accessed . . . All over the world, once they have a new sequence or new information, they quickly submit on the web.

Such participation yields the potential for significant changes, not only in the production of scientific knowledge, but also in terms of self-esteem. One entomologist granted that the Internet was responsible for his new-found assurance at scientific conferences:

> Now I am very proud when I give latest information in meetings and all. With this facility we download the latest information for the matter on what you are going to present in some forums. It increases my confidence. I have the confidence to argue with anybody on any subject. I feel the same thing when I discuss the subject with foreigners too. Once a professor from the Imperial College of London came. He says that our resources are better than that of theirs, particularly in information technology. For them, it is costly and so they cannot afford them. We are doing a lot of experiments and are ahead of them.

While such sentiments were rare, it is surely significant that a scientist in the developing world may begin to consider not merely equality, but *superiority* in scientific work.

Internet affliction

If the story stopped here there would be little question about the role of the Internet – apart from how rapidly all scientists can be connected. But as Engelhard (1999b) points out, elixirs have two problems: no one seems to know the exact ingredients that provide the magic power; and those in charge of administration often leave by the time it is found to be ineffective or worse. Even in Kerala, where many scientists are beginning to gain regular access, the Internet is viewed with misgivings that range from technical to social. Although every scientist in our interviews was familiar with the Internet – a major shift since 1994 – levels and types of access varied widely. The following agronomist at a rice research institute has used the Internet but laments the overall lack of access that he and his colleagues experience in Kerala: "There is lack of facilities here. We do not have Internet. Even the village officers are having Internet connection. But the researchers do not have it. It is a pathetic condition."

Even with access, bandwidth and cost are frequently problematic, issues raised by the following university scientist:

> We have to wait till midnight and get a full speedy download. Another problem is that the infrastructure is not developed, means power cut and all. Power cut is a big problem. There won't be enough voltage. We have everything, but infrastructure is not developed. So use of Internet is costly here. The phone charges are very high and we have to pay phone charges for using Internet. In the US, there is unlimited use. This is a hurdle here. Keeping engaged with Internet means you are paying for every minute. It is a costly business – you cannot browse that easily, carefree and without considering the amount of money required for that.

Owing to excessive demand, regular power cuts are scheduled for one or two hours each day. Infrastructural problems such as these are clear reminders that a retreat into cyberspace is not possible for most in the developing world, even if it were desirable.

This is the problem of "theoretical connectivity." Widely experienced in the universities and research institutes of Kerala, the problem of theoretical connectivity exists where a connection is planned but not available, where a connection has been established but is not in working order, where the speed of the connection is so slow that little activity is possible. Although we lack the statistics to document the phenomenon, it is remarkable how often a scientist will report access to the Internet but that now, at this particular time, it is not possible to use it. In terms of research practice, the inability is probably more significant than the reasons why.

Apart from questions of access, many informants challenged the notion that the Internet will provide only benefits to those with access to the technology. Awareness is a double-edged sword for those who are not able to retrieve information they now know exists. A common complaint among those interviewed is that full articles are often not available on the Internet. Though there would seem to be a benefit in gathering references quickly, the source itself is unavailable, or would require an expenditure of scarce resources to acquire. Sources that are accessible for downloading and uploading information are problematic for reasons often discussed by scientists in the US and Europe: reliability and peer review.

Internet publication by Kerala scientists is still extremely rare. Although it would seem to be an inexpensive means for the presentation of research results, such a venue is neither widely available nor beneficial professionally:

> Because Internet publication is not peer reviewed. The publications which are not reviewed have no value. We can publish articles in Internet. There are many sites for that. But it won't help us in any way. In the scientific world, publication in Internet has got limitations. The system of peer review for each article should be essential.

A scientist at a national agricultural research station was critical of sites that contained false or biased information that was detrimental to his research and mission:

> For example, many sites on coconut oil. They are biased ones. The oil palm lobby and soybean lobby are working against coconut. These lobbies are rich. They feed information such as ill-effects of coconut oil. We cannot compete with them as we do not have money or knowledge to start our business [working against this propaganda].

Biased information is not only a concern for professionals with a stake in certain commodities. As a university agronomist reports, Indian research is often inadequately represented:

> In most of the reviews of research on the Internet, the role of India is marginalized. [Foreigners] will project only their findings in most of the reviews . . . For instance on the Internet we will sometimes find some reviews on some specific topics such as multiple cropping, farming systems, etc. There are some sites from which we can get such information. If these reviews appear in journals, say foreign journals, there may be some bias in favour of their findings and research.

A researcher in veterinary science emphasizes that scientists must view the information received via the Internet with a critical eye:

> Adulteration is everywhere and so in this Internet also there can be such things. We cannot take everything for granted [from the Internet]. We

should also have our own perspective, ideas and then only we can be assured of the reliability of information on the Internet. We should not take everything on the Internet.

Finally, a forestry researcher is broadly critical of the changes that have occurred since the introduction of the Internet. His concern was not so much reliability as research practice, changes in habits of mind caused by the speed with which we become accustomed to receiving information. Will this affect the ability to do original work?

> Sometimes people may become lazy also. Earlier you know we were spending days in the library for references but now such reading is not there much. When you read books, although it may not have much information, you get lot of ideas, new ideas. We will think a lot. But when you use Internet, you will get lot of information very fast; but we will not spend time for thinking. We will improve our papers with the information you get from the Internet. But we will not think much and so you may not get more and more ideas. I think that is the difference. When you read something carefully you will get more ideas on the topic. But as you watch the television you get more information within a short period but your brain will not process it. This is what I feel.

In truth, the quotation above expresses no more than a prediction, but leads us to the third major perspective.

Teething troubles

As indicated in the "affliction" perspective, a pervasive theme in these materials is the extent of technical problems experienced in attempts to utilize communication technologies. Perhaps the most significant problem in the sociology of technology is the conditions under which a technology is defined as "working." A scientist who studies the biochemistry of aging described the state of connectivity in his department with a comment that summarized a variety of typical issues:

> We have a connection . . . but it is not working now for some reason. We are supposed to get this Ernet education research network. It is not working in full swing. Because of it downloading is very low. Very low download speed. So most often we won't use it other than for sending email. Now also there is some problem. Other than email, the browsers in the university are not working in good condition. The users have to

wait hours and hours. They will have to wait twenty to thirty minutes to open a site. It is not productive. So I use and depend on my personal connection.

What may not be immediately evident from such comments is that they are often not wholly negative, but imply a future in which the problems do not occur. This scientist uses a "personal" or home connection because his professional setting does not offer a comparable experience. A spice researcher reports that the problem of blocked phone lines now constituting a barrier to use will soon be resolved:

This connection I can use it. But of course, when I am using it this phone will not be free and so that problem is there. That is why we are going to get a leased line. Once leased line comes into effect this phone and all phones will be free.

Our informants were often quick to indicate their future expectations of the Internet, including its potential usefulness for collaboration:

Now I think the present facility is okay. I think if we are able to pursue on this line in future it will be a must for collaborative research rather than individualistic or institutional research projects. If we are having some collaborators outside it will be a faster way of communication and also for getting information from other institutions and scientists. I think these are the possible uses.

Such expectations represent possibilities, but not, for most, possibilities that have been realized. Some report a realization of falling behind the technological curve, as in this comment by a forestry professor, concerned with the limitations of the technology available in India:

When you are linked with Internet network to large number of people you know what is going on in some places and what they have encountered which you can avoid in your research. You can either avoid the pitfalls or take advantage of that situation . . . Many people are not knowing what others are doing and what is happening in Delhi or in other institutions. Now that problem, to a great extent, is over because of Internet. But most of the Indian information or Indian organizations are not, I think, in the forefront of this revolution. Even if we look at [our] web page this is true. It does not give the information one may require. I don't know if you have seen our website or not. Suppose a student will be visiting our site and would like to make an application to a programme, say field forestry. But how can he make an application? Is it possible through Internet? Unfortunately, it is not possible right now at our website. But, you know, these things are possible elsewhere (laughs). So we are still in that old age. That is my feeling.

Discussion

Interviews with Kerala scientists show high levels of awareness and increased levels of Internet use. Virtually all are conscious of the web as a vast storehouse of information and email as a rapid and efficient technology for communication with other scientists throughout the world. Many are eager to ensure their work does not duplicate that done elsewhere, keep up with cutting edge research, and perhaps publish their findings online as a means of participating in a global scientific community. A few have begun to address the issues of selectivity and credibility that accompany the transition from deficit to excess of information. Clearly, the Internet has begun to alter the way professionals in the educational and research institutions of south India reflect on their work.

Still, much of this story reflects sentiments of possibility rather than realized aspirations, a kind of teething trouble we have discussed as connectivity that is "merely theoretical" in the hard reality of the present. Such connectivity is still in the planning stage, established but non-working, a matter of high cost and low bandwidth that renders web browsing a curiosity or midnight obsession. But theoretical connectivity is something different from absence – it is an implied future in which these problems have been resolved, if only to the extent that they have been in the west.[13]

The summary perception of the Internet by Kerala scientists is best understood by comparison with their characteristic preoccuption with education and literacy. While it is not strictly true, "total literacy" is frequently claimed by Keralites, declared by state fiat in 1991 in the wake of a highly successful total literacy campaign led by the most prominent NGO in the state, the Kerala People's Science Movement (Kerala Sastra Sahitya Parishad, or KSSP). For professionals in Kerala, the Internet bears this constrast well. A marine scientist, asked what

---

13   As we write this, the server in the Department of Sociology at Louisiana State University has been down for several weeks, infected so badly with viruses that technical personnel have declared it unsalvageable.

motivated him to use the Internet, highlighted its importance as a basic skill:

> You get new . . . information. Interesting – and there is entertainment. Nowadays, lack of knowledge about Internet means something like a situation of lacking in education. Isn't it? It is almost like having literacy.

Such a judgment renders it close to a sociological inevitability that the Internet will diffuse throughout Kerala. The same social motivations that produced total literacy are likely to produce total connectivity, but questions of consequence remain. Total literacy has not solved the problems that have left Kerala an average Indian state in terms of economic well-being. It remains to be seen whether the Internet will do better.

References

Abbate, J. (1999). *Inventing the Internet*. Cambridge, MA: MIT Press.

Abels, E. G., Liebscher, P., and Denman, D. (1996). Factors that influence the use of electronic networks by science and engineering faculty at small institutions. *Journal of the American Society for Information Science*, 47, 146–58.

Adams, O. (2000). Falling through the net: defining the digital divide: a report on the telecommunications and information technology gap in america. *Journal of Government Information*, 27, 245–6.

Arunachalam, S. (1999). Information and knowledge in the age of electronic communication: a developing country perspective. *Journal of Information Science*, 25, 465–76.

Bhat, Mari P. N. and Rajan, S. I. (1990). Demographic transition in Kerala revisited. *Economic and Political Weekly*, 1–8, September, 1957–80.

Campion, P. and Shrum, W. (forthcoming). Gender and science in developing areas. *Science, Technology, and Human Values*.

Dedijer, S. (1963). Underdeveloped science in underdeveloped countries. *Minerva*, 2, 61–81.

De Roy, O. C. (1997). The African challenge: Internet, networking and connectivity activities in a developing environment. *Third World Quarterly*, 18, 883–98.

Engelhard, R. (1999a). *State of the art of the opportunities offered by new ICTS in the building of cooperation programmes in agricultural research for development*. European Forum on ARD. 7–8 April, Wageningen, The Netherlands.

Engelhard, R. (1999b). *Inter-networking for national agricultural systems in ACP countries: making the Internet work.* CTA (Technical Centre for Agricultural and Rural Cooperation ACP-EU).

EPW Research Foundation (1994). Social indicators of development for India-II: Inter-state disparities. *Economic and Political Weekly,* 29 (21 May), 1300–8.

Franke, R. W. and Chasin, B. H. (1994). *Kerala: radical reform as development in an Indian state.* Oakland, CA: Institute for Food and Development Policy.

Gaillard, J. (1991). *Scientists in the third world.* Lexington: University of Kentucky Press.

Gulati, I. S. (1995). Central funding agencies neglecting Kerala. *The Hindu,* 9 Oct.

Haythornthwaite, C. and Wellman, B. (1998). Work, friendship, and media use for information exchange in a networked organization. *Journal of the American Society for Information Science,* 49, 1101–14.

Heller, P. (1996). Social capital as product of class mobilization and state intervention: industrial workers in Kerala, India. *World Development,* 24, 1055–71.

Hindman, D. B. (2000). The rural–urban digital divide. *Journalism and Mass Communication Quarterly,* 77, 549–60.

Hurd, J. M. and Weller, A. C. (1997). From print to electronic: the adoption of information technology by American chemists. *Science and Technology Libraries,* 16, 147–70.

Iyer, S. R. and MacPherson, S. (2000). *Social development in Kerala: illusion or reality?* Aldershot: Ashgate.

Jeffrey, R. (1992). Politics, women, and well being: how Kerala became a model. London: Macmillan.

Jimba, S. W. and Atinmo, M. I. (2000). The influence of information technology access on agricultural research in Nigeria. *Internet Research: Electronic Networking Applications and Policy,* 10, 63–71.

Kannan, K. P. (1995). Declining incidence of rural poverty in Kerala. *Economic and Political Weekly,* 30 (14–21 October), 2651–62.

Mathew, E. T. (1995). Educated unemployment in Kerala: some socio-economic aspects. *Economic and Political Weekly,* 30 (11 Feb.), 325–35.

Parayil, G. (1996). The "Kerala Model" of development: development and sustainability in the third world. *Third World Quarterly,* 17, 941–57.

Parthasarathy, A. (2001). Between you and me. *The Hindu* (Thiruvananthapuram edn), 27 August, p. 5.

Robbin, A. (1995). SIPP access, an information system for complex data: a case study creating a collaboratory for the social sciences. *Internet Research: Electronic Networking Applications and Policy,* 5, 37–66.

Rogers, E. (1995). *Diffusion of innovations.* New York: Free Press.

Salam, A. (1966). The isolation of the scientist in developing countries. *Minerva,* 4, 461–5.

Saradamoni, K. (1994). Women, Kerala and some development issues. *Economic and Political Weekly,* 29 (26 Feb.), 501–9.

Schott, T. (1993). Science: its origin and the globalization of institutions and participation, *Science, Technology, and Human Values*, 18, 196–208.

Shrum, W. (1996). *Research for sustainable development: a study of scientific research capacity in Kenya, India, and Ghana*. The Hague, Netherlands: RAWOO. Ministry of Development Cooperation.

Shrum, W. and Campion, P. (2000). Are scientists in developing countries isolated? *Science, Technology, and Society*, 5(1), 1–34.

Sooryamoorthy, R. (1997). *Consumption to consumerism in the context of Kerala*. New Delhi: Classical Publishing Co.

UNDP (1999). New technologies and the global race for knowledge. *Human Development Report*. New York: Oxford University Press.

Walsh, J. and Bayma, T. (1996a). The virtual college: computer-mediated communication and scientific work. *The Information Society*, 12, 343–63.

Walsh, J. and Bayma, T. (1996b). Computer networks and scientific work. *Social Studies of Science*, 26, 661–703.

Walsh, J., Kucker, S., Maloney, N., and Gabay, S. (2000). Connecting minds: CMC and scientific work. *Journal of the American Society for Information Science*, 52(14), 1295–1305.

18

Social Support for Japanese Mothers Online and Offline

Kakuko Miyata

Abstract

This study explored how the receipt of social support through the Internet affected people's well-being, and how the Internet facilitated the provision of social support to friends and neighbors both on online and in "real life." In particular, it focused on the effects of childcare-related online communities on mothers' psychological well-being in Japan. The author conducted a longitudinal panel design study targeted on mothers who have preschool children and also exchange childcare information on the Internet. The appropriate participants were recruited from four electronic bulletin boards and forums to answer the questionnaires on the web site. In this paper, the data of 331 participants who answered both the first and the second surveys was analyzed. The results show the receipt of social support from weak ties via an online community promotes psychological well-being. In particular, mothers in the "posting group," who have posted a message in a supportive online community received more support from weak ties on the online community in addition to that from strong ties in real life, resulting in increased self-esteem and decreased depression than those in the "non-posting group," who has never posted any message. Moreover, those in the "posting group" were likely to provide social support to others in real life both short- and long-term because of a sense of generalized reciprocity. These findings suggest that active participation in online communities may supply "network social capital," that is, social relations that significantly provide companionship, emotional aid, goods and services, information, and a sense of belonging.

Author's Note

This chapter has profited from the advice and assistance of Barry Wellman. I thank him for having created stimulating milieux for thinking about cyber-society. Caroline Haythornthwaite made useful comments upon this paper and I appreciate her kindness. The research that underlies it has been conducted in association with my compatriots,

Professor Mitsuhiro Ura, University of Hiroshima, and Research Associate Koji Hasegawa, Hiroshima International University. It has been supported by the Telecommunications Advancement Foundation.

There is no consensus yet about the effects of the Internet on social involvement and personal well-being. Some survey research shows that Internet use, such as contact with neighbors, friends, and family by email and participation in online communities, affects people's exchange of social support (Dunham et al., 1998; Haythornthwaite and Wellman, 1998; King, 1994), their probability of having fulfilling personal relationships (Cole, 2000; Howard et al., 2001), their commitment to their communities (Wellman et al., 2001), and their psychological well-being (Kraut et al., 2002; LaRose et al., 2001; Mickelson, 1997; Turner et al., 2001; Wright, 2000). By contrast, different survey research suggests that the Internet pulls people away from other interactions inside and outside the household (Nie and Erbring, 2000).

Whether the Internet will have a positive or negative social impact may depend upon the nature of online activities (Wellman et al., 2001) and the quality of people's online relationships (Kraut et al., 2002). For instance, when the Internet engages people primarily in asocial activities such as web-surfing and reading the news, its immersiveness can turn people away from community, organizational and political involvement, and domestic life (Wellman et al., 2001). By contrast, use of email helps people build their social networks by extending and maintaining friends and family relationships (Howard et al., 2001).

I explore here how the acquiring of social support through the Internet affects people's well-being, and how the Internet facilitates the provision of social support to friends and neighbors, both on online and in "real life." In particular, I focus on the effects of childcare-related online communities on mothers' psychological well-being in Japan.

Why are Online Communities Important for Child-Raising Mothers?

Childcare networks in Japan

The boundaries of family systems are closed in Japan so that there is little involvement from outside the household. Due to traditional gender roles, mothers are likely to take a leading role in childcare (Watanabe, 1994). These circumstances sometimes cause mothers to be burdened and feel isolated during their child-raising years. Thus, childcare can be a stressor.

Mothers can reduce their stress and increase their well-being by receiving social support. Their well-being is highest when childcare networks outside the household are large, and the proportion of their kin and the density of their networks is neither too low nor too high (Matsuda, 2001). The larger a social network is, the more weak ties it contains, and weak ties with socially heterogeneous people provide more diverse information (Granovetter, 1973). On the other hand, the denser the network becomes, the more often members tend to communicate with each other and to grasp their needs for social support. When the network is densely knit, the members of the network tend to reach consensus on norms, and they exert consistent informal pressure on one another to conform to the norms and to keep in touch. Consequentially, a densely knit network may restrict members' freedom to obtain social support from outside the network (Bott, 1957). Hence, child-raising mothers with a large childcare network structure that is mixed in composition and with neither too low nor too high density will receive a variety of social support to increase their psychological well-being.

Supportive online communities

Online community on the Internet may provide enough social support to improve the well-being of mothers. Online environments can provide anonymous spaces where mothers can communicate. This anonymity protects members' privacy. The open type of community on the Internet affords access to anyone from anywhere at any time and lets them exit at will. In addition, the Internet supports interest groups that are composed of a massive and heterogeneous number of people with knowledge of certain topics. It is a cyber-place that is likely to provide useful information to solve a problem. It can also provide social and emotional support, companionship, advice, and information (Wellman and Gulia, 1999).

The proportion of Japanese homes owning computers or mobile phones that connect to the Internet has increased year over year. The penetration rate of the Internet reached 34 percent of households in 2002 in Japan. In particular, the percentage of women who use the Internet has increased since access via mobile phone first became possible in February 1999 (Ministry of Public Management, Home Affairs,

Posts and Telecommunications, Japan, 2001). Thus, online communities can become important for child-raising mothers to seek contact with others, and to obtain advice on child-rearing practices to help them cope with stress.

Four questions about social support via online communities

1   What kinds of mothers are receiving social support from online communities?

A survey of parents of disabled children by Mickelson (1997) demonstrated that parents accessing online supportive communities received less unsolicited support from their parents and casual friends than did mothers who participated in local health organizations. Mothers who posted messages on online supportive communities more often perceived more stress from experiencing their child's special needs, and less help from their husbands. In another study, cancer patients participated more within the online community when they perceived that the support received from online community was high and when the support received from one specific significant face-to-face partner in mind was low (Turner et al., 2001).

In light of these results, it can be supposed that mothers who receive a considerable amount of "Internet support" – defined as social support exchanged via online supportive communities – tend to receive less "real-life support" – defined as social support exchanged in their personal networks of the "real world," such as from family and friends. I hypothesize the following:

H1: Mothers who receive less real support are inclined to receive more Internet support.

2   Does receiving Internet support increase mothers' well-being?

A longitudinal study of Internet use, by Kraut et al. (2002) shows that users experienced overall positive effects from the Internet on the frequency of interpersonal communication, extent of community involvement, and personal well-being. In particular, extroverts who used the Internet more often reported increased psychological well-being. This included lower levels of loneliness, fewer negative effects, decreased time pressure, and increased self-esteem. Moreover, a study of college students found that the Internet led to less depression because of the support obtained through email exchanges with associates (LaRose et al., 2001).

Online interpersonal relationships bring diverse information to mothers who are seeking solutions, including suggestions about how to cope with problems. Mothers may also more easily find online someone who has similar worries or ideas about childcare. Therefore, it is predicted that a mother's well-being can be raised by gaining diverse social support from online community members sharing the same concerns, such as information on childcare, empathy with one's problems, encouragement, and consolation.

H2a: Mothers who receive more Internet support have higher psychological well-being than those who receive less Internet support.

Ikeda (1997) found that only the members of online communities who posted some messages could satisfactorily gain suitable information for their needs, because other members were likely to comment on or answer their messages. However, people did not obtain useful information when they simply read the discussion logs of online communities. Applying these findings to my study, I infer that mothers who post messages to an online community can receive appropriate Internet support. Thus, their well-being can be increased. On the other hand, mothers who do not post any message are unlikely to see benefits in their well-being. Wright (2000) also revealed that older adults' greater involvement with an online community was associated with lower perceived life stress.

H2b: Mothers who post a message are likely to gain more Internet support to increase their well-being than are those who do not post any messages.

3   Why are mothers motivated to provide childcare information and support in online communities?

One possibility is that the process of providing support and information on the Internet is a means of expressing one's identity, particularly if technical expertise or supportive behavior is perceived as an integral part of one's identity. Helping others can increase self-esteem, respect from others, and status attainment. We also know that workers will provide technical advice to an in-house community of practice because of norms of generalized reciprocity and organizational citizenship, rather than because of personal reasons such as being pleased to help others or a desire to achieve respect (Constant et al., 1997). An online community concerned with childcare is a self-help group in which norms of generalized reciprocity might be easily established. Mothers provide Internet support because of a sense of generalized reciprocity. As an online community is open for anyone to access and exit freely, the boundary between members and non-members is hard to draw. Mothers who strongly identify with a supportive online community should provide more support directly to others who have helped them in the past or to total strangers in the online community.

H3: Mothers who identify with an online community tend to provide more Internet support to other members of the online community.

4   *Are there correlations between the receipt and the provision of Internet support and real support?*

Miyata (2000) found that over 60 percent of participants in online communities shared information earned from the online community with family and friends in real life. Both strong ties (for example, with family, friends, and so on in real life) and weak ties (for example, with members of the online community) might affect behavior, psychological processes, and everyday life. Receiving Internet support may reduce one's coping in the long term, if receiving Internet support interferes with access to real-life sources of support. However, gaining Internet support may raise one's well-being, if it facilitates receiving real support. If Internet support assists in providing real support to family and friends, it may raise self-efficacy and thus increase self-esteem. Hence, this study explores the interactions between real support and Internet support, and it examines how one's well-being is affected by their interplay.

Method

Survey

To study these issues, I conducted a longitudinal panel design study of mothers who have preschool children and also exchange childcare information on the Internet. This research examines the causal relationship between people's use of the Internet, their exchange of social support, and some likely psychological consequences of exchanging social support. With longitudinal data, I can draw stronger causal conclusions than is possible in research in which the data are only collected once.

In January 2000, I recruited participants for my survey from four forums devoted to childcare and childhood education on Nifty: "Child-Rearing Forum," "Wife Network," "Forum for Working Mothers" and "Forum on Education." Nifty is Japan's biggest Internet provider and AOL-like portal, with about seven hundred forums on genres from hobbies to business. I chose these four forums because they had many participants and provided chat rooms, bulletin boards, and smaller electronic conference rooms for members of Nifty to exchange information and advice on child-raising (see table 18.1).

I posted announcements on these forums to recruit mothers with a preschool child or children to participate in my first survey after I had obtained permission from the forums' managers. I asked the mothers to answer the questionnaires on my web site. I got 416 responses to the first survey. Three months later, I conducted a second survey by sending emails to the original participants. I used almost the same questionnaires as in the first survey and received 331 responses. My investigation has been carried out by analyzing the information received from the 331 participants who answered both the first and the second surveys. Most (87 percent) came from the Child-Rearing Forum.

Sample

Participants ranged in age from 22 to 42 years old (mean = 32.6 years). Most 60.9 percent, were housewives, 21.2 percent were part-time workers, and 17.9 percent were full-time workers. As for educational background, 20.2 percent had finished junior high school or high school, 32.3 percent had finished technical school or two-year college, and 47.5 percent had finished four-year college or another form of higher education. Over half, 55.6 percent, had one child; 35.0 percent had two children; and 9.4 percent had more than three children. The mean number of children was 1.6 per household. Most of the participants' families were made up of husband, wife, and child(ren), with no parents or parents-in-law. Participants reported an average of 3.5 persons were available as babysitters. However, 11.2 percent of the

Table 18.1 The nature of online communities

Name	Purpose	Type of participants	Contents	No. of participants
Child-rearing forum	To discuss and exchange information on child rearing and consult about troubles mutually	Married persons, doctors and nurses who are interested in child-rearing	28 electronic conference rooms and information on childcare from the doctor who manages this forum	289 (87.3%)
Wife network	To exchange information on housekeeping, cooking, childcare and problems of housewives	Housewives and house husbands	15 electronic conference rooms, a chat room, a bulletin board, and information on housekeeping, cooking, and childcare	7 (2.1%)
Forum for working mothers	To discuss problems of working mothers, such as a return to work after a delivery, child rearing, and education	Working mothers	18 electronic conference rooms, a chat room, a bulletin board and a mail magazine	34 (10.3%)
Forum on education	To discuss educational practice	Teachers and persons interested in early childhood education	37 electronic conference rooms and web pages of information on education	1 (0.3%)
Total				331 (100%)

participants claimed to not have any relatives, neighbors or friends to baby-sit their child(ren) – even for half a day.

Results

How different is Internet support from real support?

To explore how participants exchange social support, I examined the amount of social support reported in the past three months at Time 1 (the first survey) and at Time 2 (the second survey).

(a) Receipt of real support was measured by asking how often the mothers gained three types of social support regarding childcare from family, neighbors and friends:

1 The receipt of informational support was measured by asking "How often do you receive the following three types of information?": information about child illness, physical development and training; useful information to come into contact with many people or to know social issues; and information on babysitter and day-nurseries.

2 The receipt of emotional support was the sum of two questions; "How often are you encouraged or gain the empathy of others about childcare trouble?" and "How often do you learn that there is someone else who has similar troubles and worries?"

3 The receipt of instrumental support was measured by "How often do you babysit?" Each question was reported on a 4 point scale: 1 = "not at all", 2 = "seldom", 3 = "often" and 4 = "usually." The score for the amount of received real support was calculated by summing up these six items. Scores range from 6 to 24.

(b) Provision of real support was measured by asking questions about the frequency of providing informational, emotional, and instrumental support to family, neighbors, and friends. I used the same six items as those measuring the receipt of real support. The score on amount of real support provided was calculated by summing these six items.

(c) Receipt of Internet support was measured by asking how often the mothers receive informational support (three items) and emotional support (two items) from the online supportive community from where they were recruited. I used the same items as those measuring the receipt of real support, except I excluded instrumental support because it is rarely provided online. The score on amount of received Internet support was calculated by summing these five items. Scores range from 5 to 20.

(d) Provision of Internet support was measured by asking how often the mothers provide informational support (three items) and emotional support (two items) to the online community. I used the same five items as those measuring the receipt of Internet support.

Table 18.2 shows that the amount of receipt of informational and emotional support through the Internet (M = 14.93, SD = 2.68) exceeds the amount of receipt of the support from friends and family in real life (M = 12.58, SD = 3.19) at Time 1 (t = −11.43, p < 0.01). Participants were likely to receive more social support from online community members than from friends and neighbors at Time 1. To take a closer look at each item of Internet support, mothers were likely to receive the most social support when they learned "I was not the only one who was worried about childcare" on the online community. Also, they felt they received social support when online community members encouraged them. Thus, they tended to receive more support, especially emotional support, from online community members than from friends. This is congruent with their accessing online communities with the expectation of finding someone who also has similar worries about childcare.

At Time 2, however, there is no significant difference between the receipt of information and emotional support in real life and the receipt of such support in the online community. The receipt of Internet support declined from Time 1 to Time 2, although the receipt of real support did not change during this period. The receipt of real support may be more stable than the receipt of Internet support because mothers in need may seek Internet support in addition to receiving real support.

Mothers tended to provide more informational and emotional support to their friends and neighbors than to other community members. The amount of informational and emotional support provided via the Internet (Time 1: mean = 7.58, standard deviation (SD) = 3.43; Time 2: mean = 6.89, SD = 2.93) is less than the amount of support provided from friends in real life (Time 1: mean = 12.36, SD = 3.02; Time 2: mean = 12.38, SD = 2.87) at both Time 1 and Time 2 (Time 1: t = 20.63, p < 0.01; Time 2: t = 26.34, p < 0.01). Mothers provided the most Internet support when they were encouraging other mothers in their online community who had childcare trouble.

Table 18.2 Means of amount of social support received and provided

Contents of social support	Time 1						Time 2					
	Receipt		t-test	Provision		t-test	Receipt		t-test	Provision		t-test
	Real	Internet		Real	Internet		Real	Internet		Real	Internet	
Informational support												
1 Receipt/provision of information about childhood illness, physical development, and training	2.76	3.44	−12.22**	2.74	1.58	18.74**	2.75	2.95	−3.72**	2.67	1.39	24.49**
2 Receipt/provision of information about coming into contact with many people or to know social issues	2.45	2.74	−4.83**	2.23	1.44	14.54**	2.40	2.40	n.s.	2.24	1.35	16.52**
3 Receipt/provision of information about babysitter and day-nursery	1.63	2.01	−6.32**	1.68	1.23	9.12**	1.70	1.66	n.s.	1.79	1.15	12.36**

Emotional support												
4 Receipt/provision of encouragement and empathy about childcare troubles	2.88	3.22	−5.29**	2.92	1.69	18.53**	2.87	2.70	2.77**	2.93	1.52	24.30**
5 Learning/teaching that there is someone else who has similar troubles and worries	2.86	3.52	−12.39**	2.79	1.49	20.99**	2.86	3.15	−5.14**	2.77	1.49	21.68**
Instrumental support												
6 Receipt/provision of babysitting	2.57			1.67			2.51			1.69		
Mean of the sum of items 1 through 5	12.58	14.93	−11.43**	12.36	7.58	20.63**	12.58	12.86	n.s.	12.38	6.89	26.34**
Mean of the sum of items 1 through 6	15.15	14.03		15.10	14.07							

** $p < 0.01$. Higher scores indicate more received/provided social support. Items 1 through 3 measured informational support. Items 4 and 5 measured emotional support. Item 6 measured instrumental support.

Table 18.2 also shows that the receipt of Internet support exceeds the provision of Internet support at Time 1 (t = 18.67, p < 0.01) and Time 2 (t = 15.28, p < 0.01). These results suggest mothers are more likely to access online communities to get informational and emotional support than to provide such support to other members. The provision of Internet support was more stable than the receipt of Internet support over time. Some mothers who participate in the online community may frequently provide Internet support to other members.

Who receives Internet support?

Who receives social support in an online community? Do mothers with more real support also gain more Internet support or those with less real support?

To examine hypothesis 1, I conducted a stepwise multiple regression analysis by setting the amount of received Internet support at Time 2 as the dependent variable. I used seven independent variables at Time 1:

(a) Amount of received Internet support at Time 1: the sum of received informational and emotional support from the online community at Time 1.

(b) Amount of received real support: the sum of received informational, emotional, and instrumental support in real life at Time 1.

(c) "Childcare stressors caused by child's health." This scale was measured by six items on a 4-point scale, asking, for example, "How often do your children not eat/drink properly?" The score was calculated by summing up these responses, and ranged from 6 to 24. See the appendix for this and other scales.

(d) "Childcare stressors caused by restraining mothers' behavior." This scale was measured by six items on a 4-point scale, for example asking "How often do you experience not having time for yourself?" The scores on this scale ranged from 6 to 24.

(e) Frequency of access to the online community. This is measured on a 6-point scale by asking how often they accessed the online community from where they were recruited to this survey.

(f) Identification with the online community. This is measured on a 4-point scale by asking the degree to which they agree with the statement: "I recognize my being a member of the online community."

Table 18.3 Multiple regression analysis predicting amount of Internet support received at time 2

Predictor variables	β	t
Amount of receipt of Internet support at time 1	0.309***	5.80
Amount of receipt of real support at time 1	0.155**	2.92
Childcare stressors caused by restraining mothers' behavior at time 1	0.187**	3.59
Frequency of access to the online community at time 1	0.146**	2.88
Perception of diversity of the online community at time 1	0.127*	2.47

*** $p < 0.001$; ** $p < 0.01$; * $p < 0.05$. $R^2 = 0.231$; adjusted $R^2 = 0.219$.

(g) Perception of diversity of the online community. This is measured by asking on a 4-point scale the degree to which they agree with the statement: "The online community comprises members with a wide diversity of ideas and thoughts so that there are a variety of comments." Results are shown in table 18.3. Mothers receive more Internet support at Time 2 when they:

1 receive more Internet support at Time 1;
2 perceive a higher level of the diversity in their online community;
3 have stronger feelings that childcare restrains them;
4 receive more real support;
5 frequently access their online community.

It was not that mothers who received less real support received more Internet support. Rather, mothers who received real support also tended to receive Internet support. Thus, Hypothesis 1 was not supported. In other words, mothers who have existing social support got more social support from using the Internet. This is a manifestation of the Matthew effect (Merton, 1968).

This result is inconsistent with earlier studies of mothers with disabled children (Mickelson, 1997) or cancer patients (Turner et al., 2001). Such mothers may have difficulty finding people who have a similar stressor in their real life, so they turn to the Internet for support. The mothers I studied can rather easily find other mothers who have similar stressors regarding childcare in real life. Hence, they can receive more support from their friends than mothers with disabled children or cancer patients. However, they may find more suitable information for their needs and seek more adequate encouragement from online community members than from friends.

Mothers who perceive diversity in the online community receive more Internet support. Online communities often have many weak ties that are formed by a network of acquaintances that reaches beyond local groups and brings information from the outer world (Wellman, 1997). The social networks work as pools of heterogeneous information sources that are sometimes useful and influential for decision-making, job changes, and so on. Weak ties also increase the probability of finding someone who has similar interests or worries (Granovetter, 1973). Taking these phenomena into account, it can be conjectured that mothers expect to get more advice and information or to find more people with childcare troubles from heterogeneous sources such as the online communities than from homogeneous sources such as their friends and family. Thus, they turn to online communities for support.

Mothers with stronger "childcare stressors caused by restraining mothers' behavior" receive more social support from online communities. However, the degree of "childcare stressors by child's health" is not related to the receipt of Internet support. Such mothers may gain enough information and advice for their child's health from relatives and childcare experts (such as medical doctors, public health nurses) to suppress "childcare stressors caused by your child's health." On the other hand, "childcare stressors caused by restraining mothers' behavior" varies from mother to mother. Moreover, these are sometimes regarded as mothers' self-indulgences. Hence, social support to deal with "childcare stressors caused by restraining mothers' behavior" might be difficult to receive in real life. Given these circumstances, mothers may seek social support from the online community. In sum, mothers with strong "childcare stressors caused by restraining mothers' behavior" are likely to receive more social support from the weak ties of these online communities as well as receiving social support from strong ties in real life.

*How does the receipt of Internet support affect depression
and self-esteem?*

Does receiving Internet support increase mothers' well-being? Some studies have shown that the receipt of social support was correlated with depression and self-esteem (for example, Cohen and Wills, 1985).

Table 18.4 Means and standard deviations of the depression and self-esteem scales by "posting group" and "non-posting group"

Depression	Time 1	Time 2
All participants (n = 331)	15.97 (4.87)	15.57 (4.69)
"non-posting group" (n = 172)	16.39 (5.17)	15.80 (4.85)
"posting group" (n = 159)	15.52 (4.50)	15.33 (4.52)
t (df = 329)	1.63	0.90
p <	0.11	n.s.
Self-esteem		
All participants (n = 331)	7.13 (1.58)	7.25 (1.59)
"non-posting group" (n = 172)	6.96 (1.68)	7.19 (1.67)
"posting group" (n = 159)	7.31 (1.45)	7.31 (1.50)
t (df = 329)	2.02	0.73
p <	0.05	n.s.

Lower scores on depression scale indicate lower depression. Lower scores on self-esteem scale indicate lower self-esteem.

Depression and self-esteem were used as indicators of how the receipt of social support affects the mothers' well-being. As shown in appendix 18.1, depression was measured using ten items of the Todai Health Index (Suzuki and Roberts, 1991). Each item was scored as 1 = Rarely, 2 = Occasionally, 3 = Most. The scores on each item were summarized into a scale, ranging from 10 to 30, with lower scores indicating lower depression. Self-esteem was measured by asking two statements from the Rosenberg self-esteem scale (1965). (1) "I feel that I have a number of good qualities." (2) "All in all, I am inclined to feel that I am a failure." Both were on a 5-point scale; 1 = Strongly agree, 2 = Agree, 3 = Neutral, 4 = Disagree, 5 = Strongly disagree. The sum of reversed score of statement (1) and score of statement (2) was used as an indicator of self-esteem. This scale score ranges from 2 to 10, and a higher score indicates higher self-esteem.

I divided the participants into two groups: the "posting group" and the "non-posting group." The "posting group" refers to the participants who had posted at least one message on the online community during the past three months at Time 1. They are considered to be more involved with the online community than the "non-posting group."

Table 18.4 shows that the "non-posting group" has stronger depression and lower self-esteem than the "posting group" at Time 1. However, there was no significant difference at Time 2 in the level of

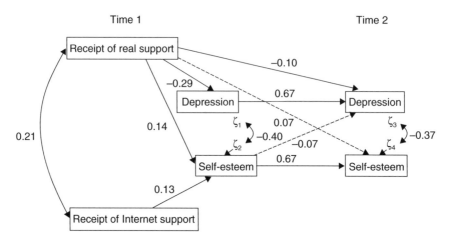

Figure 18.1 Structural equation model of correlation between the receipt of support and well-being (all participants)
Source: Solid lines illustrate statistical significance ($p < 0.05$). Broken lines indicate a significant tendency ($p < 0.1$). Unconnected variables are not significantly related

depression and self-esteem between the "posting group" and the "non-posting group." The "non-posting group" reduced depression and increased self-esteem over time. Is it because mothers in the "non-posting group" might have received enough real support at Time 2 to increase psychological well-being?

Structural equation modeling (Bollen, 1989) was conducted to examine how the receipt of real support and Internet support at Time 1 affects depression and self-esteem at Time 1 and Time 2. Figure 18.1 shows, for all participants, that receiving real support at Time 1 reduced depression and raised self-esteem at Time 1 and at Time 2. Mothers who received more real support showed greater well-being in the short and long term. On the other hand, although the receipt of Internet support at Time 1 increased self-esteem at Time 1, it did not have a direct and significant effect on self-esteem and depression at Time 2. However, Figure 18.1 also shows that receiving Internet support at Time 1 may indirectly raise self-esteem and reduce depression at Time 2 by mediating the rise of self-esteem at Time 1. Thus, H2a was partially supported.

Figure 18.2 presents the analysis of the "non-posting group." The receipt of real support by the "non-posting" mothers has some effects on reducing depression and raising self-esteem at Time 1 and also has

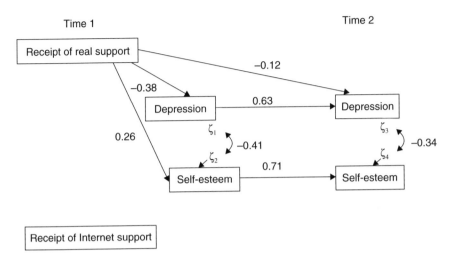

Figure 18.2   Structural equation model of correlation between receiving support and well-being ("non-posting" group)
Source: Solid lines illustrate statistical significance (p < 0.05). Unconnected variables are not significantly related

a direct effect on reducing depression at Time 2. However, there is no effect of received Internet support on well-being in the short and the long term. This implies that in the "non-posting group" the effects of received real support on psychological well-being is stronger than the effects of received Internet support.

In the "posting group," the receipt of Internet support at Time 1 correlates negatively with depression and positively with self-esteem at Time 1. By mediating the rise of self-esteem and the reduction of depression at Time 1, receiving Internet support appears to reduce depression and raise self-esteem at Time 2 (see figure 18.3). These results show that mothers who receive more Internet support demonstrate more well-being than those who receive less Internet support, but only when they communicate with the online community. Hence, H2b was confirmed. This is probably because the "posting group" can receive more diverse social support by actively exchanging communication in the online community. These activities are associated with the rise of self-esteem and the reduction of depression. Moreover, the data reveal that the receipt of real support at Time 1 reduces depression at Time 1 and raises self-esteem in the long run.

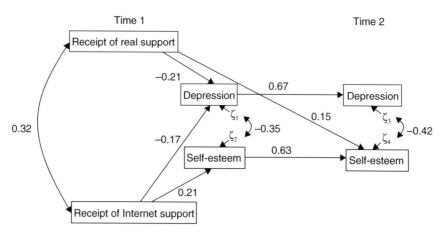

Figure 18.3 Structural equation model of correlation between receiving support and well-being ("posting-group")
Source: Solid lines illustrate statistical significance ($p < 0.05$). Unconnected variables are not significantly related

Motivation to provide Internet support

Who was motivated to provide childcare information and support in online communities? To explicate the factors that determine Internet support provision, a stepwise multiple regression analysis was performed. The amount of provided Internet support at Time 2 was set up as the dependent variable. I used five independent variables at Time 1:

(a) Amount of provision of Internet support at Time 1.
(b) Amount of provision of real support.
(c) Frequency of posting a message to the online community on a 7-point scale: 1 = not at all, 2 = rarely, 3 = monthly, 4 = a few times a month, 5 = weekly, 6 = a few times a week, 7 = daily.
(d) Identification with the online community.
(e) Perception of the online community's diversity.

Table 18.5 shows a tendency to provide Internet support at Time 2 when the participants provide a lot of Internet support at Time 1. When mothers frequently post on the online community, and have a stronger identification with the online community at Time 1, they

Table 18.5 Multiple regression analysis predicting amount of provision of Internet support at time 2

Predictor variables	β	t
Provision of Internet support at time 1	0.374***	5.44
Frequency of posting at the online community at time 1	0.281***	4.07
Identification to the online community at time 1	0.095*	2.09

*** $p < 0.001$; * $p < 0.05$. $R^2 = 0.446$; adjusted $R^2 = 0.441$.

provide more Internet support at Time 2. This indicates that the participants who provide Internet support ordinarily post messages on the online community and have a stronger identification with the online community. Therefore, H3 is supported.

This study also examines the psychological motivation for mothers to provide childcare information and support to the online community. Kollock (1999) demonstrates a list of possible motivations for providing support to online communities. One possible motivation is anticipated "generalized reciprocity" (Sahlins, 1965). Mothers are motivated to contribute valuable information to the online community in the expectation that they will receive useful help and information in return. A second possible motivation is the effect of contributions on reputations. High-quality information, impressive technical details in one's answers, a willingness to help others, and elegant writing can all work to increase one's prestige in the community. A third possible motivation is a sense of efficacy, that is, the mothers' feeling that they have some effect on this environment. A fourth is the attachment or commitment mothers can have to the online community.

I measured providers' motivation by asking them to select one reason why they gave Internet support to other members, from the nine items listed on table 18.6. Table 18.6 shows the means of providing Internet support by motivation at Time 1 and Time 2. The providers of Internet support who answered, "someone on the online community helped me before, and I wanted to help someone in turn," provided a mean of 11.19 Internet support at Time 1 and 10.92 at Time 2 (on a 6–24 scale). About one-fifth of the providers gave Internet support because they thought sharing information benefited them too. Their scores were 11.25 at Time 1 and 9.35 at Time 2. Over 10 percent of the providers did so because of an attachment for their online community.

Table 18.6 Means of amount of Internet support provided by motivation

Why did you provide social support to other members?	Time 1 Amount of Internet support provided				Time 2 Amount of Internet support provided			
	N	%	M	SD	N	%	M	SD
I want to increase my prestige in the community to present my knowledge and information about childcare to others	0	0.00	—	—	0	0.00	—	—
I feel attached to my online community	17	12.41	10.24	2.84	13	10.83	10.62	1.85
I am pleased to help others	5	3.65	10.80	3.56	8	6.67	8.13	1.96
I am pleased to solve problems	9	6.57	10.78	1.72	9	7.50	8.56	2.24
I would like to receive respect	1	0.70	14.00	—	0	0.00	—	—
Sharing information benefits me too	24	17.52	11.25	2.35	26	21.67	9.35	2.19
My duty is to help other members	1	0.70	13.00	—	1	0.83	7.00	—
Someone on the online community helped me before, and I wanted to help someone in turn	73	53.28	11.19	2.78	52	43.33	10.92	2.58
I expect that others will help me in turn if I help others	3	2.19	11.33	2.08	6	5.00	9.33	1.97
Other reasons	4	2.91	7.25	2.63	5	4.17	11.60	5.03
Total	137	100.00	10.96	2.71	120	100.00	10.10	2.62

These results show that most of the participants who provide social support to the members of the online community are motivated by an anticipated generalized reciprocity. The amount of Internet support provided by those motivated by an anticipated generalized reciprocity is larger than the support provided by those who are motivated by personal reasons, such as pleasure in helping others. This suggests that supportive online communities, such as the childcare networks studied here, may promote norms of generalized reciprocity and facilitate supportive exchanges.

Does the receipt of Internet support facilitate the provision of real support?

As described above, receiving Internet support and real support each leads to increased psychological well-being. It is essential to investigate the association of the receipt and the provision of real support and Internet support to understand the long-term effects of the two on psychological well-being. I used a longitudinal design to analyze the association of real support and Internet support.

The result of structural equation modeling indicates that participants who receive more Internet support at Time 1 receive more real support and also provide more real support at Time 1 (see figure 18.4). There is also a significant relation between the receipt of Internet support at Time 1, and the receipt and the provision of real support at Time 2. This implies that the receipt of Internet support promotes the provision of real support, and it does not interfere with the receipt of real support in both the short and the long term.

In the "non-posting group," participants who receive more Internet support at Time 1 receive more real support and provide more real support at Time 2 (figure 18.5). However, the receipt of Internet support is not related to the receipt and provision of real support during the same time period (Time 1). This demonstrates that in the "non-posting group," the effect of receiving Internet support takes a while to influence the practice of receiving and providing real support.

By contrast, in the "posting group," there is a significant positive correlation between the receipt of Internet support at Time 1 and the provision of real support only at Time 1 and Time 2. However, the receipt of Internet support was related to the receipt of real support at Time 1 (figure 18.6). This means that in the short term, mothers can

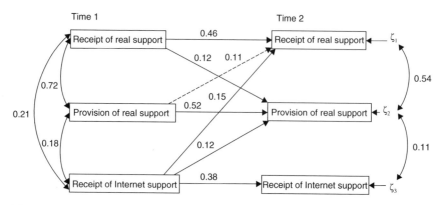

Figure 18.4 Structural equation model of correlation between receipt and provision of social support at time 1 and time 2 (all participants)
Source: Solid lines illustrate statistical significance (p < 0.05). Broken lines indicate a significant tendency (p < 0.1)

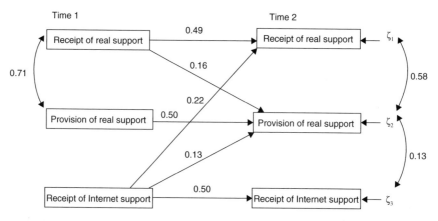

Figure 18.5 Structural equation model of correlation between receipt and provision of social support at time 1 and time 2 ("non-posting group")
Source: Solid lines illustrate statistical significance (p < 0.05). Unconnected variables are not significantly related

acquire diverse sources of support by increasing communication in the online community without hindering the exchange of support in their real lives. Perhaps they may stop receiving real support in the long-term, because they have received enough support via the online community.

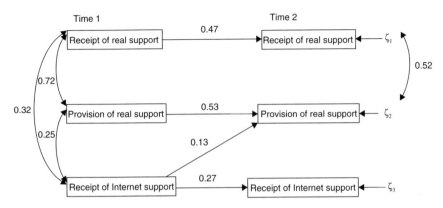

Figure 18.6 Structural equation model of correlation between receipt and provision of social support at time 1 and time 2 ("posting group")
Source: Solid lines illustrate statistical significance ($p < 0.05$). Unconnected variables are not significantly related

Discussion

This study has shown that mothers with high "childcare stressors caused by restraining mothers' behavior" accessed childcare-related online communities to find information to suit their needs and to seek encouragement from weak ties. They do this more when they perceive the online community to be diverse. The more mothers already obtain social support from their strong ties, the more they seek social support from weak ties. These findings imply that Internet support supplements existing real support rather than displaces it for child-raising mothers. This is probably because weak ties in online communities serve as information bridges across clusters of strong ties and can offer people access to resources that are not found in their strong tie relationships.

Second, weak ties on the online community help to maintain and promote psychological well-being. However, these weak ties supported by computer networks are likely to be more limited than friendships supported by physical proximity. Kraut et al. (1998) indicate that when people first go online, they are less likely than friends established at school, work, church, or in the neighborhood to be available for help with tangible favors, such as offering small loans, rides, or babysitting. Moreover, because online community members are not embedded in the same day-to-day environment, they are less likely to understand the context for conversations, thereby rendering the need for support less explicable.

However, mothers who are likely to post messages in the online community tend to acquire more Internet support and possess higher self-esteem and lower depression. When mothers express their worries about childcare, ask questions, and seek help from other members of the childcare-related online community, other participants can recognize them and try to provide information and advice.

LaRose et al. (2001) suggest that stressful interactions with the Internet itself, rather than inadequate interaction with other people through the Internet, may lead to depression. He further suggests that a sense of self-efficacy can reverse the effect of the stress. Mothers who communicate actively may have achieved the necessary degree of self-efficacy to cope with the new sources of stress that the Internet introduced into their lives. Thus, they may reduce depression and increase self-esteem by receiving Internet support. They may learn how to obtain social support through the Internet and build confidence in their ability to acquire Internet support.

Hence, mothers who contribute to the online communities can receive considerable information and advice from the more diverse resources of weak ties. They can select the most useful information and advice to fulfill their needs or resolve their troubles, and they are better able to cope with their distress and increase their well-being.

Third, mothers who provide Internet support strongly identify with the online community, perhaps because they perceive the existence of norms of generalized reciprocity and group citizenship (see also Quan-Haase and Wellman, this volume). Those online communities that have norms of generalized reciprocity or group citizenship are relatively few in comparison to the thousands of online communities that are focused on professional advice, hobbies, and entertainment. However, the childcare-related online communities I studied are formed specifically to provide support. Hence, they may have more access to the communities and provide social support to other members according to the norm of generalized reciprocity.

Fourth, the receipt of Internet support is associated with the receipt and provision of real support in both the short and the long term. This suggests that one can acquire diverse sources of support by increasing communication with an online community without ruining the exchange of support in one's real life. Some observers (Rheingold, 1993; Wellman and Gulia, 1999) have reported that individuals who regularly offer advice and information receive more help more quickly when they ask for something on online communities. This study suggests mothers who receive Internet support are also likely to provide real support in both the short and the long term. Participants in those online communities that have a norm of generalized reciprocity may facilitate provision of social support not only online but also in real life, due to the anticipation of future reciprocity.

Conclusions

As the Internet becomes more commonplace in the lives of mothers, it is important to understand the mechanisms of its impact on their lives. This study is an attempt to shed light on how the receipt and provision of social support through the Internet affects the lives of child-raising mothers. My findings show that receiving social support from weak ties via an online community increases psychological well-being. At the same time, receiving support from strong ties in real life in the short and the long term, similarly increases psychological well-being. Moreover, gaining social support through the Internet promotes the receipt and provision of social support in real life, in both the short and the long term.

Taken together, these findings suggest that participation in online communities supplies "network capital," a form of "social capital." Network capital means relations with friends, neighbors, relatives, and workmates that significantly provide companionship, emotional aid, goods and services, information, and a sense of belonging (Wellman and Frank, 2001). We have seen that those who have more "real" support receive more Internet support. Thus the receipt of support happens synergistically online and offline. It may also be the case that a gregarious personality is involved, with certain types of people "knowing" how to attract support in multiple milieux, offline and online. In the future, more detailed studies should focus on the way in which people spend their time both online and offline is related to the supply of "network capital."

Appendix 18.1   Scales used in the Study

I   Childcare stressors caused by child's health and behavior

The six-item scale was measured by asking how often participants experienced the following stressors on a 4-point scale (1 = "not at all", 2 = "seldom", 3 = "often" and 4 = "usually"): "Children do not listen to parents," "Children lose their temper," "I do not know how to bring up my children," "Children do not eat/drink properly," "Children tend to be sick," "Children are not healthy enough." Cronbach's Alpha = 0.667 at Time 1. Cronbach's Alpha = 0.689 at Time 2.

Children stressors caused by restraining mothers' behavior

This scale was measured by asking how often participants experience these stressors on a 4-point scale: "I do not have my own time," "My husband does not cooperate with childcare," "I am in a circle of my children and myself, and have no contact outside the circle," "I do not have anyone to babysit my children," "I am doing routine work every-day," and "I feel irritated about myself for not enjoying rearing my children": Cronbach's Alpha = 0.776 at Time 1. Cronbach's Alpha = 0.785 at Time 2.

The Todai Health Index: depression scale

The scale was measured by ten questions: Each question was reported on a 3-point scale: 1 = Often, 2 = Sometimes, 3 = Hardly ever or never. The questions were: "Do you feel blue?", "Do you feel that your life is hopeless?", "Do you lose interest in things you usually enjoy?", "Do you feel lonely even when you attend a meeting or are in a group?", "Do you feel lonely?", "Do you sometimes feel like not seeing other people?", "Do you feel inferior?", "Are you depressed?", "Do you feel as if your life is going badly?", "Have you had less confidence lately?": Cronbach's Alpha = 0.894 at Time 1, Cronbach's Alpha = 0.897 at Time 2.

References

Bollen, K. A. (1989). *Structural equations with latent variables.* New York: John Wiley and Sons.

Bott, E. (1957). *Family and social network: role norms, and external relationships in ordinary urban families.* London: Tavistock.

Cohen, S. and Wills, T. A. (1985). Stress, social support, and the buffering hypothesis. *Psychological Bulletin, 98,* 310–57.

Cole, J. (2000). *Surveying the digital future.* Los Angeles, CA: UCLA Center for Communication Policy.

Constant, D., Sproull, L., and Kiesler, S. (1997). The kindness of strangers: on the usefulness of electronic weak ties for technical advice. In S. Kiesler (ed.), *Culture of the Internet.* Mahwah, NJ: Lawrence Erlbaum.

Dunham, P., Hurshman, A., and Litwin E. (1998). Computer-mediated social support: single young mothers as a model system. *American Journal of Community Psychology*, 26, 281–306.

Granovetter, M. (1973). The strength of weak ties. *American Journal of Sociology*, 78, 1360–80.

Haythornthwaite, C. and Wellman, B. (1998). Work, friendship and media use for information exchange in a networked organization. *Journal of the American Society for Information Science*, 49(12), 1101–14.

Howard, P. E. N., Rainie, L., and Jones, S. (2001). Days and nights on the Internet: the impact of a diffusing technology. *American Behavioral Scientist*, 45(3), 383–403.

Ikeda, K. (ed.). (1997). *Networking communities.* Tokyo: University of Tokyo Press (in Japanese).

King, S. (1994). Analysis of electronic support groups for recovering addicts. *Interpersonal Computing and Technology*, 2(3), 47–56. Available: http://www.helsinki.fi/science/optek/1994/n3/king.txt

Kollock, P. (1999). The economies of online cooperation: gifts and public goods in cyberspace. In M. Smith and P. Kollock (eds), *Communities in cyberspace* (pp. 220–39). London: Routledge.

Kraut, R., Patterson, M., Lundmark, V., Kiesler, S., Mukhopadhyay, T., and Scherlis, W. (1998). Internet paradox: a social technology that reduces social involvement and psychological well-being? *American Psychologist*, 53(9), 1017–31.

Kraut, R., Kiesler, S., Boneva, B., Cummings, J., Helgeson, V., and Crawford, A. (2002). Internet paradox revisited. *Journal of Social Issues*, 58(1), 49–74.

LaRose, R., Eastin, M. S., and Gregg, J. (2001). Reformulating the Internet paradox: social cognitive explanations of Internet use and depression. *Journal of Online Behavior*, 1(2). Available: http://www.behavior.net/JOB/vln2/paradox.html

Matsuda, S. (2001). Childcare networks and the well-being of mothers. *Japanese Sociological Review*, 52(1), 133–49 (in Japanese).

Merton, R. (1968). The Matthew effect in science: the reward and communication systems of science are considered. *Science*, 159(3,810), 56–63.

Mickelson, K. D. (1997). Seeking social support: Parents in electronic support groups. In S. Kiesler (ed.), (2001). *Culture of the Internet* (pp. 158–78). Mahwah, NJ: Lawrence Erlbaum.

Ministry of Public Management, Home Affairs, Posts and Telecommunications, Japan. *Information and communications in Japan: the accelerating IT revolution.* http://www.joho.soumu.go.jp/eng/Resources/WhitePaper/ WP2001/2001-index.html

Miyata, K. (2000). Communication processes between consumers through the Internet. In K. Takemura (ed.), *Social Psychology of consumer behavior* (pp. 80–94). Kyoto, Japan: Kitaouji Shobo (in Japanese).

Nie, N. H. and Erbring, L. (2000). *Internet and society: a preliminary report.* Stanford, CA: Stanford Institute for the Quantitative Study of Society. http://www.stanford.edu/groups/siqss/

Rheingold, H. (1993). *The virtual community: homesteading on the electronic frontier.* Reading, MA: Addison-Wesley.

Rosenberg, M. (1965). *Society and the adolescent self-image.* Princeton, NJ: Princeton University Press.

Sahlins, M. (1965). On the sociology of primitive exchange. In M. Banton (ed.), *The relevance of models for social anthropology* (pp. 139–236). London: Tavistock.

Suzuki, S. and Roberts, R. E. (eds) (1991). *Methods and applications in mental health surveys: the Todai Health Index.* Tokyo: University of Tokyo Press.

Turner, J. W., Grube, J. A., and Meyers, J. (2001). Developing an optimal match within online communities: an exploration of CMC support communities and traditional support. *Journal of Communication,* 51, 231–51.

Watanabe, H. (1994). A sociological analysis of parent and child relations in the present day: an introduction to social theory of childcare. In the Social Development Research Institute (ed.), *Contemporary family and social security: marriage, childbirth and childcare* (pp. 71–88). Tokyo, Japan: University of Tokyo Press (in Japanese).

Wellman, B. (1997). An electronic group is virtually a social network. In S. Kiesler (ed.), *Culture of the Internet* (pp. 179–205). Mahwah, NJ: Lawrence Erlbaum.

Wellman, B. and Frank, K. (2001). Network capital in a multi-level world: getting support from personal communities. In N. Lin, R. Burt, and K. Cook (eds.), *Social capital: theory and research* (pp. 233–73). Hawthorne, NY: Aldine de Gruyter.

Wellman, B. and Gulia, M. (1999). Net surfers don't ride alone. In B. Wellman (ed.), *Networks in the global village* (pp. 331–66). Boulder, CO: Westview.

Wellman, B., Quan Haase, A., Witte, J., and Hampton, K. (2001). Does the Internet increase, decrease, or supplement social capital? Social networks, participation, and community commitment. *American Behavioral Scientist,* 45(3), 436–55.

Wright, K. (2000). Computer-mediated social support, older adults and coping. *Journal of Communication,* 50, 100–18.

19

Experience and Trust in Online Shopping

Robert J. Lunn and Michael W. Suman

Abstract

A key aspect of everyday life is consumer behavior. The Internet is increasingly being used as a tool for purchasing goods and services. In this chapter we focus on the factors influencing online shopping. We examine the role of a wide variety of variables organized around 14 conceptual themes. Using data from the 2001 UCLA Internet study, we analyze the relative importance of these different components in predicting Internet shopping frequency and dollar amounts spent. The results suggest the importance of experience as a major factor in predicting both amount and frequency of Internet shopping. Experience is conceptualized as a complex multi-dimensional construct consisting of indirect and direct components. These different components interact with the purchase process in different ways. We also discuss the advantages of a sequential modeling approach when attempting to understand predictors of amount and frequency of Internet purchases. Comparisons with other research findings are discussed. We conclude with a discussion of the importance of experience and trust as predictors of net shopping and suggest the implications of our findings for future research.

Introduction

The Internet is having a serious impact on the world's economy. Former US President Clinton asserted that one-third of all new economic growth that occurred during the eight years of his presidency was attributable to high-tech, with the Internet being a key component (Emeagwali, 2000). The value of e-commerce transactions is still small relative to the size of the American economy, and after a period of remarkable growth, the rate of expansion slowed considerably. However, even many traditionalists admit that the Internet's role in our consumer culture will continue to grow.

Beyond the dollar amount of e-commerce transactions, even more significant are the ways in which businesses and consumer activities are being changed. New business models are being created in an effort to lower business costs, improve customer service, and increase productivity and profitability (US Department of Commerce, 1999).

Both Internet-based companies and some traditional producers of goods and services are transforming their ways of conducting business. And as for the customers, they can now shop 24 hours a day, 365 days a year. They are buying computer hardware, software, books, CDs, airline tickets, flowers, automobiles, and a host of other products. They are making hotel reservations, trading securities, checking their 401 K accounts, and conducting a wide variety of other business transactions.

Consumer behavior is one key aspect of everyday life affected by the Internet and that is what we investigate in this chapter. In particular, we examine the factors influencing online purchasing behavior. Do consumers shop on the Internet because they perceive the prices there to be lower than in brick-and-mortar establishments? Do they turn to the net to meet their shopping needs because of convenience, as a way to save time in their busy lives? As Internet experience grows, do consumers buy more products and services using the Internet? Does experience with other means of remote shopping, such as phone and mail purchasing, predispose the consumer to buy online? Are Internet users deterred from online purchasing by their concerns over the security and privacy of their personal and credit card information? Do they opt out because of inferior customer service or because they would miss the social aspect of the shopping experience that they get at the local mall? Are people put off because it is difficult to assess the quality of products or the accuracy of online product descriptions? To what extent do demographic variables predict whether one will be an Internet shopper or not? Do the young shop more than the old, women more than men, the well-off more than those who are less so? Are those with faster Internet connections more likely to buy online than those with slower telephone modem connections?

Previous research

To date there has not been much empirical research on predictors of online buying behavior. There has been conceptual work on factors influencing online shopping (Alba, Lynch, Weitz, Janiszewski, Lutz, Sawyer, and Wood, 1997; Palmer, 1997). And there have been efforts to classify different types of online shopper (BMRB International, 1999; Harris Interactive, 2000). Lohse, Bellman, and Johnson (1999, 2000) have identified predictors of online buying behavior using panel data from the Wharton Virtual Test Market survey. Based on their first survey panel (WVTM1), Lohse et al. reported that people who spent more money in e-commerce had a more "wired lifestyle," were on the net more hours per week, and received more email than other Internet users. In their second study conducted one year later (Lohse et al., 2000, using WVTM2), they associated net purchasing with less concern about online privacy, more years of online experience, more email messages received per day, more purchasing from catalogs, being male, and more frequent use of the net to search for product information, travel information, financial information, current events information, and news. They identified certain variables that, though they did not predict whether one shopped online, did influence how much one spent there. These factors positively associated with online spending included income, likelihood of downloading software, number of hours worked per week, and hours per week online.

Swaminathan, Lepkowska-White, and Rao (2000) have investigated factors influencing electronic exchange using secondary data based on an email survey. They found that perceived vendor reliability, convenience of placing orders and contacting vendors, price competitiveness, and access to information had a positive influence on the number of online purchases, but did not influence the amount of money spent on the Internet. Their results showed that among females social interaction served as a shopping motivation, and that loss of social interaction deterred female consumers from frequent online shopping. Consumers who valued convenience tended to use the Internet to purchase more frequently, and they seemed to spend more money in their electronic transactions. These researchers conducted a stepwise regression to assess the relative contribution of their different independent variables. The results indicated, with both frequency of shopping and amount spent online as dependent variables, that customer characteristics, such as convenience as a shopping motive, dominated all other variables in terms of variance explained. One problem with this approach is that stepwise regression results are notorious with respect to replication problems.

Data

After a review of the literature, we selected a wide range of variables that have been implicated in predicting purchase frequency and purchase amounts on the Internet.

The source of our data is the 2001 UCLA Internet Study. In this study interviews were conducted with 2,006 households throughout the 50 states and the District of Columbia.

Sample

This was the second year of an American longitudinal dynamic panel study. Out of 2,096 people in the original panel, 1,274 answered the second year's survey. For both the original sample drawn last year and the replacement sample selected this year a national Random Digit Dial (RDD) telephone sample using an Equal Probability Selection Method (EPSEM) was used. This sampling methodology gives every telephone number in the 50 states and the District of Columbia an equal chance of being selected. In the initial call an interviewer spoke to a person in the household 18 years of age or older to obtain a roster of all household members. At this point, a computer system ("CFMC Servent" CATI) randomly selected one individual from among those 12 years of age and over in the household to be the interviewee from that household. If the randomly selected individual was between 12 and 17 years of age, the interviewer asked a parent or guardian for permission to interview the child. In the initial contact, once the selection of a household member was made, only that individual was eligible to complete the interview. Eight call attempts were made to complete an interview. If a household refused twice, it was not contacted again. In re-contacting panel members from the original sample up to 16 call attempts were made to reach them. The same household member who participated the previous year was interviewed again. The only condition in which a new household member was accepted was if the one interviewed the previous year was no longer a member of the household. Those participating in the survey for the second year were paid a monetary incentive. Interviews were conducted in English and Spanish. Interviewing took place between May and July 2001.

After the data were collected they were compared to census data to ensure that the sample was representative in terms of geographic distribution, race, age, sex, family composition, education, and household income. The sample was very close on all demographic categories except for minor discrepancies on education, gender, and race. To correct for this the data were weighted by these three factors. Sample size was preserved during the weighting process. Since some of the questions were only asked of adults, the analytical sample consisted of only adult Internet users (18 years of age or older). The analytical sample size was 1,173.[1]

Analysis

Overview of the data analysis section

The data analysis consisted of three phases: data conditioning, data transformation, and data modeling. Data conditioning was performed to remove extreme values and handle missing data. Data transformation in this circumstance refers to the principal components transformation of the set of potential regression predictor, that is, independent, variables to statistical independence. The data modeling phase involved two multivariate data analytic techniques: regression and discriminant analysis. Regression analysis provides information on what variables are reliable with respect to predicting the dependent variables of interest, that is, average purchase amount and average purchase frequency, and how important each reliable variable is in terms of predictive ability. It also provides information on the quality, that is, how well they predict, of the predictive equations. Discriminant analysis is a statistical classification procedure. Our usage of discriminant analysis in this study was confined to how well the reliable variables found in our regression analysis could predict respondents who purchase versus those who don't purchase on the Internet. The following sections describe each of the data analysis phases in more detail.

Data conditioning

The variables selected for inclusion in the analysis were examined for outliers. The presence of outliers was small. The outlier values

1 For more information on the survey and to see the questionnaire used in the study go to UCLA Center for Communication Policy's website at http://ccp.ucla.edu

were winsorized (outlier values brought in to two standard deviations from the mean). The proportion of missing data was also small. Missing data were replaced with random imputation around each variable's modal value. Missing data were not imputed for the dependent variables (dollar amount of Internet purchases and frequency of Internet purchase). If data were missing for the dependent variables, the case was dropped. The proportion of cases with missing data on the dependent variables was less than 3 percent. No pattern signifying that cases with missing data were different than cases with data was apparent.

Controlling for redundancy and conceptual confounding

The primary purpose of the research effort was the development of predictive models to help identify characteristics associated with Internet purchase behavior. Specifically, we wanted to understand what factors predict purchase frequency, and what factors predict purchase amount. One complication faced by all model builders concerns the issue of multicollinearity. Multicollinearity refers to the presence of correlations among a set of predictor variables. The presence of multicollinearity causes interpretative difficulties with respect to the size, stability, and computational accuracy of a regression model's predicative weights. There are several approaches to handling multicollinearity. We chose to apply a principal components transformation to the set of predictor variables. The following provides a brief introduction to the concept of principal components analysis.

A principal components analysis determines how a set of variables are interrelated, that is, correlated, and then demonstrates how the correlated variables could be combined into a smaller number of statistically independent "factors" that represent most of the information in the original set of variables.

A brief example will clarify the underlying concept. In our situation, people who rate themselves as highly experienced Internet users spend more time connected to the Internet, send and receive more email, and have been using the Internet more years than people who rate themselves as inexperienced Internet users. Since all these concepts are inter-correlated, we can substantially simplify our analytical task, and remove multicollinearity, by combining items that are correlated into one unified information theme. So, in our example, we can combine the four different "experience-oriented" variables into one underlying informational theme, or factor, called "Internet experience." Thus, a principal components analysis combines similar informational items by removing redundancy.

A second benefit associated with a principal components analysis is the removal of certain types of conceptual confounding. A good example of this concerns the pattern of associations between predictor variables like income, online experience, and age with a dependent variable such as average purchase amount. Income, online experience, and age are each individually correlated with average purchase amount. An interpretative confound can occur because income, online experience, and age also exhibit a pattern of correlations with each other. However, the nature of those correlations is not sufficient to consider them as measuring a unified informational theme. In this situation, the principal components analysis recognizes there are three different underlying informational themes, that is, income, online experience, and age, and transforms them to separate, statistically independent factors. Statistical independence means the resultant factors are not inter-correlated.

The end result is a set of predictor variables, that is, factors that have no correlation with each other.

Data modeling

Regression analyses were performed in two stages. The first stage was used to identify significant predictor variables. The second stage removed the non-significant predictor variables from the resultant predictive equations. This allows for a better estimate of the explanatory power of the regression equations. The predictor variables were orthogonalized factors. Because the predictor variables were orthogonal, that is, zero correlated, there was no multicollinearity present. This means the variance figures are strictly additive for higher-level conceptual interpretations.

A discriminant analysis was used to determine the ability of the significant predictor variables in the regression analysis to predict membership in groups representing the zero/one state for our dependent variables. The zero/one state for purchase amount and purchase frequency indicated those who purchased on the Internet and those who did not.[2]

Results

In this section we provide information on the results of the principal components analysis and statistical details concerning how well our different informational themes predicted online purchase frequency (model 1) and online purchase amount (model 2).

Indication of a variable's predictive strength

In a regression analysis some of the predictor variables are better predictors than others. A regression analysis provides "weights" that allow us to assess the *relative* predictive strength for each variable. One of these weights is called a "beta" weight. You would normally see a table of these weights when describing regression results.

However, one of the bonuses involved with using a principal components analysis is that the predictor variables have been transformed to independence. That substantially simplifies our reporting task. When you are dealing with independent predictor variables the sum of the squared beta weights is exactly equal to R^2.

Our results are presented in the regression table, table 19.1, which shows the percent of predicted variation in each model attributable to each of the significant predictor variables. For example, when predicting purchase amount (model 2), the average amount you spend per year making mail and phone purchases, excluding Internet purchases, accounts for 56.83 percent of all the accounted for variation in the dependent variable, that is, average amount of online purchases. With these independent predictor variables we have obtained the *absolute* predictive strength for each significant predictor variable.

---

2 The discriminant analysis classification results were obtained using a 50 percent random hold out sample. This allowed us to obtain an unbiased estimate of the classification accuracy for each set of variables. We ran the discriminant analyses to obtain classification accuracy figures to compare with the results of Lohse et al. (1999, 2000). Lohse et al.'s models demonstrated that it was possible to achieve a high degree of classification accuracy when attempting to distinguish those who purchase from those who do not purchase on the Internet.

Informational themes

The following 14 informational themes were identified by our principal components analysis: perception of the Internet, Internet experience, privacy/security concerns, negative consequences of shopping on the Internet, perceived availability of goods and services on the Internet, connection speed, age, increased likelihood of buying brand names, perceived price advantage of shopping on the Internet, structural Internet shopping difficulties, income, shop on Internet / buy elsewhere, previous purchase by mail and phone, gender.

The following describes each of the identified informational themes. We also include a brief overview of how similar informational themes have been found to predict average purchase amount and average purchase frequency in past research.

1   *Perception of the Internet*

This component includes one's evaluation of the Internet overall, perceived ease of finding information on Internet, perceived amount of relevant information available on Internet, how much of the information on Internet one believes is reliable and accurate, and the extent to which one believes that using the Internet saves time. These variables involve the extent to which one has positive perceptions of and experiences with the Internet. These types of positive feelings might be tied to higher levels of online buying.

Some of these concepts have been previously explored. For example, there is evidence suggesting the importance of perceived reliability of an exchange partner on purchase behavior (Morgan and Hunt, 1994; Luedi, 1997). Swaminathan et al. (2000) also connect online purchasing frequency with vendor reliability. And Moorman, Deshpande, and Zaltman (1993) relate the concept of vendor reliability with trust. We expect trust-oriented perceptions to positively correlate with Internet purchasing behaviors.

2   *Internet experience*

This component includes self-rated ability to use the Internet, total hours of Internet connect time per week, use of email, and number of months of Internet experience. There is evidence that these experience variables are associated with Internet purchase amounts and frequency (Lohse et al., 1999, 2000). Experience with an activity is often tied to increased levels of that and related activities. We would expect these variables to positively correlate with Internet purchasing variables.

3 Privacy/security concerns

This component includes concern about the privacy of personal information when purchasing on the Internet, concern about the security of one's credit card when purchasing on the Internet, concern that new technology will lead to loss of personal privacy, and the perception that people who go online put privacy at risk. Some research suggests that consumers are not very concerned about privacy (Milne and Gordon, 1993). Other studies suggest that they are (Bloom, Milne, and Adler, 1994; Rohm and Milne, 1999). There is also evidence that perceived lack of security is a major deterrent to online purchasing (Zellweger, 1997).

The concept of trust is obviously directly related to these concerns. Many facets of the issues of security, privacy, and trust have been extensively reviewed (Camp, 2000; Cranor, 1999; Feldman, 2000; Fox, 2000; Friedman and Kahn, 2000; Gefen, 2000; Grossman, 2000; Lohse, Bellman, and Johnson, 2000; Minahan, 1997; Olson and Olson, 2000; Sabo, 1997; Salnoske, 1998; Schoder and Yin, 2000; Sklar, 2001; Urban and Sultan, 2000; Wachter, 1999). According to Swaminathan et al. (2000) online consumers are only marginally less concerned about the security of electronic exchanges than non-consumers. But they argue that online consumers are more concerned about some aspects of information privacy. For example, consumers who purchased more on the Internet seem to be more favorable about the creation of laws protecting privacy on the Internet. And they state that another dimension of privacy, that is, consumers' beliefs that marketers want information about them for marketing purposes, has a marginally negative effect on the amount of money spent on the Internet. Despite some discrepancies in previous research, we would expect these variables to be somewhat negatively correlated with the net purchasing variables.

4 Negative consequences of shopping on the Internet

This component includes being uncomfortable with the lack of face-to-face contact when ordering on the Internet, stated concern that one would miss the company of fellow shoppers when buying online, perceived difficulty in assessing product quality and accuracy of product descriptions, perceived difficulty in returning or exchanging goods ordered on Internet, and the inverse of an intention to make many more purchases online. Some of these factors deal with the concept of convenience. There is evidence that perceived convenience is an important factor encouraging remote (from the home) shopping (Gehrt, Yale, and Lawson, 1996; Gillet, 1976; Reynolds, 1974). In addition, Swaminathan et al. (2000) provide evidence that convenience is powerfully associated with purchase amount and frequency. Research also suggests that the Internet is less attractive to consumers who value the social aspect of shopping (Alba et al., 1997). This finding was confirmed by Swaminathan et al. (2000).

One factor, the negative aspects of Internet shopping, includes a mix of two concepts: convenience and the loss of social interaction. The perceived inability of consumers to assess product quality and accuracy of product descriptions, and difficulties in returning or exchanging goods and services ordered on the Internet are inverse aspects of shopping convenience. The discomfort with lack of face-to-face contact and missing the company of fellow shoppers involve the loss of social interactions in the shopping and transaction process. As these are by their nature structural problems with shopping online, we would expect these variables to negatively correlate with the net purchasing variables.

5   Perceived availability of goods and services on the Internet

Those who perceive a ready availability of goods and services on the Internet are probably more likely to buy them. Therefore, we would expect this variable to positively correlate with the Internet purchasing variables.

6   Connection speed

The faster one's connection the easier it is to use the Internet, and by extension, the easier it is to buy online. This relates to the previously discussed concept of convenience. We would expect high-speed connection to positively correlate with the net purchasing variables.

7   Age

Some studies suggest that demographic variables influence Internet usage patterns (Hoffman, Kalsbeek, and Novak, 1999; UCLA, 2000).

Others relate demographic variables more specifically to shopping motivations and behaviors (Bellenger and Kargaonkar, 1980). Since younger elements of the population are more likely to be on the Internet, we would expect this segment to purchase more frequently online. However, older people have more money than younger people, and people with more money might be expected to spend more online and purchase more frequently. It is difficult to provide a uniform prediction of the net effect of age.

8 Increased likelihood of buying brand name products while shopping on the Internet as opposed to in brick-and-mortar stores

This speaks to a certain level of fear and lack of trust with online vendors. Since the consumer does not know if he or she can trust the online vendor, he or she turns to something that has proved to be historically reliable in their experience, and substitutes brand reliability for vendor trust. We would expect this variable to be correlated with net purchasing variables, although we would expect its role to be a negative one. If you fear something, it is a negative factor. It could be said that people buy brand names on the Internet because they are less expensive on the Internet. We would argue that one of the hallmarks of strong branding is pricing consistency. Many brand name manufacturers do not allow sale pricing of their merchandise because sale pricing detracts from the premium status of the brand.

9 Perceived price advantage to shopping on the Internet

There is evidence that the Internet supplies information that makes price comparison possible and that this information is likely to increase purchases (Zellweger, 1997). Swaminathan et al. (2000) have demonstrated a relationship between price competitiveness and online purchase frequency. We would expect this variable to positively correlate with the net purchasing variables.

10 Structural Internet shopping difficulties

This factor includes the stated position that if sales tax were charged one would probably buy less on the Internet and the belief that shipping charges for online products are too high. The first statement is a negative form of price influence for Internet transactions. The second statement is another negative aspect of Internet price influence, shipping charges. Factors 9 and 10 appear to measure similar concepts of price sensitivity. However, factor 9 is more of an overall impression of price on the Internet versus price elsewhere while factor 10 is more structurally oriented. Factor 10 involves underlying processes which might account for why overall costs on the Internet could be higher than elsewhere. We would expect these variables to negatively correlate with the net purchasing variables.

11   Income

Higher income levels are typically correlated with higher levels of buying and we would expect the same association here.

12   Shop on Internet/buy elsewhere

This factor measures whether a person seeks information about products and services on the Internet and then makes the purchase transaction in a local store. This is a strategy that relegates Internet sites to a mostly information provision status. Since beginning Internet users mostly use the Internet in an information-seeking fashion (UCLA, 2000; UCLA, 2001) we would expect a higher frequency of novice Internet users to adopt this strategy. Since Internet experience is likely to be positively associated with Internet purchase behavior, we would expect this variable to be negatively correlated with the online purchasing variables.

13   Previous purchase by mail and phone

These older forms of from-home shopping may serve as precursors to Internet shopping. This may occur through the experience of establishing a level of comfort and trust with a remote vendor. There is evidence associating online buying with catalog purchasing (Lohse et al., 2000). We would expect buying from mail and phone to be positively correlated with buying online.

14   Gender

Some studies have examined the effect of gender on the process and outcomes of the use of the Internet (Wachter, 1999). Swaminathan et al. (2000) give evidence that males are less motivated than females by social interaction as a shopping motive and are more convenience-oriented, both of which are associated with increased Internet shopping. Lohse et al. (2000) have also linked being male with increased online buying. We would expect being male to be positively correlated with buying online.

Description of the predictive models

In this section we provide a technical overview of the regression and discriminant analysis procedures. Model 1 describes the results when we are attempting to predict online purchase frequency. Model 2 describes the results when attempting to predict average online purchase amount. The explanatory power for both models is similar.

In the first regression model (model 1) we are trying to predict results for the following question: "During a typical year, how many times do you purchase products or services over the Internet? Do not include payments for your Internet connection." Ten of our 14 informational themes were significant predictors of online purchase frequency. Overall the model predicted 26.3 percent of the total variation in average yearly number of times purchased on the Internet ($F(10,1162) = 34.4$, $p < 0.000$). The shrunken R^2 was 25.50 percent.

In the second regression model we are trying to predict average purchase amount. The actual question was "During a typical year, how much do you spend ordering products or services over the Internet? Please do not include any money that you paid to access the Internet." Seven of our 14 informational themes were significant predictors of average purchase amount. Overall this model predicted 23.9 percent of the total variation in the average yearly amount the Internet user purchased on the Internet ($F(7,1165) = 36.5$, $p < 0.000$). The shrunken R^2 was 23.3 percent.

Table 19.1 provides an overview of the predictive results across both models. The second column of table 19.1 provides the percent importance in terms of predicting average online purchase frequency by the different variables. Variables that do not appear in column one were not reliable predictors. Predictive importance figures in parentheses indicate a negative association. For example, high scores on the factor "negative consequences of shopping on the Internet" reduces average online purchase frequency (see column two, row three). The third column ranks the importance of each significant predictor in terms of predicting average online purchase frequency (the table is sorted by model 1 results). The fourth and fifth columns show the results for

Table 19.1   Overview of predictive models

Factor name	Model 1 (purchase frequency) % Importance	Model 1 rank importance	Model 2 ($ amount) % Importance	Model 2 rank importance
Purchase mail/phone	41.59	1	56.83	1
Negative consequences of shopping Internet	(24.78)	2	(11.40)	3
Income	7.69	3	7.21	4
Internet access experience	6.32	4	2.02	7
Privacy/security concerns	(5.77)	5	(3.49)	5
High-speed Internet/home	5.54	6	15.71	2
More likely buy brand products on Internet	4.23	7	NS	—
Availability of good and services	1.45	8	NS	—
Gender (male)	1.32	9	3.34	6
Internet prices lower	1.31	10	NS	—

model 2. The table was designed to facilitate comparisons of differences across the two models.

Classification accuracy

The purpose of the discriminant analyses was to determine how well our reliable predictors variables from each model, models 1 and 2, could classify people who purchase from people who don't purchase on the Internet. This test was performed so classification accuracy could be compared with results from other researchers (Lohse et al. 1999, 2000). The two discriminant analyses were run using a random hold out sample (50 percent). This is done so that resultant classification accuracy is based on a set of randomly selected data (50 percent of the sample) that were *not* used to construct the classification equations. This removes a known source of bias from the classification results. The classification accuracy for the variables used in the regression model for Internet purchase frequency was 77 percent. The classification accuracy for the variables used in the regression model for Internet purchase amount was 73.7 percent.

These tell us that the set of significant predictor variables for each model can accurately determine respondents who purchase on the Internet from respondents who don't purchase on the Internet with an accuracy of 77.0 and 73.7 percent respectively.

Interpretation of Results

The results of the two models predicting different measures of Internet purchasing are relatively similar. This is not surprising since the correlation between dollar amount of purchases and frequency of purchases on the Internet is 0.59 (p < 0.000). Thus, some degree of similarity in the results of the two models is to be expected. Both models provide similar levels of predictive power. Model 1 accounts for 25.5 percent of the total variation in purchase frequency, and model 2 accounts for 23.3 percent of the total variation in purchase amount.

Experience and trust

The most important predictor of Internet annual purchase amounts and frequency of purchases is the amount of money an individual spends by mail or phone.

Previous research has demonstrated that another type of experience, that is, experience with the Internet itself, has a strong association with Internet purchase frequency and Internet purchase amount (Lohse et al., 1999, 2000; UCLA, 2000, 2001).

These findings imply that the degree of experience with non-Internet, remote shopping modalities, that is, a form of indirect experience, might substitute for direct Internet experience, that is, years of Internet experience and/or average connect time. Previous research has indicated a relatively long latency period between an individual's first usage of the Internet and his/her first Internet purchase (UCLA, 2000, 2001). If purchase experience by catalog or phone substitutes for

Internet experience, we would expect a shorter time period (that is, a shorter latency period) between an individual's first Internet access and his/her first Internet purchase for those who have phone or mail purchasing experience. This is exactly the pattern of results observed. Adult Internet users who shop by catalog or phone, on average, take 18.1 months before they make their first Internet purchase. Adult Internet users who do not shop by catalog or phone take 25.0 months. This is a reliable difference ($t = 3.10$, $p < 0.001$).

One measure of Internet experience is the individual's average connect time per week. If non-Internet remote shopping substitutes for Internet experience, then we should find lower average connect times for individuals who purchase on the Internet with alternative remote shopping experience versus individuals who purchase on the Internet with no alternative remote shopping experience. Once again, this is the pattern of results observed. Adult Internet users who do not shop by catalog or phone but do shop on the Internet have an average weekly connect time of 13.7 hours. Adult Internet users who do shop by catalog or phone and shop on the Internet have an average weekly connect time of 10.9 hours. This is a reliable difference ($t = 2.03$, $p < 0.04$).

The concepts of trust and experience are often found to be strongly associated (Gefen, 2000). In a way, trust in the retail environment is built through repeated successful transactions. In the absence of actual experience with a retailer, vendor reputation, brand reputation, or word of mouth serve as surrogates for actual experience. We now know that experience with a similar shopping modality also substitutes for experience. Without experience, the first purchase that someone makes on the Internet represents a leap of faith. The larger the dollar amount of that first purchase, the greater the risk. The greater the risk, the greater the leap of faith. Reduction of perceived risk levels has been identified as a key antecedent to relationship commitment in general (Sheth and Parvatiyar, 1995) and consumer behavior in particular (Bauer, 1960). Although we don't specifically measure a "trust" factor, the concept of trust is very likely strongly associated with how often and how much one buys in any purchasing experience.

The presence of a high-speed Internet connection in the home is another factor that is strongly influenced by experience. Only 6.7 percent of users with less than one year of connection experience have high-speed access (i.e., cable modem, DSL, ISDN, T1/T3). High-speed access is present for 13.2 percent of individuals with two to less than four years of experience, and 22.5 percent of individuals with five or more years of experience. The UCLA studies have also demonstrated that the ways in which the Internet is used change as a function of Internet experience. Those newly online primarily use the Internet in chat rooms, for general browsing, and for games and entertainment. More experienced Internet users use the Internet more for work, checking their finances, trading stocks, and shopping (UCLA, 2000, 2001). As people gain experience, they learn how to use the Internet to address and satisfy more practically oriented needs and concerns. And correspondingly, as the Internet becomes more useful, an individual is more likely to commit to a high-speed connection.

We therefore argue that at least three of the factors in our models appear to represent different aspects of a multi-dimensional construct of trust/experience. Since the different factors are independent, their predictive contributions are additive. Using this interpretive approach, trust/experience related factors account for 74.56 percent of the predicted variation in dollar amount of purchases. This compares with only 53.45 percent predictive power in model 1 where we are predicting purchase frequency. Thus, trust and experience factors account for greater predictive power when we are modeling purchase dollar amount as opposed to purchase frequency.

Major barriers to Internet shopping

The predictive power of negative consequences of shopping on the Internet are substantially stronger when we are predicting purchase frequency (24.78 percent), as opposed to when predicting purchase amount (11.40 percent). Negative consequences of shopping on the Internet include variables such as being uncomfortable with the lack of face-to-face contact when ordering on the Internet, perceived difficulty in assessing product quality and accuracy of product descriptions, and perceived difficulty in returning or exchanging goods ordered on the Internet.

The higher predictive power for frequency of purchases suggests an underlying cumulative effect. The more times you purchase, the more likely something is going to go wrong. Or the more times you purchase, the higher the cumulative shipping charges. And the more times you purchase, the higher the likelihood of having to return merchandise, and the greater the hassle involved.

Income: the more you make, the more you spend

Both models suggest that individuals with higher incomes tend to purchase more frequently and spend more money on the Internet. This finding adds face validity to the results since most retail studies demonstrate that higher incomes are associated with more purchases.

Income and age are confounded to some degree. The principal components analysis statistically transformed income and age into distinct factors. Thus, while these two variables may be naturally interrelated, after the principal components analysis, they are transformed to statistical independence. The advantages of this approach are clear in the resultant modeling efforts. The portion of variation due to age alone was not a reliable predictor of online buying behavior, while the proportion of variation due to income was.

These results suggest that any univariate association, that is, correlation, of age with online buying behavior is either spurious or represents an indirect or mediated effect. In other words, just because you are young does not mean you buy more goods and services online. By splitting income from age, we can see that it is most likely that income, and not age, is directly associated with buying behavior.

Privacy and security

Privacy and security concerns appear in both models, but their effects are relatively small. Privacy and security concerns are measured in this study on a five-point scale ranging from "extremely concerned" to "not at all concerned." Let us first look at Internet users with mail or phone shopping experience. For members of this group who have also purchased on the Internet, the mean score on concern for the security of their credit card information on the Internet is 2.74. The mean score on this measure for Internet users with no Internet purchase is 3.40. Among individuals who have made a mail or phone purchase, the Internet purchasers have reliably lower levels of concern than individuals who have not purchased on the Internet (t = 10.5, p < 0.000).

Among Internet users with Internet shopping experience but no mail or phone shopping experience, the average rating on concern about the security of their credit card information on the Internet is 2.56. For those who have made no remote purchases (mail, phone, or

Internet) the mean score is 3.31. Once again, Internet users who have made an Internet purchase express reliably lower levels of concern than individuals who have not made an Internet purchase ($t = 7.24$, $p < 0.000$).

This same pattern of results extends to concerns about the privacy of personal information. The average ratings of privacy concern among mail and phone shoppers purchasing on the Internet and not purchasing on the Internet are 2.69 and 3.23 respectively ($t = 8.75$, $p < 0.000$). The average ratings of privacy concern among non-mail and phone shoppers purchasing on the Internet and not purchasing on the Internet are 2.59 and 3.12 respectively ($t = 5.10$, $p < 0.000$).

We controlled these mean comparisons by mail and phone shopping experience to demonstrate an important finding. While previous shopping experience using mail or phone shopping modalities appears to substitute for Internet experience when considering impact on purchase frequency and amount, this effect does not extend to security and privacy concerns. These concerns appear to be mostly related to the Internet shopping modality itself.

The role of brand, product availability, price

The Internet purchase frequency model (model 1) includes three factors that do not appear in the Internet dollar amount purchase model (model 2). In modeling frequency of Internet purchases, more frequent purchases are accompanied by a higher likelihood to purchase brand-name products on the Internet, a greater perceived availability of goods and services on the Internet, and a greater perceived price advantage to shopping on the Internet.

The likelihood of those with mail and/or phone experience who are Internet shoppers to buy brand name products is higher than the likelihood of remote shoppers who only purchase through mail and/or phone. The mean score for those who purchase on the Internet is 2.93, and for those who do not the mean is 2.58 ($t = 3.67$, $p < 0.000$). This same pattern is not replicated among people without mail and phone purchase experience. In this case, the mean score for individuals who purchase on the Internet on the same statement is 2.69, while for those who do not purchase on the Internet the mean is 2.51 ($t = 1.15$, NS (not significant)). Apparently experiences drawn from mail and phone purchases predisposes one to buy brand name products. Thus, remote shopping experiences have "taught" the customer that buying brand names somehow reduces the inherent risk associated with not touching and feeling the goods.

The finding that perceived price advantage is not an important predictor of Internet purchasing behaviors might seem puzzling given the attention paid to price by many e-retailers. Examining perceived lower prices by our familiar mail/phone/Internet groupings revealed no reliable differences by any combination of these variables. Perceived price advantage does not predict purchase amounts, and is only a minor predictor for Internet purchase frequency. This finding could reflect a cost versus convenience trade-off, or Internet sites could be claiming lower prices on an item-by-item basis, but when shipping charges are added to the bottom line, prices may be seen as equivalent. Alternatively, selection and customer service often substitute for low price. In any event, price is not a major predictor of Internet purchasing behavior, and Internet sites that concentrate on trying to convince consumers that they have lower prices than local retail stores are likely to encounter a good deal of skepticism. This is particularly true when dealing with traditional (brick-and-mortar, mail and phone) retail operations that also have an online presence. If vendors selling through traditional retail operations were to offer lower prices for their online shopping outlets, they would undercut their own traditional retail outlets.

The availability of goods and services is a minor predictor of purchase frequency, accounting for only 1.45 percent of the predicted variation. There is a reliable mean difference ($t = 7.06$, $p < 0.000$) between people who purchase on the Internet (4.01) and those who don't purchase on the Internet (3.66) on perceived product availability. Apparently, this difference is irrelevant when attempting to predict the dollar amount of purchases, and is only of minor relevance when attempting to predict frequency of purchase.

The role of gender

Gender is a reliable minor predictor of purchase frequency (1.32 percent) and purchase amount (3.34 percent). Interestingly, males, on average, spend nearly three times as much on the Internet as females ($899 per year versus $311, $t = 4.25$, $p < 0.000$). Males also purchase more frequently than females (7.14 times per year versus 4.39, $t = 3.46$, $p < 0.001$). In the aggregate, the average purchase for males is $126 per year versus $71 for females.

It is instructive that our dependent variables exhibit such large mean differences by gender, yet gender itself is a minor predictor in our regression equations. One likely explanation is that gender is confounded with other predictor variables, specifically experience.

Among people who shop on the Internet, the average experience in months for males is 51.9, the average for females is 44.6 (t = 3.21, p < 0.001). In addition, males spend nearly twice as much money as females using the mail/phone order remote shopping modality, excluding Internet purchases ($758 per year versus $402, t = 2.22, p < 0.02). Thus, males have more direct (time online) and more indirect (spend more on male/phone orders) experience than females. When variation due to experience is factored out of gender, the resultant gender specific variation is a poor predictor of online shopping behavior. Another reason for this poor performance is that gender is a two-value variable, that is, male or female. A two-value variable is never going to do a good job at predicting a continuous range variable like purchase amount. Although we are not attempting a causal analysis in this chapter, it does seem logical that the more (favorable) experience you have with remote shopping, the more likely you will be to increase your remote shopping. Gender could never have that type of effect since gender does not vary beyond two values. A gender effect would have to work in an indirect fashion, influencing other variables that exhibit a range of values.

A note on location

"Location" is certainly a critical factor for real-world shopping facilities. However, it would not have a one-for-one correspondence with a similarly named concept in cyberspace. For example, distance and ease of access would probably define location for real-world shopping facilities. However, distance is irrelevant in cyberspace. We suspect a higher-level concept like convenience would encompass location in its definition, but the sub-components that define convenience in the two shopping domains would very likely be different. It would be interesting to compare models for brick-and-mortar buying behavior with different modalities for remote shopping behaviors, but that would very likely involve designing a study just for that purpose. The UCLA study contains a wealth of information about remote shopping behavior, but it has no information on brick-and-mortar shopping behavior. Thus it offers no information on location as a variable.

Classification results

We used two levels of modeling in our analysis. The regression models were used in an attempt to predict the "amount" of the dependent variables. The discriminant analysis models were used to determine accurate classification rates for a yes/no predictive model. (We could have also used a logistic regression approach in the latter case, but discriminant analysis is adequate for the task.)

The classification results were relatively strong. Each of the classification models correctly predicted over three-quarters of the modeled behaviors.

Summary and Conclusions

The single most important factor predicting Internet shopping behavior is experience. Experience is actually a complex multi-dimensional construct that consists of direct and indirect components. Direct experience refers to aspects of Internet utilization, for example, the amount of average Internet connect time per week or the presence of a high-speed Internet connection. In this study, indirect experience, such as the amount of money a person spends purchasing by mail or phone, was found to substitute for direct Internet experience such as average Internet connect time. This has important theoretical and methodological implications. For example, when predicting Internet purchase amounts or frequency using a direct measure of Internet utilization such as Internet average connect time, you will get different results depending on the amount of mail or phone shopping experience present in the sample.

Our findings with respect to experience generally support those of Lohse et al. (1999, 2000). They also associated Internet purchasing and Internet purchase amounts with more years of online experience, and more email messages received per day (that is, direct measures of Internet experience). They also found a relationship between purchasing from catalogs (indirect experience) and online purchasing and amounts spent online. Where the studies differ is in the strength of the effects. This study used a multivariate procedure to remove redundancy present in the different predictor variables, and then predicted both the Internet purchase dollar amounts and purchase frequencies. Lohse et al. (1999, 2000) predicted Internet buying or not buying using a logistic regression approach with correlated predictor variables. In their study, remote shopping experience was only the third most important predictor. In practice, it is difficult to compare effect sizes between studies predicting different aspects of the same variables. Our study modeled amounts of the dependent variables, whereas Lohse et al. (1999, 2000) modeled purchase/no purchase.

Results from our multivariate discriminant analysis agree with Lohse et al.'s (1999, 2000) finding that it is possible to achieve a high degree of classification accuracy when attempting to distinguish those who purchase from those who do not purchase on the Internet. We successfully classified 77 percent of those who purchased from those who did not purchase on the Internet using a 50 percent random hold out sample with the reliable predictor variables from the purchase frequency regression model. This is the same predictive power found in Lohse et al. (1999, 2000).

Although we did not focus on this in the results section, the predictive power of the different variables was different in the regression and discriminant analysis models. This difference clearly reflected the difference in the analytical tasks. This finding and the importance of experience-oriented factors suggest that our predictive understanding of factors that influence Internet purchases could be enhanced by a sequential or hierarchical modeling approach. That is, first understand the factors that are most predictive of making that first "leap of faith," that is, the first Internet purchase. Then model the factors that predict low to moderate levels of Internet purchases, and moderate to high levels of Internet purchases. It seems plausible that different aspects of experience and trust may come into play as the number of Internet purchases increases. For example, the positive influence of mail and phone purchases may decrease in terms of their predictive power for people who already make a lot of Internet purchases. In other words, the effects of surrogate experiences may saturate in terms of their predictive power. In this situation, the importance of having a high-speed Internet connection, a measure of direct Internet purchase experience, may be a stronger predictor for people who frequently purchase on the Internet as opposed to those who only purchase at moderate levels.

A second important conclusion from this research is that previous experience with mail and phone shopping acts to offset potential negative consequences of remote shopping on the Internet. This seems to occur because the basic structural risks are the same. For example, if you are shopping remotely, you do not have face-to-face contact, and your perception of goods and services is dependent on "descriptive" materials provided by the vendor. In addition, remote shopping involves paying shipping charges, and more hassle if products need to be returned. Apparently, people who shop remotely trade off these negative aspects of remote shopping in exchange for higher levels of convenience. However, no amount of mail or phone order experience decreases concerns about privacy of personal information on the Internet or concerns about security of credit card information on the Internet. It appears that only direct Internet shopping experience acts to reduce these types of risks. Conceptually this implies that there are two types of risks. One is a basic structural consequence of remote shopping in general; the second is specific to Internet shopping.

This raises an important question. What is there about Internet purchasing in general that makes security and privacy concerns unique to that purchase modality? The security and privacy fear might be linked to the prevalence of hackers on the Internet. Some of the largest Internet companies have experienced major security intrusions where unauthorized access to confidential information has been gained. Privacy concerns may, in part, be related to "cookies" and related technologies that track how a person uses the Internet. These types of concerns appear to be relatively unimportant in our current models.

The results of Swaminathan et al. (2000) stress the importance of perceived convenience in predicting both online purchase frequency and amount. Once again, it is difficult to compare the results across studies because the studies have different research goals and the measures are not comparable. In the UCLA study the concept of convenience was measured mostly by our "perception of the Internet" factor. This factor contained elements such as "using the Internet saves time" and "ease of finding information on the Internet." We found that this factor was not a reliable predictor of either Internet purchase frequency or purchase amount. However, Swaminathan et al. (2000) did not include any measure for mail or phone shopping. People often use mail and phone shopping for purposes of convenience, and it's possible that a good deal of convenience information was captured by our mail and phone shopping factor. This possibility will be examined in more depth in future research.

In our analysis, social interaction as a motive for shopping was (inversely) part of the "negative aspects of shopping" component. We found some predictive value here and Swaminathan et al. (2000) did as well. Those who value the social aspect of shopping appear to buy less online. Swaminathan et al. (2000) also found that perceived vendor reliability had a positive influence on the number of online purchases, but did not influence the amount of money spent on the Internet. Reliability was part of our factor on perceptions of the Internet, which was not a significant predictor. However, we also noted that reliability is related to trust which was a significant predictive factor in our analysis, especially as we related it to experience. Comparisons are especially challenging here as they do not include in their analysis the experience variables, both in terms of the Internet and other remote shopping modes, that we find to be the most important predictors.

Swaminathan et al. (2000) found that price competitiveness had a positive influence on the number of online purchases, but did not influence the amount of money spent on the Internet. We also found that perceived price advantage does not predict purchase amounts. But according to our evidence this variable is only a minor predictor for Internet purchase frequency.

In the realm of privacy and security Swaminathan et al. (2000) found that online consumers are less concerned about the security of electronic exchanges than non-consumers, but only marginally. This corresponds with our findings. On this matter Lohse et al. (1999, 2000), who found that purchasing and purchase amounts were negatively associated with privacy concerns, also agree.

In the realm of minor findings, we also mirror the results of Lohse et al. (1999, 2000) showing income predicting purchase amounts and maleness being positively associated with online shopping. The results involving the demographic variable of age, and gender as well, were interesting because they illustrate the dangers of confounding among predictive variables. Given that gender can only take on two values, it would be instructive to see if gender was an important predictor in terms of classifying people who purchase on the Internet from those who do not. Perhaps the leap of faith required to make that first Internet purchase has an association with age or gender.

In conclusion, our findings generally support those of Lohse et al. (1999, 2000), and Swaminathan et al. (2000). Discrepancies that exist are very probably the result of two factors. Lohse et al. (1999, 2000) were predicting the presence or absence of Internet purchasing and we were predicting amounts of purchase and frequency of Internet purchases. Differences with the results of Swaminathan et al. (2000) are more likely attributed to the different measures used in both studies, especially the absence of experience variables in their work. But the differences also might be due to the nature of the samples. Lohse et al.

used a large (10,180 in year one and 9,738 panelists in year two) random sample that closely matched the US online population. Swaminathan et al. used secondary data based on an email survey that respondents were invited to participate in through newsgroup and mailing list announcements, and banner ads. Based on the demographic information for this sample, it was clearly not projectable to the US population. The UCLA study was a random projectable sample.

References

Alba, J., Lynch, J., Weitz, B., Janiszewski, C., Lutz, R., Sawyer, A., and Wood, S. (1997). Interactive home shopping: consumer, retailer and manufacturer incentives to participate in electronic marketplaces. *Journal of Marketing,* 61(3), 38–54.

Bauer, R. A. (1960). Consumer behavior as risk taking. In D. F. Cox (ed.), *Risk taking and information handling in consumer behavior* (pp. 22–3). Cambridge, MA: Harvard University Press.

Bellenger, D. N. and Kargaonkar, P. K. (1980). Profiling the recreational shopper. *Journal of Retailing,* 56, 77–82.

Bloom, P. N., Milne, G. R., and Adler, R. (1994). Avoiding misuse of new information technologies: legal and societal considerations. *Journal of Marketing,* 58, 98–110.

BMRB International (1999, October 11). *Six different types of UK web shoppers.* Available online at:
http://www.nua.ie/surveys/ index.cgi?f=VS&art_id=905355333&rel=true

Camp, L. J. (2000). *Trust and risk in Internet commerce.* Cambridge, MA: MIT Press.

Cranor, L. F., Reagle, J., and Ackerman, M. S. (1999). *Beyond concern: understanding net users' attitudes about online privacy.* AT&T Labs-Research Technical Report TR 99.4.4. Available online at:
http://www.research.att.com/ projects/privacystudy/

Emeagwali, P. (2000). *History of the Internet: Emeagwali's recollections from 27 years.* Available online at:
http://emeagwali.com/history/Internet/index.html

Feldman, D. L. (2000). Public confidence in cybersystems: issues and implications for sustainability. *International Political Science Review,* 21, 23.

Fox, S. (2000). *Trust and privacy online: why Americans want to rewrite the rules.* Pew Internet and American Life Project. Available online at:
http://www.pewInternet.org/reports/toc.asp?Report=19

Friedman, B. and Kahn, P. H., Jr (2000). Trust online. *Communications of the ACM,* 43(12), 34–40.

Gefen, D. (2000). E-commerce: the role of familiarity and trust. *Omega,* 28(6), 725–37.

Gehrt, K. C., Yale, L. J., and Lawson, D. A. (1996). The convenience of catalog shopping: is there more to it than time? *Journal of Direct Marketing*, 10(4), 19–28.

Gillett, P. L. (1976). In-home shoppers: an overview. *Journal of Marketing*, 40, 81–8.

Grossman, W. (2000). Circles of trust. *Scientific American*, 283, 34.

Harris Interactive (June 8, 2000). *Six types of online shopper identified*. Available online at: http://www.nua.ie/surveys/index.cgi?f+VSandart_id=905355830andrel= true

Hoffman, D. L., Kalsbeek, W. D., and Novak, T. P. (1999). Building consumer trust online. *Communications of the ACM*, 42(4), 80–5.

Lohse, G. L., Bellman, S., and Johnson, E. J. (1999). Predictors of online buying behavior. *Comunications of the ACM*, 42(12), 32–8.

Lohse, G. L., Bellman, S., and Johnson, E. J. (2000). Consumer buying behavior on the Internet: findings from panel data. *Journal of Interactive Marketing*, 14, 15–29.

Luedi, A. F. (1997). Personalize or perish. *Electronic Markets*, 7(3), 22–5.

Milne, G. R. and Gordon, M. E. (1993). Direct mail privacy–efficiency trade-offs within an implied social contract network. *Journal of Public Policy and Marketing*, 12(2), 206–15.

Minahan, T. (1997). Internet buying is a tough sell. *Purchasing*, 122(1), 113.

Moorman, C., Deshpande, R., and Zaltman, G. (1993). Factors affecting trust in marketing relationships. *Journal of Marketing*, 57, 81–101.

Morgan, R. M. and Hunt, S. D. (1994). The commitment-trust theory of relationship marketing. *Journal of Marketing*, 58, 20–38.

Olson, J. S. and Olson, G. M. (2000). Trust in e-commerce. *Communications of the ACM*, 43, 41.

Palmer, J. W. (1997). Retailing on the WWW. *Electronic Markets*, 7(3), 6–9.

Reynolds, F. D. (1974). An analysis of catalog buying behavior. *Journal of Marketing*, 38(3), 47–51.

Rohm, A. J. and Milne, G. R. (1999). Consumers' privacy concerns about direct marketers' use of personal medical information. In J. F. Hair, Jr (ed.), *Proceedings of the 1999 Association for Health Care Research Conference* (pp. 27–37). Breckenridge, CO.

Sabo, J. T. (1997). Lessons learned: providing government Internet services with public trust. *Public Manager*, 26(3), 55–8.

Salnoske, K. (1998). Building trust in electronic commerce. *Business Credit*, 100(1), 24–5.

Schoder, D. and P.-L. Yin (2000). Building firm trust online. *Communications of the ACM*, 43(12), 73–9.

Sheth, J. N. and Parvatiyar, A. (1995). Relationship marketing in consumer markets: antecedents and consequences. *Journal of the Academy of Marketing Science*, 23, 255–71.

Sklar, D. (2001). Building trust in an Internet economy. *Strategic Finance*, 82(10), 22–5.

Swaminathan, V., Lepkowska-White, E., and Rao, B. P. (2000). Browsers or buyers in cyberspace? An investigation of factors influencing electronic exchange. *Journal of Computer Mediated Communication*, 5(2). Available online at: http://www.ascusc.org/jcmc/vol5/issue2/swaminathan.htm

UCLA Center for Communication Policy (2000). *The UCLA Internet Report.* Available online at: http://ccp.ucla.edu/pages/Internet-report.asp

UCLA Center for Communication Policy (2001). *The UCLA Internet Report.* Available online at: http://ccp.ucla.edu/pages/Internet-report.asp

Urban, G. L. and Sultan, F. (2000). Placing trust at the center of your Internet strategy. *Sloan Management Review*, 42(1), 39–48.

US Department of Commerce (1999). *The emerging digital economy II.* Available online at: http://www.ecommerce.gov/ede/

Wachter, R. M. (1999). The effect of gender and communication mode on conflict resolution. *Computers in Human Behavior*, 15, 763–82.

Zellweger, P. (1997). Web-based sales: defining the cognitive buyer. *Electronic Markets*, 7(3), 10–16.

Index